SANDERS FAMILY:
A THOUSAND-YEAR HISTORY

SANDERS FAMILY:
A THOUSAND-YEAR HISTORY

A Revised and Expanded Edition of Generations:
A Thousand-Year Family History

Ralph Sanders

with Carole J. Sanders

Peggy Sanders Van Der Heide

To order additional copies of this book, contact:
Xlibris
1-888-795-4274
www.Xlibris.com
Orders@Xlibris.com
732221

CONTENTS

Epigraph..vii

Introduction...ix

About This Revised And Expanded Edition xiii

Chapter 1   Before Leonard 1

Chapter 2   Leonard 14

Chapter 3   Sende Manor 43

Chapter 4   Sanders Place...69

Chapter 5   Quartered Arms...80

Chapter 6   Ewell.. 118

Chapter 7   Wales 162

Chapter 8   Gloucestershire 196

Chapter 9   Bristol..228

Chapter 10   Colonial Virginia 252

Chapter 11   Spotsylvania...275

Chapter 12   Kentucky..298

Chapter 13   Eagle Creek 342

Chapter 14   Leaving The Land..368

Appendix I 383

Appendix II..417

Index...433

EPIGRAPH

Cinque, a Mende slave: I will call into the past, far back to the beginning of time. I will beg them to help me. At the time of judgment, I will reach back and draw them into me, and they must come, for at this moment, I am the whole reason they existed at all.

John Quincy Adams: That when a member of the Mende encountered a situation where there appears to be no hope at all, he invokes his ancestors' tradition. The Mende believe that if one can summon the spirit of one's ancestors, then they have never left, and the wisdom and strength they fathered and inspired will come to his aid.

> We have been made to understand that who we are is who we were.
>
> —*Amistad*

INTRODUCTION

Some years back, our parents, Dorothy and Ralph Sanders, visited General Butler State Park near Carrollton, Kentucky, and happened to browse through its collection of books on subjects pertaining to that part of Kentucky. There they purchased a book by Anna V. Parker, now out of print, entitled *The Sanders Family of Grass Hills*. The book eventually made its way into our reading and touched off a set of questions that since have occupied us for nearly three decades. At the conclusion of Parker's charming account of some Sanders who lived 150 years ago near Ghent, Kentucky, lay a captivating genealogy. This genealogy traced an ancestry back to a certain Nathaniel Sanders, who Parker said came from Wales to America about the year 1700. Could we somehow be related to these people? Was this Nathaniel our first American ancestor? Were we really from Wales? We pored over the life facts that Anna Parker gave for early Sanders figures, wondering if any of these people could have been responsible for our own being.

For reasons now distantly recalled, it may have been our Aunt Marie—in truth a great-aunt, though not of the Sanders line—who piqued our interest in family history. She loved to recite tales of earlier families and made those folks now gone seem terribly compelling to us. Whatever Aunt Marie said, it seemed to us that we needed, perhaps even urgently, some greater sense of our own background.

We knew so little of our Sanders ancestors. In fact, we were certain of little more than our grandfather's name. But inexperienced as we were in genealogical research, we reviewed one source after another, writing letters here and there, hoping to find some information to link our family to those people of Anna Parker's book. Our parents helped out. After a few years, we finally found the elusive links and took great delight in discovering our American ancestry. Yes, we do indeed descend from Anna Parker's Nathaniel Sanders.

Eventually, we grew accustomed to the idea that finding our ancestors was an important part of our lives, and we embarked on a project to extend the genealogy as far back as we could. The three of us who wrote this book evolved an overlapping division of labor—Peggy principally focusing on medieval England up to about the year 1600, Ralph on the next two centuries, and Carole working mainly on the 1800s and later. But moving beyond Anna Parker's genealogy turned out to be more difficult than anticipated because the older historical times lacked the usual genealogical records of births, marriages, and deaths. We scratched for land and court records, noted odd accounts in books and journals, wrote letters of inquiry of all sorts, and found that direct, simple proofs of ancestry such as birth and marriage records only occasionally could be found. Slowly, imperceptibly, we discovered that finding distant ancestors involved reconstructing communities of persons who seemed a part of our family history while also examining the historical character of their era. We used these patterns to shape our search and understanding. This shift in research strategy produced an unintended consequence. Unwittingly, we had begun to uncover details about those whom we sought to discover. Two decades later, we find we had by degrees reconstructed the social and historical settings of all our direct Sanders ancestors for the last millennium. So now we are able to offer a somewhat biographical approach to this long family history. If in telling these ancestral stories we extend the force and excitement of Aunt Marie's narratives, the telling will repay the effort.

Most surprising for us was the amount of information we have been able to uncover about our ancestors. If they were special people—and they were—they were exceptional in the same way that all people are exceptional, but not disproportionately so. These people by and large are familiar types, not notably wealthy in the main, not especially famous or powerful, not distinguished in ways that could have produced extraordinary paper trails. And so our findings about them carry a message—that the extraordinary amount of detail we have found about our own ancestors is available to others seeking understanding of their own families. A main requirement seems to be an origin in the British Isles, where record keeping has a long tradition and the language of records is generally familiar.

No part of this work is fiction. What this book contains are facts and interpretations of facts. If there are errors, they are errors of interpretation, of the meanings we have derived from facts. But in no instance are these portraits of family figures the result of unfettered imagination or literary invention. All of what we have written is true, insofar as truth can be determined. We furthermore have not been interested in offering judgments about how our ancestors' lives were lived, and we have not offered them. Our view is that this work offers these people the chance to walk again among us. We accept something nearing a sacred obligation to develop their portraits in as faithful a manner as possible so that they appear to us as they were. We hope we have done so.

Some explanation of how we use the surname Sanders in the narration might make readers more comfortable. Surnames are the labels used to identify family. But a difficulty exists in tracing surnames through time. Surnames evolve irregularly, and the idea of standardizing surname spellings is of fairly recent vintage. It was not uncommon in the eighteenth century and before for names routinely to be spelled different ways. William Shakespeare is said to have spelled his own name at least four different ways. We uncovered numerous instances for our own family in which a single record offered more than one spelling for the person of record. To avoid confusion in our chapters, therefore, we have loosely standardized surname spellings according to most common forms, adhering to the spelling "Saunders" in England and Wales and "Sanders" in the New World, except in a few cases where exact spellings have specific meanings. But one must understand that we employed this simplification for narrative convenience. The records themselves contain far greater varieties and inconsistencies in spelling than our writing suggests.

The biggest missing piece in this family history is the story of family women. Women comprise one half the family history, but in our treatment, they are accorded only brief mention. This occurs for several reasons. First, in the historical records available from patronymic English society, the woman's name changed at marriage. That means that in most instances, a given record for, say, Ann Sanders might refer to one of two persons, either Ann (née) Sanders or Ann Sanders, a person's wife. Few of such records are amenable to useful interpretation because the identity is ambiguous. Even where we know a woman's identity, learning something of her own ancestry places her within another patronymic lineage, following the surname of her father. Thus, the enate genealogical past tends to evaporate after one generation. Beyond that, for the most part, women's activities were rarely recorded. Their roles in society typically were constricted to domestic settings, roles that produced virtually no written records. One, of course, can find books on women's history—Antonia Fraser's fine *Weaker Vessel* is a case in point—to improve one's general understanding of women in history. But such histories necessarily lack the particulars required to understand one's own ancestresses.

Ralph wrote the text using the results of research and careful outlines of findings in part produced by Carole and Peggy in their portions of the work. Together, we three are indebted to the fine collections and services of the city libraries of Minneapolis, Syracuse, and Covington, Kentucky. In addition, the libraries of the University of Minnesota, Syracuse University, the Kentucky Historical Society, the Filson Club of Louisville, and the Dyfed County Council Library at Haverfordwest in Wales were especially helpful. Also helpful was the cheerful and ready assistance of Elaine Kuhn of the Local History Department in the Kenton County Public Library in Covington, Kentucky, where all our family research papers have been placed for public use.

Beyond those invaluable resources were the unique contributions of a number of people. Mary Margaret Boyles of Chicago was a fine

Sanders genealogist before her passing, and her firm admonishments and encouragements guided our early thinking. Martha Sanders Reiner shared her acquaintance with our nineteenth-century family and events to our advantage. Greatly helpful were John Konvalinka, who unearthed useful records in both the United States and the United Kingdom, and Dr. Thomas E. Sanders of Louisville, who offered insights on the families in Virginia and Kentucky. Geoffrey Roberts, an exacting records searcher for Bristol, England, and surrounding counties, produced extraordinarily useful records that helped connect Old and New World family branches. There were others, many others, who willingly shared ideas and records in specific areas of research. Their contributions are mentioned in the appropriate places in the text and are appreciated beyond these few words of acknowledgment.

Our great debt of gratitude is to Nancy Gustin Sanders, Ralph's wife, who combed through records, generated many helpful ideas, suggested countless improvements in early drafts, and patiently endured Ralph's writing struggles through all these years.

RAS
CJS
PSV

ABOUT THIS REVISED
AND EXPANDED EDITION

This is a revised and expanded version of our original book, Generations: A Thousand-Year Family History (Philadelphia: Xlibris, 2007). We have entirely rewritten major portions of the first several chapters, correcting important misapprehensions having to do with the family's earliest recorded days. To explain, in Generations, we told a story of Leonard de Sanderstead and his ancestors and descendants in the beginning chapters of that book, but our narrative there is largely incorrect. Major errors resulted from our acceptance of the account offered by Burke (A General Armory of England, Scotland, and Ireland), in which Burke stated that the family held Sanderstead property in the time of Edward the Confessor, that is, before the Norman Conquest of 1066. This resulted in our belief that the family's early history lay in Saxon origins, as Saxon royalty held Sanderstead in those early times. That is how we tried to interpret the family's history. This new edition restates our family history in an entirely new way, as a story stemming from England's post-Conquest years in which Saxon origins played no part. Not the least gain in this new research is that we are now able to push back our genealogy another two hundred years, to the early 900s, and to learn the stories of yet earlier generations.

This new research enabled us to actually decode Leonard de Sanderstead's original coat-of-arms, dating to about the year 1179. This enduring family symbol we found contains a message from Leonard, a message now more than eight hundred years old.

We also amended our story of how the family came to Virginia in the 1600s, to better portray economic and cultural dynamics that underpinned this formative event. From that new understanding, we can better grasp how lives unfolded in our first American generations. Part of our learning about the 1600s rested upon a variety of unpublished Sanders records for Bristol and Gloucestershire, important source areas for migrants coming to Virginia. New to this edition is an appendix, publishing these British records for the first time. These may help Sanders researchers with that most difficult genealogical task, connecting family members on both sides of the Atlantic.

CHAPTER ONE

Before Leonard

Over the long march of history, we have made a choice, unknowingly perhaps, but a choice nonetheless. This choice involves how we think about the relationships between ourselves and other people in our world and experience. In centuries past, our relationships with others were generally unchosen, given by the circumstances of birth and locality; they were organic, arising naturally from their surroundings. Relationships were systematically inherited from one's family and its immediate social circle, and these remained the key dynamic influence throughout one's lifetime. However, in the past few centuries (but especially in the twentieth), we have been changing all that. Relationships with others today are largely chosen, not given. They are sometimes planned, even calculated, and frequently ephemeral. These are built on choice, on opportunity, on necessity [1].

The content of older organic relationships above all was the family, the nexus of kinship—parents, brothers and sisters, aunts and uncles, grandparents, cousins of all stripes, even descendants yet unborn, and not least, distant ancestors. As functioning entities, extended families seem largely a thing of the past, and even smaller nuclear families—parents and children—lack the force of earlier times. But even today, these family relationships can form the main human context of our lives, close enough to ourselves to be protected. They are important enough to be preserved.

For the family genealogist and historian, there is no richer lure than the idea of identifying one's distant ancestors. But greater satisfaction lies in learning these ancestors are not merely old names found in dusty records but rather real people like ourselves—real people but of other times and places, hidden from view most of our lives, yet with perhaps more influence in shaping our lives and possibilities than we might realize. It seems important to try to revive these people, not only for the sake of their own memory, but also for a clearer understanding of who our family was and who we are.

Leonard

If we were to choose one person in the last one thousand years who best symbolizes the Sanders family, that person would be Leonard, sometimes known as Leonard de Sanderstead. Because he was at times called "de Sanderstead," we find in Leonard the ultimate source of the surname Sanders. How "Sanderstead" evolved into "Sanders," however, is not a simple story, because that evolution itself took place over about one hundred years. But we do claim that the modern surname Sanders for our own line derives from the earlier form de Sanderstead, based on the unbroken sequence of names we have assembled from father to son for many generations, beginning with Leonard de Sanderstead. But except for Burke's study [2], we have uncovered only one other genealogical treatment of this line of Sanders, a wonderfully detailed but somewhat flawed account, which we necessarily exclude from further consideration [3].

As with all surnames, the surname Sanders, in any of its forms—Sanders, Saunders, Sandars, Saundre, Sawndirs, and like variations—emerged with the needs of the evolving political state and increased scale of society, the need, especially the legal need, for unambiguous identities of individual persons. Roughly speaking, we may say that surnames arose in feudal times as familiar nation-states began to take recognizable form, which for England occurred in the middle feudal period, around the early fourteenth century. The use of surnames in this early period, though, was at best occasional, and spelling in general, and for surnames in particular, was not then standardized. Standardized spelling of surnames, in fact, did not take full effect until well into the nineteenth century, both in England and America. But over long periods of time, surnames evolved complexly, often diverging from common roots and just as frequently converging from diverse origins.

For this story, we limit ourselves to the particular line of Sanders that began as de Sanderstead. However limiting that might seem, this line in fact relates to perhaps half the persons today called Sanders or Saunders, in all numbering about 345,000 in the United States and perhaps double that number worldwide [4].

Leonard's position in Sanders family tradition is further cemented by his adoption of a coat of arms bearing three bulls' heads [5]. This coat of arms began as Leonard's military shield. His shield design continues even to this day as his lasting contribution to family lore. This coat-of-arms has undergone some modification over the centuries, but his original design is known and is displayed here and on the front cover of this book.

The ancient arms of Leonard de Sanderstead. In Leonard's day, the shield would have had an elongated and narrowed form to afford better movement and protection in battle, and a knight's crest was not attached to the shield. Leonard's symbol of a sinister hand might have been depicted either in vertical or horizontal position.

In England, after Leonard and into present times, families called Sanders or Saunders are generally associated with two distinctly different coats of arms, those displaying three bulls' heads on the shield and those with three elephants' heads [6]. The argument is sometimes advanced that the bulls' heads arms are more ancient and that all Saunders are entitled to them, but that only some Saunders are entitled to the elephant arms. This implies that the elephant arms actually derive from the bulls' heads arms and that those claiming entitlement to the elephant arms are a later branch of the older bulls' heads Saunders family. But we have found no evidence whatsoever to support these claims. The assertion that bulls' heads arms are more ancient is equally unsupported, if only because no definitive study has established dating for the inception of the elephant arms or, for that matter, for the origins of that particular line of Saunders in England.

The two principal coats of arms for the Saunders of Britain.
The bulls' heads arms are those of the Saunders originating
in Surrey; the elephants' heads arms, those of the Saunders
of Northamptonshire. In later centuries, Leonard's use of
the sinister hand gave way to a demibull, forelegs extended,
attached to the shield as a crest.

The Sanders family of which we write is exclusively tied to the coat of
arms bearing three bulls' heads. In Britain, these arms apply to historical
lines mainly at Sanderstead, Charlwood, and Ewell in Surrey; in Derby at
Lullington and Little Ireton; and in and near Tenby in Pembrokeshire, Wales.
Our research shows further family dispersals of these lines, which we follow
later in some detail. In England, Sanders arms from Surrey bearing bulls' heads
are contrasted with those of the Saunders of Buckingham, Northamptonshire,
Warwickshire, Ireland, and elsewhere, which use three elephant heads. No
genealogical connection between these separate lines is known to exist, and
they have entirely different histories. These two coats of arms, each signifying a
Sanders or Saunders family, reflect the general process of surname convergence,
a process in which the modern surnames of Sanders and Saunders arose from
different origins, one from the place-name Sanderstead and the other possibly
from a progenitor named Alexander.

Brittany
    If we are to understand something of this person named Leonard, we need
first to grasp the tenor of the times in which he lived and his own ancestry. Both
indelibly shaped Leonard's life. Thus, Leonard's story begins not in England

but in Brittany. Leonard thought himself a Breton and some of his extended family remained there even in his own day. He undoubtedly knew something of his Breton ancestors and probably was instructed that his family's Breton history should not be forgotten. Leonard did not forget.

Brittany is a district in northwestern France, lying on the English Channel at its north and jutting into the Atlantic Ocean on the west. In ancient times, the area was called Armorica, home to a loose assemblage of Celtic tribes dating back to the times of the Roman Empire and before. Armorica later became known by the name "Brittany" (French, "Bretagne") after migration there in the 600s by Britons, another of the Celtic tribes, who departed western England when invading Saxons drove them out. By the 800s, Brittany had been absorbed into Charlemagne's Holy Roman Empire, in large part because Brittany's King Salaman served as one of Charlemagne's chief allies. As part of the Holy Roman Empire, Brittany adopted Charlemagne's feudal arrangements, taking on French as a unifying language and setting out strong centralized hierarchical arrangements for landholding and the administration of law. A key feature of this feudal regime was the development of military art, in which new armaments, rigorous training, and tight organization combined to produce innovative, disciplined, and highly effective military forces.

By the 900s Brittany had evolved into a unified and autonomous state, controlled by a small number of noble families. Among these were the Counts of Dol, whose influence extended over a significant portion of Brittany. Leonard's own people descended from these Counts of Dol, though by the late 900s they were counts no longer, retaining their influence rather through a series of appointments called "seneschals," a term that in official English parlance came to be called "dapifer". Around the year 1000 this title of seneschal had been declared hereditary for them, securing for this family numerous political, social, and economic advantages for its foreseeable future.

At Dol, the count possessed full power and authority over his realm and used his Seneschal to exercise that ability. The seneschal and count maintained an assymetrical relationship in which the count delegated authority to the seneschal, and the seneschal advised the count on the wisest courses of action. The seneschal was to guard the prestige, prosperity, and safety of his noble superior, and generally had free rein in how best to accomplish these things. In effect, the Seneschal was governor of the noble's realm, the face of the law, the person to whom a subject might appeal for justice or protection. And perhaps most significantly, the Seneschal organized and maintained the Count's army and sometimes led it in battle.

From the mid-900s onward, the names of these leaders of Dol, that is, the immediate ancestors of Leonard, are known [7]. A certain Ewarin was Count of Dol about 950 and married into the de Dinan family, creating a noble house called "Dol and Dinan." Ewarin's son Alan followed him as Count of Dol but appears to have died soon after, because another son, Hamo, held that title about 980. Following Hamo was his son Guienol, after whom came Alan, unambiguously stated to be the Seneschal and not the Count of Dol. Finally, Alan's son Flaad, or, as he was called by the naming convention of the time, Flaad FitzAlan [8], assumed the title of Seneschal of Dol, perhaps about the year 1040.

This Flaad FitzAlan was the Seneschal of Dol when William the Norman Conqueror invaded England in 1066. Flaad followed suit by crossing the English Channel from Brittany to Cornwall, then pressing his formidable army northward along the Welsh border to lands today that lie in Shropshire, England. Whether Flaad's attack was coordinated with the Norman attack farther east in England is not known, but their mutual advantages and successes in the same time period are clear. In victory, Flaad claimed a Shropshire manor called Oswestry, which served for many years after Flaad as a family anchor in England.

Flaad's son Alan, later known as Lord of Oswestry, augmented the family's holdings after being recruited by English King Henry I to secure the contentious Welsh border. Beyond his rewards of property for military success and loyalty to Henry I, Alan also married well, to a daughter of the de Hesdin family by whom he came into additional estates. By about 1100, Alan had become one of the most powerful barons in his part of England. Later, this family acquired Clun Castle through marriage to symbolize and fortify their superior position [9]. Descendants of Alan FitzFlaad from one of his sons eventually became the English Earls of Arundel. On another side was Alan's son Walter FitzAlan, father of Leonard de Sanderstead.

Scotland

Born about the year 1108 and growing up at Oswestry, Walter FitzAlan knew wealth, privilege, and warfare. And he was quick to capitalize on his background. In his late twenties, Walter joined forces with some of the most powerful Norman figures in England, engaging in a series of battles in which the throne of England was at stake. On one side was the claimant Stephen of Blois, and opposing him was Matilda (called "Maud"), the daughter of recently deceased King Henry I. In these contests, Walter FitzAlan linked up with Scotland's King David and also with one of King Henry's sons, named Reginald Dunstanville, a half-brother of Maud [10]. Although their cause on behalf of Maud was eventually lost, firm relationships between Walter FitzAlan, Reginald Dunstanville, and King David had been established.

In Scotland, King David was busy attempting to duplicate the Norman feudal system of centralized governance, which had been rapidly implanted on English soil following William's conquest of 1066. Many of those Norman innovations had not reached Scotland by David's time. David embarked on his program by importing a class of Norman and Breton land barons, persons of sufficient power to command the respect of local populations but who also would pledge their fealty and provide a force of trained knights for the Scottish monarch. In addition to endowing these new figures with land, David restructured ancient counties with new sheriffs and justices; created towns with specific rights, opportunities, and protections; and promoted religious uniformity and adherence with a sweeping reorganization of bishoprics. All this for Scotland was a novel ruling regime and one that long endured, but also one that generated a steady stream of resistance. From the north were ancient Scottish clans and Norsemen left over from Viking days who feared and resented David's intrusions into their traditional homelands. And from the south, from England, arose claims on Scottish territory. David, then, required above all an effective fighting force that could secure his rule both north and south to bring his revolutionary plans for Scotland to fruition.

King David recruited Walter FitzAlan as a key ally for his projects in Scotland and induced Walter to join him with promises of land and important responsibilities. Walter was a perfect fit. He was in the words of one commentator, a "Norman by culture and by blood a Breton." Holinshed opined that "Walter (FitzAlan) proved a man of greater courage and valiance than any other had been commonly found, and there reigned in him a certain stoutness of stomach ready to attempt high enterprises" [11]. He brought stature, fighting prowess, and an insider's knowledge of Norman rule in in England, and he could be relied on for steady support. About the year 1136, Walter entered Scotland with his brother Simon and settled in for good.

After a few years, David appointed Walter FitzAlan the Royal High Steward of Scotland—a position identical to a Seneschal at Dol—and rewarded him with vast land holdings in Renfrewshire, Ayrshire, and Berwickshire. David granted Walter the lands of Kerkert and Strathgryffe (much of the land of Renfrewshire), and it was here, in Paisley, that Walter established his home. He built a structure called Blackhall Manor, which served him and his descendants for generations [12]. Blackhall served as an ancestral home for subsequent generations of his family who served as hereditary stewards of Scotland. In the centuries to follow, these hereditary stewards ascended to the Scottish throne as kings, adopting the surname Stewart for themselves and ultimately forming the Stuart Dynasty that ruled Scotland, Ireland, and England during the seventeenth century [13]. Thus Blackhall Manor can be thought a cradle of kings, as the Stuart Dynasty of Scotland and England find their beginnings in Walter FitzAlan at Blackhall. Also at Paisley, Walter endowed a Cluniac monastery in Paisley in Renfrewshire, importing monks from Shropshire, which grew into Paisley Abbey in Walter's lifetime. In later years Walter would be buried there.

Blackhall Manor in Paisley, the boyhood home of Leonard de Sanderstead. Blackhall was carefully restored in 1984. Photograph copyright Wikipedia, licenced for reuse under Creative Commons Licence.

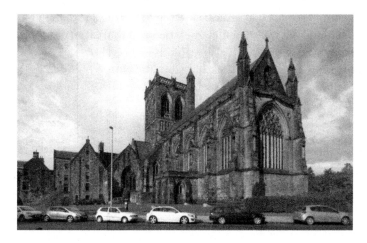

Paisley Abbey, Scotland, founded in 1163 by Walter FitzAlan, father of Leonard de Sanderstead. Photograph copyright Lairich Rig, licenced for reuse under Creative Commons Licence.

Walter thus occupied center stage in the Scottish court and provided long service as Scotland's first Royal High Steward, not only for David, but also for his successors Kings Malcolm and William (the Lion). In David's time, Walter would have marshalled Scottish forces for any number of the minor skirmishes that dotted David's reign, and he led them to an important victory over an approaching northern army led by their chief Sommerled in the so-called Battle of Renfrewshire of 1164. Walter FitzAlan's position in the Scottish court continued the long family tradition of stewardship, reaching back generations to his ancestral Seneschals of Dol. By 1157 his position as the first Royal High Steward of Scotland was made hereditary—just as it had been in Brittany— an act that cemented his own position and that of his eldest son and their descendants for a long period of Scottish history.

When Walter first entered Scotland, he did so with a close companion named Robert Croc, an Anglo-Norman knight. Croc died soon after, and around 1139 Walter married Croc's young widow, a woman named Eschyna de Londoniis (this name from her father), also at times called Eschyna de Molle (from her mother's side). Not only did Eschyna bring property to the marriage, she also brought a young son from her first marriage. He was named after his father, Robert Croc. This son Robert Croc prospered in his mother and stepfather's household and later received honors for his service to the Scottish court [14]. The ties between these Crocs and the FitzAlans remained strong; marriage connections can be found in England a generation later.

Walter and Eschyna had several children in the decade of the 1140s—sons Alan, Walter, and Simon; daughters Beatrice and Margaret; and finally a son Leonard, born about 1143 in Paisley, Renfrewshire [15]. All these, save one, are names commonly found at the time, but the choice of the name Leonard is another matter altogether. This subject is of Leonard's own life, to which we now turn.

NOTES

1. This notion of historically changing human relationships is not original. The sociologist Weber called the web of organic relationships "gemeinschaft" and modern mechanical relationships "gesellschaft." The former allows that we retain kin-based relationships in our lives, which involve both opportunities and burdens. In modern times, we are less burdened with given relationships, but we also lack the supportive context of extended family, having to build personal support on our own initiatives. American demographics today indicate that even small nuclear families (parents and children only) comprise fewer than half of all households. The economic historian Fernand Braudel (Civilization and Capitalism, 3 vols. [New York: Harper and Row, 1984]) suggests that these contradictory systems coexist, gesellschaft replacing gemeinschaft in a long, slow pace of modernization. Braudel poignantly notes that the traditional economy, that which is not monetized, still comprises up to 30 percent of the modern economy, when all forms of economic exchange are included. Economic and social systems are closely linked, so we might conclude that the institution of family, though weakened, is by no means completely undermined.

2. Burke's genealogy provides a de Sanderstead lineage for persons following the conquest, but as detailed in chapter 5, William Saunders of Charlwood married Joan Carew of Beddington. Burke's portrayal provides incorrect parentage and lineal descent for this William and fails to note that William's immediate ancestors were from Charlwood and not Sanderstead. Gaps of time between generations seem at times unusually large. Most notably, Burke fails to indicate at which point the de Sanderstead appellation goes to extinction. These and other problems call into question the reliability of Burke's de Sanderstead genealogy, although some undetermined portions of it could be correct.

3. The source in question is the following: Thomas Homer-Saunders, "The Saunders, Sanders, Sandars Family and Its Blood Connections, Under the Sprig of Alexander (Alisaunder) the Great, from which the surname is derived and which came into existence during the thirteenth and fourteenth centuries" (n.d.), p. 24. We repeat this account in detail here as

some of the facts adduced in Homer-Saunders's unpublished manuscript may inform others of their own Sanders genealogy, even though we cannot agree with his final conclusions in relation to Sanderstead.

Homer-Saunders details a lineage that follows Norman royalty through five generations, from a grandson of William the Conqueror to a person named Alexander, whom he names as a Surrey Sanders ancestor. Alexander's lineage, beginning with the death of Theobald II in France in 1152, commences not long before the birth of Sir Leonard de Sanderstead and, Homer-Saunders suggests, eventually ends up at Sanderstead.

Homer-Saunders claims that Mary—daughter of Theobald II (–1152), brother of King Stephen (c1097–1154) of England and grandson of William the Conqueror—married Eudo, Count of Blois. Their son Hugh III had two sons: (1) Eudo, Duke of Burgundy, who married Theresa, daughter of the king of Portugal, and (2) Alexander, Lord of Montague and Chagny, who married Beatrice, daughter of William, Count of Challon.

Alexander and Beatrice had a son Eudo, also lord of Montague and Chagny, who married Elizabeth, daughter of Peter II of Courtenay, Emperor of Constantinople. Eudo and Elizabeth in turn had four sons: (1) Philip, (2) Scaevola, (3) William, lord of Montague and Chagny, and (4) Alexander, a count who left France and settled in Wiltshire, England, about the year 1220. The arms of Count Alexander are said to be etched into window glass at the parish church at Wilton. Interestingly, this is the same small church that holds the remains of Athelfleda, wife of King Edgar and donor of Sanderstead lands to the Abbey of Hyde. See Ashley, British Kings and Queens, p. 800.

In Count Alexander, Homer-Saunders suggests we have located the original English Sanders ancestor. Count Alexander had two sons: (1) Sir Robert Alisaundre, who married into the powerful Baldwin family of Flanders and who during the reign of Henry III was baron of the Cinque Ports, commanding in 1224 two galleys of eighty sailors each in defense of England, and (2) John Alisaundre, first MP for Arundel, Sussex, in 1296 and, Homer-Saunders claims, the ancestor of the Sanders of Surrey. Homer-Saunders sees the newly minted surname Alisaundre used by Alexander's sons gradually evolving into the surnames Saunders, Sanders, and other variants in later generations.

But the claim that John Alisaundre was the original ancestor of the Surrey Sanders cannot be sustained. More than four hundred years of recorded Sanderstead history preceded John Alisaundre, and at least one person definitely bore the surname de Sanderstead (Leonard) a century before John Alisaundre was born. If we accept Homer-Saunders's notion that around 1300 John Alisaundre originated the Sanders line at Surrey, then we would also have to accept that an Alisaundre brought the Sanders name to Sanderstead at least four hundred years after the place was documented to exist by Duke Alfred. This is of course impossible. Homer-Saunders made other errors. His original publication, which informed our own research, names Eudo as the father of Count Alexander. But in a separately typed but undated document, he also states that Hugh de Montfort was Count Alexander's father.

The genealogy of Homer-Saunders should not be dismissed too hastily, however, as several features of his argument seem correct. Among others, Homer-Saunders's notion that the Saunders of Warwickshire descend from Robert Alisaundre makes good sense. This line of Saunders claims a coat of arms bearing three elephants' heads and is distinctly Norman in origin.

4. See David L. Word, Charles D. Coleman, Robert Nunziata, and Robert Kominski (2008). *Demographic Aspects of Surnames from Census 2000.* U.S. Census Bureau, Washington DC, 2008. Sanders is the 88th most frequently occurring surname in the United States, and Saunders the 439th. Updated estimated frequencies of occurrence in the United States for 2016 are 264,587 persons named Sanders and 80,484 named Saunders.

5. Guillam, an early cataloguer of English coats of arms, reported these arms for Sir Leonard years later, in 1611, allowing that subsequent generations of Sanders from Leonard are entitled to these insignia.

6. A small number of other shields for Sanders and Saunders also exist. See Burke, General Armory of England.

7. 7. J. H. Round, Stewart History: From Flaad Forward, Parts 1 and 2, at medievalgenealogy.org.uk, and J. H. Round, Origin of the Stewarts, in Studies in Peerage and Family History (Westminster: Constable, 1901).

8. The prefix "Fitz" is a derivation of the Latin "filius," meaning "son." Thus, for example, Walter FitzAlan is identified as a son of Alan. If Walter then had a son, that son would be called FitzWalter. There seems no equivalent term for women, who most often bore labels taken from family property. From a perspective of genealogical research, some care is advised here. A son of any person named Alan would be called FitzAlan; there are no a priori grounds for assuming any two FitzAlans would be related, since many persons named Alan might have sons bearing that label.

9. D.F. Renn, Norman Castles in Britain (London: J. Baker, 1968).

10. This history and genealogy of Walter FitzAlan, including his forebears both in Shropshire and Brittany, is given in The Stewart Society, The Story of the Stewarts (Edinburgh, 1901). See also Siege of Winchester at Tudorplace. com, describing King David's linkage with the FitzAlans. William and Walter FitzAlan were at the court of Maud, and both signed the Charter

of Houghmond Abbey at Oxford in 1141. See W. Metcalfe, History of the County of Renfrew (Paisley, 1905), p. 123.

11. A. Mackenzie, Rise of the Stewarts (London, 1935), p. 8; J. Stewart and D. Stewart, Stewarts of Appin (Edinburgh, 1880), p. 15.

12. See Scottish Castles Association website, Blackhall Manor—Its History and Restoration, 2010. The notion of a "cradle of kings" is taken from this source.

13. J. H. Round, Stewart History: From Flaad Forward, Parts 1 and 2, at medievalgenealogy.org.uk. In 1603, Queen Elizabeth named James I, the first Stuart king, as her successor.

14. Robert Croc is said to have received land in the Levern Valley by the Scottish king by 1170. Levern waters flow through Renfrewshire, home of the FitzAlans.

15. Numerous genealogies place Leonard as the son of Alan FitzWalter, and thus a grandson of Walter FitzAlan, but these are incorrect. Alan FitzWalter, born in 1140, could not have been Leonard's father since Leonard attained adulthood and achieved knighthood around 1166, at which time Alan himself would have been only age twenty-four and any son of his a very young minor. We have estimated Leonard's birthdate at 1143, placing him as a brother of Alan and the son of Walter FitzAlan. Instructively, Leonard named his eldest son Walter following the standard practice of the day for a father to name a first son after his own father. An accurate account of the names of Eschyna and Walter's children is difficult to provide because Scottish and FitzAlan genealogies vary substantially in their treatment of parents and children across two or more family generations.

CHAPTER TWO

Leonard

This is the story of Leonard de Sanderstead [1]. Leonard may be the first person in all of English history—or perhaps any history—to bear the surname Sanders, albeit in precursor form. The claim that Leonard among all people is the first of the Sanders rests on the observation that in Leonard's own time, the widespread use of inherited surnames had not yet come into being. That Leonard was sometimes called "Leonard de Sanderstead" is purely historical accident; Leonard simply owned a place of that name. He was merely "of Sanderstead." This Sanderstead label and its evolved abridgements attached to Leonard's descendants as inherited surnames of "Saunders" and "Sanders" finally came into accepted use. As a history similar to this is most unlikely to have occurred elsewhere, a claim for Leonard's first place in Sanders family history seems eminently reasonable.

Leonard entered this world about the year 1143 in a most unpropitious way. He probably was named for a saint—Saint Leonard of Nabloc—and there was a special reason for that. St. Leonard of Nabloc was an ancient French ascetic whose remains were largely forgotten until the onset of the Crusades. The Crusades commenced in the year 1090 and carried on intermittently throughout the next century. St. Leonard became known as the saint of prisoners, to whom one might pray for the safety and release of loved ones. Between the Crusades and the constant state of warfare in feudal Europe at the time, there could be found no shortage of prisoners or prayers for them, and churches dedicated to St. Leonard cropped up steadily over the whole of Europe in the twelfth century. But less appreciated is the fact that St. Leonard also offered hope for those in difficult childbirths [2]. Praying to St. Leonard might save the lives of ailing mothers and struggling babies—perhaps even including Eschyna and her infant son. In choosing to call this son Leonard, Walter and Eschyna seemed to be expressing their gratitude for the successful intercession of St. Leonard.

Leonard's earliest years were spent at Blackhall Manor in Paisley, in the Scottish county of Renfrew, an imposing structure built by his father. There is rather little to say of these early years for Leonard, except that they lasted a very short time. By about age eight, young Leonard, who at that time was called Leonard "FitzWalter" following the custom of the day, was sent away from home for schooling, perhaps initially in a monastery. This was followed by extensive training for knighthood, which, given his father's high position, probably occurred at the Scottish royal court. Here Leonard learned to read and write, including Latin, later adding lessons in comportment, honor, and loyalty. In his teens military training commenced, including horsemanship and the use of sword, lance, and battle-ax. Later on he would acquire his armor and mail and a fine steed trained for a knight's battlefield endeavors.

Leonard also learned by seeing these military skills in action. He probably accompanied Scottish knights in their travels to tournaments on the continent. In particular, he may have traveled with and even assisted Philip de Valognes, a friend of Leonard's father and Royal Chamberlain to Scottish King William (successor to David and Malcolm), in a tournament in northern France. If so, he witnessed the great tournament champion, William Marshall, as Marshall unhorsed, captured, and ransomed the unlucky Valognes before his eyes [3]. At about age eighteen, Leonard probably accompanied his father at the Battle of Renfrewshire, though as a squire, lacking knighthood, he undoubtedly remained behind the lines of combat, but here Leonard would have witnessed his father's redoubtable military leadership in action and felt some harsh outcomes of genuine warfare.

Leonard achieved knighthood in the Scottish court about the year 1163, his twentieth year. It may have been about this time that Leonard piously pledged one gold bezant annually to the convent at Durham, an act befitting his new obligations as a highborn knight [4]. Although the reason for his choice of this particular convent is unknown, Leonard's act can be seen as a political gesture underwritten by Leonard's father, a token of amity directed at Hugh de Puiset, who was archbishop of Durham, the political center of Northumbria. This region was frequently contested by Scotland and England, and Puiset played both sides in these struggles, extracting payments that allowed each army to pass through Northumbria without molestation. Leonard's gift then may have helped fill a Scottish political need to please Durham's grasping archbishop.

Marriage

Leonard's achievement of knighthood signified his readiness for marriage, at least in the eyes of those who decided such things. A choice of bride, though, was not Leonard's to make. Marriage fundamentally was viewed as a union between two families in a society organized mainly around genealogical facts. Romance played no part. The succession of national monarchs was driven exclusively by genealogy, and this same principle held throughout medieval society for awarding of noble titles, acquiring political positions, and inheriting property. Marriage was one of two main weapons in international diplomacy, whereby territories might be annexed either under force of arms or through strategic marriages that captured hereditary property rights in contested areas. Marriage was a key means by which Henry II, England's king in the time of Leonard, maintained control of much of France and other lands. And in a less grandiose way, this is the setting in which decisions about Leonard's future in marriage were sorted out.

On one side of this marriage decision was the English royal family and King Henry II himself. Henry's territorial control was large indeed, encompassing land from the Pyrenees to Ireland, but in the time of Leonard he sought unambiguous control of Northumbria in the face of Scottish resistance. In Scotland, King William (the Lion) had recently ascended to the throne and made no secret of his own desire for Northumbria. From King Henry's perspective, a marriage for Leonard offered him an opportunity to penetrate the Scottish court with new allies for his own plans, and this goal he could serve by satisfying Walter FitzAlan's demands regarding Leonard's future. One imagines that Henry's support for this marriage came at a suggestion of Reginald Dunstanville, Henry's uncle and steadfast ally in important matters of state.

The other party to the marriage plan was Leonard's parents, Walter and Eschyna FitzAlan. From Walter FitzAlan's perspective as steward to the king of Scotland and the second most powerful person in the kingdom, a wife for Leonard should possess his high social rank and offer a means for extending the family's prestige, wealth, and political influence. Beyond all that, though, Walter would have sought assurances that Leonard be placed on a path to stewardship in England. This stipulation addressed the means by which the FitzAlan's family history of stewardship might be extended. Leonard's older brother Alan was slated by inheritance to become the next High Steward of Scotland, so prospects for Leonard necessarily lay elsewhere. It mattered mainly that the bride occupied a social station equal to his own and that King Henry would honor Walter's wishes for Leonard's future in England.

All this came together when Leonard was formally betrothed to Beatrice Dunstanville in 1166 [5]. Beatrice was Reginald Dunstanville's youngest daughter, born about 1149 [6]. From the perspective of Walter FitzAlan, this match could not have been better. Reginald Dunstanville was a son of England's King Henry I. Leonard thus married the English king's granddaughter and in this limited way joined the English royal family. And so, with this new arrangement, Leonard could anticipate another life, one joined irrevocably with significant events in England's twelfth century. Through this marriage,

Leonard gained a foothold in the country's ruling elite through his linkage to the fortunes and high reach of Reginald Dunstanville.

Leonard's new father-in-law, Reginald Dunstanville, was one of about fourteen or more children of King Henry I [7]. Only three of these were "legitimate," children of Henry's legal wife, and only these three were eligible for a future crown according to established rules of succession. But Henry's two legitimate sons perished at young ages, leaving only his daughter Matilda (Maud) as a successor. As political and military events unfolded after Henry's death in 1135, Matilda managed to rule for only a few months before a cousin, Stephen of Blois, wrested away the crown for good. Reginald Dunstanville and Walter FitzAlan had been together at Maud's court.

All of King Henry I's other children sprang from his liaisons with an assortment of mistresses [8]. Henry saw to it that all his children remained close and in time arranged advantageous marriages to secure their futures. Reginald Dunstanville was one of the eldest in Henry's family and would prove to be the most influential among them as time went by. As historians of the day noted, "Assessments named Reginald and his half-brother as the most powerful men in the kingdom," and, "Both (were) men of renown throughout the country for their wisdom and power..." [9]. After Henry I died, his son Reginald had received the coveted title of Earl of Cornwall [10] and came into possession of manors and lands throughout Cornwall, Devon, Kent, Surrey, and Wiltshire. Reginald is credited with having built England's earliest lineal castle along Cornwall's south shore and having stoutly defended his step sister Maud, ultimately unsuccessfully, in her claim to royal supremacy. When King Stephen died in 1154, Reginald Dunstanville quickly allied himself with the new monarch, King Henry II, Maud's son by a second marriage and thus (by complex genealogical reckoning) Reginald's nephew.

Throughout the thirty-five-year reign of Henry II, from 1154 to 1189, Reginald remained in constant attendance in Henry's Court, often traveling with the king, acting as a personal witness to more than three hundred royal land charters, including seventy-six in which he was the sole witness [11]. Some charters were grants of manors extended to Henry's supporters, but numerous others enforced new provisions to protect and preserve existing estates as part of Henry's new and clarified legal regime. Henry named Reginald chief advisor to his "young king" Henry, a son slated for the throne before his untimely death. Even in his strained dealings with Thomas Becket, the archbishop of Canterbury later assassinated by Henry's followers, Reginald acted as go-between. Equally important, Reginald several times took the field in defense of Henry's personal rule, suppressing insurrection at home and in support of the king's dealings abroad.

Reginald Dunstanville took care in planning marriages for his daughters, almost as if he paired his daughters' marriages as a family design: Sarah and

Matilda married in France, Hawise and Joan in Devon and Cornwall, and Ursula and Beatrice in Shropshire and Surrey [12]. Matilda (Maude) married the Count of Meulan; and another daughter, Sarah, married the Viscount of Limoges. Notably, King Henry himself officiated at Sarah's ceremony in Limoges [13]. Hawise became the second wife of Baldwin, the Earl of Devon; and Ursula married Walter Dunstanville. Though both were Dunstanvilles, Ursula and Walter were not closely related, if they were related at all [14]. Daughter Joan married Ralph de Valletort, Lord of Tremonton in Cornwall, and finally, Reginald completed the last of this family responsibility in league with King Henry II, arranging for his youngest daughter Beatrice to marry Leonard FitzWalter of Scotland.

One might suppose that Beatrice Dunstanville enjoyed a favorable early life growing up in a family of high nobility, but that was not exactly the case. She grew up in Launceston in Cornwall, chief residence of the Earl of Cornwall, as the youngest daughter of Reginald Dunstanville and Mabel FitzRichard [15], but her mother was largely absent during Beatrice's childhood. Mabel "fell into insanity" in the 1140s and was nearly invisible in Reginald's later career [16]. In medieval times, the notion of "insanity" was far from a medical diagnosis of mental illness. One might be adjudged insane for something as simple as recalcitrance in marital matters. But the notion of insanity was terrifying enough in those superstitious days when mental illness was attributed to the devil or sinful acts. For Beatrice at an early age, her mother's madness suggested that the devil could be close at hand. Following common practice Mabel was probably committed to a nunnery, most likely at Chertsey Abbey; there Mabel was buried in Beatrice's thirteenth year.

A child of Beatrice's status normally would have been schooled at home until age seven; without her mother this was probably accomplished by monks or household members. Key was learning to read and write and to discover her world through religious books and stories and exposure to the arts. But after age seven, she would have been placed in another household, one associated with the royal court, where she learned homemaking skills by observing kitchen preparations, waiting on tables, making beds, and other practical matters. But also included were lessons in riding, dance, archery, and music, as well as manners and customary practices expected for her eventual place in society, including all things necessary for managing the household of a noble or aristocrat [17].

Beatrice was about seventeen years of age upon her marriage to Leonard. The ceremony itself undoubtedly took place in England at a site selected by the Dunstanvilles. By tradition, the ritual itself was not a religious affair, the couple exchanging rings and vows outside the church, entering the church only afterward for a mass. Wedding festivities lasted nine days.

Property

   After the marriage arrangement of 1166 was settled, it remained for this compact to be executed in the form of property arrangements. Now, in Leonard's time the importance of property entitlements from marriage cannot be underestimated because property ownership guaranteed access, use, and eventually inheritances for a family of nobility, and some degree of personal prestige arose from great holdings. Yet more urgency derived from the fact that property ownership represented one of very few investment possibilities in a world lacking financial institutions for savings and trade of any kind, in which coinage was always in short supply, and in which predictable returns from financial accumulation and investment were otherwise absent. A prominent exception lay in owning manors, the chief units of agricultural production in twelfth-century England. Manorial organization called for *demesne*, in which land was set aside for the manor lord's use or profit, sometimes thought to be about ten percent of land or income. Land, property, and manorial control were the feudal lord's chief assets as foundations for acquiring and perpetuating family wealth.

   At his marriage, Leonard is said to have gained "great estates in Surrey" given to him by King Henry II [18]. These appear to have been four in number. Henry's conveyance of properties to Leonard reflected the strength of his desire for this union to be made, that is, for the value Henry placed on his agenda to strengthen Scottish relations.

   One property conveyed at this time, by far the most important from the perspective of family history, was the Manor of Sanderstead. Sanderstead lay in the northern section of Surrey about twenty miles from London. That Beatrice and Leonard used Sanderstead Manor as their principal dwelling seems clear, but the exact size of their new holding is not easy to grasp. Assessments of its size before Leonard generally suggest that the Sanderstead property comprised about 1,800 acres, almost 60 percent of the parish total [19], the remainder previously dedicated to separate royal control. During Leonard's residence there, records also show numerous land transactions in Sanderstead involving persons other than Leonard or his family. Some of these might have been tenants on Leonard's lands, but as a matter of history, many were in lands for which Leonard held no entitlement. Leonard probably held only some part of the 1,800 acres, perhaps 1,500 or so. If that is at all correct, then Leonard received the equivalent of one knight's fee in Sanderstead on his marriage to Beatrice. A "knight's fee" was a parcel of land calculated in Leonard's day to be sufficient to support one knight, including his family and esquires; his horse, armor, and weapons; and other aspects of a knight's livelihood [20]. For Sanderstead a calculation of this type might well equal a holding of 1,500 acres or so. Given Leonard's knight standing, the logic of such an arrangement, if not the scant facts themselves, seems compelling.

ANCIENT SANDERSTEAD

Etymology

For the Sanders descending from Sanderstead in Surrey, the question of ultimate origins of the Sanders surname provides some interest. The name Sanders ultimately derives from Sanderstead, but how the name Sanderstead came into being has not been established. Some Sanderstead historians suggest the place-name derives from the sandy soil of its region in northern Surrey. Sanderstead in this interpretation becomes the place of sand. This explanation is plausible, but an etymology of Sanderstead is also required since the place-name springs from earlier language and not modern English usage. As the Saxons held that part of England after the sixth century, we think that the place called Sanderstead acquired a Saxon name, rooted in Saxon language, perhaps in the seventh or eighth century.

There is no doubt that the word Sanderstead derives from Saxon roots, that is, from Frisian or Old High German language. The suffix stede or stead endures today in English from the Saxon language as referring to place, but the principal root sander has more than one interpretation. In one version, the term may be a diminutive form of Alexander, referring to Alexander the Great of Macedonia. Thus, Sanderstead becomes place of Alexander, though there is little reason to suppose that seventh-century Saxons were interested in or influenced by Greek history or mythology. The term Alexander also has another meaning that may have existed in early Saxon times. Alexander is the name of an edible plant, sometimes alternately spelled alisaundre, that originated in the Mediterranean region and was brought to England by the Romans [1*]. Here, Sanderstead becomes an abridgement of Alisaunderstead, the place where the plant alisaundre is found. This possibility intrigues because alisaundre finds its way into family lore at another juncture, albeit many centuries later, as an adornment to the family arms.

Another possibility is that the term sander could be an abridgement of early Teutonic terms sand and heri, or sandheri, an expression that was elided into a single term sander. The meaning of sand in this case is true or loyal, and heri refers to army [2*]. Sanderstead, in this interpretation, acquires a literal meaning—place of the loyal army. Here we can imagine Sanderstead as an early Saxon military encampment or site of some ancient Saxon skirmish. This account nicely captures a sense of the time when Saxon conquest of Southern England was underway, in roughly the same era that we might expect Sanderstead as a Saxon settlement to have come into being. We leave this matter of Sanderstead etymology preferring the latter version but with no final conclusion as to the ultimate meaning of this ancient place-name from which our surname derives.

Ancient Sanderstead

Ancient Sanderstead was one of many settlements in the old kingdom
of Wessex in the south of present-day England, a settlement and manor
neither large nor small by the standards of the day [3*]. The settlement of
Sanderstead lay within the kingdom of Wessex, the greatest of the Saxon
strongholds, and Sanderstead holds within its own history a bit of Saxon lore.

Wessex was a particularly successful kingdom of the West Saxons, one
of a number of Saxon tribal alliances that began in England in the sixth
century and flourished thereafter in the southern part of England. Although
these early Saxon kingdoms were little more than tribal enclaves occupying
land equivalent to no more than a county or two in scale, they were neither
rudimentary in social, political, or military organization, nor were they
provincial in outlook. These kingdoms looked toward Europe and later the
Holy Roman Empire for example and leadership, and Saxon royalty routinely
visited the continent. As each local kingdom had its own royal line, often
complexly intermingled with one another, the number of kings and queens in
earliest England is astonishingly large. Ashley points out that there have been
a thousand kings and queens in Britain, and all but forty-three preceded the
Norman Conquest of 1066 [4*].

Through Wessex history, what little we know of Sanderstead is associated
with Saxon royalty. King Alfred the Great claimed the Wessex throne in the
year 871. In this same year, first mention of Sanderstead in the written record
is found in the will of a certain Alfred, often called Dux or Duke Alfred,
whose testament is usually dated to the year 871. The full text of Alfred's
will has survived [5*]. The honorific dux perhaps is useful, highlighting a
distinction between Alfred of Sanderstead and his contemporary, Saxon King
Alfred the Great.

> Duke Alfred died seized of 32 hides (one hide generally
> equals 100 to 120 acres) in Sandersted (written Sonderstede)
> and in Selsdune in Sandersted which he bequeathed with
> his livestock and all appurtenances to Werburg his wife for
> life and afterward to Aldhryth, his daughter and her issue
> and if she had none, then to his next of kin by his father's
> side [6*].

Duke Alfred also held titles of alderman in Surrey and Kent. That he
died in 871, the same year that King Alfred took command of Saxon forces,
hints that he perished at the hands of the Danes with whom Alfred and
the Saxons were at war. In this clash he had some claim to heroism. The
Stockholm Codex Aureus is a high ornate richly illustrated gospelbook, still

in existence, of eighth-century Kentish origin, and it holds an old English inscription found in the margins of an interior page. The inscription records that the book was once successfully ransomed from a Viking army for gold bullion by Ealdorman Alfred of Kent and his wife Werberh. Alfred thereupon presented the book to the high altar of Christ Church Canterbury. This event suggests why Athelred, Archbishop of Canterbury, supervised and blessed Alfred's will in later years [FT 7*].

Alfred's will makes it clear that the Sanderstead property was, in Saxon legal terminology, bookland rather than folkland. The distinction mattered. Bookland was land obtained under royal Saxon charter, in contrast to folkland, which had no such charter. Folkland could not be easily alienated, but bookland could be removed from entitlement of any landholder at the king's discretion. In Alfred's time, Sanderstead was identified as bookland, while nearby Horsley and Lingfield were called folkland. Thus, Sanderstead was under direct royal control.

Sanderstead appears in Saxon records again, this time about the year 964, nearly a century after the will of Duke Alfred. In this record, we learn the following:

Athelfleda, fifth wife and queen of King Edgar, mother of St. Edward, King and Martyr, daughter of Ordmar, gave Sandersted (written Sandalstede) with 18 hides and the church, and Lingfield and Langhurst with 2 hides, to the Abbey of Hyde [8*].

By 961, Sanderstead was the property of Athelfleda, wife and queen of King Edgar of England, he a direct descendant of King Alfred the Great. They were married about 960, but it is highly doubtful that Athelfleda was Edgar's fifth wife as this record states [9*]. She had been a childhood friend of Edgar and was sometimes known as Athelfleda eneda, the white duck. Sometime shortly after the birth of their only child, Edward, about 962, Athelfleda either died or was estranged from Edgar and in any case was buried at Wilton in Wiltshire by 964. At or near her death, Athelfleda left property at Sanderstead to St. Peter's Abbey at Winchester and not to Hyde Abbey as this record states [10*]. This gift paralleled her husband Edgar's program for monastic reform, aimed at strengthening the monasteries through endowments and other benefits.

Athelfleda's gift of Sanderstead to St. Peter's gives us our first glimpse of the property itself. Athelfleda ceded eighteen hides (one hide is about 100 to 120 acres) and the church at Sanderstead and an additional two hides from Lingfield and Langhurst to the abbey, in all about three square miles of land. The gift likely was a form of endowment for the abbey, whereby it would receive rents from the land and tithes from the church at Sanderstead. But notably, the gift did not include all the available acreage, nor did it include Sanderstead

Manor itself. From these scant records, it appears that Sanderstead Manor and fourteen hides of land (of the thirty-two hides originally mentioned by Duke Alfred) were retained for the royal family's use at Sanderstead. This arrangement held until the year 1066, when all of England underwent upheaval.

In 1066, the Normans from northern France crossed the English Channel to gain complete control of England, thoroughly routing the Saxons and other ancient tribal federations. It may rightly be said that the Normans were a colonial power in England, though they themselves speedily adopted English history as their own and settled in for good. Following the conquest, one of the first Norman acts was to survey their conquered land, to learn something of their new possessions, to identify properties for division and allocation, and to make assessments for taxation. The result was the Domesday Book, covering virtually all of England, the first survey of its kind in Europe. The Domesday record includes a detailed account of Sanderstead, the entry for which is as follows:

> Land of St. Peter's of Winchester in Wallington Hundred: The Abbey of St. Peter's of Winchester holds Sandersted. Before 1066 it answered for 18 hides (1800 acres), now for 5 hides. Land for 10 ploughs. In lordship 1. Arable land consists of 10 carrucates (or 1000 acres) of which one is in demesne. 21 villagers, one cottager with 8 ploughs, 4 slaves. Wood at 30 pigs. Value before 1066, 100 shillings. Later 7 Pounds; now 12 Pounds: however, it pays 15 Pounds. [11*]

This Domesday record of 1086 states that Sanderstead remained under authority of St. Peter's Abbey, answering for Athelfleda's eighteen hides before 1066 but only five hides by 1086 [12*]. An abrupt shift in landholding at Sanderstead took hold in the new Norman scheme. Under Norman authority reorganization took place for a large portion of Sanderstead around the time of the Conquest, removing thirteen hides previously within the abbey's purview and perhaps changing other working relationships as well. This notion is buttressed by Domesday's statement that Sanderstead contained one "lordship," a term not used before by Athelfleda, and that Sanderstead had risen in value despite its reduced acreage. The nominal manor lord then was the Abbot of St. Peter's. This arrangement seems to have carried forward without any further changes to the manor's legal status until the time of Leonard, when Henry II gave Sanderstead Manor to Leonard as a gift of marriage.

Taken together these facts produce a final arithmetic for the parish of Sanderstead in Leonard's time. Sanderstead today is said to consist of 3,151 acres, which accords with Duke Alfred's idea that the whole was thirty-two hides, assuming about 100 acres per hide. Saxon royalty following King Edgar partitioned the land such that fourteen hides, about 40 percent of the parish total, were set aside for use at royal discretion. It may be that the Manor of Purley in Sanderstead lay on these lands. The remaining eighteen hides, roughly 1,800 acres, carried forward to Domesday as heritable land, of which five (500 acres) were formally attached to Sanderstead Manor, the other 1,300 acres lying outside manorial control. Of this larger 1,800 acres, about 1,000 were arable, the other 800 suitable only for grazing or in woodland.

The historical question of Sanderstead Manor's passage from ecclesiastical to private ownership is uncertain because older deeds do not address how St. Peter's Abbey lost control of the manor that it held nearly a century before, in 1086. Most likely, the event that removed Sanderstead from abbey control was Henry II's issuance of his 1164 Constitutions of Clarendon, a pronouncement of sixteen articles that curtailed church ownership privileges [21]. This especially applied to those church properties for which no recognized ecclesiastical leader was then in place. St. Peter's Abbey by 1100 had fallen into disarray and intermittently lacked an abbot during Henry's reign. Henry gathered numerous properties and placed many of them in the hands of favored nobles. It seems that Leonard and Beatrice gained Sanderstead directly from Henry as a consequence of the Clarendon Edict, no more than a year or two after the edict was issued. After their marriage, the couple legally and unambiguously could be addressed as Leonard and Beatrice de Sanderstead, and the manor continued in family control, albeit briefly, after their demise.

Near Sanderstead is a village and parish called Warlingham in Tandridge Hundred. Leonard received lands there, as part of the marriage agreement. This Warlingham land, however, did not include the Manor of Warlingham, controlled at that time by Bermondsey Abbey. But a nearby Warlingham property called Creuses, later Creuses Manor, had been split off from Warlingham Manor at some early date. Some historians suggest that "Creuses Manor" is a corruption of "Carew's Manor," suggesting that this name arose when the Carew family gained its possession in the late 1300s. This is undoubtedly incorrect [22]. Records show that Creuses lay in Sanders family hands as early as the 1200s if not before [23]. Creuses Manor lay in Leonard's son's possession following Leonard's death and in fact remained intermittently in Sanders family hands until the late 1500s.

King Henry also conveyed a manor called Clandon Regis to Leonard and Beatrice, a holding lying in a tightly packed collection of manors near

Guildford, Surrey's most important town at the time [24]. Guildford was a center of some concentrated wealth; Henry himself celebrated Christmas there on at least one occasion. Clandon Regis, as the name suggests, was a royal property held by the king for his own profit, but after Henry's gift to Leonard and some subsequent owners, the name changed permanently to West Clandon. Clandon Regis bore Leonard's symbol of three bulls' heads, but these bulls' heads are shown sporting "ducal coronets," a heraldic symbol reserved for persons of royal descent, suggesting that this manor was held as dower land for Beatrice [25].

Yet another Surrey property given to the young couple was the Manor of Downe, lying adjacent or very near to Clandon Regis. At some previous time, the Wattevilles, a propertied Norman family, held Downe Manor and Leonard's Warlingham property as well. Downe Manor like Clandon Regis displayed Leonard's signature symbol, the three bulls' heads, and also employed ducal coronets adorning each bull, reflecting Beatrice's royal connection. This meant that Downe Manor as well as Clandon Regis were held for Beatrice's security if her marriage failed by reason of annulment, divorce, or death [26].

Time has obliterated any evidence of additional Surrey holdings for Leonard, if indeed there were more. Leonard's coat of arms can be found in manors in both Horley and Charlwood in the south of Surrey, but these probably resulted from much later family attachment to those places.

At least one additional property came to Leonard, not in Surrey, but in Shropshire. The place came to be called Leonard's Lee, part of a larger estate known as Idsall or Shifnall, controlled by the Dunstanvilles. The property lay not far from FitzAlan's holdings in Shropshire and was in all likelihood conveyed to Leonard as part of Beatrice's dowry, a gift to the new husband, supplied by the Dunstanville family on behalf of Beatrice. At the time of the earliest record, Leonard was characterized as an "early tenant" of Dunstanville. The land in question was described as a meadow or clearing, known as a "legh" or "lega" (in modern usage, a "lea"). As the property itself was called Leonard's Lee, Leonard himself entered a Shropshire legal record under the name Leonard de Lega [27]. For Leonard's own descendants in Shropshire, the label "de Lega" (later, "Lee" and "Leigh") persisted as a surname long after Leonard passed away.

So it was that Leonard on his marriage to Beatrice received not only numerous properties but also a responsibility to supervise them successfully. This involved holding manorial courts in which as lord he ruled absolutely, levying fines or other punishments and seeing that lands continued in productive use. Leonard also must have ventured across Surrey intermittently, gauging progress in crop cultivation and animal management as required to keep all his manors solvent. His continuing need was to assure personal gain from manorial production in support of his personal and social obligations and professional activity elsewhere.

Leonard's Work

King Henry's substantial property investment in Leonard as support for his marriage to Beatrice Dunstanville meant that he actively entertained ideas on Leonard's future. Though Leonard offered no immediate influence on the Scottish court, he did bring to Henry his knightly prowess, considerable education, and noble background. Leonard joined the administrative cadre who underpinned Henry's efforts to formulate and implement his new approaches to governance [28].

The reign of Henry II is most famous for having initiated legal reform, aiming to establish uniformity in laws that heretofore varied according to those administering them, usually large land barons themselves. Henry introduced juries and the notion that guilt or innocence might be determined rationally in court, rather than by forms of combat between contestants or by forms of torture intended to reveal God's will in the matter at hand. In like manner, he established rules of land ownership and inheritance that brought a modicum of order to hotly contested property claims. In all these reforms Henry gained the support of the baronial class, but it fell to others to see that Henry's legal system took hold in practice. Under Henry, the beginnings of government bureaucracy, the standardization of procedures and some consistency in their widespread implementation, came into being. Leonard among others was of great use in this scheme of things.

Henry made use of his hunting estate at Woodstock in Oxfordshire as often as he could and set aside properties for his numerous attendants and administrators to carry out their duties in locations near Woodstock. One of these was the Manor of Combe, and it appears that Leonard gained temporary possession of Combe for the duration of his royal assignments. As of about 1167 Leonard undertook work in royal administration, observing the work of royal stewards and learning procedures that routinely confronted royal governance. One focus would have been on documenting the hundreds of land transactions that dominated England's royal domestic business. Leonard's position as a trained knight also called for him to engage military actions as the king directed. Assignments were intermittent, permitting Leonard some time to manage his own manors and tend to family affairs in Sanderstead.

During Leonard's frequent and extended stays in Oxfordshire, Beatrice attended to all kinds of manorial detail back in Sanderstead. As Lady of Sanderstead Manor, Beatrice required extensive knowledge of law as it pertained to manor rights and requirements and needed to understand financial management and accounting, agriculture, and textile production. [29]. As an example, one contemporary woman in a position comparable to

Beatrice's itemized her principal efforts, which included (a) keeping tenants' houses in repair, (b) sorting out complaints and legal disagreements for local courts, (c) letting out land and property to tenants, (d) solving problems arising from troublesome workers, (e) managing a large staff of household workers, (f) supervising repairs and buying new materials, (g) overseeing food preparation for large numbers of people, (h) making medicines and watching over the sick, and (i) on occasions helping to arrange local marriages [30]. For Beatrice, the weight of these kinds of responsibilities extended beyond Sanderstead to include Warlingham, Clandon Regis, and Downe Manor.

These early times also marked the beginning of family life for Beatrice and Leonard. Among what may have been numerous children of the young couple are four sons we have positively identified: Walter, sometimes called Watkin, born about 1169; Leonard, born about 1171; Richard about 1173; and Stephen about 1175 [31]. Throughout the 1170s and 1180s, childbearing and the rearing of children eventually extended into arrangements for these sons' education, and, at least in the cases of Leonard and Richard, their training for knighthood were dominant concerns. In the 1190s marriages were arranged. In all these instances, Beatrice and Leonard would have relied heavily on their contacts in the royal court and other places in Oxfordshire as Sanderstead offered little in the way of useful social connections. Even their own manors of Downe and Clandon Regis lay about twenty miles away, distant enough to deter frequent contact. Locations for Leonard's work in Oxfordshire were about eighty miles from Sanderstead, suggesting that Beatrice must have arranged numerous extended visits there on family business following two or three days of wearisome travel.

About 1172, Leonard appears to have been placed on a path to stewardship, receiving appointment to the household of a certain Thomas Basset, an owner of numerous manors, a former sheriff of Oxfordshire, and an itinerant justice for several counties near Oxfordshire. In addition to his judicial activities, Thomas Basset was named "custos" (guardian or custodian) of the Honour of Wallingford from 1172 to 1179 [32]. The appointment was a significant one not only for Thomas Basset but, as it turned out, for Leonard as well. The so-called Honour of Wallingford began a century before as a land grant in Berkshire and Oxfordshire made by William the Conqueror. This evolved through various hands in the next century to embrace even more manors spanning several English counties. Its significance was that the Honour served as a semiautonomous political entity with advantageous tax assessments and legal preferments. By the time of Henry II, the autonomy of this Honour had begun to fade, but the term "Honour of Wallingford" in Leonard's time still retained many of these distinctions [33].

Leonard's appointment as Thomas Basset's knight in 1172 probably resulted from the initiative of Reginald Dunstanville and his particularly close ally, Richard de Lucy, England's chief justiciar, who possessed the inclination and power to make such arrangements. At least part of their motive was to join Leonard with ongoing family relationships. Thomas Basset had sometime before married Alice Dunstanville. Alice was a sister of Walter Dunstanville, who had married Ursula, daughter of Reginald [34]. So it was that Leonard's wife, Beatrice de Sanderstead, was Ursula's sister and both Walter and Alice Dunstanville her in-law siblings. This triangular relationship between Leonard's extended family, the Bassets, and the Dunstanvilles governed much of the life stories of all of them. In somewhat later years, Walter Dunstanville's son, also named Walter, married Petronilla FitzAlan of Oswestry, Leonard's close relative. Witnessing that ceremony were Dunstanville's cousins, the Bassets.

A decisive event in 1173 diverted attention away from King Henry's legal agenda when an insurrection arose involving Henry's jealous, reaching sons, another event in a long train of skirmishes that can only be described as venal [35]. A rebelling army of mercenaries organized by these sons gathered at a place in Suffolk called Fornham. There they were met by Henry's army of three hundred knights, supplemented by local fighters, a force assembled by several of Henry's leading barons, including Reginald Dunstanville, Leonard's father-in-law, and Thomas Basset. Henry's army prevailed, putting an end, however temporarily, to his sons' unquenchable ambitions. Leonard probably was among the king's forces; later events suggest that Leonard may have particularly distinguished himself in this skirmish.

Shortly after the Battle of Fornham, in 1174, Leonard, now called "a knight of Thomas Basset," acted with a certain Hugh de Bocland, sheriff of Berkshire, to assess tallages (land taxes) in that county. Eyton explains, "The great feature in the Law and Finance of the fiscal year now ended was the tax, levied on the king's demesne and on the lands of the late rebels. And it is to be noted that, in each county, the person levying the said tax was usually the contemporary sheriff, but that in very many instances the said sheriff had one or more assessors. (In this circumstance) Hugh de Bocland, sheriff of Berkshire, was coupled with Leonard, a knight of Thomas Basset" [36]. So it was that in 1174, Leonard's work as Thomas Basset's knight fell within the scope of Basset's custodianship, in which Leonard worked to levy taxes for the king under the auspices of the Honour of Wallingford.

Following his actions in support of the king, Thomas Basset's stock with Henry II rose sharply. Throughout the second half of the 1170s, Basset remained in regular contact with the king, attending him in such diverse places as Nottinghamshire, Yorkshire, Shropshire, and Staffordshire, accompanying the king on ceremonial occasions and witnessing some royal charters. The year 1179 was a particularly notable time for Thomas Basset and for Leonard. Basset resigned his custodianship of the Honour of Wallingford in this year because, as we learn, "Thomas was this year appointed Justice in Eyre for Berkshire,

Oxford and several other counties and in the list of justices errant for Pleas of the Crown and Common Pleas, and for imposing and setting the Assizes" [37]. He also was appointed a member of the Curia Regis, a post he held until 1172. All this is to say that Thomas Basset gained a lead role in Henry II's plans for implanting new justice. But more than that, Henry granted Thomas Basset the Oxfordshire Manor of Hedington in the Hundred of Bolendon and other large tracts of land outside Oxford's city gates—all this, according to Henry, for Thomas's "services in diverse wars" [38].

A New Stewardship

By 1179, Leonard had been in Thomas Basset's service for perhaps seven years, accompanying him in war, legal actions, and perhaps even in the latter's consultations with the king. But circumstances changed when Basset resigned his Wallingford custodianship. The title was then awarded by Henry II to Thomas's son, Gilbert Basset. If history is any guide here, the king also named a steward to assist the custodian, and this was Leonard. Thus by 1179 Leonard held his new title, "Steward of the Honour of Wallingford" [39], thereby satisfying Henry's promise to Walter FitzAlan and joining his family's long tradition in this kind of position. Leonard was then about thirty-four years of age. At the same time, the new Basset arrangements at Hedington probably included some manorial residence for Leonard. Stewards typically received an entitlement of half a manor in addition to direct compensation for the duration of their appointment, and at this time Leonard seems to have relocated to the Hundred of Bolendon in Oxfordshire. His location may have been at Whitfeld, a town in Bolenden not far from Hedington. In 1180 Leonardus de Whitfeld witnessed a property transfer involving the Basset family [40].

We learn that in 1187, the Steward of the Honour of Wallingford accounted to the king for several sums in pardons granted to Gilbert Basset, and to Ranulph de Glanvill, Gilbert Pepard, Alan Basset, Robert de Witefielde and William Paganell [41]. In later years, jealousies arose among Henry's other sons that fueled further conflict with their father, with the result that some factions declared their support for Prince John. Among them were the three Basset brothers and a certain Ranulph de Glanville. This evidently impolitic action by the Bassets and Glanville, whatever it was, provoked King Henry's wrath, not least one suspects because these families had been his own strong supporters in years gone by. And so in 1194 it fell to Leonard as Steward of the Honour of Wallingford to intercede again with the king, this time King Richard, on the Basset's behalf. Leonard seems to have done well here; Ranulph de Glanville and the Bassets satisfied the king by paying fines for their disloyalty of four pounds each, except for Gilbert, who as Lord of Hedington paid eight [42]. That Ranulph de Glanville, a chief adviser to Henry on legal reform, had some part in this intrigue and that he chose to be represented by Leonard is less surprising when we discover that Glanville had married a Valogne, of the same family that arranged with Reginald Dunstanville for Leonard's marriage to Beatrice nearly two decades before.

Coat of Arms

If Leonard's achievement of his Wallingford stewardship in 1179 did not represent a significant gain in his social status, which had always been high, it did provide overt recognition of his new political importance. He now exercised direct authority, delegated to him by the king, over a large set of manors spanning several counties. This new authority may have prompted Leonard to consider the fledgling but rapidly growing practice of adopting a formal knight's shield. The idea had come to England from France only a few decades before and was enthusiastically taken up by knights and higher nobility in England to enhance their own aristocratic identities. In England the practice began about mid-century [43]. As a knight, Leonard possessed a shield, but an ordinary shield reflected no personal distinction. So sometime after 1179 Leonard found reason to create his own knightly image.

Now, how Leonard designed his own shield at this time is important to us, because it presents the single opportunity we have to learn about Leonard's thinking, his private views. Leonard's shield has come down nearly intact as the Sanders family coat-of-arms, interesting even today as a family relic for those descending from Leonard himself. But what is it that Leonard chose to say? How did he represent himself? As shields necessarily employed symbols to represent ideas, we imagine Leonard must have consulted a scholar, perhaps a monk, to find appropriate symbols for a shield of his own design.

The appearance of Leonard's original shield is known [44]. It carried several very specific features. Importantly, it contained a chevron, the inverted V. The chevron signified valor in military action, denoting that Leonard served in war and in some particularly distinguished way. The Battle of Fornham seems a likely venue for that, though there were numerous actions throughout Leonard's first decade as a knight in which he might have participated. The chevron is key in determining when Leonard actually adopted his arms. As almost all of Leonard's military service took place in the decade of the 1170s, his design of a chevron-bearing shield signifying his knightly actions must have taken place after that. A strong possibility is that Leonard prepared his shield in anticipation of a new crusade to the Middle East, formal preparation for which began around 1189, the year Richard succeeded his father Henry as king of England.

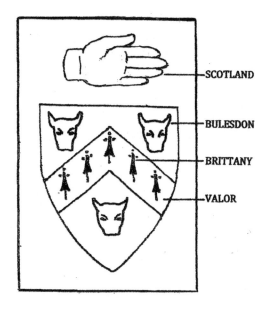

Decoded arms of Leonard de Sanderstead. See text for an explanation of symbolic representations.

On the chevron are numerous small symbols representing ermines. With these, Leonard evoked an enduring symbol of Brittany, the home of his forebears [45]. That Leonard chose these ermines to adorn his shield bespeaks a certain pride with which he held his family's ethnicity and how he wished himself to be known. The point is not small because Bretons were not Normans, and Normans dominated the landscape of English nobility. Thus Leonard used this opportunity to perhaps defiantly proclaim his own Breton background in a world riddled with Norman entitlement [46].

Leonard also selected a symbol for his knight's crest, a sinister (Latin meaning "left") hand extended. In his day, crests were not attached at the top of the shield as in later heraldry. The extended hand may have been placed in either a vertical or horizontal position, and as hand gestures were as important then as now, some specific statement was made by Leonard with this choice. Use of the hand itself generally signified the virtue of loyalty, suggesting that Leonard prized the ideal of loyalty and offered this unwaveringly to his king, his stewardship, and to his family. But his choice of the left rather than a right hand carries another meaning, one more familiar in his time than in ours. We often associate the Latin term "sinister" with some notion of "evil" or "darkness," but a secondary meaning in Latin usage referred to directionality. Today we conventionally picture directions in relation to "northernness," which means we see east on the right and west on our left. But in medieval times, directions were often reckoned relative to east, in the direction of the rising sun. Facing east, then, we find south symbolized by our right hand and north by the left [47]. In Leonard's case, he employed the sinister hand to symbolize north. "North" in England refers to Scotland, the land of Leonard's father and the place of his birth.

Finally, there is the matter of the three bulls' heads. Why Leonard chose bulls' heads is perhaps best illustrated by a parallel case. An example from Leonard's world is found in the Bolyn family (famously, Anne Bolyn, wife of Henry VIII). The Bolyn coat of arms is virtually identical to Leonard's, an inverted chevron separating three bulls' heads. "Bulls" in the Bolyn example simply reflect the sound of their own name, which in early English form was "Bullen" [48]. Leonard's choice followed similar logic. He chose bulls to refer to his own name, that is, the name he used in Oxfordshire. His shield design emerged sometime after his ascent to the stewardship for the Honour of Wallingford, the most important position he was to attain in his career of service. The Basset's Manor of Hedington, formerly a royal manor, lay in an Oxfordshire Hundred called Bolendon, earlier known as Bulesdon [49]. As Steward of the Honour of Wallingford, Leonard would have served as de facto governor of Bolendon, executing all manner of legal and managerial responsibilities as they fell upon him. One expects, then, that while in Oxfordshire and exercising his duties as Steward of the Honour of Wallingford, Leonard came to be called "Leonard de Bulesdon." If Leonard's bulls symbolized Bulesdon, they then spoke to Leonard's new identity as Steward of the Honour of Wallingford, precisely as his personal crowning achievement would warrant.

And so we grasp Leonard's full thinking in designing his shield. Using only a few symbols, he offers us a stunning recapitulation of his own life, emphasizing those things he deemed most important—his Breton origins (ermines), his birthplace in Scotland (sinister hand), his military achievement as a knight (chevron), and his ascent to an important stewardship (bulls). Thus not only is Leonard arguably the first of the Sanders (Saunders), he is also the most enduring, as his coat of arms has survived largely intact for the last eight hundred years as an encoded version of himself.

The Sanders coat of arms in modern depictions differ from Leonard's in several respects. Leonard's primitive arms were suitable for placement on a shield, as a symbol carried in battle. But as heraldry grew more formalized, so too did embellishment of arms. Derivative forms of the Sanders arms used by Burke and later authorities exhibit changes made in later historical periods [50]. Among those, most importantly, Leonard's sinister hand has been replaced with a new crest, a demibull, forelegs extended, thereby obliterating Leonard's reference to his Scottish beginnings. For the Sanders described here, modern arms typically also include an adornment of "sprigs of alexander," which are included as a canting device, an alliterative play on the Sanders surname

[51]. Mottos also are often attached, but these bear no heraldic significance. Finally, arms are sometimes "differenced," that is, emblazoned with additional symbols that reflect verified family branches. But with all these changes, the prominence of Leonard's three bulls' heads remains fully intact.

Passages

Two senior figures in Leonard and Beatrice's lives fell in the 1170s. Walter FitzAlan, Leonard's father, died in 1177 and was interred at Paisley Abbey, the Cluniac establishment of his own construction. Just two years before, Reginald Dunstanville, who had so greatly impacted the de Sanderstead marriage, also passed away and was entombed in the august Reading Abbey in Berkshire, where other royals lay. In the same decade, the three sons of Thomas Basset— Gilbert, Thomas, and Alan—grew into adulthood. These sons would lean on Leonard's support in the decade to come.

Leonard's position in the affairs of the Bassets was not only ambassadorial; it also involved family. Leonard was fifteen to twenty years senior to Basset's sons, far deeper in experience and contacts, and he became something of a central figure in their young lives. In the early 1180s Thomas Basset arranged property entitlements for his three sons. It is well that Thomas made these bequests, because he died shortly after, in 1186. His eldest, Gilbert, received entitlement to the Lordship of Hedington. His next son, Thomas, inherited some longstanding Basset holdings in Oxfordshire. The youngest, Alan, obtained, among other properties, a Wiltshire manor called Winterbourn [52].

Young Thomas Basset married Philippa Maubanc, a wealthy heiress from England's western county of Cheshire. In past decades, the Maubancs like the FitzAlans migrated to England from Brittany, and these families were likely to have known one another from their mutual west country involvements. For this reason, Leonard undoubtedly played some part in the Maubanc marriage negotiations with the Bassets. Leonard's wife, Beatrice, probably also joined in these Basset family discussions as part of their inner circle, as she was sister-in-law of young Thomas Basset's mother, that is, his aunt. Later events in Leonard's story suggests that Leonard's link—and perhaps Beatrice's—to this Maubanc family turned out to be as important for the de Sandersteads as for the Bassets.

The death of Reginald Dunstanville in 1175 had consequences for both the Dunstanvilles and the Bassets. As was not uncommon in those times, the king, Henry II, confiscated all Reginald's lands on his death, preserving for the Dunstanvilles only those lands previously given in marriage. Thus the great estates held by Reginald as Earl of Cornwall fell back to the king's possession, and all this Henry gave to his ten-year-old son, Prince John, who in time inherited the English throne.

Crusade

In 1189, King Henry II died and was succeeded by his son Richard I. Richard's passion was to launch a new—a third—Crusade to the Holy Land, and this desire he effected at once. Our question is whether Leonard joined this Crusade. It may be that Leonard produced his new coat of arms specifically for use in the Crusades, creating these arms to adorn his shield about 1188 rather than around 1179, when his Wallingford appointment initially took place. This and other indirect evidence suggests that Leonard, like so many of his cohorts in Oxfordshire, might have participated and that, if he did, he returned to England after a year or so of service. Leonard's brother, Alan FitzWalter, Royal Steward of Scotland, joined the Crusade in 1189 and was back in Scotland by 1191. Gilbert Basset, Leonard's lord for the Honour of Wallingford, became a great enthusiast and supporter of the Knights Templars, the central prop of Europe's crusading effort in the Middle East. Did Basset's contributions result from Leonard's urging? We do not know. But we do know that the three Basset brothers abandoned their support for Prince John and threw it wholeheartedly behind King Richard once the Third Crusade got underway [53]. Furthermore, we note that Leonard set aside profits from some Sanderstead lands on behalf of the Crusaders [54].

In the end, we have no certain evidence that Leonard participated in the Third Crusade, but circumstantial evidence suggests he did. He returned home for only a short continuation at Wallingford. By mid decade, King Richard appointed his own brother John (later, King John) custos of the Honour of Wallingford and placed Gilbert Basset, the former lord, in the stewardship position formerly occupied by Leonard. These reassignments suggest that Leonard dealt directly with Prince John, as he laid out the particulars of the Wallingford portfolio for Prince John and Gilbert Basset's future use. This incidental contact suggests a familiar relationship between John and Leonard that bore fruit in later years. But these changes also marked the conclusion of Leonard's ties to Oxfordshire and the occasion on which he retired to Sanderstead.

Leonard evidently passed away at Sanderstead around the end of the twelfth century, about 1199. As his time came to a close, Leonard de Sanderstead might have looked back on his years of military involvement, the changes he had seen and been a part of in the legal reforms of Henry II, his years with the Bassets, his stewardship of the Honour of Wallingford, the successes and failures of his own manors, and his three decades of marriage to Beatrice and their joint efforts to raise their sons. How Leonard felt about all these things we cannot know, but he bore something of family loyalty, military prowess, administrative skill, and knightly idealism, and that must have colored the rest.

NOTES

1. Guillam in his authoritative Display of Heraldry of 1611 provides a
    Sanders genealogy cited in the Advenie of Carmarthenshire. In this
    work Guillam referred to "Sir Leonard," and we followed that usage in
    our previous work. These are incorrect. The honorific "Sir" for knights
    had not come into use in Leonard's time; this usage was adopted by
    genealogists who assumed any knight must carry the title "Sir" as
    in later centuries. Leonard was not known as "Sir Leonard" by his
    contemporaries.

2. Wikipedia, St. Leonard, Women in Labor. "Through prayers (to St.
    Leonard) the queen of the Franks was safely delivered." See also
    Catholic Encyclopedia, St. Leonard of Limousin.

3. Knights and Tournaments—Medieval History—Scotland's History, at
    educationscotland.gov.uk.

4. J. Stevenson, Illustrations of Scottish History from the Twelfth to
    the Sixteenth Centuries (Glasgow: Maitland Club, 1834), p. 18 and
    footnote, stating that "Leonard, designed son of Alan, Steward of the
    King of Scots, who is noted in the Liber Vitae of Durham as bestowing
    a bezant yearly on the convent, was probably also a son." We elsewhere
    have corrected this genealogy but cannot closely date the record of
    Leonard's gift to Durham. Two factors suggest a date about the time
    of Leonard's knighthood. Durham lay in the contested zone between
    Scotland and England, but nothing in Leonard's subsequent life
    suggests he retained close ties to Scottish affairs. This implies that the
    gift was made at a young age while he remained linked to the Scottish
    court, a point reinforced by the fact that this record is of Scottish and
    not English origin. Second, the gift itself is of modest value, fitting
    perhaps for a young knight but probably inadequate for Leonard's
    status in later years. Bezants were unusually high-quality gold coins
    from the Middle East, brought to England by returning Crusaders.
    They generally were not used in trade but rather were reserved for
    formal or ceremonial occasions.

5. The marriage arrangement came about in part through the efforts
    of Philip de Valognes, the aforementioned royal chamberlain, who
    was Walter FitzAlan's key ally in the Scottish court. Philip's particular
    value was that his eldest brother Peter previously served as steward for
    the influential Dunstanville family. Marriage negotiations between
    the FitzAlans and Dunstanvilles were a matter the Valognes were well-
    positioned to handle. Walter FitzAlan was acquainted with Reginald
    Dunstanville from their old military alliance of the 1130s and 1140s,
    whose days were now many years past. But with help from the Valognes,
    Walter FitzAlan succeeded in finding this extraordinary match for
    Leonard, a daughter of Reginald Dunstanville.

6. Lineagekeeper's Genealogy, Reginald de Dunstanville/Beatrice FitzRichard, Family Group Sheet at famhist.us.

7. M. Ashley, British King and Queens (New York: Barnes and Noble, 1998), p. 511.

8. Reginald himself was a son of Sybil Corbet, daughter of Robert Corbet, Knight.

9. J. H. Round, Stewart History: From Flaad Forward, Parts 1 and 2, at medievalgenealogy.org.uk. The source of the second statement is from an historian of the day, Matthew Paris, found in G. Scrope, History of the Ancient Barony of Castle Combe in the County of Wiltshire (London: Nichols, 1852), p. 24.

10. Reginald Dunstanville was created earl by King Stephen in 1140, an action affirmed by Maud in April 1141. J. H. Round, Dictionary of National Biography, vol. 47, 1885–1900.

11. Many mini biographies, Charters of Reginald Dunstanville, at teachergenealogist007.com; and in R. W. Eyton, The Court, Household and Itinerary of Henry II (London: Taylor, 1878).

12. Information on all these marriages is scattered. Our focus aimed at discovering the social statuses involved and how these might reflect Reginald Dunstanville's view of Leonard.

13. R. W. Eyton, The Court, Household and Itinerary of Henry II (London: Taylor, 1878).

14. G. Scrope, History of the Ancient Barony of Castle Combe in the County of Wiltshire (London: Nichols, 1852). A more extensive treatment of Dunstanville genealogy can be found in Foundation for Medieval Genealogy: Dunstanville, at fmg.ac. Chroniclers of the age may have confused Dunstanville identities following this marriage. Reginald comes down to us in available literature as "Dunstanville," although in his time he probably was called "FitzRoi" or "FitzHenry." Ursula would have taken the Dunstanville name following her marriage, and that name was recorded for lands she acquired from her father. This may have led to past confusions. We cannot resolve the surname issue here but retain use of the label Dunstanville for Reginald in this article to be consistent with most literature.

15. For Dunstanville information, see Famhist.us/genealogy.

16. Prokasy Ancestry, Rootsweb, 2016.

17. B. Gorman, Medieval Life: Squires, Maidens, and Peasants. Yale University, New Haven Teachers Institute, 2016.

18. Advenie of Carmarthenshire, in Frances Green Papers, Havorfordwest Library, Pembrokeshire. In that collection, the statement by Geraldus (a.k.a. John Rowland) is that the Saunders "first settled in Surrey and had large grants of land and manors in that county made by the crown.

Leonard de Sanderstead had the Manor of Sanderstead given him with other great possessions in Surrey."

19. In ancient times, in the year 964, Saxon Queen Athelfleda gave Sanderstead with eighteen hides of land (perhaps 1,800 acres if we assume about 100 acres per hide) to St. Peter's Abbey of Winchester. More than a century later, in 1086, these facts had not changed. But these eighteen hides did not include another fourteen in Sanderstead set aside by a Saxon king before that time.

20. S. Harvey, The Knight and the Knight's Fee in England (Oxford, 1970). The term "knight's fee" in fact means "knight's fief," an amount of land required to fully support one knight. This amount depended upon the degree of land development, soil fertility, topography, and so on. The better the land, the fewer acres required to support a knight. In practice, some experts have suggested that this might have been any amount from two to ten hides (one hide might amount to as few as 60 acres or as many as 120) and even as many as twenty hides or more. No record has been found showing how knight's fees were limned in practice.

21. Yale Law School, Constitutions of Clarendon, at Avalon Project.com.

22. The Watteville family held Warlingham Manor among its many properties at an early date. At some point a portion of this manor was split off and given the name Creuses. This name adhered to the new Manor of Creuses after its subinfeudation from the Manor of Warlingham.

23. O. Manning and W. Bray, History and Antiquities of the County of Surrey (Wakefield: Surrey County Library, 1974).

24. Victoria County Histories. We used these sources for manorial histories in Surrey, Shropshire, Oxfordshire, and Wiltshire. All can be accessed at British History Online.

25. The entry in the Surrey Victoria County History for Clandon Regis displays three bulls' heads without coronets, but these coronets are indicated in the detailed heraldic description that follows. A dower holding preserves a woman's enduring right to dower land. A husband can use this land for profit but can sell only with his wife's permission.

26. The king had the exclusive ability to employ full crowns as a symbol of ownership, but smaller ducal coronets could be used by nonruling members of the royal family. Beatrice fit this description, but Leonard did not. See Karl R. Wilcox, Parker's Heraldry, A Dictionary of Heraldic Terms, 2011. The coronet is described as a small crown, or a crown borne by those who are not sovereigns; but generally synonymous with crown.

27. W. R. Eyton, Antiquities of Shropshire, vol. 1 (London: Smith, 1859), pp. 314–316.

28. A. Farazmand, Handbook of Comparative and Development Public Administration(New York: M. Dekker, 2001).

29. P. Knapp and M. von Zell, Women and Work in the Middle Ages, in Sandra Dodd, atsandradodd.com/sca/womenandwork, 2007.

30. From C. Adams, et al., *From Workshop to Warfare: The Lives of Medieval Women*(Cambridge: Cambridge University Press, 1983), pp. 6–11.

31. All these birthdates are our estimates, but various facts in all these sons' lives suggest a birth order as we have given it here.

32. Banks/Dean Genealogy, Thomas Basset, at GordonBanks.com, p. 210.

33. J. Hedges, History of Wallingford (London: Clowes, 1881), p. 286. Also see K. Keats-Rohan, Genesis of the Honour of Wallingford, at Academia.edu.

34. G. Scrope, History of the Ancient Barony of Castle Comb in the County of Wiltshire (London: Nichols, 1852).

35. At issue in all these struggles was vanity and greed, a warped sense of entitlement to land, wealth, and control by young royalty. In none of these cases does one find even a hint of ideology or idealism, that one might struggle for such things as country, religion, or justice.

36. R. Eyton, The Court, Household, and Itinerary of Henry II (London: Holborn, 1878), p.184. Also see E. Foss, The Judges of England: With Sketches of their Lives, vol. 1 (London: Longmans, 1848), pp. 176, 262. The timing of Leonard's cooperation with Bocland in Berkshire coincided with an effort of Reginald Dunstanville, Leonard's father-in-law, who as sheriff of Devonshire attempted to dissuade rebellious barons there. The implication is that the tallages Leonard collected were intendedly punitive, to discourage restive barons in Berkshire.

37. Banks/Dean Genealogy, referencing Basset Charters, W. Ready, ed., and E. Foss, The Judges of England: With Sketches of Their Lives, vol. 1 (London: Longmans, 1848).

38. J. Parker and W. Grey, Guide to the Architectural Antiquities in the Neighbourhood of Oxford, part 1 (Oxford Record Society, 1842), p. 285; see also B. Stapleton, History of Kidlington, Oxford Historical Society Publications, vol. 24, 1893, p. 8.

39. Our estimate of the timing of this appointment rests on the amount of experience Leonard by then had accumulated in Basset's employ and the timing of Basset's resignation of his Wallingford custodianship in favor of new appointments in 1179. That Leonard in fact became the Steward of the Honour about this time seems probable because this stewardship later defended Basset's sons against the king's accusations. The record specifically stating that Leonard was dapifer (steward) is

found in the Eynsham Cartulary, vol. 2. Oxfordshire Historical Society, vol. 51.

40. W. Stewart-Parker, The Compton Basset Charters, Methodological Problems of Standardization in Medieval Source Material,2010.

41. J.K. Hedges, History of Wallingford (London: Clowes, 1881), p. 286.

42. J.K. Hedges, History of Wallingford (London: Clowes, 1881), p. 289.

43. The Heraldry Society.com.

44. Leonard's original shield is described in the Advenie of Carmarthenshire, located in the Francis Green Papers at the Cultural Services Department, Public Library, Haverfordwest, Pembrokeshire, Wales. The record derives from Guillam's Display of Heraldry, which was published in 1611 and again in 1678. Guillam was the first to categorize and publish a work on heraldry.

45. Wikipedia, Flag of Brittany. The ermine symbols are taken from the traditional arms of the Duke of Brittany.

46. See K. Keats-Rohan. Domesday Descendants: A Prosopography of Persons Occurring in English Documents, 1066–1166, vol. II: Pipe Rolls to Cartae Baronum. The author notes the intense love of the Bretons for their native country, described as follows: "The Bretons are unusual among mediaeval peoples for having a highly developed awareness of their national and cultural distinctness, and this awareness was not confined to the predominantly Celtic Bretons of the west of Brittany. Eleventh century seigneurs of northeast Brittany, not yet part of the Norman adventure but having contact with Normans and holding Norman lands, were apt to give charters referring to themselves with clamant pride as Haimo, patria Brito or Riuallonius, Britannicus gente. This patriotic pride may account for the marked hostility towards the Bretons displayed by some Norman chroniclers, though it did not hinder, and may have helped, their advancement in England under the Norman kings. Once we are aware of this Breton particularism, the shape of the Breton settlement in England after 1066 and the subsequent conduct of Bretons in English affairs, based as these were on Breton politics, becomes immediately intelligible."

47. English Language and Usage: Sinister Hand at Stackexchange.com. In later years the sinister hand was replaced on the Sanders' coat of arms by a demibull attached to the shield, forelegs extended, and that is the symbol we see today.

48. See M. Odrowaz-Sypniewska, Boleyn Family Tree, at Angelfire.com. The principle that no two families should bear precisely the same arms was generally accepted by the fourteenth century. Disputes over ownership of arms was frequent before this time. See H. Rogers, The Pageant of Heraldry (New York: Pitman Publishing, New York, 1955), p.

65. A connection between Bolyn arms and Leonard's is not necessary to explain the origin of either.

49. H. M. Cam, Liberties and Communities in Medieval England (Cambridge University Press, 1963), p. 121.

50. Bernard Burke, A General Armory of England, Scotland, and Ireland, 1st ed. (London: E. Churton, 1842).

51. Canting is described in detail intheheraldrysociety.com.

52. J. C. Blomfield, History and Antiquities of Bicester (Oxford, 1894), pp. 150–151; and J. C. Blomfield, History of the Present Deanery of Bicester (Oxon, 1894), pp. 1–3. See also W. Kennett and T. Delafield, Parochial Antiquities, vol. 1 (London: Clarendon, 1818).

53. The Third Crusade was the greatest military effort of medieval Europe, and it failed. In 1191, Richard conquered Cyprus and sold it to the Knights Templars. Returning from the Crusade in 1192, he was captured and held for ransom by the French king. In 1194, Richard was released, but he later was killed at a siege in France in 1199.

54. "Acknowledgment by Ralph de Pappeworth (Leonard's grandson) of his obligation to secure the title of Sir Fulk Basset, bishop of London, to meadow land in Saundre, which he has granted to the said bishop, under a penalty of 40s. to the king; with renunciation by the said Ralph of the privileges granted to crusaders. Witnesses: Master William Passemer, canon of St. Paul's, London, and others. Wocking, 8 Ides 6 of November"(British History Online, Descriptive Catalog of Ancient Deeds in the Public Record Office, Record A. 4075, dated 1257). Leonard's action here cannot be interpreted as a "Saladin tithe" (a tax) for those not actually traveling to the Holy Land, which was paid once. Here Leonard provided support for crusaders as a recurring endowment from profits off the land. See Saladin tithe, wikipedia.com. For an extended discussion on Crusades taxation, see L. Blaydes and C. Paik, The Impact of Holy Land Crusades on State Formation: War Mobilization, Trade Integration, and Political Development in Medieval Europe, Working Paper (Stanford University, 2015/7).

NOTES FOR ANCIENT SANDERSTEAD

1*. The plant alexanders, previously known as alisaundre (Smyrnium olusatrum), is a stout herbaceous plant with a furrowed, much-branched stem, one to five feet high, bearing large shiny dark green compound leaves with broad, sheathing stalks and broad cut segments. It has small yellow-green flowers; its compound umbrels are pollinated by flies attracted in swarms by their heavy odor. The fruits are nearly black. The plant is native to the Mediterranean region and was formerly cultivated as a vegetable. It is now found wild throughout the British Isles.

2*. Henry Harrison, Surnames of the United Kingdom (Baltimore: Genealogical Publishing Co., 1969), p. 135.

3*. The size of Sanderstead in relation to other manors of Surrey is detailed in the Domesday record of 1086. See John Morris, Domesday Book (Chichester, Surrey: Phillimore, 1975).

4*. Mike Ashley, British Kings and Queens (New York: Barnes and Noble, 1998), p. ix.

5*. D. Whitelock, English Historical Documents 500–1042(Oxford University Press, 1955), p. 536.

6*. O. Manning and W. Bray, History and Antiquities of the County of Surrey, vol. 2 (Wakefield: E.P. Publishing and Surrey County Library, 1974), p. 568. See also Surrey Archeological Collection, vol. 4, p. 1., citing Kemble, Codex Diplomat, Cart. Anglo-Saxon, p. 492.

7*. Stockholm Reference Library, Stockholm Codex Aureus MS. A.135, ff. 9v-11r and ff. 115v-115v-116r.

8*. Manning and Bray, History and Antiquities, p. 568. Generally, a hide of land is a parcel of 60 to 120 acres depending on local practice.

9*. Records disagree on the marriage of Athelfleda to Edgar. Manning and Bray, drawing on Dugdale, suggest that Athelfleda was the fifth wife of Edgar, but Ashley (page 479) states she was his first wife, a claim enhanced by the fact that Athelfleda was Edgar's childhood friend, and that their son Edward was named king following Edgar. Had Athelfleda been the fifth wife, the previous four evidently would have been childless, leaving no heirs to the throne. Furthermore, Edgar had either one or two wives following Athelfleda. As Edgar lived only thirty-two years, the notion of his having had six or seven wives seems unreasonable. On the other hand, Edgar's dubious reputation as a womanizer was frowned upon by church figures, and it is not difficult to imagine how his escapades might have led contemporary chroniclers to a conclusion that he had several wives.

10*. Manning and Bray op. cit. p. 568. This record is one of several instances in which Sanderstead is linked to Hyde Abbey, but this is not technically correct. Hyde Abbey came into existence in the year 1110, more than a century after Athelfleda's gift. In fact she gave Sanderstead to St. Peter's Abbey in Winchester, which at a much later time became Hyde Abbey.

11*. J. Morris, Domesday Book, Phillimore, 1975. A carrucate of land is about 100 to 120 acres. Sanderstead in 1066 comprised about 1,000 acres of arable land. Land in demesne was that set aside for the exclusive use or benefit of the lord or owner.

12*. Ibid., Morris, p. 32c.

CHAPTER THREE

Sende Manor

 King Henry II died in 1189 and was succeeded by his son Richard. But Richard died in 1199 at a siege in France, and Henry's youngest son John, Richard's brother, took the throne. John continued earlier efforts to administer the law fairly, but his reign suffered uneasy echoes from times past, restive barons clamoring for better treatment. John frequently offered judgments favoring tenants over barons and held these nobles in overt contempt. John tightened forest laws [1] to deter hunting and logging and levied new and steeper taxes on them for his own income and in support of his unpopular military ventures in France. But John's inability to either address or stifle baronial dissent led finally to open rebellion and to the famous confrontation at Runnymede in 1215, the scene of the signing of the Magna Carta. In this John formally acceded to a detailed list of baronial demands, but the Magna Carta itself was not a political tract urging improvements of broader scope, standing in history more as a symbol than an act of reform. The agreement was largely ignored both by John and his successor Henry III, who came to power in 1216. Nonetheless, the term "parliament" as a notion of shared power entered the national language in 1240 under Henry III [2].

At Runnymede, standing with King John were several counsellors, including Thomas and Alan Basset, sons of Thomas Basset for whom Leonard de Sanderstead acted as steward. As we have seen, Leonard himself may have consulted directly with Prince John before his inauguration. So family fortunes were found in lofty places, and that is how we can view the family in the generations following the demise of Leonard de Sanderstead. The high political and social circles that enveloped Leonard's life persisted beyond his time. The people with whom Leonard dealt most closely remained central influences in the lives of the next generation.

But one important change occurred almost immediately. Two decades after Leonard's death, Sanderstead Manor ceased to be the family home. Following Beatrice, Leonard's widow, the focus of family history shifted away entirely from the Manor of Sanderstead to another manor in Surrey about twenty miles to the southwest, a manor called Sende. But the geographical dispersal of Leonard's family also went beyond Sende as a direct consequence of Leonard's last wishes.

Although we have no copy of Leonard's will, we can judge something of his bidding from subsequent possession of his lands. At issue is the distribution of the Surrey properties over which Leonard had direct control. These included Sanderstead Manor itself and other residual lands in Sanderstead and also his holdings in nearby Warlingham. Further, Leonard held the Shropshire property called Leonard's Lee, which lay in the Dunstanville Manor of Idsall. Finally, Leonard may have held some promise of continued family use of the Manor of Combe in Oxfordshire, which he acquired through royal administrative service. What Leonard did not control, however, were Beatrice's dower properties, the Manor of Clandon Regis near Guildford, and Downe Manor in Cobham, which abutted Clandon Regis. These holdings remained Beatrice's possessions following Leonard's death. How all these properties passed to Leonard's family is our question, as these assets underwrote opportunities for the next generation.

LINEAGE FOLLOWING LEONARD DE SANDERSTEAD

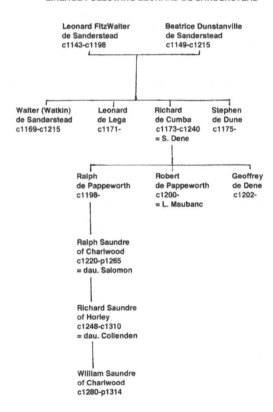

Source: Authors.

Beatrice de Sanderstead

As Leonard's wife, Beatrice was entitled to a one-third share of the Manor of Sanderstead, hers to hold for life or until she remarried. Beatrice gave up that entitlement almost immediately when she remarried about 1202, following a mourning period of a year or two. Her new husband was William Maubanc, he of Sende Manor, which lay not far from Sanderstead. Both were about age fifty at the time of marriage. But it was far more than close proximity of their manors that led to this union. William Maubanc was the son of Beatrice Maubanc and Ruald de Calne; Ruald adopted the Maubanc name after his marriage to this Beatrice. His previous identity of "de Calne" was taken from the town of Calne in Wiltshire, but at Calne he was born into a family named Croc [3]. As we recall from earlier days in Scotland, Robert Croc was Leonard's older stepbrother, suggesting that Ruald Croc (de Calne, Maubanc) was in some manner related to Leonard's own family. Thus his son William Maubanc completed a genealogical circle when he married Leonard's wife, Beatrice de Sanderstead. This link to the Croc family was not an isolated instance, as a certain Walter Croc appeared frequently in Sende records during Beatrice's time in the early thirteenth century [4].

Nor were the Maubancs strangers to Beatrice before the marriage. About 1180, young Thomas Basset of Oxfordshire had married Philippa Maubanc [5], she of this same extended Maubanc family. Leonard as Basset's steward probably had a hand in facilitating that marriage, and one might expect that in formulating marriage arrangements Beatrice collaborated with her cousin, Alice Dunstanville, Thomas Basset's mother. So a deep familiarity among all parties undergirded Beatrice's betrothal to William Maubanc.

After her marriage, Beatrice joined her new husband at Sende, bringing to this new marriage her dower properties of Clandon Regis and Down Manor [6]. But the fate of these manors following the marriage is unclear. Both may have passed to Maubanc control as a marriage settlement, but Beatrice also retained some claims as later records attest [7]. Some parts of these properties remained available for family use. In the time of Beatrice, the Manor of Downe came into the hands of a certain Deodatus de Dune, but her own son Stephen also called himself "de Dune" [8]. Likewise, the Manor of Clandon Regis was occupied alternately by the Westons and Bovills, but some part of that manor called Pappeworth was routinely used by family members from both William's and Beatrice's side. In this case, Clandon Regis and Sende shared a boundary, and Pappeworth probably lay near that intersection [9]. Some Sende lands Beatrice gave to Newark Priory (called "novo loco"), following a precedent set earlier by William Maubanc's parents [10]. But as further part of the marriage agreement, Beatrice must have received some property entitlement at Sende, either for herself or, as it appears later, for her son Richard.

After Beatrice's remarriage, Sende Manor replaced Sanderstead as a nexus for her family's activities, suggesting that Beatrice wielded some continuing matriarchal influence on her own grown sons. She died not long after the year 1212 [11].

Walter (Watkin)

The inheritance practice of primogeniture dictated that the largest share of family property is passed to the eldest son, Walter, whom we know as Watkin [12]. Watkin directly inherited the Manor of Sanderstead and adjacent Sanderstead land, as well as land of unknown extent in nearby Warlingham. When Watkin came of age in 1190, he took up residence and paid a tax at Leonard's Lee, also known as Parva Lee, in Shropshire. Before 1194, Watkin was joined there by his brother Leonard [13]. But before his father's death, Watkin as eldest son agreed to vacate Leonard's Lee following his father's wishes, conforming to prevailing law that required the eldest son to agree that some family land might pass to other siblings [14].

Watkin died without issue in 1215. In his own will, he gave Sanderstead Manor with its approximate five hundred acres to Hyde Abbey "for the souls of our ancestors" and left his other Sanderstead and Warlingham lands to his brother Stephen and Stephen's heirs [15]. Significantly, this act permanently ended family ownership of Sanderstead Manor after fifty years of occupancy and returned the manor to its ancient owner, St. Peter's Abbey. St. Peter's of Winchester previously held Sanderstead but lost control of the property after the Conquest of 1066, and St. Peter's itself later folded. But this abbey was reestablished as Hyde Abbey in the year 1110, and Watkin's gift to Hyde finally restored the ancient arrangement. Following Watkin's action, the family's link to Sanderstead Manor was forever severed.

Leonard

Watkin's younger brother Leonard received family lands in Shropshire and established an enduring presence there. Like his father, Leonard attained knighthood and probably served a succeeding generation of the Dunstanville household. In Leonard's Lee (Parva Lee) as a property owner, Leonard was called "de Lega," as was his father. But later in the century his own offspring were sometimes called "FitzLeonard" before the identity of "de Lega" attached to them for good. From this Shropshire beginning arose a branch of the Leigh family (also, Lee), a name that has persisted through the centuries. Just as the Sanders derived their name in descent from Leonard de Sanderstead, so these Leighs also descended from Leonard de Lega, these Leonards being one and the same person [16].

Stephen

Stephen inherited land in Warlingham that likely included the property of Creuses (later a manor) and added lands in Sanderstead from his brother Watkin's estate after 1216. But of Stephen nothing more is known with certainty, save that at one time he resided at a property associated with Downe Manor, a holding once in his mother's possession. But there may be more to Stephen's story than meets the eye, as in some unexplained manner he seems connected to an enigmatic figure named John de Sanderstead.

JOHN DE SANDERSTEAD

A fair amount is known about the life of John de Sanderstead, a person of some distinction and wealth. We believe he was born about 1290 and lived to 1353. John acquired property in marriage and resided in Warwickshire. About 1315 he married Elizabeth, widow of Richard de Loges, and received the Manor of Chesterton in Warwickshire and Great Wyrley and Rodbaston Manors in Staffordshire [1**] On Elizabeth's death in 1337, this manor reverted to other heirs, although John retained the right to hunt on that property. John married again in 1349 to Margaret Harcourt, acquiring interest in the Manor of Moreton Daubeney. During these times, John de Sanderstead is found in numerous records in Warwickshire and at Winchester, in part because he was appointed sheriff for the Counties of Warwick and Leicester, a post he held at least until 1350. When John de Sanderstead died in 1353, Moreton Daubeney passed to previous owners, and it is only at this point we discover that John also had owned Creuses Manor in Warlingham, the property long in family possession from the time of Stephen and his father Leonard [2**]. John's name "de Sanderstead" and his ownership of Creuses Manor point directly at an origin for John in the family we have been describing, because the historical record states that a descendant of Watkin sold Creuses to Willoughby about 1353. From Willoughby the land passed to the Carews and eventually back to the Sanders after 1430 [3**]. In addition, John's contacts in Chesterton included the de Warwicks, who were known to the Salomons of Horley. A descendant of Leonard married into this Salomon family [4**].

John de Sanderstead poses for us an interesting genealogical dilemma, because we have no record of any persons from whom he might descend after Stephen, if indeed he did descend from Stephen. But how family history unfolded here is difficult to grasp. John's use of the label "de Sanderstead" is the first instance of its occurrence since Beatrice used the label in the year 1202, and we have found no other de Sanderstead following John. But John used the name as an actual surname and not merely as a descriptive term;

this occurs about the same time that other family members adopted the name "Sanders" for their own surname. Thus the name "de Sanderstead" in John's case cannot be taken literally—that is, it carries no implication that John actually resided at Sanderstead, but does imply a descent from Leonard's line. Using this name might have helped John establish a claim to the family's coat of arms. If John descended from Stephen, he likely would have been a great-grandson. We then should expect to find evidence of this lineage at Sanderstead or Warlingham for parts of the thirteenth century, but none has appeared.

Richard

The younger sons Richard and Stephen received shares of land in both Sanderstead and Warlingham, though precise descriptions of these inheritances have not been found. But records from the deep past give us the idea that Sanderstead lands outside the manor comprised perhaps 1,300 acres, divided mainly between Watkin and Richard, Stephen receiving the bulk of Leonard's Warlingham property. If that division resulted in approximately equal shares, then Richard received about 650 acres of Sanderstead land, which held some combination of arable land, pasturage, and woodland. There is no evidence of any manor on these lands, a fact that suggests why some of Richard's inheritance came in other forms. All this is part of the larger story of Richard, Leonard and Beatrice's son, who comes down to us in family history as Richard de Cumba.

RICHARD DE CUMBA

One legacy of King John I is that despite his disagreements with the baronial class, he continued the effort, begun by his father Henry II, of improving the method of governing. This was a historical transition, from less government to more, from chaotic rule to one aspiring to greater uniformity of laws and predictability of outcomes. In extending the reforms of Henry, John facilitated the long-term transition toward more orderly English government. This goal required a body of dedicated, educated, and respected administrators, those who could help erase the lingering legal arbitrariness of former times. From the narrow perspective of family history, Richard de Cumba can be seen as working in support of King John's domestic legal agenda.

Richard was born about 1173 and, following a familiar family pattern, achieved knighthood before 1194. His parents had numerous choices in selecting a family for Richard's training for knighthood—Walter Dunstanville comes to mind—but we have no source that clearly reveals their choice [17].

He married shortly thereafter, to Sybilla Dene, a widow of Robert de Icklesham of Sussex, who died about 1192 in the Third Crusade [18]. The Denes were a wealthy Norman family with major property holdings in the Counties of Kent and Sussex [19]. Richard's marriage itself came about perhaps because Ralph de Dene, Sybilla's father, was itinerant justice in 1170 for Surrey, Sussex, and other counties. In this position he would have encountered Thomas Basset and Leonard de Sanderstead, who engaged these same duties in Oxfordshire and elsewhere.

To support his marriage to Sybilla Dene, Richard received lifetime entitlement to several Sussex properties, including of one knight's fee in Dene, one-half fee in Friston, two-thirds of a virgate and additional rent in Buckhurst, and one-third of a salt pan in Pevensel Marsh, all gifts from heirs of Robert de Dene, Sybilla's uncle. Evidently, this initial living arrangement for the young couple was not entirely suitable, because in the year 1200, the church at West Dean was granted to Richard and Sybilla in exchange for the church at Friston [20]. Their permanent new home was the town of West Dean in Sussex, a settlement originally known as Eorlscourt, later Earlscourt, then Dene, and by 1199, West Dean. Interestingly enough, in the aftermath of the Conquest of 1066, the whole of West Dean was held by the Earls of Arundel, that is, the FitzAlan family from Oswestry, the family and birthplace of Richard de Cumba's grandfather, Walter FitzAlan [21].

de Cumba

In Surrey about the time of his marriage in 1194, Richard took on a personal identifying label of "le dignu," which can be translated loosely as "the noble." As Richard "le dignu," he sold one virgate (a quarter of a hide, about twenty-five acres) of Sanderstead lands in 1196 and around the turn of the century offered his "le dignu" signature in witness to two charters for Newark Priory at Sende [22]. Though using the term "le dignu" may seem tasteless self-aggrandizement, the facts suggest otherwise. The term "le dignu" referred to an office as "royal administrator," a position Richard inherited from his father but which at the time of inheritance involved no specific property entitlement. This interpretation is consonant with the common practice of the day to refer to offices as "dignities" and to acknowledge dignities as heritable [23], permitting Richard to use the label "le dignu" according to his father's plan.

As early as the 1170s Leonard de Sanderstead served as a royal administrator under Henry II and was permitted to use the Manor of Combe in Oxfordshire to enable his work near Woodstock, the king's occasional residence. Other kings after Henry II, including Richard and John, maintained this arrangement at Woodstock [24]. Manorial entitlements such as Combe for high-level administrators in the royal household were sometimes made for life (25). In Leonard's case, some agreement was contracted for extending family use of Combe Manor to his son Richard. Leonard's hand in this is evident here, because Richard used the term "le dignu" at least two years before his father's death [26]. If Leonard negotiated family continuation at Combe Manor with King Richard, that agreement was probably suspended beyond the time of King Richard's death in 1199. Subsequently, King John would have undertaken to assemble his own administration as his reign set in, and shortly after that Richard used the name "de Cumba," the familiar term for "Combe," for the first time.

But even as his appointment at Combe was being sorted out, Richard abandoned the label "le dignu" and used the name "de Dene" for the first time, drawing on his new attachment to Sussex. In this instance, Richard witnessed yet another Newark Priory Charter, but this time under the name Richard de Dine, a spelling frequently employed for records involving the Dene family [27]. But after that, Richard's use of the name "de Cumba" became permanent [28]. For Richard's part, he would of necessity share his time between home and work, between Sussex and Oxfordshire, a pattern of segmented livelihood reminiscent of his father.

The exact nature of Richard's administrative work at Combe is unclear, but by the turn of the century, warfare and chivalry were no longer adequate for the education of a knight, and new disciplines, reading and writing, had become essential (29). The English government was evolving into one of the most advanced and professional bureaucracies of the West, staffed by well-trained men. They worked in three main areas: (i) the Exchequer, for finance; (ii) the Curia, recording judgments of the royal court; and (iii) the Chancery, authoring official documents, such as charters and writs [30]. This organizational description, however, reflects a direction of evolution more than a carefully crafted design; and overlap of functions, uncertain authorities, and frequent inconsistencies were still commonplace. Richard's work probably lay in the Chancery, which positioned him to observe, facilitate, and write charters for property, not least for those to whom he was personally linked. It was for this reason that Richard's "de Cumba" label carried weight among those who sought royal approvals, as the term itself suggested royal proximity. The usefulness of Richard's "de Cumba" label probably came into play when in 1214 he was asked to represent Say family interests in an Essex county land dispute with the Mandevilles, stemming from a previous Say–Mandeville marriage. Party to the dispute was Geoffrey Mandeville, son of England's chief justiciar in the time of Henry II, and Richard's tie to this case may also have stemmed from an earlier FitzAlan–Say marriage. The outcome, however, favored the Mandevilles [31].

In the year 1210, Richard de Cumba vacated some land in Sende, evidently ceded by him from his mother, who herself held this property by agreement of Newark Priory. Richard's holding was purchased by three persons who also called themselves "de Cumba" [32]. They included Thomas and Gilbert Basset and a certain Geoffrey (here called Galfrido), who we expect was

Geoffrey Sackville, Richard's partner in other actions. Their purpose was to acquire dower land for Thomas's "marriageable daughter" (filia maritanda), an agreement surely encouraged by Thomas's wife, Philippa Maubanc, to endow her daughter Alice with new Maubanc land at Sende. That all parties to this Sende agreement called themselves "de Cumba" is not surprising when we discover that the Bassets also held royal administrative positions in Oxfordshire [33], but the case also illustrates how administrative appointments could be used for personal purposes. About five years earlier, the aforementioned Geoffrey Sackville finally gained control of Emmington Manor in Oxfordshire after years of delay, at about the time that Richard acquired his de Cumba identity. Richard's position may have allowed him to promote prompt attention to the Emmington charter, which incidentally lay in the Honour of Wallingford [34].

After his marriage to Sybilla Dene, Richard spent rather little time in Surrey. His intermittent affairs there dealt mainly with the sale of Sanderstead land, all of which was to a family named Pirle (later, Purley and like spellings). In 1218 Richard de Cumba conveyed one hide of land with other appurtenances to Nicholas Pirle, giving the king a halfmark to schedule a hearing before an itinerant justice to establish the legality of the transaction. For this, he also left a security deposit with the sheriff of Surrey. Three years later, Richard initiated another sale to the same Nicholas Pirle, but in this instance Pirle asked the Abbot of Hyde to confirm that the land indeed was not Hyde's. Finally, in 1234, twelve years after the previous sale, Richard conveyed another parcel to Robert Pirle, perhaps Nicholas's son [35]. Though these sales did not exhaust Richard de Cumba's holdings in Sanderstead, they did exhibit his dwindling dependence on profits from old family lands.

Sussex

Despite Richard's administrative commitments at Combe Manor, the County of Sussex, which lay immediately south of Surrey, became the center of Richard's life. In the decade following his marriage to Sybilla Dene (about 1195 to 1205) and their acquisition of a Sussex home at West Dene, the couple had at least three children, as well as Sybilla's son from her previous marriage, Ralph de Icklesham. Their own offspring included Ralph, probably the eldest, named for Sybilla's father; Robert, after Sybilla's propertied uncle; and Geoffrey.

Sybilla was one of four daughters of Ralph de Dene, and probably the youngest. The eldest was Ela, followed by Idonea and Katherine. Katherine did not survive long, and Idonea's marriage took her to Gatton Manor in Surrey. But Ela remained in Sussex, and her own activity drew Richard de Cumba's attention. Ela Dene was at least a decade older than Sybilla and was principal heiress following the death of her father in 1187 [36]. She married Jordan Sackville, ancestor to the Dukes of Dorset, about 1170 and brought to the Sackvilles the Sussex Manor of Buckhurst. The Sackvilles continue at Buckhurst to this day, an extraordinary span of occupancy of more than 850 years [37]. Ela's husband Jordan died in 1175 or 1176, her son Geoffrey by then only a few years old. Ela remarried, to William Marcy, but was widowed again before Richard married Sybilla in 1194. From Sybilla's marriage, Richard de Cumba had also acquired a fractional interest in Buckhurst Manor. Richard's subsequent closeness to the Sackvilles may have stemmed from this joint property involvement.

In view of his deep family background in stewardship and his position in royal administration, it may be reasonable to guess that Richard became the Sackville's family steward, a position that may have carried forward from Ela to her son Geoffrey in later years. Direct evidence on this point is lacking, but Richard's work life in Sussex began with Ela Sackville and continuously involved both the Denes and the Sackvilles, a set of relationships that shaped much of Richard's career in Sussex.

Ela's father Ralph endowed an abbey for monks of the Premonstratensian Order at Otteham in Hailsham, but owing to frequent flooding and other inconveniences, Ela undertook to relocate the abbey, refounding it at Bayham [38]. We expect that Richard advised Ela on this process; he witnessed the new Bayham Charter in 1205. Some years later, Richard was brought before a judge for overcharging on tenement rents also in Hailsham, an accusation from which he was exonerated. The Sackvilles held Hailsham property near the former abbey at Ottenham, and Richard probably managed this tenement on their behalf [39].

One year after Ela relocated Bayham Abbey, Richard witnessed another gift from Ela, this time to the monks of Lewes Priory [40]. This marked the first of several involvements of Richard with Lewes Priory, hinting that Richard actually may have twisted Ela's arm for this second religious gift, occurring as it did only a year after her first. Ela died two or three years later, but Richard's connection to Lewes continued on. He witnessed a charter for the manor of Atlingworth, near Brighton, which came under control of Lewes Priory. Richard also was involved in a direct transaction with the Convent of Lewes, for which he is said to have held an ancient demesne in the parish of Hammes. While Richard could have purchased this demesne for himself, it seems more likely that this "ancient demesne" would have been owned by some family there from "ancient" times, for whom Richard acted as proxy. This may have been either the Say family, whose ties to Richard stemmed from an earlier FitzAlan–Say marriage, or the Bassets—and specifically in Richard's time, Alan Basset of Winterbourne in Wiltshire. The Bassets gave the church at Winterbourne to Lewes Priory and were major benefactors of Lewes after that [41]. Gilbert Basset, son of Alan, landed in Sussex Court in a contest over payments to Lewes, in precisely the same session that found Richard de Cumba blameless in the matter of tenement rents. These connections to Lewes Priory in Sussex are our clearest suggestion that Richard maintained working ties to the Basset family initiated by his father in the previous generation.

In 1220 Richard and Sybilla teamed with Geoffrey Sackville to file suit for land in Gatton, near Reigate in Surrey, against a certain Hamo de Gatton. Sybilla's father, Ralph de Dene, once held a moiety (half) of the Manor of Gatton, which passed to his daughter Idonea (sister of Sybilla) and through Idonea to her husband. But Hamo de Gatton, following the practice of his father, had long failed to honor the moiety agreement, denying benefits to the manor's other half. The suit was thus lodged to rectify the injustice. In 1226 Richard, Sybilla, and Geoffrey Sackville evidently refiled their claim or continued on with the original, but the outcome in either case is not known [42].

Later Life

In 1226, Richard's wife Sybilla passed away, and we see no evidence of Richard, then age fifty-three, having remarried after that. He remained in Sussex at their home in West Dean. One year after Sybilla's death, Richard de Dene paid forty marks to King Henry III not to be dispossessed of this property, despite a legal effort of some Dene family members to dislodge him [43]. This was one of the few instances that Richard chose to use the name de Dene, no doubt to reinforce the fact of his Dene property ownership against this legal challenge. In those later years he probably continued to shuttle between Sussex and Oxfordshire, combining his obligations for royal administration at Combe with his continuing linkage to Geoffrey Sackville. The latter might have included some management of Sackville's Oxfordshire Manor of Emmington. Richard's separate obligations conveniently fused together at Oxfordshire, and one guesses that Richard spent a good deal of time at Emmington as a consequence.

Richard died about fourteen years after Sybilla, about the year 1240, at about age sixty-seven. At that time, his remaining Sanderstead lands and any entitlement at Sende Manor would have been distributed to his three sons. But Richard also created additional opportunities in Surrey. The necessity for this action arose because Richard's properties in Sussex were held for his lifetime only and could not be passed to succeeding generations. Richard's effort on behalf of his sons probably began in the 1230s and carried forward into his final years.

RALPH DE PAPPEWORTH

Richard de Cumba's eldest son, Ralph de Dene, was at times called Ralph de Pappeworth. This label "de Pappeworth" served Ralph much the way the label "de Cumba" served his father, that is, as a functional title that had nothing much to do with residence, reflecting rather some kind of work responsibility.

The same label was also used by Robert, Ralph's younger brother. Pappeworth itself was an estate lying within Clandon Regis adjacent Sende Manor in Surrey, held originally by Beatrice de Sanderstead, then, after her remarriage, by the Maubanc family. The first person of record to hold Pappeworth was William Maubanc de Pappeworth, the son of Beatrice's second husband.

William de Pappeworth and Richard de Cumba were contemporaries, belonging in fact to the same household, though in a technical sense they were not stepbrothers, sharing no parent in common. They were sufficiently close that William joined Richard in witnessing all three Newark Priory charters in those early days, when Richard was known as "le dignu." But their cooperation ran deeper and longer than that, running parallel to a strong current of bureaucratic evolution in English government.

King Henry III assumed the throne on the death of King John in 1216, beginning a reign that would last fifty-six years. But Henry was only nine years old as his reign commenced, and Hubert de Burgh as chief justiciar served as regent until 1127. In that period, as before, the professionalization of government proceeded apace, relying increasingly on written records for judicial writs, financial dealings, and property transactions. This steady dedication to systematic records-keeping produced an important side effect, forcing higher nobility and land barons, the greatest users of these governmental services, to create records of their own. They were pressured to hire clerks and accountants who could make formal records that matched government needs [44]. Clerks in those days required an ability to read and write and to have a passable knowledge of the patchwork laws of the era. Education of that kind usually meant that clerks were drawn from the ranks of nobility. Clerks frequently appeared in land charters as witnesses for the legal proceedings of which they were part.

BASSETS AFTER THOMAS

It serves our story to give some brief detail on the Basset descent from Thomas of Hedington, as these figures touch on our story in several places. Thomas Basset, for whom Leonard de Sanderstead served as steward, had sons Thomas, Gilbert, and Alan, but only Alan (–1231) had male offspring. Three of them matter here:(i) Gilbert (–1241), a close ally of Hubert de Burgh, chief justiciar and regent during the minority of Henry III. Gilbert's escapades landed him in and out of royal hot water over the course of his life; (ii) Fulk (–1259), following other ecclesiastical appointments, was elected Bishop of London in 1241; and (iii) Philip (–1271), who acquired much land across several counties and in time won appointment as England's chief justiciar. Philip in fact was the last of these before the office was abolished.

Alan Basset's home was Winterbourne Manor in Castlecombe, Wiltshire. He was a major benefactor of Lewes Priory in Sussex, having taken on that responsibility from his uncle Walter Dunstanville, who initiated it. This suggests that Richard de Cumba was in league with the Bassets as he engaged several actions at Lewes Priory and Convent in Sussex. Alan also held lands in Surrey, notably the Manor of Woking near Guildford, where both Alan Basset's and Richard de Cumba's sons appear together in the historical record with some regularity.

Against this growing bureaucratic backdrop, Richard de Cumba joined with Alan Basset and William Maubanc to establish a working relationship whereby those at Pappeworth would function as clerks for the Bassets. William de Pappeworth, Ralph de Pappeworth, and Robert de Pappeworth all clerked for the family of Alan Basset, all of whom aggressively sought property ownerships. The clerking arrangement began with William (Maubanc) de Pappeworth and gradually passed to Ralph and Robert in the next generation. In three instances, William de Pappeworth witnessed land transactions for Alan Basset, one in Essex County and two for "meadows and pastures" at Woking in Surrey [45].

Richard and Sybilla's youngest son, Geoffrey, is the only son who did not use the "de Pappeworth" label, exclusively referring to himself as "de Dine" (Dene). The tenor of Geoffrey's records suggest he did not engage administrative tasks. In one instance after Richard had passed away, Geoffrey specifically referred to himself as son of "Richard le Dine of Sende" as he sold meadows to Fulk Basset in Woking, near Guildford. At about the same time Geoffrey witnessed a Basset charter at Woking with his brother Robert. Geoffrey also gave land near Sende to Newark Priory, a gift witnessed both by his brother Robert and by Philip Basset [46]. But Geoffrey makes no further appearance in the historical record after that.

At Sende, Richard de Cumba's son Robert de Dene married Lucy Maubanc, probably the daughter of William Maubanc de Pappeworth. After William's death, Robert may have received the Pappeworth property as a marriage entitlement. But it is also possible that Robert had some claim to Pappeworth in his own right, because Robert's brother Ralph also took on the de Pappeworth identity in the same period of time. In any case, Robert's work focused on witnessing Basset transactions, in one instance for four crofts with a field, a moor, and meadow, and in another Fulk Basset's acquisition of Hamo's Moor. He also witnessed another property addition for a Basset heir, all of which properties lay either in Woking Parish or Woking Manor itself [47].

Ralph's record at Pappeworth resembles his brother Robert's, except that he once witnessed a land purchase in Sanderstead by Gilbert Basset, and on another occasion sold some of his own Sanderstead property to Fulk Basset. This was land that Ralph's grandfather Leonard had dedicated to crusader support, and which had passed to Ralph through his father. At Pappeworth Ralph engaged a certain Henry Ford and his wife Agnes in a suit involving Pappeworth land. Otherwise his attention was directed to Basset holdings at Woking [48]. But in 1237, Ralph, specifically identified as a son of Richard, was present at Woodstock, the king's temporary palace in Oxfordshire, to witness a charter involving the Bassets. On this occasion, Ralph's objective probably was to stand in for his father, perhaps infirm at age sixty-four, rather than as clerk for the Bassets, because this record does not identify Ralph as "de Pappeworth."

The question of Ralph's marriage is a matter of some difficulty, because only one record of Ralph other than at Pappeworth has surfaced. In it, we learn that Ralph married the daughter and sole heiress of Roger Salomon, knight, of Horley in the south of Surrey [49]. Yet this record most certainly cannot be true, because Roger Salomon was alive in 1263 and cannot have left an estate to his daughter until sometime after that. But Ralph de Pappeworth was born about 1198, and so would have been age seventy or more at the time of inheritance, if indeed he was still alive by that time. Furthermore, Ralph necessarily would have been about fifty years of age to have married Salomon's daughter. These facts make clear that the Salomon marriage occurred in the generation following Ralph de Pappeworth. We are able to assert with some confidence that a person named Ralph married the heiress of Roger Salomon, because two independent sources on Sanders genealogy, each proven reliable elsewhere, agree on this fact [50]. We thus conclude that Ralph de Pappeworth had a son named Ralph, and that the latter, not the former, entered this Salomon marriage [51]. Having eliminated the possibility of a Salomon marriage for Ralph de Pappeworth, we have no inkling of his actual marriage or place of residence if other than Pappeworth.

RALPH SAUNDER

Ralph de Pappeworth's son Ralph was born about the year 1220 and probably married about the year 1242. As suggested, he married the daughter and heiress of a knight named Roger Salomon, who held land in and around Horley in the south of Surrey [52]. The fact that he married Salomon's heiress is particularly important because it tells us that Ralph received property as a result of this marriage [53]. We learn that Ralph Saundre resided in Charlwood in 1243 shortly after his marriage, undoubtedly on land provided by Roger Salomon [54].

Most importantly, Ralph Saundre is the first person we have found to use the name "Sanders" as a surname, an early version that would later evolve into the more familiar forms, "Sanders" and "Saunders." Thus the surname

Sanders enters family history in this person Ralph, who was a great-grandson of Leonard and Beatrice de Sanderstead. It is at this point that the Sanders family assumed a specific identity—the name Sanders—that has served all subsequent generations. This idea of taking on permanent surnames, just as Ralph had done, later gained traction throughout much of England around the time of Edward II, whose reign began in 1307. Some have said this adoption began as a way for titled persons to distinguish themselves from their less exalted laboring countrymen, but it is also true that as English society flourished and its court system grew, the need for more exact personal identities in legal proceedings increased as well. Although one can find earlier exceptions, such as the Bassets in our story, surnames did not come into widespread use until the fourteenth century, that is, after the time of Ralph Saundre of Charlwood. So from Ralph's time forward, all family members would be known as "Sanders," albeit often in variant and unstandardized forms such as "Saundre", "Saunders", "Sandars", and other like-sounding spellings.

Guillam states that Ralph's father-in-law Roger Salomon was "of Horley and Charthwood (Charlwood)," but the distinction between Horley and Charlwood here is not particularly helpful. These locations lie in a tangle of jurisdictions [55], and we have no specific record of Salomon properties in Charlwood. In Ralph's time, the parish of Horley held several manors, including Woodmansterne (later Kinnesley), Langshott, Bures, Horley, and Lodge, but only Lodge among these is closely associated with the Salomons. Unfortunately, Salomon records for Lodge Manor appear mainly after 1330, nearly a century after Ralph's marriage into that family [56].

Roger Salomon (later also Saleman and Salmon, but not Solomon) apparently descended from a certain Stephen FitzHamon who by 1189 had established his lordship of properties in Burstow, a parish abutting that of Horley [57]. This family, known earlier by the name Hamo and renamed as Burstow, had established itself in Kent and Essex following the Conquest of 1066 and had come to Surrey at an early date. By the early 1200s the Burstow properties, of which there were two principal holdings, then passed to Stephen's son Roger de Burstow. Roger de Burstow in turn passed one of these, called "Burstow Manor," to his nephew John, and the other, known as "Burstow Lodge," to Roger Salomon, probably Roger de Burstowe's son or nephew. Thus Roger Salomon became lord of Lodge Manor at about midcentury, the same time that John acquired Burstow Manor in 1247. In 1263, Roger Salomon, calling himself Roger "at Logge" (Lodge), sold a parcel of Burstow land to Mary, daughter of William Dammartin [58]. This William Dammartin resided at the manor of Norton in Essex, once held by the Hamo family described here [59], reinforcing the notion that Roger Salomon was intimately linked to the Hamo/de Burstowe family. This linkage furthermore suggests, however lightly, that the marriage between the Saundres and the Salomons might have devolved from the earlier ties of Richard de Cumba and Hamo de Gatton. In this instance we can imagine Ralph de Pappeworth, summoning his Dene background, arranging the marriage of Ralph to Salomon's daughter, that is, drawing on the Dene-Hamo marriage that was the subject of his family's lawsuits in the 1220s.

Burstow Lodge comprised about 360 acres which straddled the Burstow–Horley boundary, leading to some confusion about the exact location of the manor. Whether in later years a separately named "Horley Lodge" split off from the original Burstow Lodge is uncertain, but in Roger Salomon's lifetime and for some years after, Lodge Manor seems to have been a single entity.

As noted previously, Roger Salomon died some time after his land transaction of 1263, placing his daughter's inheritance some time after that. But Ralph's marriage to her probably occurred about 1242, at least two decades before Roger's death. Thus Ralph and his Salomon wife may have resided in Charlwood for much or all of their married life. It seems that Ralph's opportunity to enjoy the title of manorial lord at Lodge came rather late in life. Of Ralph Saundre we know nothing more, save that he and his Salomon wife had a son Richard, born we think around the year 1248.

RICHARD SAUNDRE

Richard, son of Ralph Saundre had the good fortune to live in the latter half of the thirteenth century. Richard Saundre's times roughly coincided with the reign of King Edward I (1272–1307), counted by many as one of England's greatest kings [60]. Notably, Edward ordered reformations in feudal jurisdictions, taxation, and the legislative apparatus, curtailing baronial abuse of traditional local authority. Yet he also more firmly established the barons' foothold in an improved parliamentary system. In his time, he brought dissident Welsh and Scot leaders to some abeyance and improved the English claims to French territories. Whether such triumphs as Edward produced were felt in localities such as Horley is hard to say, but the England of Richard's lifetime was blessed with relatively good order and prevailing peace. Though he would not have known about it, it was during Richard's lifetime that Marco Polo undertook his historic journey to the Far East, signaling the beginning of long distance European trade and broadening awareness of the world around them.

Richard probably came of age about the time that Roger Salomon left his Lodge estate to his daughter, Richard's mother, and at some point came to control Lodge Manor following his own father's or mother's death. Perhaps around 1275 Richard married a daughter and co-heiress of William Collenden, a figure who seems to have escaped the historical record altogether [61]. Thus in his lifetime Richard gathered lands recently in possession of two other families, the Salomons and the Collendens. These inheritances are evidenced by the fact that both Salomon and Collenden symbols are included in the Sanders family quartered coat of arms (see Chapter Four).

Richard seems to have put his wealth to good use. In St. Bartholomew's Parish Church in Horley lies a stone effigy of a knight bearing the arms of Salomon, which dates to about 1315. His exact identity is said to be unknown. But of this monument the historian Edward Brayley writes, "the monument has no inscription, but there is a vague tradition that it was raised to the memory of Lord Sonds, or Sanders, resident at Coulsdon Court, thought to be the builder of Horley Church" [62]. This is indeed a tantalizing tradition, one that bears close inspection, because this person, "Lord Sonds or Sanders," seems to be our Richard Saundre of Horley and the knight's effigy the person of Roger Salomon, Richard's maternal grandfather.

Stone effigy of a knight bearing Salomon arms in St. Bartholomew's Church in Horley. Source: J. G. Waller, On the Monuments in Horley Church, Surrey Archaeological Collections, vol. 7, 1880, pp. 183–191.

We know that Roger Salomon was a knight, and that his manorial lordship passed through his daughter to her son Richard, who thereupon would be called "Lord Sonds or Sanders" of Lodge Manor. Inheriting Roger Salomon's estate placed Richard in position to honor his knighted grandfather whose bequest conferred property onto him. Roger Solomon's lifespan allows that he may have been instrumental in arranging Richard's marriage to Collenden, in that both were propertied figures—social equals—in Horley.

It is not correct to say that Lord Sonds or Sanders "built" Horley church, because parts of the church date to the twelfth century. Rather he added an aisle onto the existing church, a chapel or chantry dedicated to the memory and burial of Salomon family members. This work was completed by about 1315 with the cooperation of Chertsey Abbey, but construction would have been undertaken before that date. Richard would have been about age sixty at that time [63].

Brayley's "tradition" reflects uncertainty about whether the name of this manor lord was Sonds or Sanders, but this uncertainty itself is twofold: whether it refers to two entirely different people or to one person who might be called one name or the other. The latter is more likely, because the name "Sonds" ("Saunds") itself apparently derives from the name "Saunders." A casual tracing of Sonds records for the period places that family in the same locations of other Saunders records, whether they be in Sanderstead, Gatton, or Horley, though at somewhat later dates. The Sonds established a property in Dorking near Gatton called "Sondes Place" in the fourteenth century, mimicking the earlier establishment of "Sanders Place" in Charlwood [64]. The surname "Sanders," in other words, provides a better temporal fit to Brayley's account.

Brayley's "tradition" also suggests that Richard was of "Coulsden Court," a place to the north of Horley, lying not far from Sanderstead in Surrey. But we think Brayley's Coulsden reference a mild inaccuracy, based on the fact that Richard married into the Collenden family, and probably was said in his day to be of "Collenden Court," not "Coulsden Court," property presumably lying in Horley. As Richard had indeed married William Collenden's co-heiress, he undoubtedly held Horley property once in William Collenden's possession.

By way of summary then, we believe that the Horley effigy depicts Roger Salomon, who was a knight of Horley and lord of Lodge Manor. We estimate that he was born about 1200 and died about 1265. This estimate of birthdate rests on the prior genealogy, suggesting his daughter—his heiress—married Ralph Saundre about 1242. If she was about twenty years of age at marriage, then she was born of Roger Salomon sometime around 1222. If Roger married about 1220, then he would have been born in slightly before 1200, about the same time as Ralph de Pappeworth, father of Ralph Saundre. We know that Roger was alive in 1263, but may have died shortly after, if his lifespan paralleled others of his time, who typically died in their mid-sixties.

Records suggest that Richard Saundre and his Collenden wife had sons, Ralph, Roger, and perhaps William. Both Ralph and Roger used the surname Salomon, following the name originally attached to Lodge Manor, but William did not. In later years this younger Ralph Salomon inherited Lodge Manor but died early, leaving Lodge to his brother Roger, but when a son of Ralph reached adulthood, the manor passed back to that son, named Roger Salomon. The continuation of Salomon possessions of Lodge Manor may mean that Richard had himself taken the name Salomon as a way to preserve this property entitlement and passed that usage on to his next generation. This notion is underscored by the fact that Roger Salomon, son of Ralph, in the 1330s acquired a property called Salomon's Manor in Warlingham, closely situated by Creuses Manor, long in possession of descendants of Leonard de Sanderstead [65].

Richard's probable third son William, called William Saundre, is not connected to Lodge Manor in any record, but evidently received inherited Salomon or Collenden property which lay in nearby Charlwood, touching off a wholly new chapter in family history. To William's story and that of the Charlwood Sanders we now turn.

====

NOTES

1. Forest laws applied to large swaths of England, reserving access to forested areas for royal use. By royal writ a noble might receive "free warren," the right to hunt, but those holding this right were obliged to identify or deter poachers.

2. King Henry III in Britroyals.com.

3. Ruald de Calne, Lord of Monnington Stradel at Geni.com

4. F. B. Lewis, Pedes Finium (Feet of Fines), or Fines Relating to the County of Surrey, Surrey Archeological Society, 1894.

5. A useful Basset genealogy is found at geojourney.com/basset.

6. The arms given in the record are described "Azure three bulls' heads or cut off at the neck and having crown argent." In the early thirteenth century Deodatus de Dunes held land there. Cobham Parish, Surrey, British History Online, vol. 3.

7. B. Burke, A Genealogical and Heraldic Dictionary of the Landed Gentry of Great Britain, Weston of West Horsley. A William de Weston acquired Sende, Pappeworth, and West Clandon manors in marriage to the heiress of John Dunstanville. The Dunstanville connection to these lands evidently carried on after Beatrice Dunstanville for some generations.

8. An undated charter of Newark Priory contains the signature of "Stephen de la Dune." See Calendar of Charter Rolls Preserved in the Public Record Office, British History Online, entry under "Matthew Bovill."

9. We have used F. B. Lewis, Pedes Finium (Feet of Fines), or Fines Relating to the County of Surrey, Surrey Archeological Society, 1894. This source contains records of land transactions from the time of Richard I, which we consulted to examine twelfth and thirteenth century Sanderstead, Warlingham, and Sende land records. This source also contains record of the marriage record of Beatrice de Sanderstead and William Maubanc.

10. Pedes Finium, Surrey records for John I.

11. More precisely, Beatrice's influence is most closely seen in the lives of her sons Stephen and Richard, and by extension, Richard's children.

12. Walter was sometimes called "Watkin," a common usage at the time; see W. Arthur, An Etymological Dictionary of Family and Christian Names. Sheldon, Blake, and Bleeker, 1857, but see also an updated version at surnamesdb.com. Watkin as a Norman name is first found in England in the thirteenth century. The name was a familiar form meaning "little Walter," a usage that came into play in England about the 1200s; see Surnames.enacademic.com. Likewise, the appendix "-kin" (Watkin, Wilkin, Jenkin, Dickin, Boykin, etc.) is a naming device originating in the thirteenth century, as described by T. Hoad, Concise Oxford Dictionary of English Etymology. London, 1996.

13. W. R. Eyton, Antiquities of Shropshire, vol. 1 (London: Smith, 1859), pp. 314–316.

14. Leonard de Sanderstead himself managed this same kind of transaction as Basset's steward in 1180, seeing to an arrangement that allowed a younger Basset son to acquire property, but only with his elder brother's formal consent.

15. The idea that the manor controlled five hundred acres is taken from Domesday, which states that Sanderstead had five hides, a hide consisting about one hundred acres. Manning and Bray state, "In the time of King John or Henry III (between 1199–1272), Watkin Saunders of this place, dying without issue, gave the Manor of Sandersted and the advowson of the church to the Abbot and Convent of Hyde at Winchester, and divers other lands here and at Warlingham to Stephen, his brother, and his heirs." D. Lewis, trans. Rise and Growth of the Anglican Schism, Dr. Nicholas Saunder,1585, London: Burns and Oates, 1877. This book was published posthumously but the publisher added a biographical preface using Dr. Nicholas's notes, in which Nicholas claimed descent from Watkin, who lived in the time

of John. This account is seconded by Manning and Bray, History and Antiquities of the County of Surrey, vol. 2, Wakefield: Surrey County Library, 1974, pp. 428, 568. These authors seemingly contradict themselves about whether Watkin gave manor lands or the manor itself to Hyde Abbey. Also see E. Edwards, ed., Liber Monasterii de Hyde, Cambridge Library, 2012.

16. R. W. Eyton, The Court, Household and Itinerary of Henry II, London: Taylor, 1878. Eyton provides ample detail on the generations following Leonard at Shropshire, but errs in suggesting that Thomas was the father of Leonard de Lega.

17. Walter Dunstanville, who died in 1195, was the son of Alan and heir to his uncle Robert. He inherited land in Sussex, Shropshire and chiefly in Wiltshire where he was lord of the barony of Castle Combe. Walter seems to have been a royal clerk in the early years of Henry II but disappeared from court records in later times. Walter married Ursula Dunstanville, sister of Beatrice de Sanderstead. Thomas Basset, Leonard's employer, was married to Alice Dunstanville, Walter's sister. All this suggests a tight family community in which Leonard's sons might have been educated and attained knighthood and Walter Dunstanville's prosperity and chief residence offered a suitable stage.

18. J. Dalloway, History of the Western Division of the County of Sussex, vol. 2, part 2. See also Pedes Finium, Surrey record 79.

19. M. Deane, The Book of Dene, Deane, Adeane: A Genealogical History, London, 1899. See also Some Sussex Domesday Tenants, Sussex Archeological Collections.

20. Church attendance was a legal requirement, enforced by requiring all parishioners to attend their local parish church. Richard and Sybilla required a legal process to change their church assignment.

21. At the time of the Domesday Survey, West Dean was included in the manor of Singleton. Like East Dean, it was a forest area and the park of West Dean frequently occurs among the appurtenances of the earldom of Arundel. Later the manor of West Dean was one of the manors belonging to the honor of Arundel. In 1272 it is mentioned among the manors held by John FitzAlan, Earl of Arundel. See History of the County of Sussex: West Dean, at British History online,

22. Pedes Finium, Surrey, 8 Richard I(1196).

23. See Joseph Haydn, The Book of Dignities, 1590. That dignities were heritable is shown in T. Banks, The Dormant and Extinct Baronage of England, vol. 1, pp. 222–223.

24. Woodstock—Richard the Lionheart stayed there. His brother and successor King John I—born at Beaumont Palace in Oxford and later to become the villain of the Robin Hood legends—was a regular

visitor, coming six times in one year and dropping by just after signing Magna Carta. See bbc.com/woodstock and also E. Marshall, The Early History of Woodstock Manor and its Environs. Parker, Oxford, 1873.

25. That manors around Woodstock were sometimes awarded for life for royal service, see A.P. Baggs et al., History of the County of Oxford, vol. 12, for Bladon and other manors.

26. It may be that we are over-interpreting events here, in that our dating of them is somewhat imprecise. Richard may have acquired a right to occupy Combe Manor in Oxfordshire after Leonard's passing, resulting less from Leonard's expressed will than from a simple royal decision to employ Richard for royal duties as Leonard's replacement.

27. Found in the Harleian Collection in the British Museum is a lineage of the de Dene family, indicating that the name often was spelled "de Dyne."

28. This Richard is not be confused with another of the same name and times. A contemporary Richard de Combe or Cumba, knight, was of Fittleton and Combe in Wiltshire, but this person is of an entirely different lineage. See Lansdown MS. 205. The Arms assigned to the De Combes of Fitelton are ___ Sable, three lions passant gold."

29. R. Turner, Judges, Administration, and the Common Law in Angevin England, London, 1994.

30. Farazmand, A., ed., Handbook of Comparative and Development Public Administration, vol. 41, Public Administration and Public Policy, University of Michigan, 1991.

31. Extracted by Combs Researcher Joe Kendall from Curia Regis Rolls, His Majesties Stationary Office, Public Record Office, London, 1922, vol. 1, p. 57.

32. Pipe Rolls of the Bishopric of Winchester 1210–1211. There was also a fourth purchaser who was not called de Cumba. He was called Waccelino, who was Roger Wachelino of the Winchester Bishopric. The Sende transaction was this arranged by Winchester magistrate Robert Basset, steward of the Bishop of Winchester.

33. A. Harding, England in the Thirteenth Century, Cambridge, 1993, p. 253.

34. A History of the County of Oxford, vol. 8: Parishes: Emmington, British History Online. The delay was not due to inaction at the Chancery. Geoffrey Sackville became heir to Emmington only after the intended heir Jordan Sackvillle, his half-brother, died at an early age.

35. Pedes Finium, Surrey.

36. Robert de Dena left a son Robert, who was succeeded by his son Ralph, or Ranulphus, and also a son Radulphus, who was the ancestor of various families in Kent and other counties. The younger Ralph had

two children, a son and a daughter; but the son, who was the third Ralph of the line, dying young, his sister, Ela de Dene, became sole heir to the immense estates of her father. In 1189, in conjunction with her father, she founded the abbey of Odyham, or Ottiham, and also of Bayham, where Ralph was buried. From M. Deane, The Book of Dene, Deane, Adeane: A Genealogical History, London, 1899.

37. For a worthwhile view of Buckhurst Manor, go to BuckhurstPark.co.uk.

38. Premonstratensian were a Roman Catholic religious order of canons regular founded in Prémontré near Laon in 1120 by Saint Norbert. Norbert was a friend of Saint Bernard of Clairvaux and so was largely influenced by the Cistercian ideals as to both the manner of life and the government of his order. As the Premonstratensians were not monks but canons regular, their work often involved preaching and the exercising of pastoral ministry; they frequently served in parishes close to their abbeys or priories, and were sometimes called "White Canons" from the color of their habit.

39. Calendar of Charter Rolls, Sussex, 16 Henry III (1232).

40. Descriptive Catalogue of Ancient Deeds, British History Online, Record A4221, dated 7–10 John I (1206–1209). For more on these transactions, see L. Saltzman, History of the Parish of Hailsham, Lewes, 1999, p. 179.

41. A History of the County of Wiltshire, vol. 12: Parishes: Winterbourne Bassett, pp. 184–192, at British History online. "About 1121 Reginald Dunstanville gave Winterbourne Bassett church to Lewes Priory. In the early 13th century the prior presented candidates nominated by Alan Basset. The valuable living attracted pluralist incumbents, including Fulk Basset, rector from c1214 to c1239, who was nominated to the living by his father. Walter de Dunstanville, great-grandson of Reginald (fl. c1121), granted the manor to his nephew Alan Basset in 1194. The grant was confirmed in 1199. Alan's son Gilbert inherited the manor c1232. Gilbert's estates were confiscated for his rebellion against Henry III but were restored in 1234. He died in 1241 and was succeeded by his brothers Fulk, dean of York and later bishop of London (d. 1259), and Philip (d. 1271). The manor passed to Philip's daughter Aline, relict of Sir Hugh le Despenser and wife of Roger Bigod, Earl of Norfolk."

42. Pedes Finium, Surrey, Record 4 Henry III (1221) and Record 10 Henry III (1226).

43. M. Deane, The Book of Dene, Deane, Adeane: A Genealogical History, London, 1899, p. 5 This was a family dispute in which Robert de Dene and Sibella de Harengood, his sister, were suitors.

44. J. Strayer, On the Medieval Origins of the Modern State, Princeton University Press, 2016, p. 112.

45. Descriptive Catalogue of Ancient Deeds, British History Online, Records A6930, A4058, A4060.

46. Descriptive Catalogue of Ancient Deeds, British History Online, RecordsA4034, A4059.

47. Descriptive Catalogue of Ancient Deeds, British History Online, Records A4059, A4061, A4076.

48. Descriptive Catalogue of Ancient Deeds, British History Online, Records A4032, A4034, A4075, A4022, A4055.

49. Guillam. See note 50.

50. 50.Two sources here are crucial: Guillam's Advenie of Carmarthenshire can be found in the Francis Green Papers at the Cultural Services Department, Public Library, Havorfordwest, Pembrokeshire, Wales, originally published in 1611; and D. Lysons, Magna Brittania, Derbyshire, 1817, p. clxii. Both sources ultimately may derive from Sir Thomas Sanders' confirmation of his arms in 1553. Sir Thomas appears in Chapter Six.

51. Guillam's treatment of this lineage leave a gap between these early figures, suggesting he recognized a need for additional persons to be added to the lineage.

52. That Ralph Saundre happened to marry into the Salomon family is not in itself a complete surprise. The two families are deeply linked. The name Salomon lies in the ancient history of Brittany, ancestral home of the FitzAlans. There were three kings named Salomon in ancient Brittany, the first and best known of which was Salomon, close ally and lieutenant of Charlemagne, who founded the Holy Roman Empire and implanted the feudal regime on much of medieval western Europe. That Salomon is memorialized in a stained glass window of Rouen Cathedral. Subsequent Salomons of Brittany were closely associated with Dol, and at least one person named Salomon is found in the FitzAlan lineage at Dol as late as 1182. A certain Hugh de Dol can be found at Guildford in the time of Richard de Cumba, suggesting that ancient family ties to Dol had not been completely severed. But it is unlikely that the Roger Salomon family into which Ralph married came to England directly from Dol because the Salomons had accumulated property in several locations in France before the time of Ralph's marriage, and perhaps some in England as well. Of greater interest is the manor called Britwell Salome which, as the name suggests, may have been home to the Salomons of Oxfordshire, at least for some points in its history. This manor lay adjacent to Geoffrey's Sackville's Emmington Manor. If we are correct as previously suggested

that Richard de Cumba sojourned at Emmington in pursuit of his royal obligations at Combe and otherwise served Geoffrey Sackville at Emmington, then opportunities for Richard to negotiate a Salomon marriage for his son Ralph could have presented themselves at Britwell Salome. This idea is in keeping with the Surrey historian who suggested that "the Salomons (of Horley) are thought to have come from Oxfordshire." Yet all this entails a currently unverified belief that the manor name "Salome" indicates a presence there of a family called "Salomon." In fact, what we do find at Britwell Salome in the thirteenth century is a family name "Sulham," and sometimes "Sullum," both of which bear some phonetic similarity with "Salomon," but which in no case produces any identifiable linkage to Horley or to Ralph de Pappeworth or his father Richard de Cumba. For the thirteenth century, then, we are left with little more than a feeling that those at Britwell Salome might be related to the Salomons of Horley. See Parishes: Britwell Salome, History of the County of Oxford, vol. 8, British History Online.

53. Many or most surviving female spouses are heiresses, even though many inheritances involve only minor items such as of money or jewelry. But in family records for this early period, only a small number of heiresses are identified in records. These heiresses are singled out because their inherited property passed by marriage from one family to the other.

54. M. L. Walker, The Manor of Battailles and the family of Saundre in Ewell during the sixteenth and seventeenth Centuries, Surrey Archeological Society, Guildford, 1956.

55. Confusion over the locations of property in Horley or Charlwood stems from the fact that a portion of the parish of Charlwood is not contiguous with the main body of that parish. A separate portion lies wholly within the parish of Horley and is surrounded by Horley territory. A further complexity is that "the Parish and Borough/District boundaries run through the middle (of Norwood Hill), so half the community is in Charlwood... and the other half in Sidlow and Reigate, and Banstead. It also falls within three parish church boundaries, Charlwood, Sidlow, and Leigh"; see charlwoodandhookwood.com.

56. One compilation of ancient charters lists several pertaining to the Salomons "property in Horley, Bletchingley, Newdigate and Charlwood" in the period 1240 to 1408, a span of 168 years. These were a variety of lands and tenements variously called Haderesham, Heldebregge, Hestefeld, Le Fodeslond, Welcroft, Wygodeshae, Tawheynys, Loggemore, Heneryswode, Le Bourne, Blascheny, Sandcroft or Bushefeld, and Herefeld, but presumably only some number of these lay in Horley and very few or even none of these were

held in Roger's lifetime. Thus whether Ralph of Coulsdon might have inherited any of these cannot be assessed. These charters are found in Essex Record Office, Seax Search: Estate and Family Records, Petre Estate D/DP T370, Essex Records Office, UK.

57. How Roger acquired the Salomon name in descent from the line of Stephen Fitz Hamon is not clear, but the name had wider currency in France than in England in Roger's time. We identified seven separate Salomon lineages in France, but not one of these bore heraldic arms matching those claimed by Roger. Roger's name likely derived from a maternal side in some previous marriage to a Hamo family member.

58. Surrey Feet of Fines, 1263.

59. Transactions of the Kent Archeological Society, vol. IV, 1861, p. 218. And see Norton Mandeville Manor, in A History of the County of Essex, vol. 4, Ongar Hundred, ed. W. R. Powell(London, 1956), pp. 151–152.

60. Ashley, British Kings and Queens (New York: Barnes and Noble, 1998), pp. 588–594.

61. We have been singularly unsuccessful in tracing the Collenden family, but note that a spelling of "Coulsdon" about 1270, where family members resided, is given as "Colendone."

62. 58. E. Brayley, A Topographical History of Surrey, vol. 1(Dorking, 1841), p. 279.

63. J. Morris, County Churches: Surrey(London, 1910).

64. The History and Topographical Survey of the County of Kent, vol.6. Parishes: Throwley, Kent, Pages 445–461. See also Windsor Peerage for 1890–1894, Edward Walford, which describes arms for the Sonde family at later dates.

65. A description of Salomon (Salmon) Manor of Warlingham is found at Warlingham Parish, History of the County of Surrey, British History Online.

NOTES FOR JOHN DE SANDERSTEAD

1** Victoria County History of Staffordshire, vol. 5, pp. 79–80, 121.

2** Victoria County History of Staffordshire, vol. 4, pp. 238, 335.

3** For additional information on John de Sanderstead, see British National Archives, Account and Official: John de Sanderstead. ref. E 358/2. John de Sanderstead is also found in the Victoria County History of Warwick, vol. 5, pp. 42–44 and 118–119. Specific reference to his position of sheriff is found in Calendar of Patent Rolls: 1348–1350. British Record Office.

4** Feet of Fines, Surrey, 1330.

CHAPTER FOUR

Sanders Place

In Horley, Richard Saundre was lord of Lodge Manor and about 1275 married a daughter of William Collenden. Collenden eventually left his estate to two daughters—his coheiresses. One married into the Coddington family, which received some share of Collenden property in Horley or Banstead Parish, property that may be ancestral to the Collendean Farm found on modern maps. From the other Collenden co-heiress, Richard acquired some property that lay either in Horley or Charlwood, and it is possible that the family's new home in Charlwood—called "Sanders Place" or "Sanders Place Manor"—found its origin in Collenden's bequest, a notion that gains some credence from the fact that Sanders Place lies only a short distance—a mile or two—from Collendean Farm. But it is also true that Richard's father Ralph lived in Charlwood before him, residing on land received from his earlier Salomon marriage, although in Ralph's case, the precise location of his Charlwood property is unknown. As for the origin of Sanders Place, then, we cannot provide a definite answer of how the Sanders family came to hold the property, whether of Salomon or Collenden beginnings, nor do we know whether the manor house itself was then newly constructed or merely renamed from some earlier version.

This is what we do know. The manor house of Sanders Place in Charlwood is dated to about the beginning of the reign of Edward II, that is, about 1307 [1].In the fashion of the day, the manor house itself was moated [2]. According to Manning and Bray, the manor held about six hundred acres of land, of sufficient size to maintain the family's somewhat privileged social status [3]. Perhaps a century later, this manor came to be called "Charlwood Place."

The name itself, "Sanders Place," unmistakably derived from the earlier family home of "Sanderstead," because these two names are essentially equivalent, and, one guesses, intendedly so by those who decided the matter. Thus we gather that in spite of a century of family evolution, memory of deep family roots at Sanderstead remained strong. Furthermore, recollection of

Leonard's now ancient coat of arms bearing three bulls' heads continued as
well. In later years, the Sanders family named a Charlwood holding "Bull Head
Farm" [4].

Sanders Place (by this name) came into being in the time of William
Saunder, thought to be the son of Richard Saundre or Horley and his Collenden
wife. William was born we estimate about 1280 and would have reached the
age of marriage and adult responsibilities shortly after the turn of the century,
more or less the time when Sanders Place came into being. But we have no
genealogical record that identifies William as Richard Saundre's issue or
that names William as Richard's heir. Our sole record is for the year 1314,
in which we find "William Saundre" of Charlwood bearing witness to a local
land transaction [5]. This is the only record of any Saundres in Charlwood for
the early fourteenth century, closely following the apparent establishment of
the Sanders Place property itself, around 1307. These facts, together with an
evident genealogical gap—a missing generation—between Richard and his
later descendants in Charlwood, lead us to include William as a generational
figure in the family's historic transition from Horley to Charlwood. From
William's life forward, an entirely new branch of the family came into existence,
which came to be known as the Sanders of Charlwood. This branch persisted
in Charlwood for twelve generations and more than three hundred and fifty
years [6].

This new family home in Charlwood was one aspect of a broader historical
transition. In the time of Leonard de Sanderstead, the family enjoyed close
proximity to the halls of royal power and affiliations with families like the
Dunstanvilles and Bassets whose influence was national in scope. But life at
the center and later the periphery of royal influence had slipped away, fading
generation by generation over the past century. By the time of William, these
links to power and influence had largely evaporated. For William and his
Charlwood descendants, life would take a simpler form, wresting a living from
their medieval manor and assuming the role as a leading local family in one
of Charlwood's few manors. A positive consequence of this social devolution
was a greater degree of insulation from adverse national political tides and, as
it turned out, a vital separation from natural disasters that would ravage the
whole of England in the family's not-too-distant future. However unremarkable
William's simple inheritance might seem in the larger scheme of family
acquisitions, it nonetheless ignited an entirely new and defining era of family
history.

The first two centuries of the family's tenure at Charlwood fall into what
historians sometimes call the late feudal period. In earlier feudal times, the
issue of nationhood, the notion of a unified political and military whole for
the land of England, was in serious doubt, and who might rule over the large
expanse of land and its diverse peoples was a matter of persistent uncertainty.

But all that changed. The English nation at the time the Saundre family arrived in Charlwood was fully formed, and national government itself enjoyed a broadly accepted, though still evolving, form. Through this time, parliamentary government grew by fits and starts. From a popular point of view, subjects of the Crown now were loyal to their English rulers or at least to the institution of monarchy, adopting a relatively new political culture that placed national citizenship on a close footing with earlier local and kinship attachments. People had begun to regard themselves foremost as Englishmen.

Dark History

The century following William was a century like no other, one that remade the face of England, and in fact the whole of Europe. Following William Saundre of Charlwood, whose date of death falls in the first quarter of the 1300s, the Saundre family, as well as England as a whole, fell into deep darkness, an epochal cross-current of death that upended England's progress as a nation. Disastrous plagues of the fourteenth century decimated local populations and disrupted the institutions through which personal records might otherwise have been preserved. As a result, we have virtually no family records from these times. The fourteenth century in England was a shipwreck, a century crushed on the twin shoals of famine and plague. A three-year famine in 1315–1317 killed an estimated half million people in England, and the bubonic plague of 1348–1349 killed off half the population of London, at least fifty thousand people, and hundreds of thousands more nationwide. A virulent recurrence of Black Death in 1360 wreaked further havoc. All told, the population of England was reduced by famine and plague from about five million in 1300 to about two-and-a-half million in 1377 [7], a 50 percent decline over three generations. Scarcely any place, rural or urban, went untouched, nor were any social classes, high or low, unscathed.

Early on, the plague savaged many parts of Asia, slowly making its way westward into the Black Sea region. From there merchant fleets of Venice and Genoa carried the disease back to their home ports and to Marseilles, which then diffused in all directions to the north, west, and east in Europe. By 1348 the great Bubonic Plague had all of England in its grip. Once the great infection took hold, for some it affected the bloodstream and for others the lungs, producing death in either case in one to three agonizing days. As Tuchman observed, the pestilence appeared more terrible because its victims knew no prevention and no remedy. In a given area the plague accomplished its destruction within four to six months and then faded, except in larger cities where it abated in winter only to reappear in spring and rage for another six months [8].

One account in Surrey at a manor called Lagham, perhaps ten miles from Charlwood, provides a close-up view. An Inquisitio post mortem for the Manor of Lagham in Surrey for 1349 reveals the local devastation: "There is a ruinous water mill of no value this year because all the tenants who used to grind there are dead. Prequisites of court, nothing, because all the suitors are dead. There are 200 acres of sheep pasture, formerly valued at a halfcent an acre, but worth nothing this year, for it cannot be let to farm. There are 200 acres of arable land in Lagham which cannot be farmed. Last year the rents of free tenants were four pounds; this year one-half pound because almost all the tenants are dead, and their tenements empty for default of heirs. The profits of court are nothing, because the tenants who did suit of court are dead"[9].

The darkness of the plague began to lift toward the end of the fourteenth century, but the England of this new light was a far different place from that a century before. This was a direct result of the double disasters of plague and famine in the previous century and the massive human losses that resulted. Severe shortages of labor led quickly to increases in wage rates throughout the century and a newfound ability of heretofore destitute feudal laborers to accrue wealth, at least for the most enterprising among them. The lesson that labor could now command good compensation became a thread that began to unravel the feudal cloth of vassalage. It was not unusual for tenants of the fifteenth century to buy up land, crops, and herds of manorial lords, and some number of entrepreneurs in all laboring categories maneuvered into position to amass wealth as they had never before imagined [10].

Following the plagues, wholly new categories of social standing entered the picture to fill the thinned-out ranks of the privileged. The term "yeoman" came into use to describe those whose life now combined manual labor, landholding, and civic responsibility at local levels. Above that emerged a more genteel class, the "gentleman," a noble figure placed at the lower end of nobility, a person of dignity whose improved means were inherited from below or gained through fortuitous marriage. These emerging social categories constituted new opportunities resulting from shortages of both labor and leadership and from a rising economic base in an England, gradually renewing itself on recovered agricultural production, renewed manufacture, and the resumption of trade.

Charlwood Lineage

We know little of the Sanders of early Charlwood. This is a direct consequence of England's hard times in the fourteenth century, because those institutions responsible for records-keeping, mainly offices of state and churches, failed at the same rate as the population itself. All that can be said is that the family enjoyed the quiet success of survival at times when this outcome was not assured. What we know of the family following William depends entirely on a single document, a relic of the difficult past rescued by a historical figure named Robert Harley [11]. In the Harleian collection is Manuscript Number 1433, which provides a simple genealogy of surviving Sanders family members from this early time in

Charlwood. To this Harleian manuscript we have added estimated birthdates for the Sanders lineage to suggest a general genealogical flow.

THE SAUNDRE FAMILY OF EARLY CHARLWOOD

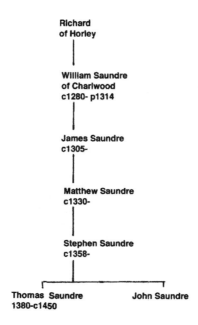

Source: Harleian Manuscript #1433, supplemented by authors.

William Saundre

As previously described, William we think was born about 1280, and married by perhaps 1305. The hardest history of England of the mid-to=late 1300s occurred mainly after William Saundre's time, but he nonetheless lived in times cursed by the weak rule of Edward II, a period marked by ineffectual military adventures and a resurgence of baronial contempt for royal authority. A punishing three-year famine of 1315–1317 made matters far worse. Of William's account we have nothing more, save that he had a surviving son named James.

James Saundre

James, born perhaps around 1305, lived in the time of Edward III, whose fifty-year reign commenced about the time that James entered adulthood. Edward III is often regarded as one of England's greatest kings, an effective monarch under whom the enduring political upsets in England were held in some abeyance. He ruled from 1327 to 1377, bringing steady statesmanship to England and limited but encouraging triumphs on the battlefield, improving the sense of competence in authority that was lost in Edward's predecessor. Of course, Edward III, for all his political skills, was entirely without means to deal with the plague and its grisly aftermath. In his waning years, James himself witnessed the onset of plague and the devastation left in its wake.

Matthew Saundre

James Saundre's son was Matthew, whose birth date can be placed about 1330. As Matthew entered the prime of his life, approaching the time of marriage and child-producing years when the Black Death struck with full fury in 1348 and churned on throughout the following year, the worst years of bubonic plague outbreak that Surrey was to experience. Whether Matthew, his wife, or any of his children were directly infected with bubonic plague is unknown, but Matthew's anguish undoubtedly mounted as he counted losses nearby and felt the threat at his own doorstep.

It may have been in the time of Matthew that Sanders Place came to be called Charlwood Place, when the Manor of Charlwood took control of Sanders Place Manor. Exactly how or why this occurred is not clear, nor is the exact timing of this action recorded. But one might guess that Sanders Place somehow declined in the wake of the Bubonic Plague, which forced or permitted Charlwood Manor to render assistance and control. It is equally possible that Matthew gave the Sanders Place to Charlwood as an act of desperation or piety. From Matthew's time or before, Sanders Place, now sometimes called Charlwood Place, became a sub-manor of Charlwood Manor. Under this arrangement, the lord of Sanders Place retained his entitlements to his own manor, but was required to offer fealty—that is, sworn loyalty and specified payments—to the lord of Charlwood Manor, and the right or obligation to hold court by one manor or the other was part of the new arrangement. At the time of this subinfeudation—subsuming a smaller manor into a larger—Charlwood Manor was held by the Prior and convent of Christchurch, Canterbury as a member of the Manor of Mersham. This meant that, as a practical matter, the lord of Sanders Place, called now Charlwood Place, was required to offer fealty to the local Rectory of Charlwood Church.

Stephen Saundre

Matthew survived long enough to have a son Stephen. Stephen was born about 1358, shortly before the Black Death recurred in England one final time in the fourteenth century. In his lifetime, Stephen saw the continuing devastation of the bubonic plague, the death of the popular and able Edward III, and the rise of Richard II. Stephen lived to see Richard's duplicitous handling of Wat

Tyler's popular rebellion [12] and ultimately the full corruption of power in Richard's later years. If these unhappy larger events disturbed Stephen, they also would have fed some evident dissatisfaction with his own life in Charlwood.

Stephen chafed under his personal circumstances. In 1388, he was formally accused of trespass. Thereafter, he appears repeatedly in court records of the period of the early 1400s documenting his refusal to offer fealty to the lord of the Manor of the Charlwood Rectory. Whether his refusal stemmed from legal, financial, or religious objections is not clear, but Stephen's recalcitrance, imperiling though it might have been, was a sign of the times. The England of Stephen Saundre was beginning to change in ways that had less to do with ancient rules of land tenancy and more to do with evolving economic freedoms at local levels.

Stephen is known to have had two sons, an older son Thomas and a younger son John.

Thomas Saundre

Into this changing world was born Thomas, son of Stephen Saundre. Thomas was born about 1378 and lived to an old age. He married Johanna Odworth, she of an old and distinguished Charlwood family, and they lived at Charlwood's Sanders Place [13]. Thomas and Joanna had four sons, William, Reynold, John [14], and Robert, and a daughter Johanna. From the Odworths Thomas received the Manor of Odworth in Charlwood, which would in later years be subject to a family dispute [15].

The main picture we have of Thomas's life, though much incomplete, is of property acquisition, land rental, and business enterprise. He became, in the adaptive language of the day, a yeoman [16], a new class of land tenants who acceded to land ownership and acquired wealth and new political rights. The idea that local persons lacking noble rank might amass sizable land holdings represented a true break with the feudal past. This was a silent and incremental revolution, one that continued to shape England for generations. Thomas thus rode the crest of genuinely new history, and he rode with some considerable success.

Thomas, acquired a number of properties and augmented his rental income by developing the local industries of iron production and timber management. He seems to have had an ironworks at Ifield [17]. But a ten-years' lease of the manor of Merstham and its member of Charlwood, made in 1396 by the prior, mentions, among other things, that the 'digging of iron at Cherlwood' was to remain the right of the prior and convent [18]. Thus, some part of Thomas's gain in iron mining was not his to keep.

We find Thomas in 1411 joining with Longehurst opposing a party named Ashurst in a Surrey land transaction [19]. In 1420, he witnessed a land transaction with Thomas Hayton involving Carshalton and also land in Newdigate [20]. Hidden in this Carshalton transaction with Hayton is the fact that sometime later, Thomas's own son would marry Thomas Hayton's granddaughter and would take legal action for control of that manor. In 1446, Thomas and a son added Sloghterwyk in Charlwood to their holdings with an additional four acres granted to them by Thomas White. Four years later, they jointly purchased an additional tract in Charlwood called Godbaldesfeldes. These transactions are unlikely to be Thomas's only land acquisitions, judging by the full extent of later Saundre family holdings in Charlwood [21].

A claim is made that Thomas had enough education to become a commissioner of the peace and a tax collector for Surrey, positions that brought him into contact with leading local families and he was able to marry his son into nobility [22]. We have found no record corroborating this claim, which seems unlikely. That a yeoman without formal education from Charlwood might ascend to this level of county government would probably be without precedent, given that such positions were normally staffed by the county's leading citizens drawn from noble classes.

As a landowning yeoman, Thomas also would have felt a personal stake in matters of the realm, and the realm was deeply troubled in his time. Henry VI, a Lancastrian king, had acceded to the throne as an infant in 1422, coming of age in 1439. Henry V, his father, had begun the conquest of France in 1415, acquiring many of the great provinces of France, but also incurring heavy debt. Following Henry V's early death and the long minority of Henry VI, the aristocracy became extremely powerful, competing and feuding among themselves for the fruits of political power. Within a few years of Henry VI's coming of age, the government was in acute difficulty. Henry's ministers, particularly, William de la Pole, the Duke of Suffolk, made serious miscalculations that led to the opening of war with France and the eventual loss of all lands in France except Calais. In England, the king's debts increased enormously, partly because of the wars but mainly due to his excessive generosity in granting lands and lucrative offices to his leading ministers. This accumulation of wealth and power by the favorites in the administration led to further feuding and polarization of the aristocracy and to charges of greed and corruption. The bulk of blame fell on the Duke of Suffolk, largely because of his abuses in East Anglia. The period of 1450–1470 was characterized by high levels of violence and lawlessness, by oppression, gangsterism, and perversion of the law in those shires that had the backing of powerful ministers.

By the late 1440s, national anger at the loss of the empire in France fused with growing discontent over internal abuses within the country. Ross [23] describes this scene, "For most Englishmen the chief social evil of the day was the ability of powerful men to defy the law, to bend or pervert the course of justice and to use violence in pursuit of their own interests or those of their followers. Records of the time abound with murders, beatings, destruction of manor houses, and the carrying away of livestock, performed by large gangs of men."

Numerous uprisings began to take place in many regions of the country, and Surrey was no exception. In 1449, Thomas Saundre and others in his family participated in an insurrection in Charlwood against these abuses and in support of the Duke of York, an heir to the throne then in exile. A record of the insurrection of 1449 identifies participants as, "Thomas Saundre the elder yoman and William Saunder gentilman, both of Charlewode, Thomas Whyte of Charlewode, yoman, one of the constables of Reigate Hundred. John Jordan, constable of Charlewode, yoman, John Saundre yoman, Richard Saundre, yoman" [24]. These are Thomas Saundre and his son William; John and Richard Saundre were either William's brothers or his nephews.

Thomas Saundre may have carried the political viewpoints and ambition of his father Stephen, and he employed them as he marched with his family for greater justice. Personal comportment in the insurrection was notably moderate and orderly. The rebels themselves were organized and led by the high constable of the hundred, and thus, the marchers paraded with local political encouragement and approval. Abuses by distant higher-ups finally had been felt at home, and the insurrection spoke directly to the loss of rights and freedom brought about by the king's favorites, notably the Duke of Suffolk. Protestors demanded his removal from power and the return from exile of the Duke of York [25]. This insurrection, it turns out, was but the beginning of larger strife throughout England.

Thomas Saundre, his family, and others were later pardoned for their participation in the insurrection at the request of the queen, Margaret of Anjou, on July 6, 1449. The charges had been that "they with others of great numbers in divers places of the realm of their own presumption gathered together against the statutes of the realm to the contempt of the king's estate" [26]. Thomas and his family seem to have concluded this affair happily enough, pardoned of any punishable offense and no doubt enriched by this new evidence of their own political efficacy. Thomas Saundre died soon after the insurrection, at an advanced age of more than seventy years. Thomas died around 1450 and the south porch of the Charlwood church was added by the family in his memory [27].

By the time of Thomas's death, the Saundre family had resided at Charlwood for nearly one hundred fifty years. In that time, the Sanders had lived through vast changes in their own lives and fortunes and seen an entirely new England come to life. By the midfifteenth century, the restrictive feudal order was on the wane. Family members now owned their own land and built wealth and gained social prominence through fortuitous marriage. They had lived through famines and relentless outbreak of plague and seen times of good and bad monarchic rule. They lived to see the rise of effective parliamentary governance and simultaneous recognition of evolving political rights. Especially in the person of William, Thomas Saundre's son, heir to this epochal history, the family found rewarding involvement in a remade England and took on roles that in the past were tightly reserved for the more highly privileged.

NOTES

1. R. Sewill and E. Lane, *Free Men of Charlwood* (Crawley, Sussex: Reprographic Centre, 1979.

2. J. Harding, Four Centuries of Charlwood Houses: Medieval to 1840, Charlwood Society, 1976, p. 36.

3. E. Brayley, A Topographical History of Surrey, London, 1850, p. 266.

4. Sewill and Lane, p. 197

5. Sewill and Lane, p. 36.

6. Charlwood Place (a.k.a. Sanders Place) was sold to another family in 1664, and records after that date imply that the Saunders did not remain there in force. The name John Saunders, however, was engraved above a door at Sanders Chancery in Charlwood in 1791 and Sanders descendants could be found in Charlwood as late as the twentieth century].

7. Nigel Saul, ed., *The Oxford Illustrated History of Medieval England*, Oxford: Oxford University Press, 1997, pp. 160–161.

8. B. Tuchman, A Distant Mirror, New York, Ballantine, 1978, chapter 5.

9. Earthworks at Lagham, Surrey Archeological Collections, vol. 20, 1907, p. 117.

10. Saul, *Oxford Illustrated History*, pp. 160–166.

11. The Harley library was founded in October 1704, when Harley purchased more than six hundred manuscripts from the collection of the antiquary Sir Simonds d'Ewes. The Harleian collection today comprises more than seven thousand manuscripts, fourteen thousand charters, and five hundred rolls.

12. The Peasants' Revolt of 1381 grew out of unpopular taxation policies and was led by Wat Tyler of Kent. His peasant force eventually grew to nearly one hundred thousand and marched on the capital, killing some members of the establishment along the way. Richard II stood before the throng, promising reforms and quelling the disturbance, but he later reneged on the promises made. See Ashley, *British Kings and Queens*, pp. 605–606.

13. G. Eyre and A. Strahan, 1827–1832. Calendars of the Proceedings of Chancery in the Reign of Queen Elizabeth, vol. 1.

14. John, whose wife Margaret died in 1477, had sons John and Richard. Sketchy records suggest this Richard may have had two sons, John Saundre, whose wife leased the property of Rowley, and Richard Saundre, who owned Le Fronge in 1502 and engaged a legal dispute over the property in 1512.

15. G. Eyre and A. Strahan, 1827–1832. Calendars of the Proceedings of Chancery in the Reign of Queen Elizabeth, vol. 1. A suit of about 1455, a few years after Thomas's death, pitted Thomas's son John against John, Thomas's brother. John's son William married Johanna, Thomas's daughter, and received Odworth in marriage, but with the stipulation that the property could remain with them only upon producing an heir. But William died before Johann gave birth to their child, leaving open the question of the property's future ownership. It seems that Thomas's son John prevailed in this case.

16. According to C. Onions (*The Oxford Dictionary of English Etymology* [Oxford: Clarendon Press, 1992]), the term *yeoman* was coined in the fourteenth century for designating a minor naval rank and later adapted in the fifteenth century to refer to "a freeholder below the rank of gentleman." Also, Francis Green suggested that this Thomas Saunders might be the same person as Thomas Saunders, wine gauger of Bristol, but our research shows that this is not the case.

17. charlwoodsociety.co.uk/the-charlwood-maps, p. 42.

18. *Victoria History of Surrey*, vol. 3, p. 185.

19. *Surrey Archeological Collections*, extra vol. 1, p. 170.

20. *Surrey Archeological Collections*, extra vol. 1, pp. 259–160.

21. The *Victoria History of Surrey* provides a thorough accounting of family land acquisition and exchange for the period in question.

22. charlwoodsociety.co.uk/the-charlwood-maps, p. 42.

23. Charles Ross, *The War of the Roses*, London: Thames and Hudson, 1976, p. 164.

24. Sewill and Lane, *Free Men*, p. 44.

25. Ashley, *British Kings and Queens*, pp. 615–616.

26. Sewill and Lane, *Free Men*, p. 44.

27. charlwoodsociety.co.uk/the-charlwood-maps, p. 42.

CHAPTER FIVE

Quartered Arms

Henry VI ruled England from 1422 to 1471. This was an unhappy period, for in Henry's time much of France was lost, popular and baronial revolts sprouted, and finally the long drawn-out War of the Roses blossomed into full flower. Much of this resulted from Henry's chronic irresolution and in later years, genuine debilitation. His legacy was the loss of much of England's strong recovery from the bubonic plagues in the 1300s that decimated much of the kingdom. This was national history as William Sanders of Charlwood found it in his adult years.

By the time William Sanders was born—we estimate about the year 1415— the Sanders had lived in Charlwood for about a century and were two centuries removed from their roots at Sanderstead. Unfolding over this extended period were two centuries of gradual family devolution, a perceptible loss of preeminence in political sway, social position, and family wealth. The Sanders remained an important family in their Charlwood locality, retaining hold of Sanders Place Manor and nearby fields for their crops and animals, but their present state in William Sanders' time contrasted starkly with their halcyon days of close royal connection at Sanderstead and Sende. The family's enduring coat of arms bore silent witness to those earlier days.

But against the tide of unfavorable English history and somewhat inglorious family obscurity came a seismic change in family fortunes. The important moment came when William married Joan, a coheiress of the Carew family of Surrey.

The Carews of Surrey belonged to an old and distinguished family of Norman descent with strong Irish as well as English connections. They were kinsmen of the influential Devonshire Carews, although their immediate ancestors lived in Berkshire and it was only during the 1300s that the Carews acquired extensive Surrey estates. Among their holdings at the time of William Sanders were the manors of Beddington, Huscarle, Norbury, Carshalton,

Woodmansterne, and Nutfield, together with land in Hoe, Chesham, Horne, Mitcham, Coulsdon, and Bensham. Other holdings lay in Kent and Berkshire. Nicholas Carew, grandfather of Joan, William's young wife, had risen to the royal court as Lord Keeper of the Privy Seal, one of the great offices of state, and in later years was an executor in the estate of King Edward III [1].

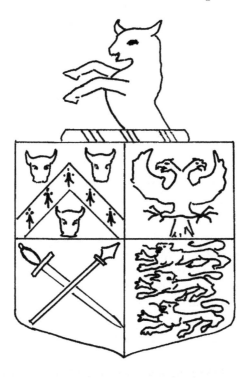

The quartered arms of William Saunder. Quartered arms represent a union of lordships from marriage. The families represented are (clockwise from top left) Saunder, Salomon, Carew, and Collenden.

The marriage of Joan and William reached far beyond mere solemnification of marriage vows. The joining required a resolution of property rights accruing to each party. The goal was to seal new entitlements for posterity. The instrument to achieve this was to create a quartered coat of arms. Hereafter, attending Joan Carew and William Sanders in their legal standing was a new and meaningful symbol, the quartered arms that held the prestigious names from which property entitlements derived—the three bulls' heads of the Sanders, the double-headed eagle of the Salamans, the crossed swords the Collendens, and now the lions of the Carews. These quartered arms symbolized a new union of lordships, a formalized and perpetuated family association of prestige, entitlement, and property. For William, the meaning of this arrangement was that his new place in Surrey lay in the elevated social and political realm of the Carews, a position reminiscent of ancient Sanderstead history. For the Charlwood Sanders, William's marriage might have seemed a restoration.

Early Years

William Saundre evidently was the youngest son of Thomas and Joanna Saundre. He was born about 1415, and no doubt lived his early years at Sanders Place Manor. We suppose William had an upbringing of some modest personal ease and social standing, as his father possessed land freely and had gained such wealth as was possible for yeomen of the time. But nothing specific is known about William until the time of his marriage.

Joan Carew was of Beddington Manor in the north of Surrey. As Carew's Beddington Manor lay adjacent to Sanderstead in Wallington Hundred in northern Surrey, the Saundres (i.e., the de Sandersteads) and Carews certainly were not strangers, having been near neighbors for generations. Even recently, William Saundre's father Thomas in 1421 had engaged property dealings with Thomas Hayton, Joan Carew's grandfather. So this marriage had its precursors and involved close families, not always the case in these times of strategically arranged marriages. But some innovations in English society equally contributed to the possibility of this match.

Following the years of devastation to the English population, English aristocracy was not on the whole entrepreneurial in style or outlook, but it did show a remarkable ability to adapt to realities. Although they closed ranks at the upper levels, the aristocratic class remained open to new entrants. There was much intermarriage among the gentry with London merchant families, and the gentry tapped a stream of recruits from the merchants, lawyers, entrepreneurs and war captains. Indeed, the ranks of the gentry were widened by the inclusion of a new category labelled 'gentlemen'[2]. This societal adaptation bore directly on William Sanders, hereafter at times called "gentleman" of Surrey.

With Thomas Saundre, yeoman, amassing what he could of personal wealth and his son William marrying well and gaining the title of gentleman, a new Saundre family of Charlwood began to find its way into prominence. William and Joan were married about 1437, when he was twenty-three and she fifteen, a not unusual early age for marriage at the time. By about 1438, the first of their many children were born.

Property

William Saundre's life was unambiguously prosperous. A fair amount is known of his property holdings. Numerous Charlwood properties came to

William directly through inheritance and others from his own enterprise. Between 1440 and 1470, he actively acquired land in and around Charlwood. In 1446, William purchased Sloghterwyk, a tract of land at Charlwood, from Richard Coleman. In 1450, William and his father purchased additional property called Godbaldesfeldes, and by around 1450, he had succeeded to Sanders Place, either anticipating or following his father's death [3]. In 1460, William acquired a shop in Charlwood from Margaret Taylor, a widow, though what kind of shop is not known. Less clear are the dates of transactions for other properties to have fallen into William's hands, but Chantersluer Farm [4], Colmannesham, and other tracts at Charlwood became his own property, if not his father's before him.

A later deed provides particulars of the family's extensive Charlwood holdings, including a capital messuage called Charlwood Place with the Great Park, the Little Park, Kewne, Great Godfreys, Lesser Godfreys, Greater Biggeshaw, two closes about Bannister's tenement Bushfield, and the Granthams, Parson Hilson, the Warren, Hither Riddles, the Middle Riddles, Farther Riddles, Skewes Mead, the Lyons, Riddlesmead, and the Andrews of three hundred acres, and lands called Telvet and Fenners Croft of forty-five acres. William Saundre in his adulthood probably had become Charlwood's principal landowner.

Rather more of William's holdings came through joint control of Joan Carew's eventual inheritance. Her inheritance involved complex arrangements that required a series of lawsuits to untangle. Joan, who was born about 1422, and her sister Mercy were daughters of Thomas Carew, the eldest son of Nicholas Carew, and his wife Agnes Hayton, the daughter and heiress of Thomas Hayton, clerk of Surrey. Thomas Carew died in 1430, leaving his young daughters as coheiresses. His widow Agnes shortly thereafter married John Exham (Hexham) and it was during this marriage that both Joan and Mercy were themselves married. Two years after the death of her father, Joan's grandfather, Nicholas Carew, died. He left property in trust for each of Thomas's daughters, to be granted to them when they attained the age of fifteen. It was also in 1432 that their maternal grandfather, Thomas Hayton, died.

When Thomas Carew died in 1430, the ages of his daughters fell in the range of seven to eleven years. We do not know who assumed their wardship at that time, though the matter had enormous significance as regards the daughters' marriages and their intended inheritances. Most likely, their grandfather Nicholas Carew either assumed these wardships himself or arranged for custody to pass to their mother Agnes. In either arrangement, the planning would not have involved simple informal arrangements but rather ones carefully drafted to ensure retention of financial control within the Carew family, no small task in the legal labyrinth that characterized feudal property regimes [5]. In all likelihood, Nicholas Carew before he died contracted for the marriages of his granddaughters to take place when they attained the age of fifteen, the age at which they were to receive their inheritances.

Following a series of lawsuits between 1448 and 1451, Joan Carew Saundre finally won the inheritance due her from her grandfather. Included in the award were a series of manors that had long lain in Carew hands. These were the manors of East Purley in Sanderstead [6] and Creuses in Warlingham [7]. She also gained the manors of Westburgh in Surrey [8] and Tullwick in Berkshire [9]. Joan inherited yet another Surrey manor called Battailes [10], in this case receiving only a third share of the manor, the remainder divided equally between her two sisters. Joan evidently also received the Manor of Aldhagh (called Esthevers) in Horley near Charlwood [11], and a share of the Manor of Woodmanstern [12]. Finally, Joan and William's legal challenges regarding inheritance of the manors of Carshalton in Surrey [13] and Purley Magna, Berkshire [14], were not successful, as these manors had been resettled on Nicholas Carew, Joan's uncle, the younger brother of Joan's father Thomas.

Joan's inheritance of these manors brought the family both wealth and responsibility, and both would color William Saundre's life in ensuing years. These manors contained lands in demesne, that is, lands used for the benefit of the lord or owner, which were a key source of wealth for the manorial lord. They often also included numerous properties at distant locations that were formally attached to the manor, constituting another important source of income. The Manor of Tullwick, for example, included eight houses in London. Battailes seemed to be connected to an inn at Southwark. All profits from these extensive properties accrued to the manorial lord.

Manors also contained lands operated by tenants, subtenants, or servants for their own use. These lands traditionally were used to produce foods for domestic consumption and for sale. Monies thus earned by domestic labor were needed for taxes, rents, and occasional purchases for personal needs. The manors themselves intendedly were self-sufficient but necessarily employed a steady supply of skilled and unskilled labor to supplement domestic staff. It fell to the owner to see that the manor was both self-sustaining and profitable, requiring careful calculations of production costs and astute analyses of market conditions for gainful trade. As time went by and Joan Carew's inherited manors—a total of six—were added to Saundre family property, William Saundre's plate was increasingly full.

The problems associated with control of these manors were by no means narrowly managerial, however. Traditional feudal manorial arrangements for using land and employing help, still a norm in William's day, lay directly in the path of rampaging new economic forces, new systems of agriculture that eventually brought feudal land tenure and agricultural production arrangements to a grinding halt. This new process involved land enclosure, a set of exclusionary practices that began in the wake of the great plagues, especially in the north of England. Slowly and systematically, manor lands were being fenced off and remade as purely private holdings, with lands used by tenants and held in common greatly reduced or eliminated. Increasingly, land was given over exclusively to wool production, and with this monoculture the need for manorial labor was greatly reduced. To William then would have come the uncertainty of managing major agricultural change and the painful process of removing land tenants whose forebears worked the land for generations.

The traditional self-sufficient feudal manor was beginning to give way to modern capitalist agriculture, a wholly new model of rural production that affected all parts of that society and economy. The extent to which enclosure engaged William Saundre's thinking is not clear, though there is no doubt that he became a player in England's burgeoning wool business. It appears that William Saundre had correctly understood the nature of economic change in his own time and acted upon it with financial success, though surely with pain. It is against this background that William and Joan released Westburgh Manor in 1466 to Henry Merland.

Beyond the management of lands and manors, William had another involvement as well. Around 1441, he and Richard Ford, his brother-in-law who had married Joan Carew's sister, engaged a legal transaction in Southwark near London, hinting that a property there might have been included in their recent marriage settlements, perhaps involving the Manor of Battailes [15]. At some point, perhaps this one, the Saundre family either gained or reaffirmed control of the Three Crowns Inn of Southwark in London, a property that would remain in family hands for some time. Ownership of this inn required royal licenses for inn keeping and wine trading and thus memberships in the appropriate mercantile houses [16]. For an extended period, perhaps beginning at this point if not before, the Saundre family name came to be associated with the Vintners Company of London. In 1498, another Richard Ford, perhaps a son of William Saundre's brother-in-law, was appointed master of the Vintners Company [17].

Insurrection

The insurrection of 1449 in which William participated with his father and other relatives did not mark the end of political conflict in England, but rather marked a beginning of the famed War of the Roses, a series of struggles that colored national life, and William's life, for two decades. In 1450, a large uprising called Cade's Rebellion, Yorkist in sympathy, turned violent and eventually was crushed by the Lancastrian king's forces, but not before Cade's well-formed contingent [18] had executed Sir James Fiennes, called Lord Say and Sele, whose practices in Kent they regarded as little better than

Suffolk's. Fiennes was related by marriage to the family of Joan Carew. The difficulties and delays surrounding Joan Carew Saundre's inheritance perhaps were attributable at least in part to this event. William Saundre himself may have felt compromised by his political compatriots as they executed his wife's relative.

An uneasy calm settled over England after Cade's Rebellion, but hostilities reemerged in 1455—the first actual battle of the War of the Roses—so-called because the Lancastrians, then in power, used a red rose as their symbol, and the oppositionist Yorkists, a white rose. Their battles over the next fifteen years were primarily struggles within the aristocracy, and the general population was little affected. William Saundre himself seems greatly affected by these events; his own offspring and their descendants chose to display roses as symbols on their own coats of arms. These seem to be political statements inasmuch as the selection of symbols at this time was not regulated, and their inclusion suggests strong family attachment to issues surrounding the conflict. As William marched for the Yorkist cause, it is instructive that his son Henry, though only a child for most of the conflict, chose a white rose for his arms. A somewhat later descendant of another son chose a red rose. In these choices, the power of symbols should not be underestimated; they reflected the kinds of allies and alliances that each family would develop in their own generations.

The last years of William's life were filled with loss. In 1470, his wife of more than thirty years died at age forty-eight. Eight years after Joan's death, their son William of Banbury died at age thirty-nine, followed in two years by the death of son Richard at age twenty-eight. William himself died eleven years after Joan in 1481. The causes of these deaths occurring in relatively tight sequence are unknown, but according to Lander, the fifteenth century has been described as the golden age of bacteria, with frequent outbreaks of bubonic plague, rural as well as urban. There were high levels of mortality in the 1420s and 1430s. The decade of the 1470s was disastrous with outbreaks of the "bloody flux." The virulence of the plague died down after the great outbreak of 1479–1480 [19]

Perspective

By the time of William's death, the Saundre family had resided at Charlwood for nearly two and a half centuries. In that time, the family had lived through vast changes in their own lives and fortunes and seen an entirely new England come to life. By the end of the fifteenth century, feudalism was fully on the wane, and the restrictive feudal order of life for the family had weakened dramatically. Family members now owned their own land and built wealth and came into social prominence through fortuitous marriages. They had lived through famines and relentless outbreak of plague and seen times of good and bad monarchic rule. They lived to see the rise of effective parliamentary governance and simultaneous recognition of their own political rights. In the person of William especially, heir to this epochal history, the family commenced commercial involvement in a new economic order and took on roles that in the past were reserved exclusively for the more highly privileged.

Though the Saundre family of Charlwood is unlikely to have appreciated the fact, the great Italian Renaissance was fully underway in the fifteenth century, ushering in a new millennium of humanistic awareness that would engulf all of Europe and eventually the globe. In time, the family would feel these changes directly. In William's own lifetime, Johannes Gutenberg printed his first book in Germany in 1454, and William Caxton followed suit with the first book printed in England in 1477. Beyond England, commercial trade was increasingly far-flung, and even the first voyage of Christopher Columbus was in the planning stages at the time of William's death. A short eleven years after William's death, Columbus landed in the West Indies [20].

Children

In his marriage with Joan Carew, William Saundre of Charlwood gained wealth, stature, and property far beyond what lay in family hands before his time. The marriage also produced numerous children. Some of the children's names have been lost to posterity because neither Joan's will of 1470 nor William's will of 1481 seem to have survived. What we do know of these children comes largely from indirect evidence resulting from the wealth and property that followed the children in their adult lives. Learning about these children matters greatly to family history because their lives intertwined fully in later years, especially when their marriages are taken into account. Understanding the life of any one of the children permits better understanding of them all since each depended upon the other in family affairs.

Records are clear that Joan and William Saundre had sons William, Richard, and Henry, and a daughter Joan [21], but it is altogether likely that they also had sons Nicholas, Thomas [22], John, and Stephen among those that survived to adulthood, and two more who are thought to have died in infancy. The eldest child William was born about 1438, and for Joan, childbearing progressed over at least an eighteen year period. In this family history, we focus on the youngest son Henry, whose life is described in chapter 4. But first we turn to the other children as their stories are rich in themselves and they cast important light on later family history. In the retrospect of history, it seems fair to guess that Joan and William would have been stunned and delighted to learn what their children made of their early advantages.

DESCENT AND FAMILY BRANCHING FROM
WILLIAM SAUNDRES OF CHARLWOOD

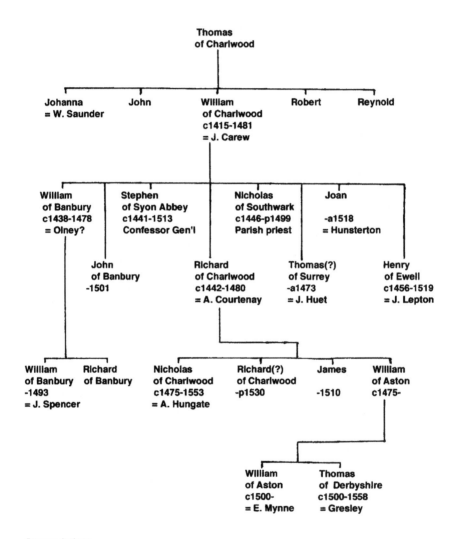

Source: Authors.

A simple genealogical recounting of names of Joan and William's children ignores a key feature of Sanders family history. For the Saundres, life after Joan and William was significantly different from what foregoing generations experienced, in part because the historical times changed, affecting how lives were lived. Equally though, this family, suddenly ascendant, possessed substantial wealth and connections to wealth, new social status, and new properties that were geographically far-flung. From this point forward in time, the Saundres family developed several enduring geographical branches, each distinct in its own location, lineage, and history, yet preserving itself as an intact, intertwined, and functioning family whole. In this respect, the Saundres family after Joan and William bore little resemblance to the family before their time.

ENDURING RELATIONSHIP BETWEEN THE CAREWS AND THE SAUNDERS

A sense of an enduring relationship of the Carews and the Saunders is given below, but this list does not include other indirect linkages involving additional families, nor does it portray continuous property exchanges between these families. Tight and enduring relationships between families such as shown in this example were common in those times.

Item	Date	Notes
Joan Carew married William Saunder.	c1427	Joan was the daughter of Thomas Carew of Beddington and heiress of numerous manors.
Richard Saunder, son of William and John Carew Saunder, married Agnes Courtenay.	c1467	Joan Courtenay, kin of Agnes, married Nicholas Carew of Mohun Ottery.
Nicholas Saunder, son of Henry of Ewell, married Joan Iwardby St. John.	c1513	Joan Iwardby was the daughter of Senchia Carew of Beddington. She had previously married Sir John St. John by whom she had a son John. This John became the ward of Nicholas Saunder.
The will of Henry Saunder of Ewell.	1518	Trustees of Henry's will included Sir Richard Carew of Beddington and his son, Sir Nicholas Carew.

Mary Saunder, daughter of sister of Nicholas (below), married Nicholas Lussher.	c1557	Nicholas Lussher was the grandson of of Ann Carew Leigh. Ann was the daughter of Sir Richard Carew and sister of Sir Nicholas (d. 1539).
Nicholas Saunder, son of William and grandson of Henry, married Isabel Carew.	1560	Isabel Carew was the daughter of Sir Nicholas Carew (d. 1539). Her niece married Sir Walter Raleigh.
Nicholas Saunder, chaplain of St. Mary Magdalen of Southwark, was a colleague of Richard Welles, clerk.	c1590	James Carew of Beddington (d. 1493) married Eleanor Welles whose mother was the daughter of Lord Welles.
		William Saunder of Banbury (d. 1493) left a legacy to Sir Nicholas Welles, priest.
Henry Saunders, son of Nicholas of Ewell (d. 1587) received a bequest from his uncle, Sir Francis Carew.	1611	Sir Francis Carew of Beddington was a brother of Isabel Carew (above).

William of Banbury

William Saundre was the eldest son of Joan and William Saundre, born about 1438 [23]. Like other eldest sons in those days, William was accorded favorable treatment, being supported in some way that elevated him quickly into high commercial circles [24]. William's lot was to become a successful wool merchant at a time when wool was emerging as England's first genuine capital (and export) crop. His life was one of capital venture, international trade, and political preferment.

In some ways, the family wealth and position produced largely from the Carew family's feudal past served merely as a precondition for further family prosperity in the late 1400s, at least for William Saundre of Banbury. Large scale economic changes had begun to grip England at the time, and one can scarcely exaggerate the degree to which all of England and the Saundres family were affected. The fifteenth century in England saw the arrival of capitalism, the greatest engine of wealth-production the world had ever seen [25]. Early forms of capital organization in the form of rudimentary corporations had developed in Italian city states, notably Venice and Florence, since the time of Marco Polo, and these inexorably pushed outward into Western Europe following refinements in corporate organization, bookkeeping, and capital lending. The result was massive concentrations of wealth among Italy's leading families, most notably the Medicis [26]. Eventually, successful European corporations provided lessons in capitalism for England, and by the 1400s, some English merchants had been brought into the international capitalist fold. The rise of capitalism in Italy in some ways underwrote the great Italian Renaissance itself as it was wealthy merchants who commissioned many of the famous advances in Renaissance art and architecture, and the same was true as capitalism advanced through Western Europe.

In England and elsewhere, for capitalism to succeed meant that older feudal forms of economy and society had to give way. In particular, the notion of a self-sufficient feudal manor producing small surpluses for local markets stood in the way of capital conceptions of land. Local surpluses could be replaced by large-scale exportable product if land were turned exclusively toward profit making. That was the capital goal, and wholesale shifts away from feudal patterns of land tenure and common fields was the result. This process was called enclosure [27]. Along with enclosure and because of it, wealth began to shift away from old-guard feudal property holders and toward those who managed and traded agricultural surpluses. New hands from the mercantile world eventually would touch the purse strings of the nation; merchants eventually commanded elevated respect in the eyes of their titled but unmoneyed brethren. But all these changes crept forward only gradually in an uncertain England habituated to old ways. In the late 1400s, in the time of Joan and William's children, we barely glimpse a capital ship that seems small and insignificant on the economic horizon.

William seems to have married around age twenty-one, probably to a daughter of John Olney, a good match for an aspiring young merchant [28]. John Olney was a successful merchant in London and in fact lord mayor of the city in 1446. Olney also held property in Neithorp in Oxfordshire, and lands in Neithorp came into William Saundre's possession in the same period, suggesting he acquired Neithorp property through marriage to Olney's daughter [29]. William probably also received the Saundre family's Manor of Tullwick in Berkshire at the time of his marriage [30].

Shortly before or after marriage, William settled in the town of Banbury in Oxfordshire, an important wool center for the region north of London. He purchased property both in Banbury and the nearby places of Grimsbury and Fenny Compton in Warwickshire [31]. The selection of Banbury as a place of residence and center of trade was well chosen because Banbury lay convenient to London and on a direct route to the port of Southampton. London and Southampton were the two principal locations for wool export, London's wool making its way to Florence (Italy) and Southampton's to Calais.

William Saundre of Banbury wasted little time developing his skills and contacts for wool trade. By the time he was in his mid-twenties, William can be found with other merchants in London recovering one hundred marks' debt from a London grocer [32]. No doubt he frequented the city regularly over the next decade, though the only record of his London business is for 1475, when he with several other merchants settled a debt with Thomas de Bardi and others at Westminster [33]. This de Bardi transaction is telling because the de Bardis worked for the powerful Medici family of Florence. William clearly was not dealing with small quantities of wool or small sums of money.

Two Florentine merchants dominated the London wool trade, Giovanni de Bardi and Gherardo Canigiani [34]. Together they jointly operated an *accomandita*, a partnership with the Medici family in which the latter remained unnamed [35]. The firm operated in London under the name of Canigiani, and capital for its commercial operations was supplied by Piero di Cosimo de' Medici and Tommaso Portarini, the manager of the Medici branch in the city of Bruges (in today's Belgium).

The Canigiani firm operated with enormous sums of money for those days and exerted their influence proportionately. In 1471, Gherardo Canigiari was creditor for King Edward IV's debt of nearly fifteen thousand pounds, a huge sum borrowed by the king during his six-month exile in France [36]. This debt forgiveness coincided with Edward's restoration to the throne. One suspects that in exchange for debt forgiveness, Canigiani, on behalf of the Medicis, extracted royal promises for the improvement of trade, and that indeed is how the later years of Edward's reign can be characterized. The historian Ashley notes, "The second half of Edward's reign lacks the glory and excitement of the first, although it was more administratively sound. It was during this period that Edward was able to carry through the reforms he had started in the previous decade, which led to better executed offices of the Crown, more effective administration of the law, and generally profitable and safe trade throughout England" [37].

Giovanni de Bardi returned to Florence in 1483 on the death of Edward IV, building a chapel for his own spiritual salvation. To adorn the chapel, he commissioned the famed Renaissance painter Botticelli for an altarpiece, which survives to this day. Parenthetically, Giovanni's son of the same name founded a music school in which Vincenzo Galilei, father of the astronomer Galileo, participated. Giovanni also is credited with creating the first Italian opera, authoring the first treatise on the rules of football, and in time was appointed chamberlain to the pope.

William Saundre, then, found himself in the company of wealthy international wool merchants and used contacts such as these to extend his commercial interests. His main attention was directed to the port of Southampton. He is first found there in 1467, selling wool and importing two butts [38] of wine from Calais [39]. By 1471, he had taken up quarters within the walled confines of Southampton, renting a tenement at the outskirts of the town's main business center. This was tenement number 26 of God's House College. But two years later, in 1473, we find William moving to larger quarters in God's House tenement number 21, just steps away from the wool market and other business establishments in the heart of the old city [40]. William had clearly moved up in his world.

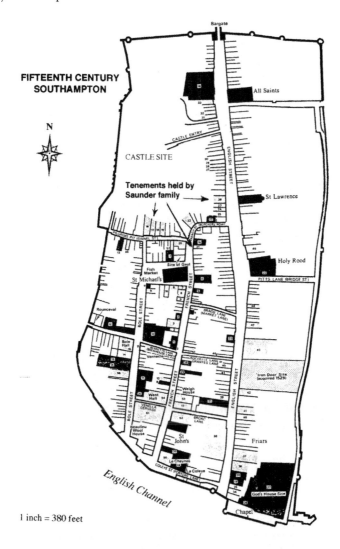

Plan of Southampton's fifteenth-century walled center, showing tenements of citizens and merchants. William Saunders of Banbury held tenements numbered 26 and 21. The wool house (bottom left) was built in 1407 as a warehouse for Southampton's important medieval wool trade with Flanders and Florence. Adapted from J. Faye, Cartulary of God's House (Southampton: University Press, 1979).

This same year, 1473, was an important one in William's life. He by then was thirty-five years old. In that year, William Saundre and Andrew James were appointed deputies of the port of Southampton [41]. Andrew James and his father, a one-time lord mayor of Southampton, dealt mostly in wines, but also in cloth, trading principally with Oxfordshire and western English centers. William and Andrew were deputized by Anthony, Earl Rivers, the chief butler of England. Anthony's title resulted rather directly from his sister Elizabeth Wydville's marriage to King Edward IV in 1464. A better claim to historical notoriety for Earl Rivers was his translation of *Dictes and Sayenges of the Phylosophers*, a manuscript that was the first book to be printed in England, off the new printing press of William Caxton in 1477.

These deputy appointments in 1473 coincide with Edward IV's decision to tighten his hold on sources of royal revenue—the chief of which were duties on Crown land, wardships, and marriages, but also customs duties "on wool, hides, and wool-fells, the custom on cloth, and the subsidy of tunnage on wine, and the petty custom and poundage on general merchandise"[42]. For some years after his accession in 1461, Edward's efforts for stricter control were tentative but following his return from exile in 1471 penalties for evasion were increased and enforcement became more rigorous. Lander notes, "In 1473, a most comprehensive commission into all sorts of evasions were issued for Devon and Cornwall, authorising enquiries into the customs officials as far back as the first days of the reign...(a)nd beginning with an experiment at Southampton and Poole in 1473, Edward imposed stricter methods of supervision upon the custom's staff" [43]. William Saundre's work at Southampton was to implement the royal program of tightened trade regulation.

William was at the zenith of his successful career in trade and port administration when he died suddenly in 1478 at about age thirty-nine. He asked to be remembered as a woolman and merchant in his will, and in addition to the usual bequests to church and community, William left money for the purchase of bells for Our Lady of Banbury Church where he was buried [44]. William's sons had barely reached legal adulthood at the time of his death. He named his younger brother Richard Saundre of Charlwood his executor [45].

The bulk of William's lands in and around Banbury probably fell to William, who from his name would seem to have been the elder son. We know little of the work of this son William, but he called himself a woolman and merchant following his father's example. He married well, into a major sheep-raising family of Warwickshire. William married Joan, daughter of John Spencer of Hodenhall, and that marriage provided entry into a social stratum that influenced later generations of the Saundres. Joan Spencer and William

Saundre had five daughters, and all were underage (one yet unborn) at the time of William's early death in 1493 at about age thirty-two [46].

Joan Spencer remarried to Sir William Cope and assumed responsibility for the five daughters Anne, Isabel, Joyce, Alice, and Joan, especially in arranging their marriages. Anne, the eldest daughter married Stephen Cope, Sir William's son, and Alice married Sir John Cooke of Gideas Hall in Essex [47]. A granddaughter of that marriage, Mildred, married perhaps the wealthiest and most influential person in the kingdom of that time, William Cecil, Lord Burghley. These marriages came to bear upon Saundres family history in the sixteenth century.

William's other son, Richard, continued his father's work in wool trading. Although records are scant, we know that in 1483, Richard met with Gherardo Canigiani, the noted Florentine wool merchant, to forgive the latter's debt to his family [48]. William evidently left Tullwick Manor to Richard, although exact succession of this property remains unclear.

In 1501, Tullwick Manor lay under the control of John Saundre, probably another son of Joan Carew and William Saundre of Charlwood and a brother of William of Banbury. John may have followed William to Banbury in his early adulthood, and he seems to have run Tullwick following his brother's death. During his tenure, John oversaw the enclosure of fifty-five acres of Tullwick land and also the eviction of four tenants who previously had worked the land under traditional arrangements [49]. These actions cleared the way for conversion of Tullwick lands to sheep raising. But by 1503, John must have died or been removed as the property lay in the hands of Richard Saundre, son of William of Banbury, and his wife Marjory Yate. In that year, ownership of Tullwick passed to John Yate of Lyford, no doubt Marjory's relative. This sale seems to have ended the Saundre family's interest in Tullwick. As for Banbury, the Saundre's family name seems to have disappeared from that location following these three generations, owing to the failure of male issue.

Sons in the Priesthood

Two sons of Joan Carew and William Saundre of Charlwood evidently entered the Roman Catholic priesthood in the latter half of the fifteenth century. Their names were Nicholas [50] and Stephen [51]. Most likely both were younger sons, born in the 1440s or slightly later. As a way to maintain family property for posterity, parents commonly denied younger sons property inheritance, concentrating their land in the hands of older sons, hoping to preserve an intact base of family landholding for later generations. Younger sons sometimes entered church service as an alternative to landownership. Priesthood was frequently chosen because the church presented important avenues for lifetimes of service and influence, at least for those sufficiently pious and talented to succeed.

The Roman Catholic Church was by far the largest single employer in England in the fifteenth century, employing as many as one in every twenty males entering the workplace. The reason for this is not hard to find. The church and the government were deeply intertwined, and many of the functions we accept today as the role of government at that time fell to the church. Church parish boundaries were used as governmental units, and parish affairs such as real estate disputes and care for the poor rested upon church authority. The church maintained courts of local jurisdiction, using ecclesiastical law to rule on family and community affairs. The church furthermore was a principal landowner throughout the realm, holding manors, agricultural lands, tenements, hospitals, almshouses, and church structures of all kinds. Finally, of course, the church exercised its monopoly on sacred matters, requiring an extensive network of churches throughout the nation. All these required church manpower. To meet this need, an extensive array of monasteries, nunneries, and schools were built to provide the large and educated workforce the church required, and education itself remained more a church than a governmental responsibility. Committing one's life to church work, therefore, presented numerous opportunities and took aspirants in any number of directions.

Nicholas Saundre was a chaplain during the 1490s at the St. Mary Magdalen Church in Southwark, a district lying at the south edge of the old city of London just across the Thames. William Saundre of Charlwood, Nicholas's father, held the Three Crowns Inn in Southwark, a property he received as part of a marriage agreement with the Carews, but so far as we know, Nicholas Saundre had nothing to do with the Three Crowns Inn. In Nicholas's time though, the Saundres family maintained other presence in Southwark, at least one family member seems to have resided there on a regular basis [52].

Of Nicholas, in fact, we know very little, but his work at Southwark brought Nicholas face-to-face with one of England's great royal mysteries. In its own peculiar way, this incident illustrates the degree to which the Saundres had begun to reach into royal circles.

When King Edward IV died in 1483, his twelve-year-old son Edward was expected to become Edward V. But in preparation for his coronation, both Edward and a younger brother Richard were duplicitously escorted to the Tower of London and thereafter remained permanently confined. Within three months, both were murdered. Richard III, uncle of the boys and brother to Edward IV, took the Crown. The question of who murdered the "princes in the tower" was never resolved and remains a persistent intrigue even for contemporary historians. Numerous theories have been spawned. Most popular is the belief that Richard III masterminded the deed as it was he who benefited most from their deaths [53]. There was, furthermore, a confession offered years later, though a highly dubious one. Nearly two decades after the fact and under severe torture, Sir James Tyrell, a knight, confessed that he had entered the tower and smothered the children at Richard III's behest. For this admission, Tyrell was beheaded in 1502.

Sir James Tyrell possessed a good deal of property, including holdings in Southwark. On his conviction in 1499 for the princes' murders, Tyrell's Southwark property was forfeited to the Crown. This land in turn was placed in the hands of Nicholas Saundre, chaplain at St. Mary Magdalen Church in Southwark, and a coworker named Richard Wellys [54]. The property itself is described as "the King's great messuage in the parish of St. Mary Magdalen by Bermondsey, Surrey, and ten small tenements adjoining and eleven gardens containing three acres . . ." Saundre and Wellys were instructed to "hold the property to the use of Cecily Whitney of Bermondsey, widow, and her heirs forever" [55]. This arrangement meant that the church itself bore responsibility for future use of the property, with Saundre and Wellys representing the church in this action.

Nicholas's role in this affair may have extended beyond conveying property because the mother of the murdered princes, Elizabeth Wydville, was confined for her lifetime to Bermondsey Abbey, to which St. Mary Magdalen Church was attached [56]. Whether Nicholas Saundre can be linked to the confinement of Elizabeth Wydville, wife of the deceased King Edward IV, is uncertain, but some connection here is plausible. Elizabeth's brother Anthony Wydville, Earl Rivers, had previously hired Nicholas's brother, William Saundre of Banbury, as his deputy for port supervision in Southampton.

Among the children who survived their parents, Nicholas may have been the family figure to whom younger brothers looked for direction after their mother's and father's deaths. The name Nicholas Saundre was echoed in three successive generations following this Nicholas of Southwark. Further, a younger brother Henry in his later life left money to St. Mary Magdalen Church, though that was not his home church, and named a curate of St. Mary Magdalen as witness to his will [57]. These actions suggest some enduring ties to St. Mary Magdalen built upon Nicholas's earlier church commitment and also Nicholas's contributions to Saundre family stability in times of turmoil [58]. But of Nicholas himself, we learn nothing more.

Nicholas's brother Stephen, if indeed he was his brother, took a different course in church affairs, opting for attachment to a monastery rather than a parish church as Nicholas had done. We cannot be certain that Stephen Saundre was a son of Joan Carew and William Saundre of Charlwood, but later events in family history do suggest the possibility. We know that Stephen was born in the same decade as William and Joan's other children. He enrolled for a baccalaureate degree in divinity before 1461 and, in that year, was named a chantry priest by a certain William Gregory, a skinner who previously had been lord mayor of London [59]. Stephen progressed through the ecclesiastical hierarchy over the ensuing decades and, by 1498, had assumed the high position of confessor-general of the esteemed Syon Abbey. He held this position until the time of his death in 1513 [60].

Syon Abbey was founded about the year that William Saundre of Charlwood was born, about 1415. It grew rapidly after that with gifts of manors and other property being added from throughout the south of England [61]. The abbey was a Brigittine monastery, designed to emulate the life of the Swedish saint Brigit who fashioned a life of piety through austerity and contemplation and who described her ideal monastery to achieve these goals. The Brigittine Syon Abbey, according to plan, would hold sixty nuns, thirteen priests, four deacons, and eight lay brethren. The confessor-general, Stephen Saundre's position, was elected by Syon brethren and charged with setting the abbey's spiritual direction. The abbey itself had cathedral-sized proportions and was probably one of England's most important ecclesiastical buildings in the fifteenth century.

We would perhaps take little note of Stephen in this narrative were it not for events in the 1500s that tied together the fates of Saundre family members and Syon Abbey itself. Two decades after Stephen's death, an Act of Supremacy was decreed, declaring Henry VIII to be the exclusive and supreme head of the church in England, supplanting papal authority in Rome. Thus, in Henry VIII's time began the Church of England and the abrupt diminution of Roman Catholicism throughout the land. Following the Act of Supremacy, representatives of several monasteries, including Syon Abbey, met with Henry's officials to try to discover a middle path whereby they could swear oaths of loyalty both to the king and the old church, but all were immediately executed. The rout of Roman Catholicism was underway. Catholic monasteries in England throughout the late 1530s were dissolved; Syon Abbey alone had refused to surrender. In 1539, numerous Syon scholars were put to death, and all other persons summarily expelled from the monastery. Henry seized the abbey and its outbuildings and even imprisoned his fifth wife, Catherine Howard, in one of them. But the fate of Syon Abbey was not fully sealed by 1539, and in this fragile but enduring Syon community, we find members of the Saundre family in the following decades. We return to this Syon Abbey story at a later point in this narrative when certain family members are seen to take refuge there.

Richard of Charlwood

Richard Saundre was born about 1442, the second son of Joan Carew and William Saundre of Charlwood. Richard among their numerous offspring was the principal heir of Charlwood property, ensuring the continuation of family presence at this traditional homeland. By the time Richard came into this property, the Saunders had dwelled at Charlwood for nearly 250 years.

By all accounts, Richard remained at Charlwood for his lifetime [62], though many details of his life story are lacking. But what is known about Richard speaks of a mercurial rise of family fortune even beyond that endowed by the Carews, a rise that elevated the family into royal affairs. About 1467, Richard married Agnes Courtenay, daughter of a distinguished old Norman family whose pedigree is a lexicon of English royal history. This union built upon an established link between the Carews and Courtenays [63] and offered the Saundres new avenues for social, political, and financial ascendancy. All these came into sharp focus in succeeding generations.

Finding Agnes in the labyrinthine Courtenay genealogy is no small task, but the effort repays itself in suggesting how the Saundres benefited in consequence of her marriage to Richard Saundre. The ancient family of Courtenay is sometimes characterized as having two main branches in England, a senior branch associated with early earldoms dating back in an unbroken line to the thirteenth century and before and a junior branch whose titles and broad prosperity commenced in the late fifteenth century. The good fortune of the junior branch of Courtenays resulted rather directly from the ill fortune of the senior. The special circumstance for Agnes, born about 1450, is that her lifetime fell within this dramatic transition.

The senior Courtenays into the fifteenth century were led by Sir Thomas Courtenay (1414–1458), the fifth Earl of Devon. He married Margaret Beaufort, whose niece of the same name was mother of King Henry VII. Sir Thomas and Margaret Courtenay had several sons and daughters, including three sons who in their time became the sixth, seventh, and eighth earls of Devon. But none survived. The sixth and seventh earls were beheaded for political opposition to the Crown and the eighth died in battle [64]. A daughter Joane first married Sir Roger Clifford, beheaded with the others, and second Sir William Knyvet. For all their offenses, King Edward IV confiscated the lion's share of extensive Courtenay property holdings throughout southern England. These events brought the senior branch of the Courtenays to a final bloody demise. Agnes Courtenay may have been a daughter in this tragic family and witness to its special horrors.

Alternatively, Agnes may have risen from the Courtenay's junior branch. Principal heir on this side was Sir Edward Courtenay (c1445–1509), designated initially as the ninth Devon earl, but later retitled the first, dimming the unhappy memory of those now gone. He regained lands lost by the senior Courtenays. A close relative of Sir Edward was Joane Courtenay, who married Nicholas Carew, he though not of the Beddington Carews. A cousin of Sir Edward's was Peter Courtenay (c1440–1492), bishop of Winchester and godfather of King Henry VIII. Agnes's age places her in this generation, perhaps of Sir Edward's family.

A Saunders genealogist writes, "Agnes Courtenay (was) of the Earls of Devon . . . (and her cousin) Sir William Courtenay married Catherine Plantagenet, daughter of Edward IV" [65]. This Sir William was the son of Sir Edward, and only slightly younger than Agnes, so it could be that Agnes was Sir William's older sister, though no records stating this have been found. In Agnes's generation also was Margaret Courtenay, who married into the Champernoun family, possessors of the Manor of Aston Rowant in Oxfordshire. The Courtenays of an earlier period also held Oxfordshire property in nearby Steeple Aston. This Courtenay presence at these locations may explain how a son of Agnes Courtenay Saundre came to reside at Oxfordshire in a village called Aston a generation later.

One cannot escape the conclusion that, whatever her exact position in that august Courtenay family, Richard's marriage to Agnes constituted a new Saundre family claim to privilege and a foothold for advancement in the political world the Courtenays long inhabited.

After their marriage, Agnes and Richard dwelled at Charlwood Place, also called Saunders Place, the moated mansion house on family lands. At least for the early years of the marriage, they shared residence with Richard's parents. Richard's mother Joan Carew died within three years of their marriage, but his father William lived on another decade there. Richard gained control of Charlwood acreage and also received from his mother the manors of East Purley and Creuses, both in northern Surrey near Sanderstead. He probably received property in Aston, Oxfordshire, from the Courtenays as well [66]. Richard's personal wealth was probably based on sheep raising and manorial incomes, though no record of wool transactions at Charlwood for this Richard have been uncovered [67].

Richard's life was lamentably short. In 1478, he served as executor for his brother William's will in Banbury, but only two years later, he himself passed away at about age thirty-eight. His father William outlived him, though only by one year.

Agnes saw to it that Richard was fully commemorated. Following Richard's death, she ordered construction of a chantry chapel to be added to St. Nicholas Church in Charlwood, an old Norman structure constructed around the year 1080. The Saunders Chapel, built to honor Richard with everlasting prayers of remembrance, is the oldest remaining structure associated with this ancient family and remains in use today, though with some changes from its original appearance. Full descriptions of St. Nicholas Church and the Saunders Chapel are available [68].

St. Nicholas Church at Charlwood. (Above) In the foreground is the section of the church structure added about 1481 to house the Saunders Chantry. (Below) View of the church facing the town of Charlwood. The Saunders Chantry is on the left. Construction of the original church was begun under Norman rule in 1080; worship in the church has continued for over nine hundred years. Photographs by Lucas Sanders.

Shortly after construction of the chapel was completed, in 1485, Agnes died and was interred with Richard. About this time, the family leased a farm in Charlwood called Chantersluer, the annual returns from which provided *chantersylver*, that is, money for the upkeep of the chantry, a means for perpetuating the commemoration.

(Above) Frieze at the entry to the Saunders Chapel in St. Nicholas Church bearing the initials "RS" to commemorate the life of Richard Saunder of Charlwood, who died in 1480. (Below) Composite mural of medieval stories on the walls of St. Nicholas Church dating from the thirteenth and fourteenth centuries. Photographs by Lucas Sanders.

Agnes and Richard's Children

Sources differ on whether Agnes and Richard had three, four, or seven sons [69], but reliable local authors claim they had only three [70]. These we can identify with some certainty. They were Nicholas, William, and James. Of James, there is little to say, other than he seems to have remained in the Charlwood area and died in the year 1510 [71].

All of Agnes and Richard's children, however many they might have been, were orphaned early in their lives [72]. Some in fact were underage as late as 1493 when a relative from Banbury addressed their continuing need in his will [73]. We have no account of wardships for these children, but responsibility for their welfare undoubtedly fell upon the few family members remaining after Agnes died in 1485. Most likely, responsibility was taken by their two uncles, Nicholas Saundre, chaplain at St. Mary Magdalen Church in Southwark, and Henry Saundre of Ewell in northern Surrey who himself had married only a year before Agnes died. Some Courtenays from the family of Agnes may have assisted as well. Thus, in the lives of these children and indeed their children, we find three distinct influences arising from their mother's death and the subsequent wardship arrangements. First, the Courtenays from the family of Agnes may have steered the children toward important political opportunities; at least that would explain how these Saundres gained some important government posts. Second, Henry of Ewell offered a base of close family support that bound together the ongoing parallel genealogies of the Saundres in Charlwood and Ewell. And third, the priest Nicholas Saundres of Southwark may have been sufficiently attentive to instill a firm commitment to Roman Catholic faith which endured in the family, even at times to the edge of fanaticism.

Probably the oldest surviving son of Agnes and Richard was Nicholas, born in the early 1470s. He lived until 1553, about eighty years, making Nicholas the person whose life tenure at Charlwood was the longest in family history. About 1504, he married Alys Hungate of Yorkshire, a match perhaps facilitated by his uncle Henry Saundre of Ewell and his wife Joan Lepton, who herself hailed from Yorkshire.

Two versions of Nicholas's life are offered in family literature, but they are contradictory. Sewill and Lane suggest that Nicholas led "a quiet and uneventful life" [74], but Edward Sandars wrote that Nicholas traveled widely and served as executor for the will of King Henry VIII in 1547 [75]. Neither view seems wholly accurate. Nicholas resided at Charlwood his entire life, engaging a variety of land transactions [76] and also involving himself in family affairs at Ewell as occasions required [77]. In these instances, Nicholas seems well settled. Furthermore, Nicholas was not an executor of Henry VIII's will as claimed. The names of the king's sixteen executors are well-known, and Nicholas Saundre is not among them [78]. Yet he may have played some role in the king's estate administration, and if so, it probably would have been to assist Sir Thomas Bromley in his executorship. Nicholas's close relative, William Saunders of Ewell, later named Bromley's nephew, also named Thomas Bromley, in his will of 1571. Additional weight for this interpretation of Nicholas's involvement lies in the fact one of Nicholas's sons eventually was knighted and came to hold an administrative position of national importance, an advancement that perhaps rested on Nicholas's earlier involvements in high government circles. We turn to this story of Sir Thomas Saunders of Charlwood in the following chapter.

Nicholas died in 1553, just days before the coronation of Queen Mary, daughter of Henry VIII. He was buried at the church in Charlwood, as was his wife Alys. The couple is memorialized in a Latin inscription on their vault at the Saunders Chapel [79]. On a brass memorial, Nicholas is shown bareheaded with square-cut hair and long beard. He is armed with sword and dagger and in full gothic armor. Alys's raiment is typical of clothing worn before her time, and their ten children are shown lined behind their parents wearing civil dress. On a wall above them are the Saundres arms quartered with the Carews. Another plaque carries arms for Alys's Hungate family, but, oddly, arms for the Courtenays are not in evidence.

The other son of Agnes and Richard Saundre was William, but with this William, our narrative departs from all other genealogies of this family. We believe that other accounts compress two generations of Williams into one, ignoring certain facts that make these past interpretations implausible [80]. The confusion over the number of Agnes and Richard's offspring, whether three, four, seven, or other number, results directly from this conflation of generations.

While we know that Agnes and Richard's son James died in 1510, and that their son Nicholas was principal heir in Charlwood, much less is understood of the third son William. He seems lost in all genealogical accounts, yet there can be no doubt of his existence. William was named as a son of Richard and brother of Nicholas of Charlwood in the 1518 will of Henry Saundre of Ewell, who was these sons' uncle. And because William was born before 1480 and alive in 1518, we can be sure he reached an age of nearly forty years. Circumstances if not actual evidence make it appear that William lived not much longer than these forty years.

William Saunders would have been born in the mid-1470s and probably married before 1500. As these life facts seem to have escaped recording in Surrey, it may be that William on reaching adulthood took up land elsewhere [81], on property brought to Saunders family possession from the Courtenays on Agnes's marriage to Richard. The most likely place was Aston, Oxfordshire. William's claim to property, if it resembled many others in these times, may have been for his lifetime only, lapsing back to the earlier owner upon death, thus denying William's own heirs an opportunity to continue dwelling there. That at least would explain why one cannot find the Saunders at Aston in the Oxfordshire records of those days.

Though no record of William's marriage has been located, it seems clear enough that he had at least four sons. One was called William, known to genealogists as William of Aston. Another was Thomas, who moved to Derbyshire. Two unnamed others traveled to the continent, one dying there in battle and the other remaining there for the remainder of his life [82]. Separate accounts of these family branches, one following William of Aston and the other Thomas of Derbyshire, are offered in the chapters that follow.

We suspect William died an early death like so many of his contemporaries, explaining perhaps why his name was lost to family recollection. Although he was alive in 1518, he probably lived only a short time after that. If this meant forfeiture of property, that would explain why his son Thomas left Aston permanently about 1520 and why the other son William seems to have returned to Surrey about the same time. In 1520, William of Aston, by then a young man, perhaps took up rental property in the Manor of Pendell in Surrey owned by Henry Saundre of Ewell and later managed by Nicholas of Charlwood, William's uncle [83].

Henry of Ewell

The youngest surviving son of Joan Carew and William Saundre of Charlwood was Henry, born about 1456. Henry, of whom mention has been made above, took up lands in the village of Ewell in north Surrey, inheriting former Carew property not far from Sanderstead. By this action, Henry continued the fifteenth- and sixteenth-century pattern of family branching, which also carried on beyond Henry's lifetime. In Henry's time and after, Henry's Ewell branch of the Saunders acquired new properties not only in Surrey, but also in Kent, Sussex, Norfolk, and in Pembrokeshire, Wales. To Henry Saunder's life we now turn.

NOTES

1. J.S. Roskell, L. Clark, C. Rawcliffe, eds., Carew, Nicholas(c.1356–1432), of Beddington, Surrey. History of Parliament: House of Commons 1386–1421, 1993.
2. Saul, *Oxford Illustrated History*, pp. 170–171.
3. Sewill and Lane, *Free Men*, p. 47.
4. Chantersluer Farm lay in the Manor of Shellwood, and rents from that property were used for upkeep of the Sanders Chantry in Charlwood in the early 1500s. Sewill and Lane, *Free Men*, p. 48.
5. Joan Carew Saundre's inheritance is surrounded by confusion, a result of the fact that the elder Nicholas Carew, Joan's grandfather, had made two property arrangements, one with his first wife and another when he married Mercy Haym, the mother of Thomas, Joan's father. Even in less confusing circumstances, the laws and practices surrounding

inheritances for minors, involving both wardships and marriage, are highly complex.

Lander explains, "In feudal society, the king possessed potentially valuable rights over his tenant-in-chief. Although the feudal system had lost its original military significance, it survived as a system of financial exploitation. The heir of any tenant-in-chief (a person holding land directly under the king) had to sue out livery for his inheritance against a fee—a kind of succession duty. If heirs were under the age of twenty-one they became royal wards. The king held their property until they were old enough to sue for livery and he controlled their marriages. Lesser lords enjoyed the same rights over their own tenants so that the upper ranks of society were thoroughly steeped in the spirit of the system. Feudal families often handled their own affairs in accordance with its existence even when they were uncomplicated by the existence of royal rights, so that the tangle of estates, wards, and widows played something like an investment system. Wardships were even bought and sold on the installment system.

"The enforcement of these feudal rights demanded eternal vigilance by the Crown. The concealment of feudal tenures both by collusion between the families concerned and the royal officials and by the creation of uses or trusts had become notorious during the fifteenth century. By the end of the fourteenth century, most wealthy families had placed a good deal of their landed property in the hands of trustees to be held to their use, thus enabling them to devise real estate by will and to evade the feudal incidents of livery, wardship, and marriage." See J. Lander, *Government and Community, England 1450–1509* (Cambridge: Harvard University Press, 1980), pp. 75–76, 89. Plowden adds, "Under English law, the wardship of any minor child who inherited landed property passed automatically to the Crown which normally gave, or more usually, sold it back to the relatives of the child concerned or some other favored applicant. The guardian was then free to enjoy the income from the property until the minor came of age—by which time he would have sold his ward's marriage to the highest bidder or else have arranged a marriage ensuring that control of the inheritance remained within the family circle." See A. Plowden, *Lady Jane Grey and the House of Suffolk* (New York: Franklin Watts, 1986), p. 6.

6.   Purley lay in the Manor of Sanderstead and, in the time of Edward IV, was divided into two parts, one being called East Purley, which retained the style of a manor, and West Purley. East Purley was acquired by the Carews in the late 1300s and was in possession of Joan Carew's grandfather Nicholas at the time of his death in 1432. His will settled

East Purley on Joan and her heirs. Recall that Richard de Sanderstead sold his lands at Sanderstead to Pirle in 1234. See *Victoria History of Surrey*, 4b, p. 329; and Owen Manning and William Bray, *History and Antiquities of the County of Surrey*, vol. 2 (Wakefield: E. P. Publishing and Surrey County Library, 1984), pp. 570–571.

7. The Manor of Creuses probably was formed by subinfeudation from Bermondsey Manor. Creuses is first mentioned in 1352 under the name of the Manor of Warlingham, but this property it seems was under preconquest ownership by the de Sanderstead family, having passed from Watkin to Stephen, his brother, before 1066. The Carews acquired the manor from the Willoughbys, no doubt reflecting the marriage of Nicholas Carew to Lucy Willoughby Huscarle in the 1300s. Upon his death in 1432, Nicholas Carew left his lands in Warlingham to Joan, one of the three daughters of his son Thomas. In default of Joan's issue, the manor was then to descend to her sister Mercy with contingent remainders to Nicholas and Isabel, son and daughter of the testator. Joan married William Saundre with whom she brought suit against William Selman (Salaman?) and William Bradford, trustees appointed by her grandfather, to oblige them to surrender the estate to her, she being more than fifteen years old, the age at which she was entitled to the estate. She deposed that in spite of this fact and of the will of her grandfather, produced by her grandmother, the trustees had refused to give it up. Creuses was surrendered to Joan in 1451. See *Victoria History of Surrey*, 4b, pp. 335–336; and Manning and Bray, *History and Antiquities,* pp. 427–428.

8. The Manor of Westburgh included land in Sandon and Essher. Thomas Hayton seized the manor in 1432. His daughter Agnes, then wife of John Exham, was his sole heir. She later married Thomas Sayer. In 1450, Thomas Sayer and his wife Agnes conveyed lands in Westburgh held in right of Agnes, to Richard Ford and his wife Mercy, William Sanders and his wife Joan, and Henry Collard. In 1466, they released the property to Henry Merland. In the period 1470–1474, the property was in some dispute, adversaries being Richard Illingworth, knight, chief baron of the exchequer John Denham, Esq., Hugh Fenn, William Essex, and Henry Merland v. Richard Ford and his wife Mercy, William Saundre and wife Johanna, and John Collard in Westburgh, Bansted, Ewell, and Sandon. See *Victoria History of Surrey*, 4b, p. 256; *Surrey Archeological Collection*, extra vol. 1, pp. 189, 194.

9. The Manor of Tullwick in Berkshire within the Manor of Wantage was held by the Carews from 1374. Nicholas Carew (d. 1432) enfeoffed John Gaynesford to hold Tullwick for his daughter Isabel for life, with reversion to his granddaughter Joan. Joan sued for these lands on

the death of Isabel and Gaynesford was ordered to make estate for her. At this time, the manor passed into Saundre hand, and in 1501, John Saundre enclosed fifty-five acres of Tullwick land, evicting four tenants in the process. John seems to have died about this time, and two years later, in 1503, Richard Saunders, son of William of Banbury, and Marjory (Yate) his wife conveyed the manor to John Yate of Lyford. See *Victoria History of Berkshire*, vol. 4, p. 324.

10. The following chapter contains background information on the Manor of Battailes in Ewell, Surrey, where Henry Saundre, surviving son and principal heir of Joan and William Saundre, long resided.

11. In 1474, Roger Huet released to Joan Saundre, widow, Richard Saundre her son, and James Base, clerk, the estate called Aldhagh (also known as Esthevers). In 1509, Henry Saundre of Ewell sold Aldhagh to Roger-att-Gate. The next day Richard Saundre, at the request of his brother Henry Saundre of Ewell, released Aldhagh to Roger-att-Gate. This record suggests that Henry Saundre of Ewell, son of William and Joan Carew Saundre, had in some fashion acquired control of Aldhagh, perhaps through his mother's inheritance, or he may have held it jointly with his brother Richard before the latter's death in 1480. Another possibility is that Aldhagh may have come into Saundres possession from a Salamon marriage many years past. The names here, however, do not refer to the family as we have described it, as Joan Carew was deceased four years before this property transfer and was never a widow. Henry's brother Richard had died in 1480, twenty-nine years before Henry sold the property with, it is suggested, Richard's cooperation. The history of ownership of this property remains unclear, and seems to contain errors under any interpretation. See Manning and Bray, p. 198.

12. The Manor of Woodmanstern was held by Nicholas Carew who died in 1432. He left one-third share of the manor in trust to Mercy Ford, daughter of his son Thomas, deceased, and her heirs, with remainder to her sister Joan, wife of William Sanders, and contingent remainder to his son Nicholas and heirs. It appears that Mercy, the second wife of the elder Nicholas Carew held a portion of this manor for her life, for in 1440 Nicholas Carew quitclaimed to Mercy (Haym) all right in the one-third part in Woodmanstern and other lands and tenements formerly belonging to his father. Toward the end of the sixteenth century, this part of the manor was held by the Skinner family. James Skinner settled it on his great nephew, John, and his wife Alice Poyntz. See *Victoria History of Surrey*, vol. 4, p. 248.

A somewhat differing account of this arrangement does exist, indicating that Nicholas Carew gave to Mercy Ford his lands in Woodmanstern,

Bansted, and Chipsted, and to Joan, who married William Saundre, he gave lands in Sanderstead and Warlingham, and then gave Beddington to his second son Nicholas. See Manning and Bray, p. 524.

13. The Manor of Carshalton was acquired by Nicholas Carew who died in 1390. His son Nicholas, dying in 1432, left Carshalton to his son Nicholas with remainder to his second son Thomas in default of issue. The manor was claimed by Thomas's daughter Mercy Ford and Joan Saundre. However, Carshalton went to the heirs of the first son Nicholas and his heir, another Nicholas, who died childless, then finally passing to his sister Senchia (sometimes Sanctia), who married John Iwardby. Their daughter Joan married Sir John St. John and then Nicholas Saundre of Ewell (c1485–1549), grandson of William and Joan Carew Saundre. See *Victoria History of Surrey*, vol. 4b, p. 182.

14. The Manor of Purley Magna in Berkshire was held by Huscarle whose daughter married Nicholas Carew (d.1390). Later, Nicholas Carew (d.1432) settled it on his wife Mercy and her heirs. However, there had been an earlier settlement, and the manor descended to the first son, Nicholas, in 1454. It seems Thomas's daughter Mercy may have held the property for a short period as there was an action in 1450 brought for assurance of remainder by Richard Ford and William Saundre in right of their wives. Purley Magna went to the last Nicholas Carew who died without heirs in 1485 and then to his sister Senchia and her husband John Iwardby. Their daughter Joan inherited this and for a short time the manor was held by Nicholas Saunders of Ewell, her second husband. See *Victoria History of Berkshire*, vol. 3, pp. 418–419.

15. The legal dispute over the period 1440–1442 regarding property in Southwark involved Robert Cawode, Thomas Kyrkeby, clerk, Thomas Wharff, John Thorley, Esq., Simon Waynfleete, clerk, William Saundre, and Richard Ford, v. John Denaway of Southwark and his wife Agnes, in the parish of St. George, Southwark. See *Surrey Archeological Collection*, extra 1, p. 184.

16. The national importance of mercantile houses in late feudal England and afterward in organizing commerce both internally and externally cannot be exaggerated. Although the advent of these establishments significantly predates William Saundre's probable involvement with the Company of Innkeepers, Taverners, or Vintners, we have found no previous examples of family association with any mercantile house.

17. Interestingly, this same Ford family, still connected to the vintners some generations later, may have remained in contact with the Sanders well into the seventeenth century.

18. In March 1450, the discontent in the realm came to a head with the impeachment by the House of Commons of the Duke of Suffolk,

followed in May by the well-supported popular rebellion of Jack Cade in Kent. Lander describes this in the following manner, "No mere rabble led this revolt. It was not a rising of peasants who felt economically repressed. At least one knight, 18 esquires, and 74 gentlemen formed part of this well-organized and well-disciplined group. They drew up a manifesto clearly stating their complaints, in part economic, but mainly political. They were overwhelmingly concerned with misgovernment and corruption at home. They also made it clear that they blamed 'not all the lords nor all those about the king's person nor all gentlemen nor yeomen nor men of law nor all bishops nor priests.' The rebel solution was to demand government by a broadly based group of peers including the Dukes of York, Exeter, Buckingham, and Norfolk." See Lander, *Government and Community*, pp. 187–189.

There was a period of uneasy calm for a few years, followed in 1455 by the outbreak of hostilities between York and the Crown—the first battle of the War of the Roses. These battles were primarily struggles within the aristocracy and the general population was little affected. Ross explains, "By choice or necessity, kings, noblemen, and gentry were the people most immediately involved in both the military and political aspects of the civil war and the effects on them were correspondingly greater. Other influential groups within the political community—the high clergy, the lawyers, and the merchants—almost entirely escaped involvement." See Ross, *War of the Roses*, pp. 157–158. By the 1460s, the stronghold of the ruling Lancastrians lay in the north while London and the commercial centers in the south of England tended toward Yorkist sympathies. Ross (p. 160) continues, "The merchant oligarchies who controlled the larger towns were largely successful in keeping their cities clear of military involvement in the conflict and commercial activities were only marginally affected. One reason why the Londoners in particular tended to favor the Yorkist cause was the hope that a change in government might bring about better commercial prospects." The poor foreign relations and the unwise commercial policies of the Lancastrian government had contributed to the decline in foreign trade and had precipitated an economic depression, which began about 1450 and lasted until about 1475.

In the war itself, the Yorkists won major battles, in 1461 deposing Henry VI. However, in 1460, Richard, Duke of York and heir to the throne, was killed, as was his eldest son. In 1461, Richard's second son acceded to the throne as Edward IV. Further intrigues and battles ended in 1470 when Edward was deposed and Henry VI reinstated.

But this lasted only one year. In 1471, Edward retrieved the Crown with his victory at Tewksbury, the final battle of the War of the Roses. After 1471, there was general improvement of conditions in England, and the king's principal concerns lay in maintaining peace and rebuilding the depleted treasury.

19. Lander, *Government and Community*, pp. 77–78.

20. The historic significance which we accord Columbus's voyage may not have seemed quite right to people at that time because stories of another land far to the west had circulated for centuries. Knowledge of the voyages of Icelander Leif Ericcson was widely shared throughout conquered Vikings territories in northern Europe and the British Isles. Stories of Ericcson's establishment of a settlement at L'Anse aux Meadows in northern Newfoundland about the year 1000 were well-documented in Icelandic and Norse literature, and these have proved to be sufficiently reliable to guide modern anthropologists to Ericcson's exact settlement site in Newfoundland. Maps and documentation of Ericcson's discovery then did exist for possible use by other seamen. New research has revealed somewhat extensive movement of Vikings throughout the northeastern portion of Canada after Ericcson, probably tied to hunting, fishing, and exploration.

Acting on Viking knowledge, Welsh sailors throughout the 1300s and before ventured to that part of the New World. Welsh trading voyages to Iceland and Greenland are celebrated in the mythical accounts of Prince Madoc's (Madog's) earlier adventures, which are repeated even in the stories of King Arthur. Some new evidence tends to support these tales. Anthracite coal from Carmarthenshire, Wales has been found in a Viking settlement in Greenland in the mid-1300s. Interestingly, in the Greenland West Settlement of 1342, excavations have unearthed evidence of the Sandres Farm there, though in this case, the name Sandres has a Danish origin, a term used by Danish anthropologists to describe the fourteenth-century "farm under the sand" that is now being excavated.

John Scolvus (a.k.a. John the Skillful, perhaps John Lloyd), who may have been a Welsh seaman with great experience in northern latitude voyaging, may have sailed directly to the New World on a venture of (further) discovery in 1477, fifteen years before Columbus's famous voyage. Scolvus is thought to have landed as far south as Maryland. Also in 1477, Columbus himself visited Bristol, England, John Lloyd's home port, perhaps learning from this experience. These accounts are detailed in a Royal Geographical Society publication. See Arthur Davies, "Prince Madoc and the Discovery of America in 1477" in *The Geographical Journal* 150(3): 363–372.

21. Although Joan is known to have been a daughter of Joan Carew and William Saundre and to have married Richard Hunsterton, research has yielded nothing more of her.

22. Thomas is not mentioned further in this chapter, but as he may have been linked to property eventually in possession of Henry, his brother, a note about Thomas is offered in chapter 6.

23. That William was the eldest son is stated in R. Sewill and E. Lane, *The Free Men of Charlwood* (Crawley, Sussex: Reprographic Centre, 1979), p. 47. See also *Visitation of Essex, 1558.*

24. How William Saundre of Banbury achieved success in the wool trade at an early age is not clear. His father had useful contacts from his own wool trade and may have endowed his son with venture capital to initiate this commerce, but we are unable to move beyond speculation on this point.

25. A full excursion into the history of European capitalism can be taken in F. Braudel, *The Wheels of Commerce: Civilization and Capitalism, 15th to 18th Century* (New York: Harper and Row, 1986). If a reader takes nothing else from Braudel, his insightful contrasts between ancient markets and historically emergent capitalism will clarify the deeply obfuscated debates about modern economic processes.

26. The Galileo Project at Rice University has this to say about the Medicis, "The Medici family dominated Florentine politics for two and a half centuries and presided over a cultural achievement that is equaled only by Athens in the golden age. The family also got its genes mixed with most of the royal families in Europe. Medici women included Catherine (1519–1589) whom married Henry II, King of France, and ruled the country after her husband's death (and) Maria (1573–1642) married Henry IV, King of France. Maria's daughters became queens of Spain and England. Cosimo Medici II's wife, Mary Magdalena, was the sister of Ferdinand II, Holy Roman Emperor." See http://www.Galileo.rice.edu/gal/medici.html. The family was perhaps the wealthiest in Europe in the sixteenth century, and two popes came from the Medicis of Florence, Leo X (1513–1521) and Clement VII (1523–1534).

27. The term *enclosure* as used in fifteenth- and sixteenth-century England refers to the process of fencing off manorial lands. Fencing these lands was useful for controlling herds of sheep, but a larger issue arose because enclosure also excluded access to the manorial land by those whose forebears lived at the manor and held certain traditional rights to farm manor lands. Their exclusion led to riots such as Kett's Rebellion in Norfolk, and enclosure eventually produced streams of migration from farm life to unemployment and hardship in towns

and cities across the land. In defense of enclosure though, severe shortages of labor in some parts of England following plagues and famines created worker shortages and higher wages, and less labor-intensive agricultural production such as sheep raising became a rational alternative.

28. John Olney, of Weston Underwood, Buckinghamshire, was a distant landlord in Banbury. We cannot be certain of this Olney marriage; another possibility is a daughter of Sir Edward Raleigh, who was an overseer of the younger William Saundre's will in 1492. In regard to Olney, see *Victoria History of Oxfordshire*, vol. 10, p. 56; and *Victoria History of Buckinghamshire*, vol. 4, p. 498. Also, the Carew arms were quartered with Olney arms at some point, indicating marriage ties between those families and suggesting that a Saunder-Olney marriage might have come about under Carew auspices. See *Visitations of Surrey, 1530, 1572, and 1623*, p. 213.

29. *Victoria History of Oxford*, vol. 10, pp. 56, 62–63.

30. See *Victoria History of Berkshire*, vol. 4, p. 324.

31. *Victoria History of Oxford*, vol. 10, p. 62.

32. Ibid.

33. *Calendar of Close Rolls, 1468–1476*, p. 383.

34. J. R. Lander, *Government and Community: England, 1450–1509* (Cambridge: Harvard University Press, 1980), p. 83. See also *Victoria History of Oxfordshire*, vol. 10, p. 56.

35. M. Kohn, "Business Organization in Pre-Industrial Europe" (working paper, Dartmouth College, Hanover, New Hampshire, 2003).

36. See Lander, *Government and Community*, p. 77. Given the timing of this record, we assume the debt was incurred during exile, though it is equally possible that this debt accumulated over a longer period.

37. Mike Ashley, *British Kings and Queens* (New York: Barnes and Noble Books, 1998), pp. 619–620.

38. Butts were large barrels, generally equal to two hogsheads each. This was no small quantity of wine, suggesting that William intended to sell wine once it reached Banbury. The wine trade from France through Calais and thence to Southampton was a centerpiece of Southampton's commerce.

39. *Brokerage Books of Southampton, 1477–1478*, pp. 22, 27.

40. Southampton Port Book listings.

41. It is possible that this appointment was made for William of Charlwood, the father of William of Banbury, as both were in their productive years in 1473. Nonetheless, we think it the latter, given his steady involvement in Southampton trade. See Calendar of Patent Rolls, 1467–1477.

42. Lander, *Government and Community*, p. 77.

43. Ibid., p. 78.

44. William's will is available at Hampshire Record Office, 43, M 48/54, and a discussion of its contents is available in *Victoria History of Oxfordshire*, vol. 10, pp. 62–63.

45. Richard Saundre was named William's executor. This could have referred either to his brother Richard of Charlwood or to his son of the same name. But the son Richard may not have been of legal adult age in 1478, or only barely so, and seems unlikely to have been prepared for this responsibility at that time.

46. For William's will of 1492, see *Some Oxfordshire Wills*, in Oxford Research Series, vol. 38–40, pp. 47–48.

47. A Cooke pedigree is available in the *Visitation of Essex*.

48. *Victoria History of Oxfordshire*, vol. 10, p. 62.

49. See *Victoria History of Berkshire*, vol. 4, p. 324; and also I. S. Leadam, *The Security of Copyholders in the Fifteenth and Sixteenth Centuries*, vol. 1 (London: Oxford University Press, 1893), pp. 108, 113–116.

50. In times of high infant mortality and a firm insistence on survival of certain family names, we find predictable repetitions of names in family lines; and in the case of Nicholas, the pattern is particularly persistent. No record we have found states directly that Nicholas was a son of Joan Carew and William Saundre, but reasons for believing this are threefold: (a) Nicholas Carew was the grandfather of Joan and was her principal benefactor following the early death of Thomas Carew, her father. Nicholas saw to it that Joan received six manors upon his death as her inheritance and he probably arranged her marriage to William Saundres as well. Traditional naming patterns in that time would have dictated a child by the name of Nicholas from Joan's personal history; (b) Nicholas is a name that persisted for generations in the Saundres family following the marriage of Joan Carew and William Saundres. This persistence suggests a Nicholas Saundre must have existed from their time forward in time; and (c) what little we know of this Nicholas points directly at other family relationships. In our record of Nicholas, we find the names Tyrell and Whitney, and Saundres marriages to Tyrell (c1560) and Whitney (c1590) suggest continuing relationships of these families. Other linkages of Nicholas to the Wydville and Wellys families virtually clinch the argument.

51. That William and Joan Saundre would name a son Stephen does not surprise because Stephen was the name of William's grandfather. It is altogether likely that William's father Thomas would have named a son Stephen after his own father. But no record has been found for a Stephen Saundre as brother of William of Charlwood, suggesting that neither this Stephen nor a record of him survived.

52. Henry's wife, Joan Saundre of Ewell, in her will of 1518, indicated that she held "moveable goods in Southwark." See M. Walker, *The Manor of Battailes and the Family of Saunder in Ewell During the 16th and 17th Centuries* (Guildford: Surrey Archaeological Society, 1956), p. 86.

53. The Richard III Society of England disputes these claims; see D. Williamson, *Kings and Queens of England* (New York: Barnes and Noble Books, 2003), pp. 54–57.

54. Richard Wellys is identified in the record as a clerk, which suggests he was probably a layperson employed by the church. Often clerks were lawyers. But the ties of Nicholas to Richard Wellys was probably no accident. Nicholas's nephew William Saundre of Banbury who died in 1493 left a monetary bequest to a certain Sir Nicholas Wellys, suggesting some remote family connection might have been at work. Years before, James Carew of Joan Carew's line had married Eleanor Hoo, whose father was Lord Wellys.

55. Patent Roll for March 16, 1503, p. 316.

56. Williamson, *Kings and Queens*, p. 57.

57. Details of the will of Henry Saundre of Ewell are given in Walker, *Manor of Battailes*, pp. 84–85.

58. There may have been other ties. Henry Merland, who acquired title to Westburgh Manor from Joan Carew, was the son of the vicar of Rochland and was resident of St. Mary Magdalen Parish in 1466.

59. S. Wabuda et al., "Preaching During the English Reformation" in *Cambridge Studies in Early Modern British History* (Cambridge: Cambridge University Press, 2002).

60. *Victoria History of Middlesex*, vol. 2, p. 190.

61. A full description of Syon Abbey is available at http://www.tudorplace.com.ar/Documents/SyonAbbey.htm.

62. Sewill and Lane, *Free Men*, p. 47.

63. Nicholas Carew (1425–1466) previously had married Joan Courtenay.

64. Nostalgia for the old days goes only so far.

65. Thomas Homer-Saunders, "The Saunders, Sanders, Sandars Family and Its Blood Connections, Under the Spring of Alexander (Alisaunder) the Great, from which the surname is derived and which came into existence during the thirteenth and fourteenth centuries." A full genealogy of these Courtenays is available in Sir Bernard Burke, *A General Armory of England, Scotland, and Ireland* (London: E. Churton, 1842).

66. This idea of Aston property persists in family lore because family genealogists agree that William (Saundres) of Aston originated in the Charlwood branch following Richard and Agnes. The matter is pursued further in chapter 5.

67. A record for 1530 for a Richard Saunders of Charlwood indicates that he was a merchant, probably in wool, but no direct evidence has been found that this Richard is a son of Richard of whom we write, beyond the matter of names. Particular interest centers on this merchant because his "mark" has been found. Merchant's marks are forerunners of today's trademarks, having been used to stamp interpretable symbols on goods for use by illiterate stevedores. Research has not revealed how these marks were read.

68. See Sewill and Lane, *Free Men*, pp. 46–51, for a description of the chapel. A good collection of photographs is available for St. Nicholas Church of Charlwood, including the chapel, at http://www.roughwood.net.

69. The principal argument in favor of seven sons comes from the *Visitations of Derby* made in 1611 and 1614, stating that Thomas Saunder of Derbyshire was Richard Saundre's seventh son. This document was produced more than fifty years after the former's death and was signed by a Derbyshire family member. Reliability of these kinds of visitation records is uncertain.

70. Sewill and Lane, *Free Men*, p. 47. This is a well-researched book based upon local reference material.

71. The name James is something of an oddity here as no earlier person bearing this name has been identified among the Saunders or Courtenays, at least for a time within memory for Agnes and Richard. The name James Carew does occur within the Beddington line, but no connection for this James to these Saunders is evident.

72. As the children were born in the 1470s and their mother died in 1485 following their father's death in 1480, none could have been adults by the time of their mother's death.

73. The 1492 will of William Saundre of Banbury states, "To such of my uncle's children as then shall be lyvyng among them 100 Pounds." See *Some Oxfordshire Wills*, in Oxford Research Series, vol. 38–40, pp. 47–48.

74. Sewill and Lane, *Free Men*, p. 51.

75. J. Edward Sandars, *The Sandars Centuries* (Oxfordshire, Henley, 1971), p. 13.

76. In 1513, Nicholas bought a house and fifty-five acres in Charlwood, adding to his property there, and he paid rent on Charlwood Place, then under control of Charlwood Manor owned initially by Sir Robert Southwell and later Henry Lecheford, gentleman. Years later, in 1550, Nicholas surrendered eleven acres in Charlwood to the use of John Bray. See Sewill and Lane, *Free Men*, pp. 47, 67.

77. Nicholas was an executor of the will of his uncle Henry of Ewell in 1518, and in 1529, he assisted in the induction of Henry's son William into ownership of a manor called Pendell in southern Surrey.

78. Henry VIII's executors are listed in the following Web site: http://www.tudorplace.com.

79. This description of Nicholas and Alys as depicted on their memorial brass is abridged from Sewill and Lane, *Free Men*, pp. 68–69.

80. Our departure from published accounts of the Charlwood lineage regarding William is made necessary by the following facts. William was born about 1475 but is said to have been appointed high sheriff of Surrey in 1556 (at about age eighty-one) and to have been knighted seven years after that (at age eighty-eight). These assertions are wildly unrealistic. Furthermore, this William is said to have been the father of Dr. Nicholas Saunder, born in 1527, and his younger sisters, making this William at least sixty when the last child was born. Other life facts reported in the text also fail to comport with the notion of a single William. In contrast, finding two Williams, father and son, one born about 1475 and the second about 1500, bring all these facts into a more normal pattern, and records for each of them do exist.

81. We believe this location to be Aston, Oxfordshire, a location near long-held Courtenay property.

82. Sandars, *Sandars Centuries*, p. 2.

83. M. Walker, *Manor of Battailes*, p. 86. Walker ascribes this record to a different William Saunders, but notes the problematic nature of his interpretation.

CHAPTER SIX

Ewell

Henry VII, the first Tudor king, assumed the English throne in 1485 and ruled for twenty-four years until 1509. Among English monarchs, his reign has drawn less attention by historians than one might expect. It produced in its comparatively few years an important new approach to governance and set England on a road to new prosperity. Henry's style broke with tradition by diminishing the role of upper nobility in government, instead calling upon minor gentry and church figures to form his main advisory bodies. Henry undercut the nobility's ability to raise private armies and control local jurisdictions, elevating Crown-appointed justices of the peace to greater power in local affairs. Subduing the ambitions of nobility was in fact a bold step toward permanently weakening the ancient feudal regime and making a beginning of a wholly new government for England. In the broadest sense, Henry's actions began to decouple the hereditary advantages of kinship and political power, heretofore the central underpinning of English feudal social organization. Into this vacuum of power, Henry interposed new figures from commercial, legal, and administrative classes. Henry's attention also turned to education and building projects, resting on innovations in Western thought then in nascent stages. In Henry's time, England, Scotland, and Wales were effectively unified, national wealth increased substantially, and peace generally prevailed [1].

In consolidating power, Henry VII relied on a relatively small circle of close advisors, the most notable of whom was a priest, Richard Foxe, a longtime ally from before his coronation. Foxe came from a family background of yeomanry in Lincolnshire and ascended through ecclesiastical ranks to high position in the church and into government over the years. On coming to power, Henry named Richard Foxe his principal secretary of state, a position roughly equivalent to prime minister in today's world, and many of Henry's key decisions were on Foxe's advice [2].

This was the world of Henry Saunder of Ewell. He touched the chords of history under Henry VII both as witness and active participant, fully devoted to his king and directly indebted to Richard Foxe for his most important accomplishments. As time went by, Henry aligned himself with the progressive elements of his society. He brought strong commitments to education and the institution of government but was not above some self-aggrandizement. Henry was wealthy and well educated, entertaining important doubts about his church, but not his religion. He was able in property and business matters, using to advantage his substantial inheritance and multiplying his wealth by further land investment. And Henry was routinely burdened by deaths in all parts of his immediate and extended families. To his story we now turn.

Early Years

Henry Saundre was born about the year 1456. He was a younger son of Joan Carew and William Saundre of Charlwood, perhaps their youngest. His mother was thirty-six when he was born and his father about forty-two. Henry grew up in Charlwood at Sanders Place, the moated manor house acquired by his family about one-hundred-fifty years earlier and inherited by his father around 1450. As a child of considerable privilege, Henry would have roamed freely over family fields at Charlwood and enjoyed a young life of deference. This privilege, shared also by his older brothers and sisters, would have been colored by the mild torments and special joys of younger brotherhood. As he grew older, Henry no doubt traveled with his family to visit Beddington Manor, home of his mother, and perhaps Battailes Manor or other Carew properties in and near Surrey. Henry would have received early lessons in responsibility, authority, respectability, and social grace, qualities necessary to those of great expectations. By all accounts, these life lessons were well learned.

Henry's father William would have viewed with some urgency the need to see to Henry's education. In this century, patronage was still more important than formal education in launching a profession [3], but from the beginning of the century, a statute declared the freedom of every man, regardless of social status, to educate his children [4]. By the last decades of the 1400s, lawyers were seen as a professional class of administrators who took up key positions in various royal councils and offices. The sons of the landed gentry were now being directed toward the law where there were growing rewards of prestige and power rather than to the church or trade [5]. So at about age seven, William undoubtedly enrolled Henry in a "song school," so-called because pupils routinely sang hymns as part of their early learning activity. Their curriculum included simple liturgical devotions, alphabet, basic prayers, the beginnings of Latin as found in religious service books, and some writing. Primary education of this type was provided in the households of aristocratic families, in religious households, and sometimes in parish churches.

Henry's first schooling may well have been with the Carews at Beddington, held at that time by Nicholas and Margaret Langford Carew. The Carews had a son and three daughters, including daughter Senchia, who married John Iwardby and whose daughter eventually married into the Saunder family of Ewell. Alternatively though, Henry may have joined the song school of the bishop of Winchester. The bishop at that time was William Waynfleet, who founded Magdalen College of Oxford in 1458 and who placed his song school alongside these college buildings. Owing to some prior contact between William Saundre of Charlwood and a certain Simon Waynfleet, a connection to William Waynfleet's school makes some sense [6]. If correct, it also suggests one reason why Henry developed a close association with the bishops of Winchester in later life.

By about 1470, Henry was of sufficient age to have completed some years of grammar school, where he would have engaged Latin grammar, absorbed Scriptures and Latin literature, participated in debates, and learned something of science and law. After that came university education, probably at Oxford, most likely at Waynfleet's Magdalen College, where the study of ecclesiastical law was required. Some time toward the end of Henry's stay at Oxford, he incurred a scrape with the law at the bishop of Winchester's court in Southwark, being accused of consorting with prostitutes, an accusation frequently made without grounds to extort money from wealthy families [7]. To Henry's seven-year Oxford education may have been added further study at the Inns of Court in London, earning additional credentials for the practice of civil law. Henry's formal education and training was finally complete by the time he reached his midtwenties about the year 1480.

Henry's Inheritance

Things happened fast for Henry as the 1480s commenced. His father William of Charlwood died in 1481, and Henry received from him a substantial bequest, despite the fact that Henry was a younger son and last in line for inheritance. Several of his brothers died before Henry completed his education, placing Henry in a position to receive more family possessions than otherwise might have been the case. This also placed Henry in a most uncomfortable position as head of the Saunders of Surrey, the family's eldest surviving male except for those in the priesthood. At the age of about twenty-five and as yet unmarried, Henry undertook the large project of seeing to the immediate welfare of his nieces and nephews, worrying over their futures of marriage and property and representing family interests to the larger world. One senses from Henry's later history that he was entirely up to the challenge.

William settled upon Henry a one-third share of the Manor of Battailes in Ewell, located in northern Surrey near Sanderstead [8]. A short time later, Henry purchased the other two-thirds shares from his maternal Carew aunts, placing him in full control of Battailes Manor, a property that became his lifetime home and an important seat of Saunder family presence in Surrey.

Henry also received properties in the south of Surrey near Charlwood, though most of the traditional Charlwood family holdings were reserved for Nicholas of Charlwood, Henry's nephew. Henry may also have inherited a manor called Aldagh, sometimes known as Esthevers. One of William's sons, Thomas, briefly mentioned in chapter 3, had married Joan Huet and acquired the Manor of Aldhagh in southern Surrey. This Thomas died quite young in 1473, the property passing to his wife and their son Richard. Many years later, Henry came to control this property, evidently having inherited a reversion of the estate following Thomas's death and Joan Huet Saundre's lifetime entitlement to residence there [9]. Also included in the bequest for Henry in the south of Surrey were holdings at Newdigate, perhaps attached to the Manor of Battailes, Charlwood, Ockley, and Nutfield, which Henry either inherited or acquired shortly after his father's death [10]. William also may have provided Henry with a substantial financial bequest because he was able to purchase property before his work in the law was fully underway. Besides acquiring full interest in Battailes and Nutfield, Henry also bought land in Tolworth and Long Ditton near Ewell before the decade of the 1480s was out [11].

William also bestowed on Henry the Three Crowns Inn in Southwark, another former Carew property [12]. Ownership of this inn was to bring Henry closer to the affairs of the city. Southwark, on the southern edge of the city of London just across the Thames, was a lively place in those days, a meeting place for roads from the south and east of the country. By the fifteenth century, Southwark held one of the city's largest immigrant populations. German, Dutch, and Flemish craftsmen filled the area because London's guilds prevented them from working within the city's confines [13].

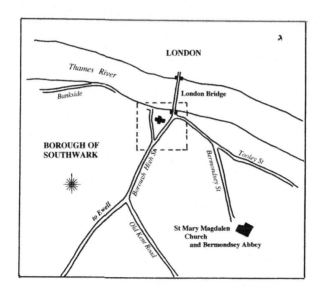

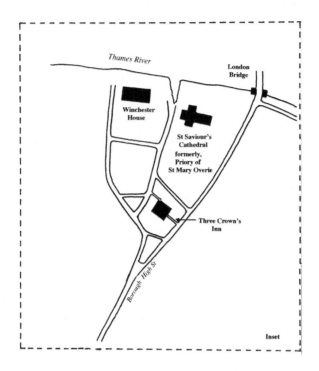

Thames River

London
Bridge

Winchester
House

St Saviour's
Cathedral
formerly,
Priory of
St Mary Overie

Three Crown's
Inn

Borough High St

Inset

(Above) Borough of Southwark, sixteenth century. Five main roads served Southwark in the 1500s. Borough High Street followed an ancient Roman highway from London to southern England through the village of Ewell, thirteen miles from Southwark. Henry Saundre's funeral procession advanced along this road. Nicholas Saundre was chaplain of St. Mary Magdalen Church and may have attended a political prisoner at Bermondsey Abbey; his brother Henry provided a bequest for this church. (Below) Inset from the Southwark map. Along the east side of Borough High Street was a row of inns, including the famed Tabard, named in Chaucer's Canterbury Tales. The Saunder family owned the nearby Three Crowns Inn, which burned in 1676. This inn is remembered on a marker in Three Crowns Square. Winchester House was the palace and residence of the bishops of Winchester. Henry Saundre left a bequest for Winchester Cathedral. Joan Lepton, Henry Saunders's wife, attended St. Mary Overie, and William Saunder oversaw the dissolution of this monastery and arranged for the care of its dispersed priests.

Owners of inns were required to join the Mystery (livery company) of Hostellers in order to conduct legal business. As hotel proprietors, they were not to be confounded with either vintners (wine importers and merchants) or taverners (alehouse keepers or publicans). Rather, their emphasis was on accommodating travelers and stabling their horses. Years earlier, in 1446, the Mystery of Hostellers had presented a petition to London's lord mayor, John Olney, for tightened innholding regulations. William Saundre, having recently acquired the Three Crowns Inn, probably participated in the conference with Olney, and this meeting could have involved personal business as well. One of William's sons married Olney's daughter two decades later. In any case, the Hostellers' petition sought new requirements for outdoor signage, rights to search for illegal hostelry, strengthened organization within the company to enforce its own rules and fine disobeying members, and certain other rules regarding the proper treatment of foreigners and servants. Olney granted the petition. By the late 1400s, the term *hostellers* had fallen into disrepute, and in 1515, a new charter under Henry VIII created the label *innkeepers*, and Henry Saundre became a charter member of the new Innholders Company [14].

Although this inn no longer stands, the Three Crowns Square on the west side of Southwark High Street marks its original site. Close inspection of today's Southwark map reveals an interesting feature near the Three Crowns site. To the west of Southwark Cathedral and adjacent Southwark Bridge lie a series of stairs and docks. The stairs descend to the river where travelers once found boats to ferry them across the Thames. One dock is called Bullhead Dock, suggestive of those days when William Saundre, he of ancient Bull Head Farm in Charlwood, owned the Three Crowns Inn and, perhaps as it appears, arranged for his patrons' need to cross over to London.

Family

Henry completed the purchase of outstanding shares of Battailes Manor about 1484, about the time of his marriage. Around age twenty-eight, Henry married Joan, daughter of John Lepton of Kipwich, Yorkshire. Although the marriage took place about three years after the death of Henry's father William, it seems likely that William arranged the union. Yorkshire had long been a leading center of wool production and export in England, and it may be that both John Lepton and William Saunder shared wool business interests. Although no record states that Henry engaged the wool business after marriage, his property inheritance and steady acquisition of land immediately thereafter strongly suggests the possibility.

Over the next two decades, Joan and Henry had a large number of children, including at least seven sons, but only four or five children survived to adulthood [15]. They were Nicholas [16], Agnes [17], William, Margaret [18] and perhaps Cornelia. In the pages that follow, we describe the life of this son William in some detail.

THE FAMILIES OF HENRY AND WILLIAM SAUNDERS OF EWELL

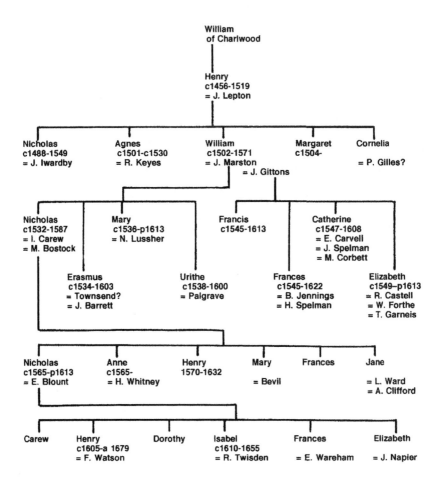

Source: Authors.

Before and during his marriage, Henry suffered an extraordinary number of family deaths. Henry lost both parents and three brothers before marriage, and he and Joan together lost perhaps ten to twelve children, judging by the age spans of those few who survived. To this number can be added several nieces and nephews and acquaintances whom we are unable to recount. To grasp the times in which Henry lived is to acknowledge the frequent mortality he and his countrymen experienced and to appreciate the extent of mourning that colored everyday life.

Career

The 1480s saw Henry develop his palette of property ownerships from inheritance and investment and also make a beginning to his practice of law. These combined in the following decade to make Henry a wealthy man. From his lands, he reaped returns from wool and other crops and rents from tenants, though not without occasional difficulty [19]. There also were profits from the Three Crowns Inn. And Henry's compensation from his legal work and perhaps some other minor preferment [20] would have further enlarged his estate, though how much each of these sources contributed to his whole wealth is uncertain.

By 1490, Henry had amassed sufficient means to build a large capital mansion on his lands in Ewell. The historian Walker [21] describes the structure as a fair mansion house with a gatehouse, a forecourt, hall, parlor, and other edifices and buildings with two backyards, stables, and barns, also a dove house, two gardens, and an orchard. Some years later, the whole covered five acres. Henry evidently purchased land (at the same time he bought the remaining two-thirds share of Battailes from his aunts) to build the large mansion house, a fitting structure for the largest landowner in Ewell. The older Battailes manor house was located on only three roods and was later retained as a dower house. Nearby a little banqueting house was built on half a rood of waste land, though this structure may have been built after Henry's death. Next to the banqueting house, a lake was created by Henry's son William, who dammed the course of a local river and walled it off from a horse pond so that fishing parties could take place from the banqueting house [22].

Besides improvements to the domicile at Ewell, Henry continued to engage land transactions in his later years, the most important of which was Pendell Manor, purchased of Thomas Uvedale in 1509. With Pendell Manor, Henry at age fifty-three consolidated his previous holdings at Nutfield and added land and property at Bletchingly, all in southern Surrey [23]. At some point, Henry also came into possession of lands at Ebbesham and Chessington in Surrey, but no record of these acquisitions seems to have survived [24].

So it was that following his marriage, Henry embarked on his career in law. To this end, he brought ever-growing wealth and considerable education, but there remained the crucial matter of patronage, sponsors who could connect Henry to the best opportunity. Of patrons, Henry had no shortage. First, there was James Carew of Beddington, a close relative of Joan Carew Saunder of Charlwood, whose surname alone was a passport to opportunity. Exactly how James worked on behalf of the Saunders of Surrey is unclear, but his contributions were significant enough for Richard Saunder of Charlwood to have named a son after him. Second, the wife of James Carew descended from Lord Welles, a family that figured prominently in the lives of both William Saunder of Banbury and Nicholas, the Southwark priest, Henry's older brother. Welles intercession on behalf of Henry would have provided high reach. Third, Henry's brother Nicholas Saunder belonged to St. Mary Magdalen Church in Southwark and probably worked closely with nearby Winchester Palace, a home base for the bishops of Winchester. Henry named his second son after this Nicholas. Finally, Agnes Courtenay Saunder, wife of Richard of Charlwood, was a cousin of Peter Courtenay. Peter was master of St. Anthony's Free Chapel and Hospital [25] and perhaps Henry's most important early supporter, even before he was named bishop of Winchester in 1485.

In 1485, the Earl of Richmond, the future Henry VII, returned to England from exile in Brittany, slew Richard III at Bosworth, and claimed the throne as England's first Tudor king [26]. Among Richmond's most important allies were two clerics, Richard Foxe, who attended Richmond in France, and Peter Courtenay, Foxe's close ally. On assuming power, Henry VII's actions were swift in replacing the stale order of contentious nobility with fresh faces from the clergy and minor gentry. Among his first appointments were Richard Foxe as his principal secretary and Peter Courtenay as bishop of Winchester. Both were particularly close to Henry VII; in later years, Foxe became the king's executor and Courtenay the godfather to Henry VII's young son, the future Henry VIII, whom Foxe immediately baptized. Shortly after these appointments, Henry Saunder of Ewell was elevated into this mix. Whether Henry Saunder first served Courtenay [27] or Foxe is uncertain, but Courtenay died in 1492, and Henry's talents and legal preparation were used by Richard Foxe after that. The sense is that Henry obtained some administrative post, one requiring legal training, connected to Foxe's responsibilities in the royal court.

Richard Foxe was no mere political associate of Henry; he also served as Henry's mentor and friend. Foxe was a lawyer, statesman, and patron of scholars and learned institutions. He was frequently criticized for being an absentee prelate—he held numerous church posts over the years—but lauded for his important diplomatic accomplishments during Henry VII's rule. One ambassador to England referred to Foxe as *alter rex*, reflecting the sweep and strength of his authority. Foxe simultaneously was thought a gentle, good, and fair man.

How Henry Saunder assisted Foxe through all his years of service under Henry VII is unclear, but as Foxe focused primarily on international affairs, we imagine Henry trailing Foxe's lead on these matters. Among Foxe's involvements were negotiations for a commercial treaty, the Magnus Intercursus, with the Netherlands in 1496 and acting as a papal commissioner for an inquiry on whether Henry VI of England should be canonized. He also negotiated betrothals of two of Henry VII's children, which involved treaties with Scotland and Aragon. There is reason to believe that Henry Saunder had a hand in developing these latter treaties as years later, Sir Thomas Saunders of Charlwood acted as attorney for Anne of Cleves during her annulment proceedings with Henry VIII. The suggestion here is that Sir Thomas may have received his appointment in part based on Henry's prior experience and reputation in such matters.

Separate from international work, Richard Foxe retained an active interest in education, frequently visiting England's two principal universities, mainly at Oxford's Magdalen College and at Cambridge's Pembroke College. These university visits followed Foxe's appointment as the bishop of Winchester in 1501. Foxe's thrust aimed to elevate the secular basis for priestly education and simultaneously to weaken the educational domination of monasteries, which he viewed as ill-directed and venal. Later events indicate that Foxe's commitment to higher education was shared by Henry Saunder.

Henry Saunder also may have had a direct role in mitigating Foxe's ecclesiastical absenteeism because after 1493, Henry's younger brother-in-law, Ralph Lepton, a priest, assumed positions in the same locations in which Foxe held office [28]. Lepton took work at Bath and Wells the year Foxe exited the post. Foxe moved on to Durham in 1494 and Lepton again followed him, accepting a position at Durham in 1497. And when Foxe was named bishop of Winchester in 1501, Lepton followed three years later to Alresford near Winchester for yet another church post. Lepton continued his close association both with Foxe and with Henry Saundre throughout his later years.

Erasmus Visits

A certain intellectual liberalism crept into England and its leaders during the time of Henry VII. This occurred in great measure from three visits to England by the great Dutch humanist scholar Erasmus, who more fully styled himself Desiderius Erasmus Roterodamus [29]. Erasmus visited England during Henry VII's reign in 1499–1500 and 1505–1506 and after the king's death in 1509–1514. One can scarcely exaggerate the importance of Erasmus's influence on scholarly thought in Western Europe and England; to many he represents the essence of Western liberal thought at a crucial juncture of change. Erasmus's influence spread in part because of his soft style, writing for broad audiences in familiar Latin to escape the parochialism of local tongues and to reach beyond narrow scholastic minds that heretofore dominated intellectual pursuits. And what Erasmus had to say was electrifying, codifying the swirl of new humanistic ideals found mostly in the literature and arts of his age. Erasmus drew on familiar but perhaps insufficiently examined examples from classical civilization to show that humanity was capable of extraordinary being in its own right, separate from the province of the divine. Secular inquiry and knowledge was needed. Though posed in gentle terms and without heretical rancor, Erasmus's words sent a dagger into the heart of scholasticism, the largely noncritical acceptance of ancient dogma by the church's clergy and its adherents, especially as found in the monasteries of Europe and England. For its part, the Catholic Church advised caution in reading Erasmus's words but stopped short of accusing him of heresy. Protestant reformers, on the other hand, disliked Erasmus's reticence at confronting church traditions.

The famed Dutch scholar Erasmus. Photograph of a Rijksmuseum statuette by Nancy Sanders.

While in England, Erasmus was particularly close to numerous progressive clergymen and reform-minded intelligensia, including William Blount, Sir Thomas More, William Warham, John Colet, John Fisher, and Richard Foxe, to whom Erasmus dedicated a book in 1501. All these were leading personages in their respective realms of endeavor, but what matters to us is the degree to which Henry Saunder was associated with them all. Mountjoy was patron of Syon Abbey and sponsored an organization called the Doctor's Commons, a loose association of ecclesiastical lawyers in London. Henry may well have belonged to this group. William Blount's daughter married into the Courtenays, and the Blounts furthermore were associated with the Gresley family into which the Saunders of Derbyshire had married (see Chapter Eight). Some years later, Sir Nicholas Saunders of Ewell, Henry's great-grandson, married Elizabeth Blunt. Similarly, Nicholas Saunders of Ewell, Henry's grandson, married the widow of Justice Jasper Fisher. These relationships may have gone even further. Erasmus's friend and publisher in Antwerp, a humanist named Peter Gilles, married a certain Cornelia Saunders, who may have been Henry's daughter [30]. Also, a certain John Palgrave of Norfolk was a scholar and a tutor of Henry VIII's children. Sir Thomas More wrote that both Erasmus and he considered "Master" John Palgrave their friend. Henry Saunder's granddaughter Urithe of Norfolk married John Palgrave, probably a nephew of this figure. Finally and as an unusually powerful tribute, Henry's own grandson was given the name Erasmus Saunders. We take it, then, that Erasmus had a modernizing influence on Henry's thinking through all these contacts and colored Henry's life and profession after the turn of the century, a powerful influence that persisted beyond Henry's own life.

Savoy and Corpus Christi

In 1505, Henry VII established the foundation for a hospital at the Savoy in London, and by 1508, funds had been allocated for the construction. The intended cruciform structure was over three hundred feet long, housing one hundred beds, sufficiently large to dominate the local landscape. Officially, the institution was to be called the Hospital of Henry VII, king of England, of the Savoy, commissioned to enhance the king's fame and that of his city and, through royal charity, to secure for the sovereign and his family everlasting glory. Henry required there be Tudor roses on the gowns of the staff and on the counterpanes of the beds and that the roof and stained glass windows embody royal qualities [31]. The hospital itself would be administered by a master and four chaplains, assisted by four paid priests and other officials and servants, including also a physician, a surgeon, and thirteen sisters [32].

Henry VII died in 1509 before the hospital sprang to life, and in his will, he charged executors to complete the project. Within a year, these officials arranged for the building to commence, remitting funds to the master of the works, a priest named William Holgill. The manner of remittance reveals much about the cumbersome procedures for financial exchange of that time. Following the king's will, his executors effected the transmission of sixty-seven sealed bags of coins to be held at Westminster Abbey, totaling five hundred marks, and later another hundred bags for constructing and fitting out the hospital [33]. As many as 165 workers labored on the construction, using the hospital's tools and working under candlelight in late hours [34].

SAVOY HOSPITAL LONDON

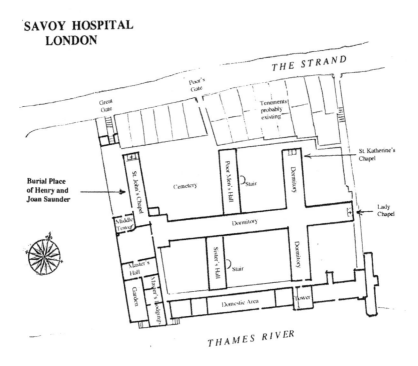

Plan of the "Hospital of Henry VII, King of England, of the Savoy." The hospital was founded in 1505, completed between 1515 and 1517, and was said in its time to be one of the great sights of London. One of the great English medieval almshouses, the hospital's appointments bore a royal touch. The structure was immense: the nave measured 200 feet, transepts 220 feet, and chancel 80 feet. Walls were three feet thick. The building was torn down in the eighteenth century; only the north wall of St. John's Chapel survives. Henry and Joan Saunders of Ewell were interred in St. John's Chapel. Adapted from R. Somerville, The Savoy (London: Duchy of Lancaster, 1960); and C. Platt, Medieval England (New York: Charles Scribner's Sons, 1978).

Construction reached completion about 1515, and in 1517, four books of statutes governing the operation of the hospital were bound under direction of Richard Foxe, an executor of Henry VII's will and by then the bishop of Winchester. These books were delivered to William Holgill, newly named master of the hospital [35]. Behind these scenes was Henry Saundre, acting in concert with Foxe, drafting hospital statutes or providing administration for the project. A relative of Henry held the position of bailiff of the Savoy [36]. There is little doubt that Henry regarded his own contribution to the creation of the Savoy as a personal crowning achievement, desiring to be buried at this site upon his death.

As Savoy Hospital neared completion, Richard Foxe turned his attention to a great love, the founding of a college dedicated to secular humanist education along the lines described by Erasmus. Here human-centered knowledge would supplant traditional religious instruction and reach as wide an audience as possible. In 1516, Corpus Christi College of Oxford was founded, giving as much satisfaction to Erasmus as to Foxe himself. Notably, Corpus Christi was created from Foxe's own resources and not from ecclesiastical spoils, as was often the case in these college foundations. To help underwrite the costs, Foxe arranged for the Manor of Milton near Egham, Surrey, to come into the hands of Henry Saunder, Ralph Lepton, and a certain William Frost, a steward of Foxe, and for this trio to donate the manor and its revenues to the new college [37].

Final Years

A virulent plague first arrived in England back when Henry VII invaded from France in 1485 to defeat Richard III at Bosworth and then claim the throne. This particular disease was unknown to England before that time, causing some to think that Henry's forces, including numerous French mercenaries, carried the sickness with them. This illness was different from bubonic plagues of earlier times, spreading more rapidly and with greater mortality. This sweating sickness [38] subsided after 1485, only to reappear again in 1507 and yet again with particular severity in 1517. This scourge claimed the life of Henry Saundre early in 1519 at age sixty-two and also his wife Joan a month later [39]. Henry had only recently resettled his estate, clarifying inheritances following the deaths of his children, perhaps even with a premonition of his own demise [40].

It was said of Richard Foxe that he would sacrifice his father to save his king [41]. The remark speaks subtly of a revolutionary age that was dawning in England, a more secular era that Foxe's humanism served to introduce. The visceral and rational importance of kinship in the lives of Englishmen ever so slightly began to slip away, yielding to the imperatives and rewards of a modern society. Henry Saunder, supporter and friend of Richard Foxe, followed Foxe's inspiration to the end. The last will and testament of Henry Saunder provided that he should be interred at the king's hospital at Savoy rather than at Ewell where others of his family lay. Henry prescribed a procession he desired, a ceremonial cortege leading from Ewell Church to Savoy, symbolically diminishing his father's legacy at Ewell for Foxe's world in London. For the ceremony, Henry provided a detailed bequest—money for each priest attending the funeral service at Ewell; money for Ewell's poor in attendance; payment for men to carry his body from Ewell, each to carry two torches in their hands; gifts to the master and chaplains at the hospital [42].

For executors of his will, Henry selected five familiar faces: Joan his wife; Ralph Lepton, his brother-in-law; William Holgill of Savoy Hospital; Nicholas Saunder, his nephew of Charlwood; and especially Richard Foxe as overseer. There were initially some personal gifts to see to, a gold cross for Nicholas of Charlwood, gowns for his son William, an annuity for Joan Hunsterton, his widowed sister, and an entitlement for Thomas Wade, chaplain and clerk, to dwell at the capital mansion in Ewell for a period of ten years. Additionally, Henry provided for several churches, including bequests for the high altars of the "mother church" at Winchester; the church at Ewell; St. Mary Overie in Southwark, which his wife seemed to attend; and for St. Mary Magdalen in Southwark, the home church of his brother Nicholas.

For disposal of his property, Henry divided his estate into two parts, each with different trustees for its conveyance [43]. His need for trustees was acute. Henry's older son Nicholas had married and was well settled. His younger son William became his prime heir, but William was underage, no more than fifteen, when the will was drafted. Care of his properties and proper administration of the entire estate by trustees until William came of age was Henry's central concern.

For properties lying in northern Surrey, his son William was to receive the Ewell capital mansion, the water mill, other Ewell lands, and property at Ebbesham and Chessington. Henry directed that the Manor of Battailes remain with his wife and, after her death, with his daughter-in-law Joan Iwardby Saunder, wife of son Nicholas, with eventual succession to his son William. The second portion of Henry's estate under separate trusteeship comprised lands in southern Surrey, notably Pendell Manor, which held lands in Bletchingly and Nutfield, but also including ownerships at Charlwood, Newdigate, and Ockley. Included under this trustee arrangement was the Three Crowns Inn of Southwark. Nicholas Saunders of Charlwood was to "have the government of" the properties of south Surrey, but all, including the Three Crowns, eventually ended up in the hands of William, Henry's younger surviving son.

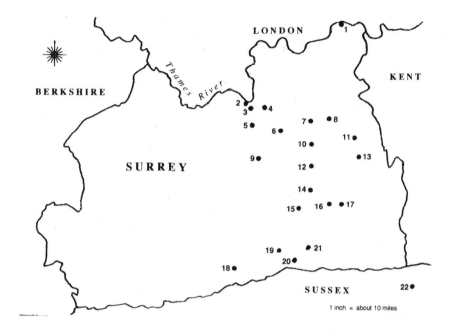

Family properties and other locations associated with the Saunders of Surrey in the fifteenth and sixteenth centuries: (1) Three Crowns Inn of Southwark; (2) Thames Ditton; (3) Long Ditton; (4) Tolworth; (5) Manor of Chessington-at-Hoke in Chessington; (6) Ewell, including the Manor of Battailes and Ebbesham of Horton Manor; (7) Carshalton; (8) Beddington; (9) Ashstead; (10) Woodmanstern;(11) Manor of East Purley at Sanderstead; (12) Chipstead; (13) Manor of Creuses at Warlingham; (14) Gatton; (15) Reigate; (16) Nutfield; (17) Manor of Pendell at Bletchingly; (18) Ockley; (19) Newdigate; (20) Charlwood; (21) Horley and Aldagh; (22) Parrock Ironworks at Hartsfield, Sussex. Not shown are family properties in Kent, including Cliff, Higham, and Frindesbury of the Manor of Cardens; and the Manor of Tullwick at Wantage in Berkshire.

Henry died in January or February 1519, and his wife Joan was swept away a month later in the sweating sickness epidemic. Joan barely had opportunity to make out a will, dying only days after its authorship. She evidently maintained three households because in addition to the Ewell capital mansion, she willed her daughters her "movable goods" at Southwark and Charlwood [44]. There was a tenement attached to the great gate of the Three Crowns Inn and perhaps this was the dwelling used by Joan when she kept residence at Southwark. One imagines Joan and Henry spent months at a time in Southwark during construction of Savoy Hospital, and she evidently had close attachments to St. Mary Overie Church there. Joan was laid to rest with her husband at the hospital.

William Saunders of Ewell

William, the younger son of Henry Saunders of Ewell, was born in the early years of the sixteenth century, a century of momentous change in life and livelihood in England. Arguably, the 1500s saw more change than any in previously recorded century. Epochal shifts in secular thought and religious belief lay at the eye of the storm. Protestant Reformations produced new religions and rejected traditional Catholic papal authority, and these ideas spread across broad expanses of Europe. Universities gained energy and momentum as inquiry into natural phenomena and human affairs became possible, and education everywhere took on secular tones. Even the scholar Erasmus's revisionist biblical interpretations made their way into English church pews.

Separately, feudal economic organization was undone as a leading force, giving way to privately held corporations operating under royal seals, and international trade on the European continent became routine and important corporate business. Feudal manors, ancient seats of power for England's landed gentry, weakened as a social and economic form, agricultural monoculture strengthened, urban markets and towns grew, and landless peasants struggled for livelihood off the land. The English countryside and political landscapes shifted in new economic tides. In the political realm, Parliament over the century cut into royal authority and began to compete on an equal footing for national power.

Architecture shed its awesome Gothic appearance in favor of smaller, human scale and lighter structures. The development of printing presses aimed at large audiences undermined parochial dialects, and language itself took on increasingly standardized forms.

And perhaps most importantly, an entirely new earth—round, large, and brimming with possibilities—became known from Portuguese, Spanish, Dutch, and English navigation. The sixteenth century had become both in fact and metaphor an age of exploration.

In individual lives, adaptation in the sixteenth century to changes of this magnitude did not come easily. Living through the bulk of this century as William Saunders did mean dealing on a regular basis with vicious and lethal competing political forces. His own time seems made less for constancy than for deftness and agility. Of a different figure in those times, it was said, "He managed to retain high office through troublous times 'by being a willow, not an oak'" [45].

In all this, William emerges as an enigma. He is a strong figure, more oak than willow, highly efficacious yet seemingly inconsistent at times in his pursuits and allies. William managed to rationalize conflicting beliefs and yet maintain decisive commitments to a singular cause—principally the Catholic cause—in part because he, like his father, probably came under the wing of Richard Foxe. Foxe lived ten years longer than Henry Saunders and may have directly influenced Henry's son William in his post-university days. Emulating the scholar Erasmus, Foxe was a voice of moderation, yet his distaste for monastic excesses set him strongly against those ancient institutions [46]. Foxe demonstrated that it was not heresy for a good Catholic to act against church excesses, and that idea may have been uppermost in William's mind as events of the mid-sixteenth century ground forward.

William Saunders is perhaps the most impressive of all figures in our family history, at least if measured by the accumulation of wealth and attainment of political position. But perhaps his greatest personal achievement was to have lived a long and full life as there were numerous others of high office who could not manage the feat, losing their heads as political tides reversed themselves with devastating regularity.

In the main, William Saunders was a product and adherent of the Catholic Counter-Reformation of the sixteenth century, a movement that embodied both liberal and conservative perspectives. The Counter-Reformation was liberal in grudgingly accepting and legitimizing secular knowledge and inquiry that sharply contrasted with the narrow monastic scholasticism of the church's past. Catholics themselves generally condemned the church for its sins of simony— making profits out of sacred things—and sought reforms for internal church improvements. But the Catholic Counter-Reformation remained conservative, reasserting the best of church teachings and traditions against the onslaught of Reformation Protestantism and afterward vigorously promoting and defending them. The crucial event of the period was the Vatican's Council of Trent, held intermittently in Italy between 1545 and 1563. Church reforms were debated and approved at the council and were then set into motion by Jesuit and Capuchin orders, eventually spurring Catholic believers into rearguard actions against Protestantism. In Spain, the Inquisition crushed any hope of Protestantism, and in sections of Western and Central Europe, Catholics regained some lost ground. In England, a fresh wave of Jesuit-led Catholic activism rose to the fore. The accession of Mary Tudor to the throne in 1553 anticipated a new Catholic ascendancy, but following Mary's death five years later, Queen Elizabeth initiated a counterattack of Catholic suppression. The Saunders, steadfast in their Catholicism and acting out the Counter-Reformation agenda of their church, were increasingly radicalized and suppressed as the century wore on. How William Saunders fared in these events is much the story of his life.

William Saunders was born about the same time that Christopher Columbus completed his fourth and final voyage to the New World in 1502 [47]. By the time William reached his twentieth year, Ferdinand Magellan's audacious three-year circumnavigation of the globe had limped to a successful conclusion. Though nothing concrete can be made of these facts as regards William's life, he is sure to have joined his colleagues in feeling the wonderment and new possibilities of overseas discovery, adding to the excitement of his times found in new books, new ideas, and new horizons. He had an opportunity in 1517 to witness the opening of the Savoy Hospital and to see his mother and father's pride of accomplishment on the day of the hospital's official founding. At age fourteen, William probably entered the university, one guesses at Magdalen College, Oxford, following his father's example, though no record of his matriculation seems to have survived. Although his educational progress may have been delayed by the simultaneous death of both his parents in 1519, by about age twenty, he entered the Inner Temple, obtaining a degree in law, as family members before him had done and as those following William also would do [48]. As William was not of age in 1519, the management of his affairs fell to Nicholas Saundre of Charlwood, his uncle, whom William's father had appointed as executor of his will. Henry's language was that Nicholas should "have government of" several properties in the south of Surrey. Nicholas was in his forties about this time and assumed responsibility for Ewell-held properties until William could mature enough to assume them for himself.

Whatever the exact timing of William's completion of studies, he emerged a very wealthy young man. From his father's will, he came into possession of the Manor of Battailes, including the capital mansion, watermill, and other structures and appurtenances; separate properties at Ebbesham and Chessington; the Three Crowns Inn of Southwark, including his mother's movable goods there; and an array of properties in southern Surrey subsumed under Pendell Manor [49]. William signed a rent roll at Pendell in 1520, an action probably having to do with his father's recent death and rental payment arrangements, though he was scarcely of age at the time [50]. In 1529 after some understandable delay [51], William asked to be formally inducted into the Pendell Manor, and this wish was granted by trustees of his father's will. This action completed William's portfolio, endowing him with yet more real estate in Nutfield, Ockley, Charlwood, and Bletchingly [52]. Induction into Pendell coincided with William's initial appointment as a member of Parliament for Gatton, the first of many political posts that William would hold.

About the same year, 1529, William married Joan Marston, a recent widow of Nicholas Mynne of Norfolk [53]. William Marston, Joan's father, held the Manor of Shalford, a submanor of the Manor of Ewell, and to this marriage, Joan brought two properties then in her possession, the Manor of Horton in Ebbesham and the Manor of Brettgrave [54]. William once commented on "my lady's grant of Somerset in Ashstead," suggesting he gained some interest in this property near Ewell by about 1530 [55].

By her first marriage to Nicholas Mynne, Joan Marston had five children, the eldest of whom was named John. William accepted the wardship for John Mynne, then age nine, an act that cemented some long-term relationships between the Saunders and the Mynnes [56]. With William Saunders, Joan had several children during the decade of the 1530s, though their birth dates are not precisely known. Following traditional naming practice, we imagine there was a son William; but if so, he did not survive. They had a son Nicholas, eventual principal heir to the Ewell estate, and another son named Erasmus, whose life in Wales we follow at a later point. In addition, there were daughters Mary [57] and Urithe [58], both of whom married well and survived their parents.

Turbulence and Opportunity

By the late 1530s, William had reaped an abundance of good fortune—fathering a growing family, engaging some practice of law, holding a great deal of wealth and property, and gaining a seat in Parliament. In 1536, he added more property by acquiring a lease for land in Gosborough Hill Wood, part of the Manor of Chessington-at-Hoke [59]; and in 1538, William gained a new and important governmental office, receiver of taxes for Surrey and Sussex [60]. This work provided William some experience in financial matters, a skill he would put to important use in later years. But turbulent years came upon William abruptly. His household was severed in 1539 by his wife's death, perhaps in childbirth, leaving him to care for his four young children from his decade of marriage. And at nearly the same moment, large events in English history landed right on William's doorstep.

In the mid-1530, King Henry VIII engaged a series of marital and extramarital affairs that strained relations with the pope as upholder of Catholic traditions [61]. Efforts to assuage both parties with a series of annulments and divorces came to nothing, and Henry finally broke with the church, declaring himself head of the church and God's representative in his English dominions. Though Henry initially was not attempting to break with the Catholic Church as Scandinavian counties had done in 1527, these events inexorably led to the establishment of the separate Church of England and to capital judgments in England against those who opposed him, notably Sir Thomas More and Bishop John Fisher. Henry then followed Parliament in 1536 in declaring small Catholic monasteries uneconomic and began closing their doors. In 1539, Parliament passed the Acts of Dissolution that disbanded all remaining English monasteries, large and small; and by 1540, the last of the Catholic monasteries in England had fallen.

The task of dissolution involved acquiring deeds, dispersing priests, nuns, and other monastery personnel, dismantling structures, and taking possession of all things of value. This work was undertaken by a court of augmentations, a revenue branch of the Crown. This court consisted of a chancellor, treasurer, legal officers and auditors, and seventeen particular receivers [62]. In 1539, William Saunders of Ewell was named one of these receivers, having jurisdiction in Surrey and Sussex. The particular receivers supervised local dissolutions and collected all assets on behalf of the Crown. The process was disheartening, messy, and utterly perfect in destroying every vestige of these ancient institutions.

On the first fateful day for each monastery, receivers assembled the monastery superior and his subjects and announced their impending demise, called for and defaced the convent seal, desecrated the church, took possession of the best plate and vestments, measured the lead upon the roof, counted the bells, and appraised the goods and chattels of the church community [63]. The following day, subordinate officers and workmen arrived to carry out the full destruction, stripping the roofs, pulling down pipes and gutters, melting the roof lead, throwing down the bells and breaking them with sledgehammers, and packing the pieces for sale to the highest bidder. Furniture was collected and sold, together with window frames, shutters, and doors until finally the stripped-out structure was abandoned, left beyond any possible use. It was William Saunders' task to certify the complete dissolution and final revenues received in each case and to repeat this process for monastery after monastery for the better part of two years [64].

Parish churches were not directly subject to the Acts of Dissolution, but monks unwilling to carry on under the circumstances created by Henry VIII were retired from churchly duties and provided with support. In one instance, William was responsible for the payment of pensions for ten monks of St. Mary Overie in Southwark, the same church remembered by his father only twenty years before in his will of 1518 [65]. One senses from scant evidence that William must have entertained some misgivings in his receivership role as he seems to have rescued two gold crosses from monasteries that he eventually bestowed on his sons as remembrances of old faith [66]. Not the least of William's struggles would have been to participate in the demise of Charles Carew, rector and last master of Beddington Chapel, and William's distant relative. The chapel and its appurtenances were forfeited to the Crown under William Saunders's authority in 1539, Carew having been accused of some unproven felony for which he evidently was executed in 1540 [67].

Finally, his work with the Court of Augmentations complete, William in 1541 was given the post of commissioner of the peace for Surrey and Sussex. How long he remained in this position remains unclear because he may also have accepted a brief stint about 1543 as treasurer of Calais, serving under Calais's governor, Henry FitzAlan, Earl of Arundel, who otherwise held the Manor of Ewell [68]. In that year, William as a wealthy landowner was required to furnish three foot soldiers for the army in Flanders for war against the French.

After five years as a widower, William finally remarried in 1544, to Joan Gittons. Joan, whose maiden name may have been Munson, first married John Spelman of Narborough, Norfolk, and second Thomas Gittons, citizen and vintner of London. Thomas Gittons in fact was the largest importer of wines in all of England in his day, and one expects wine purchases for William's Three Crowns Inn of Southwark may have brought these two together. With Thomas Gittons, who died in 1543, Joan had three children, Albey, Oliver, and Christian, all remembered in her will in later years [69]. Joan came to Ewell to live after the marriage and, with William, had four surviving children in the late 1540s, a set of twins named Frances [70] and Francis [71], and two younger daughters, Catherine [72] and Elizabeth [73]. For these younger children of William, Joan's influence on their lives seems to have been paramount because they all eventually lived in or near Norfolk, including the place of her first marriage, the Spelman home at Narborough. Closeness of the Saunders to the Spelman family after Joan's marriage to William remained particularly strong in the next generation.

Shortly after his marriage, in 1545, William was named to Henry VIII's Chantry Commission, which carried out provisions of a Chantries Act of that same year. This act extended Henry VIII's program of stifling Catholicism by targeting Catholic organizations other than monasteries, which by 1540 had been successfully disbanded. Chantries mainly were privately endowed chapels dedicated to saying masses for special occasions, such as praying for the deceased. Some chantries, like the Saunders Chapel at Charlwood, were attached to churches; others were not. The act interpreted the definition of chantries broadly, often including Catholic schools in their sweep. Resistance to the Chantries Act was widespread, having less to do with religious conviction than with the threatened loss of education for middle- and lower-class children, which some Catholic chantries heretofore had provided.

One feature of Henry VIII's dissolution of England's monasteries was the amount of monastery land released through the dissolution process. Monasteries typically held large amounts of property as endowments for income, but through Henry's actions, monastic land rapidly slipped into other hands. The enormous shift of land ownership that ensued changed the face of wealth throughout the kingdom. One historian describes the effect this way: "(Crown officers) administered the greatest social revolution in England's history since the Norman Conquest. Almost every class in England was involved in the immense, exciting scramble for the confiscated property of the church. Favourites who were being rewarded for their personal attractions, politicians who were being built up as territorial magnates for the better government of the realm, officials who had done a bit of useful work, could all look forward to enjoying the royal bounty. Land would either be given to them for nothing or sold on very favourable terms" [74].

As William Saunders undertook his involvement with the Chantry Commission, he also acquired new properties devolving from defunct monasteries. Although he may not have acquired land directly upon dissolution, he shortly thereafter purchased monastery land both in Kent and Surrey. William obtained property formerly of the London Charterhouse, a Carthusian monastery, which included the Manor of Cardens and lands in Clif, Higham, and Frindesbury in Kent. Charterhouse records show the descent of this property: "The Manor (of Cardens) had belonged to the London Charterhouse and after the suppression of the monastery, the Manor was granted to Thomas Gittons who was at once granted a license to alienate the manor to Sir Oliver Ledder." William Saunders purchased the manor and lands from Sir Oliver Ledder and David Gittons, his new brother-in-law in 1545, and the following year, he added nearby land at Harshing Marsh. Another property in Surrey called Chessington-at-Hoke, formerly held by the particularly wealthy Merton (Moreton) Abbey, fell into William's hands at about the same time [75]. In 1538, when Merton Abbey was under threat of dissolution, William also obtained an eighty-year lease on a Merton holding in Ewell, for a two-acre meadow called Entmore [76].

Separately, in 1547, William bought the Manor of Parrock, also called Parrock Inholmes, and its iron mill, known as Proke Johanna, in Sussex County. This purchase transaction was disputed by William Warner, the former owner, but litigation was resolved in favor of William [77]. More serious was the dispute over control of Proke Johanna [78]. The iron mill and forty acres had been leased from the former owner by Denise Bowyer, mother of Sir Henry Bowyer, later ironmaster to Queen Elizabeth, who claimed that William Saunders illegally seized the property. The dispute landed finally in a Star Chamber. Bowyer alleged that William came with his men and "distrained her cattle and broke up the said pools and waters so that she could not have any recourse to the said iron mill or forge." A pitched battle evidently ensued. William denied his part in any assault but claimed that Bowyer's men assailed him as he left peacefully. William added that Denise Bowyer struck the oxen drawing the wagon that was carrying tools and bellows from the ironworks and cried out,

"Down with Greybeard, down with Greybeard," until he picked Denise up and carried her out of the way. William apparently was knocked down in the melee, and Denise Bowyer alleged cried out, "Slay him, slay him, shoot at Greybeard." Although records do not describe the Star Chambers' judgment in this case, the Saunders continued to hold Proke Johanna into the next generation. Walker suggests a plausible connection between William's holdings at Proke Johanna and Chessington-at-Hoke. In 1557, William leased "woods and coppices" at Chessington perhaps to acquire fuel for the iron mill since timber in that area was in increasingly short supply [79].

Henry VIII died in 1547, ending William's involvements in his commissions. Edward VI, nine-year-old son of Henry and Jane Seymour, assumed the Crown. His uncle, Edward Seymour, Duke of Somerset, was named lord protector of the realm during Edward's minority. The reign was short, barely six years in all, but importantly it continued Henry VIII's Protestant course for the nation and acted to improve schools that the Chantry Commission had undermined.

William Saunders continued to be sought out for government assignments under Edward. In 1548, he became escheator for the counties of Surrey and Sussex, supervising the collection of properties which had lapsed to the Crown [80]. In the same year, he was also appointed commissioner for the sale of church goods in East Surrey, a commission designed to discourage "popish practices" and enforce the new religion throughout the land. For more than a year, William certified inventories of the village churches near Ewell, appropriating for the king's benefit certain valuable chalices and other goods [81].

Edward VI died at age fifteen, and a successional struggle ensued between Protestant and Catholic possibilities. Protestants prevailed, promoting Lady Jane Grey for the throne. Though Jane did become England's monarch, her reign lasted but nine days, and she was hurriedly replaced by Catholic Queen Mary Tudor. At long last, William and his fellow English Catholics had their ardently wished rout of Protestantism. William, through his numerous offices, in fact had done much to discourage Catholicism in England, but that seems a circumstance he inherited and could little change by his opportunities. To some degree, dismantling some trappings of the old church was desired by all, though William occasionally must have choked on his larger responsibilities. But no longer. Mary was now queen, and William had his Catholic monarch. For William, the future looked bright indeed.

Ascendancy

With Mary assuming the throne in 1553, England saw its return to Catholic rule. Mary's approach to overturning her father Henry VIII's Protestant reformation was initially cautious, returning to the old faith without proclaiming the pope's ultimate supremacy. But in 1554, the pope restored England to the Holy See in Rome but also required that English heretics be burned. A reign of terror under Bloody Mary thus began, and numerous famous English Protestants paid the dearest price. In the long history of vindictive English monarchs, though, the cumulative effect of Mary's actions probably lies at some midpoint on the long spectrum of executional horror [82].

Under Mary, William Saunders rose to the zenith of his career, being elevated into a central place in the English royal household. William was dubbed cofferer to Queen Mary, having responsibility to manage Mary's personal wealth. His background in legal and financial matters, as well as his persistent Catholicism in the face of numerous challenges, undoubtedly contributed to Mary's trust. Direct royal support for William also may have been responsible for his series of lucrative and prestigious appointments soon thereafter, including membership in Parliament for Surrey in 1554, knight for the Shire of Surrey in 1555, and perhaps high sheriff of Surrey in 1556 [83]. This was William's heyday, the highest point of political achievement of his own life and any of his forebears.

William's appointments concentrated in him considerable political power. On one occasion, he was able to muster six hundred men to assist the high sheriff of Sussex to keep the peace [84]. But nowhere was William's power more evident than in his actions to defend the queen during a period of disquiet [85]. In opposition to Mary's planned marriage to Philip of Spain, which many feared would reduce England to Spanish vassalage, a series of rebellions emerged, the most noted of which was Wyatt's Kentish Rebellion of 1554. Suspicions of plots were rife even in Surrey. Teaming with his cousin, Sir Thomas Saunders of Charlwood, William Saunders descended on Bletchingly in 1554 with superior force and in seventeen wagons carried off arms and other property amassed by Sir Thomas Cawarden, whose loyalty to the Crown was in doubt. Cawarden was justice of the peace for Surrey, a Protestant, and steward of the royal Manor of Nonesuch. After the confrontation at Bletchingly, William also arranged for Cawarden's eviction from Nonesuch. A few years later, following the death of Queen Mary in 1558, Cawarden sought restitution for all his property by then at Ewell, valued at more than two thousand pounds. But Cawarden died in 1559, and his widow was forced by a privy council to drop proceedings against William and his cousin Sir Thomas Saunders.

SIR THOMAS SAUNDERS OF CHARLWOOD

Sir Thomas Saunders of Charlwood joined his cousin William Saunders of Ewell in seizing the armaments and possessions of Thomas Cawarden in 1554. That Thomas and William should have joined together in this action is not surprising, because they also shared duties as commissioners for the peace in Surrey a decade before. These were just two of many instances in which the lives of the Saunders of Ewell and Charlwood intertwined.

Sir Thomas Saunders was born about 1505 as the eldest of ten children of Alys Hungate and Nicholas Saunders of Charlwood [1*]. He studied law and rose rapidly in the legal community, being appointed in 1540 as solicitor to the queen, Anne of Cleves, the fourth of Henry VIII's wives. His position lasted only briefly as this marriage failed within six months. The royal annulment was amicable however and Thomas may be due some credit for his counsel toward this outcome. In any case, within a year Thomas was selected as member of Parliament for Gatton in Surrey and appointed commissioner for the peace and also commissioner for sewers in Surrey.

About 1540 Thomas married Alice, daughter of Sir Edmund Walsingham, a marriage that anticipated ties of the Walsinghams to the Saunders of Derbyshire [2*]. Connected to the Walsinghams by marriage were the Spencers, Bolyns, and Seymours, all families involved in royal marriages, and Francis Walsingham had been the most influential figure in the court of Elizabeth.

Through his early governmental experience and family background that now included the Carews, Courtenays, and Walsinghams, Thomas secured lofty standing among the country's ruling elite. By 1545 he had been queued up by Henry VIII to succeed Christopher More as remembrancer of the exchequer. As remembrancer, Thomas's task was "to put the Lord Treasurer and the Barons of Court in remembrance of such things as were called upon and dealt with for the benefit of the Crown." The primary duty was to keep records of royal taxes, paid and unpaid. Beyond that, it fell to the remembrancer to nominate candidates for high sheriff of each county in England and Wales, and to carry out certain rituals associated with appointments to high government offices [3*]. Christopher More died within four years and in 1549 Thomas assumed exchequer duties, though by then Edward VI had acceded to the throne following Henry VIII's death. For this and other accomplishments, and through the imperatives of this period for persons in his position [4*], Thomas received a knighthood in 1550, henceforth to be known as Sir Thomas Saunders. He returned as member of Parliament for Gatton in 1553 and 1557 and received appointment as high sheriff for Surrey about this time.

As eldest son, Thomas eventually controlled extensive property holdings. At Charlwood, he owned the "great wood called Wykewood," Lorkyns Farm, and Charlwood Place. He inherited the Manors of Sanderstead, East Purley, and Creuses from his father. Other lands that Thomas acquired on his own devices were in Ewell, Chipstead, Woodmansterne, Reigate, Walton, Betchworth, Chamberlayns at Buckland, and an estate at Flanchford.

Altogether, these possessions endowed future generations of Saunders at Charlwood with ample means for their continued prosperity [5*].

Alice Walsingham and Thomas Saunders went on to have five children. These issue and further Saunders generations formed a Charlwood lineage that extended into the twentieth century, though by that time family property in Charlwood had been lost. Charlwood Place itself was destroyed in the civil war of the 1660s. At least one person from the Charlwood line dwelled in Virginia in that colony's earliest days.

Ebb of Influence

Queen Mary died in 1558 after five years of rule and her stepsister Elizabeth assumed the throne that same year. This was the beginning of nearly five decades of Elizabethan rule and the commencement of England's golden age, though not all agree that Elizabeth deserves credit for most of its glories [86]. Elizabeth returned Protestantism to England for good, though not without persistent Catholic resistance throughout her reign. In 1570, the pope declared Elizabeth excommunicated and deposed after her government demanded of its English subjects full religious conformity with the Church of England.

In 1563, despite his close and eager support of the Catholic queen just five years before, William received under Elizabeth the post of queen's surveyor, his final position in government [87]. William's substantial knowledge of escheated Surrey lands evidently outweighed his Catholic belief in procuring this appointment. Elizabeth's need for skill in property law and taxation was acute as revenues fell precipitously following her coronation. Tax assessments were static in spite of rising costs of government, and tax evasion became rampant [88]. Improving collections and selling Crown lands were imperative, but these actions depended on developing solid land inventories. William's responsibility evidently was to determine the legal status of Crown lands in Surrey. How long William continued in the post of queen's surveyor is not known, but he seems to have retired from public office after that. In 1565, William's assistance was sought on procuring grain for Ireland and for a garrison there, where needs were said to be great [89]. Old age rather than political considerations probably played the larger role in William's reduced final involvements.

Shortly after Elizabeth assumed the English throne, William and his two sons Nicholas and Francis were named on a royal pardon roll of 1559. This roll recorded those who sought "pardons of land alienation" for having acquired or repurchased Crown land originally held by monasteries, but which were originally sold without royal license. These pardons of alienation were secured by payment of fines to insulate the landowner against future claims. In William's case, his earlier acquisition of former London Charterhouse and Merton Abbey properties were henceforth protected by pardon, allowing him and eventually his sons to hold these lands legally and in perpetuity [90].

About the same time as he secured this pardon, William also purchased "animal rents" from George and William Lussher of Puttenham, an action that built upon the marriage of his daughter Mary to Nicholas Lussher some three years before. Later in the decade of the 1560s, William, despite his advancing age, purchased the wardship of young Nicholas Lussher after his father passed away.

In William's final days, the Catholic Counter-Revolution pressed ahead, heightening fears among Elizabeth's Protestant ruling elite. Arrests of recusants accelerated, and shortly after William passed away, both his sons Nicholas and Erasmus were incarcerated, as were his close allies, John, Lord Lumley, and Henry FitzAlan, Earl of Arundel. One senses that William's final days might not have been happy ones had he survived longer, but he died in his sixty-ninth year before the full suppression of his religion in England.

William's Legacy

William Saunders died in 1571 and asked to be buried "in the chapel near my tomb in the parish church of Ewell" but allowed that if he was away from Ewell, he should be interred "without any pomp in any wise (ways) to be made" [91]. Though William chose frugality with his own burial arrangements unlike his father had done, he used his generosity well on those around him. He remembered the poor at Ewell and Elsham in Surrey and at Cliffe in Kent and also his numerous servants and tenants. William's daughters and their children received money and jewels as well as debt forgiveness, and the sons of Joan Gittons were included as well. To his own son Erasmus, he left "my cross of gold with a pearl in the end thereof" and a doublet of purple satin; to son Francis, "my owch of gold with a murrion's face with a cross of mother-of-pearl" and certain tapestries. Thomas Bromley, who one day would become lord chancellor of England, received William's best coat and doublet.

Beyond personal gifts, William arranged for property succession as it had been done for generations, that is, with the eldest son to inherit the lion's share. He explained that his will should reflect his father Henry's inheritance wishes, which as a practical matter meant that his son Nicholas, who was named William's executor, should receive the properties in Ewell, Elsham, Chessington, Bletchingly, Nutfield, Charlwood, Horley, Newdigate, and Ockley, all in southern Surrey, and the Three Crowns Inn of Southwark. To that would be added the Manor of Cardens in Kent after his stepmother's decease. His son Francis received family property in Cliffe and a part of Harshing Marsh in Kent, the latter to be shared with his brother Erasmus. In William's careful legal fashion, he arranged that proceeds from the iron mill at Parrock and woods at Chessington be available as necessary to carry out provisions in the will. In selecting an overseer for the will, William chose his "especially good friend" Lumley. John, Lord Lumley, was a generation younger than William and had come into possession of the Manor of Ewell through his marriage to the daughter of Henry FitzAlan, Earl of Arundel.

Although Joan Gittons received the Manor of Cardens from William, she chose to live in Narborough, Norfolk with her daughter and near her other children for her remaining days. Joan died in 1580, nine years after William, her bequests being directed mainly at sons from her former marriage, those who benefited least from William's earlier will [92].

Through his will, William Saunders carefully programmed the perpetuation of his substantial wealth through his son Nicholas, but the legacy for Nicholas and the other children went beyond William's financial calculation. William left a high social and political orbit toward which they could reasonably aspire, a set of allegiances from marriages and political exchange that William had built over his lifetime and now left for future days.

At the center of this nexus was Sir Anthony Cooke of Gidea Hall in Essex, William's contemporary and distant relative. Cooke's mother was Alice Saunder, daughter and heiress of the second William Saunders of Banbury. He is said to have been a tutor for Edward VI, a parliamentarian and knight of the Bath [93]. Anthony Cooke among other accomplishments was said to have the best-educated daughters in England. Notably, one daughter, Anne, married Sir Nicholas Bacon, treasurer of the Court of Augmentations and lord keeper of the Great Seal of England, under whose hand royal decrees were issued. Anne was among the best translators of Latin in her day. Another daughter, Mildred, married William Cecil, later Lord Burghley, probably the wealthiest and most powerful figure in Elizabethan England, who for forty years served as Elizabeth's chief prop. Bacon and Cecil became staunch allies following these marriages [94]. The Saunders of Ewell after William drew directly upon Burghley's influence.

Another key figure was Henry FitzAlan, Earl of Arundel. Arundel held numerous lands in Surrey. He had control of Marston property belonging to Ewell Manor before William married Joan, and further control of Ashstead Manor before William acquired some interest there. There is no doubt of William's reliance on Arundel as William was once rebuked for reporting peacekeeping activities to Arundel rather than to the sheriff in charge [95]. William may have joined Arundel in Calais in earlier years, and William's good friend John Lumley married Arundel's daughter. Arundel also arranged for young Thomas Bromley to be seated as a member of Parliament for Gatton, the same seat held by William years before. This is the same Thomas Bromley found in William's will, who later become lord high chancellor of England. These figures and others of high rank formed a constellation of possibilities that William bestowed on Ewell's ensuing generations.

Later Ewell

Although our family story at Ewell ends with the death of William Saunders in 1571 and continues with William's second son Erasmus who lived in Wales, we digress briefly to describe some continuing family history at Ewell. This story is of Nicholas Saunders, William's eldest son, his marriages and offspring. But more than that, through Nicholas we discover how Ewell family wealth waxed, waned, and finally dissipated in a great scheme that undid a century of Ewell prosperity.

Nicholas was the eldest surviving son of Joan Marston and William Saunders, born about 1532, and was the prime beneficiary of his father's considerable wealth. Educated in the law, Nicholas inherited the lion's share of Ewell properties, which passed directly from his grandfather Henry Saundre through his father William. Little is known of Nicholas's professional or public life, but in his later years, he was imprisoned for recusancy, that is, for departure from the state's official faith. He spent two months in the Fleet Prison in 1578, and in his will, he left an annuity for his brother Erasmus, who likewise was imprisoned for his Catholicism.

Nicholas first married Isabel Carew, fourth daughter of Sir Nicholas Carew, knight of the Garter and keeper of the king's great seal, in St. Mary's Church at the ancient Carew home of Beddington [96]. With this marriage, the Saunders-Carew ties passed into a fourth generation, beginning with William Saunder and Joan Carew in 1439.

Isabel Carew died about 1580, and Nicholas soon remarried to Margaret, daughter of Richard Bostock of Newington, Surrey. Margaret Bostock was twice a widow before marrying Nicholas and with him bore no children, but properties accruing to Margaret from her previous marriages eventually fell into Saunders hands. Margaret first had married Richard Blunt of London and, after his passing, acquired the Manor of Bodley in Surrey, which she held on behalf of her only daughter with Blunt. The manor eventually ended up in the hands of Nicholas's offspring, who divested themselves of it in 1592. From his work in service to Sir John Leigh, Richard Blunt acquired interest in the Manor of Williton in Somerset in the southwest of England. For a short period, Nicholas Saunders may have gained some interest in this property before he died; afterward it passed to another Blunt relative in 1585.

From Margaret's second marriage to Justice Jasper Fisher, she acquired the Manor of Oldbury in Warwickshire, which in time devolved to Nicholas Saunders's son [97]. Several other properties may have been subject to the terms of Margaret's marriage to Nicholas Saunders as well, including some that may have led the family into a new presence in southwestern England [98].

With Isabel Carew, Nicholas had four surviving daughters and two sons, though one daughter, Frances, died young. A daughter Jane, born about 1567 married Luke Ward, gentleman of London, who in 1588 captained the naval ship *Tremontana* in the great English battle with the Spanish Armada. In 1590, Jane second married Sir Alexander Clifford. He was of the extended family of George Clifford, third Earl of Cumberland, who commanded an English squadron against the Spanish; Cumberland personally commanded the *Elizabeth Bonaventure*, a six-hundred-ton ship of fifty-five guns and over four hundred seamen. Jane's husband, Sir Alexander captained the *Moon*, a small vessel of sixty tons, nine guns, and forty men [99].

Born about 1568, Isabel and Nicholas's daughter Anne married Henry Whitney Jr., gentleman. Whitney served under Sir Thomas Bromley, chancellor of England, to whom William Saunders, Anne's grandfather, once bequeathed a fine coat and doublet [100]. Whitney eventually gained his family's Manor of Biggin and Tamworth in Surrey.

A younger daughter Mary, born about 1572, married Robert Bevile, and a younger son Henry, born about 1570, studied at Balliol College after 1584 and was admitted to the Inner Temple for law studies in 1589, following family tradition. Henry inherited the family's Manor of Parrock but sold this to his brother Nicholas in 1590.

Sir Nicholas Saunders

The eldest child of Isabel Carew and Nicholas Saunders was Nicholas, born in 1569. He was age eighteen when his father died in 1587, and in his will, the elder Nicholas named as overseer the wealthiest and most powerful figure in all of Elizabethan England, William Cecil, Lord Burghley. In Nicholas's words, "To Lord Burghley's honourable favour, direction, and protection," Nicholas wrote, "I commend and commit my son Nicholas." As the young Nicholas was not then of age, this arrangement evidently sought Burghley's influence and guidance for Nicholas in matters of religion and finance. Nicholas and his new wife, Elizabeth Blunt, were both named Catholic recusants in 1585, but not thereafter, perhaps reflecting Burghley's own Puritan inclinations. Burghley's influence evidently prevailed as by 1591 Nicholas was named a member of the Surrey Commission for the Detection and Suppression of Jesuits.

Nicholas attended Balliol College and, in 1586, was admitted to the Inner Temple for law studies [101]. Shortly thereafter, he became patron of a certain John Florio, who taught Italian at Magdalen College, Oxford, drafted Italian-English lexicons, and authored translations of Italian and French works. Florio dedicated a book called *Second Fruites* to Nicholas Saunders, acknowledging his patronage. In this, one sees Nicholas, with his considerable wealth, as an instrument in Burghley's orchestrations because Burghley was interested in promoting Florio's position at court, especially as language tutor for the young Earl of Southampton. Southampton was the person to whom William Shakespeare directed his sonnets, and Southampton became Florio's patron after Nicholas Saunders. Florio was a particular favorite of Edmund Spenser, author of the *Shepheard's Calendar*, and Spenser's character of Menalcas in that work was modeled after John Florio himself [102].

About 1585, Nicholas married Elizabeth Blunt, sole heiress of Richard Blunt of Bodley Manor in Surrey. They had five children, including two daughters who married into families from Dorsetshire in southwestern England and another named Isabel who married Sir Roger Twysden of Royden Hall in East Peckham, Kent. Isabel was a lady-in-waiting to Roger's mother and left a diary of those years [103]. A son Henry in 1659 sold the Manor of Battailes in Ewell.

Nicholas was knighted in 1603 and a member of Parliament for various districts until about 1626. After one particularly long parliamentary session, Nicholas wrote to a friend, "We were content to yield to anything so wee might rise . . . many of us cought such a faintnes there, so long fasting, having neyther meate in our bellies not witt in our heddes and wee shall not be able to make a wyse speeche there while wee live" [104].

One imagines the mature years for Nicholas to have been blessed with wealth and position, but in his final years, fate dealt Nicholas a different turn. While in Parliament in 1610, he served on a commission for the Wandle River that addressed difficulties in a portion of the London watershed, an experience that evidently piqued Nicholas's financial interest. A project was conceived to deliver a new water supply for the city of London, constructing a covered aqueduct to replace the fouled water of an existing open canal [105]. Nicholas invested heavily, but the project failed, bringing Nicholas to financial ruin. To help with debt, Nicholas sold the capital mansion at Ewell and most other properties. A contemporary wrote that the children of Sir Nicholas inherited his heraldic distinctions but nothing else. Overstatement though that might have been, this episode brought to an end the days of the Saunders at Ewell.

NOTES

1. Good descriptions of Henry VII are available, but the historical importance of his approach to governance seems slighted. A helpful synopsis of main themes is given in Mike Ashley, *British Kings and Queens* (New York: Barnes and Noble, 1998), pp. 624–629.
2. For Richard Foxe's personal history, see Canon S. L. Ollard, Gordon Crosse, and M. F. Bond, eds., *Dictionary of English Church History*, reprinted (New York: Morehouse-Gorman, 1948).
3. P. Ackroyd, *Life of Thomas More* (New York: Random House, New York, 1999), p. 29.
4. J. R. Lander, *Government and Community: England 1450–1509.* (Cambridge, MA: Harvard University Press, 1980), p. 155.

5. Ackroyd, *Life of Thomas More*, p. 56.
6. The connection to Simon Waynfleet is identified in a dispute regarding property in Southwark involved Robert Cawode, Thomas Kyrkeby, clerk, Thomas Wharff, John Thorley, Esq., Simon Waynfleete, clerk, William Saundre, and Richard Ford, v. John Denaway of Southwark and his wife Agnes, in the parish of St. George, Southwark. See *Surrey Archeological Collection*, extra vol. 1, p. 184.
7. Public Record Office, C, 1/64/897. Medieval Southwark, 1475–1485, p. 218.
8. 8 A share of Battailes had been his mother's Carew inheritance, but she died in 1470 about the time Henry enrolled in the university.
9. Records of 1473 and 1507 for Aldhagh are given in O. Manning and W. Bray, *History and Antiquities of Surrey*, vol. 2, p. 198. The given name of the Saunder family member possessing Aldhagh prior to 1473 is not known, but we believe it could have been Thomas, as William and Joan certainly would have had a son of that name, which was also the name of each of their fathers. Aldhagh itself evidently lay in Huet family hands before Saunder's possession.
10. Records for Nutfield for 1489–1491 and 1506 are found in *Surrey Archeological Collection*, extra vol. 1, Feet of Fines, pp. 204, 210. It is worth noting that a participant in the Nutfield land action was William Marston, whose daughter Joan married Henry's son William in later years.
11. *Surrey Archeological Collection*, extra vol. I, Feet of Fines, p. 199.
12. From the 1440 record, we know that William Saunder and Richard Ford were in Southwark presumably acquiring the Three Crowns property that was settled upon them in their Carew marriages. The setting of the Three Crowns is described by Higham, "Three Crowns Square on the west side of Southwark High Street marks the site of an inn and that an indenture of 1617 mentioned a tenement adjoining the south side of the great gate of the inn called the Three Crowns. Bryan Swynbank of the Three Crowns in Southwark was mentioned in a will of 1520." F. Higham, *Inns of Old Southwark*, pp. 416–417.
13. For further description of Southwark for the period under discussion, see T. Baker, 1970. *Medieval London* (New York: Praeger, 1970), and *Victoria History of Surrey*, vol. 2.
14. See the *History of the Worshipful Company of Innholders of the City of London* (London: Bemrose and Co., 1922). This provides the following characterizations. "The first charter granted to the Innholders' Company at the beginning of the reign of Henry VIII, was merely a confirmation of rights and privileges. The Company had then certainly been in existence, as an unchartered fraternity, for over a

century, but it probably dated its foundation another hundred or two hundred years further back" (page 7). Also on the power of these kinds of companies, "No man could hope to work in a trade or vocation that did not belong to its company, and each company was zealous in defending its prerogatives from infringement by the members of any other company. "The companies controlled the whole trade of the city"(page 6).

See also William Herbert, *History of the Twelve Great Livery Companies of London*, vol. 1 (1864; repr., New York: Kelley Publishers, 1968), pp. 110–111. "[The innholders] having been a community or society of honest friendly men, by their often meeting and conversing together, as in those days it was a matter much observed, they came to be incorporated in the 6th year of Henry VIII." Early membership can be found in the "Names of the Company of Innholders from the Record of the Chapter House," in T. Allen, *The History and Antiquities of London, Westminster, and Southwark* (London: Cowie and Strange, 1828).

15. In Ewell chapel is found a memorial to Henry, seventh son of Henry Saunder of Ewell. The memorial lies between two unnamed others, one dated 1510 and the other about 1520. This suggests a death between these two dates, and since this Henry was a seventh son, he clearly would have been underage around 1515 or so. Also, William might have been a nonsurviving first son, given traditions in naming at the time.

16. Nicholas, the older surviving son of Joan and Henry Saunder of Ewell, born about 1488, was about fourteen years older than his younger brother William. Nicholas married Joan Iwardby St. John about 1513 and from that marriage came into substantial wealth and several properties, explaining why Nicholas's father Henry had no need of including this son in his will of 1519. With Joan, Nicholas had three daughters, Ursula, who married Thomas Hungerford of Wilshire; Joyce, who married into the Woodcock family of Wilshire; and Joan, who first married Richard Bray and after his death in 1559 second married William Tyrell. Joan died in 1581.

Nicholas's wife Joan was the daughter of Sir John Iwardby and Senchia Carew. Sir John acquired the Manor of Carshalton in Surrey, which Joan and Nicholas Saunders held during their marriage. Carshalton eventually passed to the heirs of Joan Iwardby and her first husband, Sir John St. John. See *Victoria History of Surrey*, vol. 4, p. 182. In Hampshire, Nicholas Saunders came into the Manor of Farley Chamberlayne, formerly held by Iwardby. See History of St. Mary's Church, Purley, Section 33/JL1. In Ewell, the Iwardbys held the Manor of Fitznells (a.k.a. Fennelles). It is sometimes claimed that Nicholas's daughters sold Fennelles to a family named Horde in later years; see *Victoria History of Surrey*, vol. 4, p. 378. This claim seems incorrect. An alternative view is given in the *Victoria History of Surrey*, vol. 3, p. 280, in which it is stated, "In 1542 Fennelles was held by Dame Joan St. John who was daughter and heir of Sir John Iwardby, and her son sold it in 1562 to Edmund Horde." It is possible that Nicholas's daughters did inherit the property and passed it to John St. John, who then sold it to Horde. Nicholas and Joan also held the Manor of Purley Magna in Berkshire, and probably resided there. In the north wall of the Church of St. Mary the Virgin is a tablet to Jane (sic), daughter and heir of John Iwardby, wife of John St. John. See *Victoria History of Berkshire*, vol. 3, p. 422. Joan apparently became a nun and lived in a convent after Nicholas died sometime before 1549.

17. Agnes Saunder was born about 1501 and in 1519 married Richard Keyes of Greenwich, Kent. She lived only a short time, until about 1525, and bore a son Thomas, who became a captain at Sandhurst and was designated a royal gatekeeper. Thomas secretly married Lady Mary Grey, younger sister to the so-called Nine Days Queen, Jane Grey. Jane was deposed and Mary was considered by some to be the heiress presumptive to the English throne. However, Mary and Thomas Keyes were both placed under house arrest for marrying without the queen's permission, and no claim by Mary to the throne was ever made. Keyes died imprisoned and Mary Grey finally was freed before she died at age thirty-three.

18. Margaret was born about 1504 and unmarried at the time of her parents' deaths in 1519. She was remembered in her mother's will, but no record of her eventual fate has been discovered.

19. Dealing with occupants of the land occasionally posed difficulties. The following record suggests something of this. "Pardon to John Colstoke of Horsted Keynes, Sussex, yeoman, of his outlawry in Surrey for not appearing before the king to satisfy the king of his ransom by reason of a trespass and contempt of the king as well as of Henry Saunder." *Calendar of Patent Rolls*, VII, 1494–1509, p. 174.

20. Preferments were titles or offices conferred on persons of privilege, usually with few or no onerous responsibilities and generally with some compensation. The office so used gained by association with the political or social importance of the person receiving the title.

21. M. L. Walker, The Manor of Battailes and the Family of Saunder in Ewell during the 16th and 17th Centuries (Guildford: Surrey Archeological Society, 1956), p. 80.

22. This description of the fishing lake was supplied by estate agents in Ewell and Epsom at http://www.fgsales.co.uk. One rood equals about one-fourth acre.

23. With Pendell Manor, he consolidated his previous holdings at Nutfield and added land and property at Bletchingly, all in southern Surrey. See Walker, *Manor of Battailes*, p. 83 and *Victoria History of Surrey*, vol. 4, p. 259. Another property record for Henry was for Ewell in 1507, referring to tenancy, is found in Calendar of Inquisitions Post-Mortem, VIII, p. 572. Yet another of 1512 involved ancient family land in Charlwood called Colmannesham, which passed to Richard Carew. This can be found in *Victoria History of Surrey*, vol. 4, p. 268; and in Manning and Bray, *History and Antiquities*, vol. 2, p. 192.

24. Mention of these lands is made in Henry's will of 1518.

25. Peter Courtenay's position is described in the *Victoria History for London*, vol. 1, 581–584.

26. Ashley, *British Kings and Queens*, pp. 624–625.

27. That Henry was close to Peter Courtenay seems certain since he was a cousin of Henry's sister-in-law, Agnes Courtenay. That closeness continued. Henry's granddaughter Ursula married into the Hungerfords of Buckland Manor in Wiltshire, the family of Peter Courtenay's mother.

28. Records for Ralph Lepton are found in the following: (a) *Yorkshire Archeological Journal*, vol. 21, p. 488 (b) Fasti Ecclesiae Anglicanae, 1300–1541, vol. 18; (c) Calendar of Patent Rolls, Henry VII, part II, Membrane I and (d) Surrey Archeological Collection, vol. 28, p. 110.

29. J. Huizinga, *Erasmus and the Age of Reformation* (New Jersey: Princeton University Press, 1984), p. 6. Our brief characterization of Erasmus's work will have to do for the present purpose. Huizinga offers a rich portrayal.

30. The claim that Cornelia Saunders Gilles may have been a daughter of Joan and Henry Saunder of Ewell may be a reach, as we have no record specifying her origins. Cornelia either died or was married in 1515, a date that generally coincides with vital dates of their other children, and some loose connections to Henry Saunder's circle of interests can be found. Gilles evidently was from Norfolk and London, and a merchant of Antwerp. He may have been a son of John Gilles, who evidently was a vintner or innkeeper, as in 1486, an associate "fetched wine at Gilles.'" Erasmus lived with Peter Gilles in Antwerp in 1516 and greatly lamented his death in 1532; Erasmus remarked that Gilles was "so much younger than me." Further research on Cornelia's life could reveal how closely associated Henry Saunder was to Erasmus.

31. C. Stevenson, "Medicine and Magnificence: British Hospital and Asylum Architecture: 1660–1815" (New Haven: Yale University Press, c2000). Review by J. H. Baron appearing in. *British Medical Journal*, March 24, 2001.

32. The *Medieval England Encyclopedia* provides a succinct picture of these hospitals. It is cited on page 360, "Medieval hospitals differed completely from their modern counterparts; they offered little in the way of professional medical care, concentrating mainly on cleanliness, tranquility and a nourishing diet. Their principal function was to house the deserving poor in short stays."

33. R. Somerville, *The Savoy: Manor: Hospital: Chapel* (Chancellor and Council of the Duchy of Lancaster, 1960), pp. 10–11.

34. Ibid., p. 12.

35. M. Tatchell, "The Accounts of the Hospital of the Savoy for the Year 17 to 18 Henry VIII," *London and Middlesex Archeological Society*, vol. 20 (1961), p. 151.

36. Somerville, *Savoy*, p. 202. This relative was William Cope. Henry's nephew William Saunder of Banbury married Joan Spencer, and she married William Cope after William Saunder died in 1493.

37. Background on the founding of Corpus Christi College is given in T. Fowler, "Corpus Christi" in *Oxford University College Histories* (London: F. E. Robinson, 1898). The contribution of the Manor of Milton to Corpus Christi is described in *Victoria History of Surrey*, vol. 3, p. 423 and see also Walker, *Manor of Battailes*, p. 83. Richard Foxe acquired Milton from the Middleton family, placed it in the hands of Henry Saunder and others, only to have them place the manor in the portfolio of the college. Why Foxe used this indirect method for endowing the college is not clear; perhaps the action created an impression of a broader base of support for the college, if that was important.

38. Details about the sweating sickness epidemic can be found at http://www.tudorplace.com. Modern authors offer no firm conclusion on the identity or etiology of this disease.

39. Coincidental timing suggests sweating sickness as a cause of Henry's death, and Joan's soon thereafter, though no record states this directly.

40. Walker, *Manor of Battailes*, p. 83.

41. *Encyclopedia Britannica*, s.v. "Richard Foxe."

42. The Will of Henry Saunder is available at the Prerogative Court of Canterbury, Ayloffe 15. We gratefully acknowledge use of the will abstract of Tim Powys-Lybbee, published on the Internet under Powys-Lybbe Ancestry.

43. Walker, *Manor of Battailes*, pp. 76, 83 provides a thorough description of these property distributions.

44. Joan Lepton Saunder's will is also available at the Prerogative Court of Canterbury; Walker, *Manor of Battailes*, p. 86, provides a useful summary of its main points.

45. From http://www.tudorplace.com on Burghley, re the Marquis of Winchester.

46. T. Fowler, "Corpus Christi College." Characterizing Foxe's views, Fowler writes (pp. 9–10), "Whenever he had to correct and punish, he found the clergy, and particularly the monks, so depraved, so licentious and corrupt, that he despaired of any proper reformation till the work was undertaken on a more general scale and with a stronger arm."

47. Our account of William Saunders borrows heavily from the description by Walker, *Manor of Battailes*, pp. 86–93, although we provide additional detail and interpretation at certain points.

48. Although specific records for William's education are lacking, given his father's wealth and strong commitment to education, there is little doubt that he would have entered the university. Likewise, later records show that William was a lawyer, and he undoubtedly followed family tradition in entering the Inner Temple for legal studies.

49. Not all properties came immediately to William; some he gained over time following his father's will regarding successional arrangements.

50. If indeed this signature was by William of Ewell and not William of Aston, who may have returned to Surrey about this time and perhaps rented Pendell property.

51. Henry's five trustees who temporarily controlled Pendell probably received income from the property and so may have been reluctant to release the property to William. There may also have been some concern for William's marriage about this time that could have involved property entitlements, entangling Pendell in larger issues.

52. These are known Ewell properties in the south of Surrey, but there may have been others as well, including land at Newdigate.

53. Walker, *Manor of Battailes*, p. 86, documents the marriage of William to Joan Marston. A different record suggests William married Mabel Carew, but this seems incorrect; *see Visitation of Surrey for 1530, 1572, and 1623.* In this visitation record, Mabel Carew is given as the wife of William Saunder, Esq., of Ewell. She is stated to be a daughter of Sir Nicholas Carew whose other daughter Isabel married Nicholas Saunders. This marriage to Nicholas Saunders is described at a later point in this chapter. But as Nicholas Carew was married in 1514, his eldest child cannot have been born before 1515 and must have married William before his known marriage of 1529, indicating that Mabel Carew cannot have been more than twelve years of age at the time, an improbable age for marriage. Also, William's second wife outlived

him, so Mabel cannot have been a third wife. It seems reasonable to argue that the original visitation record contains an error and that the suggested marriage of Mabel Carew and William Saunders at that time was confused with the actual marriage of Isabel Carew and Nicholas Saunders. Another theory is that Mabel married an earlier William of Ewell or of some other family branch.

54. *Surrey Archeological Collection*, vol. 28, pp. 56–57. By her first marriage, Joan Marston Mynne had five children, the eldest of whom was named John. William accepted the wardship for John Mynne, then age nine, an act that further cemented some long-term relationships between the Saunders and the Mynnes.

55. How William might have gained a foothold in Ashstead property through the Marston marriage is not clear. Henry FitzAlan, Earl of Arundel, at one point had control of both Ashstead and Shalford, home of the Marstons. Later events show that William Saunders had close ties with Arundel. See *Victoria History of Surrey*, vol. 3, pp. 248, 279, 281 and vol. 4, p. 376.

56. John Mynne was about nine years old when his father died in 1528, and his wardship and subsequent marriage rights were acquired by William Saunders of Ewell, John's new stepfather. For this, an annuity of four pounds was paid William from the Manor of Horton in Surrey. See *Surrey Archeological Society*, vol. 28, pp. 56–57. Exactly how John's siblings, William, Nicholas, Francis, and Elizabeth Mynne, were cared for in subsequent years is unclear. The tight relationship between the Saunders and Mynnes extended to the Saunders of Aston (chapter 5) and even to a later generation (chapter 6).

John Mynne acquired the Manor of Horton in Ebbesham and also the Manor of Brettgrave from his mother's possession and married Dorothy Curzon of Croxall in Derby. See *History and Gazetteer of Derby*, p. 333, which provides a pedigree of the Curzons of Croxall. In 1557, Dorothy's stepsister Joyce Curzon was burned at the stake for her religious conviction. A moving tale of Joyce Curson's religious experience, her ordeal, and her final demise is given in *Foxe's Book of Martyrs*, pp. 398–402.

57. The first daughter of Joan Marston and William Saunders, Mary was born about 1536. About 1557, she married Nicholas Lussher, son of Robert Lussher and Elizabeth Leigh and grandson of Nicholas Leigh and Anne Carew, see Manning and Bray, *History and Antiquities*, vol. 2, p. 20. With Nicholas, Mary had four daughters, Elizabeth, Mary, Margaret, and Jane, the last of these born after her father's death, and one son, Nicholas. Mary's father William Saunders purchased the

wardship of Nicholas about 1567 after the elder Nicholas Lussher died. The younger Nicholas was knighted in 1603.

The Lusshers held the Manor of Sherland in Puttenham, Surrey, and other property in Hampshire; see *Victoria History of Hampshire*, vol. 2, p. 510. In later years, the Sir Nicholas Lussher seems to have acquired Hollingrove Manor, Sussex; see *Victoria History of Sussex*, vol. 9, p. 229.

58. The second daughter of Joan Marston and William Saunders was Urithe, born about the year 1538. About 1564, she married John Palgrave (1531–1610), having a daughter Jane who married Robert Lawrence, and a son, Sir Augustine, who married Elizabeth, daughter of Sir John Willoughby of Risley, Derby. John Palgrave was a bencher of the Middle Temple and later appointed to the Suffolk or Norfolk bench, and a justice from 1579 and 1610; see A. H. Smith *County and Court: Government and Politics in Norfolk, 1558–1603* (Oxford: Clarendon Press, 1974). An earlier John Palgrave (c1485–1554) was tutor to Queen Mary and was part of the inner circle of humanists with Erasmus; see J. D. Mackie 1952. *Earlier Tudors: 1485–1558*. Clarendon Press, Oxford.

59. Manning and Bray, *History and Antiquities*, vol. 2, p. 684.

60. Francis Green, *Saunders of Pentre, Tymawr, and Glanrhydw*, Historical Society of West Wales Transactions, 1911–1912, vol. 2 (1911), p. 169.

61. This brief sketch of the dissolution borrows from Ashley, *British Kings and Queens*, p. 633.

62. F. Gasquet, *Henry VIII and the English Monasteries*, 2 vols. (1988).

63. This description is paraphrased from "Suppression of English Monasteries under Henry VIII," http://www.newadvent.org./

64. See *Surrey Archeological Collection*, vol. 4, pp. 136–141, 180–183, for the financial accounts given by William and his signatures on each.

65. Walker, *Manor of Battailes*, p. 87; see also *Victoria History of Surrey*, vol. 2, pp. 107–112.

66. Ibid., p. 87.

67. *Surrey Archeological Collection*, vol. 8, pp. 302–303.

68. Arundel served in Calais in 1543. The claim that William was treasurer there is found in Burke's Peerage and Baronage in a pedigree for the Keyes family, but no date for this assignment is given.

69. Joan Gittons' will is found in Prerogative Court of Canterbury, 27 Darcy, and notes on her will are given in Walker, *Manor of Battailes*, p. 91. In this document, she refers to "Mother Munson," who may be her natural mother.

70. Frances was born about 1545 and probably was a twin of her brother Francis. Shortly after 1560, she married Henry Spelman, esquire of Congham, Norfolk, whose first wife was Anne Knyvet, daughter of Sir Thomas Knyvet of Buckenham Castle and his wife, Muriel, Viscountess

Lisle. Issue of Frances and Henry Spelman were Sir Henry Spelman, a noted antiquarian who is buried in Westminster Abbey, and Erasmus Spelman, whose son Henry was a scout and linguist in early Virginia, who is described more fully in chapter 6. Frances's husband Henry's grandfather, Walter Ford, once held the post of remembrancer of the exchequer, the same position held later by Sir Thomas Saunders of Charlwood.

Records sometimes indicate that Frances had also married Bernard Jenens (Jennings) of Streteham (Streatham), Surrey; but as his will was written in 1550, this marriage of 1547 seems impossible unless we have greatly missed the mark on Frances's birth date. We think it more likely that this Jenens marriage to Frances, a daughter of William Saunders, refers to the Saunders family of Aston; see *Surrey Archeological Collection*, vol. 52, p. 40.

71. Francis is the youngest surviving son of William and his only son by Joan Gittons. Born probably as a twin in 1545, Francis either never married or had a family in which no other member survived. In his will of 1613, he was called a gentleman of Ewell in Surrey but held property in Congham, Norfolk, and seems to have resided there. In his extensive will of 1613, calling himself a "miserable and sinful caytiffe," he made bequests to a large number of family members, naming a son of his brother Erasmus his executor and principal heir. Included in his will was mention of the young Henry Spelman in Virginia.

72. Catherine was born about 1547 and died in 1608. She married three times, first about age twenty-one to Edmond Carvel (Kervyle, Kyrvill), of Sandringham, Norfolk. Edmond died after only two years of marriage but had one daughter Anne, who about 1570 married Sir Clement Spelman of Narborough, Norfolk, a justice. Second, Catherine married John Spelman of Narborough, stepson of Joan Gittons before she married William Saunders. By an earlier marriage this John Spelman fathered Clement Spelman of Narborough who married Catherine's daughter Anne. John Spelman was a Norfolk justice in 1579–1580. Third, Catherine married at age thirty-five, about 1582, to Sir Miles Corbett of Sprowston, Norfolk. He too was a justice of Norfolk from 1590 to 1606. Miles was knighted for service at the battle of Cadiz. Their son Thomas Corbett, a Norfolk justice from 1607 to 1615, married Ann Barret of Belhouse in Alveley, Essex, a marriage paralleling that of Catherine's older brother Erasmus, who married Jenet Barrett of Pembrokeshire, Wales.

73. Elizabeth was the last surviving child of William and Joan Gittons Saunders, born about 1549. She married three times, first about 1570 to Roger Castell of Ravenham, Norfolk. Roger's mother was

Ann Townsend, sister of Sir Roger Townsend, knight of the body to Henry VIII and commissioner for the survey of monasteries in 1537, work that anticipated their dissolution shortly after. Elizabeth Saunders's husband died in 1581, and she second married William Forth (Ford),esquire of Hadleigh in Suffolk. He died before 1613, and Elizabeth third married Thomas Garneis of Horningtoft, Norfolk, who died in 1562. Thomas probably was the son of Nicholas Garneis and his wife Margaret Tyrrell who held Mendelham and Bayland Hall in Horningtoft.

74. A. Simpson, *Wealth of the Gentry: 1540–1660* (Chicago: University of Chicago Press, 1960), pp. 36–37.

75. William had a twenty-one-year lease for this property from as early as 1536; see Manning and Bray, *History and Antiquities,* vol. 2, p. 684.

76. Merton Priory Records, p. 3.

77. Walker, *Manor of Battailes,* p. 89.

78. Ibid., p. 89. Our description of these events is abridged from Walker's treatment.

79. Ibid., p. 90.

80. Ibid., p. 86.

81. Ibid., p. 87.

82. See K. Morgan, *The Oxford Illustrated History of Britain* (Oxford: Oxford University Press, 1984), pp. 261–263. Mary executed about 274 heretics in all, but many would have been executed under her father as well, their beliefs falling outside the Church of England as well as Roman Catholicism. Mary deserved her dubious reputation, but she was particularly strongly vilified by Protestant writers after her death.

83. That William Saunders of Ewell was appointed high sheriff of Surrey is not certain; some suggest this was William Saunders of Aston.

84. *Surrey History Center Collection,* Loseley Papers, LM/COR/3/13, p. 11.

85. Walker, *Manor of Battailes,* pp. 87–88.

86. Historian John Guy remarks that Elizabeth allowed England to become ungovernable; see K. Morgan, *Oxford Illustrated History,* p. 264.

87. *Surrey Archeological Collection,* vol. 8, p. 302.

88. Our brief background on William's surveyor position is interpreted from information in Morgan, *Oxford Illustrated History,* pp. 272–273.

89. *Surrey History Center Collection,* Loseley Papers, LM/COR/3/58, p. 19.

90. Elizabeth's Pardon Rolls are given in LocalHistorian.doc.

91. William's will is found in Prerogative Court of Canterbury, 42 Holney, dated October 2, 1570, and proved November 10, 1571. Extensive notes on its provisions are found in Walker, *Manor of Battailes,* pp. 90–91.

92. Prerogative Court of Canterbury, 27 Darcy.

93. See Sir Anthony Cooke of Gidea Hall at http://www.tudorplace.com.

94. Simpson, *Wealth of the Gentry*, p. 40.

95. *Surrey History Center Collection*, Loseley Papers, LM/COR/3/13, p. 11.

96. Sources for Nicholas's marriage to Isabel Carew and their family are London marriage records, *Surrey Archeological Society*, and *Visitations of Surrey for 1530, 1572, and 1623*.

97. *Victoria History of Warwickshire*, vol. 4, p. 121.

98. Margaret Bostock Saunders held Horeston Grange following the death of Fisher and sold this to Edward Blunt in 1599. In Hampshire, the Manor of Stoke Charity was leased by Nicholas Saunders, though whether this was Nicholas of Ewell is unknown. And in Somerset, we learn that a prosperous merchant named Nicholas Saunders held South Petherton Manor from 1575, though again the specific identity of this Nicholas is not given.

99. "Ships Masters, Captains and Officers of the England Fleet in the Armada" found at http://geocities.com/heartland/ridge/2216/text/ARMADA.TXT./.

100. *Victoria History of Surrey*, vol. 4, p. 231.

101. Walker, *Manor of Battailes*, p. 96.

102. A. Acheson, *Shakespeare's Sonnet Story: 1592–1598* (1988) at http://members.fortunecity.com.

103. A. Fraser, *Weaker Vessel* (New York: Alfred A. Knopf, 1994), pp. 210–214; see also *Visitation of Kent* 1619. Sir Roger Twysden, antiquary and member of Parliament for Kent, played a significant role in preparing the Petition of Kent in support of the monarchy during the period leading to the Civil War. He was arrested by Parliament and remained imprisoned for four years, his estates having been sequestered. During this difficult period, Isabel Saunders Twysden showed great strength and courage, traveling to London numerous times while pregnant, seeking her legal one-fifth share of the estates to maintain her home for her six children and seeking help for her husband. Isabel kept a diary of these years, which is extant.

104. Walker, *Manor of Battailes*, p. 98.

105. Ibid., pp. 98–100. Walker provides a detailed account of this aqueduct scheme and other details of Sir Nicholas's life; our account here rests on these descriptions.

Notes for Sir Thomas of Charlwood:

1*   This description of Sir Thomas rests heavily on materials from R. Sewill and E. Lane, *Free Men of Charlwood* (Crawley, Sussex: Reprographic Centre, 1979), pp. 51–73.

2* Katherine Walsingham (1559–1585), niece of Alys Walsingham, wife of Sir Thomas Saunders of Charlwood, married into the Gresley family of Drakelow, Derbyshire. This is the same Gresley family that supported the movement of Thomas Saunders, formerly of Charlwood, to Derbyshire around 1524.

3* See Wikipedia.com under "Remembrancer of the Exchequer" for an expanded list of responsibilities for this position.

4* For persons in high government positions and with significant wealth, knighthood was a virtual requisite. It conveyed weight and produced respect. Knighthood in this situation differed from that conferred for valor on the battlefield in that battlefield honors were awarded after the fact, while knighthood from the public service was awarded in anticipation of, and as a means to, future accomplishment. Thus, for Sir Thomas Saunders, knighthood followed quickly, in 1550, upon his formal appointment as remembrancer in 1549.

5* Sewill and Lane, *Free Men*, p. 65.

CHAPTER SEVEN

Wales

After centuries of struggle, Wales was formally annexed by England in Henry VIII's Act of Union in 1536 [1]. This action created some asymmetric colonial-type relations between the two formerly separate countries, setting in motion a set of new administrative arrangements in Wales whereby England's governance could be firmly implanted. Whether Wales benefitted from the Act of Union and subsequent administration is a matter of differing opinion, but change in Wales came rapidly after Henry VIII's rule. Shift in agriculture toward sheep raising and revised rules of land tenure changed the Welsh landscape. English law and politics washed over the countryside. The work of creating and managing these changes fell to the English government, which deployed some especially favored sons to do its work. This is how Erasmus Saunders, son of William Saunders of Ewell, came to live in Wales.

Named after the famed Dutch scholar and reformer Erasmus Desiderius, this particular son of William Saunders lived less by the light of that famed personage than his father might have wished but rather chose on occasion to inhabit shadows where ill-bred opportunities could be found. Erasmus was both opportunist and recalcitrant, an odd blend of dispositions. His talent for scheming found a particularly inviting setting in which to survive, an unrefined Welsh hinterland newly exposed to untested English administration. His knowledge of law enabled him to exploit the edges of legality for personal gain, and he seems never to have paid for his waywardness. Yet despite his deftness in politics and law, Erasmus was swallowed up for perhaps his least transgression. He was a determined subterranean Catholic in a world intolerant of his beliefs, and for this Erasmus paid dearly.

Early Years

Erasmus Saunders was born about the year 1534 of William Saunders of Ewell and his wife, Joan Marston Mynne, probably their third child and second son. That this couple chose the name Erasmus reminds us how powerful and extended was the Dutch scholar's influence on England's minor gentry. William's father Henry of Ewell was particularly enamored of Erasmian ideals, no doubt imparting these to his son. The scholar's final visit to England ended only twenty years before Erasmus Saunders was born, and William was prepared to forsake traditional family naming patterns to express his esteem for the scholar's lofty ideals that swayed English thought in his time.

Erasmus was five years old when his mother died and about ten when his father remarried to Joan Spelman Gittons. His stepmother seems to have strongly influenced Erasmus as well as her own children in establishing that Norfolk as much as Ewell constituted a family home. Erasmus came to know Norfolk well.

Nothing more is known about Erasmus from these early years, but he entered Oxford University at age fourteen in 1548 and seems to have completed his studies about the time that Catholic Queen Mary assumed the English throne in 1553. This was a major event in Erasmus's life not only because his family was Roman Catholic, but also because his father at this time joined the royal household as Queen Mary's personal treasurer. In all likelihood, Erasmus spent time in royal circles after leaving Oxford, perhaps in minor tasks assigned by his father. As Erasmus was now of adult age, he would have come to know Henry FitzAlan, Earl of Arundel, and other luminaries from Surrey in his father's close acquaintance. It was fashionable in Erasmus's time for young gentlemen to tour the Continent after their studies were complete, and it may be that Erasmus did see parts of Europe at this time, an idea his wealthy father surely would have encouraged.

Mary's reign came to an abrupt end in 1558, and with her demise came a permanent end to Catholic rule in England, and just as importantly, individual Catholics themselves fell from national grace. In the year after Mary's death, Erasmus enrolled in the Inner Temple for legal studies, following his father's example [2]. Practicing law had become a family tradition by this time, but it may have been equally important for Erasmus to seek the cover of studies to reduce his Catholic profile in London's suddenly Protestant outlook. He did complete this legal preparation about 1562 when he was twenty-eight years old and began the life of a gentleman in London.

London

Erasmus lived in London for about five years after leaving the Inner Temple and was described as "of London, gentleman" and "learned in the Law." His family and connections from the royal court would have assured him some success in law practice and enabled him to marry. That he did marry at this time seems beyond doubt, though no record of his marriage in London or Surrey seems to have survived [3]. A cluster of family interrelationships in Norfolk suggests a possible marriage for Erasmus into the Townsend family. Though a guess, a Townsend marriage would have firmly cemented Erasmus's ties to Norfolk and satisfied the need for a Catholic marriage [4]. Following usual practice, his father probably arranged for Erasmus to receive on marriage some London property, perhaps at Southwark [5].

What is certain about Erasmus's marriage is that he had a son named Richard, born about 1565, and that his wife died shortly after. Erasmus evidently sent the infant to live with his stepmother or a married sibling, and the young Richard seems to have resided permanently in Norfolk after that. In no instance do we find this son Richard in the company of his father over all their years. No details of Richard's adult life are known, although he surfaces much later as executor of the 1613 will of his uncle Francis Saunders, Erasmus's younger stepbrother of Norfolk. From Francis, who had no family of his own and considered himself a "miserable and sinful caytiffe," Richard inherited Francis's properties in Congham, Norfolk, Cliff in Kent, and at Ewell in Surrey [6].

Following the death of his wife, Erasmus continued his London legal activity, but before long, he received favorable attention from some political superiors. By 1567, Erasmus was awarded a coveted post of justice of the peace for the Carmarthen (Wales) Circuit, which included Pembrokeshire. These positions had been made locally powerful in the reign of Edward VII and carried forward undiminished in ensuing years. As justice of the peace, Erasmus would hold the most important administrative post in the county, administering the burgeoning laws of the Elizabethan period, those designed to facilitate the shift of feudal justice in Wales into the English jurisprudential mold [7]. So great was this infusion that justices of the peace were issued handbooks that encapsulated new law to guide their judgments.

Justice of the peace appointments could not be acquired without significant influence from friendly superiors, and for that, Erasmus lacked nothing. His father had connections from his days in the royal household and probably managed to generate support both from William Cecil, Lord Burghley, the second most powerful figure in England after Queen Elizabeth, and also Henry FitzAlan, called Arundel, a close friend and ally, who also sat on the Carmarthen Circuit. So it was that Erasmus Saunders in 1567 received the blessings of his superiors, closed the doors on his London engagements, and struck out for new territory, becoming in the process the first in his family line to reside beyond England's historical boundaries.

Wales

About 1568, Erasmus Saunders traveled to Wales to take up work and residence there. He probably took the so-called high road overland through Gloucestershire and across the Severn, rather than traveling by sea. He left his brother and sisters' homes in Norfolk for Pembrokeshire and passed through Brecknock in Wales along the way, perhaps with a brief sojourn at that place [8]. As a newly appointed justice of the peace, he may have stopped at Shrewsbury, the de facto political capital of Wales and seat of the Council of the Marches. He also probably visited Haverfordwest once arriving in Wales, as that is where the Great Sessions worked as the center of English legal authority in Pembrokeshire. Erasmus eventually settled in Tenby, a small port city that had passed its heyday as the chief port of Pembrokeshire. It nonetheless had an accessible harbor, and fishing and maritime trade continued to support the local economy at the time Erasmus arrived in Wales. Its waters "swarmed with privateers and pirates" [9].

1 inch = about 7 miles

Southern Pembrokeshire and southwestern Carmarthenshire, Wales, including places of residence for Erasmus and Philip Saunders' families.

Yet another early stop for Erasmus may have been to visit a Saunders cousin. Records suggest that the Saunders "originally from Surrey" came to Pembrokeshire as early as 1527, about forty years before Erasmus arrived there [10]. Exactly who this earlier migrant might have been is unknown, but one expects he was either from Ewell or Charlwood [11]. If that is correct, then the migrant likely was a nephew or son of Henry Saundre of Ewell or of that same generation from Charlwood, born perhaps about 1500, arriving in Wales in his late twenties.

The exact identity of this original migrant need not detain us here because it was a daughter (or possibly granddaughter) of this person who undoubtedly had some influence on Erasmus's future [12]. About the time of Erasmus's arrival in Wales, there was born a child named Saunders Barrett, the offspring of a father named Barrett and a mother surnamed Saunders. We surmise this mother sprang from the family of the original Saunders migrant of 1527 to Pembrokeshire and thus was a cousin to Erasmus. Erasmus knew this couple well [13] and, through them, evidently gained broader knowledge of the several Barrett branches of Pembrokeshire and Carmarthenshire and their extensive land holdings [14]. It may have been from them that Erasmus first learned of Jenet Barrett, his future wife.

Jenet Barrett was quite a catch. She was born about 1550, daughter of William Barrett, shipowner and merchant, and Ann his wife, daughter of Thomas Lougher of Tenby. Jenet was said to have been of "very tender years" when her father died in 1553 and was to be sole heiress of her father's large estate when she came of age or married [15].

Prosperity

Erasmus was getting on in years for a now-unmarried man, having traveled to Wales in his thirty-fourth year. The prospect of an available young heiress confronted him at an opportune moment, about a year or so after his arrival. Erasmus we believe acted quickly and probably unscrupulously. We learn from the records that a certain Peter Voyle (Veale) abducted Jenet from the custody of her uncle, James Barrett, and then sold her lucrative wardship to Erasmus Saunders [16]. But this account seems contrived. As Voyle cannot have held a legal wardship for an abductee, Erasmus cannot have purchased it from him. Nor would Erasmus have purchased this from her custodial uncle since we know her uncle later sued Erasmus to recover Jenet and her intended inheritance. Neither can one imagine Voyle abducting a young heiress and then, as if without plan, casting about for a taker. The record itself, probably gleaned from friendly court records, makes us believe that Voyle was a kidnapping villain and Erasmus Saunders a hero in rescuing the distressed maiden through payment that amounted to ransom. But the whole business makes greater sense if Erasmus himself arranged the plan and paid Voyle for his part. Managing subsequent legal wrangles and portraying facts other than they were would have been the easier part. Erasmus as justice of the peace held the reins of local justice and counted among his allies another of the Voyle family, who at the time was mayor of Haverfordwest and yet a third Voyle who had married another Barrett. In any case, in early 1570, Erasmus and Jenet were married [17]. Jenet's uncle James Barrett sued unsuccessfully to regain her custody or property, but Erasmus's countersuit for Jenet's land held in trust by Barrett succeeded completely [18].

As Jenet Barrett's husband in 1570, Erasmus Saunders, after about two years in Wales, became one of the wealthiest men in Pembrokeshire. His new land holdings from Jenet's inheritance were substantial, including three large properties in Tenby: a messuage and lands called the Great House, another messuage and lands in Market Street, and a house and gardens in Frog Street. Near Tenby, he acquired Barrett lands at Jordanston in St. Florence. Just to the north of Pembrokeshire lay Carmarthenshire, and here, in and around Eglwyscymmin and Pendine, Erasmus acquired extensive holdings—manor houses, tenements, and fields—separately numbering more than twenty properties in all. In time, some of these properties became residences for Jenet and Erasmus's children [19].

THE FAMILIES OF ERASMUS AND PHILIP SAUNDERS OF WALES

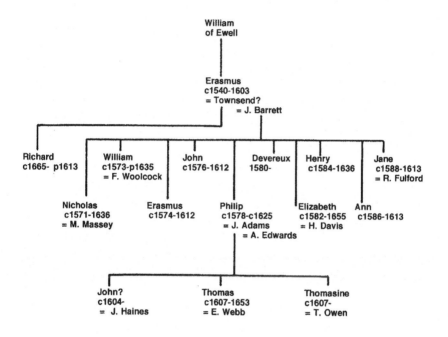

Source: Authors.

Jenet and Erasmus began a large family at once, eventually having seven sons and three daughters. Although the precise sequence of all these births is not known, the first, Nicholas, was born in 1571, and others followed in regular succession. Their span of childbearing covered about sixteen years in all. Jenet bore children at her ages twenty-one to thirty-seven, and Erasmus reached the age of fifty-three by the time the last child appeared. These children were Nicholas [20], William [21], Erasmus [22], John [23], Devereux [24], Elizabeth [25], Henry [26], Ann [27], and Jane [28], and one other son Philip, whose life we review in detail at a later point in this chapter.

Nicholas was the only child born outside Wales, being born at Ewell as Jenet and Erasmus visited during Erasmus's father William's final days. William died in 1571, naming Erasmus in his last will and testament written the year before. Erasmus received "a cross of gold with a pearl in the end thereof. And my best doublet of purple satin. And one hundred Pounds to be paid to him by my Executor [29]." William also gave to "Johennet" (Jenet) five old angels (coins). Erasmus received one-half interest in Harshing Marsh in Clif, Kent, and was second in line to receive the Manor of Cardens, the Manor of Chessington, and the Parrock Iron Mill. None of these latter properties, however, ever devolved to Erasmus, though with his extensive Barrett holdings in Wales, he scarcely needed them.

For Erasmus, the years immediately following his marriage were golden times. Even as his new family grew, he too grew steadily in wealth and influence. He retained his post as justice of the peace for the Carmarthen Circuit, being named on published lists for 1567, 1571, 1573, 1575, and 1577. In 1575, Erasmus was mentioned as among the "ablest gentlemen of the shire" for serving as justice of the peace. His appointment, which was made before this date, was for Castlemartin in southwest Pembrokeshire. To facilitate his work in Castlemartin, Erasmus acquired some property at Monkton.

Shortly after his marriage, in June of 1570, Erasmus was named on a list of Pembrokeshire property owners to furnish light horsemen "to be ready by August 8 and from then to be ready for service at commandment." This list applied to those who received an income of twenty pounds or more from lands [30]. Two years later, he was appointed bailiff of Tenby without relinquishing his justice position. In 1574, "Erasmus Saunders of Tenby" was appointed a commissioner to execute new regulations regarding tanning houses [31]. Sometime before 1577, he received appointment as mayor of Tenby, replacing James Barrett, Jenet's uncle. Having already lost so much to Erasmus, this mayoral succession must have been particularly galling to the unlucky Barrett [32].

About 1577, Erasmus acquired an ancient property once in possession of the Carews and is said to have lived there while holding the Tenby mayoralty. This was Bonville Manor (also called Bonville Castle and Bonville Court) in Saundersfoot, a small village a few miles north of Tenby in Pembrokeshire. A local historian suggests that Saundersfoot may have acquired its name from the family of Erasmus Saunders, though further particulars on this point are not offered [33]. Bonville Court is one of the few properties in Erasmus's portfolio not previously in Barrett family possession.

Erasmus probably commanded sufficient resources to acquire Bonville Court through his legitimate income, that is, rents from properties and compensation for his official appointments. But this may not have been entirely the case. Within Erasmus's actions in 1577 and after, one finds darker involvements. Erasmus was sued for trespass by Griffith White, Esq., former mayor of Tenby, at the Great Sessions held at Haverfordwest [34]. Although the alleged facts and trial outcome have not been found, Erasmus probably overstepped the bounds of his authority in some matter well-known to the former mayor. Mention of this suit means little except that it was followed by another the same year. In this, Erasmus was accused of smuggling "forbidden and unaccustomed wares" to Portugal [35], perhaps in league with a familiar figure, John Voyle of Haverfordwest, that town's mayor. There was little victims or local officials could do about such "unaccustomed" (unrecorded, untaxed) concealment except report smuggling to the privy council, but most commonly no actions were taken against offenders, and those willing to identify smugglers often were subjected to threats of personal violence [36].

We learn further that Erasmus was closely allied to Richard Vaughan, a sub-vice admiral for Pembrokeshire. This pair together were active enemies of Sir John Perrot, whose appointed task as commissioner of piracy was to root out piracy in the region [37], though by most accounts Perrot regularly colluded with pirates himself [38]. Erasmus's personal enmity for Perrot is easy to understand. Perrot was a member of the Commission for the Marches, a militant Protestant, a ruthless subduer of Catholic Munster in Ireland, and recently an acquirer of old family property at Carew. He was thought an illegitimate son of Henry VIII, and he fared well under Queen Elizabeth's hand, receiving his knighthood from her. Perrot had once captured and jailed at Carew an alleged French smuggler, but the prisoner escaped to Erasmus Saunders' house, who then arranged for his transport to London to testify against Perrot in a pending proceeding [39].

A Welsh historian provides a vivid account of one encounter with Perrot involving Erasmus Saunders: "Saunders, with Admiral Vaughan, headed a faction against Sir John Perrot of Laugharne. Sir John Perrot, who was a Pembrokeshire man, as well as the Lord of the Manor of Laugharne, was accused on many occasions—at least once by the Privy Council itself—of encouraging and harbouring pirates. In March 1578, two ships were wrecked close by Pendine. The ships were carrying valuable cargo and the spot on which they foundered was sufficiently close to Pendine to warrant Sir John considering the wrecks to be under his jurisdiction. Saunders, with his friend Vaughan, determined to intervene, however, on the owners behalf—and their own! Saunders rounded up some sixty men from Tenby and Saundersfoot, and proceeded to the scene of the double disaster in a fleet of small boats. They were too late, however, for Perrot's men were already in the area. Vice-Admiral Vaughan managed to secure eight bags of spices and two pieces of brass ordnance, but, in his absence in an effort to get further help, Sir John Perrot's men had appropriated the entire spoils" [40]. In a fruitless inquiry concerning the Pendine affair, Erasmus remarked about his friend Richard Vaughan, "the Vice Admiral carried thence nothing but shame and repulse" [41].

In 1577, an English privateer named Luke Ward, carrying "sufficient warrant from the Queen's Council," steered a French prize, the *Greyhound*, into Milford Haven, Pembrokeshire, with the intention of gaining four hundred pounds from sale of the ship and cargo of fish [42]. Competing plots ensued between Richard Vaughan and Sir John Perrot to gain the ship and constrain Captain Ward while the cargo was secreted away, Sir John eventually prevailing. The aggrieved Richard Vaughan with Erasmus Saunders sought to involve the French ambassador before the English government in Ward's *Greyhound* case to expose Perrot's illicit activity, but Vaughan overplayed his hand. Vaughan was sufficiently aroused to declare that "Sir John better deserved hanging than any thief" and that he "deserved hanging upon some one or two or three or four points." Their stratagem failed, and Perrot profited nicely from the *Greyhound* affair. An odd twist to this misadventure is that Erasmus Saunders' niece, Jane, daughter of his brother Nicholas of Ewell, married Captain Luke Ward some twelve years later [43].

Years of Struggle

Erasmus's involvements on both sides of the law in Wales came to an abrupt halt in 1578, when he and his brother Nicholas of Ewell, along with other "papists in divers places in the realm," were placed in London's Fleet Prison [44]. Erasmus was immediately stripped of his justice of the peace appointment but was referred to as "nobilis" (gentleman) at the time of his imprisonment [45]. Erasmus's brother Nicholas remained in Fleet Prison only two months in 1578, perhaps recanting his Catholic belief, but Erasmus remained steadfast and stayed in the Fleet for some time [46].

Erasmus's strong adherence to Catholicism in one sense was a simple extension of longstanding family tradition, but there was now greater urgency in the matter. Erasmus's close relatives were intimately involved in promoting Catholic causes, especially his cousin, Dr. Nicholas Saunders of Aston, a prominent voice in English Catholic resistance on the Continent. Elizabeth's most trusted advisor, William Cecil, Lord Burghley, a staunch Protestant, knew the Saunders well, and Dr. Nicholas Saunders' growing threat may well have pushed Burghley to act against the Saunders of Ewell at this time [47].

THE SAUNDERS OF ASTON

Erasmus Saunders' enthusiasms for Roman Catholicism were by no means isolated in family history; another branch of the family found itself at the leading edge of resistance to English Protestantism in Erasmus's time. These were the Saunders of Aston. The Aston Saunders and Erasmus's own family were particularly close, linked by marriages to a family named Mynne [1*].

The story of the Aston Saunders is a testimony of family faith, of piety and devotion, of firm resolve to maintain religious belief in the face of state persecution. Yet one also finds in this family a strain of zealotry, a certain fanaticism that risked lives and fortunes, an unwillingness to embrace religious differences in soft tones. Other branches of the Saunders at Charlwood and Ewell managed a religious balance in uncertain times and flourished as a result. Nonetheless, one member of the Aston Saunders through his fundamental commitment to Catholicism has claimed a place in English history above all others in the family, the much celebrated and equally reviled Dr. Nicholas Saunders [2*].

The Aston branch of the Saunders emerged at the start of the sixteenth century. William Saunder, son of Agnes Courtenay and Richard Saunder of Charlwood, came to Aston in Oxfordshire about the year 1500, evidently taking up former Courtenay property. William had a son William, probably born at Aston and raised there. This son is known to genealogists as William Saunders of Aston. Coming of age about 1520, this younger William returned to Charlwood, perhaps taking up rental property at the nearby Manor of Pendell, then in possession of the Saunders of Ewell.

About 1525 William of Aston married Elizabeth, she of a Norfolk family named Mynne. Together Elizabeth and William had twelve children, among whom were two especially notable daughters, Margaret and Elizabeth, the latter a decade younger than the former, and also a son Nicholas, who was born at Charlwood in 1527 [3*]. Elizabeth Mynne and William Saunders evidently maintained property both in Surrey and in Oxfordshire as late as 1544, when William, called a gentleman of Surrey, was called upon to furnish two soldiers for the war in France. Yet he is also said to have held property at Ewelme in Oxfordshire [4*]. One record reveals that William was appointed high sheriff of Surrey in 1556, a position formerly held by William's cousin, Sir Thomas Saunders of Charlwood, though whether this record refers to William of Aston or William Saunder of Ewell is uncertain [5*]. But the larger story of the Aston Saunders begins with the children, whose lives intersected with decisive religious events in England, especially those which impacted Syon Abbey.

Both Margaret and Elizabeth Saunders were nuns at Syon Abbey, though because of their age differences, they experienced somewhat different histories in that fated institution. Syon Abbey had been dissolved under Henry VIII in 1539 as part of his English religious reformation, and at that time residents of the Catholic abbey scattered widely to escape persecution. About eight nuns, including Elizabeth Yate, fled to the Yate estate at Buckland in Berkshire [6*]. Others of Syon exiled themselves to a sister convent at Dendermonde in Belgium. There they remained for eighteen years, waiting out the long reign of Henry VIII, praying to return to a Catholic England after that. Among them was Margaret Saunders Pitts, wife of Henry Pitts of Alton, Hampshire, whom she had married about 1550 [7*]. At this time, Margaret served as prioress under Catherine Palmer, long the Abbess of Syon [8*].

Opportunity finally came with the coronation of the Catholic Queen Mary in 1553, but the Syon community was unable to return to England until 1557. Syon Abbey finally was restored at its original location, owing mainly to an endowment provided by a sympathetic Sir Francis Englefield [9*]. Mary's Catholic reign, however, lasted only another year and England abruptly returned to Protestantism as Elizabeth assumed the throne. Syon Abbey once again hurriedly disbanded, its residents fleeing back to Belgium in 1558.

Joining Margaret in Dendermonde after Syon's second dispersal was her younger sister Elizabeth and their widowed mother Elizabeth Mynne Saunders. The younger sister Elizabeth had married into the same Pitts family, to John Pitts of Oxford, and by him had a son in 1560, perhaps born in exile. He came to be called John Pittsaeus, a Catholic priest of considerable fame in his own right [10*].

Nicholas Saunders, the brother of these Syon nuns from Aston, earlier had studied at Winchester and New College, Oxford. He completed his Oxford studies in 1551 and assumed a fellowship there in ecclesiastical law, eventually being named a Professor of Divinity. But with Elizabeth's accession to the throne, events in England overtook him. He joined Sir Francis Englefield about 1558 in fleeing to Louvain in Belgium, a leading center of English Catholic exiles [11*]. Some say Nicholas never returned to England after that, often acknowledging his debt for Englefield's unfailing support in his exile [12*]. He soon traveled to Rome, earning a Doctor of Divinity degree and Jesuit ordination there which credentialed him for several important church assignments. Nicholas attended the landmark Council of Trent, a papal convocation designed to counter Protestant revolts in western Europe and England.

The Council reaffirmed the authority of the Pope and Church tradition in all Biblical matters, rejected the principles and doctrines of Protestantism, and undertook to reform certain aspects of church administration and discipline [13*]. Nicholas then joined Cardinal Hosius in a papal legation to Prussia, Poland, and Lithuania, shoring up Catholic commitments in these places against the rising tide of Protestantism to their west.

By 1567, Nicholas returned to Louvain, meeting his mother and sisters there, and took the Regius Professorship of Theology at the University of Louvain. While there, Nicholas wrote numerous tracts on Catholic belief and an important history of the period entitled "De Visibili Monarchia Ecclesiae," a work characterized by one author as "grave, solid, and learned, without conceit or affectation, showing the simplicity and directness of (Nicholas's) nature" [14*]. Perhaps his most famous work, published posthumously, was "De Schismate Anglicano," a brief history of the Anglican schism, in which Nicholas among other points claimed that Elizabeth, born of Henry VIII and heir to his throne, was illegitimate because Henry's numerous marriages and divorces lacked Church sanction. As a consequence of his rising influence within the exiled Catholic community, Pope Pius IV granted to Nicholas "'bishoply power in the court of conscience' to receive back those who had lapsed into heresy." By this time, Nicholas came to be regarded as the "chief English Catholic leader" [15*].

In 1572 Nicholas returned to Rome to advise the Pope on English matters [16*]. The following year he traveled to Madrid, there to remain for six years, working with Spanish authorities to provide support for Catholic exiles. During this period, his sister Margaret died in France. In 1579, King Philip of Spain, with Pope Gregory's support, outfitted a ship with arms to support a Catholic uprising against Anglican rule in Ireland, and Nicholas accompanied this expedition. The action itself, a prelude to the great Spanish Armada attack on England in 1588, failed to achieve its goal. English agents in Ireland pursued Nicholas for two years, and he eventually died there a hunted man about 1581. It was perhaps from this episode, if not from all his years of passionate Catholicism, that Nicholas has come to be remembered in English history as the "Notorious Traitor."

What Nicholas may not have known is that, before his death, his younger sister Elizabeth surreptitiously returned to England, and became an object of controversy in Hampshire. Genealogist Francis Green described the event, "Elizabeth, sister of Doctor Nicholas Saunders, and the wife of Henry Pitts (sic), was arrested on the 1st of December 1580. She was found with certain 'lewd and forbidden books,' thought to have been supplied by Sir Francis Englefield. The Bishop of Winchester and others were directed to examine Elizabeth Saunders, a professed nun and Richard Hoord, a server abroad of seditious Challenge" [17*]. "She refused to say where she had been harboured since she came to England, and the Bishop was ordered to retain her in the House of Correction and examine her straightly as to the place of her residence when in London" [18*]. Elizabeth remained in confinement for at least five years. In December 1585, the bishop wrote to Sir Francis Walsingham [19*] begging that no favor might be shown to Mrs. Pitts of Alton, who at his instigation had been sent up to London and committed by the Council to the Clink. He wrote that she was a very obstinate person and sister of Nicholas Saunders, the traitor. But Walsingham considered that her return to Winchester would do more harm than ten sermons would do good, and as regards her husband who had conformed, he laid down the ruling that no man whose wife is a recusant could possibly be himself sound" [20*]. During her confinement, Elizabeth wrote letters to Sir Francis Englefield in France, describing the troubles for Catholics in England [21*].

At some point after 1585, Elizabeth regained her freedom and rejoined the exiled Syon community. By that time, the convent had lost all hope of returning to England, and sought out a new home. Syon moved from Belgium to France, probably at Rouen, then to Spain, and finally by 1594 to Portugal. Englefield remained near Syon, dying in Valladolid, Spain in 1605. Elizabeth died within her Syon community in Lisbon in 1607 [22*].

The legal device for Catholic repression in England was the crime of recusancy, the failure to attend the new English Protestant church [48]. Recusants included Quakers and those of other fledging religions but mainly Roman Catholics. Elizabeth's advisor, Lord Burghley, offered anti-Catholic counsel to the queen in clear terms; he argued convincingly that recusancy was treasonous. Catholics thus faced a dire choice of allegiance to church or sovereign. Burghley himself was both the voice and arm of repression. The decision to stifle Catholicism was reluctantly adopted by Queen Elizabeth initially, but the movement to persecute recusants gained pace during the 1580s and accelerated after that.

By 1580, Erasmus won his release from prison and took up residence at East Jordanston in St. Florence Parish, just south of Tenby in Pembrokeshire. But his cousin, the Catholic nun Elizabeth Pitts, sister of Dr. Nicholas, had recently returned to England from Louvain and Rouen on the Continent along with other Jesuit missionaries and was immediately placed under arrest, an internment lasting five years. Within a year of Elizabeth's arrest, his cousin Dr. Nicholas Saunders died a hunted man in Ireland, where he had joined a Spanish effort to foment a Catholic uprising against English rule. At this time, Erasmus's wife Jenet was convicted of recusancy and was assessed a punishing fine for not attending Anglican services. The amount for this offense previously was twelve shillings, but through an Act of 1581, this increased to twenty pounds per month.

Despite frequent punishments of himself and his family, Erasmus remained defiant. About 1581, he sent his son Erasmus abroad, perhaps to Louvain, for university education and training for the priesthood [49], an act that had become strictly illegal. Years past, in 1571, an Act Against Fugitives Over the Sea forbade Catholics to leave the country or to be trained overseas for ordination. Those overseas were given six months to return and repent or forfeit their possessions. But the younger Erasmus nonetheless achieved ordination and returned to Wales a priest. Yet harboring priests in England or Wales also was illegal. Priests caught offering a mass were fined as much as two hundred marks (nearly $30,000 today), and even attending a mass incurred fines half that amount [50]. The young Erasmus seems never to have been convicted under these laws and remained in Pembrokeshire until his death in 1612.

By 1582 or 1583, Erasmus was back in Fleet Prison for continued recusancy, and several of his lands were confiscated by the queen for debt. These included properties in Monkton and Tenby [51]. It appears by this time that Erasmus had lost much of his wealth and position, as by 1587, his brother Nicholas bequeathed "to my brother Erasmus 6.13.4 pounds yearly until he be restored with some better living" [52].

Religious matters came to a head in England toward the end of the 1580s. A complex plot to depose Elizabeth and place Mary, the Catholic queen of Scots, on the English throne illuminated the growing dangers of royal toleration and largely put an end to them. A key figure in the plot was Thomas Howard, the Duke of Norfolk. Norfolk was brother-in-law of William Saunders' "especially good friend" John, Lord Lumley, of Ewell and a son-in-law of the Earl of Arundel, who held the Manor of Ewell. Lumley, Arundel, and Norfolk were Erasmus Saunders' contemporaries, and all were intimately linked by their desire to replace Elizabeth on the throne. Norfolk himself became romantically involved with Mary, Queen of Scots, and used his advantage to plot Elizabeth's ouster and replacement with Mary as queen of England. This and subsequent plots were exposed and foiled, however, resulting finally in Mary's execution in 1587. These failed schemes were a key if not final blow to Catholic hopes [53].

Shortly after Mary's execution, a great naval armada assembled by the Catholic Philip of Spain sailed to England, aiming again to restore Catholicism there. But the combination of English naval skill and stormy seas routed the Armada, dispelling any lingering hope that Spanish intervention in English affairs could reestablish their religion. Following the defeat of the armada, in 1588, Erasmus Saunders landed in London's Clerkenwell Prison for his third internment [54].

Erasmus's torment continued through the decade of the 1590s. By 1592, when Erasmus was age fifty-eight, he removed himself from danger in Wales, fleeing to family properties in Norfolk. Erasmus took refuge at Ravingham, the former home of his sister Elizabeth before her first widowhood [55]. Although family claims to Ravingham are unclear following the death in 1581 of Elizabeth's husband, Roger Castell, it may have been Erasmus's son Richard, now age sixteen and perhaps residing at Ravingham, who assisted in offering Erasmus asylum at this time. Perhaps because of his absence from Pembrokeshire, Erasmus's name again was entered on 1592 Pembrokeshire Recusant Roll, where it appears no less than six times and also on the Carmarthenshire Roll three times [56].

When Erasmus returned to Wales from Norfolk is not known, but in 1594, he again was indicted for recusancy at Great Sessions in Haverfordwest [57]. In the following year, continuing his recusancy, he with two yeomen was declared to have been "absent from church" [58]. Little else is known of these troubles that dogged Erasmus for a decade and a half, but it is unlikely that he ever returned to any kind of normal productive life after that.

Erasmus's last appearance in Welsh records is for 1597, at about age sixty-three, when he and Jenet leased a property called Tremoillet with twelve cows, eight oxen, and one hundred sheep to John White for five years at twenty-two pounds per annum [59]. Erasmus disappears entirely from the Welsh and English records after making this lease. We know that Erasmus died about 1603 at about age sixty-nine because Jenet Saunders alone that year sued John White for recovery of rents due her from the Tremoillet lease [60]. Erasmus evidently left no will, and no estate administration has been found. Erasmus may have left Wales before his death, but evidence of late residence in Norfolk or elsewhere likewise has not been located.

Jenet, who was sixteen years younger than Erasmus, lived on another twenty-five years after her husband, living at Eglwyscymmin near Pendine in Carmarthenshire where some of her children resided, engaging in another land transaction in 1613 [61]. Jenet died in 1628, leaving the bulk of her estate to her son William. She lies interred at the St. Margaret Marloes Church in Pendine following what necessarily was a Protestant funeral. Of Jenet's final resting place, we learn that "the families of the Saunders and Prices who belonged to Pendine had their tombstones within the altar rails of this church and placed over the spot in which they were interred, the Saunders on the south side of the altar and the Prices on the north side. When the church was repaired in 1869 their tombs were removed and the stones were placed outside the church against the south wall of the church, and on the left of the porch as you stand with your face to the sea" [62].

Philip Saunders

The life of Philip, son of Jenet Barrett and Erasmus Saunders, in some important respects was different from the lives of all the previous generations of Saunders. Philip's life above all was a life of transition, of changes that reached deep into his life and livelihood. Heretofore in the Saunders family, certain patterns or currents of life persisted over great spans of time, even from the earliest moments we have been able to uncover. Among the most important of these were stability, continuity, and longevity in geographical location, social position, systems of belief, careers, and patterns of livelihood. Anchoring all this was the persistence of kinship, of extended family as the chief organizing principle of society itself. To be sure, past times were not static, and one can find certain family transitions throughout its history. But with Philip, his unique experience was that all these patterns gave way at essentially the same time within his lifetime. For Philip, no single event altered his everyday life; rather, events and circumstances accumulated that together changed Philip's life in ways that he felt personally, and that altered his family's future forever.

Over generations of this Saunders family, one constant theme has been a sense of solidarity of family, of tight family linkage in economic, social, and political arenas. This solidarity perpetuated and strengthened family identity, a functioning label under which one built one's life and opportunities. Family identity for the Saunders was powerfully embellished by the acquisition of titles and coats of arms. These proclaimed one's entitlement to privilege, honor, and occasionally lofty obligation. This sense of identity was a bulwark against all historical tides of adversity and over time produced waves of opportunity for family members. The Saunders family in Philip's time was fundamentally medieval in its basic modes of existence.

Philip Saunders's early life seems an effortless continuation of earlier times. He lived on his father's property at Tenby and enjoyed some fruits of family wealth. Following in other's footsteps, Philip acquired the title of gentleman— "gentleman of Pembroke" was the expression—and reaped benefits that routinely flowed to this advantaged position. Philip for a time held the title of bailiff of Tenby, a position his father held nearly forty years before. He married well into a family whose social position was the equal of his own. Philip had begun his adult life well in the old family modes, a young life attuned to the weakened strains of ancient feudalism.

But in his later years, we find a very different Philip, living no longer in Tenby but splitting time between a Pembrokeshire town called Amroth and the city of Bristol in England. Philip was by then a merchant or trader and a mariner, making a living on devices no longer resting on family economic tradition. He became something of an urbanite. For at least one of his sons, Philip arranged for an apprenticeship in a trade, an abrupt departure from the family's reliance on the profession of law. Although Philip undoubtedly maintained contact with his immediate family, he nonetheless set in motion some new processes that would permanently dilute the power of his family solidarity in Wales.

The best sense of Philip's life comes from realizing that this transition from one mode of living to another was perhaps less notable, less exceptional, in his daily living that it might seem to us in retrospect. These changes were taking place all around him; they were gradual, intermittent, unsteady, but at the same time also familiar in that Philip was not alone in struggling with change. These were the times that Philip lived in, and in one way or another, everyone experienced them.

Philip Saunders was born about 1578, perhaps the fourth son of Jenet Barrett and Erasmus Saunders of Tenby, Pembrokeshire, Wales. He had three sisters and seven brothers but seems to have been especially close to his sister Ann and brothers John and Henry, perhaps those siblings closest to his own age. His earliest years were those of his father's heyday, but that changed abruptly with accusations of recusancy against his father and the legal bludgeon brought to bear upon him. His father was jailed three times for recusancy before Philip reached his teenage years. Philip learned early that religious belief was political and potentially very dangerous.

About the same time that Erasmus lay in jail, the Spanish government launched their great naval armada in the direction of England. Their goal was the conquest of England and the restoration of Roman Catholicism throughout the land. The great naval attack occurred in 1588 when Philip was about age ten. English naval resistance was victorious, and the armada returned to Spain in ruin. The Saunders family in Wales as much of England was perhaps euphoric over their national victory, but the euphoria was surely dampened by their realization that English Catholicism had been dealt a severe, nearly fatal, blow. This was beginning to seem a too-familiar story. A few years before, family religious recalcitrance had been undermined on learning of the ignominious death in Ireland of their distant uncle and hero, Dr. Nicholas Saunders of Aston, regarded by many as the leading Catholic in England. Nicholas had traveled to Ireland to assist the Spanish in overthrowing that government in favor of Catholic rule. The mission failed, and Nicholas died there a hunted man in 1581.

What was Philip to think? His family had given their lives and fortunes to the old religion, but now with the Spanish defeat, the prospects for a revival of Roman Catholicism in England were dimmer than ever. Even Philip himself may have been named for the Spanish king who married Mary, the Catholic queen of England so faithfully served by his grandfather. If Philip Saunders wavered on his religion as he came of age, events of the early 1600s may have been decisive. The year 1603 was the end of a great era in England—the five-decade reign of Elizabeth I came to a close. Though much can be said about the golden age of England under Elizabeth, for Philip and the Catholic Saunders family in Wales, her demise offered some hope that a softening of attitudes and actions against Catholics might finally occur. The new monarch, James I, indeed initially offered that hope, but subsequent pressures to strengthen the Puritan hold on England largely dashed the hopes of persecuted Catholics. A series of desperate failed Catholic plots against the throne, notably the Gunpowder Plot of 1605, raised suspicions against Catholics once again and crushed any last hope for reconciliation under James [63].

So it was that Philip Saunders' views on religion, and especially its practice, left him teetering between the illegal and even dangerous Catholicism of his father's family and the ascendant Protestantism surrounding him at all turns. If Philip remained Roman Catholic, he followed his belief surreptitiously and was almost certainly the last Catholic of his line. More than likely, though, Philip acquiesced and adhered to the requirements of the new Church of England, a path enthusiastically adopted by later Saunders in the Wales line [64].

Tales of naval affairs cannot have escaped Philip's ears in his early years. He certainly heard stories of courageous and skillful Portuguese navigation following the notable voyages of Diaz, da Gama, and Magellan. Philip's father had dealings in Portugal, and an aunt, Elizabeth Saunders, a Catholic refugee, resided in Lisbon as Philip grew into manhood [65]. By the time Philip was born, the Spanish also had stories to tell of extensive New World empire and fabulous riches brought home from exotic places. Such profitability added to the lure of distant exploration, and lessons such as these were not lost on the enterprising classes in England. England had been slow to join the westward hunt, but Philip certainly heard tales of John Cabot's voyages to North America, and he probably learned every detail of Sir Walter Raleigh's attempts to establish an English colony on Roanoke Island in the 1580s.

In 1584, Elizabeth I of England granted Raleigh a patent to colonize America, and by the next year, Raleigh had founded the Roanoke Colony with one hundred settlers. But lack of supplies and hostilities with local Indians caused this colony to struggle, and the party returned to England with Sir Francis Drake, who had shortly before attacked the old Spanish colony of St. Augustine, in Florida. Roanoke was resettled in 1587, but the entire party disappeared before 1590, never to be heard from again. Tantalizing clues left behind by those settlers continue to be investigated to this day to discover their fate [66]. For Philip, Raleigh's efforts at Roanoke were virtually a family concern [67], and Philip could easily have grown up imagining himself an explorer or pioneer in that distant part of the world.

For Philip, events moved rapidly after the turn of the century. His father Erasmus Saunders had died, and Philip engaged to marry into a Pembrokeshire family with a strong naval history. Philip himself might have seemed a good catch. He was at that time styled "gentleman of Pembroke," suggesting that some dimensions of family status, otherwise threatened by recusancy, remained intact for the sons of Erasmus Saunders. In 1603 or early 1604, Philip married Jane Adams, daughter of Henry Adams and relict of John Knethell of Castlemartin, Pembrokeshire. Jane's uncle, Nicholas Adams, was at a time vice admiral for Pembroke, and the Adams owned a twelve-ton vessel called the *Anne*. A few years later, in 1607, Robert Adams, of uncertain relation to these Adams, commanded the fourth English voyage to the new settlement at Jamestown in Virginia.

Over these same years, Philip spent a fair amount of time in court between 1603 and 1604, perhaps resulting from strains in religion, politics, personal passions, economics, or all of them. One lurid event is described in Papers of the Great Sessions for 1603. At Cresswell in Lawrenny Parish, in June of that year, a quarrel occurred between Philip and a certain Gelly Laugharne, with the result that the latter accosted Philip and, with a knife, cut off the little finger of Philip's right hand [68]. Whether Laugharne was a disappointed suitor of Jane, a religious zealot, or perhaps an unhappy tradesman we cannot know, but for Philip, this untoward event did not end his business in court. In the same session, a Richard Bateman brought suit for nearly five pounds against Philip to recover goods that Bateman had allegedly supplied. Although details are lacking, this suit provides the hint that Philip had undertaken some mercantile activity about the time of his marriage. Shortly after their marriage, in 1604, Jane and Philip were back in court once again, suing a certain Henry Bowen for recovery of some property due Jane as relict of John Knethell. Whether the suit was successful, we do not know.

Jane and Philip Saunders had at least two children, and circumstantial evidence suggests a third. There of course may have been others, but no record of them seems to have survived. Born to Jane and Philip was a son Thomas and a daughter Thomasin [69]. Thomas was born about 1607 and Thomasin not long before or after. Another son may have been John, if later records can be interpreted in this way. Both sons Thomas and John, if indeed there were two, would later follow in their father's mercantile footsteps.

Over the first few years of Philip's marriage, records are mute on the subject of his main occupation. We know only that in the year 1612, he was named bailiff of Tenby. As bailiff, it would have been Philip's duty to carry out the will of the court, executing writs, processes, distraints, and arrests, serving as chief magistrate in a town under authority of the county's sheriff [70]. The bailiff position was one held by his father nearly forty years previously and more recently by Philip's brother John, whose appointment was made by 1607. John died in 1612, the same year Philip took on the bailiff's duties, suggesting that some family entitlement or tradition was at work in these appointments. As Philip left Tenby just a year or two after receiving this post, his appointment to the position may have been as temporary replacement for John. Not long after, in 1616, Philip's brother Henry became yet another bailiff in Tenby. Philip's primary occupation at this point in his life seems more likely to have been in commerce than government [71].

Philip's marriage to Jane Adams was lamentably short. She died about the year 1611 or 1612, about the same year as Philip's brother John. These years were devastating. Philip lost yet another brother Erasmus, the priest; in 1612, a sister Ann in 1614; and an uncle Francis Saunders in Norfolk in 1613. Another of Philip's brothers, Devereux, may also have died in this period [72]. Philip was the only brother mentioned in Ann's will, and Philip was also named in the will of his wealthy uncle Francis Saunders of Norfolk, receiving from Francis one Double Ryall, a somewhat valuable coin. Yet even in the face of family tragedies and Francis's generosity, Philip and his brothers and cousins sued Richard Saunders, their elder stepbrother and Francis's executor, over some aspect of the will [73].

Philip, remarried about 1615, to Alice, daughter of John Edwards of Tenby, a coastal merchant and colleague of Philip's father Erasmus [74]. Alice previously had married Saunders Barrett, whose family was well-known to Erasmus as well [75]. It was about the time of this marriage to Alice that Philip took up residence in Amroth, a small village just north of Tenby. The Edwards marriage could have gained Amroth property for Philip, though slivers of evidence also suggest that Amroth may have been inherited by Philip from some earlier Barrett possession [76].

Whether Alice and Philip had children of their own is uncertain, though one record suggests the possibility [77]. A son William and daughter Jenet, recurrent names within the Wales family, years later both married into the Woolcock family, yet another familiar Wales name for the Saunders. Nothing more is known of this Jenet, but it may be that this son William is the same person as William Saunders who died in 1627 in Alice Edwards's later home village of Wiston in Pembrokeshire [78].

In 1617, Alice and Philip Saunders were sued by John Barrett for payment of a debt Alice incurred before her marriage to Philip, this John Barrett evidently a relative of Alice's former husband, Saunders Barrett. This suit records the last year in which Philip can be found in Wales; after that, Philip seems to have resided in Bristol, England, at least intermittently.

That Philip might have gone to England, or shuttled between Bristol and Amroth for an extended period, is in itself not all that surprising. For the period in which Philip lived, Bristol dominated Tenby's coastal trade [79]. The ports were separated by less than one hundred sea-miles. Two of Philip's cousins, Erasmus and Henry, sons of his uncle William Saunders of Tenby, are known to have moved to England, probably to Bristol, at about the same time that Philip was there [80].

It should be recalled that Philip's mother, Jenet Barrett Saunders, had years before been sole heir to her father's estate, which included "my bote and my gayne" (my boat and its profits). Although the boat went to James Barrett, the experience, contacts, and encouragement of the Adams family may well have propelled Philip to engage in maritime trade. That at least would explain why, in 1621, in Bristol, England, Philip Saunders was identified as a mariner. The occasion was an agreement to establish an apprenticeship for Philip's son Thomas in Thomas's fourteenth year [81].

Philip arranged this Bristol apprenticeship for his son with a certain John Mynne in 1621. John Mynne was himself a cousin, or rather a stepcousin, if such a term can be used, of Philip. The relationship goes back to Ewell in Surrey. Philip's grandfather William Saunders of Ewell had first married about 1529

Joan (née Marston) Mynne, who by her first marriage had a son John Mynne, born in 1519. William Sanders took on the wardship of this John Mynne. John Mynne and Erasmus Saunders thus were stepbrothers by the same mother, though nearly a whole generation of age separated the two of them. Given the timing of all this, John Mynne of Bristol in 1621 probably was close relative of John Mynne of Ewell but of the next generation. In the apprentice arrangement, Philip posted a bond ensuring the faithful performance of his son's work for Mynne, the bond to be forfeited if young Thomas proved inadequate for the work over the seven-year obligation.

Circumstances surrounding Thomas Saunders' apprenticeship reveal that Philip Saunders (and perhaps John Mynne as well) died before the seven years were up because Thomas did not conclude his training as planned. He completed his apprenticeship in 1628 under different supervision. Thomas's new master was William Roach, also known as Roche, who resided in the village of Wiston, Pembrokeshire [82]. This arrangement came about through the effort of Philip's widow Alice.

Shortly after Philip's death, Alice Edwards Saunders remarried, and the new apprenticeship was one result of this union. Alice (Thomas's stepmother) remarried about the year 1628, and she went to live in Wiston, Pembrokeshire, home of her new husband, Hugh Wogan. William Roche of Wiston and Hugh Wogan must have been business associates or at least in sufficient contact to conclude an agreement for the young Thomas Saunders, an agreement probably financed by Philip's estate by then in the hands of Alice Saunders Wogan. Alice's faithfulness to her stepson seems to have been rewarded as she was remembered in the 1628 will of Jenet Barrett Saunders, Philip's mother [83].

About the time, Thomas completed his apprenticeship in England, Jane Adams and Philip Saunders's daughter Thomasin married Thomas Owen, he of a well-known family in Pembrokeshire. If Thomasin married at about age eighteen, a common age for the time, then she wed about 1625, near the time of Philip's death. This marriage also seems to have been arranged by Alice Saunders, Thomasin's stepmother. Through Alice were several connections to the Owen family. In fact, her husband Hugh Wogan had first married an Owen. Sir Hugh Owen was a colleague of Philip's father Erasmus when both were justices of the peace in Pembrokeshire. Thomasin's marriage to Thomas, son of George Owen, argues that family social status had not been seriously injured through punishments to the devoutly Catholic Erasmus [84].

Of Philip we hear nothing more, except a single comment in the 1636 will of Henry Saunders, Philip's brother. Henry wrote, "I give and bequeath unto my sayd nephew William a bond of three score pounds upon my late brother Mr. Philip Sanders" [85]. That bond—perhaps a security for business dealings—is the last trace of the Saunders in Wales for this particular family line, though other branches have remained there to this day [86]. Owing to

Philip's limited opportunity in Wales and his maritime enterprise, his family's future lay elsewhere, in the west of England and later in lands across the seas.

NOTES

1. A brief account is given in Mike Ashley, *British Kings and Queens* (New York: Barnes and Noble, 1998), p. 636.

2. Surrey Archaeological Collection, vol. 14, p. 20.

3. Evidence for Erasmus's marriage, admitted indirect, lies in his age, education, and social station, all of which suggest that he was particularly eligible and prepared for marriage. Further, his son Richard never appears in Welsh records, suggesting he was born before 1568 when Erasmus resided in London.

4. The notion that Erasmus married a Townsend, though a speculation, helps assemble a picture of how Erasmus's son was supported in Norfolk and how and why Erasmus was able to return to Norfolk in times of duress. Of course, the matter requires further research, but a starting point for this is to investigate whether Erasmus married a daughter or sister of Richard Townsend of Raynham, Norfolk, a marriage that would have been arranged by Erasmus's stepmother. Joan Spelman Saunders first married John Spelman of Narborough, near Raynham. The Townsends were recusants. There are strong connections between the Townsends, Kervilles, and Castells, families into which Erasmus's younger stepsisters married. Roger Castell's grandmother was Ann Townsend whose brother Sir Roger was a commissioner on the Court of Augmentations. Erasmus's father William served as a particular receiver for this Augmentations Court.

5. We think that Erasmus married about 1563 and received some London property from his father. The bulk of William's property bequest in 1571 went to Erasmus's brothers, Nicholas and Francis. William's will, however, made no mention of possessions in Southwark or London, and it is possible that Erasmus had received a grant of property there before William's death. This explains how Erasmus lived in London after 1563 and why Erasmus received so little property in William's bequest of 1571, by which time he had remarried in Wales.

6. The 1613 will of Francis Saunders, Ewell, Surrey, is available in *Virginia Magazine of History and Biography* 15 (1907–1908): pp. 304–306.

7. Many accounts of this period are available. The following sources are particularly helpful: J. R. S. Phillips, *The Justices of the Peace in Wales and Monmouthshire, 1541–1689* (Cardiff: University of Wales Press, 1975), pp. xiii, xiv, and 205; A. L. Rowse, *Expansion of Elizabethan England* (New

York: St. Martins Press, 1955), especially chap. 2, "Borderlands: Wales," p. 53 on the justice of the peace system; and F. Heal and C. Holmes. *Gentry in England and Wales 1500–1700* (Stanford: Stanford University Press, 1994), pp. 166–170.

8. H. A. Lloyd, *The Gentry of South-West Wales* (Cardiff: University of Wales Press, 1968), p. 188. Records faithfully repeat that Erasmus went to Wales "via Brecknock," but the significance of this observation escapes us.

9. A. L. Rowse, *Expansion of Elizabethan England* (New York: St. Martins Press, 1955), p. 64. See also R. Howells, Tenby: Old and New (Llandysul: Gomer Press, 1981), p. 1.

10. Sir Bernard Burke, *A General Armory of England, Scotland, and Ireland* (London: E. Churton, 1842).

11. One is tempted to guess that this migrant was from Ewell in view of the fact that Erasmus went there later. But we have found no concrete evidence pointing to this conclusion.

12. The earliest Saunders record we have located in Pembrokeshire is for a John Saunders, who in 1581 leased lands in Steynton for a period of twenty-one years. This John may well be a son of the original migrant. See E. A. Lewis and J. Conway, eds., *Records of the Court of Augmentations relating to Wales and Monmouthshire* (Cardiff: University of Wales Press, 1954), p. 500.

13. In later years, Erasmus's own son would marry the widow of Saunders Barrett who died in 1611.

14. There may be more here than meets the eye because both the Barrett connection and the appointments to justice of the peace positions can be found in family records of Norfolk. See chap. 4, note 71. Erasmus's sister Catherine married at age thirty-five, about 1582, to Sir Miles Corbett of Sprowston, Norfolk. He was a justice of Norfolk from 1590 to 1606. Their son Thomas Corbett, a Norfolk justice from 1607 to 1615, married Ann Barret of Belhouse in Alveley, Essex.

15. Francis Green, "Saunders of Pentre, Tymawr, and Glanrhydw," *Historical Society of West Wales Transactions, 1911–1912*, vol. 2, p. 175.

16. There were three branches of Barretts in Wales, at Pendine, Gellyswick, and Philbeach. The Voyles were proximate to the Barretts of Philbeach; Erasmus's wife Jenet was of the Pendine branch.

17. Jenet and Erasmus were married shortly before October 1570. This marriage date is known because William, father of Erasmus, included Jenet in his will of October 1570, yet William's will named no children for them. But their first son Nicholas was born in 1571 at Ewell, suggesting a marriage in early 1570.

18. Green, "Saunders of Pentre," pp. 170–171. Barrett's suit cost him forty pounds but came to nothing.

19. In Carmarthenshire, Erasmus held a large number of properties. In Eglwyscymmin, he owned Tremoillet, where his daughter Ann died in 1614. He held Newbourne in Newton, Laugharne Parish, which was later occupied by his son Nicholas and also in Laugharne a tenement called Prictarow and a parcel of land called Great Hill Burrows and East Marsh. In Llanstephan, Erasmus held a tenement in Llangunnock and one called Yr Hendre.

    His holdings in Pendine were most extensive. These included tenements called (1) Dewes, (2) John Thomas the Younger's, (3) Wilkin's in the fields of Penhowe and Pendine, (4) Margaret Blake's, and (5) Robert Poyer's on the west part of Pendine Church. He also held two cottages in Pendine, a messuage called Wytewye's Tenement, and the Great House on Pendine Green. The last of these is perhaps the same as Big House, which he held during his mayoralty of Tenby. This is described as being in Pendine, situated behind St. Margaret Marloes Church where a number of the Saunders in this line are buried.

    In addition, Erasmus held much acreage in the area. These lands were (1) four acres in the fields of Pendine near Fabanthes Well, (2) seven acres in the east fields of Pendine, (3) one acre on Cantes side in Willway and one acre in the fields of Willway, (4) mountain ground called Pent y Wrath, (5) Skrynckill Mountain from Kreege sideward of a portway unto Tremoillets Mountain, (6) a close called Great Cline, and an additional seventeen acres.

20. Erasmus's eldest son Nicholas was born at Ewell in Surrey in 1571. Later of Newton in the Parish of Laugharne, Nicholas held a messuage called Newbourne. Nicholas married Mary Massey and with her had six children, who are described in Francis Green 1911. "Saunders of Pentre, Tymawr, and Glanrhydw," *Historical Society of West Wales Transactions, 1911–1912,* vol. 2, pp. 161–188. Although Nicholas was the eldest son, typically the principal heir to family properties, Nicholas evidently was bypassed in favor of his younger brother William. The reason may have been religion. The names and marriages of Nicholas's children suggest Protestantism in this family. For example, their daughter's name of Temperance was a popular choice for Puritans and is not a Catholic name. Also, their daughters married Protestant clergy. If Nicholas became a Puritan, he certainly would have incurred the wrath of his parents.

21. William was the second son of Jenet Barrett and Erasmus Saunders and principal heir to their estate. William married Florence Walcot (a.k.a. Woolcock), and they resided at Pendine, Carmarthenshire. He

is ancestor to an enduring line of Saunders in Wales, known as the Saunders of Pentre. This line is richly described in Green, "Saunders of Pentre."

22. Born about 1574, Erasmus's son Erasmus entered the Catholic priesthood, studying abroad to achieve his ordination. Erasmus's name surfaces in a list of those studying for the priesthood in Europe, probably at Louvain, Douai, or Verdun; see Lloyd, *Gentry of South-West Wales*, p. 174. Erasmus returned home in the wake of other Jesuit missionaries, arriving in England after 1580, but in view of Elizabethan repression, could not practice his religion openly. Erasmus died in 1612.

23. John Saunders is suggested by Francis Green to be a son of Erasmus, but no record unambiguously states this. John, like several others in Erasmus's family, was bailiff of Tenby in 1607. John died in 1612, and in his will of that date, he left a bequest to Henry, another of Erasmus's sons, suggesting this family relationship. John probably married Elizabeth Griffith and had a son Thomas, who he placed under the guardianship of Thomas Griffith when he died, bequeathing to his son twenty-two pounds and forty sheep.

24. Among all of Erasmus's children, least is known of his son Devereux. He may have been named for Devereux Barrett. His date of death is not known, but he evidently was deceased before 1613, as, unlike his siblings, he was not named in his uncle Francis Saunders's will of that year.

25. Elizabeth was the longest lived of all the children of Jenet and Erasmus, dying in her seventies in 1655. She married Harry Davis, whose identity is unclear. There are many Davises in Wales, but in view of her sister Jane's marriage to Fulford, one might suppose this Harry Davis was kin to Capt. John Davis. The conjecture is further supported by noting marriages involving Elizabeth's Ewell cousins, which connected that branch of the family both to Wales and to maritime adventures. The matter requires further research.

26. Erasmus's son Henry was styled gentleman and in 1616, like others in the family, was bailiff of Tenby. Henry never married and in his will of 1636 left all his possessions to his brother William, including "a bond of three score pounds upon my late brother Mr. Philip Saunders."

27. Erasmus's daughter Ann died unmarried at about age twenty-seven in 1613. Of Eglwyscymmin, Carmarthenshire, Ann named her brother Philip executor for an estate of more than thirty-six pounds.

28. Jane probably was the youngest daughter of Jenet and Erasmus. She married Robert Fulford before 1613. This may be the same person as Robert Fulford of Great Fulford, Devon. Her sister-in-law, Faith

Fulford, was wife of Capt. John Davis (1543–1605), noted for his search for a northwest passage through North America.

29. William's will is found in Prerogative Court of Canterbury, 42, Holney, dated October 2, 1570, and proved November 10, 1571.

30. Calendar of the Register of the Council in the Marches of Wales, Cym Rec. Ser. #8, 1535 in 1569–1591, pp. 72–74.

31. Ibid., pp. 124–127.

32. J. Phillips, "Glimpses of Elizabethan Pembrokeshire," *Archeologia Cambrensis* 5, no. 16 (1898): p. 279.

33. T. G. Stickings, *The Story of Saundersfoot* (Tenby: Walters Publishers, 1970), pp. 36, 120.

34. Green, "Saunders of Pentre," p. 169.

35. Lloyd, *Gentry of South-West Wales,* p. 89.

36. Ibid.

37. Phillips, "Elizabethan Pembrokeshire," p. 279.

38. A. L. Rowse, *Expansion of Elizabethan England* (New York: St. Martins Press, 1955), especially chap. 2, "Borderlands: Wales," pp. 63–64.

39. Phillips, "Elizabethan Pembrokeshire," p. 306.

40. Stickings, *Story of Saundersfoot,* p. 37.

41. Phillips, "Elizabethan Pembrokeshire," p. 311.

42. This account is greatly abridged from Phillips, "Elizabethan Pembrokeshire," pp. 307–310.

43. In London Marriage Records is found the following entry: "2-26-1589/90. Luke Warde of the City of London, gent., and Jane Sawnder, spinster, of same, dau. of Nicholas Sawnder, gent., late of Ewell, co. Surry, dec." Luke Ward had an interesting naval career following the *Greyhound* episode. Commanding the *Tremontana,* he sailed for England against the Spanish Armada; and before that, he had a voyage of 1582 that included a conference at sea in the mid-Atlantic to determine longitude. See Katherine Neal, "Mathematics and Empire, Navigation and Exploration," *Isis* 93 (2002): pp. 435–453.

44. John Strype, *Annals of the Reformation,* vol. 2, part 2, n.d.

45. Erasmus is routinely listed as a justice of the peace for Pembrokeshire throughout the 1570s but is missing from the list in 1579 and thereafter.

46. Nicholas, brother of Erasmus, was committed to Fleet Prison on April 30, 1578, and was freed June 23 of that year; see M. L. Walker, *The Manor of Battailes and the Family of Saunder in Ewell during the 16th and 17th Centuries* (Guildford: Surrey Archeological Society, 1956), p. 80. Erasmus was in prison longer than Nicholas. Our suspicion that Nicholas recanted his Catholicism is based not only on the fact of his abbreviated prison stay, but also because Nicholas asked the powerful

Puritan Burghley to supervise his son, acting as overseer of Nicholas's 1578 will.

47. Cecil knew the Saunders well. His wife's grandmother was of the Banbury Saunder family, and he routinely interacted with many of the same families as did the later Saunders. As noted, in 1587, Cecil was asked to oversee the will of Nicholas Saunders of Ewell.

48. For a penetrating look at recusancy in Wales, see Lloyd, *Gentry of South-West Wales*, pp. 188–191.

49. Our dating here is inexact because the age of the younger Erasmus is not precisely known; see Lloyd, *Gentry of South-West Wales*, p. 174. The University of Louvain is where Dr. Nicholas Saunders taught and wrote during his years in exile.

50. See the First Missionaries (1571–1581) at http:users.globalnet.co.uk.

51. Lewis and Davies 1954, p. 497. One of the confiscated properties was a messuage called New Inne.

52. Particulars of the will of Nicholas Saunders are given in Walker, *Manor of Battailes*, pp. 95–96.

53. See K. O. Morgan, 1984. *Oxford History of Britain* (Oxford: Oxford University Press, 1984), for a short history of the Catholic struggle in England and Elizabeth's views on Catholicism. For the role of Lumley, Arundel, and Norfolk in the Ridolphi plot involving Mary, Queen of Scots, see N. Williams, *All the Queen's Men: Elizabeth I and Her Courtiers* (New York: Macmillan Company, 1972), pp. 131–132.

54. Walker, *Manor of Battailes*, p. 94. Walker notes that Erasmus's name was given on a recusant list for Clerkenwell, which was a prison near the old Charterhouse in London. Erasmus was not convicted for recusancy in Clerkenwell as he did not reside there; rather, he was placed in prison there for recusancy elsewhere.

55. Erasmus is described as "having lived at Raveningham in Norfolk," where his sister Elizabeth lived, she having married Roger Castell of that place; see Walker, *Manor of Battailes*, p. 82. It seems Elizabeth must have retained some claim to this property after Castell's death.

56. Lloyd, *Gentry of South-West Wales*, p. 190.

57. Walker, *Manor of Battailes*, p. 94.

58. Lloyd, *Gentry of South-West Wales*, p. 191.

59. Francis Green Papers, n.d., the Francis Green collection, encompassing thirty-five volumes of wills, marriage licenses, parish registers, and related materials, together with some eight hundred envelopes containing sheet pedigrees of Dyfed families, can be consulted at the Dyfed County Council, Cultural Services Department, Public Library, Dew Street, Haverfordwest, Dyfed, SA61 1SU. See p. 171.

60. Green, Papers, p. 171.

61. Llwyngwair Deeds and Documents, no. 13967, National Library of Wales. Jenet granted a twenty-one-year lease to David Palmer, yeoman, for a parcel of land at Portland and a house and garden at Hemlock Mill, in the town of Laugharne.

62. Green, Papers. A Saunders family residence, always known as the Big House, was located behind the church; see also Stickings, *Story of Saundersfoot*, p. 36.

63. Bruce Robinson, *The Gunpowder Plot*, 2004. Robinson describes a series of minor Catholic plots at the turn of the century, culminating in the Gunpowder Plot, a scheme designed to blow up the Parliament, the king, and the lords to pave the way for installing a Catholic monarch. The conspiracy was uncovered before it could be effected. See http://www.bbc.uk/history/state/monarchs.

64. Several of the later Saunders of this line served the Anglican church, including Erasmus (1670–1724), vicar of Blockley, rector of Helmdon, and canon of Brecon. This Erasmus produced a particularly important history of religion in Wales prior to the Methodist revival. The work of 1721 was called "A View of the State of Religion in the Diocese of St. David's about the Beginning of the Eighteenth Century, with some Account of the Causes of its Decay." Some others were Erasmus (1717–p1757), canon of Windsor, prebendary of Rochester, vicar of Wantage, St. Martins-in-the-Fields, and Mapiscombe; and John (1731–1814), rector of Woodford, Woodham Manor, and Witford. David Saunders (1769–1840) was a Baptist minister, poet, and hymn composer, and another David Saunders (1831–1892) preached, lectured, wrote, and composed as a Calvinist Methodist minister. See T. R. Roberts, *Eminent Welshmen* (Cardiff: Educational Publishing Co., 1908).

65. Elizabeth Saunder was of the Saunders of Aston, a branch of the Charlwood family. Her brother was the famous (or infamous) Dr. Nicholas Saunders, whose life is described elsewhere in this narrative. Elizabeth was harassed for her Catholic enthusiasms and sought refuge on more than one occasion. She died in Lisbon in 1607.

66. Ralph Lane, *Preface to The Colony at Roanoke*, 1986, at http://www.nationalcenter.org/Colony of Roanoke.html.

67. Raleigh's attempt to establish a permanent settlement on Roanoke Island off the North Carolina coast was well publicized in its day. In part the effort failed because of English preoccupation with war with Spain. The Roanoke colony foundered for lack of supplies; the threat of imminent attack on England by the Spanish Armada undercut English naval support for Raleigh's project.

These events were particularly well understood by the Saunders because the Saunders and Raleighs were related to each other through their marriages to the Throckmortons. Sir Walter Raleigh's wife was Bess Throckmorton, whose uncle through marriage was Nicholas Saunders of Ewell, brother of Erasmus.

68. Philip Saunders involvement in these court cases was uncovered by Francis Green, whose papers reveal a great deal about the Saunders in Wales and their earlier lineage. See note 59.

69. The particular naming of these children, Thomas and Thomasin, suggests twins. But the larger question is why Philip and Jane chose these names at all since no Thomas Saunders is found in the family of Erasmus, nor in the Ewell branches of the family. Philip's brother John also named a son Thomas.

70. Bailiff responsibilities at the time of Philip are reviewed in Wikipedia.org.

71. Found among the papers of Sanders genealogist Anna V. Parker (author of *The Sanders Family of Grass Hills, Kentucky*) at the Filson Club in Louisville, Kentucky, is a remarkable letter written to Ms. Parker by a Kentucky attorney in the 1950s, in which this attorney claimed that Philip Saunders came to Virginia in the year 1613. The author provided no source for his claim, making it easy to conclude that the claim was mere speculation since very few records of Virginia migration prior to about 1620 exist, and none of these name Philip Sanders as a migrant.

But what makes this letter so remarkable is that the author could not have known that Philip was indeed the ancestor of this Kentucky line of Sanders who lived at that particular time. The earliest established ancestor of these Kentucky Sanders had been Nathaniel, who came to Virginia about 1700.

The attorney's claim goes further. He suggests that Philip traveled in 1613. This is a particularly well-aimed claim. Just prior to 1613, Philip had been widowed, and his second marriage probably occurred a year or two after this date. This is perhaps the one year among all possibilities that had Philip unengaged in family matters. Furthermore, Philip's uncle Francis's will of 1613 mentioned that the young Henry Spelman was then in Virginia, and Philip might have sought out Spelman regarding family matters.

Although our evidence suggests Philip remained in Wales in 1613, Sanders family researchers perhaps should remain open to any new evidence in support of this attorney's astonishing claim.

72. Francis Saunders of Congham, Norfolk, stepbrother of Erasmus, whose father was William Saunders of Ewell, left an extensive will in 1613 in which he named all his surviving brothers and sisters and their offspring. Children of Erasmus are included, but the name Devereux

is not. See Will of Francis Saunders, Ewell, Surrey, gent. Will 17 August 1613; proved 25 August 1613, available in *Virginia Magazine of History and Biography* XV (1907–1908): pp. 305–306.

73. Francis named Philip's brother Richard; as his executor, Richard received a significant portion of Francis's considerable estate. Richard is not named as a son of Erasmus in Francis Green's marvelously detailed account of the Saunders in Wales, no doubt because records in Wales for Richard evidently do not exist. The lesson here is that although the family branches of Wales and Norfolk were geographically distant, family relationships remained strong.

Strong relationships notwithstanding, plaintiffs in the suit of 23 November 1613, three months after probate of Francis Saunders's will, were Sir Nicholas Saunders and Nicholas Saunders, Esq., and Philip and William Saunders, gentlemen.

74. A John Edwards was master of the Vintners Company in 1609, but he is unlikely to have been the father of Alice. A more likely candidate is John Edwards of Tenby, who was involved in Welsh coastal maritime trade during Erasmus's lifetime; see Welsh Port Books, 1550–1603, p. 138.

75. As a former husband of Alice Edwards, Saunders Barrett was an approximate contemporary of Philip Saunders, born perhaps about 1575. That would suggest his parents' married about 1570, more or less exactly when Erasmus Saunders married Jenet Barrett. A second Saunders/Barrett marriage in this same generation suggests that Erasmus's marriage resulted from extended relations between these two families.

76. Records suggest but do not clinch this possibility. Amroth had a castle whose fourteenth-century gate is still standing; the castle today is a hotel. In the fourteenth century, David Elliott was a burgess of St. Florence, Pembroke, and became founder of the Elliotts of Earwere (Amroth Castle) and Narberth. They held Earwere at least until the 1500s. The Elliotts evidently had come to Pembroke through the marriage of Jenkin Elliott to an heiress of the Barretts of Pendine in nearby Carmarthenshire. These Barretts are the same family into which Erasmus married.

77. A handwritten entry was at some later time entered into the Saunders genealogy in the Advenie of Carmarthenshire. This entry was placed under the name of Philip as if to suggest lineal descent and reads as follows: "William Saunders married Ann, daughter of Thomas Woolcock of Walton East in Pembrokeshire which TW died in 1635 by whom he had John Saunders, Philip Saunders, David Saunders and Elizabeth Saunders and Thomas Woolcock son of the above married Jennet Saunders of the same Saunders as these." The expression, "of

the same Saunders as these," could refer either to Philip or to any of the other Saunders depicted in the genealogy, although proximity of this record to Philip favors the former possibility.

78. But if William Saunders was born to Alice and Philip Saunders about 1615, and it cannot have been much earlier than that, his death in Wiston in 1627 would have occurred at about age twelve. If that were true, then this William could not have married into the Woolcock family as the record suggests. Better evidence is needed to conclude that William and Jenet were Alice and Philip's children.

79. Margaret Davies, *The Story of Tenby* (Tenby Museum, 1911), p. 17.

80. Green, "Saunders of Pentre," p. 175.

81. Bristol Apprentice Registers 1616–1624. 1620/1 January 20. "Thomas son of Philip Saunders, mariner of Abbots Leigh, Somerset, bound Apprentice to John Mine of Bristol mariner and Martha his wife, for 7 years. His father bound in 20 Pounds for his son's service and truth."

82. Bristol Burgess Books, 1627–1628. On "1628, June 23 Thomas Saunders, mariner, is admitted to the liberties of the city, for that he was the Apprentice of William Roach." William and John Roche (a.k.a. Roach) were of Wiston, Pembrokeshire. See William Roach, International Genealogical Index, Latter Day Saints.

83. Will of Jenet Saunders of Eglwyscymmin, 1628, Probate Index for Carmarthen, National Library of Wales, Aberystwyth.

84. Thomas Owen, whom Thomasin Saunders married, traces his descent from William Owen of the Henllys branch of that family. William Owen built a virtual empire in Pembroke, which holdings became the barony of Cemaes. As Lord of Cemaes, he held the castle of Newport, seven manors, six advowsons, two thousand eight hundred acres of land and over two hundred tenements. William Owen married into the powerful Herbert family and had a son George, who in time became lord of Cemaes. George had several illegitimate children by Ancred Obilit, whom he eventually married in 1607. Thomas Owen, husband of Thomasin Saunders, was born of this marriage.

85. Will of Henry Saunders, 1636. SD/1636/88. National Library of Wales, Aberystwyth.

86. Extensive genealogies of various Welsh Saunders lineages are provided in Green, "Saunders of Pentre."

NOTES FOR SAUNDERS OF ASTON:

1* William of Aston married Elizabeth Mynne. Her brother Nicholas Mynne married Joan Marston, but he died young. Joan Marston

Mynne then married William Saunders of Ewell, father of Erasmus of Pembrokeshire, Wales. This surname is also spelled Mynde and Mynes in the records of the day.

2*   Most accounts of Nicholas spell the name Sander, but all sources agree that Nicholas Saunders came from the Aston Saunders, a branch deriving from the Charlwood family.

3*   The *Catholic Encyclopedia* states that Nicholas was born in 1530, but Burke, in a treatment of the Sandars of Gate Burton Hall, gives this date as 1527. Both sources agree that Nicholas was born in Charlwood.

4*   Francis Green cites a record as follows, "In 1544, —— Saunders of Ewelme is mentioned in a muster roll as being liable, among the gentlemen of Surrey, to supply soldiers for the army against France." The devil is at work in this record. Green remarks that this "no doubt is William of Ewell," but it certainly can refer to William of Aston as well. These two Williams were the same age, both married a woman named Mynne, and both resided in Surrey. One seems to have been in Ewell, and the other in Ewelme, if indeed these are thought to be two different places and not merely one with different spelling variations. Green, writing in 1911, may not have been aware that Ewelme is a village in Oxfordshire lying in the deanery of Aston.

5*   It is more likely that William Saunders of Ewell was high sheriff of Surrey in 1556. He previously served as commissioner for the peace in that county, and in other respects, his career paralleled that of his cousin, Sir Thomas Saunders of Charlwood. Sir Thomas at one point held the power of nominating sheriffs for all of England's counties, and he more than likely used this influence on behalf of his particularly close cousin. Erroneous claim is sometimes made also that William of Aston was knighted in 1563, but that record clearly refers to William Saunders of Ewell. In this instance, however, the claim is doubly incorrect as neither William was ever knighted.

6*   This is the same Yate family into which Richard Saunders of Banbury married and which acquired Tullwick Manor from the Saunders. John Yate, who acquired Tullwick, collected pensions for the nuns each quarter. See Syon Abbey history at http://www.tudorplace.com.

7*   Sources disagree on these marriages between the Saunders and the Pitts. We take the view that Margaret married Henry Pitts of Alton, Hampshire, and Elizabeth married John Pitts of Oxford, following the *Victoria History of Surrey*, vol. 3, p. 183, a view affirmed in the *Victoria History of Hampshire*, vol. 2, p. 77. But the reverse case is given by genealogist Homer-Saunders. Confusion may have resulted from the identification of Elizabeth as "Mrs. Pitts of Alton," a name normally reserved for Margaret rather than Elizabeth; see *Victoria History of*

Hampshire, vol. 2, p. 80. But Margaret had died in France before this statement of 1580; therefore, Mrs. Pitts in this record is Elizabeth.

8*   Syon Abbey history is given at http://www.tudorplace.com.

9*   Sir Francis Englefield held a large estate in Berkshire and married Catherine Fettiplace of that county. The Fettiplace family also held Swinbrook Manor in Ewelme, Oxfordshire. This home in Ewelme may suggest how Englefield came to know the Saunders, who seem to have held property in Ewelme as well. See note 4* above. One of these Fettiplaces also married into the Carew family of Beddington.

10*   For background on John Pittsaeus (1560–1616), see *Victoria History of Surrey*, vol. 3, p. 183.

11*   David Lewis, trans., *Rise and Growth of the Anglican Schism*, by Nicholas Sander (London: Burns and Oates Company, 1877), originally published in 1585. The preface to this translated version of Nicholas's *De Schismate Anglicano* errs in suggesting that Nicholas left England in 1561. Nicholas was already in Rome the year before. More likely, Nicholas left England when other Catholic exiles did, in 1558 or the year after. See the New Catholic Encyclopedia.com.

12*   The idea that Nicholas never returned to England after his exile is lightly disputed by Sewell and Lane, *Free Men of Charlwood* (1979), p. 78, in writing that, "It has been suggested that sometime Dr. Nicholas may have returned secretly to Surrey as a Jesuit emissary and while hiding at Leigh Place scratched the faint words on the mantlepiece there."

13*   See Wikipedia.com for a brief description of the Council of Trent.

14*   Lewis, *Rise and Growth*, preface.

15*   Catholic Encyclopedia.com/Dr. Nicholas Sander.

16*   Many believed that Nicholas's return to Rome in 1572 was to receive a cardinalate, but Pope Pius had died in the interim and with him, evidently some appreciation of Nicholas's many contributions and substantial reputation.

17*   Francis Green Collection, c1911. Dyfed County Council, Library Cultural Services Department, Haverfordfwest. Green provides a large set of genealogical and historical materials on the Saunders, both before and after their arrival in Pembrokeshire.

18*   *Victoria History of Hampshire*, vol. 2, p. 77.

19*   Sir Francis Walsingham was the nephew of Sir Edmund Walsingham, and thus first cousin of Alice, wife of Thomas Saunders of Charlwood. He served as principal secretary under Elizabeth and was chief architect of her policy to suppress Catholicism. Walsingham confiscated Sir Francis Englefield's considerable estate in Berkshire for his own use.

20*   *Victoria History of Hampshire*, vol. 2, p. 80.

21* Francis Green Collection c1911. Green recorded that Englefield about 1590 sought copies of Elizabeth's letters to him from the bishop at Lyon, France. Evidently, these letters carried broad interest since Englefield shared them with others.

22* The Lisbon community finally returned to England in 1861, more than three hundred years from its first exile, settling in Dorsetshire and later Devon. The Abbey of Syon holds the distinction of being the only English religious community founded in medieval times to have maintained an unbroken lineage to the present time.

CHAPTER EIGHT

Gloucestershire

When in 1621 Philip Saunders took his young son Thomas from Wales to England to engage his apprenticeship with John Mynne, Philip probably foresaw the expanding opportunities for Thomas in overseas commerce. For the young and impressionable Thomas, this adventure probably lay in the forefront of his imagination. Excitement for Atlantic crossings reflected the historical times in which they lived; such possibilities would have captured any number of young minds or adventurous souls. Yet for Thomas Saunders, the notion that the New World might hold some exceptional opportunity was his distinct and obliging inheritance. By the time Thomas had reached his teens, Saunders relatives could count numerous visits to Virginia and their returning tales undoubtedly fueled Thomas's eagerness for New World adventure. Philip's decision to apprentice his son into the Bristol mariner community set Thomas directly on a westward path.

If Thomas were to become a mariner of Bristol, he was sure to lose a sense of homeland in Wales, and his contact with immediate family back home necessarily would have weakened. But at the same time, Thomas joined another community, a community very much including mariners to Virginia, with some of his own relatives among their number. This was a different kind of future than generations of Sanders had ever known, a future in a newly created personal community that built its identity and solidarity on oceanic risks and overseas gambles. Over the course of his life, Thomas followed this path, a path which began in the founding of Virginia itself. Earliest Virginia was a world that Thomas carried in his heart and head. And so we begin Thomas's story with Virginia narratives that Thomas was sure to have known and dreamed about.

Virginia Company of London

Around the time of Thomas's birth, in 1606, a collection of entrepreneurs in London petitioned King James I for a charter to explore and harvest the resources of the new land called Virginia. The proposal was instructive. It signaled a new and different beginning for England in the larger European contest for influence in the New World, a world in European perspective that was now more than a century old. The Spanish and Portuguese were first in the era of discovery, developing a formula for wealth based on conquest, exploitation, slavery, and Christian conversion for native populations. The New World in their approach represented foremost a military challenge, the establishment of Spanish rule over large provinces. The French, on the other hand, sent out teams of explorers to North America to discover the breadth of the new land and the best routes by which it might be traversed. The French brought neither substantial military commitment nor an ambitious policy of settlement, though conversions of native peoples to Christianity was a constant theme of their explorations.

But from the outset, the central thrust of the English approach to the New World lay in commerce, the desire for gainful trade made possible by minor fortifications, limited colonization and settlement, and mainly a desire for absolute control of trade in whatever valuables might be discovered. Great armies and navies were not put forward for this goal, nor was extensive exploration beyond North America's eastern coastline undertaken. Missionary work was important though in the end secondary to the main effort. The key is that the English New World and its riches were to lay essentially in private hands.

The difference between Spanish and English approaches to New World opportunity lay in their own histories. At the time of Spanish discoveries and conquest, that nation remained firmly committed to its centuries-old system of feudal monarchy. Wealth accrued to the monarch through a system of fealties that captured the nations wealth, amassing the capabilities of the state in a single regal institution. The purpose of New World conquest was to augment that feudal arrangement. But in England, feudalism was strongly on the wane, a new system of privately held capital institutions having percolated up to northwest Europe from earlier beginnings in the Mediterranean region [1]. By 1600, significant wealth lay in private hands, and the English monarchy, though by no means powerless at this point, nonetheless found itself increasingly beholden to a rising mercantile class.

So it was in 1606 that James I granted a charter to the Virginia Company, a collection of adventurers whose dual aspirations in about equal measure seemed to be advancement of the kingdom and their own personal gain [2]. The charter described a Virginia that covered much of the east coast of North America, from the northern edge of Spanish-controlled Florida northward to what is today mid-Maine. The original charter granted monopoly power to the Virginia Company for purposes of trade, but retained strong royal control of company affairs through a Virginia council, whose membership was appointed and strictly supervised by royal authority. The sharing of powers between company and council proved unwieldy, however, and a second Virginia Charter was instituted in 1609 consolidating greater power in the company itself. This arrangement held for the ensuing fifteen years until 1624. By that time, internecine strife within the company, weaknesses in Virginia colonization and trade, and significant losses from continuing low-grade warfare with the Powhatan Confederacy all combined to undercut the Virginia Company's position in England's larger expansionary interest. The company was disbanded, and Virginia, by then a reasonably well-established colony, was made over into a Crown colony, subject directly to the king's rule and supervised by the regular instruments of English national governance.

Through this period of Virginia Company rule, life in Virginia for its earliest settlers was difficult and dangerous, and little progress was made in creating profitable movements of Virginia's resources to the home country. Visions of Spanish-style success at wealth building quickly paled as one effort after another to produce something of value fell to the ground [3]. Settler survival was a recurrent issue, as was finding new devices to encourage investment and settlement. Lotteries were established in London, and company shares were put on an open market. Advertisements touting Virginia's sunny climate and bright future were put into play, and a Virginia lottery house was built in London to accommodate whatever attention it could garner [4]. Perhaps the most successful scheme of the company to induce settlement was the adoption of the "headright" policy, whereby every person paying either their own or another's way to Virginia gained entitlement to fifty acres of land. The measure proved so popular with all parties that it was continued by the Crown long after the demise of the Virginia Company itself. Ownerships of unclaimed headrights were assets in themselves, and headright claims often were traded among the owners for other valuables. Despite some fraud and inadequate accounting, much of seventeenth-century Virginia was populated under this arrangement [5].

As for Virginia trade, tobacco alone was shown to be profitable, and the "noxious weed" quickly assumed a central position in the colonial economy. Tobacco itself was used as a medium of exchange in company transactions in Virginia, given a shortage of specie. Perversely, this crop by itself was sufficient to ensure unsteady but real progress in land acquisition and settlement.

All efforts to show Virginia in a positive light to encourage investment came to a halt, however, following a devastating massacre of settlers in 1622, in which about 330 people died, nearly a quarter of Virginia's English-speaking population. Following the massacre, a scathing broadside written by Virginians was distributed in London, exposing the harsh conditions of life in Virginia and the company's unpreparedness to make improvements or to defend itself against enemies. The protest was worth the effort in that it led to a formal examination of the company's record. Shortly thereafter, in 1624, the Virginia Company of London was finally disbanded.

Yet despite Virginia's sometimes desperate condition and the company's inability to succeed unequivocally at trade and colonization, the colony did manage to grow, and land speculation and acquisition continued apace. The shape of later Virginia was significantly conditioned by the experience of the Virginia Company and by the people who endured and fueled such progress as Virginia could show. Some of those souls were family members, and they paved the way for their next generations.

Family in Earliest Virginia

Several persons named Sanders resided in Virginia from its earliest days when Virginia was a fledgling enterprise of the Virginia Company of London. Although we cannot pin down these Sanders precisely as to their family origins back in England or Wales, we can be certain that their names and Virginia activities were entirely within the minds of family members back home. The experiences of these Sanders of early Virginia, however briefly lived, shaped the imaginations of those back across the ocean, their excitements, their fears, even their own opportunities, and life prospects. Thomas Saunders, apprentice mariner of Bristol, would have been among the foremost to be captured by the lure of Virginia.

Undoubtedly, the first Sanders in Virginia was an unidentified person who accompanied Captain John Smith in Virginia during the initial days of Jamestown's founding, beginning in 1607. Smith explored the Chesapeake Region in 1609 and produced a detailed map, published in 1612, that records a place called "Sanderses Poynt" on the eastern shore of the Chesapeake. Who among the extended Sanders family might have been this early adventurer at Sanderses Poynt is unknown, but a reasonable guess is that he hailed from the Saunders of Derbyshire, because Joseph Saunders of that line opened a warehouse precisely at Sanderses Poynt in 1623 [6].

The first of the family in Virginia whose identity is known to us was Henry Spelman who, though not a Sanders by name, was a close relative of the Sanders of Ewell and Wales. Henry's father was Erasmus Spelman who was named after Erasmus Saunders of Tenby, Thomas's grandfather. Erasmus Spelman's mother was Erasmus Saunders' sister. Erasmus's brother Francis Saunders of Norfolk mentioned young Henry Spelman of Virginia in his will of 1613 [7]. Details of Henry Spelman's adventurous life in Virginia were well-known to the Saunders in Ewell, Norfolk, and Wales. Young Thomas Sanders would have counted him a cousin.

Henry Spelman was sent to Virginia in 1609 at the age of fourteen as punishment for some youthful indiscretion. Shortly after his arrival, he was taken by Capt. John Smith to an Indian encampment, an auspicious and perhaps too immediate beginning for Henry Spelman's career as Indian interpreter and local diplomat. In his first days, weeks, and months, Henry Spelman developed close relations with native leaders but all too quickly found himself snared in intrigue. In 1610, the powerful Indian chief Powhatan induced Spelman to convince colonists to engage in a trading expedition for desperately needed Indian corn. But trusting Spelman and following his instructions, thirty colonists in the expedition were slain from ambush by Powhatan's tribe. Fearing severe punishment, even hanging, from charges of betraying the colony, Spelman quickly fled north, taking up with Indians friendlier to the English. Spelman eventually did return to Jamestown, narrowly escaping yet another attack that took the life of a traveling companion. For Spelman, the lesson was clear, and it was learned repeatedly for the next decade. As an interpreter and reluctant go-between for cultures at war, Henry Spelman and other interpreters in his position were often useful but frequently mistrusted by both sides. A contemporary wrote that "we have sent boies (boys) amongst them to learn their language, but they return worse than when they went" [8].

By 1613, Henry Spelman had returned to England and wrote a personal memoir of his time in Virginia called *Relation of Virginia*. This piece, though not published until 1872, is said by historian Frederick Fausz to be "one of the most sensitive, intimate views of the Chesapeake Indians in the annals of English colonization" [9].

Spelman continued to shuttle between two worlds after his return to Virginia although his precise movements before 1619 are not clear. But by 1620, we find him in Jamestown, on trial against the accusations of another interpreter, an unscrupulous one at that, named Robert Poole. Poole claimed that Spelman spoke disparagingly of the Virginia governor in his meetings with native leaders. Spelman seems to have been exonerated of the claim, though he was spared not so much by direct evidence as by his continuing value in the colonial struggle against the Powhatans [10].

In 1623, Henry Spelman, by now called "Captain" Henry Spelman [11], just a year after the great massacre of 1622, led a trading expedition along the Potomac, to the north of secure colony lands. But again, he had been deceived by a promise of safe trade, and Henry with nineteen other colonists were slain in an attack involving about sixty Indian canoes. Their ship, the *Tiger*, narrowly escaped capture, carrying only four survivors. Henry Spelman died in the ambush, it was said, "because he presumed too much upon his acquaintance amongst the tribes of the region" [12].

Henry Spelman was not the only family member to perish at Indian hands. Fate dealt equally harshly with Lt. Edmond Sanders. Edmond came to Virginia before 1622, though his ultimate purpose there is unclear. His title of lieutenant suggests an appointment as subordinate of Capt. John Martin, who at that time was master of the ordnance in the colony.

Edmond lived at Martin's Brandon, a large estate on the south side of the James River above Jamestown owned by one of that era's most controversial figures. John Martin was a merchant tailor, a sea captain, and vigorous adventurer in Virginia enterprise. Martin's ambitions frequently put him at odds with Virginia Company policies regarding land acquisition, headright entitlements, cattle raising, and Indian affairs. His actions and opinions in fact provoked vitriolic responses by company members [13].

One of Martin's treatises written for the benefit of the Virginia Company was entitled "How Virginia May Be Made a Royal Plantation," a scheme to convert Virginia tribal areas under native rule into thirty-two shires corresponding to those of England in which English shire governments would supply manpower and support for their mutual relations and trade advantages. The suggestion was resented. Any endorsement of a plan such as Martin's was tantamount to an acknowledgment that the Virginia Company was not succeeding in its charter obligations. Martin further described how to capture the Indians in another work entitled "The Manner How to Bring the Indians into Subjection," a paper whose main point identified the need to avoid a tedious Indian war and develop profitable trade with them, thereby forestalling further acute shortages of supplies for the colonists and strained relations between these peoples. In Martin's words, "Reasons why it is not fitting utterly to make an extirpation of the savages yet. My reasons are grounded twofold. First upon Holy Writ and my own experience. Secondly other necessary uses and profits that may return by the same" [14].

An argument over land and cattle at Martin's Brandon in 1622 caused John Martin to return to England and to leave his cattle, the ownership of which lay in dispute, in the care of Lt. Edmond Sanders. But while Martin was in England, on March 22, 1622, a large Indian attack burst forth, resulting in the death of 330 settlers in Virginia. The massacre missed few areas in England's Virginia, and among the many casualties, including women and children, was Lt. Edmond Sanders.

Shortly after, Samuel Argall, a former governor and leading figure in Virginia, surveyed the destruction at Martin's Brandon, leaving an account of the scene of Lt. Edmond Sanders's demise. Argall had "certain news that the houses and all things else therein were burnt." Little besides "some small trompery" remained, "the Indians having carried away all other things as it should seem by their strewing of old chests and barrels about the field" [15].

Henry Sanders sailed to Virginia in 1623 aboard the Southampton, accompanying Abraham Piercey, a cape merchant to whom Henry was indentured. By 1625, Henry had reached the age of twenty years, and he resided at Piercey's Hundred in Virginia [16]. Nothing more is known of this Henry, save that he experienced a mutiny aboard the *Southampton* during his Atlantic crossing.

The *Southampton* originally had been instructed to sail to Virginia, then to Canada for a lading of fish, and from there to "Portucall, Biscay, or France" and then home to England. But Capt. John Harvey of the *Southampton* seems to have changed this plan en route, much to the displeasure of his crew and passengers. Struggles aboard the ship ensued, and the matter was thrown to an English court on their return.

In an ensuing inquiry, Captain Harvey claimed that Robert Guyar, the ship's master, and master's mate John White, "hath most pernitiously framed a mutynie or devision among the shipps company and hath been so impudent, yea, insolent, as to deliver into the hands of your said petitioner (by whose bread he liveth at all) of ther names, whose myndes he hath seditiously alienated from their duty, for the utter overthrowing of ye voyage." Guyar and White denied the accusation, explaining, "For muteny (if any be) Robert Guyar holdeth it to be against himself by Captain Harvey and his Confederates, that Harvey claimed he knew none of the ship to have command above him, esteeming himself Master and Commander" [17].

Although the final disposition of this suit is unclear, the cause of the conflict probably lay with Harvey since he destroyed invoices describing the ship's cargo as worth more than four thousand pounds sterling, and he erased the shippers' names upon its lading.

This *Southampton* mutiny demonstrates an important and persistent command flaw in seventeenth-century maritime commerce, a flaw that added immeasurably to the great risk of sailing in hazardous Atlantic waters. The ship's master, in this case Guyar, served as principal representative of the ship's owner and the specifically delegated agent for the ship's lading, both as regards carrying passengers and freight. His instructions from the owner were to deliver goods and passengers to predetermined destinations, there to conduct the business of sale and trade, and then to acquire goods and passengers for the return journey. On the *Southampton* in 1623, this was exclusively Guyar's business as ship's master, and John White was there to assist him.

A ship's captain or commander, on the other hand, hired the crew and made all final navigational decisions once underway. But precisely where a captain's authority ended and a master's began was always unclear. A captain's decision to take on additional passengers and goods to make free with wares on board or to change a port of call, such as Captain Harvey evidently did, jeopardized the master's ability to carry out his instructions on behalf of the ship's owner. As Guyar claimed, Captain Harvey in effect usurped his master's position. No clear means for deciding such disputes were available since these arose far from home, and legalities underwriting these separate authorities not widely observed. Under this system of dual empowerment, antagonisms such as those on the *Southampton* in 1623 were an inevitable, even predictable, outcome. As servant to an influential merchant on the *Southampton*, Henry

Sanders probably sided with Guyar and White; at least both he and Piercey managed for themselves a safe landing in Virginia.

Alexander Sanders arrived in Virginia in 1623 aboard the *Truelove*, a ship named for its owner Richard Truelove. Francis Lathbury, a close associate of London vintner and merchant Joseph Saunders (of whom more later), had once assumed responsibility for goods carried on the *Truelove*, a hint that Alexander Sanders was part of a London business association involving the Vintners Company and the Saunders. The name Alexander Sanders does not occur again in any records for the period, however, either in England or Virginia. Much the same is true for George Sanders, who lived at Archer's Hope along the James River in Virginia in 1623. At a later time, in 1653, a George Sanders lived in Barbados, though we cannot discern whether this might be the same person. Given the thirty years of separation in these records, this identity seems unlikely.

Rev. David Sanders, a name suggesting Welsh origins [18], lived at Hogg Island in the James River near Jamestown in 1623. There can be no mystery as to the reason for his coming to Virginia. From its earliest moment, the London-based Virginia Company saw need to furnish Protestant services to colonists far from home and to "propagate the Christian religion to such people as yet live in darkness and miserable ignorance of the true knowledge and worship of God" [19]. Yet the Virginia Company noted as late as 1619 that Virginia by then had eleven boroughs but not more than five ministers in all. A proposal therefore was advanced in the company to provide at least one minister for each borough. As an inducement to serve in Virginia, the company proposed to advance to each willing cleric one hundred acres of glebe land and six men as tenants to work this land. Rev. David Sanders was recruited under such arrangements, but the length or success of his Virginia service is unknown.

In London, Richard Sanders was apprenticed to Richard Lee in 1608 and by 1617 gained free admission to the London-based Vintners Company [20]. Before 1624, he took passage to Virginia aboard the *Francis Bonaventure* and at that date was living in the Main in Virginia. A year later, Richard was referred to as one of the governor's men at Pasbyhaigh and the Main, James City. At some point, he married a woman named Margaret. Richard died about 1636 at Neck of Land, a small spit of land near Jamestown, and Margaret shortly thereafter married William Morgan. Following the marriage, Morgan acquired land on the Chickahominy River, claiming fifty acres each for two headrights originally acquired by Richard Sanders that passed to Margaret on his death and then to Morgan through marriage [21].

The lives of these earliest Sanders in Virginia of course were far richer than we have been able to discover, but we know nothing more of their families or their Virginia experiences. Their contemporaries in England and Wales no doubt learned more as tales of the colony drifted back across the Atlantic, and many of the survivors in Virginia did return eventually to the home country. But in one particular instance of an early Sanders in Virginia, we learn a great deal more and in fact discover a main pathway by which numerous Sanders made their way to Virginia in later years. In terms of what we learn about family history, the story of Edward Saunders, not to be confused with the deceased Lt. Edmond Sanders, is by far the most important of these early Virginians.

Edward Saunders was born about 1595 in Charlwood, Surrey, and descended in the Charlwood line probably from a son of Thomas White Saunders [22]. He came to Virginia in 1619 at age twenty-four and resided there intermittently for nearly two decades. He may have returned to England about 1621 after an initial Virginia tour and returned to Virginia the following year. During his early Virginia years, Edward stayed both in the peninsular settlement at Accomack and on the mainland near Jamestown. Edward developed some familiarity with the entire colony, at least as far upriver as a place called Pasbyhaigh on the James River. His movement about the colony certainly would have brought him into some regular contact with Richard Sanders, not only because of some family relationship but because both were intimately involved in Virginia business interests of the Vintners Company.

Edward Sanders' first son, Thomas was born in England in 1622. If Edward was in Virginia in March that same year, he witnessed the great destruction and loss of life resulting from the lethal Indian attack on the colony. Many of his acquaintances and business associates were among the dead and injured.

Although he was not specifically enumerated as a resident in Virginia in a 1624 census, Edward was identified as a Virginia inhabitant during a legal inquiry in that year in London. The occasion was an investigation of a document produced by one Edward Waterhouse, a Virginian who drafted an indictment of conditions in the colony at the time of the massacre. In that inquiry, a Captain Butler elaborated on the colony's problems in a document called "The Unmasked Face of Our Colony in Virginia as It Was in the Winter of the Year 1622," read before a Privy Council in London. Edward Sanders was one of three persons named as Virginia residents at these proceedings, and Edward provided his mark signifying agreement with Butler's main message.

Edward probably returned to Virginia before his second son, Edward, was born in 1625. Edward also had another child, a daughter, but neither her name nor year of birth have been discovered.

Saunders Warehouse in Virginia

Edward's work required his regular presence in Virginia and frequent Atlantic crossings. As early as 1622, he had been joined in Virginia by a relative named Roger Saunders, called a mariner in one instance and a gentleman in another [23]. In time, Roger would serve regularly on a newly established Virginia Court, and he became a burgess in the colony's weak legislative authority. Together over the next decade, Edward and Roger assisted others in managing the lands and cattle of Lady Dale, the ex-governor's wife, and in establishing their own plantations.

Far more importantly, Edward and Roger Saunders collaborated to operate a colonial warehouse to facilitate some transatlantic trade. This warehouse was among the first, or even the very first, private commercial establishment in English America [24]. The exact site of this warehouse is not known, but it lay at the southern end of Accomack County on its Chesapeake side, near a place on today's maps called Cape Charles [25]. In 1609 this place, as previously mentioned, was called "Saunderses Poynt." This was also the location selected by Roger Saunders for his plantation in 1628, where his wife joined him after the plantation house was constructed [26]. This may be the first instance of a married couple named Sanders living together in the New World, if the marriage of Richard and Margaret Sanders was not.

The warehouse itself was part of a larger family scheme designed to profit from Virginia trade. Principal support for the Sanders warehouse at Accomack was supplied by Joseph Saunders, a well-to-do merchant, shipowner, and member of the Vintners Company of London [27]. Joseph was of the Saunders of Derbyshire, an offshoot of the Saunders of Charlwood. Joseph married Anne daughter of William Smith of Mitchum, Surrey. At one point, William Smith, probably Joseph's brother-in-law, joined Roger and Edward Sanders in Virginia, and he obtained land in Accomack near Roger Sanders in 1629. There is no evidence suggesting that Joseph himself ever traveled to Virginia.

THE SAUNDERS OF DERBYSHIRE

Thomas Saunders' excursion to Virginia in the 1640s reflected Saunders family interests in overseas commerce that began a generation or more before Thomas's time. All Saunders branches in one way or another found a role in extending England's global reach, exploiting emerging opportunities in the nascent English capitalist regime of the early 1600s. But from a family perspective, one branch of the Saunders in particular engaged international trade. They were the Saunders of Derbyshire. And within the Derbyshire line, one figure contributed most significantly to Virginia's early development; he was Joseph Saunders, merchant of London.

Virginia in its earliest days was a colony of the Virginia Company of London, a collection of wealthy investors operating under Crown sanction as a licensed monopoly. None but Company members could prospect in Virginia's future except by purchasing Virginia Company shares and hoping for Company success. But the Company failed in 1624 after seventeen years of struggle and Virginia thereafter became a Crown colony, subject only to the broad rules of trade that governed all commerce in England's economy, both at home and abroad. By a stroke of good fortune Joseph Saunders' early training in business ended in 1623, just at the time the Virginia Company collapsed, and his mercantile career began at the same moment that Virginia's new economic arrangement got underway.

Trade in earliest Virginia floundered in part because the colony lacked ports and commercial development. Ships arriving from England landed at individual plantations along Virginia's rivers, carrying goods consigned to individual colonists. What was missing was a center for collecting and distributing goods, a marketplace for exchange. Joseph Saunders' particular genius was to recognize this need and act upon it, establishing the first, or one of the first, private businesses in Virginia. Joseph built a warehouse at the southern tip of the Accomac peninsula, a strategic site where Chesapeake Bay enters the Atlantic Ocean. All shipping to and from Virginia passed this point. But just how Joseph acquired the entrepreneurial initiative, contacts, and resources to act on early Virginia opportunity is a question whose answer lies in his own family history.

The Derbyshire Saunders

In their earliest days, the Saunders of Derbyshire maintained close relations with the Saunders of Surrey, but they departed in significant ways from longstanding family patterns. Notably, they drifted away from the trenchant Roman Catholicism of the Surrey Saunders and frequently chose military over civilian careers. It may be the latter that ultimately fostered this family's concentration on international commerce.

The Derbyshire branch of the Saunders originated with a certain Thomas Saunders, whom we interpret to be a grandson, and not a son, of Richard Saunder of Charlwood, born about the year 1500. We think him the son of William Saunder who acquired property at Aston, Oxfordshire about 1500 and who raised his children there [1*].

Thomas first appears to us in 1522 in military service in Flanders. In that year Henry VIII sent an expeditionary force against France to help Spain defend the Low Counties, which Spain then controlled. Thomas served in this army under a certain Sir John Gresley of Derbyshire [2*]. On this occasion English forces besieged the walled medieval settlement of Montreuil-sur-mer, a town lying on the French border and guarded by a royal French castle. The siege failed, and we are told that a brother of Thomas died there, though his name is unknown [3*]. Thomas returned to England by 1524, taking up property at the Gresley estate of Lullington in Derbyshire [4*]. Whether this property came to Thomas for military service or from marriage is unknown, but the latter is more likely.

Thomas probably married into the Gresley family in the 1520s, perhaps to a daughter of Sir John Gresley, whose children were of Thomas's generation [5*]. Such a union accounts for Thomas's possession of Gresley property, gained in 1524 [6*], that remained in the family for generations. Thomas evidently also married a second time, having a child late in life [7*]. Evidence shows that Thomas maintained contact with his Charlwood roots; Sir Thomas Gresley of this same line married Katherine Walsingham whose aunt Alice had married Sir Thomas Saunder of Charlwood. But nothing more is known of Thomas, save than that he died in 1558 and rests at Lullington [8*].

Thomas's son, also called Thomas, was born in 1548, ten years before his father died. He eventually succeeded to the Manor of Lullington, probably through inheritance, and married Alice Toone of Clifton about 1575. Alice seems to have died in childbirth [9*], and Thomas remarried about two years later to Marjory, daughter of Peter Collingwood, she an heiress with properties in Staffordshire and Derbyshire [10*]. In his later years, Thomas could count among his holdings, besides Lullington, properties at Caldwell and Little Ireton in Derbyshire, and at Barton and Collingwood in Staffordshire. From his two marriages, Thomas had four daughters and at least five sons, their ages spanning nearly two decades.

The eldest son of Thomas Saunders of Lullington was named Collingwood Saunders, born in 1578. Collingwood inherited the Manors of Caldwell and Ireton, Derbyshire. He married Elizabeth, daughter and sole heir of Edmund Sleigh of Little Ireton, a London Vintner [11*]. Collingwood's elder sister Alice also married into this Sleigh family, to a Vintner named Richard. These marriages seconded existing ties to the Vintner Company found in the Saunders of Surrey [12*].

The Company of Vintners had ancient roots, having been founded as early as 1364, receiving at that time a grant of monopoly for wine trade with Gascony, including exclusive rights for purchasing English fish and cloth for export to Gascony. By the mid-1440s, wine constituted nearly a third of all England's imports, from which trade the Vintners built wealth and political power. By 1515, the Vintners were considered one of England's great twelve livery companies. Their influence ebbed and flowed after that, however, with steady erosion of its monopoly status. The great Fire of London of 1666 eventually destroyed the Vintners' Hall and several other Company properties, resulting in financial disaster [13*]. The Company's influence abated after that.

Collingwood Saunders acquired the coat of arms for his family, affirming its origins in the bulls'-heads arms of Charlwood and retaining its ancient family motto, but differencing these arms with a red rose on the shield. The Derbyshire arms illuminated the bright military career of Collingwood's son,

Thomas Saunders, called the "Celebrated Roundhead," who was knighted for his service to the Puritan cause under Cromwell [14*].

Another son of Thomas of Lullington was Major Henry Saunders whose family nearly encircled the globe. Henry captained the Cripplegate Ward Company, active during the English civil wars. In later years, Henry and two of his sons were silkmen, trading in imported cloth from Italy and afar. Another of Henry's sons named Thomas was a factor for the British East India Company. Thomas died at Bantam, a major port and trading center at the western end of Java in the East Indies, established by the British in 1603. Two other sons, George and Christopher, crossed the Atlantic and settled permanently along the Connecticut River in New England [15*].

A daughter of Thomas of Lullington, Katherine, married John Bloodworth, an opulent London dealer in Turkish goods. Their son, Sir Thomas Bloodworth, was admitted into the Vintner Company in 1645, knighted at the Hague in 1660, and became both Master of the Vintners and Lord Mayor of London in 1665. His performance on behalf of the City during the Great Fire of 1666, however, earned him no praise.

Joseph Saunders

Joseph Saunders was the youngest son of Thomas of Lullington, and he was as enterprising as all the others. Joseph's interest lay primarily in Virginia, and his effort there reflected his family's well-honed commercial talents. Born about 1598, Joseph apprenticed as a Vintner under Richard Sleigh, his sister's husband. He received Free Admission to the Vintners Company in 1623, providing him entitlements and contacts to pursue international trade, a pursuit he lost no time in engaging. Before the decade was out, Joseph purchased two ocean-going trading vessels, the *Flower de Luce* and the *Bonny Bess*, and opened three warehouses, one in London, another in Rotterdam, and the third in Virginia on that colony's eastern shore, a triangle of strategic commercial value. Joseph conducted his business in St. Mildred's Poultry of London, using the Three Cranes Inn as a place of meeting.

He held residential quarters in the Poultry, renting space to his brother Henry and Henry's son Daniel, and to John White, whom Joseph called his "brother." Joseph married Anne Smith of Mitcham, Surrey, and her brother William joined in Joseph's business dealings. William Smith traveled to Virginia in the 1630s and died there. Joseph contracted with a wine merchant named Norden to carry wine to Virginia, and imported Virginia tobacco both to Rotterdam, where terms of trade were usually advantageous, and to London for more than a decade. At one point he offered the *Bonny Bess* for sale to Leonard Calvert, Lord Baltimore, Governor of Maryland [16*].

Beyond trade itself, Joseph's mercantile ventures provided an avenue of Virginia settlement for many in his acquaintance, certainly including the Saunders of Charlwood and Gloucestershire and no doubt numerous others whom we have not positively identified. Edward Saunders of Charlwood worked for Joseph in Virginia, and Joseph's hand can be detected in the Vintner apprenticeship of Edward's son Thomas. A certain Roger Saunders, unidentified as to his English origin but called a burgess, gentleman, and mariner [17*], managed the Virginia warehouse, and Thomas Sanders of Gloucestershire evidently picked up the slack in the 1640s following the deaths of earlier partners. Joseph himself died in that same decade.

Joseph and other Sanders in the colony may have had another inducement to involve themselves in Virginia trade other than their own entrepreneurial spirit. A sense of duty to the national interest was in the air and rather nobly embodied in a distant relative. Sir William Throckmorton, knight and baronet, a heavy investor in the Virginia Company, had ties to the Saunders of Charlwood; his own son or nephew, another Sir William Throckmorton, married Dorothy Saunders of Charlwood, Surrey, and acquired the entire property there. The acquisition brought to a close more than four hundred years of Saunders residence at that ancestral home.

The elder Sir William Throckmorton brought a certain idealism to the Virginia endeavor, no doubt born of his education in the Middle Temple of London, an educational establishment dedicated to inculcating into their young students "ideals of public service, breadth of vision, and a national outlook" [28]. His desire to see the Virginia Company succeed extended beyond his own fifty shares in the company stock. He once "out of his own purse" sought to care for an Indian maiden suffering from "consumption" who had been brought to England by Sir Thomas Dale, the Virginia governor [29]. Throckmorton joined with three others in an early plan to build a town in Virginia, "to place preachers, build churches, schoolhouses, and such like works of charity" [30]. Later, this plan transformed into an idea for a large plantation. Throckmorton and the others eventually outfitted a ship and recruited thirty men for the venture [31]. Whether Throckmorton might have invested Joseph Saunders with his vision and enthusiasms, of course, remains unknown, but we recall that Edward Sanders assisted in managing the property of Lady Dale, the former governor's wife, who was a Throckmorton by birth [32].

Joseph Saunders owned two ships used for Virginia trade. One, an aging vessel of two hundred tons bore the interesting name, the *Flower de Luce* [33]. This was large enough to carry 130 to 140 passengers on a single voyage. But on one voyage, the aging *Flower de Luce* leaked so badly that the crew plugged the holes with beef to keep her afloat [34]. Joseph's smaller ship of fifty tons was called the *Bonny Bess*, which had sailed to Virginia by 1623 if not before. This ship Joseph eventually sold to a mariner, Richard Orchard, in Virginia. In the 1620s and 1630s, Joseph did business out of St. Mildred's Poultry in London, and his ships plied the waters between Virginia, Rotterdam, and London, often carrying "strong waters" and other supplies to Virginia, returning a cargo of tobacco to London, and occasionally to Rotterdam where profits sometimes excelled. Profits, though, were often elusive, in part because England placed stringent restrictions on how and where goods could be marketed, occasionally denying traders the opportunity to sell in Holland. Worse yet, obtaining marketable products from Virginia was fraught with difficulty. Joseph Saunders in one instance ventured two thousand pounds sterling for a single voyage and received back from his investment a shipload of rotten unmarketable tobacco [35].

Even finding a reliable captain and crew for his ships proved a challenge. Joseph hired a captain named Henry Weston for the *Flower de Luce*, a decision that landed all of them in court in later years. It seems on one voyage, Weston destroyed the ship's papers, using them to "light his tobacco" and casting others overboard, destroyed the merchants' marks on lading, and broke open passengers' trunks destined for the colony. Whether Joseph or others recovered damages from Weston's antics is unknown, but his business venture itself did carry on throughout the 1630s and into the 1640s.

Between about 1625 and 1635, activity at the warehouse involved importing goods such as linen and powder from England for colonists' use and amassing valuables for shipment to England and Holland. The bulk of the valuables were hogsheads of tobacco, but Roger Sanders collected wildcat skins and beaver hides as well. At one point, he ordered more padlocks for the facility, though whether these were needed for expanding business or simply improved security is not known. What is clear is that trade became sufficiently routine after the demise of the Virginia Company that hardships in the colony eased considerably.

Roger Sanders died about 1632 [36], and William Smith in 1636 [37]. Edward Sander seems to have managed Joseph Sanders' business affairs in Virginia after that. About 1635, Edward returned from England, escorting his daughter to Boston in New England [38] and his two sons, Thomas and Edward to Virginia at ages thirteen and nine aboard the *Safety*. Two years later, he shipped goods from England to the Virginia warehouse on the *Flower de Luce*. But in 1639, Edward and three of his coworkers in Virginia died aboard the *Flower de Luce* on a return journey to England [39], ending the tight working relationship of family members across the Atlantic that had lasted for nearly two decades.

The community of merchants and mariners at Accomack, united for a decade or more at least partly by their mutual interests in Saunders' trade, became after 1640 a nexus of Virginia connections for Joseph Saunders and his London trading contemporaries. Over the next generation, those in Accomack built upon earlier successes, seeing to the importation of new settlers including several Sanders and using these headrights for more Accomack land and newly settled lands in Virginia's coastal tidewater. But for all practical purposes, Edward's death ended the warehouse venture at Accomack.

Virginia eventually would hear again from Edward Sanders' young sons, but for their immediate well-being, the boys were returned to England after their father's death. Following the loss of all his longtime partners in Virginia, Joseph Saunders henceforth sought new partners in the colony. Not the least important of these, as we shall see, was Thomas Saunders, who by that time had become a well-established young mariner of Gloucestershire.

Thomas Saunders

While the Saunders in Virginia and England were organizing and carrying out their interests in transatlantic trade, young Thomas Saunders, son of Philip Saunders of Amroth, Wales, was beginning his apprenticeship in 1621 among the quays, warehouses, and ships of Bristol harbor under the watchful eye of Thomas's distant relative, John Mynne. At the age of fourteen and away from his own family, Thomas cannot have relished either his new surroundings or his enlarged responsibilities. Bristol was a far larger and more confusing city than anything he had experienced in Wales, and expectations placed on the new apprentice probably seemed burdensome and unjust.

Apprentices usually lived with their masters in some small quarters and served their masters needs not only in work but also in household chores. These multiple duties lasted from early morning until late at night. Apprentices usually came to know their adopted families well, and sometimes built relationships upon them. Thomas's master John Mynne had married Avis Cox in 1601 [40]; later events suggest that Thomas maintained good relations with the Cox family [41].

Thomas Saunders' formal mariner training was by mimicry; apprentices learned mainly by doing. The drudgery that Thomas experienced probably differed little from many on the docks, except that his master's treatment may have been fairer than other apprentices who had no family history to protect them from excessive expectations or punishments. In time, Thomas learned mariner routines and the underside of the shipping business, hiving about Bristol's waterfront in his blue coat so that all parties knew his business there [42].

On occasions, ships arrived at Bristol from distant places, strange sounding in name and exotic in detail, sources of new tales of an unfolding world. Thomas's geography was that of an unlettered but increasingly experienced young man. Merchant ships from the East India, Muscovy, and Virginia Companies brought tales and unfamiliar wares from afar, and news of mercantile gains and losses a long away from Bristol. Ships, passengers, and goods were lost at sea with alarming frequency, and that too would have imprinted Thomas's psyche and aspirations. But as Thomas tended John Mynne's affairs, his learning would have been directed mainly toward Virginia and the Caribbean, places that dominated Bristol's overseas portfolio and which presented the port's most immediate commercial opportunities.

Thomas served John Mynne as an apprentice for about four or five years until Philip Saunders, his father and sponsor, passed away [43]. How apprenticeship agreements were handled in such circumstances is not clear, but in this case, Thomas moved rather abruptly into a different apprentice arrangement. Within a year or so, he was serving under a new master in Bristol, William Roche (also Roach), who hailed from Wiston in Pembrokeshire, Wales. This apprenticeship evidently was arranged by Hugh Wogan of Wiston, whom Thomas's stepmother married after the death of his father. William Roche was a mariner also and no doubt held interests in Virginia. A relative, Edward Roche, possibly a brother, conducted business in Accomack throughout the 1630s until his demise there about 1638 [44]. Edward Roche's commercial activity in Accomack engaged merchants well-known to the Sanders on both sides of the Atlantic [45].

Losing his father at about age eighteen in a land not his home would seem to have devastated Thomas, and perhaps it did, but he was not without some family support. Not far from Bristol was the mariner community of Abbots Leigh, Somerset, which Thomas's father Philip called home when away from Pembrokeshire [46]. With Philip in Abbots Leigh lived Henry Saunders, also a mariner, who may have been a son of William Saunders, Philip's older brother [47]. Yet another mariner at Abbots Leigh was a different Philip Saunders, about the same age as Henry, whose origins have not been uncovered [48]. Being nearby, this mariner Saunders would have known of Thomas's apprenticeship and his father's death. For Thomas, they might have offered some sense of continuity in times of drastic change.

In 1628 at about age twenty-one, Thomas Saunders completed his mariner's apprenticeship under Roche and six months later was admitted to the liberties of the city of Bristol [49], a certification that Thomas was now prepared for active citizenry, having mastered a useful trade. Exactly what his business interests were at this point in Thomas's life is not clear, but at least part of his involvement was in cloth manufacture or sale. This pursuit evidently sprang from earlier family contacts going back to Wales. William Nicholas was a clothier of Bristol and frequently traded at Tenby during the 1580s and later [50]; he may have been a trading partner with Thomas's father. Indeed, it was intensive trade between Tenby and Bristol that fostered numerous contacts between these places. Relations built on trade inevitably produced tighter family linkages as well and new opportunities to migrate from the hinterland to the commercial center. All this may explain how, some years later in England, a younger William Nicholas became Thomas Saunders' lifelong friend, a trusted ally, and one suspects a business partner as well.

The clothiers, probably including the Nicholas family, played some part in inducing Thomas to move to Gloucestershire, the county to Bristol's immediate north. Gloucestershire had become a rising hub of English cloth making at this time [51]; and before the seventeenth century was over, the county became the center of England's textile trade. In this preindustrial era, however, clothiers' work was to service a woolen cottage industry scattered throughout the county, buying small bolts and bundles of cloth in various producing locations and marketing it for profit in the county's larger towns and cities. The work was not always benign. Some years after Thomas left Gloucestershire, the county erupted in riots and clashes between weavers and clothiers, mainly over clothiers' stringent weaving requirements and ungenerous compensation for the weavers' tedious labors.

It was in Gloucestershire that Thomas met Anthony Webb, a clothier of Wotton-under-Edge. Within a year of the time Thomas completed his apprenticeship, at age twenty-two, Thomas met and married Anthony Webb's daughter. Thomas Saunders and Elizabeth Webb were married in 1629 in a town called Kingswood near Wotton-under-Edge. Their wedding in December of that year occurred just one month after the recently deceased Anthony Webb's estate was distributed. Anthony Webb left Elizabeth one hundred pounds sterling [52]. Thomas Saunders thereupon began a life in Gloucestershire as a clothier in this highly productive region increasingly famed for its textiles, with Anthony Webb's reputation preceding him and with Elizabeth Webb's support and resources at his side.

THE FAMILY OF THOMAS SAUNDERS OF GLOUCESTERSHIRE

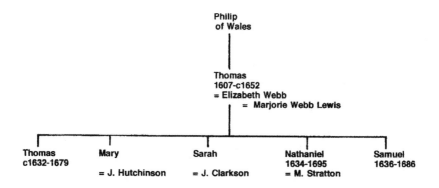

Source: Authors.

During the 1630s, Elizabeth Webb and Thomas Saunders had at least five children. They named a son Thomas, following the ancient tradition of echoing the father's name. A daughter was Mary, and another was Sarah, though their birth dates or birth order are not known. In 1634, Elizabeth and Thomas's son Nathaniel was baptized in Wotton-under-Edge; and in 1636, a son Samuel was born there. The names they chose for their children reflected just how far Thomas's life had led away from his Welsh origins. These were unfamiliar names in a Saunders family from Pembrokeshire, but Thomas was a new person in a new land, carrying less and less of his inherited identity as time went by. How Thomas and Elizabeth actually chose these latter names is cause for some curiosity. Neither name, Nathaniel or Samuel, can be found in the family of Anthony Webb or in any branch of the Saunders of Wales. We do not know their inspiration, but some tantalizing evidence suggests a hitherto unappreciated family link to a certain Nathaniel Saunders of Keynsham, Somerset [53].

There seems a richer story of how Thomas Saunders landed in Wotton-under-Edge, but an obscure one. Thomas's move may have been part of some limited family migration to Gloucestershire. As previously noted, no evidence in Wales identifies siblings for Thomas other than a sister Thomasin, who married and remained there. Nonetheless, we find a Rebecca Saunders marrying Thomas Osbourne in Wotton-under-Edge just a year before Thomas's marriage. In 1627, Sara Saunders married Henry Stokes in Tetbury, just eight miles away. More interestingly, in Wotton-under-Edge, a John Saunders married in 1638, naming sons Nathaniel, Samuel, and Thomas, a coincidence of naming sufficiently great to suggest close kinship with Thomas. It appears that Thomas accompanied some of his relatives to Gloucestershire, though their genealogy remains a mystery [54].

Sometime in the 1630s or 1640s as his own family was growing, Thomas Saunders acquired property in Berkeley, Gloucestershire, which became his family's principal residence after the children were born. The property comprised a house, outbuildings, and a garden [55]. But the family that Elizabeth and Thomas built did not endure. Elizabeth Webb died before the decade of the 1630s was out.

Following Elizabeth's death, Thomas remarried in 1640. His new wife was Marjorie Lewis of Tetbury, where Sara Saunders had married in 1627. Marjory Lewis's maiden name was Webb; she probably was a cousin of Elizabeth Webb. Marjory's family originally was from Deptford, Kent, but both she and her brother Giles Webb had resided in Tetbury for some time. Marjory and Thomas Saunders evidently had no issue, but Thomas's five or more children, then still quite young, no doubt lived with them.

Virginia Years

By the time of his second marriage, Thomas had reached the age of thirty-three years, and he had spent his adult years in Gloucestershire trade as a clothier. But this settled life was soon to be overtaken by larger events. By 1642, political and economic events in Gloucestershire and England had begun to push at the edges of Thomas's livelihood, and the pull of Virginia became increasingly irresistible.

Festering political and religious differences in England broke out into open hostility in 1642 between King Charles I and the English Parliament in what came to be called England's First Civil War. Military clashes broke out sporadically across England, though these were mainly skirmishes between small armies of the opposing forces, involving the citizenry and normal life only to a small degree. Few citizens felt the issues affected them greatly, and most were neutral, except when local circumstances compelled them to declare loyalties. Morrill explains the situation further, "Trade up the Severn (River, in Gloucestershire) was seriously affected by royalist occupation of Worcester and parliamentary occupation of Gloucester. Bad weather added to other problems to make the harvests of the later 1640s the worst of the century. High taxation and high food prices depressed the market for manufactures and led to economic recession" [56]. For the most part, those in commerce leaned toward supporting Parliament rather than the monarch [57], not least because Charles I had levied new taxes on ships to finance his position against Parliament.

If times at home had become trying for Thomas, they also offered new possibilities abroad. In London, Joseph Saunders of the Vintners Company had begun casting about for new contacts in Virginia, seeking to continue trade that was well begun with his Accomack warehouse. But with Edward Sanders' death in 1639, Joseph needed new colonial representation for his trading business, and for this purpose, he contracted with a certain Peter Knight of Virginia [58]. Peter Knight arrived in Virginia about 1638, residing at Accomack, and shortly thereafter amassed a sizable plantation on the James River. In 1643, Knight underwrote the costs of transportation for William Nicholas, Thomas Sanders' good friend, to come to Virginia and undertake trade there. Knight's engagement of William Nicholas on behalf of Joseph Saunders suggests that Joseph actively sought partners from the Bristol maritime community. It seems likely that Thomas Saunders traveled to Virginia a year before William Nicholas under a similar arrangement [59]. If so, he spent a year or two in Virginia before returning to England.

Whether or not Thomas visited Virginia earlier in the decade, he definitely committed to the colony very shortly after that. Thomas Saunders sailed to Virginia in 1646 under sponsorship of Joseph Croshaw. Using this and other headrights, Croshaw acquired land in a newly settled area at the head of the

York River, formerly called the Charles River, a large estuary to the immediate north of the James [60]. Thomas Saunders adopted this location as his Virginia home upon arrival. Along with Thomas on the 1646 voyage was William Smith, perhaps Joseph Saunders' nephew and son of William Smith of Accomack. Smith perished a year or so after arrival [61].

Thomas's years of preparation for overseas trade in cloth (and Joseph Saunders' wines?) had come to fruition, though his Virginia commitment meant a long separation from his family in Gloucestershire. For the remainder of the decade, Thomas engaged in the commerce that brought him to Virginia [62], selling English wares in the colony in exchange for exportable hogsheads of tobacco [63].

The Virginia of Thomas's time was not a comfortable place. Fischer describes it thus, "When Sir William Berkeley (a future Governor) reached Virginia in February 1642, it was a sickly settlement of barely 8,000 souls. The colony had earned an evil reputation 'that none but those of the meanest quality and corruptest lives went there.' The quality of life in early Virginia was more like a modern military outpost or lumber camp than a permanent society. Its leaders were rough violent men . . . The colony was in a state of chronic disorder. Its rulers were unable to govern, its social institutions were ill-defined, its economy was undeveloped, its politics were unstable, and its cultural identity was indistinct" [64]. Fischer might have added physical discomfort and early death as constant companions of these early Virginians.

Thomas's location along the York River was at the frontier of the Virginia colony, an area hotly disputed with local Indian tribes during Thomas's tenure there. Initial English settlement on the north side of the York River took place as early as 1642, but a fierce Indian attack in 1644 took the lives of 350 settlers in the region. A truce agreement was struck that ostensibly preserved land north of the York for Indian use, but English retaliation against Indians led to their removal from the area, and by 1649, settlers reestablished earlier claims and new settlement north of the York took place after September 1649. Thomas Saunders acquired his land at about this time, probably in 1650, land said to lie on Arracaico Creek lying north of the York, near the mouth of the Mattaponi River, part of a new land bonanza in that part of Virginia.

Most plots acquired by traders at that time covered about one hundred to four hundred acres. Thomas's plot probably amounted to four hundred or more acres, judging by the size of adjacent land holdings. Whether Thomas obtained his land as a personal homestead or more simply for tobacco production is not clear, but inadvertently or otherwise, Thomas's purchase in 1650 provided ready acreage for Virginia settlement by later family members, including some not yet born in Thomas's time. Thomas's sojourn in the colony thus provided an enduring Virginia legacy that benefitted his family for a half century or more.

Initial settlement in Virginia centered on the lower
Chesapeake. Earliest family properties there were Joseph
Saunders' warehouse at Accomac (early 1620s) and Thomas
Sanders' land on Arraciaco Creek (mid 1640s). "Sanderses
Poynt" in Accomac, identified by Captain John Smith in
1609, lay at the same location as Joseph Saunders' warehouse.
Locations shown here are approximate.

Between 1646 and 1648, Thomas is found moving among his new community in Charles River County. Some members of this community undoubtedly were known to him from the old country; others were new business acquaintances. But his contacts were of no small consequence as it turns out. This small Virginia community that Thomas helped build comprised friends whose descendants eventually intertwined with the Sanders. Edward Watkins, Thomas Harwood, and John Clarkson were Thomas's especially close associates. In time, Clarkson and Harwood had much to do with Thomas's children; and many years later, Thomas's yet unborn grandson would join the Watkins family in this part of Virginia.

We do not know whether Thomas ever returned to England. After 1650, he disappears from sight. Finally, we learn by 1653 that Thomas Saunders, a merchant of Berkeley, Gloucestershire, was deceased. Whether Thomas died in England, Virginia, or on an Atlantic crossing is not known, but he was in his early forties at the time of death [65].

Arranging Thomas's affairs in Berkeley fell to Thomas's friend and fellow Virginian William Nicholas, whose main responsibility was finding support for Thomas's wife and children. Thomas Saunders' wife of about a decade, Marjorie Webb Lewis Saunders, soon married a person named Cox, a family connected with Thomas's uncle John Mynne. By 1653, Thomas's children had aged nearly enough to join productive society. The eldest son Thomas was by then at least twenty-one and probably trained for a trade. Ann and Sarah were approaching marriageable age. The youngest sons entered apprenticeships, Nathaniel as a mariner and Samuel as a mercer, each reflecting their father's own background. And like their father, all of the children, except Samuel, eventually made their way to lands beyond Gloucestershire's horizon.

NOTES

1.   Fernand Braudel, *Civilization and Capitalism*, 3 vols. (New York: Harper and Row, 1984), vol. 2, "The Wheels of Commerce," makes this case.

2.   Wesley F. Craven, *The Virginia Company of London: 1606–1624* (Baltimore: Clearfield Press, 1957), p. 57.

3.   This was not for want of trying. Inventories of Virginia natural resources were compiled by the company, identifying the base for economic exploitation. Among the resources identified were animal skins (sables, otters, luzernes, martins, wildcats, fox, muskrats, and beaver), ship supplies (masts, cordage, pitch, tar, turpentine, rosin, wax, and various woods), and foodstuffs and spices (walnut oils, linseed oil, saffron, honey, alum, sweet gums, berries, and sarsa parilla). Of this last item, readers may recall a drink sold in fabled Western saloons

disparagingly called sasparilla, a soft drink not unlike root beer. See Susan Myra Kingsbury, ed., *Records of the Virginia Company of London*, 4 vols. (Washington DC: Government Printing Office, 1906–1935). See especially vol. 3, pp. 237–239.

None of these separately or as a collection comprised anything near what the colony sought or required as an economic base. For that reason, significant efforts were put forward to establish a silk industry. Books on the subject were sought and translated into English, silk houses were built in Virginia, French experts on silk making hired, native mulberry trees planted, and even a shipload of silkworms sent. Unfortunately, all the worms were dead on arrival, and the colony ultimately failed to make a go of this heroic effort. See Kingbury, *Records of the Virginia Company*, vol. 1, pp. 91, 309–310, 353, 422, 431–432; vol. 3, pp. 116, 301–302, 448, 661–663; and vol. 4, p. 143.

4.   Virginia Company lotteries were established at an early date, but irregularities in their accounting caused them to be examined in Chancery Court in 1619. One party to this examination was a person named Carew Saunders, or Matthew Carew Saunders, whom we cannot further identify, though the name Carew Saunders carries a certain Ewell aroma. The Company lotteries were discontinued following this examination. See Kingsbury, *Records of the Virginia Company*, vol. 1, p. 93; and vol. 3, pp. 44, 57.

5.   N. Nugent, *Cavaliers and Pioneers*, 3 vols. (Baltimore: Genealogical Publishing Company, 1957). See vol. 1, pp. xxiv–xxvi.

6.   J.M. Thompson, The Journals of Captain John Smith, National Geographic, Washington DC, 2007. We have no direct evidence that Joseph Saunders was somehow connected to this early Saunders figure, but an interesting coincidence occurs. While this early Sanders figure is linked to Captain John Smith, it also happens that Joseph Saunders married the daughter of a William Smith, and another William Smith—probably Joseph's brother-in-law—obtained land near Sanderses Poynt in 1629. Thanks are due to Nancy Sanders for discovering the existence of Sanderses Poynt.

7.   The 1613 will of Francis Saunders, Ewell, Surrey, is available in *Virginia Magazine of History and Biography* 15 (1907–8): 305–306.

8.   J. Frederick Fausz, "Middlemen in Peace and War: Virginia's Earliest Indian Interpreters, 1608–1632," *Virginia Magazine of History and Biography* 95(1): 41–64. See p. 64.

9.   Fausz, "Middlemen in Peace and War," p. 58.

10. Kingsbury, *Records of the Virginia Company*, vol. 3, pp. 174–175.

11. The basis on which Henry Spelman acquired the title captain is not clear because he had no history of maritime involvement, and he

evidently was not in a local militia. The title may have been a simple honorific for the responsibilities he bore, though he was formally stripped of the title in 1619 as punishment for speaking against the governor. See Kingsbury, *Records of the Virginia Company*, vol. 1, p. 310.

12. Fausz, "Middlemen in Peace and War," p. 58.

13. Seven company members in Virginia signed a complaint against Martin, using strong language to excoriate Martin to the London Company: "We have been ready to yield him all lawful favor for the settling of him at his plantation, which his own disabilities hath hindered. We cannot but praise your charity in forgiving and forgetting those many and foul injuries whereof he hath boasted, yet hold it our duties to inform you how much you are mistaken in him and what he hath retributed for so great a favor, being besides his many slanders, whereof we send you some particulars under oath, a sower of dissention and disobedience amongst us . . . the rather because, being a man of so light repute and credit in the Colony where he hath been so long discovered and known, we hope yet the venom that precedes him will produce no dangerous effect." See Kingsbury, *Records of the Virginia Company*, vol. 4, pp. 517–518.

14. Kingsbury, *Records of the Virginia Company*, vol. 3, pp. 704–710.

15. Ibid., vol. 4, p. 516.

16. Peter C. Coldham, *Complete Book of Emigrants* (Baltimore: Genealogical Publishing Company, 1987), 2 vols. See vol. 1, p. 50.

17. Kingsbury, *Records of the Virginia Company*, vol. 4, pp. 459–461.

18. St. David is regarded as the patron saint of Wales, and St. David's Parish in Pembrokeshire is proximal to the locations of several Saunders families in that area in the sixteenth and seventeenth centuries.

19. Craven, *Virginia Company of London*, p. 5.

20. "Register of Freedom Admissions and Apprentice Bindings for the Vintners' Company, 1602–1660," manuscript #15211/2, Guildhall Library.

21. Nugent, *Cavaliers and Pioneers*, vol. 1, p. 94.

22. That Edward descended from Thomas White Saunders (c1545–p1590) of Charlwood is unproven, and our incomplete Charlwood genealogy for that period may preclude identifying better possibilities. Genealogical information on Thomas White Saunders and the later Charlwood line is provided in the appendix.

23. We have been unable to identify Roger from English records either in terms of his home county or his relationship to Edward Sanders of Charlwood and Virginia or Joseph Saunder of London. The name Roger occurs with some frequency in various English lines, but none we have found match the life dates for Roger of Accomack. Records

for him are surprisingly extensive, given his early date of arrival in Virginia. See Peter C. Coldham, *English Adventurers and Emigrants, 1609–1660* (Baltimore: Genealogical Publishing Company, 1984); and vol. 1 in Beverly Fleet, *Virginia Colonial Abstracts*, 4 vols. (Baltimore, Genealogical Publishing Company, 1988).

24. This claim may seem extravagant but our search has yielded no evidence of other such establishments in Virginia, and this warehouse predates any such development in New England.

25. Attempting to track down the exact location of this warehouse produced a startling coincidence. In investigating modern maps for place-names in this location in Accomac, the name Bull Farm appeared at once. This name is stunningly reminiscent of the old Charlwood farm known as Bull Head Farm. Could Edward Sanders have carried this ancient family property name with him to Accomac? Alas, we found that Bull Farm in Accomack was named for the Bull family which held the property in the late nineteenth century.

26. Roger's plantation at Accomac seems the best clue as to the warehouse location.

27. Joseph supplied the capital in the form of ships and inventory for the warehouse, and he also provided staff for managing the trade at home in London. Some of these staff later migrated to Virginia, notably the Lathbury and Ellsey families.

28. Eric Gethyn-Jones, *George Thorpe and the Berkeley Company: A Gloucestershire Enterprise in Virginia* (London: Alan, 1982), p. 34.

29. Kingsbury, *Records of the Virginia Company*, vol. 1, pp. 338–339.

30. Ibid., vol. 3, p. 131.

31. Ibid., vol. 3, pp. 138–139; 212–215.

32. Gethyn-Jones, *George Thorpe*, p. 57.

33. The ship's name *Flower de Luce* perhaps was inspired by a Charlwood family property of the same name in Surrey. "Henry Leigh died seized of a house called the Flower de Luce . . . lying in the parish of St. Dunstan . . . (received) of the gift of Thomas Arundel, Knight, and Henry Saunders, as by deed (of 1549)." Calendar of Inquisitions Post Mortem (London: Stationery Office, 1955), pp. 88–89.

34. Coldham, *English Adventurers and Emigrants*, p. 79.

35. Ibid., p. 76.

36. Following Roger Sanders's death, some ungentlemanly folk in Accomack traded bets on whether the widow Sanders would marry William Burdette. See Fleet 1988, vol. 1, p. 7. It seems she did, as Burdette soon thereafter acquired Roger's plantation. See Nugent, *Cavaliers and Pioneers*, vol. 1, p. 121.

37. Fleet, *Virginia Colonial Abstracts*, vol. 1, p. 37.

38. Lacking information on the age or name of Edward's daughter makes it difficult to guess whether she was taken to New England for a betrothal or to place her with guardians. One gets the sense that Edward brought all of his children across the Atlantic about 1635 because conditions at home made it impossible to leave them there. Perhaps his wife died. It seems likely that his daughter was underage and that he left her in New England to live with relatives. Numerous persons named Sanders migrated to New England about this time.

39. Fleet, *Virginia Colonial Abstracts*, vol. 1, p. 62. This record incorrectly identifies the victim as Edmond rather than Edward Sanders. Careful examination of additional records, however, reveals that other persons in this same record, namely Searchfield (Joseph Saunders's accountant) and Dodsworth were business associates of Edward in Virginia. We have seen the loose interchanging of the names Edmond and Edward in records of the Saunders at Charlwood, and note that these two names appear almost identical in the original old-style handwriting.

40. The marriage of Avis Cox to John Mynne is recorded in an Internet listing of the Church of the Latter Day Saints.

41. After Thomas Saunders's death, his second wife, Marjorie Webb Lewis Saunders, remarried into the Cox family.

42. David H. Fischer, *Albion's Seed: Four British Folkways in America* (New York: Oxford University Press, 1984), p. 357. Fischer explains, "In the seventeenth century, English servants and apprentices commonly wore blue. 'Blue cloaks in winter, blue coats in summer,' wrote Alice Morse Earle, 'Blue was not precisely a livery; it was their color, the badge of their condition in life, as black is now a parson's.'"

43. The exact date of Philip's death is not known. Only two pieces of evidence are available to estimate this date. First, Thomas's apprenticeship was interrupted sometime between 1622 and 1627, perhaps by the death of Philip. Second, Philip's wife Alice Edwards evidently remarried during this apprenticeship, before 1628.

44. Fleet, *Virginia Colonial Abstracts*, vol. 1, p. 71.

45. Ibid., vol. 1, pp. 15, 33, 55. These records contain references to persons named Hort and Pettit. The name Hort is associated with mariners named Saunders in Abbots Leigh, Somerset, and the Pettit family later rendered assistance to Edward Sanders's sons.

46. For purposes of contracting the apprenticeship, Philip Saunders identified himself as a mariner of Abbots Leigh. This does not preclude his retaining his principal residence in Amroth.

47. This Henry Saunders of Abbots Leigh was a shipwright, born about 1595, dying in 1665. Henry may have been the son of William Saunders, son of Erasmus, and brother of Philip, of Pembrokeshire. Francis

Green noted that William's son Henry went to England. Henry was too old, however, to have been the Henry who served under Abraham Piercey in Virginia. In his 1660 will, witnessed by John Horte, William Browne, and Liddi Horfrenton, Henry Sanders left "to my son John Sanders all my wearing apparel, one table board, one feather bed that the maidens do lye upon." Holy Trinity, Abbots Leigh Parish Registers, Burials, 1656–1567.

48. Philip Sanders, a mariner of Abbots Leigh wrote his will, witnessed by Arthur and Thomas Maskall, in 1662. He left "to my daughter Frances Hort one shilling in money as a token and my best cot; to my grandson John Jones a bedstead, bed and bolster and a cupboard and stools; and the rest and residue to my grandchild Martha Jones whom I make sole Executrix." Philip died in 1665. Holy Trinity, Abbots Leigh Parish Registers, Burials, 1656–1567. Note that the name Hort also appears in the Will of Henry Saunders of Abbots Leigh as well as in early Accomack County, Virginia.

49. The exact meaning in 1628 of being "admitted to the Liberties of the City of Bristol" is not clear, but the event marked the end of Thomas's apprenticeship with appropriate entitlements for his new station in life.

50. Welsh Port Books, 1570 to 1603.

51. The historian Fernand Braudel, in the first volume of his Civilization and Capitalism trilogy, entitled *The Structures of Everyday Life*, argues that three material necessities for human survival—food, clothing, and shelter—have not yet been met by the world economy. Only efforts at clothing the world's people can be said to have succeeded. That success in no small part stems from heavy capital investment in the cloth industry in the sixteenth and seventeenth centuries, particularly in England, and even more particularly in west England. To have worked as a clothier in Gloucester in the seventeenth century is to have toiled on a brighter side of history.

52. Kingswood Marriage Register, 1628–1638, and Prerogative Court of Canterbury, Wills, 1620–1660.

53. Nathaniel Saunders of Keynsham, Somerset, is found in Somerset records for the period. Keynsham itself is not far from Bristol, and Nathaniel was contemporary with Thomas's father Philip, suggesting that he could have been in position to support Thomas as occasions required. Nathaniel Saunders of Keynsham married Edith, daughter of Samuel Weaver, in 1602, and sometime following this marriage acquired property in Tetbury, Gloucestershire. If Thomas named his son after this Nathaniel, it follows that he could have adopted the name Samuel for his younger son after Samuel Weaver. In Virginia during

the 1630s and after, Samuel Weaver is found in close proximity with the Sanders there.

One name found in sixteenth-century Keynsham preceding Nathaniel is Richard Saunders, perhaps Nathaniel's father. This is grounds for suspicion that Nathaniel's family might descend from Richard Saunders, son of Erasmus Saunders, who was executor of the will of Francis Saunders in 1613. If all of this were correct, then Nathaniel would have been Philip's first cousin. None of the above is proven, however, and is offered here as a starting point for future research.

54. Francis Green, the authoritative turn-of-the-century Welsh genealogist, labeled among his Saunders papers a section called Saunders of Tetbury (Gloucestershire), though these papers themselves provide no description of Saunders having left Wales for that destination. Yet it seems improbable that Green would have adopted this label without some evidence of precisely the migration to which we refer for the 1620s and 1630s. On the other hand, the names Sara and Rebecca are not found among descendants of Erasmus Saunders in Wales, and so a point that these may not be sisters of Thomas is well taken.

55. Gloucester Record Office: D2957/P630 (41 [34])—Berkeley, Glos. 1665 Deed (in Latin). The sense of this record seems to be that Thomas owned one property, consisting of a messuage (dwelling house and outbuildings) and a garden, even though the record itself actually describes two such properties.

56. John Morrill, "The Stuarts," *The Oxford Illustrated History of Britain*, ed. K. O. Morgan (Oxford: Oxford University Press, 1984), p. 320.

57. Ibid., p. 318.

58. Coldham, *English Adventurers and Emigrants*, p. 86; also Nugent, *Cavaliers and Pioneers*, vol. 1, p. 166.

59. Nugent, *Cavaliers and Pioneers*, vol. 1, p. 131. This record states that a headright for Thomas Sanderby was claimed by William Barnard in 1642. This could be an error because the name Sanderby cannot be found in Virginia after 1642, although an earlier instance of a 1635 migrant to Nevis of the name Thomas Sandby can be found. Instructively, William Barnard acquired land adjacent William Tookey, a family with whom Thomas's son had close dealings in later years. Even more significantly, the Barnard family in 1647 rented land on the Charles River from an early settler there, William Prior. Thomas Sanders later would witness the execution of William Prior's estate and himself take up lands near Prior's original plantation. Prior's daughter married a Thomas Edwards, perhaps a relative of Thomas Sanders's stepmother, and this Edwards held the Prior plantation that the Barnards eventually rented. Taken together, these facts argue

that Barnard's headright claim for Thomas Sanderby was in fact for Thomas Saunders.

60. Nugent, *Cavaliers and Pioneers,* vol. 1, pp. xxxiv and 166–167. Croshaw's land was in Charles River County. The Charles River itself, named after the monarch, was hastily renamed York in 1642, a political bow to Parliamentary sensibilities during the first civil war in England. Charles River County was renamed York County in 1642 and relabeled again as Gloucester County ten years later.

61. Fleet, *Virginia Colonial Abstracts,* vol. 3, pp. 69, 109.

62. Numerous records for Thomas Saunders for the period 1646–1648 are sprinkled through York County records in Fleet, *Virginia Colonial Abstracts,* vol. 3, pp. 49–98, and records pertaining to his land can be found in Nugent, *Cavaliers and Pioneers,* vol. 1.

63. Thomas was required to master knowledge of tobacco in order to trade legally and successfully. Not all tobacco produced in Virginia was considered exportable. Special safeguards were put into place to protect the reputation of Virginia's tobacco, and punishments were exacted for those who jeopardized the scheme. As an example, in 1656, Michaell Fletcher removed good tobacco from hogsheads and substituted tobacco stalks and dirt. Tried and convicted of this offense, Fletcher was ordered for an hour each day for a year to stand on the courthouse steps and display the following message on the front of his hat, "Behold and Beware by My Example How Ye Cheate and Abuse Tobb'o Already Rec'd." Fleet, *Virginia Colonial Abstracts,* vol. 3, p. 162.

64. Fischer, *Albion's Seed,* p. 210.

65. No will or estate administration has been found, either in England or Virginia. As a property owner in Berkeley, Thomas's estate would have been treated in the courts had he died there, so one suspects the lack of documents indicates a death overseas. Few wills have survived from those early days in Virginia.

NOTES FOR THE SAUNDERS OF DERBYSHIRE:

1* The beginning of the Derbyshire line is less certain than most genealogists imply. All accounts suggest that the original migrant to Derbyshire was Thomas Saunders, claimed to be the seventh son of Agnes Courtenay and Richard Saunders of Charlwood. As their son, he must have been born before 1480. Thomas died in 1558, thus making him nearly eighty years old at death. And as his son was born in 1548, Thomas would have been nearly seventy at his birth. A further awkwardness exists. Thomas's military involvement in 1522, prior to his marriage and acquisition of property, would have occurred in about his forty-fourth year, near the end rather than the beginning of a military career. These and other claims about this Thomas are available in J. E. Sandars, *The Sandars Centuries* (Henley, Oxfordshire: Mercers Solicitors, 1971), p. 33.

Statements concerning the time of Thomas's birth and subsequent life events rest ultimately on the documented *Visitation of London of 1633*, which mimicked an earlier *Visitation of Derby* in 1611 and 1614. In this visitation, Edmund Saunders of Charlwood attested that Thomas was Richard's son. But Edmund was describing events that occurred nearly a century and a half before his time, as Richard was his great-grandfather. We are loath to question original records, but Edmund simply may have been wrong. Taken as a whole, a better interpretation is that Thomas was born later than this record allows. As records for Richard of Charlwood indicate the existence of a hitherto unknown son William, born about 1475, a useful guess is that Thomas was a son of this William, and thus Richard's grandson, born around 1500. This interpretation accords with facts ascertained for the origins of the Saunders of Aston, described elsewhere.

The matter is not closed. What we suggest here is the need for a reexamination of existing records and a search for more. Our statements here are meant to reflect apparent but not final conclusions.

2* Sandars 1971, p. 33. At one point Sandars incorrectly identifies this Gresley military figure as William rather than John.

3* Sandars, *The Sandars Centuries*, p. 2.

4* Ibid., p. 33.

5* We have not been able to identify the children of Sir John Gresley by name, but they were part of the Gresley's of Drakelow, Derbyshire, whose genealogy is otherwise well documented.

6* Sandars, *The Sandars Centuries*, p. 33.

7* Thomas's son was born in 1548 when Thomas was nearly fifty years old or, if we accept other published versions, when he was seventy.

8* Thomas's death is given as 1558, which may exclude him as a candidate for the death of (another?) Thomas Saunders in 1557. One hopes so. A Captain Thomas Saunders was executed in 1557 for his part in a plot to capture Scarborough Castle. Thomas and co-conspirators were beheaded, drawn and quartered, and finally boiled, and their heads mounted on bridge and gate posts. No doubt their evil was thoroughly expunged. All this is detailed in the *Diary of Henry Machyn, Merchant Taylor, 1550–1563*, pp. 81–82, 134–137.

9* His daughter Alice, born in 1576, evidently issued from his first marriage to Alice Toone.

10* The Staffordshire Historical Collection, vol. 5, part 2, pp. 259–262. The collection provides an annotated reproduction of the *Visitation of Staffordshire of 1614 and 1663–1664.* Included is a genealogy for the Sanders of Barton-under-Needwood and also the Sanders of Little Ireton in Derby. They explain the Saunders' marriages this way, "Thomas married Alice Toone and had a child in 1576... Peter Collingwood had a wife Alice who was mother by a previous husband of Thomas Saunders de Lullington. It would therefore appear that Peter Collingwood married the widow of Thomas Sanders, senior, and that Collingwood Sanders was the son of her son Thomas by Alice Toone." But why would Alice Toone and Thomas Saunders name a son Collingwood unless Collingwood was actually his mother's name (from a second marriage for Thomas)? That would be the case if Thomas had actually married Marjory Collingwood, daughter of Peter, a notion that makes particular sense because Thomas eventually acquired Peter Collingwood's property in Staffordshire. On these grounds, we have suggested that Alice Toone did not survive long after bearing the daughter Alice and that Thomas remarried about 1578. As before, we believe this matter requires further research, and our suggestion of two marriages for Thomas cannot be thought a firm conclusion.

11* Sandars, *The Sandar Centuries*, pp. 33–34.

12* William Saunders of Surrey acquired interest in the Three Crowns Inn from the Carews in the mid-1440, and this may have initiated a family association with the Vintners Company as this inn passed through several generations of Surrey Saunders. William Saunders of Ewell married into the Gittons family, who were vintners.

13* Vintnershall.com.

14* Sandars provides an interesting biographical sketch of this Sir Thomas Sandars. See Sandars, *The Sandar Centuries*, pp. 34–41. A "roundhead" was a familiar term applied to Puritans because they wore their haircut short.

15* Henry married Susanna, daughter of Christopher Alleston. The Allestons equally may have been involved in international trade. At least two persons of that name were present in Virginia in the 1650s; see N. Nugent, *Cavaliers and Pioneers*, vol. 1 (Baltimore: Genealogical Publishing Company, 1983), pp. 255, 315.

16* Facts about the life and business of Joseph Saunders are adduced largely from the accounts given in P. W. Coldham, *English Adventurers and Emigrants.*

17* For details on Roger Saunders of Virginia, see Fleet, *Virginia Colonial Abstracts*, vol. 1.

Chapter Nine

Bristol

Nathaniel Saunders rose as a phoenix from the ashes of his own feudal ancestry and built a different world of family, work, church, and community. The medieval trappings of the Saunders family of Gloucestershire had nearly evaporated with Nathaniel's father. This son of a Gloucestershire and Virginia tradesman emerged, inheriting little of privilege and expectations that his forebears routinely received. Nathaniel's advantages lay in his own capacities, his wit, and his skills. Among the family we are describing, we can say Nathaniel Saunders was perhaps the first among modern men.

In our family history, Nathaniel Saunders' life marks the point in time where within a single person *gesellschaft* replaced *gemeinschaft* as a dominant theme in personal existence [1]. From this point forward, Nathaniel would have to construct his life for himself, being both advantaged and burdened by an abundance of personal freedom. He inherited no title and little property, but also few expectations in service to old traditions.

Nathaniel's personal freedoms, such as they were, by no means derived from any sort of broad renaissance in English society; rather they emerged from an accident of birth placing him apart from traditional kinship support. Medieval feudalism was indeed on the wane and even on the run with the onslaught of new mercantile and parliamentary successes. Cumulative changes in social, political, and economic sectors were slowly eroding the base of ancient English culture, but modern society as we know it today by no means had overtaken the older order. Nathaniel Saunders inherited a society that still took most of its cues from an older, unforgiving world. This meant that ancient but faltering feudal social, economic, and political institutions remained stubborn facts in Nathaniel's life, and they circumscribed the opportunities that he could seize for himself.

A Father's Son

Nathaniel was baptized in 1634 in Wotton-Under-Edge, probably the third child and second son of Elizabeth Webb and Thomas Saunders, and he lived his early days there. He had siblings: Thomas, who seems the eldest, Mary, and Sarah, and a younger brother by two years named Samuel [2]. Sometime during the 1630s, the family moved to Berkeley in Gloucestershire, just a short distance north of Wotton-under-Edge, a new location upriver on the Severn more conducive to Thomas Saunders' maritime trade. His mother died before 1640 when Nathaniel was no more than five years old, and in 1640, his father married Marjorie Webb Lewis. The children evidently lived in Berkeley with their stepmother throughout the 1640s while their father worked in Virginia [3].

By 1648, Nathaniel's father Thomas had been in Virginia for two years or more, and Nathaniel, like so many his age of fourteen, probably entered an apprenticeship for a trade akin to his father's. Although no record of an apprenticeship has been uncovered, we can surmise from family history that Nathaniel's father enjoined a commercial ally in the Bristol-Gloucestershire maritime community on behalf of his son. Thomas Harwood, mariner and Virginia contemporary of Thomas Saunders, is a likely candidate for such sponsorship [4].

When Nathaniel was about eighteen years old, about 1652, word came through William Nicholas that Thomas Saunders, the absent father that Nathaniel cannot have known very well, was dead. His father before him experienced exactly the same trauma and disruption that Nathaniel now faced, and the original apprenticeship that his father once underwrote unraveled before his eyes. But William Nicholas fairly soon arranged another, and Nathaniel at age nineteen began his second apprenticeship, this time with Thomas Stratton, a Bristol mariner, and Mary his wife [5]. This agreement began a relationship with the Stratton family that lasted Nathaniel's entire life.

Into Adulthood

Thomas Stratton was part of a Bristol family that had strong ties to Virginia. A Joseph Stratton dwelled in Virginia as early as 1628. A different Thomas Stratton was in Accomack County as early as 1634 [6], and John and Henry Stratton were situated in other parts of Virginia's tidewater by the late 1630s [7]. Joseph Croshaw, who in 1646 acquired the headright for Thomas, father of Nathaniel Saunders, a year later claimed Richard Stratton's headright [8]. Though the relationship between Richard Stratton in Virginia and Thomas Stratton of Bristol is not established, the Stratton family produced a large number of shipbuilders who served Bristol maritime needs for over a century, and one can easily imagine busy communication between these members of the same nautical family.

Nathaniel Saunders served his apprenticeship under Thomas and Mary Stratton for probably not more than two or three years, perhaps until 1656. After that, he seemed to have taken up trade immediately, though we find only a single instance of Nathaniel's work following his apprenticeship. In 1658, Nathaniel acquired an indenture of one Theophilus King, an agreement for seven years of King's labor in Barbados [9]. But five months after signing King's indenture, he sold the contract to William Tuckey, a merchant whose colonial family was instrumental in bringing Saunders relatives to Virginia in 1664 [10]. Thus in a single instance, we find Nathaniel looking outward to the Atlantic, with one eye on the burgeoning sugar trade in the Caribbean and the other on Virginia's tobacco.

In these days following his apprenticeship, Nathaniel operated with less than a free hand. It may be recalled that Nathaniel's father Thomas was granted admission to the liberties of the city of Bristol just a few months after completing his apprenticeship with William Roche Yet no such reward was visited upon Nathaniel, who would have to wait years to receive this privilege. Good reasons can be cited for the delay, resting as they did on a greatly unsettled England at this time of Nathaniel's young life.

Monarchic power had been a deep fact of English governance from as early as the Norman Conquest nearly six centuries before, and it had endured a variety of challenges over its long history, albeit with modest changes. The most successful challenge to monarchy actually arose during Nathaniel Saunders' lifetime. Nathaniel was but eight years old when the First English Civil War began in 1642. Events in the war generally were not momentous; one doubts whether Nathaniel would have remembered or felt much of it by the time warfare ground to a halt in 1646, though Gloucestershire was one of the most fought-over regions. Popular feeling generally favored peace over either royalist or parliamentary forces [11]. But following its limited victory in 1646, Parliament positioned itself for greater authority, much to the dissatisfaction of ordinary citizens. Armed resistance to Parliament and its military rule rose in the counties, giving rise to the so-called Second Civil War [12]. Parliament again held sway however, and King Charles I was eventually executed in 1649. The fall of Charles I was especially significant because his execution was state-sanctioned, the first time in English history that a monarch was deposed in that fashion. Even more significantly, the collapse of the monarchy sent royalists scurrying for cover, many of them leaving for Virginia to find new positions of privilege and authority. The resultant "cavalier" immigration colored Virginia's history thoroughly and indelibly [13].

An English republic was born. From 1649 to 1653, Parliament ruled England directly but somewhat unsuccessfully. In 1653, Parliament declared Oliver Cromwell to be lord protector and head of state, ushering in an era of Puritan rule under a singular titular head.

Nathaniel Saunders was by then nineteen years old and nearly ready to take his place in the larger world of commerce. But Cromwell had placed military supervisors in charge of local jurisdictions, and these "major generals" interfered in every aspect of local government [14]. Nathaniel's instatement into Bristol citizenry would have to wait for local government to find its new bearings. Nathaniel, as other tradesmen, probably swore the oath of allegiance to the new Commonwealth, a Cromwellian foil against insurrection in a time of uncertain authority and unpopular Puritan austerity. The Cromwell era lasted until 1660, when at last a chastened monarchy was reinstated with Charles II as king. Shortly thereafter, Nathaniel was finally admitted to the liberties of the city of Bristol as life returned to normal.

Beginnings

In spite of Thomas Saunders' premature death around 1650, the sons and daughters of Thomas Saunders of Gloucestershire were left with modest means to begin their adult lives. We have no record of a will or estate administration for Thomas, but subsequent records make clear the sons inherited Thomas's property. The youngest son Samuel evidently received some property at Wotton-under-Edge and in time became a successful mercer there. He married a woman named Catherine and in the 1680s acquired additional land, forming an estate called Upton Grove that remained in his own family for some years [15].

Nathaniel, the middle son, whose life we follow here, became owner of the family home at Berkeley, which seemed to have consisted of two messuages with gardens. He held this until 1665, selling the properties to Giles and Ursula Machin and to William and Alice Margretts [16], the sale providing means for Nathaniel's new home in Bristol.

Thomas, Nathaniel's older brother, traveled to Virginia to take possession of his father's land in Gloucester County. Their father Thomas died before 1653, but references to "Thomas Saunders' land" appear with some regularity throughout the 1650s. Thomas's original land claim has not been found. From records of adjacent properties in the period, we deduce that Thomas Saunders' land lay on the north side of the Mattaponi River and upon a creek or swamp called Arracaico (also Arakeyaco and similar spellings), today known as Burnt Mill Creek. Thomas's land lay first in Charles River County, then Gloucester, and then New Kent, as the county name evolved.

The decade of the 1650s provides an availing history of Thomas's property. In 1654, at least two years after Thomas Saunders' death, a Virginia patent was granted to Toby West for land on the northern boundary of Thomas Saunders' land in Gloucester County. In 1659, West's holding was sold to Joseph Croshaw, the same person who originally owned Thomas's headright. Separately, in 1655, John Hudson (Hodson, Hodgson) and John Garrett jointly claimed land at the "southmost corner" of Thomas Saunders' land, also lying upon Arakeyaco Swamp.

Not long after, in 1658, Hudson and Garrett passed their land to Nathaniel Bacon, uncle of the famed rebel. By the end of the decade, then, we can identify a single property lying in Thomas Saunders' possession on Arracaico Swamp, abutting the land of Joseph Croshaw on the north and Nathaniel Bacon on the south. But what is not certain is whether these records of "Thomas Saunders' land" taken from the 1650s describe the father or the son [17]. At issue simply is exactly when Thomas's son Thomas took up Virginia residence.

This son Thomas, Nathaniel's brother, did travel to Virginia and make a home there, at least temporarily. He evidently lived on the Arracaico land of his father, though at some point he also acquired a parcel of land slightly larger than forty-three acres on a creek called Assatians [18], this lying upstream along the Mattaponi not far from his father's original land patent. A forty-three-acre parcel of land is typical of many headright grants, and so it may be that Thomas paid his own way to Virginia. But Thomas's headright seems also to have been claimed by a group of investors in Mattaponi lands in 1665 [19], suggesting that Thomas may have journeyed to Virginia on more than one occasion. In any case, Thomas held his smaller parcel of land until John Lane acquired the forty-three acres "purchased of Thomas Saunders" sometime before 1675, about the time that Thomas left Virginia for good. The size of this acreage and the timing of its sale suggests that Thomas gave this land in exchange for passage back to England or to Barbados [20]. Thomas later surfaced as a planter in St. Philip's Parish, Barbados about 1675. Both his sisters lived there by that time, and his brother Nathaniel visited that island several times in the decade of the 1670s.

Thomas, Nathaniel's brother, married a woman named Elizabeth probably during the 1660s, but little more is known of her, save that she bore a daughter and a son [21]. Mary Saunders, sister of Nathaniel, married John Hutchinson, probably in England. Scant evidence suggests Hutchinson may have visited Virginia, perhaps briefly as a mariner, but he seems never to have lived there. In later years, these Hutchinsons are found in Barbados.

Sarah Saunders, the other sister, married John Clarkson, a marriage somehow resulting from a particularly close association between John Clarkson and Thomas Saunders, Sarah's father, in Virginia. Clarkson acquired land in Charles River County in the 1630s before Thomas Saunders arrived there, and the two were near neighbors and joined in business transactions in the late 1640s. Because Sarah's age in uncertain, we cannot guess when she married John Clarkson, but her husband was clearly of her own generation since he survived beyond 1682. While the marriage would seem to have resulted from an agreement or encouragement from their two fathers, this might not have been precisely the case. Sarah had two daughters, Alice and Elizabeth, the latter born in 1680 in Barbados. This birth date suggests Sarah's marriage to Clarkson occurred much later than could have been arranged by her father, deceased by 1653. On the other hand, her older brother Thomas, living in Virginia in the 1660s and 1670s, may well have brokered the marriage arrangement on Sarah's behalf.

A Segmented Life

The adult life of Nathaniel Saunders differed significantly from those Saunders who came before him. The difference lay in the segmentation of his domestic and work lives, the wide separations in personal experience that make multifaceted men out of one whole person. Compartmentalized life, of course, is familiar and routine today, but in Nathaniel's time, the experience was new. The pattern of Nathaniel's life resulted directly from his detachment from his extended family and its support apparatuses, which for past generations would have been undesirable and even unimaginable. Nathaniel's domestic life in his own time seems private, unconnected, even unaware, of the affairs of his distant extended Saunders family, and it was shaped largely by opportunities that befell him as much by chance as by design. In spite of struggles at home in Bristol, his domestic life conveys a sense of good settlement, even insularity, of placidity and moral certainty, and a degree of simplicity.

Contrarily, Nathaniel Saunders' work life was fraught with dangers, built and rewarded on risk and uncertainty. Above all, it was geopolitical and hemispheric in scope, large and unpredictable, and not serene in the least. Nathaniel's work life devolved from his association with Thomas Stratton and his community of mariners and had only a hint of Saunders family underpinning in the abbreviated and mostly absent life of his father Thomas. All this is to say that Nathaniel offers us two stories of his life, each with an independent sense of being, as if one depended not at all on the other.

At Home

Nathaniel Saunders was twenty-eight years old when he was finally admitted to the liberties of the city of Bristol in 1662, and his life improved considerably thereafter. He was at this point deemed a free man, able to fully engage commercial activity and also able to marry.

For a marriage partner, Nathaniel did not have far to look. In 1665, he sold his family's property in Berkeley and married Mary Stratton, daughter of Thomas and Mary Stratton of Bristol, master and mistress of his apprenticeship [22]. The marriage took place at St. Michael's Church in Bristol, Mary's father posting the marriage bond. Both Thomas Stratton and Nathaniel were identified as sailors on the marriage certificate, providing us some idea of Nathaniel's work during and after his Stratton apprenticeship.

The Strattons likely had come from an old family in Wiltshire, who were originally of Norfolk [23]. Thomas Stratton, Nathaniel's new father-in-law, seems a successful mariner, having maintained in his lifetime a messuage in

Gloucestershire called the Grange in Olveston Parish and another called the Glass House in Redcliff Street, St. Mary Redcliff, Bristol. In addition to their daughter Mary, Thomas and Mary Stratton had a daughter Joyce, who married an Edwards, though whether this Edwards was related to Philip Saunders's second wife in Pembrokeshire is unknown. The Strattons had sons Thomas, William, John, and Richard, the last of these bearing the same name as Richard Stratton whose passage to Virginia in 1648 was paid by Joseph Croshaw. Perhaps to stretch a point, the evident linkage of both Thomas Saunders and Richard Stratton to Joseph Croshaw in Virginia hints that Nathaniel's apprenticeship to Stratton may have been by Thomas Saunders' design.

In their first year of marriage, Mary Stratton, and Nathaniel Saunders witnessed an outbreak of bubonic plague, the intractable scourge of the Middle Ages, that lasted for about a year. Though the plague apparently had no immediate consequences for them, this outbreak at the start of their marriage seems ominous. Their marriage was riddled with trauma [24].

THE FAMILY OF NATHANIEL SAUNDERS OF BRISTOL

Source: Authors.

A year after they married, a daughter named Mary was born to Nathaniel and Mary, but the daughter survived only a year. Then a son Thomas was born in 1668 in their third year of marriage, but Thomas lived only two years. Yet another son Nathaniel, born about 1670, survived no longer than the others. Seven years after their marriage, they had another son named Thomas, repeating the name given to their first son. This son survived into adulthood.

But another son whose name is unknown seems to have died shortly after childbirth in 1674 and another daughter repeating the name Mary was born in 1677, living but five years. By this time, Nathaniel and Mary had had six children in eleven years, but five of them suffered early deaths. Finally, a daughter Elizabeth, born in 1678, lived to adulthood, as did a son again named Nathaniel, born in 1681. Their ninth and last child, Alban, was born in 1682. After sixteen years of childbearing, Nathaniel and Mary's surviving children were precious few in number: Thomas, nearly a decade older than his siblings, and three youngsters—Elizabeth, Nathaniel, and Alban.

Mary and Nathaniel lived for thirty years in Bristol after their marriage, moving about the city as life circumstances required. On marriage they first lived in St. Nicholas Parish, home of the Strattons, but shortly after found residence in adjacent St. Michael's Parish, where they attended church and where their first four children were baptized, three of whom failed to survive. All were buried at St. Michael's, as were Mary, Mathaniel and a daughter Mary in later years. Nathaniel and Mary remained in St. Michael's until 1677 when new developments in Nathaniel's employment allowed them to move to St. Augustine Parish, a district where many of the wealthy and higher-ranking of the maritime community made their home. It was in St. Augustine Cathedral that Mary and Nathaniel's last three children were baptized. In 1681, after all but the last child was born, Nathaniel's greater means allowed him to acquire another indenture of property in St. Augustine, a forty-one-year lease at forty shillings per year due to the mayor, burgesses, and commonalty of Bristol. This indenture, or lease, included A lower messuage and tenement lately erected and new built by Nicholas Sexton, being formerly a stable together with a washhouse and lodging chamber over, divided and separate from the now dwelling house of Rowland Thrupp, together with a court adjoining and also a great court lying before the said messuage, toward Frog Lane, with the hospital orchard on one side and dwelling house of the said Rowland Thrupp on the other. [25]

In this dwelling, Nathaniel, Mary, and their surviving children lived out their years. In all their years together, Mary seems never to have left Bristol for any extended period.

One striking feature in Nathaniel's domestic life was his loyalty to his church, to Anglicanism and Protestantism in general, and to his Bristol community. His commitment and activity in church matters rivals the commitment to Roman Catholicism found in his ancestors, though extreme action in defense of his belief seems never to have been required.

His new dwelling on Frog Lane was only a short walk from the Cathedral. His attachment to the Cathedral's broad viewpoint in matters of charity seems to reflect in him a liberal outlook. In 1678, Nathaniel contributed one shilling toward the rebuilding of St. Paul's Cathedral in London that had been destroyed in the great fire of 1666 [26]. The fire itself destroyed eighty-nine churches and over thirteen thousand houses, affecting about four-fifths of England's largest city [27]. In 1669, Christopher Wren designed an extraordinary new St. Paul's, which after much debate was approved in 1675. The actual rebuilding took another thirty-five years [28].

Nathaniel was named a "sideman" of St. Augustine Cathedral in 1681, a position of significant church responsibility [29]. As sideman, Nathaniel's task was to "walk the boundaries of the parish"—that is, to survey the entire parish—reporting back to the church on conditions and circumstances worthy and needful of church attention. The position made Nathaniel something of an intermediary between the church and parishioner, and no doubt a sought-after figure in his church community.

In 1685, events in France touched off a massive emigration of French Protestants (Huguenots) to England and other points of safety. A century of persecution had been visited upon these people, but in 1598, the Edict of Nantes granted Huguenots religious freedom and civil rights. Catholic extremism in France returned, however, and in 1685, Louis XIV revoked the Edict of Nantes, spurring the flight of as many as half a million Huguenots from France. A year later, Nathaniel contributed one shilling for Huguenot relief in England [30].

Though these records are few, one is left an impression of Nathaniel as a man of some piety and with sufficient resolve to act conscionably and regularly on behalf of his church and community. He was, in his own locale and by modest means, a pillar of his Bristol community. This person, we shall have to remind ourselves, is the same Nathaniel Saunders whose life on the high seas bore no resemblance to his secure existence at home.

Mariner

In his early thirties and finally able to pursue trade freely, Nathaniel slowly worked his way into positions of responsibility. As a Bristol sailor, he no doubt first worked on smaller ships that plied their trade up and down the Severn and to nearby English ports. Junkets to Wales and Ireland were probably undertaken. Judging by historical records, Nathaniel in time probably became a masters mate and may well have experienced more distant voyages, perhaps even to ports of call across the Atlantic. Although there is no record of Nathaniel in these days, subsequent records suggest that such experience was requisite to the kind of work he engaged in later years, and one senses that Nathaniel was particularly successful in his early marine and business undertakings.

In 1671, at the age of thirty-six and after eight years of free citizenry, he found himself in control of a much-noted Dutch and English merchant ship. Nathaniel Saunders was named master of the *Golden Lion* [31].

The *Golden Lion* was no ordinary ship and had no ordinary history. We first learn of the *Golden Lion* in 1652 as she lay in Virginia's James River near Pagan Creek [32]. The *Golden Lion* was at the time accounted a Dutch ship with Dutch ownership, and it often carried goods from Amsterdam, though its most recent passage to Virginia had originated in London [33]. Its master was John Jasperson of Zealand in the Netherlands. The *Lion's* steersman, Jacob Saunders, also hailed from Zealand. Jasperson served at the pleasure of the ship's owners, Peter de Leeun, Govert Lachard, and others who dwelled in the Spanish dominion of Flanders [34]. In 1647, the ship had been purchased by Richard Ford and James de Ham, whose brother Tobias de Ham kept her books [35]. Others involved in the *Lion's* business were Abraham and Seger de Ham, London and Rotterdam merchants with family ties to Norfolk. The *Golden Lion* had an international pedigree.

By 1651, the British Commonwealth under Oliver Cromwell had come into being, and under Cromwell, Parliament, responding to London mercantile interests, enacted a set of navigation acts, declaring that the singular purpose of British colonies was to serve the mother country, consequently ordering that the colonies be debarred from trade with foreign countries. The legislation was unpalatable for colonists in Virginia and elsewhere as prices charged for London goods were higher than those of the Dutch [36]. Thereupon, in February of 1652, the Dutch *Golden Lion* was surrounded by three English ships and seized at Pagan Creek. This provocation was part of what came to be called the First Anglo-Dutch War, a set of naval skirmishes between 1652 and 1654 designed to reset the terms of maritime trade between the contesting nations. The *Golden Lion* itself was a considerable merchant prize for its English captors, a ship of two hundred tons carrying up to eighteen cannons and twenty-seven seamen, a formidable opponent to those who would seize her lading at sea.

Confiscation of the *Golden Lion* and its cargo hit close to home. Among shippers on the *Golden Lion* was Giles Webb, Nathaniel Saunders' uncle, brother-in-law of Nathaniel's father Thomas by his second marriage. Webb had placed his tobacco aboard the vessel for London and planned to take passage aboard her to return to England. But he was forced by the *Lion's* capture to lose his tobacco and to sail to England on a New England ship. Unluckily, this ship was captured by the French on the homeward voyage, and Giles Webb was imprisoned at St. Malo on the coast of Brittany [37]. How long Webb endured imprisonment and how he finally effected a release is unknown, but he eventually returned to life in Virginia [38].

The *Golden Lion* afterward for a time sailed under the English flag, even after the end of the Cromwell era and the return of monarchy to England. In 1660, Thomas Harwood, friend and Virginia business associate of Thomas Saunders in the 1640s, became her captain [39]. During the 1660s, the *Lion* under Harwood sailed regularly out of the port of Bristol to Virginia and the Caribbean [40]. It is not unreasonable to suppose that after 1660, young Nathaniel Saunders, then age twenty-six, at this time might have served on the *Golden Lion* under Harwood. That at least suggests how a decade later Nathaniel would become master of this particular ship.

In 1671, Nathaniel Saunders, perhaps for the first time, bore primary responsibility for the *Golden Lion's* passengers and cargo sailing to Barbados, one of his several voyages to that colony. Aboard the *Lion* on this voyage were persons indentured for four years of service in Barbados and the wares of Bristol merchants to be exchanged mainly for hogsheads of Barbados sugar. In November of that same year, Nathaniel visited Virginia on Golden Lion business, in this instance carrying thirty-one hogsheads of Virginia tobacco weighing 13,284 pounds to Bristol on behalf of Richard Yearbury and Company. Nathaniel sailed under a cloud of uncertain ownership, however, because the *Golden Lion* soon after 1671 returned to Dutch control.

By 1672, the *Golden Lion* again carried the Dutch flag. Prior to this decade, a second Anglo-Dutch War had flared up, producing no clear resolution to conflict, and in the 1670s, yet a third trade war between the English and Dutch commenced. The Third Anglo-Dutch War was a more serious affair with large naval battles raging between the nations in the North Sea, culminating in 1674 with the Treaty of Westminster, which ceded Dutch possessions in New Jersey and New York, including the city of New Amsterdam, to the English [41]. A key engagement in that final war featured the *Golden Lion* and its eighteen guns, flying the Dutch flag and under the command of Dutch Adm. Cornelius Tromp, towering over its tormentors in the 1673 Battle of Texel, a scene preserved for posterity by Dutch painter Willem van de Velde the younger.

The Golden Lion (largest ship, left center) in the Battle of Texel (Kijkduin) in 1673 during the Third Anglo-Dutch War. Nathaniel Saunders was Master of the Golden Lion in the same decade. From a scene painted by Dutch artist Willem van de Velde the Younger (1633–1707).

The end of these Dutch-English conflicts saw the return of the slightly damaged *Golden Lion* to mercantile service, probably back under the British flag, though, as before, its ownership and service retained an international flavor. By 1674, Nathaniel Saunders was again master of the *Golden Lion*, and trade for Barbados sugar was his main intent. But sailing the Atlantic was no safer after 1674 than it was before that time. The so-called Anglo-Dutch Wars had been part of a larger and continuing quadrilateral dispute over territories and trade involving the Dutch, English, French, and Spanish militaries. At sea, merchant ships regularly fell prey to these national adversaries, causing disruptions in trade as far away as Virginia, Caribbean, and, at times, even the Pacific [42].

The control of trading ports throughout the Caribbean and Middle America changed hands often, reflecting the inability of European governments to establish and maintain authority and trade. State-sponsored privateering as a means to keep national control was a favored instrument, but privateering frequently led to unaligned and disloyal piracy by renegade commanders and abused and idle sailors. The chaos that resulted produced an environment where high-seas piracy blossomed [43]. A piratical Brethren of the Coast was formed with a sworn strict code of conduct, organizing buccaneers into a "roving sea republic" that served its own purposes alarmingly well [44]. Sir Henry Morgan, perhaps the most famous pirate of the era, operated throughout the lawless Caribbean in the decade of the 1670s, in the same decade that Nathaniel Saunders endeavored to do the *Golden Lion*'s business there.

Dangers on the high seas for merchantmen were by no means restricted to attacks by hostile naval forces, privateers, or pirates. Unfavorable winds often extended voyages to extra weeks and even months, incurring shipboard privations and illness. These struggles, together with insect-borne island illnesses and ravaging windstorms, imperiled every voyage and at times must have seemed limitless. Though a ship's problems at sea fell to the captain rather than the master to resolve, each decision by a captain—to change course, to make for safe land, to ignore advice—in turn jeopardized the master's mission. Occasionally, circumstances required landings at places other than the intended destinations, forcing the ship's master to negotiate new deals for his lading to supplant those that had been planned. As master of the *Golden Lion* engaged in Caribbean trade, Nathaniel Saunders routinely faced circumstances that jeopardized his mission, his ship, and his life.

In October 1674, Nathaniel Saunders lingered in Barbados long enough to witness the last will and testament of his friend and colleague, Capt. James Hayman. The Saunders and Hayman families were to remain close in Virginia in later years. Also witnessing Hayman's will was Capt. Edward Ditty, another of Nathaniel's close associates. William Lane, whom we found in conjunction with Nathaniel's indenture of Theophilus King in Bristol in 1658 [45], had acquired the headrights of Edward Ditty and Joseph Stratton for land in Virginia in 1662 [46]. Likewise, the Ditty family held a Virginia headright for Mary Worly, with whom Nathaniel's son had Virginia land dealings in the first decade of the 1700s [47]. Nathaniel's mariner community maintained a tight triangle of familiarity and mutual support between Bristol, Barbados, and Virginia.

This community extended to immediate family as well. About the time that Nathaniel witnessed James Hayman's will, Nathaniel's brother Thomas, who recently had sold some of his land in Virginia, arrived in Barbados to take up sugar cultivation. In 1675, Thomas joined his sisters Mary Hutchinson and Sarah Clarkson and their husbands in St. Philip's Parish in the southeast of Barbados. It even may be that Thomas sailed with his brother on the *Golden Lion* in yet another voyage to Barbados in 1675 if, as it seems, Thomas spent time in England after leaving Virginia [48]. If Thomas sought greater prosperity in moving to Barbados, he might have chosen better than St. Philip's Parish because those lands were marginal, the rainfall sparse, and the farms small; the parish was among the least prosperous in the entire island [49]. Thomas Saunders died four years after reaching Barbados, leaving his wife Elizabeth, a daughter Mary and a son John, his sisters and brothers-in-law also surviving him [50].

Nathaniel made one more voyage as Master of the *Golden Lion*, sailing in 1677 to Barbados [51]. It was perhaps the last time he saw his brother alive, though he may have seen his sisters at least one more time after 1677. This was Nathaniel's final voyage on this ship. After that, Thomas Stratton, probably Nathaniel's nephew, took over as the Golden Lion's Master.

Commander

About 1677, Nathaniel was named Commander of the Globe, a large merchant vessel in the fleet of the Micajah Perry Company, one of London's largest overseas shippers. At the time of Nathaniel's new appointment, Perry had merged his interests with Thomas Lane, an old maritime family well-known to Virginia. A ship called the Perry and Lane plied Virginia's waters. Many years earlier, Ralph Lane of this same family led the ill-fated Roanoke Colony, the first English attempt at settlement in the New World. Later generations of these Lanes crossed paths with Nathaniel in Barbados, and William Lane purchased land from Thomas Sanders, Nathaniel's brother, in Virginia. The Lanes lived in St. Augustine Parish of Bristol at the time Nathaniel took residence there. It seems likely that Thomas Lane was instrumental in convincing Nathaniel to accept a new position with Micajah Perry.

Nathaniel's new title of Commander brought with it some high level of respect and prestige, and undoubtedly greater personal compensation, enabling him in 1681 to acquire his new abode on Frog Street and endowing him with some amount of personal authority in his work at St. Augustine Cathedral. As

Commander, Nathaniel assumed full control of the Globe, include all matters of navigation as well as responsibilities for crew, passengers, and cargo. Even more, as a commanding presence, Nathaniel would find easy access to governors and other leading figures in the colonies on whose cooperation Perry depended heavily. For Micajah Perry, this was no small matter.

Perry once complained to the English parliament that vessels sent by Scots were crewed by captains and factors authorized to pay good prices in Virginia which enabled them to obtain full cargoes. He and other English merchants argued that the only way the Scots could afford to pay such good prices was their ability to avoid paying duties on the tobacco at home. Micajah Perry later appeared before Parliament to provide statistics of the duties paid by his firm in earlier years and the far smaller amounts paid in the past several years because his ships could not obtain full cargoes in Virginia [52].

To address the problem of acquiring cargo, part of Perry's strategy was to trade with colonial governments in Williamsburg and also county authorities. Micajah Perry dealt directly with Virginia Governor Nicholson, and with Colonel Spotswood, and engaged transactions in all parts of Virginia, frequently in probate issues for land and debt in King and Queen and Essex counties. To represent Perry in Virginia meant that Nathaniel carried Perry's money for tobacco purchases at a rate they had agreed on, and then transported the tobacco on the Globe to Perry's warehouses or buyers in England. As these colonial governments collected taxes in the form of tobacco levies, the goal was to capture the amassed levies as overseas shipments from which profits could be taken. But to forge agreements, Perry's representative—Nathaniel in this case—should command the respect and attention of the colony's leading figures, and to be able to offer credible assurances that business would be conducted on high standards of honesty and reliability. The title of Commander undoubtedly served both Perry and Nathaniel well in these arrangements.

As Commander, Nathaniel also was entrusted to conduct royal business with colonial rulers, the fledgling English navy lacking the capacity for such tasks. Armed merchantmen owned by private individuals still comprised a large proportion of ships conducting official business. In 1686, Nathaniel as Commander of the Globe carried an official message regarding security of the "Bermudas"—in this case, St. Kitts and Nevis—to be delivered to Sir William Stapleton, Commander in Chief of the Leeward Islands, instructing that "he was ordered to call at the Bermudas and enquire into the condition thereof, and during the stay there, to give all the assistance... to the Government for the security of those islands" [53].

While at St. Kitts, Nathaniel also attended to company business. St. Kitts was an epicenter of sugar trade in the seventeenth century, lying about 150 sea miles to the north of Barbados. Nathaniel's goal was to acquire a shipload of muscovada sugar, a thick dark brown crude sugar, partly refined in the canefields, suitable for shipment in sealed hogsheads and additional refinement back in England. For this arrangement, Nathaniel dealt with John Hutchinson, not his brother-in-law, who we learn had died three years earlier, but a nephew in this same family [54].

From this visit, we learn something of a Commander's work [55]. Nathaniel drafted buyer invoices for seven lots of muscovada sugar, aggregating to a total of 135,765 pounds, nearly sixty-eight tons, loaded on the *Globe* for England. John Hutchinson himself shipped ten hogsheads, ranging in weight from 1,124 to 1,533 pounds each and three barrels, each weighing from 216 to 308 pounds. Thus, Hutchinson accounted for 14,201 pounds of sugar, which was liable for a duty of 4.5 percent. Trimming and fitting the hogsheads additionally was assessed at eighty pounds, bringing the total weight to 14,920 pounds. Nathaniel added a 10 percent commission for invoicing and shipping this lot, which added another 1,492 pounds to Hutchinson's final weight. The 10 percent commission for the entire lading of the *Globe* came to more than £13,500, a hefty gain for the entire effort, if it could be successfully delivered [56].

Virginia

Family land in Virginia was sometimes said to lie on Assawaymansecock Creek [57], a branch within the well-water tidewater. As with all other aspects of life in the Virginia colony, land on the Assawaymansecock was more than a simple endowment; it represented both a symbolic and real continuation of family and business associations that began in England.

An early landholder on the Assawaymansecock was John Pettit, who obtained a patent of land there in 1658 [58]. Pettit was a London vintner and chirurgeon who became the guardian of Thomas and Dr. Edward Sanders after their father Edward's death in 1639. Following Pettit, Thomas Sanders became a vintner himself, and the younger Edward a chirurgeon under Pettit's tutelage. Pettit's Assawaymansecock land eventually passed to the Watkins family into which family Nathaniel married. In 1673, some of the original Pettit land fell to Robert Bagby, who owned headrights for Thomas Else [59], and Samuel Hoskins, whose daughter would one day marry Nathaniel's son Hugh. Pettit's life thus bridged two branches of the Sanders family in Virginia—that of Edward Sanders of Charlwood in Surrey and Thomas Saunders of Wales and Gloucestershire.

Other such associations existed as well. During the 1680s, Edward Chilton acquired portions of the original Pettit land. The Chiltons were closely tied to the Edwards family [60], believed from accumulated evidence to be the same family as the Edwards of Wales into which Philip Saunders had married about 1615. In the 1690s Edward Chilton's Assawaymansecock land passed to Peter de Shazo, Nathaniel Sanders' neighbor by 1702. Philip Saunders, evidently

Nathaniel's cousin, obtained Westmoreland County land in 1705 from John Chilton, undoubtedly a relative.

John Coleman, probably the grandfather of Robert, who one day would marry Nathaniel's daughter Sarah, acquired Assawaymansecock land during the 1670s, portions of which eventually fell into the hands of Bartholomew Fowler. An earlier figure and one suspects a relative, Francis Fowler, once exchanged merchandise at the Three Cranes Tavern in St. Mildred's Poultry, London, a place of business for Joseph Saunders, Virginia merchant and shipowner in the colony's early days. In 1700, Bartholomew Fowler sold his Assawaymansecock land to William Edwards, gentleman, of the same Edwards mentioned above.

These brief accounts, of which there are many more for the Assawaymansecock settlement, leads one to understand Nathaniel Sanders' original location as the product of longer-term historical processes by which the immediate and extended Sanders family community in Wales and England reproduced itself on Virginia soil. Nathaniel's early years of family building in Virginia took place among neighbors known to him and who shared his lifestyle, his language and religion, and his enterprise.

As late as 1685, more than thirty years after the elder Thomas Saunders' death, the land on Assawaymansecock, or a branch called Arracaico Creek, still lay in family hands. Thomas Saunders' eldest son Thomas had taken possession of the land and held it during the decades of the 1660s and 1670s. But Thomas left Virginia around 1675 and this land passed to Nathaniel, Thomas's younger brother and Commander of the Globe, either when Thomas departed Virginia or on his death in Barbados in 1679. Information on the land is scant:

> Patrick Gillmore, 24 ac., New Kent Co., in Stratton
> Major Par., Nov. 1685. Beg. on Arracaico Cr., nr.
> Gough's and Pride's line, nr. Sanders' line, etc. [57]

The question arises as to how Nathaniel could manage his acreage in absentia while conducting business for Perry, and the lack of records for the period does not permit unambiguous answers. But they do suggest some strong likelihoods. He probably appointed a trusted acquaintance to work the land, providing Nathaniel some profits for any successful crop, either in tobacco or grains, the usual crop rotation scheme. Such an arrangement was perhaps offered to Theophilis King, Nathaniel's former indenture who by this time had migrated from Barbados to Essex county, Virginia [58] or to Thomas New, friend of Thomas Harwood, one-time Master of the Golden Lion before Nathaniel.

Nathaniel sailed to Virginia as Commander of the Globe in 1689 no doubt to conduct business on behalf of Micajah Perry, but also to tend to some personal affairs. He brought along his son Thomas, then age seventeen, and perhaps also his son Nathaniel, merely eight years old at the time. While there, Nathaniel Saunders witnessed a land transaction involving Nicholas Langford and Thomas Watkins in Old Rappahannock County, Virginia [59], and sent his son Thomas to witness probate proceedings for the will of the above-mentioned Thomas New in Essex County. The combination of these events suggest that Nathaniel named Thomas Watkins to oversee his land after 1689, because the Langford-Watkins transaction was for land acquired by Nathaniel's young son Nathaniel in later years. The idea of a working relationship between Nathaniel and Thomas Watkins is also suggested by the fact that William Lane, who previously purchased forty-three acres of family land about 1675, also sponsored Thomas Watkins passage to Virginia in 1670. A decade later, Nathaniel's son Nathaniel married Thomas Watkins's daughter as the new century dawned.

Bristol

Nathaniel's father-in-law and mentor, Thomas Stratton, died in Bristol in 1690. He left to Mary his daughter, Nathaniel's wife of twenty-five years, one-half interest in his messuage in Redcliff Street and a silver beaker [60]. Mary's interest in the property perhaps passed to her own children in time.

Of Nathaniel and Mary Saunders we learn little more, except that Nathaniel died in 1696 at age sixty-two and was buried at St. Michael's Church. Following his death, Mary continued on at St. Augustine Cathedral, attending with her sons Nathaniel and Oburn (Alban) in 1696 [61]. Mary died four years later, in 1700, and was interred beside her husband [62]. For the family line we follow, the deaths of Mary and Nathaniel Saunders in the last days of the seventeenth century forever closed the door on Saunders life in its British homeland.

NOTES

1. The terms *gemeinschaft* and *gesellschaft* are explained more fully in chapter 1. They refer specifically to a state or condition of society, and not to individuals within the society. But history proceeds irregularly, and disjunctions between historical processes in any place are more the rule than the exception. So it seems that, among many others of his day, Nathaniel's life pattern anticipated later societal development, and his experience was more akin to that we would find in later persons, and more perfectly fit to a later society to which the term *gesellschaft* applies.

2. Baptismal records for Thomas's sons Nathaniel (December 30, 1634) and Samuel (January 19, 1637) are found in Wotton-under-Edge,

Gloucestershire Baptism Register: 1630–1645 (unpublished). Birth or baptism records for the other children have not been located; their ages relative to Nathaniel are gauged from known dates of experiences in their own lives.

3. Unless they lived in Tetbury at their stepmother's home, if in fact she retained one there after her marriage to Thomas Saunders.

4. At a guess, Nathaniel's initial apprenticeship may have been with Thomas Harwood. As was common, apprentices partnered with sponsors in later life, and Nathaniel's life in important respects shadowed the life of Thomas Harwood. Thomas Harwood from the earliest time worked with Thomas Saunders, Nathaniel's father, in Charles River County, Virginia, and later both Harwood and Nathaniel Saunders held command positions on the same ship.

5. This interpretation of Nathaniel's apprenticeships, if indeed there were two, draws upon his age as the major clue to his experience. Nathaniel's acquiring an indentured servant for four years of service in Barbados in 1658 is not the work of an apprentice and realistically cannot have been undertaken if his apprenticeship begun in 1653 at an age of nineteen had lasted for the requisite seven years. An initial apprenticeship undertaken at age fourteen is far more likely. The record of Nathaniel's apprenticeship with Thomas and Mary Stratton as arranged by William Nicholas on May 12, 1653, is found in Bristol Apprentice Books: 1650–1655; see Appendix II.

That William Nicholas would have arranged this apprenticeship for Nathaniel Saunders with Thomas Stratton is not surprising because William Nicholas, friend of Thomas Saunders, had married Alice Stratton in 1633, and thus was a member of that family. See Berkeley, Gloucestershire Marriage Register: 1620–1653, Appendix II. Sadly, William Nicholas died shortly after arranging Nathaniel's apprenticeship.

6. Beverly Fleet, *Virginia Colonial Abstracts*, vol. 3 (Baltimore: Genealogical Publishing Company, 1988), pp. 35, 46.

7. Nell Nugent, *Cavaliers and Pioneers*, vol. 1. (Baltimore: Genealogical Publishing Company, 1983), pp. 92, 125.

8. Fleet, *Virginia Colonial Abstracts*, p. 88.

9. Peter W. Coldham, *Complete Book of Emigrants*, vol. 1 (Baltimore: Genealogical Publishing Company, 1987), p. 388.

10. Coldham, *Complete Book of Immigrants*, p. 67. Philip and John Sanders were indentured to John Tucke(y) for seven years of Virginia labor in 1664. This pair were in some manner close relatives of Nathaniel, thought, though incorrectly, by Sanders genealogist Anna Parker to have been Nathaniel's brothers. John took up lands in Essex County

and Philip in Lancaster County in later years. The lives of John and
Philip are described in other sections of this book.

11. Kenneth O. Morgan, ed., *The Oxford Illustrated History of Britain* (New
York: Oxford University Press, 1984), p. 318.

12. Ibid., p. 323.

13. David H. Fischer, *Albion's Seed* (New York: Oxford University Press,
1989), pp. 207–418. Fischer calls this section of his important work,
"Distressed Cavaliers and Indentured Servants, 1642–1675." He
outlines the crucial role of Sir William Berkeley in recruiting royalists
to Virginia and placing them in high positions, granting them large
estates, and creating the ruling oligarchy that ran the colony for many
generations.

14. Morgan, *Oxford Illustrated History*, p. 328. On August 8, 1662, Nathaniel
Saunders was finally "admitted to the liberties of the City, for that he
was the apprentice to Thomas Stratton, a freeman." Bristol Burgess
Books: 1652–1662; see Appendix II.

15. A brief history of Upton Grove is available in the *Victoria History of
Gloucestershire*. Later records for this line are found in Ralph Bigland's
"Gloucestershire Collections," Memorial Inscriptions (publication
information unavailable).

16. In 1665, Nathaniel sold two properties in Berkeley, each consisting of
a messuage and garden, to Giles and Ursula Machin and to William
and Alice Margretts, but the record fails to produce a clear sense of
the nature of the transaction. The record itself is written in Latin
and is found in the Schedule of Berkeley, Gloucestershire Records at
Gloucestershire Record Office (unpublished). Translation and notes
were supplied by Bristol Records Office, Research Service, April 1998.

17. These land records are found in Nugent, *Cavaliers and Pioneers*, pp.
232, 310, 361, and 381. No record directly describing Thomas's original
land acquisition has been found. The persistence of references to
Thomas Saunders's land on Arakeyaco Creek through the 1650s can be
explained simply as geographical indicators in other land acquisitions.
The land clerk's office had no means to coordinate information about
deaths in or departures from Virginia with land information unless
specific claims were made for or against the property ownership as
originally recorded.

18. Nugent, *Cavaliers and Pioneers*, p. 541. Confusions in these records
are substantial, including wide variations in the spelling of Assatians
(Tassitomps, Tassatians, etc.) and whether the lands in question lay
to the north or south of the Mattaponi River. They are on the north
side, falling into King and Queen County after it was formed in 1693.

19. Nugent, *Cavaliers and Pioneers*, p. 538.

20. Nugent, *Cavaliers and Pioneers*, vol. 2. Virginia State Library, Richmond, pp. 166 and 240. That John Lane would have purchased land from Thomas Saunders is not surprising since this Lane family is found in Nathaniel Saunders's indenture record of 1658 involving Theophilus King; Nathaniel is Thomas's brother. Furthermore, William Lane, brother of John, acquired headrights for Strattons and Watkins, names tightly tied to later Sanders in Virginia, for land near John. See also Nugent, *Cavaliers and Pioneers*, p. 4.

21. Joann M. Sanders, *Barbados Records: Wills and Administrations, 1639–1680*, vol. 1. (Marceline, Missouri: Walsworth Publishing Company, 1977), p. 316.

22. Bristol Marriage License Bonds: 1637–1700, April 19, 1665. The marriage license provides residential information. See Appendix II.

23. Thomas Stratton (–1581) held the estate called Haseland in Bremhill, Wiltshire, and had numerous children. Notable among them was John Stratton (–1624), gentleman of Seagry, Wiltshire, and the Manor of Kinggrave, Gloucestershire. He possessed several Gloucestershire properties, including lands in Sodbury, Old Sodbury, Doddington, and Chipping Sodbury. Proximity of these lands to that held by Thomas Stratton of Bristol, Nathaniel Saunders's new father-in-law, suggests a likely relationship of these Strattons. The *Victoria Histories for Wiltshire and Gloucestershire* provide more background on this family.

24. Baptism and death records for Nathaniel and Mary's children are found in St. Michael, Bristol, Baptism (1665–1690) and Burial (1665–1700) Registers. See also St. Augustine Cathedral. See our Appendix II.

25. Ancient Leases, Counterpart of Lease, Bristol Records Office, Accession 1309(1), April 2, 1681 (unpublished).

26. St. Augustine, Bristol, Baptism, Marriage, and Burial Register, Appendix: List of Contributors toward the Building of St. Paul's Cathedral, London, October 29, 1678. See Appendix II.

27. St. Paul's Cathedral at http://www.avlewoncities.com/london/stpaulscathedral.html.

28. Ibid.

29. St. Augustine, Bristol, Baptism, Marriage, and Burial Register, Appendix: List of Sidemen and Waywardens 1680–1700. See Appendix II.

30. St. Augustine, Bristol, Baptism, Marriage, and Burial Register, Appendix: Moneys collected for French Protestants June 21–24, 1686 (unpublished). On two occasions we find Nathaniel contributing one shilling toward charitable causes. The size of these contributions can be gauged from the fact that his lease agreement for his home near Frog Lane was for forty shillings per year, or about three and a half

shillings per month. Nathaniel's charitable donations of one shilling then were about the same as a week's rent in each instance.

31. Coldham, *Complete Book of Emigrants*, vol. 2, p. 171.

32. Peter W Coldham, *English Adventurers and Emigrants, 1609–1660* (Baltimore: Genealogical Publishing Company, 1984), p. 134. A legal proceeding provides basis for this description.

33. Coldham, *Complete Book of Emigrants*, p. 262.

34. Flanders today is located in Belgium but at the time was one of several independent provinces of the Netherlands. Over a short period, Spain waged war in the region and captured Flanders, but its gain was short lived. Spain was permanently expelled before the end of the seventeenth century.

35. Elizabeth Saunders, sister of Erasmus Saunders of Wales, married into the Ford (or Forth?) family of Norfolk in the decade of the 1570s. As the *Golden Lion* was purchased by members of the de Ham family also of Norfolk, it may be that some distant Saunders-Ford relationship bore on the eventual appointment of Nathaniel Saunders some ninety years later to his post on the *Golden Lion*. If so, this is the only instance in which we can identity an influence of the Saunders extended family on Nathaniel's life, and it is an improbable one at that.

36. Cyril Hamshere, *The British in the Caribbean* (Cambridge: Harvard University Press, 1972), pp. 57–58.

37. Coldham, *English Adventurers and Emigrants*, p. 134.

38. Nugent, *Cavaliers and Pioneers*, p. 450. Giles Webb and his wife sailed to Virginia at least twice in the decade following his capture in 1652.

39. Coldham, *Complete Book of Emigrants*, p. 462.

40. Coldham, *English Adventurers and Emigrants*, pp. 462, 484; and Coldham, Peter W. 1990. Complete Book of Emigrants, vol. 2 (Baltimore: Genealogical Publishing Company, 1990), pp. 70, 169, 171.

41. This brief portrayal of Anglo-Dutch hostilities is based on "The Contemplator's Short History of the Anglo-Dutch Wars," available at http://www.contemplator.com/history/dutchwar.html. The Battle of Texel (a.k.a. Kijkduin) in the Third War is described in http://www.fact-index.com/b/ba/battle_of_texel.html.

42. David Cordingly, ed., *Pirates—Terror on the High Seas—from the Caribbean to the South China Sea* (North Dighton, MA: J. G. Press, 1998), p. 64.

43. Ibid., p. 64.

44. Ibid., pp. 41, 48.

45. Recall that John Lane bought Thomas Saunders's land in Virginia, 1674.

46. Nugent, *Cavaliers and Pioneers*, p. 391.

47. Fleet, *Virginia Colonial Abstracts*, vol. 2, p. 113; Nugent, *Cavaliers and Pioneers*, p. 398; also see Essex County, Virginia, #031171, Book D&C, vol. 2, pp. 65–66.

48. Nathaniel's 1675 voyage is noted in Coldham, *Complete Book of Emigrants*, vol. 2, p. 257. We have no record of Thomas Saunders's actual passage to Barbados, but records indicate an active business life in England for Thomas in the 1660s, suggesting that he shuttled between England and Virginia as occasions required. See Coldham, 1990, pp. 29, 35, 61, 121, 122.

49. Richard S. Dunn, *Sugar and Slaves* (New York: Norton and Company, New York, 1972), pp. 91, 95.

50. Sanders, *Barbados Records*, p. 316.

51. Coldham, *Complete Book of Emigrants*, p. 277, 278. Although this is the last instance we have found of Nathaniel Saunders aboard the *Golden Lion*, it was not the last of her transatlantic sailings. Voyages for the *Golden Lion* are recorded through the 1680s and 1690s to Virginia, Maryland, and Barbados. Interestingly, the commander of the *Golden Lion* on a 1688 Barbados voyage was William Stratton. The final voyage we have located is for 1697, when bound for Virginia, the *Golden Lion* was captured by French privateers and taken to Martinico (Martinique). See Coldham, *Complete Book of Emigrants*; and also Coldham, *English Adventurers and Emigrants*.
    A question emerges as to how long a wooden ship of those days might last. The *Golden Lion* in our records sailed for at least half a century. According to Iain MacKenzie of the Maritime Information Centre of the National Maritime Museum of Greenwich, England, we could be looking at a "fairly extreme longevity that rebuilding programmes could bestow on a ship. This longevity, however, is on the principle of 'Grandfather's Axe'—the name remains the same, without necessarily a vestige of the original fabric of the ship being present." Personal communication, 15 February 1994.

52. Price, Jacob M. Perry of London: A Family and a Firm on the Seaborne Frontier, 1614–1753. Cambridge, MA, and London: Harvard University Press, 1992

53. Sir John Lefroy, Memorials of the Discovery and Early Settlement of the Bermudas, vol. 2, pp.546–547. The security matter involved uprisings on the island.

54. The relationships between these Hutchinsons in St. Christopher's and Barbados are described in Sanders, *Barbados Records*, p. 316, and careful analysis of multiple Lovell family records in this source helps determine exact relationships.

55. This information is contained in the William Hearn Ledger, details of which were kindly supplied by Jay Hearn, to whom we extend our gratitude. See http://www.cragun.com/brian/hearne/history/hh029m.html.

56. Notice that all reckoning of value, whether hogsheads of sugar, labor, customs duties, or shipping costs, was made in terms of pounds of sugar, the price for which would be set in England. This is the same arrangement for Virginia with its tobacco. Thus, the value of labor (wages) or services (handling, shipping) was unknown at the time rendered, and was entirely dependent on market conditions and mercantile reckoning half a world away. This rudimentary and volatile international economy, which shortchanged the colonies, no doubt played a large part in colonial dissatisfaction over the years and the subsequent desires for improved representation or independence. The cry for "no taxation without representation" occurred in Barbados long before it was heard in America. See Dunn, *Sugar and Slaves*, p. 82.

57. During the period in question, Assawaymansecock Swamp or Creek was also irreverently called Whorecock Creek, a name which made its way into official records. See Nugent, *Cavaliers and Pioneers*, p. 130.

58. Nugent, *Cavaliers and Pioneers*, p. 387. Researchers should be aware that the name Pettit is subject to wide spelling variations in the records of the time, such as Peteete and Poteete.

59. This name Else is otherwise shown as Ellsey, a family of vintners in England, associated with Joseph Saunders's mercantile operations.

60. In 1660, John Edwards of Lancaster County, chirurgeon, married Elizabeth Chilton.

61. Nugent, *Cavaliers and Pioneers*, p. 293.

62. See note 20.

63. Essex County, Virginia, #031172, Book D&C, vol. 13, p. 21.

64. Bristol Record Office, Genealogical Abstract of Will of Thomas Stratton of Bristol, Mariner. The will was made December 24, 1687, and proved July 12, 1690. See our Appendix II.

65. The Inhabitants of Bristol in 1696, Bristol Record Society Publication, vol. 25, p. 35.

66. Death records for both Mary and Nathaniel Saunders are given in St. Michael, Bristol, Burial Register 1665–1700. See Appendix II. Nathaniel's burial date is January 24, 1696, and Mary's is April 19, 1700. For the record, St. Michael's Church still exists, but today's church is not the structure Nathaniel and Mary would have known. The earlier structure dated to the twelfth century and measured seventy-three feet between the tower at one end and the altar at the other. It had a tiled

roof and a painted glass window showing two figures at a communion table. On the east side of the tower was a niche containing the figure of an abbot, perhaps an abbot of Tewksbury, whose abbey controlled St. Michael's. We are grateful to Cynthia Stiles of About-Bristol.co.uk for this description.

CHAPTER TEN

Colonial Virginia

Nathaniel Sanders, son of Nathaniel Saunders, master and commander of Caribbean trading ships out of Bristol, and his wife Mary Stratton, is often regarded as an original ancestor of large numbers of Sanders whose American ancestry began in Virginia. That is because Nathaniel was indeed the first of the line to settle permanently in Virginia, to have survived into reasonably old age, and to have married a Virginian and raised a large family from which numerous descents have been drawn. But this simple portrayal suggests that the person we have in Nathaniel is somehow a singular heroic migrant whose life circumstances, whatever they might have been, directed him to depart the Old World for the New, and to build from his own wit and devices a new livelihood and prosperity that would later launch a large New World family. Insofar as we hold this view, that Nathaniel's migration was a solo act, a first seed of the Virginia Sanders, a genuine new beginning for an Old World family, we are quite misled. Nathaniel in fact was a participant in something larger, a longer-term migration process flowing westward in a stream of interconnected English and Virginia history for the better part of a century. And it is this larger historical context that gives explanation and meaning to Nathaniel's Virginia years.

Nathaniel Sanders' life in the retrospect of family history contains a sense of inevitability that he would live and die in Virginia. His grandfather Thomas Saunders of Gloucestershire lived for a time in Virginia in the 1640s and probably died there. His father, the mariner Nathaniel Saunders of Bristol, traveled to Virginia in the late 1680s and perhaps other times, and his uncle Thomas lived on family land in Virginia through the 1660s and 1670s. Even Nathaniel Sanders' elder brother Thomas took up permanent residence in the colony during the 1690s.

Nor were Nathaniel's immediate family the only Sanders in Virginia known to him. The two sons of Edward Sanders of Accomac, Thomas and Edward, migrated to the colony in the 1650s. Thomas, credentialed as a member of the Vintners Company of London, arriving with his new wife Grace Anscombe from Merstham near Charlwood [1], and Edward, a practicing chirurgeon [2], both took up new lands on the north side of the Rappahannock River. Edward Sanders in time married Mary Webb, daughter of Virginian Giles Webb whom we met in a previous generation as the brother of Thomas Saunders' second wife in Gloucestershire. Another relative, Hugh Sanders, from his name probably from Wales, came to Virginia in the mid-1660s and acquired property on the south side of the James River [3]. A John Sanders, perhaps from the Abbots Leigh maritime community near Bristol, settled along coastal Virginia's Skiff's Creek in the 1660s [4]. Yet two others, most likely brothers and certainly well-known to Nathaniel's family, Philip and John Sanders, found lands on the south side of the Rappahannock in the 1660s [5]. All these Sanders were a generation older than Nathaniel, and though many were deceased by the time of Nathaniel's arrival, their offspring constituted a New World resource that would give Nathaniel's life in Virginia a familiar base of personal support.

Beyond the Sanders' substantial presence in Virginia before Nathaniel's time, there were also relatives on his mother's side, the Strattons, who had long experience in the colony, and those from his grandfather's marriage, the Webbs. Finally, Nathaniel's father's maritime community and his grandfather's trading partners, including among many acquaintances such names as Watkins, Wetherby, Ditty, Hayman, Harwood, Lane, Pettit, and Edwards, all had their own Virginia histories. In all, Nathaniel Sanders' circle of friends, relatives, supporters, and acquaintances guaranteed that Nathaniel Sanders would arrive in Virginia as nearly a native son as any newcomer could be.

Yet there was a great deal more in his Virginia predecessors that colored Nathaniel's life. These Virginians no doubt acted on specific occasions to assist the young Nathaniel, but far more important than specific actions on behalf of Nathaniel, these people's uncalculated but rich embodiment of transplanted English culture and folkways in the Virginia countryside were Nathaniel's ultimate resource. They were exactly the kinds of people Nathaniel left behind on the Atlantic's eastern side. By the close of the seventeenth century, it can be said that most Englishmen migrating to Virginia would have found a familiar home away from home, an England transplanted. The fact is that for all its differences from England, Virginia was purposely designed to replicate the mother country's most salient features. Nathaniel did not arrive in a strange land, and he was no stranger to it when he stepped ashore in the New World.

Virginia in Nathaniel's Time

The Virginia that Nathaniel adopted as his home took its early eighteenth-century form much earlier, beginning in fact about the time that Nathaniel's grandfather Thomas arrived in the colony. The occasion then was the appointment of Sir William Berkeley of Berkeley's Castle in Gloucestershire to the royal governorship in 1641, the beginning of what would be Berkeley's thirty-five-year rule. During Berkeley's time, Virginia's population increased from eight thousand to forty thousand, and by the governor's careful design, the colony developed a ruling elite and a coherent, well-crafted, if rigid, social order.

The principal instrument of Berkeley's policies was colonial immigration [6]. Virginia's migrants came from the higher and lower ranks of Englishmen while New England drew mainly from the middle [7]. About three-quarters were indentured servants. The overwhelming portion of Virginia migrants came from the culture area in England that was ancient Wessex, the old Saxon stronghold in the southern and western tiers of England's counties. The greatest single source for this stream was the Severn Valley in Gloucestershire. Between 1642 and 1666, the Gloucestershire wool trade was greatly disrupted, and its old cloth towns lost population and saw poverty increase substantially, pushing its population toward new opportunity.

This migration fully shaped Virginia's cultural base, producing a distinctive character in Virginia's people that can be felt to this day. Migrants brought with them distinctive habits of speech, dress, food and cooking styles, work ethics, and architectural preferences. Their way of living was heavily patriarchal as regards family, marriage, and inheritance. Male children were named not from biblical sources as in New England but rather for Teutonic warriors, Frankish knights, and English kings. Girls received the names of Christian saints [8]. Place-names in the region were frequently taken from English royalty, eschewing Indian names for counties and parishes, preserving for Virginia's cavaliers some sense of their royalist origins.

The beginnings of Virginia's ruling elite, Berkeley's recruits, can be found in the royalist migration from England following Parliamentary successes against English royalty. Berkeley seized the opportunity to recruit younger sons of royalist families, and these instantly became Virginia's leading families in part because Berkeley saw to it that they received massive land grants. All of these royalist families find their Virginia origins within a decade of 1655 [9]. Of 152 Virginians who held top offices in 1600s and early 1700s, 101 were sons of baronets, knights, and rural gentry [10]. Many had entered maritime and mercantile industry from roots in the English countryside, country gentlemen [11] who hailed mainly from southwestern England. Their genealogies were a "tangle of fishhooks, so closely interlocked that it is impossible to pick up one without drawing three or four after it" [12]. An author comments, "It is difficult to think of any ruling elite that has been more closely interrelated since the Ptolemies" [13].

In religion, Virginians clung to orthodox Anglicanism, and dissenting sects were actively discouraged from settling in. The Anglican establishment held a middle position between the churches of Rome (Catholic) and Geneva (reform-minded Protestants). The going religion of England was part of the life of the English gentleman of America. Virginia was no place for religious refugees or utopian schemers as in other colonies [14]. In Virginia, as in England, the emphasis of Anglicanism was on institutions and ritual rather than doctrines [15].

Perhaps the most distinguishing part of seventeenth-century Virginia was the system of deference based on social class. It was exceptionally difficult for any person to cross these social demarcations, and observing these customs was a requirement that fell to both high- and low-born citizens. Virginians lived where people acquiesced in government by the rich and well-born and where the rich and well-born did not overbear the people. As ruling Virginians particularly admired the ideal of the English country gentleman, the genteel canon they followed most closely was moderation [16]. Only freeholders could vote. The gentry chose a sheriff from among themselves, and the sheriff managed elections [17]. By 1670, Virginia society was beginning to be frozen, and Negro slaves had largely replaced white indentured servants [18]. During this period, no prerevolutionary political tracts or theories of government were offered. How Virginians should be governed was simply not at issue.

Though the system of government rooted in social privilege was solidly established in the time of Sir William Berkeley, not all of his policies were universally supported. In Berkeley's later years, signs appeared that his iron control of the colony was slipping away. The end came quickly in the form of an armed uprising. In 1676 and mainly in Old Rappahannock County, popular discontent exploded when Berkeley's government refused to act against Indian provocations (as the colonists saw them), causing citizens to take matters into their own hands. A large well-supported citizen force grew under a young Nathaniel Bacon, and Berkeley was unable to raise a substantial force against the popular Bacon. Bacon then moved against the governor [19]. Undergirding popular unrest was heavy farmer indebtedness resulting from a punishing Navigation Act [20].

Bacon's early initiative against the government forced Berkeley to abandon Jamestown, taking refuge on Virginia's eastern shore, but Bacon himself died later that year while camped on Dragon Swamp in Old Rappahannock, and the rebellion was crushed soon after that. Conspirators were indicted at the governor's mansion called Green Spring, and several were hanged. Among those named was John Sanders, a ship's carpenter of Essex County, who narrowly escaped the gallows when Berkeley was recalled to England [21]. Bacon's rebellion brought an end to Berkeley's long rule. Of Berkeley's end, it has been said, "This was not a cruel man by nature, but rebellion made him pitiless. His allegiance was a craze which warped his whole nature. To that superstition this loving husband, warm friend, and courtly gentleman sacrificed everything—his old friends, his peace of mind, his name in Virginia and in history" [22].

In some senses, Virginia's tight hold on English social and political traditions in the late seventeenth century was stronger than England's own grasp. Important changes in English civil society in this period largely escaped Virginians' attentions. In the reign of William and Mary (1689–1694), fundamental changes were wrought in England through a peaceful so-called Glorious Revolution. A new Bill of Rights was enacted in 1688 that overrode the hereditary monarchic right of rule, replacing it with rule by the will of the nation expressed through parliament. After this time, the monarch was to rule by de facto decisions of parliament and not the de jure ordinance of heaven. The Glorious Revolution was a fundamental turning point involving the decisive rejection of an entire conception of government and replacing it with a social contract in which the will of the ruled became sovereign [23]. The Glorious Revolution of 1688 was followed shortly after by new Toleration Acts, providing new freedoms in religious expression. It would take nearly another century before similar changes found their way to the colonies.

Nathaniel's Early Years

Nathaniel was born of Mary Stratton and Nathaniel Saunders of Bristol in the year 1681. He was their eighth child but only their third among those that survived beyond infancy. An earlier son also was called Nathaniel, but he died in 1672 in his second year. Among the surviving children, Thomas was the eldest brother of Nathaniel, nine years his senior, and he had a younger brother Alban and an older sister Elizabeth, born in 1679. In the year of Nathaniel's birth, his father acquired a forty-year lease on a Bristol property that was Nathaniel's home for all his younger days. Nathaniel was baptized in St. Augustine Cathedral, Bristol, and no doubt in his early learning was endowed with Anglican beliefs following his father's devoted service to that church. So it was that Nathaniel Sanders spent his earliest years in Bristol, England, as if in exile from a Virginia that expected his arrival. The exile would not last long.

From his earliest years in Bristol to the time of Nathaniel's marriage in Virginia at about age twenty, we unfortunately have not one shred of direct evidence to describe his whereabouts or activities for the intervening period. From the time of his birth in 1681 to the year 1702, we have not a single record describing Nathaniel's youth or young adulthood. Family historian Anna Parker provides the only known statement about Nathaniel's migration to Virginia. Working from private family papers, Parker states simply, "Nathaniel Sanders, who emigrated from Wales to the colony of Virginia in the early part of the eighteenth century, is the first Sanders to be mentioned in the family records in America" [24]. Research has shown, however, that Nathaniel did not emigrate from Wales, though Wales is the place of his own distant ancestry, and there are reasons to believe that Nathaniel came to Virginia before the end of the seventeenth century, at least two or three years before Parker asserts. Though the difference of years in these two interpretations seems small, it is fundamental to understanding Nathaniel's story in Virginia because his initial Virginia experience greatly influenced his life thereafter.

Considering his considerable stature in his Bristol maritime community, we can suggest that Commander Nathaniel Saunders made provision for his sons' futures within that maritime world. Judging by what little we know of Thomas, the eldest son, Nathaniel probably initiated his training by 1686, at Thomas's age fourteen. One might guess a junior officer position on one of Micajah Perry's ships might have been a goal. For the younger son Nathaniel, we can be more certain that he was brought under Perry's wing about 1695, to receive some business-oriented education for eventual employment in Perry's overseas ventures. Young Nathaniel's schooling here would have included knowledge of tobacco and sugar prices and how those prices were set; some elements of bookkeeping and taxation laws; some specific knowledge of traders on both sides of the Atlantic; something of how lading and stowage on ships insured fair passage of products; these and many other dimensions of trade that enabled profits to be gained. The decision about Nathaniel's future was cemented when Commander Nathaniel died at the end of that same year. The young Nathaniel's personal course was set in the final years of the 1690s as a member of Micajah Perry's entourage.

As previously described, about 1689, Nathaniel's mariner father and brother Thomas traveled to Virginia. During their stay, Commander Nathaniel probably arranged a tobacco shipment on the Globe, but also to make arrangements for continued production on the family's original land patent on Arraciaco Swamp [25]. Nathaniel's land would have been a continuing source of personal revenue, if a sound arrangement for land tenancy could be held in place. During the visit, Nathaniel's son Thomas, though only seventeen at the time, witnessed the Old Rappahannock County probate of the estate of a certain Thomas New, a friend or sailing companion of his father [26]. If Thomas New had managed Nathaniel's land before 1689, then some new arrangement was now called for. Shortly after, in 1690, the elder Nathaniel witnessed a land transaction between a family named Langford and Thomas Watkins, another long-standing family friend [27]. It may be that Thomas Watkins assumed responsibility for Nathaniel's land at this point. If the younger Nathaniel traveled with them on this visit, he would have been between eight and nine years old. It may be that, while the others tended affairs in Old Rappahannock County, the young Nathaniel lodged with Hugh Sanders and his family in Isle of Wight County south of the James River [28].

Shortly after 1690, Nathaniel and his son(s) sailed back to Bristol, but the older son Thomas returned to Virginia again in 1695, this time for good [29].

Thomas thereafter married Jane, widow of Thomas Blanton, before 1699, the same year in which he accepted a wardship for Sarah, an orphan of Brian Ryly, until she reached the age of eighteen [30]. Although young Nathaniel did not return to Virginia in the company of his brother, he did permanently migrate to the colony before the century was out.

Before he died, the Commander would have treated the question of the family's Virginia land in Old Rappahannock County. After 1691, this land fell into the newly created Counties of King and Queen and Essex. Judging by subsequent events—again records are lacking—Nathaniel probably subdivided his holding, a portion in Essex County for son Thomas, and another in King and Queen County for Nathaniel. Such an arrangement at least accords with land records of later years.

Nathaniel in Virginia

Nathaniel Sanders married the daughter of his father's friend, Thomas Watkins, in 1701 or before. The only surprise in this is that the marriage took place in Nathaniel's twentieth year—very soon after he migrated to the colony. This is the earliest marriage we have found in the long documented history of this family [31]. The timing of this marriage is the best evidence that Nathaniel arrived in Virginia before the turn of the century, since one expects the marriage to have been preceded by some period of acquaintanceship.

In January of 1702, Thomas Watkins devised his last will and testament, naming Nathaniel Sanders as his son-in-law, though not naming his daughter, and leaving Nathaniel a "young horse or mare." Watkins's will was not proved until 1704, and the estate administration took another three years [32]. Also in 1701, James Boughan of Essex County claimed the headright of Elizabeth Saunders, Nathaniel's sister, following their mother's death in Bristol in 1700. Of Elizabeth we learn nothing more, save that she might have been a servant of William Merrick, son of Captain Sir William Merrick, while still in Bristol [33].

Thomas Watkins did not provide his daughter's given name in his will, and her name appears nowhere in available records. But we can venture a guess based on the traditional practice of that time of naming a daughter after the mother, in the same way that sons were named for their fathers. Nathaniel and his wife did name a daughter Sarah, and inspecting the names of female grandchildren, we found that the given name "Sarah" occurred most frequently among the children of Nathaniel's offspring. We use this name "Sarah" in the narrative that follows, but this name remains simply a guess.

More complicated is the question of why Nathaniel married at such a young age, and so soon after his arrival in Virginia. One possibility is that Nathaniel and "Sarah" were guilty of an indiscretion and a resultant pregnancy required his immediate taking of vows. But another circumstance suggests Nathaniel's hand might have been forced by a different necessity. The question revolves about a figure named John Wynell Sanders.

John Wynell Sanders is said by two family genealogists, Walter Sanders and Anna Parker, to be Nathaniel's "eldest son." Said to be a "seafaring man" by Walter Sanders, John Wynell Sanders is the only child of Nathaniel to have routinely used a middle name, an unfamiliar name at that. Middle names were not in the least vogue in Virginia at the time; in fact, one is hard-pressed to find any other example of this practice in Virginia records for the period. And for Nathaniel to have chosen the name "John" would be highly unusual, especially for a first son, as the name "John" is nowhere to be found in Nathaniel's family background [34]. Thus the notion that John Wynell was Nathaniel's eldest son seems dubious. Another possibility seems more likely—that "Sarah" was a widow at the time she married Nathaniel, having previously married a man named John Wynell, who imparted his name to a new son. If this conjectured husband John Wynell died soon after, his son would have been further endowed with the name "Sanders" after his widowed mother "Sarah" married Nathaniel. Without further records, this idea remains largely speculation. Following this line of reasoning, then, "Sarah" Watkins would have been in dire straits without a husband and with a young child when Nathaniel arrived in Virginia. Nathaniel may have been urged into this marriage by her solicitous father, who of course was Nathaniel's father's close friend.

Separate from questions about John Wynell, Nathaniel Sanders and his wife began their child-rearing years on family land in King and Queen County. By 1704, we find Nathaniel paying taxes on two hundred acres of land in King and Queen County not far from John Watkins, Thomas's son or brother [35]. One land patent provides a description:

> Henry Pigg, 122 acres, King and Queen County;
> on the back road; about one mile below John Watkins'
> plantation; adjacent Sanders' line; corner of Peter
> de Shazer; 2 Nov., 1705. [36]

Although this record does not identify Nathaniel by name, no Sanders other than Nathaniel owned land in King and Queen County at this time.

As to children, we are offered in family literature two versions of their offspring. One is provided by Anna Parker, who from unpublished family papers states that Nathaniel had four sons and several daughters. She indicates that only the son's names are known: Philip, Nathaniel, Hugh, and John [37]. The other version, authored by genealogist Walter Sanders, provides additional detail, stating that from Nathaniel's will five names are known. He lists Fanny,

Sally, Nathaniel, John, and Hugh [38]. We have determined that both lists are
accurate but incomplete.

THE FAMILY OF NATHANIEL SANDERS OF COLONIAL VIRGINIA

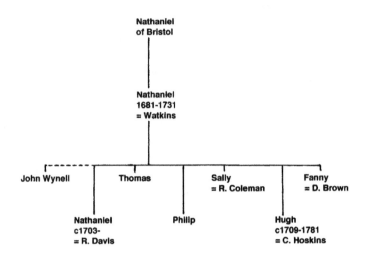

Source: Authors.

Judging by his name, the eldest son would have been Nathaniel; both
writers agree on this name. The name is expected, being taken from both
grandfather and father. Nathaniel also had a son Thomas, as that was the
name of his brother, his uncle, his grandfather, and his wife's father. Following
traditional naming patterns and sequences, this Thomas was probably the
second son. Though not named in Nathaniel's will of 1731, Philip was probably a
middle son of Nathaniel. He may have been named for a certain Philip Sanders
who lived in Essex County in the 1680s before Nathaniel arrived in Virginia,
as this Philip was in some manner linked to Nathaniel's brother Thomas.
Philip's exact relationship to Nathaniel's family, however, is unknown. Probably
the youngest son of Nathaniel and "Sarah" was Hugh, whose life we follow in
detail at a later point. Hugh Sanders is a comparatively rare name, found only
once in Virginia before the eighteenth century and not at all in this family
line in west England in the time of Nathaniel. If Nathaniel named a son after
Hugh Sanders of Virginia, it was probably because, as recounted previously,
the young Nathaniel lived with Hugh Sanders and his family in Isle of Wight
County at about age ten perhaps until Hugh died in 1691. Less is known about
Nathaniel's daughters, said by Anna Parker to be "several" in number. One was
Sarah Ann (Sally) and another was Fanny. Any other daughters have escaped

our detection. Birth years in all cases are unknown, but most if not all surviving children would have been born in the first decade of the 1700s, or very shortly thereafter. All these children are especially notable as the first native-born Virginians in this family line.

Nathaniel's Work

Nathaniel began his married life with land in King and Queen County, on land that may have been part of the family's original plot from the 1640s, or, as it lay adjacent to a Watkins property, it may have been dower lands for "Sarah" as her entitlement upon marriage. A record in 1704 suggests something of Nathaniel's nearby community. In that year, Nathaniel witnessed a land sale between Mary Worly Langford and John Crow in adjacent Essex County. Particular interest attaches to this record because Mary Worly was brought to Virginia by Edward Ditty, a ship's master who accompanied shipmaster Nathaniel Saunders in Barbados in 1674 [39]. Both Edward Ditty and the elder Nathaniel Saunders witnessed the will of James Hayman in Barbados and in Essex County, one of Thomas Edmondson's daughters married into the Hayman family. Nathaniel's involvement in Essex County affairs more than anything else reflected his own extended family's settlement history.

Nathaniel surely put his own land to use in tobacco or other crops for personal income, but whatever the extent of his total acreage from family sources, he seems not to have enlarged his holding to any great degree in the ensuing decade.Land issues and exchanges dominated the Virginia courts. Nathaniel provided legal witness for title changes to land in 1702, 1704, twice in 1709, 1713, and 1722, a slave sale in 1722, and a last will and testament in 1715. But his sole land acquisition in the decade following his marriage was a purchase of two 150 acres plots from his brother-in-law Thomas Watkins. This was the same land whose trade by Thomas Watkins was witnessed by Commander Nathaniel Sanders in his visit of 1689–1690 [40].

At least part of the reason he did not aggressively push his agricultural effort further was that Nathaniel's main interest and skills lay not in producing tobacco, but in handling it. That was a product of his early training with Micajah Perry's Company. In the language of the day, Nathaniel was Perry's "factor" in Virginia. Over his first decade or more in Virginia, Nathaniel's principal responsibility was to see that Perry's ships had holds full of tobacco on their return to England.

Ships arrived from England replete with goods in high demand in the colony—bolts of cloth, shoes, cookware, dinnerware, cutlery, numerous objects of fine manufacture not otherwise available in Virginia, and not least, wines and spirits from England and the continent. Nathaniel would see to the distribution of these objects, no doubt steering objects of great desire to his favored contacts who could afford them, many the same people who produced heavily in or controlled the local tobacco market. Among them were elected county commissioners. Nathaniel's linkage to these community leaders was immediate and thorough. Nathaniel witnessed numerous legal actions in Essex County, most involving government officials and in every instance, these were persons holding elected or appointed offices. Officeholders identified in records involving Nathaniel were Thomas Edmondson, James Boughan, Richard Covington, Francis Gouldman, Thomas Meriwether, Benjamin Moseley, and Robert Coleman. All were named Commissioners for the Peace for Essex County in 1705 and other years. These persons constituted a significant part of Nathaniel's community and endowed Nathaniel with mercantile advantage [41]. For example, Thomas Edmondson as sheriff of Essex County was charged with collecting a hundred-thousand-pound tobacco levy by Virginia's Governor Francis Nicholson [42]. Capturing the Essex levy for one of Perry's ships would be a good start toward filling its hold.

In 1715, Nathaniel and Capt. William Covington were awarded payment of debts in the probate of Thomas Edmondson's will [43]. Nathaniel was not named in the original will, but from this probate document, we learn that Edmondson engaged in the tobacco trade with England. Edmondson's debts to Nathaniel and William Covington suggest that Nathaniel has not yet been paid for tobacco, which earlier had been marketed by Edmondson. This probate yields he interesting background that Edmondson's money was in the hands of Mr. Micajah Perry and Company and Mr. Richard Lee, merchants of London. Transactions for this tobacco were conducted by Leonard Hill, a merchant, at the Virginia Coffee House in St. Michael's Alley, Cornehill, London. In Virginia, a servant named Jane Peacock worked for both Leonard Hill and Richard Covington, William's son. Perry, Lee, and Hill all were names of families in the Rappahannock region of Virginia; all were well-known to Nathaniel as part of his commercial repertoire.

Not long after 1715, a notable shift in Nathaniel's involvements is evident. His involvement with Essex County Commissioners and tobacco dealing in general seems to have ceased, and he began an entirely new commitment. A new focus lay in establishing and operating "ordinaries." In the space of a decade, Nathaniel had a hand in at least five ordinaries. He opened his own Essex County Ordinary in 1719 and supported Purkins (1722), Pettit (1723), Edmondson (1724), and Coleman (1729) in other licensing [44].In the cases of Edmondson and Coleman, their licenses allowed them to operate at "Sanders Ordinary" in Essex County. For all these, Nathaniel acquired licenses to legalize their establishment, receiving some portion of their earnings in return. It seems that Nathaniel no longer worked as Perry's factor after this time. This dramatic change suggests that Nathaniel passed on his knowledge and contacts for tobacco trading to his son John Wynell Sanders, who came of age in this period. John Wynell's later years make clear that he was a trader rather than producer of tobacco. He engaged tobacco trade with England as Master of two ships in later years.

Ordinaries were rudimentary inns established under license in private homes to accommodate travelers in sparsely settled areas. Licenses were issued by county governments and the requirements for keeping an ordinary were clearly spelled out: the proprietor must "constantly find and provide good wholesome and cleanly Lodging and Dyet for Travellers and Stableage fodder and provender or pasturage and provender as the season shall require for their horses . . . and shall not suffer or permit any unlawfull gameing in his house nor on ye Sabbath day suffer any to tipple or drink more than is necessary" [45]. It seems from Nathaniel's effort to acquire licenses that ordinaries provided a steady income from the growing stream of entrepreneurs and settlers anxious to explore opportunities in interior Virginia's sparsely settled new lands. Beyond travelers, ordinaries also served in some cases as local public houses, as the sparcity of towns and villages in the newer counties of Virginia provided little opportunity for socializing beyond what ordinaries could offer.

AN ORDINARY STORY

In 1719, Nathaniel obtained his first license to open the ordinary in Essex County. This Ordinary evidently was located at the site of his deceased brother Thomas's dwelling. Thomas's estate inventory following his death in 1708 provides a glimpse of this home. Thomas's estate after ten years of work reveals little in the way of accumulation beyond livestock (a few cows and pigs), kitchen utensils, basic furniture, rugs, and two guns. A chest with lock and key provided a modicum of security. His small collection of one large and six small cider casks hints at one source of income. The feather bed was the prized possession, although Thomas and his wife Jane possessed trundle and cattail beds as well. Items that might be thought luxuries were a few old books, a looking glass, a parcel of flax, another of pewter, and eight old swords. The inventory lists no tools of any kind. In all, this estate was valued at just over twenty-one pounds, more than half of which lay in his livestock and the feather bed [1*]. But in the details of Thomas's inventory lies a hint of a larger story.

Thomas immigrated to Virginia permanently in 1695 at age twenty-three, and acquired land in Essex County near a certain Philip Sanders. This Philip Sanders had been in Virginia for nearly thirty years by the time Thomas arrived. Philip's exact relationship with the family of Nathaniel and Thomas is unknown, but he was of an age to make him contemporary with their father, Commander Nathaniel Sanders of Bristol. Loosely, then, Philip can be imagined as a kind of "uncle" to brothers Thomas and Nathaniel.

In 1698 Thomas Sanders married Jane Blanton in Essex County. Family records erroneously state that Jane was the daughter of Thomas Blanton. In fact, Thomas Blanton was Jane's first husband, who died in 1697. Jane Blanton was born Jane Maguffey about the year 1671. Her own background is complex [2*], but she brought six Blanton children to her new Sanders household. To this total was added Ann, a daughter to Jane and Thomas, and Sarah Ryly, daughter of deceased Brian Ryly, whose wardship was accepted by Thomas until Sarah reached the age of eighteen. After two years of marriage, by the year 1700, Thomas was twenty-eight years old and a Virginia resident for five years. His household consisted of eight children and Jane, age twenty-nine. No doubt all these children remained in Thomas's household during his marriage years because Thomas owned one feather bed used for the adults, and several trundle and cattail beds for the children.

We have no settled ideas on how Thomas supported his household except perhaps as a paid seaman, but as he was in possession of six cider casks at the time of his death, at least part of his income probably derived from cider production. This activity was not unusual for the time, because cider was the principal drink in colonial Virginia except for those who could afford to import wine from Europe. The cider itself was produced from apples, which trees were planted in Jamestown's earliest years. The apples themselves were small and tart and not used for eating directly. In later years Thomas Jefferson introduced improvements based on other European stock, and from these early beginnings some modern apples have evolved. Thomas's cider presumably would have been distributed to individual families and local ordinaries if any existed in his time or locale.

Thomas Sanders died in 1708 at age thirty-six, and his widow, Jane Blanton Sanders, married Richard Hill the following year. Jane and Richard had a son Richard, who in later years called Ann Sanders his "sister." All but two of Jane's children entered the Hill household as well. The eldest Blanton child and Sarah Ryly Sanders (as she was call by then) had reached the age of eighteen, and took on independent lives after that [3*].

Sarah Ryly Sanders married Henry Bate within a year or two of Thomas Sanders' death. From the perspective of deep family relationships, this marriage comes as no surprise. Henry Bate evidently grew up in Essex County and in some way was related to another Bate named Nathaniel. Nathaniel Bate's father, probably William Bate, died in Essex County in 1684 and his younger son Nathaniel became the ward of Philip Sanders, Thomas's "uncle," by 1685. Recall here that Sarah grew up in Thomas Sanders' household, a near neighbor of his "uncle" Philip Sanders [4*]. But this Sanders-Bate relationship had even deeper roots, because in previous years in other parts of Virginia the sister of an earlier Henry Bate married Edward Stratton—the name of Nathaniel Sanders' grandfather—and another Bate married into the Watkins family. So it was that after about 1710 Sarah Ryly Sanders and Henry Bate resided in Essex County and in time had three children, Henry, Humphrey, and Ann.

By 1709 Thomas Sanders' house stood empty. This poses an interesting prospect, sketched here. As Thomas's legatee, Jane Sanders Hill could decide on the house's use. It seems she allowed her daughter's family, the Bates, to assume possession of the property, either freely or under some rental arrangement, as she had moved into the Hill residence. No sale of the property seems to have taken place. Thomas's brother Nathaniel maintained personal and perhaps commercial interest in this particular arrangement because in 1719, Nathaniel obtained a license to open an ordinary in Essex County. Given the timing, one can suggest that this ordinary was established at Thomas's house, occupied and operated by Sarah and Henry Bate. By 1719 their children had grown a bit. One might even guess the Bates may have continued Thomas Sanders' cider-making to provision the ordinary. Nathaniel's ordinary continued to operate until 1724, in which time the Bates left Essex County for North Carolina. Nathaniel abandoned his management of the ordinary the same year, giving it over to Thomas Edmondson. Two years later, Nathaniel saw the ordinary shift from Edmondson to James Coleman, who was licensed to keep his own ordinary at "Sanders' Ordinary."

So it appears that Nathaniel Sanders maintained close contact with Sarah and Henry Bate between the years 1710 and 1724 in Essex County, Sarah and her children representing the last vestiges of his brother Thomas's short life in Virginia. These fourteen years were enough for Nathaniel to see the Bate children reach their teenage years before the family departed for North Carolina.

But the Bate story does not end at this point. The Bates were Quakers, and being Quakers in colonial Virginia was by no means easy, though they were not directly persecuted. They were vilified by Anglican churchmen, jeered, mocked, and often disadvantaged in court proceedings. Most disliked was Quaker aversion to armed warfare and their refusal to swear secular oaths. Their numbers were relatively small. The nearest Friends Meeting House in the time of Henry and Sarah Bate was in Caroline County, too great a distance from their home in Essex to permit frequent attendance. Around the year 1724, a large migration of Quakers, mostly from Virginia's southern counties, was undertaken. They ended up about one hundred miles south of the Virginia border in Birtie County, North Carolina. At that time, North Carolina was a neglected colony, offering little in the way of governance of any kind, but also offering greater freedom in religious matters.

A certain Nathaniel Bate, after whom Philip Sanders' ward of 1685 ward was named, is often named as the original English settler in North Carolina. He lived with Indians of the area and established a fur trade. Nathaniel Bate was visited in the 1670s by English missionary George Fox, founder of the Society of Friends (Quakers). Fox developed a particularly strong following in Isle of Wight County in Virginia which later formed the nucleus of Quaker migration to North Carolina some decades later. Exactly how Henry Bate was connected to this earlier Nathaniel Bate is not clear, but the dual themes of Quakerism and North Carolinian freedoms evidently dominated Henry Bate's life. Henry, Sarah and their three children left Essex County about 1724 for good, and took up a successful life in Birtie County after that. Henry Bate died early and by 1740 Sarah had residence with her son Henry. This younger Henry, in his own will, provided his "honorable (or honored) Mother Sanders" with land and money to build her a house. The expression "honorable Mother" derives from Biblical origins and was frequently used by Quakers. Sarah's other son, Humphrey, was given land by Nathaniel Sanders in his 1731 will, at which time his nephew Humphrey was coming of age [5*].

Joining the Bates in this migration was Nathaniel, eldest son of Nathaniel Sanders of King and Queen County. He is said in family records to have been a preacher and to have moved to North Carolina. That is only partly accurate. Nathaniel was a Quaker and did move to North Carolina in his early twenties, but as Quakers do not have preachers, we can impute only that Nathaniel migrated for religious reasons. Nathaniel was a cattleman and died intestate, probably in the 1740s, leaving his estate to his son, Thomas William Maximilian Sanders. This odd name had Quaker inspirations, because Quakers strongly admired a third-century figure named Maximilian, who refused to take up arms as ordered by his Roman superiors. In 1729, Nathaniel listed his cattle "earmarks" among those farmers filing this information to a new colonial administration in North Carolina. In later years, in the 1730s and 1740s, Nathaniel can be found in Northampton County, North Carolina after Birtie County was subdivided into smaller county units [6*].

In the same year that Nathaniel opened his ordinary, he also began to acquire land on a larger scale. The year before, he had sold seventy acres in Essex County to Thomas Wethersby, land he took back three years later [46]. But in 1719, Nathaniel joined with Thomas Chew to acquire four hundred acres of new land in the unsettled northern reaches of King and Queen County at a location called Piney Lick. An exact location for this land has not been determined, but it undoubtedly lay upstream in the tributaries of the Mattaponi or Rappahannock Rivers. This they sold to Colonel Gawin Corbin in 1722 [47].

In 1726, Nathaniel, by now age forty-five, purchased 1,200 acres of new land in King William County. This transaction reflected the uncertainty of county boundaries for new lands because this same acquisition was shown elsewhere to be in Caroline County. The question of how Nathaniel was able to acquire this large amount of land is addressed in Caroline County records, where Nathaniel is said to have been a "favorite" of Governor Drysdale [48]. Favorites were minor gentry (Nathaniel is called a "planter" here) who were held in some esteem by governors or their lieutenants. They were granted land of one thousand acres or more, provided they actually seated the land; those who failed to do so were in danger of losing the grant. Grants to favorites were land entitlements that went beyond the normal strictures of homestead laws and were a logical extension of the process by which Virginia's gentry maintained its hold on colonial wealth and governance. One suspects that his long-term involvement with several of Essex County's leading citizens may have resulted in Nathaniel's good fortune in this instance. In any case, that Nathaniel was now regarded as a "planter" and a "favorite," suggesting perhaps more vertical social and political mobility in Virginia than historians of the period suggest we might expect.

At risk of feeding the geographical confusions of the day, we can add that Nathaniel's same twelve hundred acres are also later described as land on Glady Fork in Spotsylvania County, land that remained in the family for another generation. Nathaniel paid six pounds sterling for that land. And to this sizable holding Nathaniel added yet another adjacent 1,000 acres in 1728, land which unambiguously fell into Spotsylvania [49]. This brought Nathaniel's holding to 2,200 acres of new land. The purchase of 1728 was to be Nathaniel's final land acquisition.

Final Days

Nathaniel Sanders died at age fifty, his last will and testament being proved on August 4, 1731 [50]. Although the will has not been found, some records of bequeathed land have survived, given us a partial idea of Nathaniel's wishes. We have no record of a specific bequest for John Wynell Sanders, but he offers a story of some success, with or without a provision in Nathaniel's will. By 1740 John joined a consortium of businessmen to purchase more than 500 acres on land in Caroline and Spotsylvania Counties, farmland which they managed for sixteen years. That he was heavily involved in tobacco trading is certain, as he was master of the ships London in 1742 and the Industry in 1751. He is found in numerous Spotsylvania records into the 1760s, but without land purchases. John did acquire land in Culpeper County, where he obtained 335 acres in 1749 "because of service in the French and Indian War," land which lay at the Great Fork of the Rappahannock River beginning on the south side of Butler's Swamp [51]. John Wynell Sanders evidently died in Fauquier county in the 1780s, his will being witnessed by Thomas Sanders, his brother.

In his will of 1731 Nathaniel gave his eldest son Nathaniel four hundred acres of land in Spotsylvania County, but Nathaniel never took up this property. As previously described, he owned land in Northampton and Edgecombe counties, North Carolina. In 1743 Nathaniel ceded these four hundred acres to Robert Coleman, husband of his sister Sarah, for payment of overdue taxes, John Wynell Sanders witnessing. In 1731, Nathaniel also left two hundred acres to Humphrey Bate, son of Sarah Ryly Sanders of North Carolina, at which time this Humphrey was coming of age.

For his son Thomas, Nathaniel left four hundred acres of Spotsylvania land, though it is unlikely that Thomas put that to his own use. In the 1730s Thomas worked as a stonemason, working with William Philips in Caroline County. Subsequent generations of these Philips are credited with stonemasonry in a property called called Estouteville (1827–1830), now on the National Register of Historic Places, and again later acting as stonemason at Thomas Jefferson's new University of Virginia. In 1743 Thomas, declaring that he was a mason (stonemason), mortgaged his Spotsylvania land [52] to build a racetrack in Front Royal, Fauquier County. Whether the racetrack was built is unknown, but Thomas remained there long enough to witness his brother's will in the 1780s.

We have no record of Philip being included in Nathaniel's 1731 will, perhaps because Philip is found only in Caroline County records throughout his adult life. But he may have received some portion of Nathaniel's 1,200 acres purchased in 1726, as some of this fell in Caroline County. Philip was called a "Planter," living with his wife Mary in Drysdale Parish through the 1760s [53]. Similarly, no specific records of bequests for daughters Sarah and Fanny have been located. Sarah married Robert Coleman. This couple is found in records of Essex, King and Queen, and Spotsylvania counties for three decades, from the 1730s to 1759. Of all Nathaniel's children, least is known of Fanny. She is said to have married Daniel Brown, and that seems probable, because a Daniel Brown held property adjacent to land that Nathaniel purchased in 1726. The couple may have moved to Culpeper County, though we have been unable to confirm this assertion [54].

Evidently the largest portion of Nathaniel's land was inherited by Hugh, his youngest son. Hugh received all of the one thousand acres that Nathaniel bought in 1728, which in fact Nathaniel had placed in Hugh's hand at the time of purchase. Hugh Sanders' inherited lands provided a solid base of settlement for the next generation of his family. It is to Hugh's story we next turn.

Of Nathaniel's life, we can reflect that he arrived in Virginia a young man, both parents deceased, and married well, building a life of some prosperity. He fathered and supported at least seven children who survived into adulthood, beginning with a few hundred acres and ending with more than three thousand. In that time, he joined in the inexorable move toward the Virginia interior as new lands open up, and established a reputation and status as a planter, no small accomplishment in a colony that admitted very few to its exclusive middle and upper social classes. Nathaniel's acquired social standing and substantial property gains underwrote the more comfortable lives of the next generation of these Sanders.

NOTES

1. Nell Nugent, *Cavaliers and Pioneers*, vol. 1 (Baltimore: Genealogical Publishing Company, 1983), p. 247.
2. Beverley Fleet, *Virginia Colonial Abstracts*, vol. 1 (Baltimore, Genealogical Publishing Company, 1988), p. 603.
3. Nugent, *Cavaliers and Pioneers*, vol. 1, p. 480.
4. Ibid., vol. 2. Virginia State Library, Richmond, p. 71. A John Sanders is named in the will of Henry Saunders, mariner, of Abbots Leigh, Somerset, a maritime center near Bristol. Henry died in 1665 and it may be that his son John is the same person who went to Virginia in 1667. Timing seems about right for him to be the same person as John Sanders of Warwick County, Virginia, though the matter is far from certain.
5. Peter W. Coldham, *Complete Book of Emigrants*, vol. 2 (Baltimore: Genealogical Publishing Company, 1990), p. 67.
6. David H. Fischer, *Albion's Seed* (New York: Oxford University Press, 1989), pp. 211–212.
7. Ibid., p. 227.
8. Ibid., p. 307.
9. Ibid., p. 214.
10. Ibid., p. 216.
11. Ibid., p. 218.
12. Ibid., p. 220.
13. Ibid., p. 222.
14. Daniel Boorstin, *The Americans: The Colonial Experience* (New York: Vintage Books, 1958), p. 123.
15. Ibid., p. 124.
16. Ibid., p. 122.
17. Ibid., p. 116.
18. Ibid., p. 101.
19. Jane Carson, *Bacon's Rebellion: 1676–1976* (Jamestown: Jamestown Foundation, 1976), pp. 4–11.
20. Boorstin, *Colonial Experience*, p. 102.
21. John Sanders was a ship's carpenter by trade and arrived in Virginia in 1664 with Philip Sanders, thought to be his brother. He is found

occasionally in records of Old Rappahannock County but no records of land ownership for John have surfaced. As a sailor, John would have chafed under the Navigation Acts that can be seen as one provocation for Bacon's Rebellion. See Carson, *Bacon's Rebellion*, p. 39. Following the collapse of the rebellion, John was indicted and sentenced to the gallows, but Berkeley's recall to England forestalled this action, and rebels were released after that. We extend our gratitude to Dr. Tom E. Sanders of Louisville, Kentucky, for pointing out the narrowness of John's escape from the noose.

22. Carson, *Bacon's Rebellion*, p. 51.

23. Kenneth O. Morgan, ed., *The Oxford Illustrated History of Britain* (Oxford: Oxford University Press, 1984), p. 354. The importance of Morgan's remark can scarcely be overstated. The notion that people should be thought capable of agreeing without coercion to be governed is revolutionary. That they should be governed by someone of their own choosing is more revolutionary yet and can be thought the main impetus of modern society as we understand it.

24. Anna V. Parker, *The Sanders Family of Grass Hills* (Madison, Indiana: Coleman Printing, 1966), p. 1.

25. Nugent, *Cavaliers and Pioneers*, p. 293.

26. Nathaniel's brother Thomas witnessed legal action concerning the estate of Thomas New of Old Rappahannock, later Essex, County in 1689. Thomas New was indentured in Bristol for service in Virginia in 1672. He was in Old Rappahannock County by 1681 and in 1687; after his death, New's land passed to Francis Gouldman who previously sold land to Philip Sanders, perhaps Thomas's uncle. But this family interrelationship was older than that because Richard New held land near Capt. Thomas Harwood, erstwhile master of the *Golden Lion*, and lived near John Sanders, probably of Abbots Leigh, Somerset, who married Susanna Ravenett of Warwick County, Virginia.

27. See Essex County Deeds, #031172, Book D&C, vol. 13, p. 21.

28. Hugh Sanders of Isle of Wight County died in 1691, his lands passing to his son Henry. Nathaniel's selection of the name Hugh is unlikely to have drawn upon the family naming tradition in Wales, but rather may have honored Hugh Sanders of Isle of Wight County, Virginia, as their lives overlapped. Hugh Sanders died when Nathaniel was about age ten.

29. Nell Nugent, *Cavaliers and Pioneers*, vol. 3 (Richmond: Virginia State Library, 1979), p. 2. Edwin Thacker of Middlesex County acquired 2,634 acres in Essex County for fifty-three headrights, including that of Thomas Sanders. Our review of these headrights found that the young Nathaniel was not among these fifty-three names.

30. Essex County Deeds, #031162, Book D&C, vol. 9, pp. 341–342. Thomas Blanton evidently arrived in Virginia around 1682, after that acquiring two hundred acres or more on three separate occasions in what later became Essex County. Thomas Saunders's acceptance of Sarah Ryly's wardship may be tied to Thomas Blanton's earlier history of importing Irishmen to the colony. See Nugent, *Cavaliers and Pioneers*, pp. 238, 240, 315.

31. Thomas Watkins wrote his will on 10 January 1702, identifying Nathaniel Sanders as his son-in-law, indicating that Nathaniel was married as early as 1701. See Essex County Deeds, #031172, vol. 13, p. 30. He named his sons Lewis, Thomas, Benjamin, and John, a daughter Margaret Coats, a godson Will Bristodine, sons-in-law Nathaniel Sanders and William Cole and his wife Ann.

    Watkins records in early Virginia are tightly correlated with Sanders records throughout the period, leading to the conclusion of a longstanding relationship between these families, evidenced early in the 1640s in Virginia with the relationship between Edward Watkins and Thomas Saunders, Nathaniel's grandfather; See for example Fleet, *Virginia Colonial Abstracts*, vol. 3, p. 82.

32. Confusion about Nathaniel's arrival date in Virginia, his date of marriage, and the probable birth dates of children may stem from the fact that five years elapsed between the time Watkins authored his will and the time it was finally probated.

33. Nugent, *Cavaliers and Pioneers*, p. 41. Elizabeth Sanders's headright was claimed by James Boughan, a close associate of William Covington, in 1701, the date incorrectly claimed by Anna Parker to have been Nathaniel's year of arrival in Virginia. Both Boughan and Covington held local government posts in Essex County. Elizabeth's employment with Merrick before traveling to Virginia is suggested in The inhabitants of Bristol in 1696, Bristol Record Society Publication, vol. 25. We have misplaced a record we believe stated that after arrival in Virginia, Elizabeth Sanders married into the Ironmonger family.

34. Well, almost nowhere. Edward Teach's (a.k.a. Blackbeard) ship, the *Queen Anne's Revenge*, was found recently in shallow waters off North Carolina's outer banks. A handwritten note in Anna Parker's papers states that John Sanders, brother of Hugh, was thought to have been one of Blackbeard's men. John Sanders's indictment for piracy is found in Essex County Deeds, #031163, Book D&W, vol. 10, pp. 49A–49B. But we find no connection of this John to the family we describe here.

35. Annie L. W. Smith, *The Quit Rents of Virginia* (1704). (Richmond, Virginia: Chesterfield Press, 1957), p. 78.

36. Nugent, *Cavaliers and Pioneers*, p. 99.

37. Parker, *Sanders Family*, p. 108.
38. Walter Sanders, unpublished papers (Sanders Genealogy), n.d. Held at the Litchfield, Illinois Public Library.
39. Essex County Deeds, #031171, D&C Book, vol. 12, pp. 65–66.
40. Essex County Deeds, #031172, D&C Book, vol. 13, pp. 388–390.
41. Ibid., pp. 108, 118, 233.
42. Essex County Record Book Number 11, p. 15.
43. Fleet, *Virginia Colonial Abstracts*, vol. 2, pp. 62, 82.
44. Ibid., pp. 144–146. Records of Nathaniel Sanders's involvement with ordinaries are found in Essex County records for the years 1722 (Purkins), 1723 (Pettit), 1724 (Edmondson), and 1729 (Coleman).
45. The requirements for keeping an ordinary are described in J. R. Mansfield, *A History of Early Spotsylvania* (Orange, Virginia: Green Publishers, 1977), pp. 141–142.
46. Essex County Deeds, #031165, D&C Book, vol. 16, pp.24–28; 296–300.
47. Nugent, *Cavaliers and Pioneers*, p. 233.
48. Nugent, *Cavaliers and Pioneers*, p. 303. Caroline land grants to favorites are listed in T. E. Campbell, *Colonial Caroline: A History of Caroline County, Virginia* (Richmond, Virginia: Dietz Press, 1954), p. 303.
49. Ibid., p. 355.
50. We have been unable to locate the 1731 will of Nathaniel Sanders. Walter Sanders apparently saw it but failed to note its location. The will probably provided the basis on which Walter identified Nathaniel's children, but Walter made no mention of Nathaniel's wife.
51. Mike Sanders, Early Sanders Records from the Library of Virginia. Rootsweb.com 2007.
52. William A. Crozier, *Spotsylvania County Records: 1721–1800* (Baltimore: Southern Books Company, 1955), record for 1743.
53. Philip Sanders of King and Queen County had three daughters, who are as follows: (1) Frances, born in 1740, married in 1762 to Capt. John Sale, and died in Amherst County, Virginia in 1832; (2) Clara, who before 1772 married Thomas Sale, brother of John, and died in Amherst County; and (3) Mary, who is found in Essex County records. See Essex County Court Orders, 1749–1751, pp. 179, 254, inter alia. Also see D. S. Goodman, *Root and Branch of the Sale Tree in America* (1939), Appendix p. xii. We are grateful to Muriel Gregory of Raton, New Mexico, for sharing this information.
54. We appreciate the assistance of family researcher Nancy Josue of Santa Rosa, California, for her advice regarding Sanders family records for Culpeper County.

NOTES FOR AN ORDINARY STORY

1*. Thomas Saunders's wife was Jane Blanton. He died in 1708 in Essex County. Jane Blanton, Thomas Munday, and Francis Graves were bound to James Boughan, gentleman, for two hundred pounds sterling, for the faithful execution of Thomas's will. See Essex County Deeds, #031172, vol. 3, p. 159. The inventory of Thomas's estate was completed on October 11, 1708. Essex County Deeds, #031172, vol. 13, pp. 175–176.

2*. Jane's mother, also called Jane, was born about 1645, but her maiden name is unknown. This elder Jane married four times, to:

   (a) a person named Davenport about 1663, and he died about 1667;

   (b) John Maguffey about 1668 and he died in 1676. With John, she had two children: John and Jane Maguffey, born about 1671;

   (c) Francis Graves (1630–1691) about 1677, having three children, Francis, Richard, and Thomas. This husband died in 1691; and

   (d) John Doughty about 1692 who died in 1704.

The younger Jane Maguffey (from marriage #2 above) married three times, to:

   (a) Thomas Blanton about the year 1690 and had six children, Richard, John, William, Thomas, Jane, and Elizabeth (order of birth not known). Thomas Blanton died in 1697;

   (b) Thomas Sanders in the year 1968, having a daughter Ann. Thomas died in 1708; and

   (c) Richard Hill, having a son Richard.

Note that there were a total of seven marriages for this mother and daughter, reflecting the high mortality rate for these husbands and importantly, the fact that in Virginia at that time, males outnumbered females by a factor of about four-to-one. Wives were in short supply.

3*. Our estimate of the age of Sarah Ryly is based on the following argument: in 1731 Nathaniel left Humphrey Bate, son of Sarah Ryly Sanders, two hundred acres of land in Spotsylvania County. Humphrey must have been of adult age, or very nearly so, to be so named in his will. This suggests Humphrey was born about 1712 or so, implying that Sarah was already married by that date. If Sarah was eighteen to twenty years old at her marriage, then she was born about 1690. The Blanton children's ages would have ranged from about ten to eighteen at the time of Thomas's death, and his daughter Ann was probably nine at that time.

4*. It may be that Philip resided on Commander Nathaniel's land that fell into South Farnham Parish, Essex County, the same general location for the Commander's son Thomas. As Thomas arrived in Virginia not long after Philip died, Thomas could have taken up Philip's abode. Note that a Bate is found in both Philip and Thomas's houses. They may have been and the same structures. See Essex County Deeds, #033649, Order Book 1, p. 209. This record indicates that Philip Sanders was involved in a legal contest regarding custody of a certain Nathaniel Bate in 1686.

5*. Henry Bate's Will is found in The North Carolina Historical and Genealogical Register, vol. 1, p. 28. The full text is extant. See also Crozier's Spotsylvania County Records, Deed Book F: 1761–1776, p. 224.

6*. Abstracts of Edgecombe County, North Carolina: 1759–1772, Deed Book 00, p. 20. See Also Birtie County, NC Deeds for Nathaniel's cattle records. Nathaniel gave his son the full name Thomas William Maximilian Sanders. On the use of the name Maximilian, see Hodgson, William, Select Historical Memoirs of the Religious Society of Friends, Commonly Called Quakers. Philadelphia: J. B. Lippincott Co. 1867.

CHAPTER ELEVEN

Spotsylvania

Hugh Sanders lived his entire adult life in Spotsylvania County, Virginia. Born about 1709 as a young, perhaps the youngest, son of Nathaniel Sanders of King and Queen County, Hugh grew steadily into a life of land acquisition and exchange, tobacco farming, and tobacco trade. In his own family, Hugh was part of the first generation born in Virginia, and his later life held nothing of English or overseas concerns, save his marketing of tobacco. His father won recognition as a planter, an important designation in status-conscious colonial Virginia, and Hugh was accorded the same title as an adult. His property entitlement came early on. In 1728, when he was eighteen or nineteen years old, his father gave Hugh a thousand acres of unsettled land in the upper reaches of the Mattaponi River in the newly minted county of Spotsylvania. This was frontier country, full of hardship, full of opportunity, full of speculation.

The system of impenetrable social ranks engineered so effectively by Sir William Berkeley decades before perpetuated itself brilliantly in colonial Virginia in the many years since Berkeley's rule and into the life of Hugh Sanders. This English system of titles and social labels deeply stabilized colonial Virginia society. Titles dictated one's entitlements, the rationale, form, and content of social interactions, the sense of one's place in the larger scheme of things. Hugh as a small planter commanded some local esteem from his title and married well, living a life of modest prosperity though without any strong likelihood of upward mobility.

The driving force behind Virginia's social order lay in the near-universal acceptance of social stratification as inherently right and proper. Most vital was that Virginia's peoples accepted these defined positions as inevitable and useful and believed them profoundly correct and moral as a way to order their world [1]. This belief attached not only to those in the highest tiers of society, those very people who could accept such positions most easily, but also those below them who would think elevated ranks justified and would find equal justification in their own ranks, mean though they sometimes might have been. So it was that a blacksmith ought not to judge himself fit to rule, nor a slave fit to be free. This principle of profound rightness in the existing social order, applied to the Virginia of the early eighteenth century, explains why the monstrous institution of slavery persisted so successfully. Hugh Sanders had a number of slaves and had routine concerns but probably little remorse about their life condition. The deep personal inculcation of moral instruction about social difference, or social inequality, for all parties in all strata in society provided the means for its members to maintain a coherent social order despite its wildly unequal outcomes. Enforcement of the status quo by and large was self-enforcement.

This does not mean that upsets, bothers, never occurred. Slaves did rebel and try to escape, and nonconformists or recalcitrants occasionally had their day. Tempests of the minor sort can indeed be found at that time in Virginia, but these generally veered away from attacking society's foundations. Upsets tended to be of two kinds. First, there were actions that attempted to right some wrongs that disturbed the rational order—actions that were deeply conservative, aiming to maintain society's best traditions of church, economy, and polity. Second, there were protests rooted in the inconveniences of expanding frontier settlement, circumstances in which the proper social order was threatened by weak infrastructures and institutions in the colony's newest counties.

Beneath the surface of moderate protest throughout the 1700s, though, lay more insidious realities that wormed their way into Virginia's fragile psyche. From the perspective of Virginians, the two main pillars of colonial society, its government and its established religion, had never been set straight. After Bacon's Rebellion of 1676 and the demise of Sir William Berkeley's governorship and a few others that followed, the English government for sixty-eight years decided not to appoint another royal governor for Virginia. Rather, it named a succession of deputy governors whose power and prestige were insufficient to command full respect in the colony and any meaningful political clout back in England. Effective representation in the halls of English government was sorely lacking for two generations of Virginia's citizenry, and they knew it.

England further compounded this insult to the colony's sense of self-importance by rejecting its requests for an Anglican bishop. All ecclesiastical affairs for the colony were decided by bishops across the Atlantic in ignorance of colonial church needs, oblivious to the falling hopes for effective ministry during the colony's time of great physical expansion. In Virginia, the established church simply did not keep up and failed to show that Virginia's needs mattered very much. A Virginia bishop never was appointed.

The American Revolution, when it finally did come in 1776, was not initially very revolutionary in Virginia, in large part because Virginians had no culture of dissent rooted in alternative belief. Among Virginians of that time, the sorest point in the long train of aggravations was that they were denied an Englishman's rights, which grievance if properly addressed would have restored a more perfect earlier state. English taxation was vexing and personally costly but was not a cause over which to discard one's government. But to be denied a respect accorded routinely to one's peers in England was another matter altogether. The Virginians' objection was not to "taxation," but "taxation without representation," a prevailing sense that Virginians were not seen as fully English, not equally entitled to representation in an Englishman's government. So it was in Hugh Sanders' life that things eventually fell apart in Virginia; the center of English culture could not hold.

Early Years

Hugh Sanders spent his earliest days in King and Queen County at his parents' farm. While still a youth, he perhaps and chored in Essex County at the family's ordinary that offered travelers room and board. Hugh would have seen to guests' horses and moved about the stable and guest lodgings according to instruction. If he was particularly responsible in these growing-up years, that might explain why Hugh seems to have been favored among Nathaniel's sons with the largest gift of land any of the children received. His father had purchased twelve hundred acres of new land in Spotsylvania County in 1726 and two years later added another thousand acres. On the same day of purchase in 1728, Nathaniel placed this latter acreage in Hugh's hands [2]. Nathaniel's act was to fix Hugh's future in Spotsylvania County, a location from which he never ventured long. Hugh's new land lay on Gladys Fork of the Po River, one of the four main tributaries of the Mattaponi River [3].

Hugh's father Nathaniel died three years later, in 1731, leaving Hugh with even more land in Spotsylvania County than the initial thousand acres. Of Nathaniel's 2,200 acres that we know about, Hugh came into possession of at least 1,657 acres of it. Little seems to have gone to Hugh's brothers, perhaps because they had other interests. Other than Philip, who evidently farmed in Caroline County, Hugh's other brothers had different ideas. Thomas, who resided in Spotsylvania County in 1743, mortgaged his personal estate for fifty-three pounds currency and aimed to open a race track in Port Royal. Nathaniel abandoned his inherited property and joined a Quaker migration to North Carolina, and an older brother John Wynell, following his grandfather's example, had gone to sea [4].

In the 1620s and 1630s in Virginia, new land purchases required seating, that is, establishing some form of domicile or other evidence that new land was not being used for speculation alone, a rule promulgated to serve the colony's goal of expanding its agricultural export base. Legal ownership lapsed for lack of seating and could be claimed by farmers or opportunists alike. But Hugh probably was in no position to seat his first inheritance of 1628. He was young and unmarried, and as things turned out, it was just as well that he did not try. The year 1728 was a year of plagues, three in all, that washed over frontier Caroline and Spotsylvania counties. The year began with a severe caterpillar infestation that laid waste to crops and trees. The resulting loss of natural forage led to deer invasions and destruction of field and kitchen crops. Deer carcasses abounded from starvation, and weakened deer attracted large numbers of wolves, which took not only deer but domestic livestock as well. Against these odds, stacked with caterpillars, deer, and wolves, any effort to begin farming operations in Spotsylvania County in 1728 would have come to naught [5].

Matters grew no easier in the following decade. Frontier road building had begun in the 1730s in Caroline and Spotsylvania counties. Its main goal was to link tobacco-growing lands with new warehouses on the Rappahannock River to assist growers in avoiding difficult and unreliable transportation on the shallower Mattaponi to the south. But as this progress moved forward, the British government changed the rules of tobacco trade. A Tobacco Transportation Act passed in 1732 required owners to pack hogsheads with whole unstripped leaves of tobacco, reducing growers' return on these devalued shipments. Farmers responded by disobeying the act and burning warehouses, but the profit from tobacco cultivation had been significantly reduced [6].

Though this disobedience was small in the larger scheme of British colonial rule, it was part of a growing sense of discontent among the colonials. In 1735, an election for burgesses in neighboring Caroline County challenged the longstanding canon of genteel politics in the colony. The contest pitted a candidate of small farmers and artisans on one side against a royalist, large planter candidate on the other. The campaign erupted in rancor as opposing nominees ran particularly unscrupulous campaigns. The small farmer candidate finally tallied more votes, but a court invalidated the result on evidence of cheating. Though the election furor eventually died down, partisan lines had been drawn clearly along economic and social classes, a political division from which there was to be no retreat [7].

One gets a sense that Hugh never seated much or any of his father's Spotsylvania land during the 1730s because in 1739, a suit was filed alleging that Hugh's claim to sixteen hundred acres had lapsed [8]. Lapsed land, land unseated for a period of ten years, was fair game, and a certain William Bartlett tried to claim it. But Hugh found the perfect device to withstand Bartlett's suit. He sold his land to a certain Ambrose Foster, in effect stopping the clock on his own title, and later reacquired it from Foster to begin a new term of ownership beginning in 1740 [9]. This manipulation cost Hugh two hundred pounds paid to Foster for the transaction, which Hugh partly defrayed that same year by selling two smaller tracts of land for a total of thirty-nine pounds currency [10].

In 1735, Catherine Hoskins and Hugh Sanders were married. Catherine, affectionately known as Caty through all her years, was only about seventeen years old at marriage and Hugh about twenty-six. Caty is recalled as being a "small woman, having been injured in a horseback fall which caused her to limp, but of great energy" [11]. She was the daughter of Samuel and Mary Brereton Hoskins of Essex County. Caty Hoskins bore a distinction of descending from one of Virginia's "ancient planters," that small cadre of surviving adventurers who came to Virginia under the auspices of the Virginia Company of London. Bartholomew Hoskins came to Virginia in 1616 as a boy; over the years, he found his way into some prosperity. Hoskins Creek near today's Tappahannock in Essex County takes its name from Bartholomew Hoskins' early land claim in that area. Decades later, Samuel Hoskins or his father of the same name held land on Assawaymansecock Creek where Hugh's father Nathaniel eventually resided [12].

Frontier Years

Hugh and Catherine Hoskins Sanders planted their joint lives in Spotsylvania County on a fork of the Po River and lived through numerous lean and good years on family land. The years of the 1740s and 1750s, though, were not simple as change rippled through Virginia and Spotsylvania in ways that altered those places permanently. If measured by area of settlement, Virginia's size about doubled in two decades, and the character of Spotsylvania County changed quickly from rough frontier to established agricultural community. In short order, Orange County was split off from the western side of Spotsylvania, and a decade later, in 1749, Culpeper County was separated from Orange. In a matter of few decades, frontier Spotsylvania County became a mere stepping-stone to an advancing western periphery.

Government in those times was relatively benign. George II was popular with all classes throughout his long reign [13], and his wife, Caroline of Ansbach, after whom Caroline County was named, was particularly popular for her staunch defense of the Protestant faith in Europe [14]. The 1750s, the last decade of George's reign, were sedate years in England [15]. Under George, the administration of Sir William Gooch as deputy governor of Virginia was generally moderate. Gooch encouraged tolerance for Quaker and Presbyterian dissenters along the frontier, particularly as the established church did poorly at following western settlement. Gooch was especially enamored of new settlement, approving the formation of no less than six land companies for developing unsettled lands in western Virginia and lands "over the mountains." Most prominent among these organizations was the Ohio Company, formed in 1748 of wealthy investors, whose license entitled them to claim lands on behalf of company's privileged membership [16].

In the last years of Gooch's rule, economic panic and loosened credit led to severe indebtedness of small farmers. Tax evasion became rampant. This in turn led to farm foreclosures and consolidation of smaller farms into fewer larger holdings and acted as a spur to westward migration for those needing a fresh start. In 1749, Gooch was replaced by Robert Dinwiddie as deputy governor. Dinwiddie proved a particularly competent administrator whose policies stimulated production and trade, the growth of new warehouses, and a vastly improved system of courts. He imposed a 5 percent tax on imported slaves, retarding the rapid growth of that institution. But perhaps most importantly, Dinwiddle shared his predecessor's enthusiasm for western development, granting a half million acres to the Ohio Company in a single act. His encouragement of westward migration was seconded by a devastating drought in 1754 and 1755 that squeezed eastern agriculture and by his sanctioning of bounty payments for western Indian scalps. Scalping became a source of supplemental income for those scratching out a living on the distant frontier.

The period of westward expansion under Gooch and Dinwiddie ran into trouble toward the end of Dinwiddie's decade-long tenure as deputy governor and undermined his popularity with ordinary Virginians. At the heart of trouble was the outbreak of the Seven Years' War between England and France, and resultant hostilities in the colonies, known on the western side of the Atlantic as the French-Indian War. The French had previously occupied the Ohio Valley, and in 1756, they ignored diplomatic attempts to make them respect western Virginia territory. Indian massacres occurred with some frequency for the few Virginians who had ventured that far westward. But equally serious for the colony, hostilities in Europe dried up the tobacco market, the result of a French naval blockade in the Atlantic. Economic hardship predictably followed for Virginians, and taxes were left unpaid. These unpaid taxes in turn made forming and equipping a militia impractical, initially rendering Virginia impotent in its western dispute with the French.

By 1758, however, the British government provided new financing. Virginia militias were formed, and under duress, the French finally withdrew from the Ohio Valley. Though British-French struggles continued in Europe until 1763, the British regained naval control of the Atlantic by 1759, easing Virginia's barriers to its tobacco trade and its western land ambitions [17].

For Hugh and Caty Sanders, events of the 1740s and 1750s, though troubling for the colony as a whole, had remarkably little impact on their livelihood. They seem to have prospered reasonably, at least insofar as Hugh's land dealing reveals this. Land sales might be expected where droughts, taxes, and other setbacks might have occasioned debt and financial need, but Hugh is known to have sold land only twice in a decade, both times to a family named Gatewood [18]. In 1742, they sold 207 acres to Henry Gatewood of King and Queen County for eleven pounds, and in 1752, another 267 acres to Dudley Gatewood for slightly more than forty-five pounds. Hugh and Caty's daughter Sally eventually married Peter Gatewood, and Peter was named executor in Hugh's last will and testament in later years [19].

Besides selling land, Hugh joined the rush for new land by acquiring property in new Culpeper County, though the date, amount, and exact location of this property is undetermined. From other family records, we surmise that in the 1750s Hugh purchased Culpeper land on Cedar Run, about twenty miles or so northwest of his home in Spotsylvania [20]. For Hugh, these decades of the 1740s and 1750s were good ones, resulting in a net gain of land and a large and growing family.

These were the childbearing, child-rearing years for Caty and Hugh. They had twelve surviving children, born between the late 1730s and the early 1760s, an unusually long span of childbearing [21]. Among these twelve, some reached adulthood before the others were born. They had four sons: John, Nathaniel, Robert, and Charles, and eight daughters: Sally (Sarah), Elizabeth, Molly (Mary), Millie (Mildred), Ann, Catherine, Abigail, and Rosie [22].

THE FAMILY OF HUGH SANDERS OF SPOTSYLVANIA

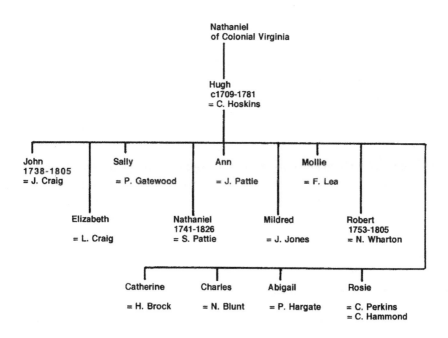

Source: After A. V. Parker 1966.

From the perspective of family history, this selection of names is startling in its novelty. From these children's names, we find an important new feature of Hugh and Caty's life and times. Family naming from earlier times in England was driven by strict cultural rules, rules that perpetuated family solidarity by institutionalizing its naming patterns. Given names, as well as surnames, were badges of family identity, social position, and economic entitlement. But after all those centuries of family reproduction—of children and their familiar repeating names—the English cultural mold was cracking in frontier Virginia. This line of Sanders before Hugh never had a Robert or a Charles, nor were women ever called Mildred, Abigail, or Rosie [23]. Hugh and Caty not only found new names for their children, they chose to ignore old ones. We find no children named for Hugh's generation—Thomas, Philip, Hugh, or Fannie— nor any Samuel from the Hoskins' side [24].

English cultural tradition and Virginia frontier life were beginning to uncouple. This is an important dimension of the so-called frontier hypothesis about the origin of distinctly American culture—that in the crucible of American frontier life, we find the birth of strong individualism, and ultimately its individualistic form of democracy. In the life of Hugh Sanders, kinship as the first principle of social organization was suddenly seen to pale in favor of what others envisioned as individual self-reliance [25]. At whatever level these opposing notions warred within Hugh and Caty, they were forced to choose between competing cultural imperatives as they brought children into their world. In choosing names, connecting with extended family became less important to them than finding new names somehow suited to their frontier circumstance. The distance between frontier folk and their compatriots back in England was ever-widening, a cultural breach expanding in direct proportion to their increasing physical separation.

Though their family was a large one, their twelve children were not the only family that Hugh and Caty possessed. Another family, less formalized as an institution but still a functioning whole, was their collection of slaves. Hugh and Caty owned fourteen slaves at one time. With their children and themselves, and with the slaves in residence, Hugh and Caty's farmstead near the Po River counted a population of twenty-eight persons, a virtual small village. Hugh and Caty's Spotsylvania home produced a thousand small stories that have not been told, a rich concoction of twenty-eight human contrasts and allegiances.

The slave collectivity itself embodied two sets of relationships, those among themselves and those with Hugh and Caty's own family. These latter relationships were many things, sometimes good and sometimes bad, but always and without exception, they were asymmetric and subordinated. Any picture we might conjure of this village—bucolic harmony or harsh bondage—cannot erase the fact that we have no certain knowledge of either master or slave in this Spotsylvania setting on Gladys Fork. These slave and nonslave families were forcibly melded together by a condition that faced them all, the certain and immediate need for farmstead self-sufficiency. They all had to eat.

One small glimpse of family economy can be distilled from the few facts known about these slaves—their names and their market value [26]. Field crops, principally tobacco, wheat, and corn, being the family's cash crops, would have been produced under Hugh's hand from the manual labor of Sellar, Caesar, Big Bristo, Sus, and perhaps Ralph. If as it seems Sellar was the fittest among these men, he probably worked behind a span of Hugh's best oxen; Caesar or perhaps another steering the second oxen team. Big Bristo might have used the plow horses. Younger slaves probably tended other animals, at one time numbering sixteen head of cattle, twenty sheep, ten hogs, two sows, and fifteen younger pigs. Hugh and Caty's young slaves evidently were Isabel, George, Wyatt, Little Bristo, Unice, and Davy. Though their ages are not known, Rachel was referred to as a girl and Wyatt and Davy boys in 1781 [27].

Tending the garden and meeting kitchen, cleaning, weaving, and child-rearing needs under Caty's direction probably fell to Phyllis, Little Phyllis, and perhaps Rachel. Producing cloth for all its purposes was a main effort. In the farmhouse were a cotton gin, cotton cards and wheels, a spinning wheel, and a loom. Sacks of feathers for the home's four feather beds were kept ready.

The names Big Bristo and Little Bristo and Phyllis and Little Phyllis suggest slave parentage at the farm and perhaps even a marriage between Phyllis and Bristo. If that is correct or even partly so, then some of these slave children may have been born at the farmstead as were Caty and Hugh's own children. A special tragedy of slavery was the permanent forced separation of slave parents and children, and that indeed may have happened when Rachel was given to Catherine Sanders as she undertook marriage, and Wyatt and Davy to Abigail Sanders as her own marriage approached.

Into the Maelstrom

In 1760, after thirty-three years of rule, King George II passed away, the crown passing to George III, whose reign was to last six decades. George III's first few years were successful enough. Following his accession to the throne, England enjoyed a decade of vibrant prosperity [28]. In Virginia, Francis Fauquier was kept on as Virginia deputy governor, and a buoyancy of good times under George III and Fauquier was felt throughout the colony. Large planters enjoyed their particularly good fortune with excessive extravagance, and frontier conditions improved as well. Strides were made in improving roads, bridges, warehouses, and courthouses, all the result of reinvigorated trade with England. In Caroline and Spotsylvania counties, ecclesiastical boundary reform was undertaken, modestly improving access of people to churches and churchmen to people. A sense of civilization was beginning to settle in on the increasingly prosperous outer counties despite another drought in 1760 that pushed more marginal farms out of existence. After 1760, the Rappahannock agricultural region saw some shift away from tobacco and

toward new concentrations in grains. Wheat and corn production resulted in
new mills being erected on streams, and a small distilling industry emerged
[29]. Hugh is known to have built his mill on Gladys Fork before 1751 since it
appears on the survey map of Peter Jefferson, the future president's father, and
Joshua Fry, published in that same year [30].

In the western parts of Virginia, peace along the mountainous frontier
had been secured after the French and Indian War ended in 1758. Yet despite
a negotiated peace with the Cherokees, Virginia land speculators and settlers
continued to encroach on those same Indian territories that the colonial
government had promised to respect. As a result, for a period of four years,
from 1758 to 1762, low-grade warfare with the Cherokees smoldered in the area
that is today's southwestern Virginia and eastern Kentucky. Hostilities dogged
Indians and settlers alike until a well-organized, well-armed militia under the
command of William Woodford negotiated an end to Cherokee resistance. It
seemed finally that western settlement could begin in earnest.

After a decade of struggle to gain access to lands beyond the mountains,
having aided the Crown in its quest to remove the French, and recently having
quelled Indian resistance, Virginians saw their land of opportunity finally
begin to open up. This was the chance for great landlords to grow rich through
speculation, for homesteads to be built by the sons of small landowners, and
land made available for indentured servants who completed their terms of
service. But at just this moment of apparent victory in 1763, George III issued the
so-called Hillsborough Proclamation, a royal decree that denied all residents of
British coastal colonies in America the right to patent additional land beyond
the Alleghenies. Outrage in Virginia was instantaneous, but protests to the
Virginia government in the end were unavailing [31]. After a time, this noxious
edict by George III was allowed to lapse.

On the heels of the Hillsborough Proclamation came the Stamp Act of
1765, which placed a new tax on all legal documents, newspapers, pamphlets,
and almanacs. The goal of the tax was to make defense of the colonies self-
financing [32]. But the main result was to create a howl of protest throughout
Virginia, widespread resignations of local government positions, and a
disinclination to accept appointments made by Governor Fauquier to vacant
county offices. Though the Stamp Act was repealed in 1766, hostilities toward
English government never fully abated after that.

Upsets to the established order continued. The 1760s saw an unanticipated
eruption of Baptist preaching in rural Virginia, utilizing homes, barns, and
fields, wherever an eager religious following could be assembled. In 1761,
Craig's Baptist Church was established in the village of Paytes, not far from
Caty and Hugh's homestead. The established Church of England's poorly
developed system of parishes and parish churches finally produced its barren
seed. Religious dissenters in the rural counties flocked to the words of ministers

such as the Craigs, the Wallers, and even the Sanders [33]. They soon developed large and loyal followings.

Caty Sanders and her family were among them, joining with other Spotsylvania families to follow and support the ministry of Lewis Craig. In short order, Caty and Hugh's daughter Elizabeth married Lewis Craig, founder of the Baptist church at Paytes, and their eldest son John married Lewis's sister Jane Craig about 1762. Throughout this period of religious conversion, Hugh Sanders is said by some to have remained with the Church of England, but evidence suggests otherwise. Just a few years after Craig's arrival in Spotsylvania, in 1766, Hugh gave Lewis Craig three hundred acres of his own land [34].

The appointment of Norborne Berkeley, titled as Baron de Botetourt, to replace the deceased Francis Fauquier in 1768 was cause for some celebration in Virginia because Botetourt was the first royal governor of Virginia in sixty-eight years, the previous ones being styled deputy governor and lacking the status of peerage. The objective in Botetourt's appointment was to reassure the colony's restive population that the Crown appreciated its needs by elevating the stature of the governor's office and of the person occupying it. Botetourt of course was a thoroughgoing royalist and, in his three years of rule, did little to improve conditions or attitudes in the colony. Though he was popular enough with Virginia's aristocrats, Botetourt promptly distanced himself from smaller landowners and tradesmen by attempting to impose new taxes and strengthening the hold of the established church on all religious matters. His religious intolerance extended that of his predecessor to persecuting and arresting Baptist and other dissenting ministers, stifling religious dissent as best he could. But Botetourt was too late; the Baptists had been worshipping in Spotsylvania and other counties for nearly a decade and by then were well established. Lewis Craig was arrested more than once in Spotsylvania and Caroline counties. Craig's claim, and that of other Baptist preachers, was that they were entitled and licensed to preach under the English Toleration Acts, but these licenses, lacking Episcopal ordination, were deemed invalid by Botetourt. By the time Botetourt died in 1770, the battle for religious freedom in Virginia was in full flame [35].

In the 1770s, as Hugh Sanders reached his sixties, a broad new liberalism swept across all of British colonial America, certainly including Virginia. The accumulation of economic, political, and religious grievances of Virginians finally produced a clear sense that separation from England was necessary and inevitable. For a time, a political division between loyalists (Tories) and separatists (Patriots) festered throughout the colony. Tories accused Patriots of seditious speech; Patriots responded with litanies of English injustice. But before the decade was out, Virginians of all stripes had largely united in their resolve to deal with British injustice. The Declaration of Independence of 1776 gathered the sentiments of all the colonies, and organized armed hostilities ensued. The Revolutionary War was on, though this was a war for Hugh and Caty's children, a war for the next generation, having not much to do with senior planters whose old orderly world was now crashing down.

Hugh's heart probably lay with the class of small planters whose political grievances mounted over the years, no doubt producing their revolutionary sparks. But against those feelings would have been a countervailing sadness at the impermanence of the world he gave a lifetime to building on traditional English foundations, a world now fully exposed of its frailty. However Hugh's feelings played out as the Revolution ground forward, he began to prepare for things ahead.

In 1780, with the war still in progress, Hugh and Caty joined with their son John and his wife Jane Craig to sell nine hundred acres of their Spotsylvania farmland to Thomas Bartlett for six thousand pounds currency [36]. Evidently, they were beginning a process of selling out, giving up a large portion of their land and income for a different future. What exactly was Hugh's intention with this sale remains unknown, however, because a decisive event overrode the plan. Within a year of the sale of this large part of the family farm, Hugh Sanders died at about age seventy-two.

Shortly before he died, in August of 1781, Hugh authored his last will and testament [37]. In his will, he left the now-reduced Spotsylvania farm to Caty, his wife of forty-six years, with the provision that it pass to their son Nathaniel after her death. He previously gave his son John some land in Spotsylvania County, and for his sons Robert and Charles, he left equal shares of his lands on Cedar Run in Culpepper County. He named his eight daughters, of whom five were by then married, and he specifically provided for two, Catherine and Abigail, both of whom had impending marriages. Of the unmarried daughters, only underage Rosie received no bequest, though Hugh knew that his principal bequest to Caty would underwrite Rosie's future as well.

In October 1781, the Spotsylvania County Court ordered an inventory of Hugh's estate. The inventory was completed five months later, documenting a personal estate, excluding land, of £735. The value of his fourteen slaves constituted more than 80 percent of that total and farm animals most of the rest [38]. A close reading of this inventory yields an impression of incompleteness; no money or notable valuables, no luxury items, no tools, no riding horses, and only a few old pieces of furniture were included. Some items of value clearly had gone elsewhere in the six months following Hugh's death.

Into the Wilderness

Around the time of Hugh's death in the autumn of 1781, life in western Spotsylvania County was unusually hectic. Beyond the normal activity of fall harvest, Hugh and Caty's friends and neighbors were preparing for a great trial and greater reward. The occasion was the beginning of what is now called the Traveling Church, a large exodus of rural Baptists from their Spotsylvania homeland to lands over the mountains to Kentucky. There seems little doubt that Hugh and Caty planned to join the Traveling Church in that fall of 1781, but Hugh's death changed all that.

The idea of leaving Spotsylvania for land over the mountains did not occur overnight. In the 1760s, western Virginia and Kentucky County, as it was then called, remained dangerous Indian territory despite numerous attempts to clear the land for settlement. In 1768, both Iroquois and Cherokee tribes signed a treaty permitting white settlers to move west of the Appalachians into lands not occupied by those tribes. But that agreement failed to match growing demands for new territory, and by 1774, Virginia's Governor Dunmore had initiated yet another campaign against Indian tribes in the Ohio Valley. A decisive battle at Point Pleasant in today's West Virginia resulted in the expulsion of large Indian tribes from lands south of the Ohio River. After 1774, settlement in Kentucky began in earnest. Land claims along the Kentucky and Ohio rivers skyrocketed, and there is some evidence that Lewis Craig and others in the Traveling Church had arranged for Kentucky lands during this period well before 1781 [39].

The wagon train of the Traveling Church assembled first at a Baptist church about twenty miles west of Fredericksburg on September 28, 1871, and immediately made a day's journey to Paytes, where a large gathering of wagons, people, and animals were waiting at Craig's church. The entire assemblage left the next morning, the twenty-ninth, a great train of wagons followed by pack horses with slaves and white youth driving livestock at the rear. The party held more than two hundred Baptists and twice as many other eager migrants. A key organizer was Caty's son-in-law, the firebrand, oft-arrested preacher Lewis Craig, the founder of Craig's church at Paytes who had married Caty's daughter Elizabeth. For Lewis Craig and the Baptists, the only reason for going west was religious freedom, freedom from the persecutions of the past two decades. Others in the party saw migration as an opportunity to obtain cheap unsettled lands and an unfettered new livelihood. But they all traveled together for mutual support and safety. The long journey was to consume about two and a half months, covering about six hundred miles.

For Caty Sanders and her family, the journey to Kentucky would have to wait. In September of 1781, there was Hugh's death to deal with, the bequests of his will, an inventory of his estate to undertake, and arrangements for maintaining the farm, its livestock, and slaves. For the present, the Traveling Church would have to go on ahead.

The Traveling Church made rapid progress in the first miles of wagon roads through the rolling hills of central Virginia [40]. But as the train approached western Virginia, the terrain steepened and roads worsened. Progress toward a new home would not be easy from this point, but with struggle, determination, and heavy doses of reaffirmed faith, the group finally reached Fort Chiswell in Virginia's southwestern corner around the end of October, the last outpost of permanent settlement on the road west.

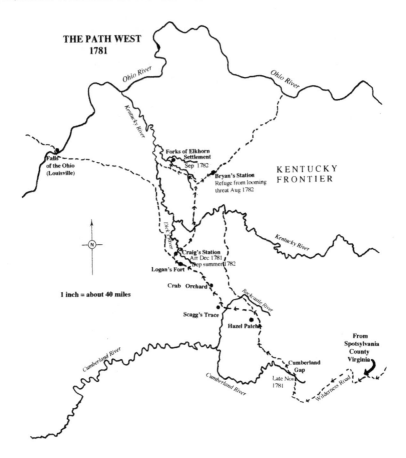

The Traveling Church left Spotsylvania County, Virginia on September 29, 1781, and traveled nearly four hundred miles in about six weeks, following the Shenandoah and Holston Valleys to reach Cumberland Gap. On reaching their Kentucky destination on Gilbert's Creek in December 1781, they wintered over and built the first church structure in Kentucky. Caty Hoskins Sanders with other family members was delayed in her Virginia departure by the death of her husband, but joined the church at Craig's Station in early summer of 1782. Following the siege at Bryan's Station, the travelers finally settled at Forks of Elkhorn in September 1782.

At Fort Chiswell, they learned that beyond Cumberland Gap, no wagon roads in Kentucky existed, that their wagons and possessions therefore would have to be abandoned, save what few items could be loaded onto pack animals. This was the place where the frontier began in earnest. Unburdened of many possessions, the Traveling Church forged ahead, reaching Wolf Hills, the last of the simple settlements on the Virginia frontier, in mid-November. There they overtook another traveling church that had bogged down and also learned that Gen. George Washington had trapped the main force of the British army at Yorktown, signaling the end of the Revolutionary War. This was not the Baptists' war, however, because it articulated no promised land in victory, and so the party forged ahead. In late November, the procession moved through Cumberland Gap and stepped for the first time onto Kentucky soil. Although without wagons the going was difficult, the passage in Kentucky became more swift as gentler landscapes and broad valleys opened before them. The Traveling Church made its way past a series of small Kentucky stations, nothing more than crude houses with livestock pens, first Hazel Patch, then Skagg's Trace, westward then past Crab Orchard, and finally past Logan's Fort in central Kentucky.

By the second Sunday in December, the Traveling Church had settled into a camp on Gilbert's Creek, a small tributary of Dick's River. There they proceeded to construct a small church and outbuildings, eventually to be called Craig's Station. Craig's Station held the first church house built in Kentucky [41]. The Traveling Church had finally arrived at a new Kentucky home in time for the winter of 1781–1782.

Caty, her son John and his wife Jane Craig, and others of her family left Spotsylvania early in 1782 after the winter eased up. Sons Nathaniel, Robert, and Charles remained behind in Spotsylvania or Culpeper at least for a time. No account of their migration in 1782 is found in records of the period, but Caty's party, including some Gatewoods, Bledsoes, and Leas among many others, would have followed the route of the Traveling Church through the Cumberland Gap and along the Wilderness Road into central Kentucky. Their travel would have found the same risks, experienced the same hardships, and borne the same hopes as the Traveling Church before them. But for Caty, now age sixty-four, her odyssey began too unceremoniously. As the group departed in the spring of 1782, Caty abandoned the land of her birth and family. She traveled overland to Kentucky in a horse-drawn wagon, shorn of most comforts, carrying great faith but little else, save some lingering memories of her husband, her homestead, and a rapidly fading Spotsylvania landscape.

Kentucky Years

Caty and her family traveled two months or more and, by early summer 1782, overtook the Traveling Church at Craig's Station, where that group had wintered over [42]. By midsummer, members of the Traveling Church, including Caty and her family, left Craig's Station, heading north, presumably to take up family lands that had been purchased before the migration [43]. They traveled as far as Bryant's Station, near today's Lexington, and took refuge there against looming Indian threats in the region. Those threats became real in August of 1782 when the infamous Simon Girty and his band of renegade Wyandotte and Huron outcasts attacked Bryant's Station [44]. Killed in the attack was nineteen-year-old Hugh Lea, Caty's grandson, son of Molly Sanders and Francis Lea her husband [45].

Bryant's Station was vulnerable to siege, lacking an internal source of water, a fact that did not escape Girty's attention. The renegades surrounded the station, but several women, fully vulnerable to Girty's band, voluntarily drew water at a spring outside the station, allowing the settlers inside to survive until help arrived. These women's bravery in the face of severe peril is commemorated today in artists' drawings and historical markers near the site.

Girty's party was eventually routed and Bryant's Station rescued. Caty, her family, and others resumed their travel soon thereafter. They journeyed onward another thirty miles or so to the South Fork of the Elkhorn River near today's Frankfort to settle for good. Though the exact date of their arrival is unknown, this settlement on the Elkhorn marked the final stop in Caty's odyssey, about a half-year after she left Spotsylvania County.

Catherine Hoskins Sanders resided for more than a dozen years in Kentucky near the forks of the Elkhorn, seeing the growth of strong settlement around her and a thriving Baptist church nearby. Sometime after the Revolutionary War had concluded, Caty lived with her son Nathaniel and his wife Sally who had migrated to the Elkhorn area. She witnessed the birth of numerous grandchildren. In time, Caty and Hugh's grandchildren would number a staggering eighty-three in all. All things surrounding Caty—family, church, and settlement—provided the satisfactions she found at the forks of the Elkhorn. Her son Nathaniel took care of lingering business back in Spotsylvania County, seeing to the final payment of debts and sales of land and slaves in 1787 [46].

In 1793, Caty, by then age seventy-five, relinquished the legacy from her husband, leaving any last remnants of farmland and possessions in Virginia to Nathaniel, as Hugh asked. But she held back those things she still required, which she described as "a Negro wench named Nicey, choice of one horse bridle and saddle, and choice of one bed and furniture and eleven pounds Virginia money paid every six months" [47]. This is our last view of Caty Sanders, making arrangements to continue riding at age seventy-five.

NOTES

1. Daniel Boorstin, *The Americans: The Colonial Experience* (New York: Vintage Books, 1958), p. 109.
2. Nell Nugent, *Cavaliers and Pioneers*, vol. 3 (Richmond, Virginia: Virginia State Library, 1979), pp. 355–356.
3. If we ever have an opportunity to rename our rivers, we might consider following the example of the Mattaponi. The Mattaponi has two main tributaries, called the Matta and the Poni. Each of these tributaries in turn has two main feeders, the Mat and the Ta for the first, and the Po and the Ni for the second. Thus we cannot miss if, downstream in a canoe, we hope to reach the Po on our first try.
4. Key records for Thomas Sanders are found in William A. Crozier, ed., *Spotsylvania County Records: 1721–1800* (Baltimore: Southern Book Company, 1955). See records of 1733 and 1743. See also T. E. Campbell, *Colonial Caroline: A History of Caroline County, Virginia* (Richmond: Dietz Press, 1954), p. 115. For Nathaniel Sanders, see Crozier, *Spotsylvania County Records*, record of 1742.
5. Campbell, *Colonial Caroline*, pp. 71–73.
6. Ibid., pp. 73–75.
7. Ibid., pp. 83–90.
8. In the 1739 Council of Virginia Executive Session Minutes, the following entry can be found: "William Bartlett's petition, ordered that the petitioner give notice to Hugh Sanders to cause the life of the patent to run out and concluded or to appear before this Board to show cause." See *Virginia Magazine of History and Biography*, April 1907. Though William Bartlett's suit to claim Hugh's land did him no good, it seems that much later a relative accomplished what William could not. In 1780, Hugh sold nine hundred acres of this land to Thomas Bartlett. We are grateful to Nancy Josue for bringing this record to our attention.
9. Crozier, *Spotsylvania County Records*, record of June 3, 1740.
10. Hugh sold a 235-acre tract of his land for twenty-four pounds in 1740 and another of 105 acres for nearly fifteen pounds that same year. See Crozier, *Spotsylvania County Records*, records for October 4 and November 25.
11. Anna V. Parker, Unpublished Sanders Family Papers, located at the Filson Club Library in Louisville, Kentucky, n.d.
12. On this family, see Nell Nugent, *Cavaliers and Pioneers*, vol. 1 (Baltimore: Genealogical Publishing Company, 1983), p. xxxiv; and other references. Also see Nell Nugent, *Cavaliers and Pioneers*, vol. 2. (Richmond: Virginia State Library, 1977), p. 126.

13. Campbell, *Colonial Caroline*, p. 181.

14. Ibid., pp. v–viii.

15. Kenneth O. Morgan, ed., *The Oxford Illustrated History of Britain* (Oxford: Oxford University Press, 1984), p. 374.

16. The bulk of our portrayal of history at the scale of the county rests on Campbell's fine history of Caroline County. Also helpful in its assemblage of topics and facts for Spotsylvania County is the work of J. R. Mansfield, *A History of Early Spotsylvania* (Orange, Virginia: Green Publishers, 1977).

17. British success in the Atlantic and the Ohio Valley matched that elsewhere. General James Wolfe captured Quebec in 1759 to fulfill William Pitt's plan to expel the French from Canada, a period when creation of the global British Empire was gaining momentum. See Mike Ashley, *British Kings and Queens* (New York: Barnes and Noble Press, 1998), p. 677.

18. A few other Spotsylvania records involving Hugh are not mentioned in this chapter. They are the following: (1) 1744, June 5, when Hugh Sanders witnessed a Spotsylvania County land sale between Edward Ware and Erasmus Allen; (2) 1747, April 4, when Hugh Sanders witnessed a Spotsylvania County land sale between William Hensley and Robert Spilsby Coleman. This Coleman was probably Hugh's brother-in-law; and (3) 1755, when Hugh Sanders and William McWilliams with Joseph Collins posted a two-hundred-pound bond for Joseph's guardianship of the orphans of Thomas Collins.

19. Crozier, *Spotsylvania County Records*, records for July 3, 1742, and May 6, 1752.

20. This acquisition is known from Hugh's will as he left Culpeper land to his sons. The Culpeper County seat was established at town of Fairfax, more commonly known as Culpeper Court House. Robert Coleman was said to have owned the land on which Fairfax was founded. Robert Coleman and Daniel Brown, contemporaries of Hugh and sons-in-law of Nathaniel, were at Culpeper perhaps before Hugh purchased land there.

21. This portrayal of Caty's history of giving birth is discomforting. John, the eldest son but probably not the eldest child, was born in 1738, suggesting that Caty's firstborn came about 1736 or 1737. From other family records, we learn that the two youngest daughters were unmarried by 1782, suggesting they may not have reached their twenties by that time. Thus, the youngest, Rosie, probably was born in 1762 or 1763. This means that Caty's childbearing years spanned about twenty-six years, from her age eighteen to about age forty-four.

22. Marriages of children were: John married Jane Craig about 1762, Nathaniel married Sally Pattie in 1776, Robert married Nancy Wharton, Charles married Nancy Blunt, Sarah (Sally) married Peter Gatewood, Elizabeth married Lewis Craig, Mary (Molly) married Francis Lea, Mildred (Millie) married James Jones, Ann married John Pattie, Catherine married Henry (Harry) Brock, Abigail married Peter Hargate, and Rosie married first Constant Perkins and second Charles Hammond. All these are taken from Parker, Unpublished Sanders Family Papers.

23. The names of the youngest daughters, Abigail and Rosie, may have been chosen from a family source. Nathaniel Sanders, brother of Hugh who moved to North Carolina, married Rosanna, daughter of Robert and Abigail (Lewis) Davis. The coincidence of these names Rosanna and Abigail is clear, and may suggest that these two families remained close. On the other hand, Abigail Lewis Davis was scarcely a family member by any calculation, and the concurrence of these names may be simple coincidence.

24. Some children might have died young, of course, eliminating familiar family names from the list of survivors. But it seems unlikely that so many survivors would carry "new" given names and those who failed to survive were those carrying "old" family names.

25. The importance of the frontier in shaping the American character is a theme first or at least best described by Frederick Jackson Turner. Among other authors, Ralph Waldo Emerson identified the importance of self-reliance in American culture.

26. The inventory of Hugh's personal estate in 1782 provides the information used to describe both slaves, animals, and tools at the farmstead. The inventory tries to state the market value for the slave in anticipation of sale, a reckoning of the slave's ability to do useful work, calculated in such things as age, physical strength, acquired skills, and agreeable personality. But market value fails to distinguish adequately between the very old and the very young as both require support and neither contributes much to the farm economy.

Hugh and Caty's slaves and their market value in pounds currency in 1781 were as follows:

Name	Stated Value
Sellar	110
Caesar	75
Phyllis	65

Little Phyllis	60
Big Bristo	60
Sus	50
Rachel	45
Ralph	40
Isabel	25
George	25
Wyatt	20
Little Bristo	20
Unice	20
Davy	15

Our attempt here to distill some meaning from these values may be too ambitious; indeed, it is not even clear whether Sus is man or woman.

27. Hugh Sanders's last will and testament of August 5, 1781, is found in Spotsylvania County Will Book E, p. 418.
28. Morgan, *Oxford Illustrated History*, p. 380.
29. See *Virginia Magazine of History and Biography*, October 1985, pp. 409–426.
30. The Jefferson-Fry map provides locations of mill sites in Virginia's streams and indicates a mill on Gladys Fork. The map produced by Peter Jefferson and Joshua Fry, published in 1751, provided the first comprehensive survey of the colony.
31. Campbell, *Colonial Caroline*, pp. 182–183.
32. Ashley, *British Kings and Queens*, p. 679.
33. Numerous Baptist ministers were harassed and jailed at the time, including Nathaniel Sanders. This Nathaniel was the son of John Wynell Sanders, Hugh's brother. See http://www.ourworld.compuserve.com/homepages/jkonvalinka/sandhome.htm.
34. This gift of three hundred acres may have been dower lands set off by Hugh for his daughter Elizabeth's marriage to Lewis Craig. Subsequent events especially in the life of Caty, Hugh's wife, make clear that relationships between the Sanders and the Craigs were strong.
35. Of course, vices grew in these counties too and betting on horses was chief among them. Hugh's (probable) brother Thomas Sanders benefitted as owner of the Port Royal racetrack. In view of later Kentucky history, it is worth noting that John Baylor, perhaps the

wealthiest man in Caroline County, imported thoroughbreds, which raced at Port Royal.

36. The amount received for this sale of land that contained no structure seems very large. Evaluating the worth of six thousand pounds currency at that time in Virginia is difficult. Campbell, *Colonial Caroline*, pp. 382–383, explains this difficulty. He identifies five types of currencies then simultaneously in play: (a) British money, (b) Virginia specie, (c) Spanish gold coins, (d) bills of exchange, and (e) tobacco certificates. British pounds sterling and Spanish pistoles, both desirable, were chronically in short supply. Virginia specie was prone to inflationary pressure, limiting its value in exchange, and bills of exchange were only as valuable as the credit worthiness of the issuer, which tended to be known only locally. That left tobacco certificates, issued at the point of sale or exchange, as the main useful currency. The need for tobacco certificates for many transactions tended to promote tobacco agriculture at the expense of other crops.

    The land in question lay in Berkeley Parish of Spotsylvania County. Berkeley Parish was created in 1769 by a subdivision of St. George's Parish where Hugh's original land was located. At this stage in his life, Hugh's known gifts and sales of land since 1740 totaled 2,115 acres, considerably more than his original inheritance. These sales probably reflect at least partly the financial strains on small planters that occurred over the previous three decades, although his acreage in Culpeper County is not known to us.

    We have not commented specifically on two other records involving Hugh Sanders as neither contained any significance that we could identify. These are as follows: (a) 1769, February 18, when Hugh and Catherine Sanders sold 101 acres in Spotsylvania County to Benjamin Mastin for twenty-five pounds; and (b) 1771, John Winal (as spelled) Sanders, Daniel Brown, and Hugh Sanders were the complainants against William Jerdon and Richard Tunstall on a Bill of Injustice brought in Caroline County Court.

    The case was dismissed, but an appeal granted. The substance of the complaint and the final outcome are not known, although, given the names of all parties, the sense is that this suit involved neighbors of the original land grant of Nathaniel, Hugh's father. Again, we thank Nancy Josue for sharing her find of this latter record.

37. The precise death date of Hugh Sanders is not known, but it occurred between August 5, 1781, when he authored his will, and October 18 when a court ordered an inventory of his estate. The court order is found in Spotsylvania County Will Book E, pp. 419–420.

38. Hugh's Estate Inventory, completed on February 28, 1782, is found in Spotsylvania County Will Book E, pp. 446–447. This inventory raises questions about how Hugh's will was followed. In his will, he gave his daughters three slaves, Rachel, Wyatt, and Davy who are found in Hugh's estate inventory a half year later. It seems that, for unknown reasons, these slaves were never given to the daughters as they evidently were included in a Virginia slave sale five years later. We therefore may be wrong in suspecting that Hugh broke up the slave family by giving young slaves to his daughters in spite of his stated will.

39. See Philip Fall Taylor, *A Calendar of the Warrants for Land in Kentucky, Granted for Service in the French and Indian War* (Baltimore: Clearfield Company, 1991). Taylor notes that a certain George Frazer, a familiar Spotsylvania County name, had two thousand acres surveyed in 1774, which thereafter was transferred to Lewis Craig, though the date of the transaction is not given.

40. The complete story of the Traveling Church is richly described in Thomas D. Clark, *Kentucky: Land of Contrast* (New York: Harper and Row, 1968), pp. 41–54.

41. Clark, *Kentucky*, p. 49.

42. Caty's traveling contingent should have reached Craig's Station by early summer, before that party moved on. But if they were delayed, then they caught up with Lewis Craig's group at Bryant's Station not later than July of 1782.

43. The reason for leaving Craig's Station is not clear, but the desire to take up newly purchased family land is a plausible one. Both John and Nathaniel Sanders, sons of Caty, purchased Kentucky land before the Traveling Church left Virginia. This land was on Locust Creek near today's Carrollton, as described in Virginia Grants and Surveys, 1774–1791: Treasury Warrant #3537, May 22, 1780.

    Nathaniel purchased five hundred acres at a cost of two hundred pounds on Locust Creek adjacent Thomas Brown and John Sanders. The family never resided there. We surmise that Locust Creek was inaccessible in 1782 and that Caty's party decided rather to settle on the more accessible Elkhorn. Several French and Indian War land grants awarded in 1774 and 1775 were for lands on the Elkhorn River. That area by 1782 was ripe for settlement. The Frazer family of Spotsylvania County obtained an Elkhorn grant for two thousand acres in 1774 that was later passed to Lewis Craig and Nathaniel had dealings in Virginia in 1787 with this same Frazer family.

44. This attack was part of a larger Indian offensive to remove white settlers in Kentucky and was abetted by British forces, which remained in the area for some time after the Revolution. Simon Girty was for

a time in British employ, though he acted independently in 1782. He is perhaps the most reviled character in Kentucky's early history. A lesser known fact is that Simon Girty's father was killed in 1750 by a Samuel Sanders, not of this family, although in a Supreme Court trial in Philadelphia, Sanders was convicted of a lesser charge of manslaughter; see K. Scott and J. Clarke, *Abstracts from Pennsylvania Gazette* (Baltimore: Genealogical Publishing Company, 1977), p. 123. Had Girty realized that several Sanders were trapped within Bryant's Station, the outcome might have been different. We thank Dr. Tom E. Sanders for bringing the Samuel Sanders record to our attention. The name Nathaniel Saunders appears on a memorial list of defenders of Bryant's Station, but this was not Nathaniel, son of Caty and Hugh, whom we believe remained in Virginia at this time. This Nathaniel Saunders may be a cousin, the son of John Wynell Sanders, who was a Baptist preacher, but we do not know if this Nathaniel was with the Traveling Church.

45. Parker, Unpublished Sanders Family Papers.

46. In March of 1787, Nathaniel arranged for all debts and accounts to be paid in Spotsylvania County. This evidently involved the sale of slaves for £620, the precise valuation of Hugh's fourteen slaves as given in his estate inventory. The sale was handled by the firm of Somerville and Mitchell of Fredericksburg, merchants. Nathaniel also conferred power of attorney to assist in transactions to Thomas Towles of Spotsylvania, and on March 6, he sold just over nine acres of land in Spotsylvania to Anthony Frazer for eleven pounds. See W. Crozier, Spotsylvania County Records, Deed Book L, p. 404; and Crozier, *Spotsylvania County Records*, records for 1787.

47. Fayette County, Kentucky, Burnt Records, vol. 7, p. 488.

CHAPTER TWELVE

Kentucky

The American Revolution is usually understood as an American rebellion against English authority, a military victory of struggling colonies against an overbearing ruler. That is how the event is celebrated today. But to see this revolution solely in terms of military victory and the earning of national independence, important though those achievements were, is to miss the wider revolutionary character of the age. The American Revolution began a larger process whereby numerous colonies in the western hemisphere eventually became independent states. Geopolitical relations spanning the Atlantic took on a wholly new character, and for a considerable period, alliances between the New and Old World became substantially disentangled. The Revolution of 1776 set these processes in motion by its successful outcome and through its democratic inspiration.

The new United States of America chose a political course, a political philosophy, that drew upon the liberalized politics in European monarchies that had been underway for nearly a century. Notable in this process was the so-called Glorious Revolution in England of the 1680s under William and Mary, which replaced the religious rationale for monarchy—rule by divine right—with a parliamentary arrangement in which government was chosen to some degree by popular will. The new United States enshrined the notion that mankind possessed natural rights—rights to life, liberty, and the pursuit of happiness—as a constitutional foundation. A novel form of government rooted in a new social contract was decreed, an explicit constitutional agreement that the form and content of government existed only by consent of its citizens, and not by any other rationale. Significantly included in this declaration was provision for religious freedom, the right to religious practice without interference of government.

This sense of newness and opportunity that began with political change was further enlarged by a social revolution of great importance. The new American society endorsed an ideology of equality among citizens, the notion that none should be born with social advantage conferred by the political state. Most important was the abolishment of inherited titles, the ancient feudal legacy that proclaimed and cemented unequal social relations based on titles and supported by institutionalized advantages. Heretofore in the new United States, social advantage would be earned and not assumed, and political expression and economic opportunity should accrue to individuals without regard to their social standing. The United States offered this daring dream as a concrete reality in a new constitution, though perhaps with less-than-perfect confidence that an untried form of government could ensure its success.

The founding of the United States in the mid-eighteenth century was particularly fortuitous in that its governing ideas, and the tenor of the times in general, took their cue from Enlightenment principles, the collective rationale for a new Age of Reason. The established church in Europe had lost control of the agenda of intellectual inquiry, allowing new protocols of thought—divergent, scientific, and secular in tone—to elbow their way to the fore. So it was that this new country began its life by sloughing off the yoke of colonial paternalism with a new confidence in the value and power of reason, a ratification of the notion that ideas, inventions, and technologies could arise from unfettered imaginations and unlimited inquiry.

There were, of course, many things that were not changed by the war.

Slavery remained an established institution, and the triumphantly proclaimed rights of man lacked universal application. Trade relations with England were surprisingly durable after the war. Prerevolutionary debt was generally honored, and the general market economy retained its Old World flavor. English culture retained its preeminent position in language, literature and leading ideas, in the systems of weights, measures, and money, and in the established institutions of education and law.

The Revolutionary War was waged by colonies of a distant England. The colonies themselves dated from the earliest days of North American settlement, and as physical entities, they were by and large the same territories before and after the war. In this sense, the victorious new nation was a simple geopolitical restatement of old territorial arrangements. But that reality would not last long. The Revolutionary War commenced at a time when the dam to westward migration was giving way. Westward development pressures had reached a peak, and within a short time, the new nation erupted onto new western lands. In western Virginia, for example, about a quarter million people poured through the Cumberland Gap to Kentucky in less than three decades following the war [1]. The new nation was founded with an immense untapped land resource that seemed virtually infinite in unexplored possibilities.

National independence and western frontier life were the twin progeny of the revolutionary age. A sense of discovery, opportunity, and optimism undergirded the national prospect from its earliest days and provided essential fodder for a unique expansive national culture to emerge. The new nation in many respects became, at least symbolically, a frontier America, a nation of outward prospects and a strong people willing to engage the rigors of movement and privation for later reward. Frontier life and political independence converged into a culture of personal independence, a culture self-confident and self-reliant, a frontier motif that colored the national identity and its sense of unbounded domain.

Nathaniel Sanders was a child of this revolutionary period. His life is a chronicle of the age, its war and its frontier life. Nathaniel grew up a contemporary of many famed American Revolutionary figures, several of whom were born within a decade of Nathaniel. Among Virginia's revolutionaries of that period, Thomas Jefferson was born two years after Nathaniel, and George Washington only nine years before. Like them, Nathaniel lived a large life, full of opportunities and rigors, a close witness to the revolutionary age. And like those famed figures, Nathaniel's life, beyond its panoply of adventure and achievement, reached mythic proportions in the eyes of those who knew him.

Early Years

Nathaniel Sanders was born in 1741, the second son and third child of Hugh and Catherine Hoskins Sanders of Spotsylvania County, Virginia [2]. Nathaniel was named after his grandfather, the first permanent settler in Virginia for this family. His grandfather, Nathaniel Sanders, died a decade before his grandson Nathaniel was born. This younger Nathaniel's parents Hugh and Caty lived their adult lives in Spotsylvania County, and that is where the first years of Nathaniel's life were spent.

The earliest of Nathaniel's years were lived on the family's nearly two thousand acres of land along Gladys Fork, a small easterly flowing stream that entered the Po River a few miles from the family plantation [3]. As an older child, Nathaniel shared his upbringing with John, an older brother, and Catherine, a sister not more than a year his elder. New brothers and sisters came along with some regularity until all the surviving children eventually numbered an even dozen. The plantation itself was relatively isolated as scattered large-acre plantations were few and widely spaced in that part of Spotsylvania County. Nathaniel's exposure to the wider world was limited—his family, their slaves, and occasional visitors, together with regular churchgoing, provided him with the only sources of knowledge and worldly exposure he could obtain. How much education Nathaniel might have received is uncertain, but whatever formal education he did acquire undoubtedly came from his mother. Practical education in crop growing and livestock raising no doubt dominated his early learning.

Nathaniel's life on Gladys Fork, though, came to an abrupt end about 1755 when he ran away from home at about age fourteen [4]. He evidently fled to a Cherokee Indian settlement somewhere in south central Virginia and lived for a period of seven years on the unsettled frontier [5]. Though no record of these years of Nathaniel's life exists, it is clear that numerous white Virginians interacted routinely and intermarried with the generally peaceful, amicable, and well-educated Cherokees of the region. In fact, the surname Sanders was fairly common in the Cherokee nation in the nineteenth century [6]. One gets a sense that Nathaniel's flight from home was not unique among younger Virginians. Escape from the isolation of frontier farms and relief from dreary youthful apprenticeships offered young men exciting if not improved prospects [7].

Whatever the reason for Nathaniel's flight, he found a new kind of education beyond the fringe of Virginia settlement. In league with other young fugitives, Nathaniel learned Cherokee ways of surviving, hunting, and earning a living in unsettled lands and about the geography of unmapped western Virginia territory. In all likelihood, Nathaniel knew Nathaniel Gist, son of noted early Kentucky explorer Christopher Gist, who had charted Kentucky lands as early as 1751. The younger Gist lived with the Cherokees for seventeen years and may have been the father of the famed Cherokee linguist Sequoia [8].

In the western parts of Virginia, peace along the mountainous frontier had been secured after the French and Indian War ended in 1758, an English (and Virginian) victory gained in part with Cherokee assistance. Yet despite a negotiated territorial agreement with the Cherokees, Virginia longhunters [9] and settlers increasingly encroached on Cherokee land. As a result, for a period of four years, from 1758 to 1762, when Nathaniel was between seventeen and twenty-one years old, intermittent warfare with the Cherokees emerged in the area that is today's southwestern Virginia. Hostilities dogged Indians and settlers alike until a well-organized Virginia militia under the command of William Woodford negotiated an effective end to Cherokee raids in 1762.

Nathaniel's movements and activities in his late teenage years are difficult to project, but by about 1760, rising tensions between Virginians and Cherokees would have diminished Nathaniel's ability to remain with his adopted people. Nathaniel's frontier apprenticeship at midcentury in Virginia, such as it was, lay directly in the path of those colliding worlds. By the turn of the 1760s, if not before, Nathaniel probably found life with the Cherokees no longer feasible and necessarily would have sought other frontier employment or attachments. Nathaniel may have latched on to a hunting party, such as the famed first longhunt into Kentucky by Elisha Waller in 1761 or other hunting parties with more limited goals [10].

A strong possibility is that Nathaniel acted as an Indian scout in William Woodford's campaign of 1762 [11]. Woodford's success in dealing with the Cherokees, it has been written, depended heavily on "pioneer scouts" to reach the Cherokees and conclude a peace [12]. Nathaniel was perfectly educated and experienced for such a responsibility. Friendships with William Woodford and some of his Caroline militiamen from the 1762 campaign, furthermore, might explain why Nathaniel later visited or resided in Caroline County before the Revolutionary War.

Nathaniel managed to maintain himself on the Virginia frontier into his twenty-first year. In that year, 1762, he returned home to Spotsylvania County [13], perhaps at the conclusion of Woodford's campaign. His family barely would have recognized him after seven years, having left as a youth and returned as a frontier-hardened man. Nathaniel too would have been amazed to find siblings nearly grown and seeing for the first time two young sisters not born when he left home.

How long Nathaniel remained with his family at this time is unclear, but it cannot have been very long. No record of Nathaniel Sanders in Spotsylvania County can be found until the Revolutionary War had nearly come to a close in 1780.

Thirteen Lost Years

Nathaniel's years between the time he returned home at age twenty-one and age thirty-four, up to the year 1775, are lost to family history. We have no record whatsoever of these thirteen years. As noted, one gets a sense from later records that Nathaniel lived in Caroline County before the Revolution, though no Caroline records reveal when or how long Nathaniel's sojourn there might have lasted. At least part of the time Nathaniel served as an Indian spy in western Virginia, though whether this scouting might have been done as a service to pioneer settlers or for a peacekeeping militia is anybody's guess [14].

After the Woodford campaign of 1762, peace between the Cherokees and the Virginians lasted for a decade. This peacetime corresponds perfectly with the period in which Nathaniel's location is unknown. If as it seems he spent several of these years on the frontier, then we cannot discount the strong possibility that Nathaniel married and lived with a Cherokee woman, sometime between 1762 and 1775. Albert Goodpasture, a Cherokee authority, writes of such white-Indian marriages as follows, "It was a general, almost a universal, practice for white men living, even temporarily, in the (Cherokee) nation, to take Indian wives; not generally 'until death do us part,' but during the residence of the husband in the nation" [15]. Such a marriage, if indeed there was one, explains Nathaniel's long absence from Spotsylvania County and furthermore underpins an enduring myth that Nathaniel had a Cherokee son [16].

Opportunities to explore the wilderness of southwestern Virginia or eastern Kentucky would have routinely surfaced in the late 1760s and early 1770s. Among other events, this was the time of Daniel Boone's excursions into Kentucky through the Cumberland Gap and the period in which the Bledsoe brothers of Culpeper County, Virginia made their lucrative longhunts along Kentucky's Cumberland River. Nathaniel could have engaged either of these opportunities. In 1772, a body of "Clinch (River) Scouts" was organized to monitor Indian activity in the region. One of these scouts was a twelve-year-old boy. Nathaniel at age thirty-one might have been another.

One party of later Kentucky exploration seems likely to have included Nathaniel, though no proof of his actual participation exists. In 1774, John Floyd of North Carolina explored central Kentucky as far west as the falls of the Ohio River, near present-day Louisville. Nathaniel may well have traveled along on this expedition because John Floyd was Nathaniel's distant relative [17], and because Nathaniel's first large purchase of Kentucky land, some eight years later, was at Floyd's Fork, very near John Floyd's initial two-thousand-acre plot [18].

Despite the dearth of information about Nathaniel in the period 1762 to 1775, what seems certain is that he had years of frontier experience and a rugged disposition to match. Nathaniel is remembered as having stood "five feet ten inches in height, (being) very stout and strong (and is) said to have been equal to two men in a fight" [19]. These words seem well chosen to represent a figure living in the untamed lawless frontier and are almost prescient in describing Nathaniel's preparedness for a future of soldiering. Nathaniel was by 1775 in his thirty-fourth year.

Beginnings of Independence

Around the first week in July, 1775, Nathaniel gathered up his belongings, some provisions, and his long Kentucky rifle, saddling his horse for a long ride to Winchester, Virginia. From Caroline County, the ride was just shy of a hundred miles and would take the better part of three days. Just weeks before, the fledgling nation's breakaway Continental Congress in Philadelphia had asked the middle colonies to form ten rifle companies, and Virginia's rebellion-minded House of Burgesses agreed to form two of them. In charge of one of those companies was Daniel Morgan of Winchester. Morgan's charge was to assemble a formidable force and move as quickly as possible to support the Patriot cause in Massachusetts.

In Nathaniel's mind as he rode to Winchester that July was the hopeful knowledge that the Minutemen of Massachusetts had fought well just two months earlier against the British in the Battle of Lexington and Concord. More recently—just three weeks previous—the Patriots also had given a good account of themselves at Bunker Hill. So now war was upon the land, and Nathaniel was riding directly into it.

Exactly how Nathaniel became linked to Daniel Morgan's effort to form his rifle company is not clear. In 1774, Morgan had distinguished himself in the Battle of Point Pleasant (now West Virginia) in what has come to be called Dunmore's War [20]. The paths of Nathaniel Sanders and Daniel Morgan may have crossed in 1774 on Virginia's western frontier. Or Morgan may have sent word to William Woodford of Caroline County to seek out solid recruits for his new effort. If that were the case, one suspects that Nathaniel's name would have surfaced at this point.

In either event, Nathaniel reached Morgan's camp in Winchester before the fourteenth of July 1775, and if he was like other recruits, he agreed to a six-month tour of duty [21]. Morgan managed to assemble his rifle company of ninety-six men in just ten days. The company immediately began a march north, leaving Winchester on July 14 and arriving in Boston August 6, completing the march of six hundred miles in about three weeks.

Once in Massachusetts, they joined other elements of the Continental army in a siege of Boston. This army eventually grew to a force of between six and eight thousand men, nearly doubling the number of British regulars housed in Boston. The siege, undertaken in late June, was to last for ten months, involving only sporadic and generally inconsequential military confrontation. In the end, the British were forced to evacuate that strategic port city. Morgan's Virginia Rifle Company held its position on the hills surrounding Boston for only a month during this period until a more pressing need for the Virginians suddenly surfaced.

As the siege of Boston dragged on, a plan was concocted to bring military force to bear on Quebec. By the time of the Revolution, Quebec lay entirely in British hands, French control having been permanently dislodged by force more than a decade before [22]. At this revolutionary moment in history, in 1775, neither the United States nor Canada yet existed, and Quebec was sometimes regarded as simply a "fourteenth British colony" of the North American eastern seaboard. Patriot success in Quebec would shut off British access to the St. Lawrence River and negate the possibility of British attacks from the north. Revolutionary fever also ran high among some English-speaking Quebecers, though that colony sent no representative to the Continental Congress and produced no ad hoc government to organize an attempt at independence. The lack of widespread revolutionary enthusiasm in Quebec stemmed in no small part from the British Act of Quebec of 1774, which provided important civil guarantees for French-speaking Quebecois and laid useful groundwork for cooperation between Quebec's English and French populations [23].

The Continental army provided one thousand soldiers under Benedict Arnold's command to engage the British at Quebec, and Daniel Morgan eagerly volunteered his Virginia Rifle Company for the attempt, at least in part to escape the boredom, filth, and disease at the Boston encampment [24].

In assembling the Quebec force, George Washington, by then in command of the Continental army, laid out two requirements for volunteers, that they be "active woodsmen and well-acquainted with bateaux" [25], requirements that fit Nathaniel particularly well. A graphic description of the Virginia woodsmen in Boston gives us a picture of Nathaniel as we might imagine him then: "Known as excellent marksmen, (the Virginians) carried long rifles, much more accurate weapons at long range than smoothbore muskets but more difficult to reload, thereby reducing any tactical superiority in pitched set-piece battles. The woodsmen also had tomahawks and scalping knives strapped to their belts; and to set them even further apart from musketmen, their standard dress consisted of fringed hunting shirts, Indian leggings, moccasins, and broad-rimmed hats. It is said that the Virginians received special orders from Washington for the Quebec campaign not only because of their special skills, but because of their obstreperous behavior in camp. They resented military discipline and reveled in brawls with New England soldiers" [26].

On September 19, the column for Quebec got underway, sailing northward along the coast from near Boston to the mouth of the Kennebec River, a sea voyage of about one hundred miles. From there, the route led inland toward the northwest, following the irregular course of the Kennebec River, known from scouts to be free of British control. In the lead were Morgan's men, including his Virginia riflemen. At the upper reaches of the Kennebec, the column planned to negotiate several long portages, make their way to the Dead River, then cross the rugged highlands separating Maine from Canada, and finally make its way in haste and by stealth across the remaining lowlands to the fortified city of Quebec.

The trek itself was an epic of hardship and is richly described in Kenneth Roberts's historical novel, *Arundel* [27]. The expedition began in hastily made bateaux, 220 in all, which were constructed from unseasoned pine. These slowly disintegrated on the rocky shallows of the upper Kennebec. Before the journey was half-completed, men were forced to wade alongside boats that were barely afloat. On one occasion, seven bateaux capsized in rapids, losing valuable supplies and armaments. Soon, freezing weather set in, and the sodden soldiers fell ill in great numbers. Before arriving at Quebec, as many as four hundred men, nearly half the contingent, had given up the venture—through illness, frostbite, lost boats, wet weapons, rancid food, unseasonable floods, and finally through discouragement born of an enervating boggy wilderness. Those remaining finally got their first view of Quebec in a driving snowstorm, nearly two months after embarking on a trek thought to require no more than three weeks in all [28].

In view of the Patriots' epic two-month struggle to gain its position, the Battle of Quebec from the Patriots' perspective was anticlimactic. The city was better fortified and manned with more volunteer soldiers than Arnold had anticipated. Given the sorry state of his bedraggled column, Arnold grimly retreated to a location across the St. Lawrence about twelve miles from the city. There he waited for reinforcements from the south, which after much delay finally arrived. The combination of deteriorating winter weather and lapsing enlistments allowed little further delay for the planned attack.

After yet another month of preparation, the attack finally commenced on New Year's Day 1776 but ended quite abruptly. The city of Quebec held firmly with few casualties, and the Patriots fell in utter defeat. They counted fifty-one of their own men dead, thirty-six wounded, and two-thirds of the remaining column, some 372 men, became prisoners of war [29].

What became of Nathaniel in the Quebec venture we cannot say. He may have been among those never arriving at Quebec; he may have fought and escaped capture; he may have been captured and released. We have no reason to think him injured in battle, and any illness that befell him in Maine or Quebec seemed not to have produced any long-term debilitation. It seems his enlistment was up by mid-January if not before, and his desire to return home after unrewarding military effort in the north cannot be doubted. After Quebec and probably on his own devices, Nathaniel returned to Caroline County, arriving before the summer of 1776, his revolutionary fervor still very much undimmed.

Revolution in Virginia

The house of James and Sarah Pattie of Caroline County, Virginia was areel with revolutionary and matrimonial excitement in June of 1776 [30]. Nathaniel Sanders had only recently returned from military service in the north with stories of war and had asked for the hand of James Pattie's daughter Sally in marriage. Though Sally Pattie was only seventeen years of age in 1776 and Nathaniel thirty-five, the bargain was agreed. The Reverend Abner Waugh conducted the ceremony at the Pattie homestead.

Reverend Waugh was a controversial figure in that part of Virginia for his enthusiastic support of the Revolution despite his standing in the Anglican church. Waugh had joined Caroline County's Committee of Safety, the ad hoc revolutionary county government, resigning from the committee only reluctantly after protestations by the Anglican church hierarchy that his revolutionary sentiments were inappropriate. Waugh was a particularly close friend of William Woodford, who lived in Waugh's parish in Caroline County, and served as chaplain for part of Virginia's militia before 1776 [31]. Nathaniel's relationship with William Woodford may have played some part in Abner Waugh's agreement to marry Sally and Nathaniel. One imagines Waugh's wedding ceremony for Sally and Nathaniel to have been grounded in equal blessings of holy matrimony and political liberty.

Evidently, Nathaniel came to know Sally Pattie through his sister Ann, who earlier had married John Pattie, Sally's brother. The Pattie family itself had been established in Caroline (formerly Essex) County for only one generation before James. A certain Sylvester Pattie, perhaps the father of James, seems to have been the first of his line there, taking up land in Essex County in 1715 [32].

Sanders family records suggest that the Patties were a family of some prominence in Caroline County, but that seems incorrect. James Pattie was an artisan, known to have taken in four apprentices between 1755 and 1761 to teach them skills in carpentry and weaving [33]. However skilled or honorable James Pattie might have been in his work, artisans of his kind could not gain significant social prominence in Virginia's rigidly class-conscious society in the prerevolutionary era.

The Declaration of Independence was issued by the Continental Congress only a few weeks after Sally and Nathaniel's wedding. And so it happened in 1776 that fate unwound two ribbons of new life, a new family for Nathaniel and Sally and a new war for their Virginia and their emerging nation. These were simultaneous and richly interwoven.

Caroline County sprang to immediate action after the declaration and, by 1777, had organized its militia for service on the frontier [34]. Nathaniel joined this fighting force in Caroline County in 1777 [35] and with them journeyed back to familiar Virginia frontier territory. The goal was to forestall threats of British and Indian attacks from that quarter, threats that in the end never materialized. How long or in what way Nathaniel served this militia is unknown, but in his wife's later recollection, he was accounted an Indian spy and fighter and to have served at least two years after his marriage [36]. Nathaniel evidently returned to Spotsylvania County by 1779 if not before.

In the midst of the Revolutionary War, Sally bore their first two children, a daughter Catherine born in 1779 and a son Hugh born in 1780, named for Nathaniel's parents. After their marriage and with regular news of war reaching them, Nathaniel and Sally took up some land, their first home together, though exactly how they acquired it is uncertain. Most likely, they lived on the land of Nathaniel's aging parents and dwelled at their home in Spotsylvania County for at least their first few years of marriage.

THE FAMILY OF NATHANIEL SANDERS OF KENTUCKY

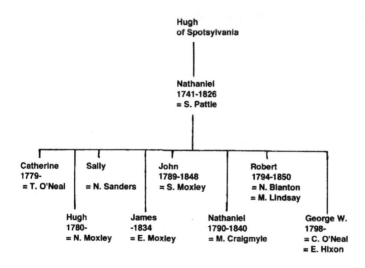

Source: Adapted and extended by authors from A. V. Parker 1966.

In 1780, four years after marriage, Nathaniel Sanders of Spotsylvania County managed to purchase 207 acres of land from William and Elizabeth Nelson for five thousand pounds [37]. This may have been the same 207 acres Nathaniel's father Hugh sold to Henry Gatewood nearly four decades before. If so, then Nathaniel established his own family's presence on lands long in family hands and near his own parents' home.

Land acquisition, however, did not translate into farmwork for Nathaniel. During the entire Revolutionary War, we know that Nathaniel cultivated no crops, or did so only irregularly, and that this responsibility devolved to his wife alone [38]. In all likelihood, Nathaniel's acquisition of land in Spotsylvania County at this time represented something of an insurance policy in a period of great uncertainty. From Nathaniel's perspective, the war, then in its fifth year, had no certain outcome, and Nathaniel's own survival cannot have seemed assured, given his past (and probable future) military involvement. If he did not survive the war, or if the British prevailed, his wife and children at a minimum would own some Spotsylvania farmland for their future support. Those 207 acres were all that Nathaniel could guarantee in these uncertain times.

The Southern Campaign

In the early months of 1780, disaster struck. British forces captured Charleston, South Carolina, resulting in the loss of the entire Continental army of the south. In all, 5,400 men were captured, along with several ships and a large cache of arms. In desperation, the Southern Department of the Continental army was hastily reconstituted and placed under the command of Gen. Horatio Gates, hero of the Patriot victory at Saratoga. Gates accepted the southern command in June of 1780 and two months later engaged an advancing British army at Camden, South Carolina. Gates's forces at Camden were decisively routed, however, and Gates himself undertook something of an unsoldierly retreat that later cost him his command.

Learning of these disasters, Daniel Morgan, who led Virginians in the earlier northern campaigns, came out of brief retirement to join the southern command as brigadier general under Gates. Morgan accepted this command in October of 1780. In that same month, Nathaniel Sanders provided "1 waggon, 4 horses and harness compleat for use of army under Maj. Gen. Gates" [39]. As Nathaniel at this time was designated a "revolutionary soldier of Virginia," we can surmise that Nathaniel served under Morgan in South Carolina and fought alongside him in subsequent action, notably at the Battles of Cowpens and Guilford Courthouse.

From the time that Nathaniel joined the southern forces in October, action against advancing British troops was assured, and it was not long in coming. In January 1781, British and American forces met in the Battle of Cowpens, a place on the North and South Carolina border. Here, Morgan used his Virginia long rifles and other sharpshooters to good effect, targeting British officers from long range to induce confusion and employing innovative tactics of strategic retreat and attack to outwit his enemy. The result was a solid victory, though a gain perhaps less significant as a military outcome than as a psychological one for the harried Patriots. Two months later, at Guilford Courthouse, North Carolina, Virginia sharpshooters again played a key role, though the final outcome was mixed. It may be on this occasion that Nathaniel lost use of his gun, a loss for which he later received compensation [40]. Although the British won the field that day in Guilford Courthouse, they did so at greater cost than paid by the Americans. A strategic withdrawal from Guilford left the Continental army fresh for the months ahead while exhausted British troops soon thereafter abandoned the Carolinas.

About the time that Morgan's Carolina campaign was winding down, Nathaniel may have learned that his father passed away. Hugh Sanders wrote his will in early August 1781 and died soon thereafter. If Hugh held any resentment toward his son having left home at an early age and delayed his return for so long, that resentment evidently evaporated with the war. Whatever Hugh's exact thoughts, he favored Nathaniel in his will by endowing him with the family farm in Spotsylvania to be Nathaniel's full possession upon the death of his mother [41].

In August 1781, the British general Charles Cornwallis massed his eight-thousand-man army in Virginia with a goal to subdue Patriot resistance in that colony. He established a large base at Yorktown, a site served by access to the sea for supplies. But American forces from northern and southern commands, eventually numbering over seventeen thousand men, converged upon him, and French naval allies arrived by sea to form a blockade from which Cornwallis could not escape. Sometime during this movement, Nathaniel lost two horses, according to War Department records [42]. The siege of Yorktown got underway in September, and on October 19, the noose now tightened beyond endurance, and the British stacked their arms in surrender. That was the end of it all. Nathaniel had the good fortune to personally witness the end of the Revolutionary War at Yorktown [43].

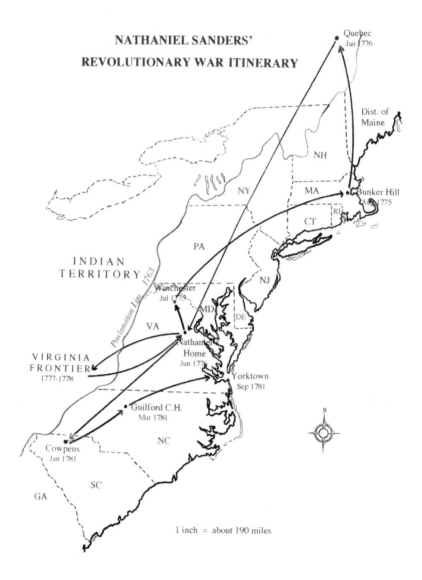

NATHANIEL SANDERS'
REVOLUTIONARY WAR ITINERARY

Quebec
Jan 1776

Dist. of
Maine

NH

NY

MA

Bunker Hill
June 1775

RI

CT

PA

INDIAN
TERRITORY

Winchester
Jul 1775

MD

DE

NJ

VA

Nathaniel
Home
Jun 1776

VIRGINIA
FRONTIER
1777-1778

Yorktown
Sep 1781

Guilford C.H.
Mar 1781

NC

Cowpens
Jan 1781

SC

GA

1 inch = about 190 miles

Nathaniel Sanders' participation in the Revolutionary War
spanned six years, from 1775 to 1781, and covered nearly
all the fledgling nation as it then existed. The western
boundary as shown was proclaimed by George III in 1763,
but frontiersmen, longhunters, and a few intrepid settlers
occasionally crossed this line. The precise location and timing
of Nathaniel's service in the Virginia frontier is unknown. His
home during this six-year period alternately was in Caroline
and Spotsylvania Counties.

For Nathaniel, the Revolutionary War began with his marriage to Sally Pattie and ended with the death of his father. In war, he had seen firsthand virtually all of his new nation, from beyond its northern border in Quebec to one of its southernmost states in South Carolina, and also from Virginia's western frontier to the nation's eastern shore at Yorktown. Nathaniel undertook his part in the war a somewhat solitary frontier woodsman and returned from it a married military veteran. War-weary but victorious after six years of revolutionary struggle, it was finally time for Nathaniel to seek some peace. He was at this time forty years old.

Spotsylvania

Following the war, life in Spotsylvania County began to return to normal for Sally and Nathaniel, though normal for those times in Virginia was anything but settled. Virginia struggled to cope with new political, economic, and social realities. Following the surrender at Yorktown and an end of hostilities, the 1783 Treaty of Paris gave international recognition to American independence [44]. Of this time, Boorstin writes that the Revolution of 1776 amounted to the suicide of the Virginia aristocracy. The turmoil of the war, destruction by British troops, disestablishment of the church, disruption of commerce, and the dismantling of tobacco culture all spelled the decline of the aristocracy and its institutions [45]. Massive change in Virginia was underway, but little of this affected Nathaniel on the plantation in Spotsylvania County. Struggles in the immediate postwar period, such as they were in Spotsylvania, were appreciably dimmed by the fact that Nathaniel had no intention of remaining in Spotsylvania for long. Sooner or later, with his growing family in tow, he would head for Kentucky.

Nathaniel's idea of migrating to Kentucky was a firm plan even before the war ended, at least insofar as we can infer intentions from Nathaniel's land transactions. In 1780, just after he returned from service with the Caroline militia and before the southern campaign of the war, Nathaniel purchased a treasury warrant in Virginia for five hundred acres of Kentucky land on Locust Creek on the Ohio River. This plot lay adjacent his brother John Sanders' land claim in what was then Jefferson County, Kentucky, lying not far from today's Carrollton. The land itself was not surveyed until 1784, and a certificate of ownership finally was drafted in 1787. But by the time this certificate was issued—six years after purchase—Nathaniel had already assigned this Locust Creek property to John Pattie, his brother-in-law [46], probably because he had already bought a larger plot of land elsewhere in Kentucky.

By late 1781, Nathaniel had learned he inherited his parents' plantation on Gladys Fork [47] and shortly thereafter the full contents of his father's estate [48]. But just months after his father's death, and with his parents' plantation far from his mind, Nathaniel had seized an opportunity to acquire a large tract of land in Jefferson County on Floyd's Fork of the Kentucky River. In November 1781, Nathaniel paid two thousand pounds for three Virginia treasury warrants, acquiring a total of six thousand acres in a single transaction [49].

Even as this purchase was being transacted, Spotsylvania's Traveling Church was heading into Kentucky, with Nathaniel's sister Elizabeth and her husband Lewis Craig at the fore. Before another year was out, in early 1782, Nathaniel's widowed mother and his younger sisters, his brother John and his wife, and several other relatives had left for Kentucky as well. By 1782, Nathaniel may well have been the only family member still residing in Virginia.

Sally and Nathaniel remained in Spotsylvania County for six rather uneventful years during the 1780s, perhaps waiting to receive unambiguous title to their Kentucky land. Through this period of immense change in postrevolutionary Virginia, we learn only that Sally and Nathaniel's middle children—Sally and James—had been born [50]. In 1783, Nathaniel's name was included on the Virginia tax list, indicating that he held five slaves at this time [51]. In 1784, he received the hopeful news that his large Kentucky land claim on Floyd's Fork finally had been surveyed. The next year, Nathaniel obtained a wagon and team of horses from a William Jenkins at a cost of one hundred pounds, perhaps replacing the wagon and team lost under Morgan in the war's southern campaign [52].

Finally, following receipt of the land certificate in January of 1787 for his six thousand acres, Sally and Nathaniel made ready to leave for Kentucky [53]. In the month of March 1787, as winter was losing its grip, Nathaniel hurried to complete some legal transactions. After a delay of nearly six years, he sold off nine acres of land to Anthony Frazer for eleven pounds [54] and conveyed power of attorney to a Mr. Towles to oversee final disposition of his mother's Virginia possessions [55].

Settlement in Kentucky

In the spring of 1787, Sally, Nathaniel, and their four children followed the path of many others, entering Kentucky through the Cumberland Gap and making their way along the Wilderness Road to a new home near present-day Frankfort, Kentucky. They arrived in summer at the south branch of the Forks of Elkhorn, a tributary of the Kentucky River that flows northwesterly to the Ohio. In the words of a contemporary, "By about 1787 the Forks of Elkhorn began to be settled. Mr. Nathaniel Sanders and others had moved down" [56]. Before long, in 1789, a son John was added to Nathaniel and Sally's family. John bears the distinction of being perhaps the first native Kentuckian in this line of Sanders.

Nathaniel curiously chose not to continue on to Floyd's Fork but rather to remain at Forks of Elkhorn. This decision seems an abrupt change of plan. Floyd's Fork, fully in Nathaniel's possession, lay only about fifty miles to the northwest from Folks of Elkhorn, but was considerably less settled at the time and more prone to Indian attacks. Perhaps more importantly, Nathaniel's mother, brother, and numerous other relatives had made a beginning of settlement at Forks of Elkhorn, and these family members may have induced Nathaniel with his own young family to remain with them. Further, Nathaniel's wartime contacts were busy promoting land sales at Forks of Elkhorn and planning a town at Frankfort. These contacts may well have been decisive because Nathaniel evidently purchased land from them soon after his arrival at Forks of Elkhorn [57].

By summer of 1787, Nathaniel bought property on the South Fork of the Elkhorn River, on acreage cut out from the holdings of Gen. Andrew Lewis, by then deceased. Andrew Lewis had received military grants totaling five thousand acres for his service in the French and Indian War [58], during which action he had collaborated with Nathaniel's future wartime mentor, Daniel Morgan. Both Morgan and Lewis held command positions in Dunmore's Battle of Point Pleasant in 1774. Daniel Morgan himself received Kentucky land for this service, and although Morgan never took up the land, his relatives were active in Kentucky land surveying through the 1780s. Charles Morgan in fact surveyed part of Andrew Lewis's military grant. By the time of Nathaniel's arrival at Forks of Elkhorn, the Lewises were selling off the deceased general's estate, and Nathaniel was among those buying Lewis land in 1787.

Nathaniel's brother John seems also to have obtained land from Andrew Lewis's holdings. The Lewis family later sued both John and Nathaniel over payment for lands acquired [59], though court judgments in these cases have not survived. Such suits commonly arose during Kentucky's early settlement, a result of Virginia's inexperienced land granting process that led to uncertain property boundaries and overlapping land claims [60].

In 1787 or the year after, Nathaniel also purchased a parcel of land in the newly platted town of Frankfort. Developing the town of Frankfort was the brainchild of another of Nathaniel's wartime contacts, Gen. James Wilkinson. Wilkinson was present at the Battle of Quebec with Arnold and Morgan and served with Horatio Gates and Daniel Morgan at Saratoga. Wilkinson was complicit in the so-called Conway Cabal, a conspiracy to replace George Washington with Horatio Gates as commander-in-chief of the entire Continental army in the Revolutionary War. Around 1786, Wilkinson traveled to Kentucky and contrived to build a town at Frankfort, laying off plots of land for quick sale and encouraging those who knew him from his wartime exploits to join the venture. Nathaniel purchased one of Wilkinson's Frankfort parcels, plot number 69, near the center of the planned town [61]. Wilkinson, ever the schemer, shortly moved on to other ventures, and the plans for Frankfort failed to advance very far in the late 1780s. It remains unclear whether Nathaniel ever occupied the Frankfort land, but he later sold it to Joseph Craig [62]. For most of the time that Nathaniel lived in the Elkhorn area, he seems to have lived along the South Fork and probably never resided in the undeveloped town of Frankfort for any appreciable length of time. At some undetermined point, a brick house was constructed on plot 69, though whether it was built by Nathaniel or Joseph Craig, the ensuing owner, is unknown [63].

Once established at Forks of Elkhorn, Nathaniel threw himself into public affairs with no hesitation and before long found himself deeply immersed in local developments. The Elkhorn community was growing explosively. Developing land, agriculture, roads, basic manufacturing, and governmental infrastructures all were urgent needs. Among Nathaniel's first acts in 1787 and 1788 were to erect a mill and fish dam on the Elkhorn's South Fork [64] and to sign petitions for the improvement of government in the area. One petition sought the establishment of a tobacco inspection warehouse to facilitate tobacco trade, an establishment that would benefit all tobacco growers in the area, certainly including Nathaniel himself. Another petition asked for the rapidly growing large county of Fayette to be subdivided [65]. Woodford County was shortly thereafter cut out from Fayette County territory, and Nathaniel's land lay in Woodford. Whether Nathaniel had any hand in naming the new county is unknown, but naming the new county after Nathaniel's frontier compatriot from Caroline County cannot have displeased him.

Such development continued apace; in 1789, the county formed a commission to establish an improved road to serve the area of the Elkhorn's South Fork, later called the Sanders Mill and Steele Ferry Road. A few years later, a gallows was built along Sanders Mill Road [66].

Similarly, the spiritual requirements of Baptists in the Elkhorn community were largely unserved before Nathaniel arrived. Remnants of the Traveling Church and also the party of Baptists who followed them to Kentucky the next year, including Nathaniel's mother and sisters, all settled at Forks of Elkhorn, but they never were able to construct a permanent church or find a resident pastor. Though Rev. Lewis Craig—principal organizer of the Traveling Church—remained in the area until 1792, his leadership in the Elkhorn Baptist community evidently waned. After 1792, Rev. Lewis Craig and his wife Elizabeth, sister of Nathaniel, moved to Maysville, Kentucky, in Bracken County to pursue other church work [67].

The task of creating the church long desired by the Elkhorn Baptist community fell squarely on Nathaniel's shoulders. Nor did he delay in making a start. In 1787, only months after his arrival in the area, Nathaniel proposed that Rev. William Hickman of the Marble Creek Baptist Church be brought in to form a Forks of Elkhorn church. With church community assent, he and John Major invited Reverend Hickman to become pastor, and as inducement, Nathaniel offered Hickman one hundred acres of his own land on which to live [68]. Hickman agreed, and in 1788, the Forks of Elkhorn Baptist Church was founded. Shortly thereafter, Nathaniel was baptized by Reverend Hickman and named a deacon of the church [69]. Nathaniel then accepted responsibility for erecting the church structure itself [70].

Reverend Hickman recorded his recollection of these events as they unfolded. Hickman wrote, "Mr. Sanders, who has a slight acquaintance with me, mentioned my name (as a prospective pastor). This seemed strange, as he was a very thoughtless man about his soul. They tendered me the call, and Mr. Sanders tendered me the farm on which I now live, a part of his own estate. He was not a professor (i.e., one who openly professed his faith), but I found that his wife was a devout Baptist. I said to him one day: 'Sir, you don't care for religion, I want to know why you wish me to come.' He replied, 'If it is never any advantage to me it may be so to my family.'" Hickman added later, "To my great pleasure, Mr. Sanders came forward and gave his experience, and soon thereafter he found peace with the Lord. The dear man I so much dreaded I baptized, and the church chose him as one of her deacons" [71].

About the same time Nathaniel concentrated on building the church, he also opened a tavern for food and drink along Sanders Mill Road [72]. This enterprise, juxtaposing religion and liquor selling in nearly simultaneous actions, was perhaps less controversial then than now. In fact, the Reverend Elijah Craig—he of the same religious Craig family of the Traveling Church—is generally credited with inventing the famed Kentucky bourbon by aging rough whiskey in charred oak barrels. As for Nathaniel Sanders, one suspects this tavern-owning, newly named deacon of the Forks of Elkhorn Baptist Church continued to be "thoughtless about his soul" in the eyes of fellow churchmen.

Nathaniel also, in 1790, filed a petition for leave to build a water grist mill on the North Fork of Elkhorn. The petition was successful, reflecting Nathaniel's expanding base of agriculture over a large territory. This mill eventually ceased operation by 1809 [73]. In 1790, he purchased from Benjamin Craig one acre of land beginning at "Brown and Hickling's line, to Montgomery's line, to Settles' line" in Woodford County [74] and followed this with a significant expansion of his original holding in Andrew Lewis's original military survey. At a cost of one £125, he obtained 157 acres of land in Woodford County from Ovid McCrackin of Allegheny County, Maryland, this land lying between Lewis's original holding and Andrew Steele's preemption [75]. And again, one year later, Nathaniel added to his holdings, purchasing another six hundred acres from William Lewis of Botetourt County, Virginia, for seven hundred pounds, this land also part of Andrew Lewis's original military tract [76].

A New Kentucky

In the four years since his arrival, Nathaniel had amassed more than seven thousand five hundred acres of land (including that he purchased previously at Floyd's Fork), a plot of town land in Frankfort, a grist mill on each of the main branches of the Elkhorn, and a tavern. He had built a church and became its deacon, worked toward a county division and establishment of a tobacco inspection station, and purchased as many as seventeen slaves and numerous cattle and horses [77]. By 1791, Nathaniel had established himself in Woodford County as a leading citizen and wealthy planter. There were satisfactions in those achievements, but gains such as Nathaniel and his fellow Kentuckians won meant that the earlier character of Kentucky was fast eroding. The frontier Kentucky of Nathaniel's youth emphatically was not the Kentucky in which he now dwelled.

In 1789, the new United States Constitution was adopted, replacing the ineffective Articles of Confederation that bound the new country together only loosely and ineffectively. Of this, John Adams would later remark, "The Constitution was extorted from a reluctant people by grinding necessity." With the new constitution came the inauguration of George Washington as the country's first president. And shortly thereafter, petitions for new states to be added to the union were received. Vermont and Kentucky stood first in line.

The legal basis for Kentucky's move toward statehood lay in the Virginia Constitution of 1776, which described a procedure by which separations of new states in Virginia's historic western domain could be achieved. During the 1780s, Kentucky came to be viewed as a liability to the Old Commonwealth, and Kentuckians saw little advantage of remaining in servitude to its neglectful master. The so-called Virginia Compact of 1789 resolved most points of contention between these parties, and this compact provided the base upon which Kentucky's application to the United States government was presented. Within two years, Congress decreed that Kentucky would become a state—a "commonwealth" in Kentucky's own language—on June 1, 1792, the fifteenth state of the union, following Vermont.

The winning of statehood, however, placed an obligation on Kentuckians to develop a constitution. Constitutional conventions—ten in all—were held exposing deep divisions among all classes of Kentuckians, and it fell largely upon George Nicholas, a prominent transplanted Virginia lawyer and friend of James Madison, to find the needed political compromises. Nicholas earned a sobriquet as the father of the first Kentucky Constitution [78]. A son of John Sanders, brother of Nathaniel, would eventually marry into this Nicholas family [79].

Nowhere was the need for effective local government more apparent than in the matter of settler safety. Just a month before statehood was officially conferred, in May of 1792, a group of twenty-five Indians kidnapped a settler near the Forks of the Elkhorn. Nathaniel Sanders, called by his friends "Captain" Sanders, and Captain Anthony Foster with their men gave chase, but all the Indians save one escaped. To quote from Woodford County History: "The respective friends of Colonel Grant and Captain Sanders claimed for their commander the honor of shooting this Indian" [80]. The kidnapped settler was rescued. In the same year, Nathaniel and others pursued Indians who attacked Haydon's Station. Nathaniel was particularly remembered for killing several Indians with the "big gun" he brought along [81].

Several towns in Kentucky competed for the opportunity to become the state's capital, Frankfort among them. Although in 1792 Frankfort had little to offer in the way of urban amenity, the town proposed an existing structure as a temporary capitol building and the promise of its leading citizens to offer land and financial support for its beginnings. Nathaniel was among eight leading citizens pledging three thousand dollars in specie—gold or silver—for the effort [82]. The hope was to stimulate the growth and importance of Frankfort to create new opportunities for its entrepreneurs and citizens. The plan prevailed, and Frankfort was named the state capital in the last days of 1792. For his part in the financial plan, Nathaniel sold 2,500 acres of his land at Floyd's Fork to Robert Floyd [83].

The new state capitol was temporarily located in the house of Andrew Holmes of Frankfort, a large structure Holmes had purchased from James Wilkinson. The town immediately laid plans for a new capitol building, and Nathaniel agreed to build twelve benches for Kentucky's new legislators at a cost of thirteen pounds [84]. The government sprang into action at once, and Nathaniel's name arose again in 1793 as one who could see to road building. The first road act of the Kentucky legislature appointed Bennett Pemberton, Nathaniel Sanders, and Dan Weisiger commissioners to receive subscriptions in money, labor, or property to raise a fund for clearing a wagon road from Frankfort to Cincinnati [85].

The decade of the 1790s were filled with changes to Sally and Nathaniel's family. In 1791, Nathaniel turned fifty years of age and Sally thirty-two. Nathaniel served as executor in 1792 in the estate of his friend and neighbor, Dr. Thomas Lloyd [86]. The next year, Nathaniel's mother Caty at age seventy-five relinquished her dower, retaining modest means for herself and otherwise providing the inheritance due Nathaniel from his father Hugh [87]. No record of the estate's content in 1793 seems to have survived. In 1794, Sally bore another son, Robert, the couple's seventh child and fifth son.

When young Robert was but two years old, his two older sisters married in Franklin County within a few months of each other. Sally married her cousin Nathaniel Sanders, a son of John, and Catherine married Thomas O'Neal, Nathaniel giving his permission [88]. Nathaniel probably provided dowry land for his daughters, but no record of this seems to have survived. Another family marriage took place, in 1800, when their son Hugh married Nancy Moxley, whose family lived adjacent Nathaniel and Sally's home on the South Fork of the Elkhorn [89]. And notably, in 1798, Sally and Nathaniel had their final child—born twenty-one years after their eldest child—a son they named George Washington Sanders.

The High Price of Statehood

From the moment Kentucky came into being as a state, life for Nathaniel seems to have taken a substantially different turn. Suddenly gone after statehood were Nathaniel's heady initiatives of buying land and building structures and institutions, of fighting Indians and leading civic causes, of contributing to the common good. In place of that, beginning about 1794, Nathaniel's attentions turn to selling property and confronting legal challenges. For the next decade, the robust Nathaniel of earlier days seems to have given way to a different person. How can this have happened? The answer seems to lie in the actions of the Kentucky legislature itself, though a full answer is by no means clear.

Political battle lines formed in Kentucky even before the state constitution was drafted. On one side were the Democratic Republicans, populist in tone and overwhelmingly favored by the majority of Kentuckians, and on the other were the Federalists, who supported a somewhat more traditional and autocratic approach to government, not unlike that of Virginia before the Revolution [90]. Issues of land policy, slavery, and taxation were fundamental points of dispute as the legislature carved out its initial approach to statehood.

Following the first elections, Democratic Republicans won a substantial majority in the Kentucky legislature and soon passed laws unfavorable to large landowners. In its first year, 1793, new taxes were laid on lands and slaves. The best lands, called first-rate land, were taxed at a rate roughly seven times higher than poorer third-rate lands [91]. All of Nathaniel's Elkhorn lands were regarded and taxed as first-rate, and together with his remaining property at Floyd's Fork, his taxable land totaled more than four thousand acres [92]. Furthermore, the legislature laid a new tax on persons, slaves and nonslaves alike, excepting only female slaves under age sixteen. In 1795, Nathaniel's titheable household consisted of his family of ten and also seventeen slaves, although in 1797 Nathaniel agreed to set one slave free [93]. Together these new taxes took their toll. In 1794, Nathaniel sold land totaling 138 acres in four separate transactions, raising £370 in sales [94].

In 1796 Nathaniel conveyed four acres of land in Franklin County near the Forks of the Elkhorn to Robert Barr and Company, which land included the tavern he opened four years before. This agreement with the Barr Company enjoined Nathaniel from ever again opening another tavern on the same land [95]. Two years later, he placed his Woodford County mills and plantation for rent in a Kentucky news magazine [96]. In the six years following statehood in Kentucky, Nathaniel had divested himself of much of his land around the Elkhorn region and rid himself of important sources of income from his mills and tavern. Nathaniel evidently pictured some better future than he could imagine at Forks of Elkhorn. In 1801, he sold another sizable plot of land, conveying ninety acres for forty-five pounds of current money [97]. Yet the records leave unclear the question of exactly when Nathaniel did leave the area or why. As late as 1801, Nathaniel is known to have supplied plank wood to John Major to enclose the latter's garden [98]. This is the last year that Nathaniel appears in the Franklin County Tax List.

Toward the end of Nathaniel's years on the Elkhorn, legal matters intruded upon him. He was ordered to grand jury service in the United States Federal Court in 1797 [99]. In 1798, he undertook with Charles Patterson to construct two bridges across the Elkhorn near the forks together with an agreement to keep the bridges in good repair for a period of seven years. These bridges fell into disrepair well before the term of agreement expired—whether from poor construction, heavy use, or high water we cannot say—and the county ordered suit to be brought for redress [100]. On behalf of the county, the United States sued Nathaniel for recovery of costs in 1798 and again in 1802, evidently winning both cases [101]. How strong an effect these verdicts against Nathaniel might have had on his finances is unknown, but these cases represent the last known instances of Nathaniel residing at the Forks of the Elkhorn.

By 1802, Nathaniel had reached his sixty-first birthday and by that time had resolved to leave the Forks of Elkhorn. Legal problems and onerous taxes undoubtedly influenced his decision, but one gets a sense that insidious longer-term detractions were equally important. Nathaniel undertook a process of selling land and buying none from as early as 1794, steadily reducing his assets and commitments to the Forks of Elkhorn over nearly a decade. Tobacco growing probably reduced the fertility of some of his fields, rendering them less productive and less valuable as time went by. But more than those things, particularly heavy expectations had been placed upon Nathaniel by his community; he was asked to play the roles of a wealthy planter and slave owner, political actor and contributor, and community builder and protector. Nathaniel became engulfed in community responsibility, ensnarled in the close and confining forces of settlement and civilization. This may have been a burden this frontiersman could not carry. He chose to leave and, in leaving, to find a relatively undeveloped frontier in a different part of Kentucky.

Eagle Creek

Sometime between 1802 and 1804, Nathaniel moved himself and his family to a lightly settled part of the state, northward into Gallatin County. The county lay along the Ohio River to its north, and forming its southern boundary was a westward flowing stream called Eagle Creek that paralleled the Ohio. Eagle Creek emptied into the Kentucky River not far from where the Kentucky flowed into the Ohio, allowing settlers along Eagle Creek convenient access to points along the Ohio River and also the nation's interior on the Mississippi. Equally, one could travel from Eagle Creek upstream on the Kentucky River to the rich central Kentucky bluegrass lands, including the area around Frankfort that Nathaniel had called home for nearly two decades. Eagle Creek itself was navigable up to the spot Nathaniel chose for his new home, about eight miles upstream from the Creek's confluence with the Kentucky River.

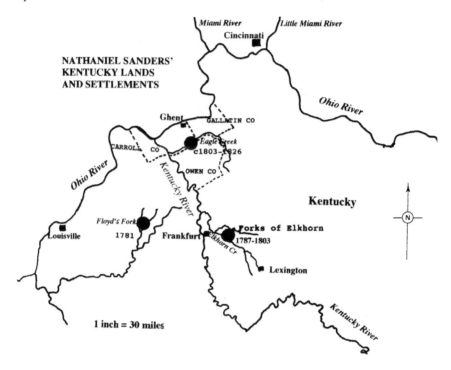

Nathaniel Sanders first acquired six thousand acres of Kentucky land at Floyd's Fork, but he never settled there, and that purchase remained in litigation for years. He purchased numerous tracts of land at Forks of Elkhorn after arriving there about 1787, residing on the South Fork but holding land on the North Fork as well. After the turn of the century, Nathaniel moved to a location on Eagle Creek in what later became Gallatin County and established a settlement that eventually became known as Sanders, Kentucky. The town of Sanders was annexed by Carroll County in 1872.

We find no clear record of Nathaniel's initial purchase on Eagle Creek, but by 1806, he had acquired two hundred acres on Eagle Creek from J. C. Richardson, perhaps his first actual land holding in the area, and quickly added another 667 acres from Richardson that same year [102]. It is possible that Nathaniel occupied the Richardson land before 1806 as a land transaction can precede an officially recorded date of it. Alternatively, these 1806 purchases may have added to an earlier holding for which no record has survived.

Nathaniel settled not far from his brother John, who lived at Ghent in Gallatin County and who is remembered as an original settler of that place. Nearby also was his brother Charles, who had purchased a farm on McCool's Creek just outside Ghent. If part of Nathaniel's decision to relocate to Gallatin County was to reunite with his brothers, then in this Nathaniel found immediate disappointment. John died within a year of Nathaniel's arrival. Six years later, Nathaniel became legal guardian of John's son Samuel [103].

Life at Eagle Creek quickened Nathaniel's pulse. Reinvigorated by the challenges of this undeveloped land, Nathaniel's activity resonated with new energy despite his advancing years, reminiscent of his early days at Elkhorn. We first discover Nathaniel's whereabouts in a record of 1805, where we learn that he already owned a tan yard [104] on Lick Creek, a small branch of Eagle Creek, and that he also had been appointed overseer of the road leading from McCool's Creek to the County line. This thirty-five-foot-wide road led directly to Nathaniel's property [105] and assured Nathaniel handy access to activities in his section of the county.

Nathaniel's home soon became the gathering place for neighbors and a focal point for public business, not least because of Nathaniel's reputation and past experience at road clearing and similar responsibilities at the Forks of Elkhorn and Frankfort. In 1806, an act of Kentucky's General Assembly called for the inspection of tobacco, hemp, and flour to be located at Nathaniel's property on Eagle Creek, the establishment to be called Sanders Inspection (also Saunders Landing). This act specified that Eagle Creek to its confluence with the Kentucky River shall be declared a navigable stream and public highway for passage of boats. Five dollars per month was assessed for anyone establishing an obstruction such as a fish dam until the obstruction was removed [106]. In short order, Nathaniel's home fixed the intersection of a county road and a Kentucky "highway," a central point at which the local agricultural community could gather for business and discussion. Nathaniel was also called upon in 1806 to serve as a road commissioner through yet another act of General Assembly of Commonwealth, this to open a "waggon" road from New Castle to the mouth of the Licking River, a distance of about sixty miles. The road itself followed the spine of the high land dividing the watercourses of the Ohio River and Eagle Creek [107].

In 1809, Nathaniel erected a substantial two-story stone house on Eagle Creek, an uncommonly large and sturdy structure for that time in northern Kentucky. The house instantly became a community resource. The year after its completion, the house was named by the Kentucky legislature as an election polling place, called Eagle Creek Precinct, which was employed in a three-day

election in 1810 [108]. It also served as a Gallatin County postal station, and
Nathaniel was named its postmaster.

Nathaniel Sanders' stone house on Eagle Creek was built in
1809. The structure was dismantled about 1916 and its stones
used to build a dam. Original painting by a descendant of
Nathaniel, Emily Hayes Beale, whose sister, Mary Margaret
Hayes Boyles, shared a copy with the authors.

The term Sanders Inspection or Saunders Landing used by the Kentucky
legislature appears to be the first instance of a place-name attached to
Nathaniel's location on Eagle Creek, and Eagle Creek Precinct was another.
Whether his post office might have borne one of these names or some other is
unknown. Place-names for Nathaniel's homestead would change several times
in ensuing years.

Public duties notwithstanding, it was land that lay at the forefront of
Nathaniel's attentions from the time he arrived in Kentucky and especially
in his later years in Gallatin County. Above all other things, Nathaniel was a
landowner. In his time in Kentucky, Nathaniel at one time or another, though
not simultaneously, held title to as many as eighteen thousand acres, totaling
more than twenty-five square miles of Kentucky land. This was his business
and his pleasure. Nathaniel's land probably provided his chief source of
income from farming and produced further revenue when it was eventually
sold. Other properties he bought and sold purely on speculation, a profitable
Kentucky business in its own right. In a time of rapid growth such as Kentucky

experienced in Nathaniel's time, such gains were not negligible. But all his lands represented more than simple wealth. In Nathaniel's grassy meadows and rolling hillsides, he could see testimonies to his own accomplishments, the tangible fruit of his long and varied labors following the Revolutionary War. Yet this same land over time also became Nathaniel's bridge to his children's future. He gave good land and its future prospects to all his children, declaring in one instance that his gift of land was made with "natural love and affection." Landowners such as Nathaniel inevitably gained political influence as well, whether they overtly sought it or not. In Nathaniel's case, his land ownership crowned him the paterfamilias not only of his own offspring but, in a larger sense, of his rural community as well.

Nathaniel's first priority for land in Gallatin County probably was to add to his modest beginnings on Eagle Creek. In the decade following 1810, Nathaniel purchased more than thirty-two hundred acres in three transactions, all Eagle Creek lands that would eventually pass to his family or close relatives [109]. He financed these purchases in part by ridding himself of two properties he had to that point retained at the Forks of Elkhorn [110].

Other land dealings in Gallatin County were not so straightforward. Shortly after arriving in the county, Nathaniel teamed with a certain John Scott on several land transactions that evidently were speculative in nature. With the backing of Nathaniel and others, John Scott had been appointed surveyor for Gallatin County [111], an office that positioned him well for identifying promising opportunities in real estate, buying unoccupied land in still-budding Gallatin County and selling at a profit as settlers streamed in. Nathaniel and John Scott teamed up to buy forty-four hundred acres along the Ohio River in 1807 and another thousand acres at this location a decade later [112]. These properties lay five to ten miles distant from Nathaniel's homestead, of no apparent use to him for his farming operations. In later years, Nathaniel and Scott sold several of these Ohio River lands in smaller plots to individual buyers, some at considerable profit [113]. Other plots he gave to family as occasions required.

Floyd's Fork

We recall that before Nathaniel moved to Kentucky in 1787, he had six years before paid the Commonwealth of Virginia two thousand pounds for six thousand acres of land at Floyd's Fork. This land had been surveyed in 1784, and Nathaniel received title to the acreage before leaving for Kentucky. Nathaniel held this property without actively using it until, finally in 1792, he sold twenty-five hundred acres of it to Robert Floyd. But another fourteen years passed before Floyd's final payment permitted an actual conveyance of the land from Nathaniel's possession to Floyd's hands [114]. That sale was perhaps the lone instance of Nathaniel receiving benefit of his original purchase, although about 1801 his son Hugh received a gift of between 250 and 500 acres of this land from Nathaniel. In 1807, the year following the conveyance to Floyd, a legal inquiry was launched concerning Nathaniel's original survey—triggered by the consummation of the sale to Floyd—and a Louisville court received several depositions regarding the matter [115]. In court, several claimants and witnesses deposed that this land on Floyd's Fork had been cleared and occupied by them well before Nathaniel's purchase and that Nathaniel's survey of 1784 exaggerated his boundaries and overlapped their long-settled land entitlements. Nathaniel sued for restitution of his lands, and the result was a legal proceeding that lasted for at least thirteen years. The case held extraordinary complexity, revealing much of the anatomy of land transactions in that part of early Kentucky and generally reflected badly on its contestants, whether rightly or wrongly.

Nathaniel's original survey of 1784 provided only a broad and somewhat vague description of the property he purchased, using marked trees and stream courses to sketch the lay of his land. That description, however, was the basis upon which Robert Floyd in 1792 purchased twenty-five hundred of Nathaniel's six thousand acres. But Floyd was aware, given the vagueness of boundaries, that surplus land beyond the six thousand acres lay within Nathaniel's survey, and at the time of sale, Nathaniel—making a grievous mistake—agreed that Floyd was entitled to half of any surplus land found. Floyd seized his opportunity. In 1793, less than a year after the sale was signed, he dumped the unsurveyed "surplusage" (their term) and some of his recent purchase on unsuspecting buyers, completing a total of fifteen transactions involving more than eighteen hundred acres in under six months. The land he sold lay within the boundaries of Nathaniel's survey but also contained lands held by others even before Nathaniel had arrived in Kentucky. During the court proceeding, deponents claimed that the surplusage of Nathaniel's survey amounted to between two and four thousand acres above his original six-thousand-acre claim.

Several deponents thought they detected fraud in the whole scheme, a collusion between Nathaniel and Robert Floyd, to sell lands that Nathaniel had no legitimate title to, pointing particularly to the "blood relationship" between Nathaniel and Robert Floyd. This accusation was difficult to refute because Robert Floyd died before the case went to court [116]. Nathaniel answered that he and Floyd were but distant relatives and that he had seen nothing of Floyd for years as they lived at a great distance. Claimants pointed out that Hugh Sanders, Nathaniel's son and intermittently his representative at court, knew as early as 1801—or even before that—that Nathaniel's land contained a great deal of surplusage and that other valid land claims lay within his boundaries. Others claimed that Nathaniel refused offers of compromise. And yet Nathaniel on one occasion during these proceedings told one affected party to be at ease, to go home, and to cultivate as good a crop as he could. One land claimant threatened to shoot any surveyor who stepped on his land.

Sensing uncertainty in the legal outcome of these disputes and also his own perhaps failing health, in 1816, Nathaniel clarified who was to eventually inherit his Floyd's Fork land, which he said amounted to six thousand acres less that acreage conveyed to Floyd. He left equal shares to each of his seven surviving children and a fractional share to the heirs of his deceased daughter Sally. In the same year, his son Hugh sold off two plots of Floyd's Fork land totaling 276 acres from his original holding. In 1818, Nathaniel sent his Gallatin County friend, surveyor John Scott, to represent him in court—Nathaniel was said to be too ill to attend—and to inspect the survey lines in dispute. Scott testified in court that numerous boundary markings on trees were too fresh to have been made in the original survey of 1784.

No final resolution of the case has been located in the records, but in 1820, Nathaniel was ordered to pay court costs for several claimants whom he had sued, suggesting he lost the suit and retained no more than his thirty-five hundred acres not in dispute. On the other hand, no subsequent land sales at Floyd's Fork by any of his heirs have ever been discovered, and the land itself was not mentioned by Nathaniel in his last will and testament some years later, suggesting that he might have lost his entire claim through these legal proceedings [117]. This outcome is plausible, as Kentucky courts in this period exhibited some hostility to earlier Virginia-based land claims, favoring those originating in Kentucky itself [118].

The Children Grown

The home of Sally and Nathaniel Sanders on Eagle Creek remained a busy family gathering place even as late as the decade of the 1810s, when Nathaniel was in his seventies and Sally in her fifties. At the start of that decade, four children still remained with them. Robert had attained age sixteen by 1810 and the youngest son George Washington—called Wash in later years—was then age twelve. Samuel, John's son whose wardship was accepted by Nathaniel, was probably in his early teens by then, and a free boy of color named Reuben, about age seven, lived at the house. Reuben was apprenticed for thirteen years to learn the trade of blacksmithing "in all its varying branches" until his age twenty-one. Reuben also was to receive education in reading, writing, and "common arithmetic including the rule of three." Oddly, Nathaniel himself was called a blacksmith on this occasion; he received three pounds ten shillings for accepting Reuben into apprenticeship from Percival Butler, clerk of the Gallatin County Court [119].

Some children of Sally and Nathaniel reached marriageable age in this decade, and weddings were something of a common occurrence. Robert, though only twenty-one, married first in the decade, in 1815, to Nancy Blanton, the second marriage of the Sanders to this Blanton family, though the first in more than a century [120]. Nancy was the daughter of William Blanton who lived near Nathaniel at the Forks of Elkhorn, and in anticipation of this union, Nathaniel provided Robert with more than five hundred acres of his land on the Ohio River in 1814 [121]. Just months after Robert married, John wed Sally Moxley—the second Moxley marriage in the family—in Franklin County where the Moxleys lived. John too received five hundred acres as a wedding gift. And in 1818, Nathaniel Jr. married Mary (Polly) Craigmyle in Gallatin County, Nathaniel receiving the same gift as the others [122].

Finally, in 1820, son James married Elizabeth Moxley in Franklin County, and James received Eagle Creek land near his brothers [123].

In 1823, as if to satisfy all parts of his family, Nathaniel gave some Ohio River lands to Thomas O'Neal, the husband of Catherine, his daughter, who had married years before. In the same year, he sold Eagle Creek lands to his four grandsons by his deceased daughter Sally [124]. By this time, among all the children, only underage Wash had not received his due.

Final Years

In September of 1824, Nathaniel, at age eighty-three, authored his last will and testament. Included in his estate was his wife and all their children except Sally, who by then was deceased, and one granddaughter Lydia Smith, who was Sally's daughter by a second marriage. He added a codicil the following year, specifically benefiting Wash by giving him slaves, and also Kitty O'Neal, who received money beyond that received by her siblings. [125]. The codicil seemed suspect to other beneficiaries because Nathaniel had recently given Wash power of attorney over the estate; and within a year, Wash married Kitty O'Neal in Switzerland County, Indiana [126].

In 1826, Nathaniel, "for diverse and good causes" arranged for the emancipation of two of his older slaves, Daniel (alias Old Daniel) and Nicey, his wife [127]. Nicey had attended Nathaniel's mother in her final years until she died shortly after 1795. Nathaniel empowered Wesley Minor to effect the emancipation as he was too ill to complete the task himself. This manumission, seemingly a kind act in Nathaniel's old age, set Daniel and Nicey free to find their way in the world although Little Daniel, perhaps their son, remained a slave. Henceforth, Daniel and Nicey would seek their own food, clothing, and shelter and other requirements as they met them, though with their productive years behind them, one struggles to imagine how Daniel and Nicey survived long, if indeed they did [128]. In his will, Nathaniel also granted freedom to other slaves after his death, including Edom, David, and Wyatt, though Wyatt would have to purchase his freedom for fifty dollars payable in three installments.

Finally, on October 26, 1826, Nathaniel died at age eighty-five, his obituary being published four days later in the *Lexington Reporter* in which he was simply remembered as a "soldier in the Revolution" [129]. Nathaniel left behind sixty-seven-year-old Sally Pattie Sanders, his wife of exactly fifty years. Nathaniel's estate was administered on Sally's behalf, providing for her amply for the years ahead. The task of estate inventory and appraisement fell to son Robert, who also arranged two sales of Nathaniel's personal property for his mother's benefit [130]. Included were two land sales stemming from prior agreements and a release of the new mill property [131]. Most important were court rulings that laid off Sally's dower land and the conveyance of this to her possession [132].

In his will, Nathaniel provided that Sally should have her choice of properties, either the plantation containing the old mill and stone house on the upper portion of Eagle Creek—lying on the original two hundred acres Nathaniel purchased of Richardson in 1806—or the new plantation and mill downstream on the south bank of Eagle Creek, on land purchased from Beale in 1819. Wash then should have a choice of either property, though if he wanted the plantation his mother chose, he would have to wait for her passing to receive it. Sally chose the stone house and old mill as well as another four hundred acres of Ohio River lands. The Gallatin County Court formalized this election as dower land [133]. The court also gave Sally ownership of Edom, who evidently lost his claim to freedom in this action. In 1832, Sally renounced Nathaniel's bequest to her, clearing the way for Wash to claim her plantation as he wished [134].

Robert's inventory and appraisement of Nathaniel's estate, excluding real estate, provides some insight into Nathaniel's life and affairs in his later years [135]. The first items listed were a coffee pot and cups [136]. The whole estate was valued at more than $5,000, nearly 80 percent of which lay in slaves [137]. Other value was found in livestock, including a fine grey horse worth eighty dollars—undoubtedly Nathaniel's own. Overall, the inventory counted three horses, sixteen head of cattle, four pairs of oxen, thirty-five sheep, twenty hogs, and four pigs. Surprisingly, at the time of his death, Nathaniel held forty barrels of corn and seven thousand pounds of pork [138], evidently acting as a collector of local produce for marketing elsewhere. A wide array of farm implements and basic household furniture, appliances, cutlery, and glassware conveys a sense of a busy and comfortable, if not elegant, life on the banks of Eagle Creek.

Sally lived on for some years, dying fifteen years after her husband in 1841 at age eighty-three. Before her death, she had applied for a Revolutionary War Pension, describing in some detail Nathaniel's movements and exploits at that time [139]. Action by the government on her claim was delayed until 1844, three years after her passing, when the claim was finally paid to a Kentucky pension agent, who evidently distributed this to her heirs.

A Further Tale

The story of Nathaniel Sanders of Spotsylvania County, Forks of Elkhorn, and Gallatin County did not end with his death and estate dispersal but rather grew in proportion to Nathaniel's substantial reputation over the following decade. A tale of Nathaniel Sanders remains in his part of Kentucky and its literature even today [140].

Nathaniel was a large man in all respects, having the kind of largeness that burned itself into the psyche of those who knew him or knew of him. Nathaniel possessed an aura, a frontier charisma that captured others' imaginations. They held images of Nathaniel—a young man daring to run off into the wilderness and to survive, learning savvy frontier Indian ways, possessing the strength of two men, wielding a scalping knife and especially his long Kentucky rifle, fighting the British and the Indians, protecting friends, intimidating enemies, and building communities. Nathaniel in his lifetime was so many things— frontiersman and scout, Revolutionary soldier and militiaman, churchman and road builder, tavern owner and merchant, carpenter, miller, tanner, blacksmith, farmer, postmaster, deacon, Indian fighter, family man, landowner, slave owner—and he touched the lives of many people. That a remarkable story, apocryphal or not, should become part of his memory is understandable. This tale requires a bit of history to understand.

Ten years after Nathaniel's death, the war for Texas independence erupted. In 1836, Texas settlers and supporters—including many from Kentucky— undertook to separate Texas from Mexican dominion and to establish their own country, free of what they perceived as Mexican corruption and misrule. The Mexican army under Antonio Lopez de Santa Anna as commander-in-chief marched on the Texans and defeated—some say slaughtered—rebels at Goliad, including Samuel Smith Sanders, a youth of nineteen from the family of John Sanders of Ghent. Santa Anna then marched to San Antonio to eliminate rebels garrisoned at the Alamo. Defenders of the Alamo numbered more than two hundred, including the well-known figures of Davy Crockett and Jim Bowie, a Kentuckian. Most Americans at the Alamo were killed resisting the Mexican onslaught, and those that were captured were immediately executed, and their bodies burned. America was furious. Santa Anna at that time was perhaps the most reviled figure in America. Shortly after the Alamo, Santa Anna's forces were defeated by Texans under Sam Houston at the Battle of San Jacinto in 1836, and Santa Anna himself was taken prisoner.

A detachment of soldiers was directed to escort Santa Anna to Washington for proper justice—though Texas was then not part of the United States—and to achieve this, the escort placed the general in leg irons and from Texas carried him up the Mississippi and then the Ohio River to Kentucky. They stayed over at Frankfort before completing the trip east along the Wilderness Road to

Virginia and Washington. All that is undisputed fact. But it is at Frankfort that a remarkable story unfolds, about which there is little agreement [141].

One version goes like this. Fearing for the general's safety, the military escort secretly moved Santa Anna to a tavern just outside of Frankfort, but word leaked out and before long, an angry mob of Kentuckians gathered at the tavern, demanding that Santa Anna be turned over to them [142]. Discussions or violence followed, and eventually, the escorts agreed to allow three members of the crowd into the tavern to speak with Santa Anna. They entered and met the prisoner, but what they heard next was stunning. Speaking in a pure Kentucky drawl without a hint of Spanish accent, Santa Anna let out words to this effect, "Rest easy, gentlemen, I'm one of you. My name is Nathaniel Sanders, and I'll be coming back to claim my land." Amazed and confused at Santa Anna's portrayals of his background and parentage, the Kentuckians eventually retreated, and the hostile crowd melted away.

From their experience, those inside the tavern later gave a more detailed explanation of what they heard. It seems that Santa Anna was an Indian son of Nathaniel Sanders—he of our family—whose name was also Nathaniel Sanders but who was usually called Bull Sanders, owing to his violent temper. Bull Sanders at a young age was sent off to West Point—just newly in operation after 1802—but later got into difficulty with a young local girl. Her enraged father, a ferryman on the Hudson River, confronted Bull Sanders. The ferryman was found murdered the next day. Bull Sanders proclaimed his innocence to other cadets but was not seen around West Point after that. He eventually made his way to Mexico and from there up a ladder to high position in the Mexican army as Antonio Lopez de Santa Anna.

Whether the person in the tavern that night was indeed Santa Anna or perhaps a double artfully substituted by Santa Anna's escort as a ruse we cannot know. Santa Anna scholars tend to scoff at this story, citing records of Santa Anna's family and his birth at Jalapa in the province of Veracruz and his record of service in the Mexican military. These scholars, however, have been unable to account for the name "de Santa Anna," which place evidently cannot be found either in Mexico or in Spain. A land deed bearing Santa Anna's name, authenticated in a county court and reported in a recent local newspaper, has been found in Tennessee, and a Sanders relative claims to have seen another such deed among records of the elder Nathaniel Sanders' Kentucky transactions. Some claim these deeds were created to lure Santa Anna back to the United States, where local justice could be extracted upon him.

Claims and counterclaims, facts and opposing facts, beliefs and disbeliefs continue to wander through this story even today, leaving us with but one certain truth. A regional myth has intrigued Kentuckians for nearly two centuries, and Nathaniel Sanders has been chosen to stand at the center of it.

NOTES

1. United States National Park Service, Cumberland Gap (brochure), Cumberland Gap National Historical Park, Kentucky, 2005.
2. Anna V. Parker, *The Sanders Family of Grass Hills, Kentucky* (Madison, Indiana: Coleman Printing, 1966). Some vital dates of Nathaniel's siblings are uncertain, but Nathaniel seems the third child, based on his birth date, his parents' marriage date, and the knowledge that John and Catherine were older.
3. The term *plantation* in this chapter conforms with the term's usage in the eighteenth century and before, meaning generally a "place of planting, a farm," usually one established in a new clearing. *Plantations* in the antebellum period commonly referred to grandiose structures and extensive property holdings, a meaning we do not intend here.
4. Although we do not know exactly when Nathaniel left home, his age fourteen seems about right. He could not easily have survived the wilderness at an earlier age, and if he were much older, his leaving home would not be regarded as "running off." Age fourteen was the usual age for the start of a six- or seven-year apprenticeship, often a dreadful prospect for a lad emerging from childhood.
5. Parker, *Sanders Family of Grass Hills.*
6. See Bob Blankenship, "Cherokee Roots," in *Eastern Cherokee Rolls*, vol. 1 (1992), cited in *Sanders Siftings*, no. 36 (January 2004), p. 4. Blankenship lists numerous Cherokees bearing the surname Sanders among those east of the Mississippi River for the period 1817–1924.
7. Benedict Arnold ran from his apprenticeship. A description of how these arrangements were viewed by teenage boys at the time is given in J. K. Martin, *Benedict Arnold: Revolutionary Hero* (New York: New York University Press, 1997), pp. 27–31.
8. Nathaniel Gist, son of noted early explorer of Kentucky, is thought by some to be the father of the famed Cherokee linguist Sequoia.
9. The term *longhunt* was commonly used to describe wilderness hunting expeditions, which often lasted for months at a time and resulted in prodigious numbers and varieties of hides brought back. Individual longhunters were known to take along four horses on a hunt, one to ride and three to carry hides. Kentucky longhunts took varied game, returning hides of bison, wolves, deer, elk, and smaller animals at considerable profit.
10. Exploration and settlement in the 1700s focused on the southwestern fringe of Virginia, in part because the Blue Ridge mountains were relatively penetrable there and because a well-worn trail to the west called the Warrior's Path, later known as the Wilderness Road,

traversed the area. The Warrior's Path lay in Cherokee territory and did much to encourage early trading and exploration with the Cherokees throughout the first half of the century. By midcentury, the first longhunt by Elisha Waller passed through the area, and the explorations of Christopher Gist in the 1750s and Daniel Boone (1769) later covered the same land. Gist's son Nathaniel lived with the Cherokees for more than a decade. Initial white settlement in southwestern Virginia took place along this path, commencing toward the end of the 1740s.

11. That Nathaniel might have served in Woodford's campaign is not idle conjecture. Several events in Nathaniel's life after the completion of that campaign in 1762 point to his probable acquaintance with Woodford, notably Woodford's acquaintance with Daniel Morgan and Abner Waugh, both well-known to Nathaniel, and Nathaniel's presence in Caroline County despite his Spotsylvania origins. It may not be simple coincidence that Nathaniel returned home after seven years' absence in the same year that Woodford's western campaign ended.

12. T. E. Campbell, *Colonial Caroline: A History of Caroline County, Virginia* (Richmond, Virginia: Dietz Press, 1954), p. 169.

13. The claim that Nathaniel returned home after seven years is given in Parker, *Sanders Family of Grass Hills*. Parker's source was Sanders family papers, which came to her through Lewis Sanders, nephew of Nathaniel. These papers can be found at the Filson Club, Louisville, Kentucky.

14. Application for Revolutionary War Veteran's Pension, United States Government GSA Form 6751, Rev. 8–71, Sanders, Nathaniel—W8703. Details of this application are also found in Parker, *Sanders Family of Grass Hills*.

15. See Albert V. Goodpasture, "The Paternity of Sequoya: The Inventory of the Cherokee Alphabet," *Chronicles of Oklahoma* vol. 1, no. 2 (1921), pp. 121–130. Oklahoma Historical Society and Oklahoma State University, Stillwater, p. 129.

16. Details of this alleged Indian son and that son's exploits are described later in the chapter.

17. This relation is not easy to explain, but that Nathaniel and John Floyd would have known each other through their family relationship seems clear. Abigail Davis Floyd (née Lewis) was the mother of Rosanna Davis and from a second marriage also the mother of John Floyd. Rosanna Davis married Nathaniel Sanders of North Carolina, he the uncle of Nathaniel of Spotsylvania County. Imprecisely, then, we can say that John Floyd was Nathaniel's uncle through marriage.

18. Detail of Floyd's expedition is available in L. Harrison and J. Klotter, *A New History of Kentucky* (Lexington: University Press of Kentucky, 1997), p. 19.

19. Parker, *Sanders Family of Grass Hills.*

20. Daniel Morgan's military career is described in several sources, but a useful brief chronology is found at http://www.patriotresource.com/people/morgan/page4.html. Morgan's leadership in the Battle of Point Pleasant during Dunmore's War led to his command appointments during the Revolution.

21. No record directly stating enlistment terms for the Virginia riflemen has been found; probably none exists. The notion that they had six month enlistments stems from statements to that effect by commanders of the American force at Quebec. See Martin, *Benedict Arnold*, p. 158.

22. Ashley provides the background to British control of Quebec. In 1759, the British gained a victory over France in the Battle of Quebec. James Wolfe captured Quebec to fulfill Pitt's plan to expel the French from all of Canada. France surrendered Canada to England in 1763. See Mike Ashley, *British Kings and Queens* (New York: Barnes and Noble, 1998), p. 677.

23. The Act of Quebec of 1774 stimulated strong feelings in both directions as regards separation from the mother country, stirring Tory support among the gentry but provoking anger among others in Canada. Americans overestimated support for separation, and that contributed to the failure of their invasion.

24. Martin, *Benedict Arnold*, pp. 114–128. Martin provides a description of Arnold's force including its Virginians, travails of the march northward, and the Battle of Quebec.

25. Ibid., p. 115. Bateaux were double-ended, flat-bottomed rowboats suitable for river transportation. Arnold ordered two hundred bateaux for his thousand-man expedition but found the boats were smaller than he had requested, and so requisitioned another twenty to be built.

26. Ibid., p. 116.

27. Kenneth Roberts, *Arundel* (Greenwich, Connecticut: Fawcett Publications, 1963).

28. Martin, *Benedict Arnold*, pp. 123–128.

29. Ibid. This contains a full account of the battle and its aftermath; see pp. 151–182.

30. James Pattie died in 1787 in Virginia and his wife Sarah followed the Pattie children to Kentucky. Later, Ann Sanders Pattie resided in Bracken County, Kentucky, which was also home to the Reverend Lewis Craig and his wife Elizabeth Sanders Craig, Ann's sister. In later years,

noted writer-mountainman James Ohio Pattie also called Bracken County his home. One might guess that he was named after James Patty of Virginia. See also Patrick Wardell, Virginia/West Virginia Genealogical Data from Revolutionary War Pension and Bounty Land Warrant Records, vol. 5 (n.d.), p. 8.

31. Campbell, *Colonial Caroline*, pp. 258, 431–432. Also see Otto Lohrenz, "The Reverend Abner Waugh: The Best Dancer of the Minuet in the State of Virginia." *Kentucky Review*.

32. Beverley Fleet, *Virginia Colonial Abstracts*, vol. 2. (Baltimore: Genealogical Publishing Company, 1988), p. 62. Immigration records for Sylvester Pattie or his forebears have not been found. Beyond timing and locational coincidences, evidence that Sylvester is the father of James Pattie derives from the fact Ann Sanders and John Pattie named a son Sylvester.

33. Campbell, *Colonial Caroline*, p. 446. Note also that James Pattie was executor for the estate of Caleb Lindsay in 1764, presaging later close links between these families; see p.479.

34. If Nathaniel was in Spotsylvania County at this time, he may have returned to Caroline for this purpose; see Campbell, *Colonial Caroline*, p. 370.

35. Wardell, Virginia/West Virginia Genealogical Data, vol. 5 (n.d.), p. 8.

36. Application for Revolutionary War Veteran's Pension, United States Government GSA Form 6751, Rev. 8–71, Sanders, Nathaniel—W8703.

37. William A. Crozier, ed., *Spotsylvania County Records: 1721–1800*, vol. 1 (Baltimore: Southern Book Company, 1955), p. 366.

38. The meaning of this statement is that Sally rather than Nathaniel directed their slaves in farming.

39. Revolutionary War Service Claim L136-19-8, Library of Virginia Archives, Court Booklet, Spotsylvania County, p. 15.

40. Revolutionary War Service Claim, p. 18.

41. Spotsylvania County Will Book E, p. 418.

42. Revolutionary War Service Claim, Library of Virginia Archives, Court Booklet, p. 19, Spotsylvania County, Virginia. 1781, August (claim of 1782, May 1), War Department certificate granted to Nathaniel for two horses lost, August 1781, certified by James Decamp, DWM, L75.

43. Application for Revolutionary War Veteran's Pension, United States Government GSA Form 6751, Rev. 8–71, Sanders, Nathaniel—W8703.

44. Ashley, *British Kings and Queens*, p. 680.

45. D. J. Boorstin, *The Americans: The Colonial Experience* (New York: Vintage, 1958), p. 143.

46. Nathaniel purchased Treasury Warrant #3537 in Virginia for five hundred acres at a cost of two hundred pounds. On May 22, 1780, he

entered his land selection, for five hundred acres on Locust Creek in Jefferson County, adjacent Thomas Brown and John Sanders. On April 18, 1785, the land surveyed, survey number 4499 and then assigned to John Pattie. In September 1787, the certificate of ownership was granted with assignment to John Pattie. See Virginia Land Grants and Surveys, 1774–1791. Original records are retained by the Kentucky Secretary of State Land Office.

47. William A. Crozier, ed., Spotsylvania County Records: 1721–1800, Deed Book L, 1785–1788 (1955), p. 4.

48. Spotsylvania County Will Book E, pp. 419–420.

49. Nathaniel purchased three Virginia treasury warrants for six thousand acres on Floyd's Fork, Jefferson County, in 1781. These treasury warrants previously had been held by Benjamin Holladay, who was distantly related to Nathaniel. Both the Sanders and the Holladays had married into the same Coleman family; see J. R. Mansfield, *History of Early Spotsylvania* (Orange, Virginia: Green Publishers, 1977), p. 179.

50. The exact birth years of Sally and James are not known. Older siblings Hugh and Catherine were born before 1780, and John was the firstborn in Kentucky in 1789. Sally's and James's births fell between these dates.

51. Virginia Tax Records, p. 354. One might guess that these slaves came from his father's plantation.

52. Spotsylvania County Deed Book K, 1782–1785, p. 388.

53. The Virginia legislature granted three law office treasury warrants dated November 6, 1781 (numbers 8505, 8506, 8514) to Nathaniel Sanders, for six thousand acres on Floyd's Fork in Jefferson County, this act signed by Edmund Randolph, governor of Virginia, on this date in 1787. Nathaniel had entered six thousand acres on June 6, 1782, on Floyds Fork, labeled Entry A-246 in Jefferson County, adjacent the lands of Quirk and Stephens. The land was surveyed by November 17, 1784, the survey bearing number 7189. The land itself was formally granted January 10, 1787; see Kentucky Secretary of State Land Office and Jefferson County Records, vol. 2, Book A, pp. 86, 246. The Virginia treasury warrants were not for military service, and the idea that Nathaniel might have received acreage for Revolutionary War service is incorrect. Military warrants in Kentucky for Virginia army privates were usually about one hundred or two hundred acres.

54. William A. Crozier, *Spotsylvania County Records: 1721–1800*, vol. 1 (1955), p. 409. This is the first transaction for family land in Spotsylvania's Berkeley Parish. This parish was newly formed at the time of this transaction.

55. Ibid. Deed Book l, p. 404.

56. J. H. Spencer, *A History of Kentucky Baptists* (Lafayette, Tennessee: Church History Research and Archives, 1886).

57. A possibility exists that Nathaniel purchased this land before leaving Virginia, but if he did, we have no record of it.

58. This purchase by Nathaniel is not recorded in Taylor, P *Calendar of the Warrants*. Warrants for Land in Kentucky, Clearfield, Baltimore, but the early grants of Andrew Lewis are given, together with some subsequent dispositions of those lands.

59. 1788: *Rowland Madison v. John Saunders* re debt; Nathaniel agrees to pay the fine if John defaults. William Lewis was an assignee of Madison. See Virginia Superior Court District of Kentucky Order Book, June Court, p. 449. Also in 1789, *Thomas Lewis v. Wm. Hickman (Rev.) and Nathaniel* re debt. In this case, it should be noted that prior to this suit, Nathaniel had given Hickman one hundred acres of his own land. Virginia Supreme Court District of Kentucky Order Book, September Court, p. 116.

60. Harrison and Klotter, *New History of Kentucky*, pp. 53–55.

61. No record of Nathaniel's purchase of this Frankfort land has been located, but his ownership of this is clear from other records. Many Frankfort deeds were destroyed by fire at Fayette Court House in 1803. See W. R. Jillson, *Early Frankfort and Franklin County, Kentucky* (Louisville: Standard Printing, 1936), p. 59.

62. Nathaniel sold this property including a brick messuage and brick kitchen to Joseph Craig by 1797; see Kentucky Court of Appeals Deed Book D, p. 12.

63. It should be noted that by 1788, the town of Frankfort had but two houses. By 1795, the population had grown to around sixty-five people, but the houses there were said to be rude log structures or small framed buildings unlike the brick house described for plot 69. See Robert Haydon, *William Haydon: Kentucky Adventurer, 1740–1819* (Arkansas: Little Rock, 2002), p. 231.

64. *Kentucky Ancestors*, vol. 10, no. 2 (October 1974), p. 57.

65. Hening's Statutes at Large, The Laws of Virginia, vol. 12, Petition Numbers 40 and 52, pp. 580, 663.

66. R. E. Wells. Abstract of Woodford County Order Book A, 1789–1790. See also L. F. Johnson, *History of Franklin County, Kentucky* (Frankfort, Kentucky: Roberts Publications, 1912), p. 8.

67. E. J. Darnell, *Forks of Elkhorn Church* (Baltimore: Clearfield Company, 1993), p. 112.

68. William E. Railey, *History of Woodford County*, p. 223, and J. H. Spencer, *History of Kentucky Baptists*, vol. 1, p. 149.

69. The Forks of Elkhorn Church was established in June of 1788. See Spencer, *History of Kentucky Baptists*, vol. 1, p. 151.

70. A permanent site for Forks of Elkhorn Church was chosen four miles east of William Haydon's Station at the intersection of Lexington-Leestown Road and Steele's Ferry. See Robert Haydon, *William Haydon: Kentucky Adventurer, 1740–1819* (Arkansas: Little Rock, 2002), p. 194.

71. Spencer, *History of Kentucky Baptists*, pp. 149–151.

72. Haydon, *William Haydon*, p. 202.

73. Woodford County Order Book A, p. 121.

74. Woodford County Deed Book A, p. 154.

75. Woodford County Deed Book A, p. 197.

76. Woodford County Deed Book B, p. 21.

77. Franklin County Tax List of 1795.

78. Harrison and Klotter, *New History of Kentucky*, pp. 60–61.

79. Parker, *Sanders Family of Grass Hills*. Lewis Sanders married Anne Nicholas and one son of this marriage was George Nicholas Sanders. He was a particularly notorious actor on behalf of the Confederacy in the Civil War and one of only five Confederates for whom rewards for capture were offered. After the war, he made his way to Europe and allied himself with revolutionaries there.

80. Lewis Collins, *Historical Sketches of Kentucky* (Cincinnati: Collins and James, 1847), p. 555.

81. Taken from Alexander Hamilton's comments for Shane, State Historical Society of Wisconsin, Draper Files; see also Haydon, *William Haydon*.

82. Kentucky Historical Society, *The Register*, vol. 43 (1945), p. 178.

83. Jefferson County Deed Book 4, p. 5.

84. Lewis Collins, History of Kentucky, vol. 2 (Frankfort: Kentucky Historical Society, 1966), p. 245.

85. Littell's Laws 1809–1814. The Statute Laws of Kentucky, vol. 1, p. 185.

86. Woodford County Will Book A; See also Taylor, *Calendar of the Warrants*, p. 121.

87. Fayette County Burnt Records, vol. 7, p. 488.

88. Kentucky Historical Society, *Kentucky Marriage Records from The Register* (1983), p. 206.

89. Ibid., p. 216.

90. Harrison and Klotter, *New History of Kentucky*, pp. 72–75.

91. Kandie Adkinson, *Researching Early Kentucky Tax Lists: 1792–1840* (Land Office, Kentucky Secretary of State, Frankfort, n.d.).

92. Franklin County Tax List for 1795. Nathaniel appears in this list owning seventeen slaves, seventeen cattle, seven horses, and 4,132 acres.

93. Franklin County Deed Book A, p. 41.

94. Woodford County Deed Book B, pp. 380, 382, 383, 386.

95. Franklin County Deed Book A-2, p. 54.

96. *Kentucky Gazette*, vol. 11 (July 18, 1798).

97. Franklin County Deed Book B, p. 205.

98. Kentucky Historical Society, *The Register*, vol. 69 (1971), p. 317.

99. United States District for Kentucky Order Book B, 1798–1800.

100. L. F. Johnson, *History of Franklin County*.

101. United States District for Kentucky Order Book B, 1798–1800, pp. 132, 346. *United States v. Nathaniel* on debt, 1798. The plaintiff recovers $233.18 to be discharged by payment of $111.59 and costs. For the second legal action, see United States District for Kentucky Order Book B, pp. 219, 233. James Morrison for the use of the *United States v. Nathaniel* on debt, 1802. Clement Bell of Franklin County undertook bail for the defendant. The plaintiff recovers against the defendant and Owen Powell his appearance bail, $125.86 to be discharged by the payment of $62.53 with 6 percent interest from June 12, 1800, and costs.

102. These deeds were produced by Richardson in 1808. See Gallatin County Land Records, 1806–1825, Book A., pp. 1–12; 409–424. Also, Nathaniel Sanders, age sixty-nine, appears in the Gallatin County Census for 1810. See Kentucky 1810 Census by R. V. Jackson and G. R. Teeples, Accelerated Indexing Systems, Inc., 1978, Bountiful, Utah.

103. Parker, *Sanders Family of Grass Hills*.

104. The existence of a tanning yard suggests something more than would be required for occasional tanning for home use. Nathaniel probably maintained a tanning yard as a cottage industry for hides taken from wild game as well as domestic animals, and hides were probably brought to the yard by neighbors as well as from his own household.

105. C. R. Bogardus Sr., *The Story of Gallatin County* (n.d.). Bogardus's work was edited and reproduced posthumously by J. C. Claypool; a copy is held at Ft. Thomas, Kentucky Library.

106. Littell's Laws 1809–1814, vol. 3, p. 513. Also see Sandra Gorin, *Early Tobacco Warehouses and Millages*, part 2, http://www.rootsweb.com/~usgwqury/ KY/TIPS.

107. Ibid., p. 365.

108. Ibid., vol. 4, p. 106.

109. Transactions were (a) 450 acres for $500 on waters of Big Lick Fork of Eagle Creek from John Pelley and Daniel Epps (see Gallatin County Deed Book C, p. 127); (b) N. D. Beale conveyed to Nathaniel 2,500 acres for $2,500 on Eagle Creek (see Gallatin County Deed Book C, p. 543); and (c) in 1819 Nathaniel bought 339 acres for $949 on Eagle

Creek from Robert Jones of Virginia (see Kentucky Court of Appeals Deed Book T, p. 378).

110. In 1813, Nathaniel conveyed twenty-one acres to the heirs of John Logan, Polly Blume, Jane Ballinger, David Logan, Betsy Harris, Theodcin Tompkins, Sally Logan, and Letia Logan for 108 pounds, ten shillings in Franklin County on Elkhorn Creek near his South Fork mill; see Franklin County Deed Book D-1, p. 133. He also in 1815 sold forty acres of land for $400 to George Smith at Forks of Elkhorn. See Kentucky Court of Appeals Deed Book Q, p. 4.

111. Nathaniel and others posted a security bond in 1807 in the amount of $3,000 to Gov. Greenup for John Scott's faithful performance as Gallatin County's surveyor. See Gallatin County Deed Book A-1, p. 520.

112. The land itself was purchased of William French of Dinwiddie County, Virginia. He sold 4,400 acres in Gallatin County for $2,200 to Nathaniel and John Scott, the final conveyance of the deed taking place in 1811. See Gallatin County Land Records, 1806–1825, Book A, pp. 1–12; Gallatin County Deed Book B, p. 214; and Gallatin County Deed Book E, p.139. They jointly acquired the one thousand acres for only $200; see Gallatin County Deed Book E, p. 139. In 1814 they swapped parcels, Nathaniel receiving from Scott two lots of five hundred acres each in exchange for Scott's receiving 883 acres from Nathaniel. See Gallatin County Deed Book C, pp. 43, 70.

113. Together they sold 250 acres of land in 1816 for $250. See Gallatin County Deed Book C, p. 259. A year later they sold another one hundred acres of this land. See Gallatin County Deed Book C, p. 441. In 1823, Nathaniel received five tracts of land from Scott, though details of locations, lot sizes, and purchase prices are not known; see Gallatin County Deed Book E, p. 330. Other transactions detailed in the records are as follows: (a) in 1814, Nathaniel conveyed 870 acres on the Ohio River to Robert Montgomery for $1,870, this being part of French's original survey of 15,918 acres (see Gallatin County Deed Book C, p. 55); (b) in 1815, Nathaniel conveyed two hundred acres on the Ohio River to Joel Ellis (see Gallatin County Deed Book C, p. 170); (c) in 1823, Nathaniel conveyed a tract of land on Ohio River to Thomas O'Neal for $1 (see Gallatin County Deed Book E, p. 333); (d) In 1823, Nathaniel conveyed 104 acres to Lewis O'Neal on the waters of Stephens and McCool's creeks for $300 (see Gallatin County Deed Book E, p. 332); and (e) in 1824, Nathaniel conveyed sixty-nine acres on Stephens Creek to John Knox (see Gallatin County Deed Book F, p. 5).

114. Jefferson County Deed Book 4, p. 5.

115. M. and B. Cook, *Jefferson County, Kentucky Records*, vol. 2 (Evanston, Indiana: Cook Publishing Company, 1987).

116. But of course if Nathaniel had a hand in this fraud, he would have been most unlikely to have filed suit for recovery of lands, opening a legal door to discovery of his alleged machinations.

117. Records in this case are scattered widely and no single source provides a good summary of the proceedings. But see especially Old Chauncery Court Records, Case 753, 1815, Jefferson County, Kentucky. Also helpful are Kentucky Court of Appeals Deed Book R, p. 3; "Heirs in Court of Appeals Deeds," in *The Register of the Kentucky Historical Society*, vol. 42, no. 140 (1944), p. 257; R. C. Jobson, *History of Early Jeffersontown* (Baltimore: Gateway Press, 1977), pp. 24–25.

118. Harrison and Klotter, *New History of Kentucky*, p. 78. The authors cite *Kenton v. McConnell* in 1794 as a case in point.

119. Gallatin County Deed Book C, p. 7.

120. Recall that Thomas Sanders, brother of early Virginia migrant Nathaniel Sanders, married Jane Blanton shortly after 1695.

121. Gallatin County marriage certificate. Nathaniel's conveyance to Robert is given in Gallatin County Deed Book C, p. 150. Robert sold this land in 1824. See Gallatin County Deed Book B, p. 38.

122. Franklin County Marriage Bond Index, 1811–1831, and Merrifield, Dorothy: Gallatin County Marriages 1799–1820, from Owen County Abstracts and Deeds, 1980. His gifts of land are given in Gallatin County Deed Book E, p. 334, 340; and also Owen County Deed Book B, 1826, p. 297.

123. Franklin County Marriage Bond Index, 1811–1831, and Gallatin County Deed Book D, p. 225.

124. Parker, *Sanders Family of Grass Hills*. These grandsons were Lewis Sanders Jr., Bennett Sanders, Lemuel Sanders, and Nathaniel Sanders Jr. of Franklin County, all sons of Nathaniel's deceased daughter Sally. The transcription of this record gives the name Lemuel, but his name was Samuel. In contrast to his other gifts of land to family, Nathaniel sold these 339 acres of land on Eagle Creek to these grandsons at profit, selling for $1,356; just four years before, Nathaniel bought this land for $949. See Owen County Deed Book A, p. 301.

125. Gallatin County Will Book C, pp. 570, 574. In this year, Nathaniel's brother Charles died. See Will Book C, p. 157.

126. Owen County Deed Book B, p. 11. Kitty O'Neal actually was George Washington Sanders's niece, although they were nearly the same age. Kitty was the daughter of Catherine Sanders—Wash's much older sister—and Thomas O'Neal, who married in 1796. By 1825, both Wash and Kitty had reached adulthood. A few years later, a legal contest

arose over Nathaniel's will, Robert and his older brothers believing that its terms were unduly beneficial to Wash, and Wash in turn noting that Robert tore Nathaniel's signature from the document, attempting to invalidate it. The court upheld the document.

127. Gallatin County Deed Book F, pp. 182, 194, 212.

128. At least from a material point of view, it seems Daniel and Nicey in old age might have been better off unfree, retaining familiar surroundings, proximity to Little Daniel, and some continuing rudimentary personal support.

129. See G. Clift, Kentucky Obituaries 1787–1854, Register, April 1938–October 1940.

130. Gallatin County Will Book C, pp. 232, 242. Also in 1833, Nathaniel's estate conveyed one hundred acres on the Ohio River to Samuel Ross. See Gallatin County Deed Book H, p. 407.

131. Gallatin County Deed Book F, 256, 281. Sons John and Nathaniel Jr. relinquished their five hundred acres on Eagle Creek, including the new mill, to joint heirs. See Owen County Deed Book C, p. 46.

132. Gallatin County Court, May 14, 1827.

133. Ibid.

134. Gallatin County Will Book C, p. 582; This transaction was completed in 1844. See Deed Book L, p. 479.

135. Gallatin County Will Book C, p. 232.

136. The evident priority for coffee in Nathaniel's household is a legacy that endures.

137. Nathaniel had given slaves to all his children on their marriages. Those remaining at the time of Nathaniel's death and their monetary value were the following: Edom ($350), David ($400), Wyatt ($500), Daniel ($500), William ($500), Wilkinson ($500), Harrison ($400), Trulove, the only woman in this list ($400), and boys Thomas ($200) and Greenup ($200).

138. This pork, more than three tons of it, was valued at two dollars per hundred weight, or two cents per pound.

139. Application for Revolutionary War Veteran's Pension, United States Government GSA Form 6751, Rev. 8–71, Sanders, Nathaniel—W8703.

140. The widest airing of this story resulted from the 1912 publication of *Exit Laughing* by Irving Cobb, a writer from Paducah, Kentucky. The book provides the most extensive, if not the most analytic, approach to the subject, but Cobb makes clear his disbelief. Further discussion of Cobb's story is found in Lee Hoover's "More About Mexican General Santa Anna and Jimmy Dry Sanders," *Sanders Siftings*, no. 23 (October 2000): p. 4. A thorough description of the legend is found in the unpublished "The Sanders' Santa Anna Legend," dated June 15, 1994,

by Martha Sanders Reiner, now deceased. Reiner's account provides an up close treatment of the subject as recalled by family members who received stories from earlier generations. This story of Nathaniel Sanders's connection to Santa Anna is also mentioned in Forks of Elkhorn Church records. See Darnell, *Forks of Elkhorn Church*, p. 112. Edward Dotson verified Santa Anna's deed of land in Tennessee. See Dotson, Edward, "Yesteryear," *Hickman County (Tennessee) Times*, 1995. Dotson states that Santa Anna's land in that area is revealed in a trial record of the state of Tennessee, Hickman County Circuit Court, November Term 1847—*Winfield Scott v. Antonio Lopez de Santa Anna*. Santa Anna was represented in court by Murphree, the landowner of record, and advised that Santa Anna was making no claim on the subject property. Numerous Sanders have claimed that Santa Anna's name appeared on a deed for Kentucky land held by Nathaniel Sanders of Gallatin County, but this alleged deed cannot be found.

Two useful biographies of Santa Anna provide a resource for further research. See W. H. Callcott, *Santa Anna: Story of an Enigma Who Once Was Mexico* (Norman, Oklahoma: University of Oklahoma Press, 1936); and O. L. Jones Jr., *Santa Anna* (New York: Twayne Publishers, 1968).

141. Variations on this story are too numerous to recount. No two seem to agree perfectly, but all versions hold that Nathaniel Sanders (a.k.a. Bull Sanders) was the person in the tavern that night in Frankfort, representing himself as Santa Anna at the same time that Santa Anna was in the area.

142. Jillson, a Franklin County historian, describes the tavern as follows: "William Stephens kept a brick tavern on the left of the Lexington Road, about one-half mile from the Forks (of Elkhorn), at Green Hill. The celebrated Mexican, General Santa Anna, a prisoner of war, was held in confinement there for a time on his way to Washington in 1837." W. R. Jillson, *Early Frankfort and Franklin County, Kentucky* (Louisville, Kentucky: Standard Publishing Company, 1936), p. 101.

CHAPTER THIRTEEN

Eagle Creek

Nathaniel Sanders was of advanced years when he settled on Eagle Creek in Gallatin County about 1804. There he created a home that in time would hold three more generations of his family. What Nathaniel began at Eagle Creek, in fact, was the longest span of family dwelling in any one place since Ralph Saundre left his home at Sanderstead in the year 1234—nearly six hundred years before—to take up residence at Charlwood. Nathaniel's substantial legacy at Eagle Creek comprised land, measured in thousands of acres, and slaves in sufficient number to build his wealth and to serve all his children in later years. Land, slaves, and Nathaniel's own good reputation provided the foundation upon which the next generation of Sanders stood.

Robert Sanders

History progresses in fits and starts, or so it seems for Kentucky in the time of Robert Sanders, Nathaniel's son. The Kentucky that Nathaniel Sanders knew emerged after a great revolution and was launched in an era of aggressive exploration, conquest, and early Western settlement. At the turn of the nineteenth century and for fifty years hence—after statehood arrived and largely after Nathaniel's heyday—Kentucky seems to have settled into a slower pace, almost resting, as if digesting what had been wrought in earlier days. Kentucky pushed its way forward cautiously but steadily in those years. In this respect, the gradual flow of Robert's life and times paralleled those of his grandfather Hugh Sanders back in Spotsylvania County before the Revolution [1]. The time for rapid turbulent change in Kentucky would come soon enough, but not right away, not in the time of Robert Sanders.

In the half century of Robert's lifetime, the population of Kentucky advanced steadily from almost a half million in 1800 to nearly a million at midcentury. Settlers made their way westward from Maryland, Virginia, and North Carolina, overland through the Cumberland Gap, and down the Ohio

River from Pittsburgh, migrating from places as distant as Pennsylvania, New York, and New Jersey. People arrived at a modest rate of about ten thousand persons each year. Kentucky's early settlements inexorably grew into towns. Towns became cities; the land infilled with new settlement and farmsteads. Roads and bridges began to crisscross the state, and rudimentary public transportation—ferries and stagecoaches—expanded service. New counties formed routinely, courthouses sprang up, schools were built, and with them churches, banks, and commerce grew as well. Kentucky acquired in this period a more cultivated look, the old rough-hewn frontier giving way to the needs of its larger and more diverse nineteenth-century population.

But just as Kentucky had become a destination for westward-moving Easterners, so too it had become a source of migrants who were moving to new places yet farther west, places like Indiana and Illinois [2]. Not all earlier Kentuckians had prospered on arrival there, and for those whose new life in Kentucky failed to match their hopes or expectations, destinations to the west, particularly downriver as far as Missouri, represented renewed hope and fresh opportunity for them and their children.

In 1803, when Robert was just nine years old, President Thomas Jefferson negotiated the purchase of the Louisiana territory, acquiring much of the continent's interior, stretching from the Gulf of Mexico to the Canadian frontier, from the Mississippi River to the Rocky Mountains. In time, this purchase would free vast Western land resources for the nation's expanding population. A more immediate impact, however, was to create unfettered access to the Mississippi River, solving the vexing problem of moving goods from west to east. The Louisiana Purchase created an accessible sailing lane from Kentucky to major markets on the eastern seaboard via New Orleans. The result created new agricultural potential west of the Appalachians, an economic opportunity to match the growing exertions of its frontier people. Kentucky by midcentury had become a nexus of migration and trade. This is the Kentucky that Robert Sanders knew.

Robert, fifth son of Nathaniel and Sally Sanders, was part of the first generation of this family born in Kentucky. He was born at Forks of Elkhorn, and he was old enough—about ten years old—to remember his family with all their possessions leaving their home at Elkhorn, floating downstream on the Kentucky River and into Eagle Creek, making their way upstream a final eight miles to their new homestead in Gallatin County around 1804.

For Robert, these early years along Eagle Creek must have seemed isolated and remote. There were few settlements around, in contrast to the busier home he would have remembered at Elkhorn, and companionship for Robert was less than one might imagine for a large family, owing to the large age differences that separated them all. Three of his older siblings were already married, and his nearest older brother, John, was five years older than Robert. Likewise, his sole younger brother George Washington Sanders, called Wash, was younger by four years. Much of the time, Robert would have to find his own entertainment. At home, Nicey was perhaps as much a mother as a slave to him, and the free black boy Reuben, who lived in their home, was undoubtedly a young friend at times. Robert's amusement as a youngster would have been toying at the gristmill and fish dam when daily chores and home education [3] did not interfere.

In 1809, when Robert was fifteen, his father built the large two-story stone house on Eagle Creek that must have seemed a castle in his eyes. The pace of home life picked up after that as regular visitors frequented the homestead for official inspections of their farm produce, for debating road courses, bringing hides to the "tan yard," stopping by for postal business, and casting votes in an election. Those frequent adult business and civic conversations around the homestead, coupled with his relative isolation, probably helped catapult Robert into his own adulthood at an early age [4].

Marriage

The family of William Blanton lived at Forks of Elkhorn at the same time Nathaniel Sanders did, and they moved north to Owen County, which lay just south of Gallatin County, about the same time that Nathaniel brought his family to Eagle Creek. The Blantons took up residence at New Liberty, a village just a few miles south of the Sanders homestead. In 1815, a new link between these families was forged. Robert married Nancy, daughter of William Blanton [5], and he maintained particularly close relations with the Blantons in later years. Scarcely had this marriage been made when Robert accepted custody of his young cousin Samuel, an orphan of the Sanders of Ghent [6]. At age twenty-one, Robert suddenly was married and supporting a small family of his own.

As early as 1820 and probably before, Robert had gained possession of 256 acres of land in Owen County [7], probably lying close to Blanton land on the south side of Eagle Creek. No record of how or when Robert acquired this first property seems to exist, but probably this Owen County land was given the young couple as Nancy's dowry by William Blanton. Within four years, this holding grew to more than six hundred acres [8].

Robert had other land as well. In anticipation of Robert's marriage, Nathaniel gave his son more than five hundred acres of land in Gallatin County near Ghent, land that Robert sold ten years later [9]. One doubts that Robert and Nancy ever lived on this property, which lay inconveniently far from their Eagle Creek homeland. In 1816, Nathaniel also named Robert and his other sons as heirs to his extensive land holding at Floyd's Fork, but no record of conveyance of this property to heirs after Nathaniel's death in 1826 has ever surfaced [10]. But by some undetermined means, Robert had acquired a substantial holding approaching fifteen hundred acres along Eagle Creek in

Gallatin County by 1820, and this seems to have been the home of Nancy and Robert their entire married life [11].

For Robert and Nancy, children came along with some regularity after marriage. Probably first was a daughter named, interestingly enough, Elizabeth Craig Sanders [12]. She apparently was named for Elizabeth Sanders Craig, Robert's aunt—Nathaniel's sister—who had married Rev. Lewis Craig and with him entered Kentucky with the Traveling Church in 1782. The Craigs lived at Forks of Elkhorn until 1792, when, two years before Robert was born, they moved to Bracken County some distance up the Ohio River east of Gallatin County. How Elizabeth Craig might have impressed Robert is not clear, but choosing her name for his daughter suggests a continuing relationship between the families of Elizabeth Craig and Nathaniel Sanders that is not apparent from the records of the day. In later years, Nancy and Robert's daughter who married Frank Sandford would be known to family members as Auntie Craig.

THE FAMILIES OF ROBERT AND ELIJAH SANDERS OF EAGLE CREEK

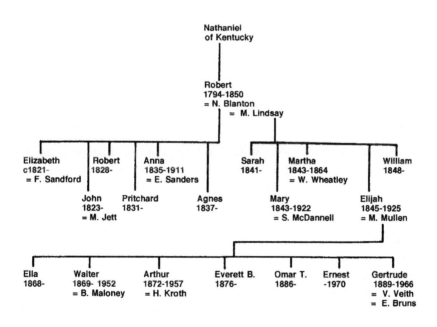

Source: Authors

Through the 1820s and 1830s, Nancy and Robert had several other children, though all their names and birth dates are not known. After Elizabeth Craig came three sons John, Robert L., and Pritchard. In the 1830s, daughters Ann and Agnes were born, and perhaps another daughter named Nancy as well. Although there are hints of other children, records of their names seem not to have survived [13]. As Nancy Blanton's childbearing years spanned a twenty-two-year period, from 1816 to Agnes's birth in 1838, during which time we can identify only three sons and three daughters, the supposition that she bore more children than we can name seems well grounded.

Fathers' Estates

Robert's father wrote his last will and testament in 1824, added a codicil in 1825, and died in 1826. Nathaniel provided no executor for the will, merely empowering his youngest son George Washington Sanders to see to his affairs in his final years. It fell on Robert's shoulders to administer the estate and to arrange for his mother's well-being, though why this responsibility fell to Robert rather than Wash, or to an older brother, is not clear. For the task of administration, Robert hired the use of a slave at a cost of $150 per year [14]. Robert sold most of his Owen County land at this point, evidently maintaining residence in Gallatin County either with his mother Sally, then age sixty-seven, or nearby [15]. The next year, Robert conducted an official inventory of his father's substantial personal property and conducted two sales of these possessions for his mother's benefit.

Nathaniel's will eventually went into probate six years after his death in 1832, and this probate was contested in a lawsuit launched by Robert and his older brothers against Wash regarding the legality of the will. Behind the suit evidently were the plaintiffs' beliefs that Wash benefitted excessively from their father's will, which was vague about Wash's intended land entitlement. In a clumsy attempt to negate Wash's perhaps exaggerated claims, Robert tore off Nathaniel's signature from the document and claimed in court that the will, lacking a signature, was invalid. He then substituted a different will without signature. Robert asserted that his father was aware of these actions and approved them. Wash counterclaimed that his aged father was insensible at the time and could not have approved. In the words of the deciding judge, "There is not only no proof that he authorized or sanctioned the act of his son Robert, but there is good reason for inferring from his quiescent, torpid, and almost senseless condition at the time, and from other facts that have been proved, that he did not even know that his signature was to be or had been torn off." The judge concluded, "If the (original) document was then his will, it is yet his will," and the case was closed in favor of Wash [16].

Following this judgment, Sally renounced her legacy from Nathaniel, freeing Wash to claim lands left to his mother until her death, including four hundred acres near the Ohio River and the stone house and mill on Eagle Creek. Presumably, Sally's requirements for renouncing her entitlement were met in subsequent arrangements. Wash and Robert also exchanged several tracts of their inherited lands following the court judgment, trading land on Eagle Creek at no cost to either of them [17].

At the time Robert was contending with his father's estate, he and Nancy dealt with her father's death as well. In 1832, they received a bequest from William Blanton's estate, a 119-acre plot in Owen County. This land they sold immediately to Paschell Green, husband of another daughter of William Blanton [18]. At the same time, Robert received title to a 153-acre plot across Eagle Creek in Gallatin County from Carter Blanton, another heir to William Blanton's estate [19]. The following year, Robert and Nancy conveyed land in Owen County to Edward Blanton [20]. Finally in 1837, several heirs of William Blanton, including Nancy and Robert, sold the dower land of Elizabeth Blanton, William's widow, amounting to more than five hundred acres, completing the disposition of the Blanton estate [21].

Livelihood

The inexorable surge of population westward after the American Revolution was driven by opportunity, mainly a chance to own land in greater amounts than was possible in the east. Land west of the Appalachians was superabundant, vastly greater in fact than the pioneering population could consume. Slowly, imperceptibly, this great abundance caused a change—a radical change—in the purpose of land ownership itself. In Virginia and early Kentucky, land generally was regarded as a resource, a physical exploitable base that made agriculture and livelihood possible. The resource served not only immediate needs, but also was transferable as a form of family security, an inheritable resource for ensuing generations. But reasons for buying land were shifting in Kentucky. Gradually, land in Kentucky came to be seen routinely as a simple commodity, an object like any other that could be bought and sold. In this idea, trade was the only intent in land acquisition; no thought was put to the land's immediate use. Reckoning its exchange value became the central idea in purchasing land; assessing its exchange value for profit depended on correctly anticipating future demand for the land [22].

Nathaniel Sanders's later years in Gallatin County of intermittently buying and selling land marked a beginning for family engagement in this type of land ownership. The lesson was not lost on Robert. In 1830, Robert teamed with John Scott, his father's former business partner, to sell one hundred acres of land on Eagle Creek for $150 [23]. This would be their first joint transaction, a launching point for a profitable business association built on land speculation. In the next five years, they jointly completed seven land sales involving more than one thousand acres, netting them about $1,000. Scott also separately conveyed several tracts to Robert at this time [24]. Although their pace of collaboration slowed down somewhat after that, another five joint transactions with Scott were completed over the ensuing decade [25].

Perhaps the most venturesome transaction was Robert's 1835 collaboration with both John Scott and Lewis Sanders of Grass Hills. Together they purchased land for $1,200 on the banks of the Ohio River "fronting the town of Ghent on which the ferry across the Ohio from Vevey, Indiana is established." The purchase included "two certain lots and the ferry boats, skiff, and crafts and ferry rights, appendages, and appurtenances" [26]. Purchasing a ferry business to shuttle persons and goods across the Ohio seems a rather unusual involvement for Robert, providing a transportation service alongside his agricultural pursuits. But this was not his only public activity. In 1835, Robert was named postmaster of Big Lick, a postal station site located in or near his house and close to Eagle Creek. The postal position itself had been held previously by Robert's brother Wash. Robert held the position for more than a year before this post office was closed [27]. The name Big Lick applied to his post office is perhaps the first place-name given to the family location on Eagle Creek since it had originally been dubbed Sanders Inspection or Saunders Landing more than thirty years before. Yet another public position fell upon Robert after his postal work ended. In the late 1830s, Gallatin County first organized its county court and the court convened initially in 1838. During that session, Robert was named an associate justice, along with Benjamin Tiller, Richard Lindsay, and William Scruggs [28]. No records have surfaced depicting Robert's exercise of this responsibility; perhaps he was never called upon to do so.

Robert's land dealings were by no means confined to collaboration with John Scott. He also dealt with relatives, particularly those from the family of his uncle John Sanders of Ghent. John's son Lewis Sanders built a homestead in Gallatin County called Grass Hills, a new plantation set high above the Ohio River lands of his father. From Grass Hills, Lewis launched several enterprises including the importation of purebred shorthorn cattle, the creation of a county fair, building a manufacturing complex in Lexington, and promoting Mississippi trade from a base in Natchez, Mississippi [29]. His son, George Nicholas Sanders, was equally enterprising, though for George interest fell mainly on politics and later on the Southern cause in the Civil War. All these Grass Hills efforts required money, however, and both Lewis and George looked to Robert and his brothers for support. In 1829, Lewis Sanders, then of Franklin County, mortgaged several plots of land on Eagle Creek to Robert and his brothers for $1,000, the agreement to be voided when the debt was repaid [30]. A decade later, Lewis, then of Natchez, Mississippi, repeated the arrangement with Robert's brother Nathaniel for $750 [31]. A year later, George Nicholas Sanders, son of Lewis, mortgaged his seventeen thousand acres on McCools and Eagle Creeks to Robert and a Richard Hawes for $4,000, this agreement also to be voided when the amount was repaid [32]. In 1845, Robert acquired 158 acres from Lewis Sanders in a direct purchase and then evidently took out a mortgage on the property with the Northern Bank of Kentucky [33]. In 1848, Lewis Sanders conveyed interest on various tracts and lots in Carroll and Owen counties along Eagle Creek to Robert for an immense sum of $10,500, by far the largest transaction of Robert's life [34]. An outlay of this size suggests either that Robert chose to risk his own financial stability on behalf of his cousin or that his own wealth had grown considerably during the 1840s.

THE SANDERS FAMILY OF GRASS HILLS

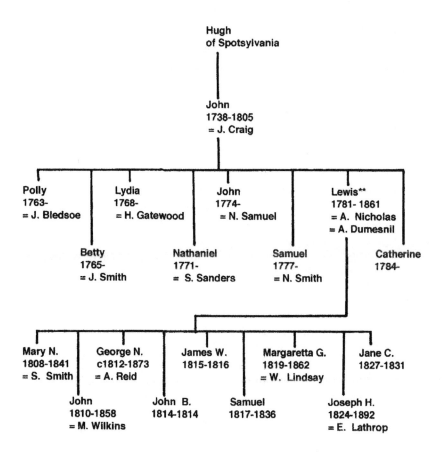

** builder of Grass Hills in Carroll County, Kentucky.

Source: A. V. Parker 1966.

Quite apart from land transactions involving inherited or estate lands, joint transactions with John Scott, or his dealings with the Sanders of Grass Hills, Robert completed numerous other purchases and sales. Overall, in the two decades of the 1830s and 1840s, he was involved with no less than fifty separate land transactions, making this enterprise probably the most important aspect of his livelihood [35]. In this period, the number of his purchases roughly equaled the number of sales, and his evident success in land speculation underwrote his lifelong modest prosperity.

A survey of Robert's land in 1850, taken after most of Robert's land dealings had concluded, showed that Robert owned 870 contiguous acres along Eagle Creek and an additional 68 acres elsewhere, totaling 938 acres. Roughly three hundred of these acres were improved, the remainder being unimproved woodland. Two unimproved plots of 127 and 129 acres were identified as dower lands for his wife. But in addition, the survey reveals that Robert had built a south-facing "mansion house," which overlooked Eagle Creek, and within view just a few hundred yards away was the large stone house of Robert's youth [36].

If land dealing was the principal source of Robert's income, farming lay not far behind as another. He maintained horses, cattle, sheep, and pigs and cultivated crops of wheat, corn, and tobacco. Some of his cattle were purebred shorthorns imported from England by his cousin Lewis Sanders, which Robert received as breeding stock in 1837 [37]. Robert also operated a sawmill, producing weatherboarding for houses and barns, scantling (studs and rafters), sheeting, and flooring, at one point holding an inventory of more than ten thousand linear feet of lumber [38]. For all these economic pursuits, and for domestic needs as well, Robert relied heavily on the work of slaves.

Slaves

There were in Robert's time in Kentucky no impediments to slave ownership so long as one had sufficient resources to buy and to maintain them. Robert managed this well enough. By and large, Kentucky had few large slave plantations; the average number of slaves in slave-owning homes in the Commonwealth was five, about the number Robert usually maintained [39]. But slave owning was becoming controversial and troublesome in Kentucky and around the nation by the 1830s, and these controversies emerged in the same decade that Robert purchased most of his slaves. The arguments of abolitionists regularly rang in his ears.

By the 1830s, the antislavery movement in the United States was well underway. Nat Turner's slave rebellion in Virginia took place in 1831, and though that rebellion was ruthlessly crushed and failed to produce other uprisings, the so-called underground railway also sprang up at that time to assist slaves in escaping to northern states and Canada.

The growing antislavery movement had deep roots. In England, slavery had been abolished by the Wilberforce Act of 1807 and all slaves in British dominions, notably in the Caribbean and Canada, were freed twenty-six years later in 1835 [40]. By 1822, a new American Colonization Society (ACS) organized a migration of free blacks to Liberia on the West African coast, a plan expected by some to constitute an answer to the vexing problem of how free blacks were to live in white American society. During its active period, only about thirteen thousand free blacks returned to Africa. Henry Clay of Kentucky served as ACS president between 1836 and 1849. The ACS administered the colony until 1847 when Liberia declared its independence, and the settlement scheme ended shortly after that [41].

In Kentucky, the legislature passed the Kentucky Non-Importation Act of 1833, forbidding the importation of slaves into the state, though leaving the practice untouched for those already present. As black slaves constituted nearly one-fourth of the state's population, there was no danger of slave shortage, and newborn slaves would eventually fill any unmet demand. The act was allowed to lapse in 1850.

Arguments about slavery grew steadily in Kentucky, and societies were formed to promote each view. Arguments against slavery in the 1830s and later were generally of two kinds—abolitionist and emancipationist. Abolitionists called for the immediate uncompensated freeing of slaves to rid the society of an intolerable moral evil. Emancipationists, on the other hand, sought a more gradual process to allow time for needed social and economic adjustments to take place, aiming to establish a coherent workable social order for whites and free blacks alike. Oddly, though all these societies generally agreed on the goal of freeing slaves, disagreements over strategies and competition between them limited their overall effectiveness in bringing others to their cause [42].

No doubt Robert opposed both kinds of antislavery arguments as the institution of slavery itself constituted for him a kind of national and family heritage, and slaves were absolutely essential to his agricultural livelihood. Throughout the decades of the 1830s and 1840s, Robert bought and sold slaves with some regularity. Robert's first known slave purchase occurred in 1827, when he acquired a woman or girl named Sarah and three boys named Charles, Gabriel, and Frank [43]. Between 1832 and 1834, in numerous transactions, he acquired Malinda, a young woman with an infant child named Elijah; a twelve-year-old mulatto girl named Polly; a child Hariett, age five; and two boys aged twelve or thirteen, Sanford and Charles, the latter perhaps the same person bought in 1827 [44]. On one unidentified occasion in 1832, Robert joined with his brother James to buy slaves; and in 1834, Robert obtained from his brother Wash two adult slaves, Harris, age twenty-six, and Betsy, age twenty-eight [45]. Some years later, in 1842, Robert sold his slave Charles, by then age twenty-one, and a girl named America, age fourteen, to his longtime business partner John Scott for $1,000 [46]. In 1848, Robert mortgaged an unnamed number of slaves and land for $603 [47]. One gets a sense that Robert exercised a certain strategy in slave trading, purchasing underage slaves at relatively low cost and obtaining higher prices for them as adults as time passed. How that strategy might have meshed with the need for strong and experienced field and mill hands, however, is an unanswered question. In all likelihood, Robert held older slaves whose names have escaped the records.

Remarriage

After twenty-two years of marriage, Nancy Blanton Sanders died in 1837 when she was about forty and Robert forty-three. She died the same year that her last child Agnes was born, suggesting that complications from childbirth could have been the cause. Shortly after Nancy's death, Robert appointed James O'Hara guardian for his children in the event of his own demise [48]. O'Hara was Robert's brother-in-law; he also married a Blanton.

In 1839, Robert remarried. His new wife was Mary (Polly) Lindsay Thompson, at this time age thirty, widow of Matthew Thompson whom she had married in Dearborn County, Indiana, in 1831 [49]. With Matthew Thompson, Polly had two children: Nicholas, born about 1832, and Margaret, about three years younger than Nicholas. Polly's two children thereafter were raised in Robert and Polly's household.

The Lindsay family of Polly Lindsay was long known to the Sanders, from as early as the days of Nathaniel Sanders in Caroline County, Virginia. Anthony Lindsay, five years older than Nathaniel, migrated to Kentucky in 1784, settling near Haydon's Station, and his family belonged to the Forks of Elkhorn Church [50]. The Lindsays eventually moved to Indiana. A family cemetery lies in the town of Aurora in the southern part of the state. Indiana's "barefoot poet" Vachel Lindsay descends from this branch of the Lindsay family [51].

Robert and Polly began their second family with the birth of twins about 1840, but neither survived. A year or two later, a daughter Sarah Ella was born. Yet another set of twins, Mary and Martha Ann, were born in 1843, and they survived into adulthood. A son Elijah Lawson arrived in 1845, and finally a son William was born in 1848, but he died in infancy, their third infant lost [52]. Shortly after Elijah was born, Robert again appointed James O'Hara as guardian for his children in the event of his demise. They now numbered eleven, though the eldest among them had reached adulthood in the 1840s [53].

Death

In the summer of 1850, Robert traveled by road from Eagle Creek to the mouth of the Licking River across the Ohio River from Cincinnati, the same road constructed some forty years before under the supervision of his father Nathaniel. His purpose was to complete a buying trip at Cincinnati, but he never completed the journey. Robert fell ill of cholera and died in Cincinnati in July of 1850. Robert was then fifty-six years of age. Robert's son John arranged for Robert's burial in Gallatin County [54].

An inventory of Robert's estate conducted in November by Frank Sandford, husband of Robert's eldest daughter, listed Robert's assets at about $10,000 [55]. As usual for that time, livestock and slaves accounted for most of the value. The estate held three slaves in 1850, all girls, by name America (valued at $450), Nice ($450), and Mary ($350). An estate sale the next month netted nearly $3,500, including $365 for America, $600 for Nice, and $430 for Mary, each sold to a Sanders family member. Other than slaves, the main items for sale were fifty-five sheep and fifty-three hogs [56]. Robert also had invested in the Eagle Creek Turnpike Road Company, buying twenty shares at $50 each, though he had made only one payment on these shares by the time of his death [57].

Separate from his personal estate, Robert's lands in Gallatin County were valued for tax purposes at $13,690 in 1850, and he held land in Owen County as well. [58]. Some of this land in and near Ghent was disposed of in an 1850 sale at the house of Samuel Sanders, Robert's one-time ward [59]. Much of his remaining property was passed to Robert's children. Polly, then age forty-two, received her dower land in the estate settlement of 1850. This amounted to two woodland parcels of more than one hundred acres each and most importantly, the mansion house situated on eighty acres of improved land lying directly on Eagle Creek [60]. That house would remain in family hands for another generation.

Robert's heirs must have received land jointly because over the next two decades following their father's death, his children steadily sold off land that lay in common to them. Between 1859 and 1863, they sold nearly six hundred acres of land in five transactions, gaining about $2,500 in the sales [61]. In 1868, some family circumstance inspired a series of land trades within the family; a total of seven transactions reshuffled family holdings. These may have been triggered by their mother's advancing age or a recognition that joint possessions could not finance separate plans [62]. Three more of these sales by joint heirs took place the following year [63]. By that time, the supply of jointly held ownerships was nearly exhausted.

Elijah Lawson Sanders

The years following the death of Robert were the most traumatic that the nation was ever to experience. States of the South seceded from the national union in 1860, creating a new Confederate States of America. The North-South rift so severely challenged the nation that a civil war to restore unity was inevitable. In the minds of many in the North, what was at stake was more than simple national unity. The need for war was driven by a sense of protecting the constitution and the universal dream it embodied, a dream, in the words of President Lincoln, "That this nation, conceived in liberty and dedicated to the proposition that all men are created equal, shall not perish from the earth." At the outset of war, Lincoln's stated goal was to restore the union, whether or not the slavery question could be resolved. But toward the end of that great conflict, his national emancipation of slaves in 1864 settled that issue permanently.

From a Southern perspective, the war was equally necessary. At stake was Southern culture itself, a style of living different from Northern ways in crucial respects. In the North, social and political norms bore a certain horizontal ideal in which citizen equality was paramount. All parties ideally possessed an equal voice in public affairs, and their governments were subject to careful scrutiny and grudging trust. They bought into the notion of a social contract that government exists by citizen consent alone. For them, the United States Constitution of 1789 embodied that contract. Beyond governance, the notion of equality carried over into society as well in which social deference was disliked and limited. Aside from ideals, the North by 1860 was rapidly capitalizing, industrializing, and urbanizing. This was a program of wealth building, and it succeeded brilliantly, though not necessarily happily for every citizen. Long work hours and low wages brutalized the least fortunate. Northern influence in national governance expanded in proportion to its greater wealth, an insult and injury to Southern gentility and aspirations.

In the end, differences in Southern culture provided contrasting, even antithetical, emphases for society and government. Principally, Southerners held fast to a kind of end-stage feudalism, a style of living held over from Sir William Berkeley's seventeenth-century Virginia. Central to this culture were hierarchical arrangements of society and political life. In the South, deference to local authority, those legitimized to rule by family origin and tradition, was particularly strong [64]. Kinship ties remained vibrant and tightly linked to social and political entitlements. Southerners as a rule also remained closer to the land in their agricultural economy. Southern plantation agriculture, the dominant form of production on both large and small scales, was especially amenable to slavery since slave populations were more easily ruled in sparsely settled landscapes. The ideal Southern plantation itself was imagined as a self-sufficient entity, an imposing feudal manor surrounded by the cruder structures of latter-day serfdom. From just this kind of arrangement, Thomas Jefferson articulated the idea that society's virtue derives from its closeness to the land, a ringing endorsement of Southern agrarian morality set against the suspect pattern of the North. The final testimony of regional enmity was the South's abiding loyalty to region and state, a loyalty that in the end superseded allegiance to the still-young national constitution.

Kentucky remained officially neutral on the question of succession, its people deeply divided. Volunteering for military service on one side or the other was commonplace. The four-year war itself was horrific, bloody beyond comparison with any past example and on both sides, the wounds of war spared no families. An entire generation of Americans bore the scars of conflict. But the greater pain lay in the South, where massive personal and property losses, postwar military and political domination by the North, and the scourge of cultural disruption devastated Southern society. The line of Sanders who we follow here felt this pain directly.

Elijah Lawson Sanders was Robert and Polly's youngest surviving son, born in 1845. He was a child when his father died. Heirs of Robert, all their sons and daughters, arranged a settlement for Robert's land in 1852 and Elijah, then only seven, received entitlement to two land parcels on Elk Creek in Owen County. These were sold immediately, presumably on Elijah's behalf [65].

After Robert died, Polly Lindsay Sanders was left largely on her own to create a living from her husband's personal estate and her dower land. At the time of Robert's death, his surviving children born by Nancy Blanton had reached adulthood, or nearly so. The children of Polly Lindsay, on the other hand, were still young. By 1850, the children by her first marriage, Nicholas Thompson was age eighteen and his sister Margaret fifteen. Her twin daughters with Robert had reached the age of seven, and Elijah was only five. Polly seems not to have inherited any slaves as all of those owned by Robert were sold to other family members in 1850.

It fell to Polly to see to the raising of the five younger children on her own devices. This she did by building a small hotel adjacent to her home, calling the establishment the Eagle Creek Hotel [66]. The structure was sufficient to house perhaps twenty guests at a time, and Polly operated the establishment personally. This constituted the main source of Polly's income for the next twenty years. Years later, the house would pass to Elijah's possession, and the hotel was given to his sister Mary [67].

The Blue Lick Springs Hotel of Sanders, Kentucky. Built in the mid- to late nineteenth century by Robert or Polly Lindsay Sanders, the hotel prospered in that century's final years. Not visible here is a two-story extension projecting rearward from the left side of the structure. The hotel was damaged by floodwaters in 1997and razed soon thereafter.

Much of Elijah's upbringing would have been spent at the hotel and the house next door. Notably, in all those years after his father died, Elijah received virtually no male guidance or companionship from his family. His stepbrothers were much older and gone from home. The other siblings were all girls. As a consequence, with Robert's demise, generations of family knowledge about land and the skills to earn a living from it died as well. These parts of the family's traditions Elijah did not inherit. What he did inherit was a whirlwind of war, death, devastation, and despair.

Civil War

Elijah was age fifteen when the Civil War commenced in 1860. He saw none of the four-year conflict directly. But he lived fully the war's aftermath, which hit home forcefully. Neighbors and friends disappeared in war or returned home shocked and maimed. His own family fared particularly badly. Robert, his brother, serving in the Confederacy's Kentucky's Fourth Volunteer Cavalry, saw action in Tennessee, but was ambushed and murdered traveling home from the conflict. His older brother John committed suicide. One of his twin sisters, Martha, died shortly after marriage at age twenty-one, and his unmarried sister Sarah Ella died of cholera about this time [68].

If all these losses were not dispiriting enough, all the slaves were gone too. In short order, the family lands of Robert became instantly valueless, or nearly so. Deprived of the means of production—the work of slaves—the agricultural potential of land largely evaporated. Small slave-owning crop farmers in the South quickly became subsistence farmers, scratching out meager livings on small plots cultivated by their own unaided toil. The traditional economic base of Elijah's family vanished overnight in Elijah's youth.

Loss of family and economy were punishing agonies, but they were not the only ones. The demise of the Confederacy at war's end signaled the beginning of Northern domination of the South, less a military occupation than an economic, political, and cultural program of transformation. Predatory bank schemes deprived Southerners of land and homes, and Northern industrial cartels appropriated much of Southern agricultural production. These were supported or at least condoned by a post-Lincoln administration in Washington. But the greatest hurt was that Northern ideas ruled. The message was clear. Rebelling against the Union was wrong, slavery was evil, the ideals of Southern society were erroneous, traditional Southern leadership was traitorous, and those who followed them were guilty as well.

One senses that Elijah perhaps never recovered from all these blows, fully disenfranchised from his own beginnings, choosing finally to go forward in the only small steps that seemed available to him.

Marriage

Elijah Sanders married Mary Mullen (called Molly) in 1867. She was the daughter of Elizabeth and Rev. John Mullen of Vevay, Switzerland County, Indiana, a small town across the Ohio River from Ghent [69]. It seems Robert's Ohio River ferry service from Ghent to Indiana paid an unexpected dividend, finding a wife for his son. She was their fifth of seven children [70]. The Mullens had migrated from New Jersey to Indiana, where John Mullen served both as a Methodist minister and school teacher [71]. Molly herself became a school teacher after marriage.

Over the next two decades, Molly and Elijah had seven children. The eldest was Ella, born in 1868. Following Ella were five boys, Walter, Arthur Lee, Ernest O., Everett Brown, and Omar Thomas. Their youngest was a daughter Gertrude Lee, born in 1889 [72]. Everett Brown was born with some mental deficiency and depended on Elijah and Molly into his adulthood.

We learn that in 1873 Elijah's mother, Polly Lindsay Sanders, died at age sixty-four. Her youngest son Elijah by then had reached his twenty-eighth year. Polly left her hotel and seventy-eight acres on Lick Creek, near Eagle Creek, to her daughter Mary McDannell, with whom she had lived in her final years [73]. The McDannell's then sold for $400 their portion of Polly's dower land to Elijah, including the brick house—Robert's "mansion house"—and other improvements. Included was about four acres of land abutting the Eagle Creek Hotel on its eastern side and another acre west of the hotel [74]. How long Elijah and Molly remained in the brick house is uncertain, but Molly maintained a house near the school in Sanders, and the brick house itself is thought to have burned [75].

Sanders, Kentucky

Before the time of Elijah, the settlement at Eagle Creek grew slowly, being known in early times as Saunders Landing, Sanders Inspection, and Big Lick. In time, the settlement came to be called Rislerville after a general store owner named John Risler. This name held until the coming of the railroad in the late 1860s, when Rislerville was dropped in favor of Liberty, then Liberty Station [76]. Land for the rail depot was leased by the company from Elijah [77]. Near the station lay a series of tobacco warehouses and stock pens, and with the employment that these and related railway services provided, the town of Sanders quickly reached a population of about three hundred.

In 1872, the town was shifted administratively from Gallatin to Carroll County as a condition set out by the latter to finance a bridge over Eagle Creek [78]. By 1884, the settlement acquired its current name of Sanders, Kentucky, named in honor of George Washington (Wash) Sanders. He was, we may recall, the youngest son of Nathaniel and brother of Robert, Elijah's father. Wash was said to "have been known over a large section of the Commonwealth. He is also said to have been famous for his huge burgoo and barbeque parties which he often gave before important elections. On one occasion, John C. Breckinridge, a United States senator and later vice president, was the guest of honor and after the dinner was over, gave a stirring address under an elm tree in the town. Many years later James Tandy Ellis wrote a delightful poem, which he named 'Whar John C. Spoke' to commemorate the occasion" [79]. Larkin Sanders, evidently a son of Wash and a member of Kentucky legislature, initiated the idea that the town be named in honor of his father [80].

For several years after 1880 and into the early 1900s, the railway provided an economic boom for Sanders, shuttling tourists from Louisville and Cincinnati to indulge the restorative springs in the area. Sanders by then had two hotels, the Darbro Hotel, named for a doctor who owned the structure and maintained his office there, and Polly's old Eagle Creek Hotel, renamed the Blue Lick Springs Hotel [81]. Waters at the adjacent springs near Lick Creek were believed particularly healthful, one called the Blue Lick and the other lithuia water [82]. Later, an annual tricounty fair near the town was added, and horse racing became the favored attraction. A map of Sanders published in 1884 provides fine detail of the layout and appearance of Sanders at that time.

If the rail era brought with it new growth to the town, it also provided impetus for erecting churches. The Sanders Baptist Church was established in 1874 on land donated by Mary McDannell, Elijah's sister. Not to be outdone, in 1880, the sons of Robert gave land on Eagle Creek for a "Christian or Reformed" church, to "erect a building for a school house and an academy of education; to use said building for the purpose of holding meetings where God's Holy Word may be read and expounded by all Christian denominations" [83]. In 1883, the Sanders Christian Church was founded and built. Elijah and others went into the woods to get logs to have them sawed into lumber [84].

Later Years

After his marriage, Elijah commenced to sell his inherited property in small parcels, financing his future by selling off capital that had accrued to the family over the years. These sales involved smaller and smaller plots of land over time, frequently involving only village lots. This tendency toward land dealing in small lots reflected the growing subdivision of land from ongoing settlement in the railroad era, and also the fact that Elijah disposed of several larger holdings in earlier years. These sales were Elijah's only evident source of income other than subsistence farming, though he also may have engaged carpentry on a limited basis.

In 1870, the family heirs conveyed to Elijah a total of six numbered lots in Liberty Station, as the Eagle Creek settlement was then called [85]. Elijah sold five of these Liberty Station lots in 1871 and four additional properties a year later [86]. He is recorded as buying plots on three occasions after that

and selling seven others at the same time. All transactions involved four acres
or fewer in Sanders or along Ghent Turnpike just outside the town. These sales
generally netted Elijah about $250 per sale [87]. For Elijah, financing survival
for himself and his family was a matter of drawing down his inheritance, used
not as an endowment for some gainful venture, but as a set of semiregular
payments in a lifetime installment plan, a plan where despair and aimlessness
trumped hope and expectation.

There is from the records some sense that Molly and Elijah drifted apart in
later years. Even as early as 1872 and 1873, Molly bought and sold land on her
own. She acquired a two-acre parcel adjacent the home of Mary McDannell,
Elijah's sister [88]. In the 1880s, she bought a three-acre plot in Sanders, land
formerly owned by Elijah's father, and also a four-acre parcel on Eagle Creek.
Finally in 1897, Molly purchased another lot within the town of Sanders [89].
It may be that Molly learned to fend for herself and the children after the brick
house was lost. By about 1891, Elijah, bereft of property sales as a means of
support, finally abandoned his birthplace. The town of Sanders held nothing
more for him, and he made his way to Cincinnati.

Molly seems to have spent some of her later years in Sanders after Elijah
moved to Cincinnati. Molly died of consumption in 1900 at age fifty-five and
was buried in Spring Grove Cemetery in Cincinnati [90]. By that time, Elijah,
calling himself a carpenter, had been living with his son Arthur in Cincinnati
for a decade, evidently having left Sanders, Kentucky for good [91]. In 1925,
at the age of eighty, Elijah died of pneumonia at the Cincinnati home of his
daughter Gertrude [92].

NOTES

1.   Robert was born thirteen years after the death of his grandfather
     Hugh Sanders in Spotsylvania County, Virginia. Both were fifth sons.
     Like his grandfather, Robert owned land initially acquired by his
     father, land that would eventually produce years of livelihood for
     himself and his family. And like his grandfather, his permanency
     in one place assured that familiar rhythms of life would comfort his
     existence, even as the world changed around him. That was exactly
     how it was for Robert and for Robert's grandfather. Years back, Hugh
     Sanders saw his Spotsylvania County change from a rough frontier to
     a settled steppingstone for newer opportunity in the West. Hugh had
     built a life on the assumption that life's most important underpinnings
     were fixed and that, on an immutable foundation of familiar culture
     and solid institutions, he could anchor his life and his family. But in
     his later days, Hugh saw that familiar pattern of life crumble in the

Revolutionary War, though he did not survive long enough to actually witness the emergence of the new and perhaps better world. Robert lived the same life. The newness of Kentucky in Robert's youth gave way to an advancing Western frontier in Indiana, Illinois, and other places; left behind was a more settled Kentucky. And in later years, the established ways of Robert's Kentucky life ultimately were crushed in another great war, the Civil War, which Robert never saw.

2.   The family of Abraham Lincoln comes to mind.

3.   Robert's home education would have resembled that for the free black boy Reuben living at Sally and Nathaniel's home. That education amounted to reading, writing, and "common arithmetic including the rule of three." Stating the arithmetic requirement in this way suggests the use of a standard primer as if saying that the arithmetic book should be followed through a specific chapter. See Gallatin County Deed Book C, p. 7.

4.   Robert seems to have grown up quickly, marrying at age twenty-one and assuming responsibility immediately thereafter for his young nephew. Soon after, he shouldered responsibility for administering his father's estate, even though he was a younger brother, and Robert's older brothers relied on Robert to launch their suit against their father's estate. During those early days, Lewis Sanders of Grass Hills chose to rely on Robert in matters of finance. In all, Robert's early adult life held a good deal of responsibility, which he seems to have borne well.

5.   Marriage Files, Gallatin County Court House, Warsaw, Kentucky.

6.   Robert's father Nathaniel originally accepted custody for Samuel, but presumably because of his advanced age, he passed this custody to Robert just after Robert's marriage. Samuel was the son of Robert's first cousin Nathaniel, son of John Sanders of Ghent.

7.   Tax List for 1820, Owen County Court House, Owenton, Kentucky.

8.   Owen County Court House, Tax Lists for 1821 through 1824. In 1821, Robert held 300 acres. In 1822, he is shown owning 500 acres valued at $2,300. In 1823, he held 650 acres valued at $3,650, and in 1824, Robert held 650 acres valued at $3,350.

9.   Nathaniel gave Robert 525 acres in Gallatin County in 1814, this land being part of French's original survey on or near the Ohio River. See Gallatin County Deed Book F, p. 128, and compare with Gallatin County Deed Book B, p. 38. In 1824, Robert conveyed five hundred acres to Elliston in Gallatin County on Stevens or Eagle Creek for $500. Also in 1824, Robert conveyed to James Knox a tract of land on Stevens Creek in Gallatin County where Knox currently lived, also part of French's original survey for $10. See Gallatin County Deed Book F, p.

4. This could have been the extra twenty-five acres not sold to Ellison, a small plot reflecting the small sale price.

10. See Kentucky Court of Appeals, Deed Book 4, p. 3. The land was tied up in litigation for years and may never have been released to Nathaniel's heirs.

11. Gallatin County Court House, Tax List for 1820, Warsaw, Kentucky. Robert's land at that time was valued at $5,620.

12. Martha Sanders Reiner in an unpublished manuscript provided a list of children of Nancy and Robert, noting that Craig was probably the eldest daughter. But an Owen County record of 1838 provides a different list of these children, including a daughter named Elizabeth. We assume that this Elizabeth is the same person as Craig and that her full name was Elizabeth Craig Sanders. See Owen County Deed Book F, p. 138; and Martha Reiner, *Robert Sanders* (unpublished manuscript, Fairfield, Ohio, c. 1998).

13. As indicated in note 12, some of the children's names in the Owen County list are not named by Martha Reiner. These names are Elizabeth, Nancy, and, oddly, a person called MJ. Whether MJ was a child is uncertain, as use of initials for given names at this time was virtually unknown. Also, the Owen County list omitted the names Craig and Ann, both known daughters of Robert and Nancy. The best listing of children is given in the United States Census of 1850: John G. (age twenty-seven), Robert L. (twenty-two), Pritchard M. (nineteen), Ann B. (fifteen), Agnes (thirteen), Sarah Ella (nine), Martha A. (seven), Mary A. (seven), Elijah (five), and William O. (two). Older children, such as Elizabeth, would have left the household by this date, and of course, nonsurviving children would not be named in the census.

14. Robert mortgaged to Nicholas Lindsay his household and kitchen furniture. If Robert pays to John English a debt of $150, which he owes as administrator of estate of Nathaniel for the hire of a black man for the present year, and if the note is paid to Nicholas Lindsay, then this sale will be null and void. See Gallatin County Deed Book L, p. 174.

15. In 1825, Robert's Owen County land was valued at $2,900, but by the following year, its value had dropped to $75, indicating that he sold most of his holdings in that county by 1826, the same year that Robert's father died. See Owen County Tax Lists for 1825 and 1826.

16. J. J. Marshall's Reports, Gallatin County Court, Case 157, *Robert Sanders et al. v. George W. Sanders* (1832), pp. 504–550.

17. Owen County Deed Book D, pp. 405, 483. Other brothers were involved in the settlement as well. Robert and James jointly accepted a mortgage of land in Owen County for $493; see Owen County Deed Book D, p. 383. Also, in 1835, John P. Sanders of Gallatin County conveyed to

Robert two hundred acres on Eagle Creek, the same land purchased of Nathaniel's estate by John; see Gallatin County Deed Book J, p. 233.

18. Owen County Deed Book D, p. 70.
19. Gallatin County Deed Book K, p. 212.
20. Owen County Deed Book E, p. 17.
21. Owen County Deed Book F, pp. 206, 279.
22. The matter goes beyond simply buying and selling. Land also began to be frequently used as collateral for loans to acquaintances, and second mortgages on land were taken out with banks to raise immediate cash.
23. Gallatin County Deed Book H, p. 323.
24. These joint transactions are given in the following sources: Gallatin County Deed Book H, pp. 165–166, 464; also in Owen County Deed Book D, pp. 256, 444. Scott's conveyances of land to Robert in this period are given in: Owen County Deed Book D, p. 485 and Gallatin County Deed Book K, p. 13.
25. See Gallatin County Deed Book K, p. 15; Deed Book L, pp. 85, 86; Deed Book M, p. 51; and Deed Book N, p. 473.
26. Gallatin County Deed Book J, p. 107.
27. Carl R. Bogardus, *The Story of Gallatin County, Austin, Indiana,* n.d.
28. Ibid.
29. The life of Lewis Sanders is described in Anna V. Parker, *The Sanders Family of Grass Hills, Kentucky* (Madison, Indiana: Coleman Printing, 1966).
30. Owen County Deed Book C, p. 223.
31. Carroll County Deed Book L, p. 227.
32. Ibid., p. 245.
33. Dates for these transactions seem confused, as Robert seems to have obtained a mortgage on this property (1845) before he acquired it from Lewis (1848). More than likely these actions were essentially simultaneous, but the official recording of them varied. See Carroll County Deed Book 2, p. 226 and Carroll County Deed Book 3, p. 113.
34. Owen County Deed Book J, p. 275. See also Carroll County Deed Book 3, p. 113.
35. Transactions not mentioned previously include both Robert's acquisitions and sales. Acquisitions are given in Gallatin County Deed Book H, p. 120; Owen County Deed Book D, p. 486; Owen County Deed Book J, p. 400; and Carroll County Deed Book L, p. 235. Sales and other conveyances are found in Owen County Deed Book F, p. 281; Owen County Deed Book G, p. 151; Carroll County Deed Book 2, pp. 101, 227; Gallatin County Deed Book N, p. 476; Carroll County Deed Book 3, pp. 33, 335, 416, 423.

36. A survey map of Robert's land following his death in 1850 by James Sayer provides the best picture of Robert's property on Eagle Creek. See Gallatin County Will Book F, p. 303.
37. "Mr. Smith returned from Lexington, brought to Robert Sanders last evening three full blooded heifers from Suttons." Signed, George Nicholas Sanders. See Parker, *Sanders Family of Grass Hills*, p. 45. For brief allusions to Robert's farming activity, see Gallatin County Deed Book L, p. 174 and Gallatin County Deed Book M, p. 51.
38. Robert's cache of lumber is revealed in his estate inventory completed in 1850. At that time, he also held eight "saw logs," basic stock for lumber production.
39. L. H. Harrison and J. C. Klotter, *New History of Kentucky* (Lexington: University of Kentucky Press, 1997), p. 168.
40. Mike Ashley, *British Kings and Queens* (New York: Barnes and Noble, 1998), p. 681.
41. Harrison and Klotter, *New History of Kentucky*, p. 176.
42. Harrison and Klotter, *New History of Kentucky*, pp. 175–176.
43. Owen County Deed Book B, p. 447.
44. Owen County Deed Book C, p. 270; Owen County Deed Book D, pp. 294, 297, 495.
45. Gallatin County Deed Book H, p. 294.
46. Gallatin County Deed Book L, p. 145. Although Robert sold America at age fourteen to Scott in 1842, Robert was in possession of her by 1850.
47. Gallatin County Deed Book M, p. 489.
48. Owen County Deed Book F, p. 138.
49. Gallatin County Court House, Marriage Files, 1839, Warsaw, Kentucky. Matthew Thompson died in 1835.
50. Darnell, E. J. 1993. Forks of Elkhorn Church, Clearfield Company, Baltimore, Maryland, p. 188.
51. Vachel Lindsay's grave site is situated near Abraham Lincoln's tomb in Springfield, Illinois.
52. Reiner, *Robert Sanders*. This unpublished manuscript provides a list of the surviving children of Robert and Polly: (a) twin daughter Mary (1843–1922), who in 1861 married Solomon McDanell; (b) Martha Ann "Mattie" (1843–1864), who married William Wheatly; and (c) a son Elijah Lawson (1845–1925).
53. Owen County Deed Book L, p. 442.
54. Gallatin County Court House, unpublished original records, Warsaw, Kentucky.
55. Gallatin County Will Book F, pp. 283–285.
56. Gallatin County Deed Book F, pp. 296–304.

57. Gallatin County Court House, unpublished original record, 1852. Affidavits showing Robert had purchased twenty shares of stock in Eagle Creek Turnpike Road Company, each share being worth $50. The said stock became due as follows: 12 percent, April 1850; 5 percent August 1850; and 5 percent each month till the total amount was called. No payments had been made except $10 at the time of first call.

58. 1850 Gallatin County Tax List 1850.

59. Gallatin County Court House, unpublished original record, 1852. Family Mirror advertisement for a commissioner's sale of Robert's property at the home of Samuel Sanders in Ghent, selling land conveyed to Robert by Lewis Sanders Jr. excepting the tavern property now occupied by Samuel Sanders. This action was recorded in 1854; see Carroll County Deed Book 5, p. 325.

60. Gallatin County Will Book F, p. 303.

61. See Owen County Deed Book O, pp. 150, 341; Gallatin County Deed Book P, p. 209; Carroll County Deed Book 8, pp. 303, 319.

62. See Gallatin County Deed Book R, p. 640, 642, 643; Carroll County Deed Book 10, p. 186, 187, 188, 265.

63. See Carroll County Deed Book 10, p. 415; Gallatin County Deed Book 1, p. 116. Also one final sale took place almost a decade later, in 1878. See Carroll County Deed Book 14, p. 68.

64. Despite national laws to the contrary, the conferring of titles, though informal, remained a distinctly southern attribute. Kentucky "colonels" are a case in point.

65. Parcels of seventy-seven and forty-six acres were involved, fetching a total of $371; see Owen County Deed Book L, pp. 77, 111, 296.

66. That Polly built the hotel is uncertain, but she did own and operate it after Robert's death, and the hotel sat on Robert's former lands; see Reiner, *Robert Sanders.*

67. Reiner states that Polly passed the ownership of the hotel to her daughter Mary. Mary's grandchildren danced at the hotel to amuse hotel guests who threw coins in approval. These coins were kept in a special box for the children's later use. See Reiner, *Robert Sanders.*

68. The source of information on sibling deaths is Reiner, *Robert Sanders.*

69. It seems Robert's Ohio River ferry service from Ghent to Indiana paid an unexpected dividend, finding a wife for his son.

70. John Mullen died in 1890 and was remembered in a Kentucky newspaper, as follows: "Some of our older citizens will remember Rev. John Mullen and wife who lived near Worthville many years ago, he being a Methodist preacher and teacher. Mrs. Mullen died recently at St. Joseph. Missouri, aged 78 years." *Carrolton Democrat,* June 14, 1890, p. 8, column 11. The 1850 United States Census for Gallatin

County provides information on the Mullens' other children, who were Thomas, Elizabeth, John, Leander, Henrietta, and Margaret.

71. The children's ages are shown in the United States Censuses for Carroll County, for 1870, 1880, 1900, and 1920. Walter eventually worked on the Ohio River and lived in Louisville, marrying Bridget Maloney. Ernest married a woman named Bessie. Omar married Hannah O'Neil, and Gertrude first married Veit Veith and second Edward Bruns, both of Cincinnati.

72. United States Census for Gallatin County, 1870. Reel number 462, circa p. 301. Birth years were: Ella, 1868; Walter, 1869; Arthur Lee, 1872; Ernest O., 1881; Everett Brown, 1884; Omar Thomas, 1886; and Gertrude Lee, 1889.

73. The McDannell's then sold for $400 their portion of Polly's dower land to Elijah, including the brick house—Robert's "mansion house"—and other improvements. Included was about four acres of land abutting the Eagle Creek Hotel on its eastern side and another acre west of the hotel; see Carroll County Deed Book 12, p. 71. See also Gallatin County Deed Book R, p. 640.

74. Carroll County Deed Book 14, p. 412.

75. Whispers of a previous generation are that Elijah burned the house to collect insurance money. We find no record of a house fire nor of insurance coverage or payment.

76. Evidently, locals called the place Dixie about this time, though that name never won official recognition.

77. Carroll County Deed Book Number 13, p. 476; Book Number 19, p. 9.

78. Long, *History of Kentucky Counties.*

79. Parker, *Sanders Family of Grass Hills.* Also see *Kentucky Historical Society Magazine*, vol. 80 (1982), p. 389.

80. The account is probably accurate but the name Larkin as a son of Wash is not given in the unpublished genealogy of Martha S. Reiner.

81. Mary McDannell sold to the Jacobs family in 1881 for $4,000.

82. The term *lithuia water* is a source of curiosity, especially as it occurs in rural Kentucky. It refers to the Lithuanian folk notion that certain waters held restorative power. But how the term made its way to Kentucky is uncertain, as no Eastern European settlement occurred in that area at that time. A clue lies in the naming of the nearby town and Gallatin County seat of Warsaw. Warsaw's name derives from a popular book of the day, called Thaddeus of Warsaw, and Poland shares a border with Lithuania. It may be that lithuia (Lithuanian) water was mentioned in that book.

83. Gallatin County Deed Book 1, p. 427 and Carroll County Deed Book 14, p. 452.

84. See article by Mrs. G. W. Shirley, secretary-treasurer of Sunday School, Sanders Christian Church, filed at the public library in Carrollton, Kentucky.

85. Gallatin County Deed Book 1, p. 374.

86. Carroll County Deed Book 11, pp. 232, 342, 347, 395, 396; Gallatin County Deed Book 1, p. 509.

87. Carroll County Deed Books Number 11, p. 430; Number 13, pp. 293, 435; Number 14, pp. 435, 601, 602; Number 24, p. 303; Number 25, pp. 314, 361; and Number 28, p. 107.

88. Carroll County Deed Books Number 11, p. 403; and Number 12, p. 70.

89. Carroll County Deed Book 17, pp. 174, 175.

90. Death Certificate, State of Ohio, Cemetery Record.

91. Williams Cincinnati City Directories, 1891 through 1901. Elijah appears residing with his son Arthur each year, except 1898.

92. Elijah is buried in Evergreen Cemetery, Southgate, Kentucky. Death Certificate, State of Ohio, Cemetery Record.

CHAPTER FOURTEEN

Leaving The Land

Arthur Lee Sanders was born eight years after the Civil War mercifully ground to a halt in 1864. He heard war stories from the previous generation and knew firsthand how crucial the war was in shaping the world into which he was born [1]. By the time Arthur reached adulthood, the rural economy had nearly collapsed from the aftershocks of war and reconstruction [2]. Life in Sanders, Kentucky, was no longer viable for a hopeful young man and Arthur, like so many others, left his homeland for Cincinnati, Ohio. Above all, Arthur needed employment, but that required building his life on a wholly new urban basis and without effective family guidance. Except in the lightest way, family had virtually nothing to offer Arthur; his family offered no traditional occupations, skills, contacts, property, or money. In Arthur's life, we can detect some hesitation in his footsteps toward his uncertain future, but the hard demands of livelihood reduced his chance of backsliding and made his move away from Sanders largely irreversible.

Arthur Sanders grew up under the wings of Elijah, who struggled in his own life, and Molly, his mother, who taught school and seemed to have provided key support for her children. Arthur probably learned about the importance of education and religion as these were key themes of his parents' existence. But neither proved decisive in the years ahead for Arthur.

By the time he was nineteen, his father had already moved to Cincinnati, and Arthur joined him there in 1892. For the next five years, Arthur worked first as a porter and then as a streetcar conductor in the city [3]. In 1897, Arthur purchased four acres of land back in Sanders from his father, paying him as he could until he finally received the deed in 1903. His intention evidently was to leave Cincinnati and return home, though his financial circumstances, particularly with a marriage in 1897, seem not to have permitted this [4]. In 1902, Arthur tried again, purchasing a residential lot on the south side of the railroad in Sanders for $300, but he sold this five years later without having lived there [5].

Arthur's idea of returning to Kentucky had little chance for success. The depressed state of rural Kentucky at that time made finding gainful employment nearly impossible, especially in the tobacco-growing regions of the Commonwealth. Large tobacco cartels drove tobacco prices to dismal levels, and their schemes to bankrupt dissenting farmers had reached a peak by the turn of the century. Farmers finally reacted, organizing a large band of horsemen, as many as three thousand, to intimidate farmers who complied with cartel business and to resist civil authority which stood in its way. This episode, called the Black Patch War of 1906, failed to return tobacco farms to viability, and farm families continued to desert the land in droves [6]. At the time Arthur was seeking a return to Sanders, the tobacco economy of the region lay in ruin. The town of Sanders had experienced a mild turn-of-the-century recovery in its emerging tourism centered on mineral springs, hotels, and fairs, but nothing in these developments seems to have captured Arthur in his thought of returning home.

In 1897, Arthur married Henrietta Kroth, a first-generation Cincinnatian born of German parentage [7]. They married in Louisville [8]. Both of Arthur's parents, Elijah and Molly, lived with the young couple in Cincinnati after their marriage. Molly died in 1900, three years after Arthur married [9]. Elijah evidently moved out after Molly's death, returning for a period to Sanders, and finally joined Arthur's sister Gertrude in Cincinnati until his death in 1925. At the same time that Elijah left Arthur's small household, Sarah Kroth, now a widow, moved in with Arthur and Henrietta in 1901 [10]. Arthur and Henrietta had their first child, a daughter called Eugenie, in 1899, and a son named Ralph was born seven years later.

After sixteen years in Cincinnati, Arthur amassed enough savings by 1907 to purchase a house across the Ohio River in Newport, Kentucky; the sale of his lot in Sanders this same year undoubtedly helped [11]. He continued on as a streetcar conductor and motorman for four years, and finally by 1912, Arthur was able to establish a small grocery store, first in his home; then later, he built a stand-alone store at the edge of his lot.

The grocery store became the family's main occupation for more than a decade. But during this time, Arthur and Henrietta's daughter Eugenie contracted tuberculosis and died in her seventeenth year. Eugenie's story was carried in the Newport newspaper, which noted that she caught cold during a rainy excursion to see the Liberty Bell, then on a national tour by railroad flatcar from Philadelphia [12]. She died shortly after that, leaving in 1917 an extraordinary legacy of drawings and paintings for so young a person.

Examples of painted China by Eugenie Sanders. Both pieces were completed shortly before Eugenie's death at age seventeen. Photographs by Lori and David Van der Heide and Nancy Sanders.

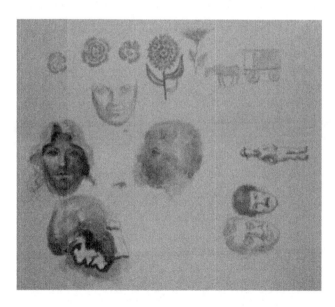

Pages from Ralph L. Sanders' sketchbook. Photographs by Nancy Sanders.

Pages from Ralph L. Sanders' sketchbook. Photographs by Nancy Sanders.

Arthur sold the grocery store in Newport in 1924 and purchased a home in Fort Thomas, Kentucky, a town lying a few miles south of Newport [13]. There he maintained an income working in the grocery business on his own and later for a larger store in town [14]. Arthur and Henrietta remained in Fort Thomas until 1937 when they sold their home [15] and followed their son Ralph to Erie, Pennsylvania. While in Erie, Arthur is thought to have sold formal photographic portraits on a door-to-door basis. Arthur eventually moved to Jamestown, New York, where he lived with an old acquaintance [16], and he died there in 1957. Henrietta remained in Erie, living with her son and his wife, where she stayed until her death in 1968 [17].

Ralph Lee Sanders

Ralph was the only son of Arthur and Henrietta Sanders. He grew up in Newport, Kentucky, working in the family grocery store and cavorting with neighborhood friends [18]. The streets of Newport at that time were filled with streetcars, horses, and wagons of all sizes. There were green grocery peddlers, milk wagons, a waffle man, a hot tamale and hot dog man, all noisily selling their wares. An icehouse business near Arthur's grocery store carted large ice blocks around town, using an extra team of horses for steep grades. Once an ascent was complete, the extra horse team was freed to find its way back to the stable on its own.

Arthur had his own horse, named Joe, and a grocery wagon used mainly for weekly visits to wholesalers in Cincinnati to stock his store. The first stop at the wholesale market was for coffee, where beans were ground to order, then fresh greens and fruit, and finally the meat market with sawdust strewn on the floor where rows of bacons, hams, sausages, bologna, and leona all hung from hooks. The store in Newport was a gathering place for the neighborhood's older gentlemen, who gathered for war stories, games of checkers, and cheese and crackers. Shortly before the store closed, Arthur purchased a T-model Ford touring car with side curtains at a cost of between five and six hundred dollars. Ralph's job was to attend to the car's water, oil, and grease and to hand-pump the tires when necessary. But his failure to mind the oil in one instance resulted in engine damage costing sixty dollars in repairs.

Ralph's mother Henrietta routinely worked in the store, and the family hired a black woman named Emma to do household chores of cooking, laundry, and cleaning. Emma was a large strong woman with scars on her arms from scuffles with her husband, and Ralph took orders from her without hesitation.

Ralph's friendships formed initially in grade school and lasted through the high school years. Memories of Oscar Rummel, Lee Grasfeder, Fred and Eldon Warren, Wayne Bowman, Harry Ahrand, Harry's cousin Earl Bradley, and Otto Wolf echoed through Ralph's later life. These recollections suggest something about the times in Newport. Many of the families in that area were

German. Oscar Rummel's father, a strict disciplinarian, was from Germany and owned the first car in the neighborhood—an Oakland. Fred Warren was the leader of the pack, a maverick with a penchant for wearing uniforms. His brother Eldon was more subdued. Lee Grasfeder was a big strong kid who broke an arm playing football and later lost the full use of it. Wayne Bowman was thought particularly sophisticated, and his parents sent him to Cincinnati for high school. Harry Ahrand contracted a fatal bone marrow disease and was bedridden, but the group rallied to him, helping him construct and operate a crystal radio set before he passed away. Harry's father had a newspaper route, delivering papers in a two-wheeled chariot pulled by an old nag. Earl Bradley, Harry's cousin, generally followed the group. Otto Wolf was the butt of too many jokes about his freckles, red hair, and shy demeanor. Ralph noted of himself that he always carried candy and marbles, largesse no doubt from the grocery store. For amusement, the group would go to the movie theater most weeks to see a Wild West show or shoot pool or on rare occasions take a riverboat across the Ohio to visit Coney Island, Cincinnati's amusement park. But a more common pastime was to play shinny, a form of street hockey using homemade sticks and crushed tin cans.

All these friends lived on Third Street, just a block from the grocery and near the bottom lands that were susceptible to annual flooding. No floodwalls by then had been constructed, and as often as twice a year, residents in the lower parts of the city took refuge on their second floors from floods. Arthur and Ralph made boat deliveries on these occasions, tying baskets of groceries to ropes, which were hoisted to grateful customers. Houseboats often anchored nearby, but this itinerant group often obtained their groceries on credit and sailed away before paying their bills.

During the First World War, street parades in support of the war effort were a weekly Newport event, and neighborhood rallies were held regularly. Platforms were hastily erected, sopranos sang the national anthem, and politicians offered speeches on patriotism. Afterward, the speaker would read telegrams about the progress of the war and welfare of the local men in uniform. Noisy crowds chanted, "Kill the Kaiser." After the war, parades and memorials for men lost in battle were commonplace.

Ralph graduated from Newport High School as class valedictorian in 1924. The honor was less than it might appear. A teacher nominated about ten students for the position, and Ralph's friends combined to elect him. This election was akin to receiving the shortest straw since the valedictorian was required to give a graduation speech, something all struggled greatly to avoid. Ralph managed finally to deliver a stirring valedictory address after freezing in mid-oration [19].

A local directory listed Ralph's occupation as artist about the time he entered adulthood [20]. The label was earned. As occasions in the past had allowed, Ralph studied art and made the acquaintance of a fellow named Murphy who studied at the Cincinnati Art Academy. Together they drew and painted in their high school years until their school homework assignments suffered. Ralph provided numerous freehand drawings for his school yearbook. Later, he drew with a neighbor, an art professor at the University of Cincinnati. He provided Ralph with some free art lessons, and together they sculpted a fountain for Arthur and Henrietta's pond on their eight acres in Fort Thomas.

Ralph remained with his parents after high school, helping to dig trenches for the house's water supply in Fort Thomas and seeing to their twenty or so chickens. But twice, the chicken coop and all the birds were consumed in flames, once from spontaneous combustion and a second time from errant fireworks.

In those times, he frequently rode the trolley back to Newport to visit with friends and to play tennis. At tennis, he made the acquaintance of Bill Poate, who in time invited Ralph to his home. There he discovered the excitement and confusions of a large family and met Dorothy Poate for the first time. In stark family contrast, only rarely did Ralph travel back to Eagle Creek to visit his grandfather Elijah and other relatives. Once, with a newfound friend in Sanders, he shot at turtles from the covered bridge over Eagle Creek. While visiting, Ralph tried biscuits and sorghum molasses but resolved that food in Newport was far better.

Ralph and Dorothy Poate went together for about seven years before finally marrying in 1937. Dorothy and five siblings were raised by her mother and aunt following the early death of her father [21]. William Poate, Dorothy's father, originally from Philadelphia, traveled widely in his work, setting up brick manufacturing plants throughout the eastern half of the United States and Canada, living about two years in each place until each brick operation was satisfactorily underway. Working in Newport in 1910, William met and married Lauretta Grizzle, she of a family originally from southwestern Virginia [22]. Dorothy was born in Winnipeg, Manitoba, in 1913. Her father died suddenly in 1920 at age forty in Acme, North Carolina, near Wilmington, leaving his wife Lauretta and their six children, who shortly thereafter returned to Newport. Roger Moore of the brickmaking firm in Acme assisted their return, selling the family's 1913 Cadillac and forwarding the proceeds to Lauretta, who had no benefit of life insurance on her husband.

For a short period, Ralph worked as a railroad messenger and file clerk, then for a printing company called Donaldson's Lithograph in Newport during the Great Depression of the 1930s. Donaldson's was bought out by a larger company and its doors closed, but several employees of the Newport operation were offered transfers to Erie, Pennsylvania, to work in what became the United States Printing and Lithograph Company. Ralph accepted that offer and, over the ensuing years in Erie, worked principally as foreman of that company's Art Department, in which small drawings or photographs were enlarged and printed for display as outdoor billboard advertising. His work in printing spanned four decades.

The marriage of Dorothy and Ralph lasted their lifetimes. They began married life in the city of Erie in 1938, first in rented apartments, then in a nearby house they purchased within the city. A decade later, they moved to the suburbs near the shores of Lake Erie where their children were raised and held that property into the 1970s. They returned to Cincinnati and later Fort Thomas in their retirement years. Ralph died in 1987 at age eighty-one and Dorothy in 1999 at age eighty-six [23].

THE FAMILIES OF ARTHUR AND RALPH SANDERS

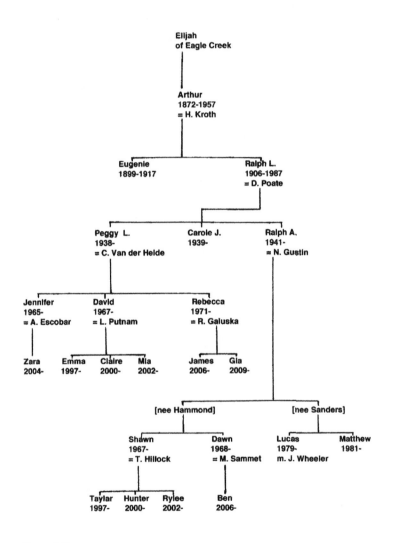

Source: Authors

After Dorothy and Ralph Sanders

The three children of Dorothy and Ralph, named Margaret (Peggy), Carole, and Ralph, graduated from high school in Erie in the decade of the 1950s, and all received advanced education after that. All three prospered modestly, traveled widely on several continents, and have lived in numerous locations throughout the United States. This family history and genealogy is the result of their close collaboration in research and writing.

The grandchildren of Dorothy and Ralph numbered seven in all. Each has some level of university education and reside in such disparate locations as Washington DC, Minnesota, California, Texas, and Germany. Two have married internationally. From them, great-grandchildren are emerging in the new millennium.

Perspective

The decision by Arthur Sanders to leave Sanders, Kentucky, as a young man to seek a livelihood in Cincinnati was momentous in ways he could not have imagined. He bowed to the imperatives of political, economic, and social disruptions such as they affected rural Kentucky in his time. But those disruptions reflected much larger changes set in motion centuries before, diffusing to different locations over time, first to cities and then to rural areas, initially to the centers of culture and then to their peripheries. This constellation of forces comprises modern life and livelihood, and in concert, they undercut the extended family as an institution as it had been constituted and understood for a thousand years. The last remnant of that ancient institution slipped away as Arthur made his way to Cincinnati, and a new strain of family life emerged in its place. The family after Arthur became now fully of the modern order, sharing its unique experiences and common interests largely among a tightened circle of relatives and a broadened circle of acquaintances. Tales of these later generations, engulfed in modern opportunity and mobility, separated from the lands and places and experiences of ancestors, have limited bearing on the longer Sanders family history and so receive little accounting here.

We have seen the Sanders family, the branch that we have described, from the moment of its inception, or rather, before it began. In Sanderstead, Surrey, England in the 800s were some prefamily beginnings, a series of related persons whose identities arose from their traditional ethnic or tribal origins. Those traditional societies undoubtedly contained social forms that we might account as families today, but they are largely inaccessible to us; records are rare and surnames for those protofamilial units did not exist. In this sense, explorations of family history can trace no deeper than the traditional society from which it emerged, though lineages of certain prominent tribal leaders may still survive in ancient documents. For our own family, we learned that the Sanders were sired by a person named Leonard. Not Leonard Sanders, just Leonard, a figure of traditional origin.

After about the year 1000 in England, as tribal conflicts ground forward into ever-enlarging territorial domains, early forms of feudal society emerged. From this feudal period, for seven hundred years or so, the European and English nation-states inexorably emerged; and with them, the institution of family blossomed. Family surnames were adopted, and they flourished, principally because these names carried powerful social meanings. Surnames were borne by individuals and signified in coats of arms, but more than that, they representing extended families, spoke of land entitlements, created political attachments, demarcated social class, and determined economic position, the whole of society's interactions playing out through a complex web of enduring and determinative genealogies. Marriage was a key instrument of social mobility for any family as merged genealogies represented some multiplication of social reach. As extended families grew, they branched out to new locations; but ties between members scarcely weakened because the binding forces of society, economy, and polity that cemented feudal families together remained intact and even strengthened throughout the feudal epoch. So it was that the Sanders family after Sanderstead eventually located in Charlwood, Ewell, Derby, Wales, Gloucestershire, and even Virginia and Kentucky. But for all that dispersion, the notion that extended family was paramount in people's lives was never fully challenged. The family's many members continued to share grand commonalities of interest and purpose, and society at large accepted such commonalities as a central organizing principle for societal affairs.

What began in Sanderstead, Surrey, effectively ended in Sanders, Kentucky, a thousand years later. The feudal history of this family ended around the beginning of the twentieth century when the Sanders extended family no longer could supply most of the meaningful social relations that frame any one person's life activity. When at the end of the nineteenth century Arthur Sanders left his home for a new urban world, he declared that this family was finally done with the last thousand years of its existence and must now step forward into modern society. What remains after Arthur by and large is a series of small households and nuclear families, principally child-rearing institutions that mainly binds mother, father, and children. Under this scheme of modern life, the nuclear family has no powerful institutions that promote extended family solidarity between and across generations. As extended family, we do not work together or share property or make ourselves known to others through a large functioning family whole. We replaced all that with the individually based challenges and opportunities of modern culture.

The institution of family seems less determinative of one's future now than ever before. Yet we all travel on a path that arcs toward the future. That path is the main subject of history. Where we have been tells us something of where we collectively are headed. If we look back, we come to know ourselves better, to know who we are and how we are influenced. We are imbued with thousands of continuities from the past that lie within ourselves and our culture. These can be discovered and interpreted. The main message we receive from family history is direct enough, however, and amounts to this: the people we are, for the most part, are the people we were.

Henry Marsh offers a final thought:

> So few lives divide us; a hundred years
> Carry three lives, and when the party's over,
> The century drained dry, it yet appears
> For patient spade suddenly to uncover,
> Frail, and a little chipped, the perfume gone
> Of the dead wine. But in the bottle yet
> We see the vanished ruby that glowed and shone
> During those faded years when the wine was set
> In those three glasses. Thirty men at most
> Fill out a thousand years, each with his glass,
> Laughing at table, no unbodied ghost
> But a friend speaking, though the hours pass
> So swiftly from the bottle to the tomb;
> Their faces shine within my shadowed room.

NOTES

1. Owen County (and Gallatin County to its north) developed a cash crop economy based on tobacco. Given the low tobacco prices between 1890 and 1914, some county residents migrated to the urban areas of the north, mostly Cincinnati and northern Kentucky. See John E. Kleber, ed., *The Kentucky Encyclopedia* (Lexington: University of Kentucky Press, 1992).
2. Not least were the dispiriting effects on the rural population, finding their postwar homeland in deep depression.
3. Cincinnati City Directories, 1891 through 1901 (Williams Directory Company, Cincinnati).
4. Carroll County Deed Book 24, p. 303.
5. Carroll County Deed Book 27, p. 191; and Carroll County Deed Book 28, p. 468.

6. Events in the Black Patch War of 1906 actually took place in central Kentucky, but the conditions and anger that gave rise to the conflict were found in northern Kentucky as well.

7. Eugene and Sarah Kroth migrated to Cincinnati from Germany about thirty years before. Sarah is believed to have come from Baden and Eugene from Bavaria. Eugene listed his occupation as a "molder" in Cincinnati.

8. The marriage of Arthur Sanders and Henrietta Kroth of Cincinnati was solemnized on December 1, 1897, at Portland Methodist Episcopal Church Parsonage in Louisville, with Rev. J. Y. Rushing officiating. The marriage was probably an elopement as the ceremony was conducted in the church parsonage and Rushing was not the pastor for this church. If so, a reason for eloping was that the two families differed on religion, Henrietta being Roman Catholic and Arthur a Protestant.

9. Death Certificate, State of Ohio, Spring Grove Cemetery, Cincinnati.

10. Williams Directory of Cincinnati, 1901. Both parties gave their address as 4044 Eastern Avenue.

11. The property lay on lot 91, on the northwest corner of Third and Berry streets in the Mansion Hill addition to Newport. See Campbell County Deed Book 102, p. 16.

12. *Kentucky Post,* January 7 or 8, 1917.

13. See Campbell County Deed Book 144, p. 617. The property he purchased was lot 27 of Hawthorne Addition of Fort Thomas at 53 Hawthorne Avenue. See Campbell County Deed Book 145, p. 575.

14. Stegner Grocery Store, Ft. Thomas.

15. See Campbell County Deed Books Number 177, p. 433 and Number 178, p. 133.

16. This person's name was Paul Christ. Although his prior relationship with Arthur is not known, Arthur sold his house in Fort Thomas to Fred and Matilda Christ.

17. Both are interred with their daughter Eugenie in Evergreen Cemetery, Southgate, Kentucky.

18. Ralph wrote a brief memoir of his early days in the form of a letter in 1987. This and other early Newport accounts are based on that and other letters. He recalled this group enjoyed their pranks, which were numerous. A favorite among them was perpetrated on the streetcar which regularly passed the neighborhood on a slight uphill grade. These trolleys used electric power from overhead wires. The ploy was to wait for the trolley to near the top of the ascent, then sneak behind and pull the trolley ropes off the wires, disconnecting the vehicle from its source of power, having first soaped the tracks. No account was given of how the trolley finally gained its objective. On one occasion,

a member of the group waited at the scheduled trolley stop; and as it came to a halt, he put his foot on the first step of the streetcar, tied his shoelace, and left, thanking the motorman for his help.

19. Ralph gave the valedictory address to the class of 1924. Within the speech, he offered these words, "Dear friends, we who are passing out of High School life into a more active citizenship today, feel that we have a place in national life. We feel that each one of us has work to do in demonstrating the spirit of patriotism that is within us. Reconstruction is still going on all over the land and much indeed needs to be reconstructed and much to be destroyed. We can all have a part in it, women as well as men, girls as well as boys. Whatever makes our nation better and nobler; whatever serves to elevate the people of the land to any higher plane of life; whatever in any way makes America or any portion of it better worth the living in, is helping on the great work of reconstruction; and remember, whatever elevates the individual, to a greater or lesser degree, elevates the community in which he lives."

20. Covington and Newport and Vicinity Directory, 1928–1929. Williams Directory Company, Cincinnati.

21. William Poate (1880–1920) of Philadelphia, Dorothy's father, was born in Worthing, Sussex, England. He was one of ten children of Clara Griffin (1857–1927) and William Richard Poate (1857–1898). They migrated with all the children from Worthing to Bromley in London about 1883 and to America in 1886 or 1887. William Richard Poate's parents were Rosetta Richards and Richard Poate (1803–) of Midhurst, Sussex. They were married about 1836, then moved to Albion Street in Southwick where their eight children were born. Richard himself was the son of John Poate (c1770–1840), a laborer of Midhurst. Earlier generations of the Poates are found in the vicinity of Catherington, Hampshire, near the Sussex county boundary.

    Earlier versions of the surname Poate are found as Pote and Port. An interesting account of the evolution of this surname is given in an unpublished account by Walter Poate of St. Leonards-on-Sea, written in 1910, "Up till about 1200 it was generally spelt Port or Porte; soon after that date, when the pronunciation of the 'o' became more like 'oo,' the 'r' was frequently omitted. Towards the end of the 16th century the 'a,' which at the time was frequently pronounced 'r' in Hants and Sussex, was added, no doubt to make it phonetically correct. It has always been pronounced Port until quite recently; in fact some old villagers still continue to do so."

22. Lauretta Grizzle (also Grizzel, Grizzell), wife of William Poate whom she married in 1910 and mother of Dorothy Poate, was born in Persimmon

Grove, Kentucky, in 1882. She and her four siblings were born of Sarah Margaret Randall (c1850–1927) and Elam Grizzle (1853–1915). Elam was born in Russell County, Virginia, in the state's southwestern corner, the son of Elizabeth Artrip (1817–1901) and George Grizzle (1819–1896). George was the son of Rebecca Hamon (1782–1857) and William Grizzle (1780–). Both Rebecca and William were born in North Carolina, perhaps in Rutherford County, and migrated to Virginia as part of a larger family movement to that location. William's father evidently was William Grizzle, born about 1730 in Pittsylvania County, Virginia. Earlier generations of Grizzles are found in and near Henrico County, Virginia, in the 1600s, though precise relationships between all these persons have not been determined. We are particularly grateful to James O. Grizzell of Hendersonville, Tennessee, for sharing with us his extensive collection of materials on the Grizzells.

23. Both are interred in Evergreen Cemetery, Southgate, Kentucky alongside Arthur, Henrietta, and Eugenie.

Appendix I

This appendix provides a more complete Sanders genealogy than is described in the foregoing chapters. Genealogical information given below is arranged as family branches and employs certain other conventions, as follows:

Dates

In 1582, Pope Gregory initiated a new calendar that simplified and modestly shorted the reckoning of months and years to replace the old Julian calendar. This Gregorian calendar was adopted slowly over the next decades and gradually became the standard measure of the year's progress. The result is that records of specific events from that historical era often contain both new and old dates. For these cases, we report here only the latter of two dates from the competing systems, in effect reporting all dates in terms of the modern calendar for this Sanders genealogy.

Vital dates of persons or events, when known, are given without prefixes; but where uncertainty exists, the following prefixes are used to convey available information:

- c indicates circa; a date estimated from records to be accurate within about five years before or after the given date.
- Generally, the later the historical period, the more accurate these estimates area.
- a indicates ante; an event occurred before the given date.
- p indicates post; an event occurred after the given date.

Numbering

We numbered each generation as a genealogical sequence. One number following another reflects a father-son relationship. For example, Sc3 Walter FitzAlan is the son of Sh2 Alan FitzFlaad. Numbering also allows us to track generations across different family branches. This means, for example, that Henry of Ewell (E14) is of the same generation as William of Banbury (B14).

Family Branches

To organize our genealogical research, we identified family branches, that is, portions of the family which adopted new geographical homes and established enduring presence there. Some judgment was required to determine whether a given circumstance merited designating a new branch or merely continuing an existing one. No hard and fast rule was adopted; rather, we identified and retained those that most effectively aided us in trying to understand our family history.

Here family branches are identified by geographical location. Branches are indicated with the following prefixed letters in the genealogical listings, as follows:

Old World

Br	-	Brittany
Sh	-	Shropshire
Sc	-	Scotland
S	-	Sanderstead
C	-	Charlwood
B	-	Banbury
E	-	Ewell
A	-	Aston
D	-	Derbyshire
W	-	Wales
G	-	Gloucestershire

New World

Ac	-	Accomack
KQ	-	King and Queen
K	-	Kentucky

OLD WORLD GENEALOGY

This genealogy begins in Brittany, a region in the northwest of (today's) France and focuses on a place called Dol. Numerous genealogies and family histories have it that some early figures at Dol belong to the genealogy described below, but these arguments rest largely on *historical* rather than *genealogical* facts. We include here only established genealogical facts, agreeing though that these earlier figures undoubtedly contributed to this family's history. In temporal sequence, these figures were Counts of "Dol and Dinan" (a single entity), namely Ewarin, Hamo, Guienoc, and perhaps Alan, unless the last of these was a seneschal and not a count. Later family members within this genealogy were seneschals, as follows:

BRITTANY (Br)

Br1   Flaad (c1045–), Seneschal of Dol, who entered England.

SHROPSHIRE (Sh)

Shropshire is a county in west England that shares a boundary with Wales.

Sh2   Alan FitzFlaad (c1070–), whose issue was:

1.   Jordan, Seneschal of Dol.
2.   William (–1160), ancestor of the Earls of Arundel.
3.   Walter (see Sc3).
4.   Simon, who entered Scotland with his brother Walter.

SCOTLAND (Sc)

Sc3   Walter FitzAlan (1108–1177), Born in Shropshire, he entered Scotland by invitation of Scotland's King David and became Scotland's first Royal Steward. About 1138, Walter married Eschyna de Londoniis, widow of Robert Croc, by whom she had a son Robert.

Walter and Eschyna's had issue:

1.   Alan, Second Steward of Scotland, by then a hereditaryposition.
2.   Walter.
3.   Leonard (see S4).
4.   Simon.
5.   Margaret.
6.   Beatrice (perhaps).

SANDERSTEAD (S)

S4   Leonard de Sanderstead (c1143–c1198), born as Leonard FitzWalter, also
at times known as Leonard de Lega. He married Beatrice Dunstanville,
granddaughter of King Henry I, and had known issue:

1. Walter (c1169–1216) Also known as "Watkin." On his death, he gave
   Sanderstead Manor to Hyde Abbey.
2. Leonard de Lega, who held land in Shropshire. In time, this line
   carried the permanent surname Leigh (Lea and other spellings).
3. Richard de Cumba (see S5).
4. Stephen le Dune, a sometime occupant of Downe Manor who received
   Warlingham and Sanderstead lands in his brother Watkin's will.

A much later figure probably from Stephen's line was John de
Sanderstead (g1290–1353). John is the last person we found to refer
to himself as "de Sanderstead." Probably of our ninth documented
generation, John resided principally in Warwickshire. His father was
Nicholas.

S5   Richard de Cumba (c1173–c1240), also known as Richard "le dignu" and
Richard de Dene. He married Sybilla Dene (–1226) and had known issue:

1. Ralph (see S6).
2. Robert de Pappeworth married Lucy Maubanc of Sende. Their son
   was Thomas.
3. Geoffrey le Dine (Dene) who held land in Sanderstead. His son was
   Henry.

S6   Ralph de Pappeworth (c1198–). Ralph was the son of Richard de Cumba
and Sybilla Dene. He evidently took up residence in Coulsdon, Surrey, but
his marriage is unknown.

S7   Ralph Saundre (c1220–p1265). Ralph married the daughter of Roger
Salomon, knight of Horley in Surrey, acquiring by inheritance the Manor
of Lodge in Horley.

S8   Richard Saundre (c1248–p1310). Richard is the son of Ralph and was
lord of Lodge Manor in Horley. He is credited with building a chantry
at Horley Church and creating an effigy of Roger Salomon, dated c1315.

Richard married a coheiress of William Collenden. His son probably is William (see C9).

CHARLWOOD (C)

Charlwood is a village and parish lying at the southern reaches of Surrey and became a Sanders home for a long period. The family held property at Charlwood called Sanders Place, the first known use of the name "Sanders" for the family.

C9   William Saundre (c1280–p1314), perhaps. He is credited as being first in the family to reside at Sanders Place in Charlwood.

C10 James Saundre (c1305–).

C11 Matthew Saundre (c1330–).

C12 Stephen Saundre (c1358–). Stephen's issue:

1.   Thomas (see C13)
2.   John, who had issue:

   1.   Richard, who married his cousin Johanna Sanders.
   2.   John.
   3.   Stephen (perhaps).

C13   Thomas Saundre (1380–c1450). Thomas married Johanna Odworth, with issue:

1.   William (see C14).
2.   Reynold.
3.   John, whose wife may have been Margaret died in 1477. His issue may have been:

   1.   John (–1530)
   2.   Richard.

4.   Robert.
5.   Johanna, who married her cousin Richard (see C12.2.1).

C14 William Saunders (c1415–1481).

William was of Charlwood and in about 1438 married Joan (c1422–1470), daughter of Thomas Carew of Beddington in Surrey. The children of this marriage were to establish new family branches in Oxfordshire and Ewell in Surrey as a result of William's marriage into this propertied Carew family. Issue of Joan and William were as follows:

1. Henry (see E15).
2. William (see B15).
3. Richard (see C15). The line at Charlwood continued with Richard.
4. Thomas (–a1473) (probably), who evidently married Joan Huet and had a son Richard.
5. Nicholas (c1446–p1499) a priest of St. Mary Magdalen, Southwark.
6. John (–1501), said by one source, probably incorrectly, to be the eldest son, who died without issue in Banbury.
7. Stephen (c1441–1513) perhaps, a priest and confessor general of Syon Abbey in Middlesex.
8. Joan (–a1518), who married Richard Hunsterton (–1500).

C15 Richard Saunders (c1442–1480).

Richard married Agnes Courtenay (–1485), but sources differ on the number of their children. Richard was buried at Charlwood, and a memorial screen bearing his initials still stands in the Saunders Chapel there. Children of Agnes and Richard are understood to be:

1. Nicholas (see C16)
2. James (–1510)
3. William (see A16)
4. Richard (perhaps). No direct evidence has been found that Richard is a son of Richard, but beyond the similarity of names, a Richard Saunders of Charlwood is recorded as a merchant in 1530. Particular interest centers on this merchant, because his "mark" has been found. Merchant's marks are forerunners of today's trademarks, having been used to stamp interpretable symbols on goods for use by illiterate stevedores. Research has not revealed how these marks were read.

C16 Nicholas Saunders (c1475–1553).

Nicholas was of Charlwood and is buried there with his wife, Alys Hungate, who he married in 1504. She was the daughter of John Hungate of

Saxton, York, a merchant of London. The couple is memorialized in a Latin inscription on their vault at the Saunders Chapel. According to this inscription, they had ten children, although uncertainty exists about all their names:

1. Sir Thomas (see C16).

2. Henry (–p1549). Nothing is known of Henry except that he appears with Thomas Arundel, Knight, to have made a gift of property in 1549 to Henry Leigh (–1568), gentleman of the parish of St. Dunstan in Fleetstreet, London, as follows:

   "Henry Leigh was seized of a house called the Flower de Luce, now or late in the tenure of John Harward and now occupied by Anthony Hickman, lying in the said parish of St. Dunstan, to the late Monastery of the Blessed Mary Overey in County Surrey sometime belonging: which said house the said Henry (Leigh) purchased to him and his heirs forever of the gift of Thomas Arundel, Kt., and Henry Saunders, as by deed thereof made dated 24 February, 3 Edw. VI (1549) more fully appears."

   This record is not without significance, as Arundel is a name associated with Charlwood history, Flower de Luce is a name carried by one of Joseph Saunders's ships, and William Saunders of Ewell oversaw the dissolution of the Monastery of St. Mary Overey in 1539.

3. Richard (p1518–)

4. John (perhaps) (p1518–)

5. Margaret, who married John Poyntz (–1545) of Iron Acton, Gloucestershire. He previously married Catherine, daughter of Matthew Brown of Betchworth Castle, Kent. Margaret later married James Skynner.

6. Anne, who married Richard Browne, third son of Sir Matthew Browne of Betchworth and his wife, the daughter of Sir Richard Guildford, knight of the Garter. The children of Anne and Richard Browne were Edmond Browne and William Browne who had a son Richard. Richard Browne's sister married Sir Edward Bray.

7. A daughter, who seems to have married Robert Bathurst of Horsmanden, Kent, and become an ancestress of the Bathursts of Leclade, Gloucester.

8. A daughter, who may have married Sir Thomas White, described as a close friend and brother-in-law of Sir Thomas Saunders. Records of Sir Thomas White are contradictory and sketchy. He is alternately said to have been a clothier of Reading, Berkshire; a merchant tailor who founded the Merchant Taylor School while lord mayor of London; and to have founded St. John's College, Oxford.

9. A daughter, who married into the Goring family.

C17 Sir Thomas Saunders (c1505–1565).

An illustrious figure about whom much is written, Sir Thomas verified the coat of arms for Charlwood and vastly extended family properties. He married Alice, daughter of Sir Edmund and Elizabeth Gunter Walsingham, providing access to the royal court and some of England's most prominent families of the time. Connected to the Walsinghams by marriage were the Spencers, Boleyns, and Seymours, and Francis Walsingham was at a time the most influential figure in Henry VII's court. Sir Thomas was knighted in 1550. In the time of Edward VI, he served as remembrancer of the exchequer.

Katherine, sister of Alice Walsingham, married Sir Thomas Gresley and Thomas Saunders, uncle of Sir Thomas, had migrated to Derby in the train of Sir John Gresley. The children of Alice and Sir Thomas were as follows:

1. Edmund (see C18)

2. Margaret, who married Sir Thomas Goodyere. She inherited a tenement at Blackfriars from her father.

3. Elizabeth, of Flanchford in Reigate, Surrey.

4. Walsingham (–1587), of Charlwood, who entered the Inner Temple for the study of law in 1561.

5. Thomas White (c1545–) of Charlwood and London. He held the Manor of Creuses, long in family possession, which he sold in 1590

to a Surrey family named Weston and took up residence in Estcombe. Thomas White Saunders married —— Haynes, having issue:

1. William
2. Christian
3. Philip (or Philippa), who married into the Cooke family.
4. Thomas (c1570–), whose issue may have been:
    1. Edward, an important family figure in early Virginia (see Ac20).

C18 Edmund Saunders (1542–1615).

Edmund (occasionally referred to as Edward) was of Charlwood and entered the Inner Temple for the study of Law in 1561. He married Philippa, daughter of Sir Edward Gage, lieutenant of the Tower, and his wife Elizabeth, daughter of John Parker. The Gages were of Firle, Sussex, and were one of the wealthiest and most devoutly Roman Catholic families in that county. Issue of Edmund and Philippa were:

1. Thomas (see C19)

2. Anna, who married John Drewry of Essex.

3. Elizabeth

4. Dorothea, who married Sir John Throckmorton, but authorities disagree on who this person is. One possibility is Sir John Throckmorton of Lincoln, who came from a strongly Protestant branch of a generally staunch Catholic family, and was governor of Flushing in the Netherlands. Another is Sir John Throckmorton of Gloucester (–1586) whose niece married Sir Thomas Dale, governor of Virginia. From this line, we find the Throckmorton interests in Virginia.

5. Alice, who married Thomas Amyce of Essex who was a captain at Breda in the Netherlands.

6. Jane, who married Thomas Joscelyn of Horsley, Essex, he apparently the son of Henry Joscelyn and his wife Anne Torrell (Tyrrell) of Essex. An earlier Thomas Joscelyn of Essex had a daughter Anna who married Stephen Bagot. Their nephew Richard Bagot married Maria, daughter

of William Saunders of Welford, he of a different line of Saunders than described here.

7. Philip, who died at Breda. The Spanish captured Breda in 1581, which was recaptured by the Dutch in 1590. Philip had a daughter Justine (perhaps) who married William Palmer in 1621.

C19 Thomas Saunders (c1570–1623)

Thomas was of Charlwood and first married Elizabeth, daughter of Lancelot and Judith Randolph Bathurst, he an alderman of London. Judith's father was Bernard Randolph (–1583), brother of Sir Thomas Randolph (1523–1590), diplomat and relative of the Walsinghams. Their children were:

1. Elizabeth (c1600–1665). She married —— Bradshaw and is said to have sold Charlwood Manor to her nephew, Sir William Throckmorton. He may have been the son of Sir William Throckmorton, investor in the Virginia Company who on one occasion saw to the care of an ailing Indian girl at the Blackfriars in London. In view of the uncertain records involving Edmund and the sale of Charlwood, it seems possible that the manor was sold by this Elizabeth rather than by her aunt of the same name. The sale of Charlwood in 1664 ended nearly four hundred years of Saunders residence at this location.

2. Judith

3. Edmund (c1600–1661). Edmund held the Manor of Charlwood at his death in 1661, which property is said to have devolved to his sister Elizabeth, Edmund having no issue. But conflicting evidence allows that Edmund married Priscilla, daughter of the "worshipful" Edward Cropley, Esq., and his wife Priscilla, daughter of Thomas Moore, alderman deputy for Aldersgate Ward, and that they did have issue:

    1. Edward (1636–), Edmund's only son unless another was born after 1648.
    2. Elizabeth
    3. Priscilla

Thomas Saunders (C19) second married Elizabeth Hopkins, daughter of a Norfolk merchant, having issue:

4. Thomas
5. Anna (Anne)
6. Jane
7. Dorothea
8. Philippa, who married Rev. Thomas Mulcaster (1609–), whose father in 1616 purchased Shiremark in Charlwood. In 1625, Mulcaster sold Shiremark to Edmund Jordan, and the property was absorbed into the Manor of Charlwood.

BANBURY (B)

B15 William (c1438–1478).

William acquired property in Banbury, Oxfordshire, and probably married a daughter of John Olney. He was a wool merchant and port administrator at Southampton. His is buried at Our Lady of Banbury Church, which he endowed with bells. His issue:

1. William (–1493), who married Joan daughter of John Spencer of Hodenhall, Warwickshire, and with her had five daughters:

    1. Anne
    2. Isabel
    3. Joyce
    4. Alice
    5. Joan

2. Richard, who held the manor of Tullwick, inherited previously by his father, which he sold to Yate in 1503.

EWELL (E)

Henry Saunders of whom we write below was the first of the family to settle in Ewell. Ewell is a village in the north of Surrey not far from the ancestral home of Sanderstead and near Beddington, home of Henry's mother, Joan Carew Saunders. Ewell property came into the Saunders possession about 1450 following the Carew marriage, and Henry Saunders and his son William added greatly to family holdings during their lifetimes. At Ewell, two family properties are notable, although these no longer exist. The Saunders owned the Manor of Battailes until 1659, and the Manor of Fennelles was added to the Ewell family property through the marriage of Nicholas Saunders, son of Henry, to Joan Iwardby about 1510.

E15 Henry Saunders (c1456–1519).

The son of William and Joan Carew Saunders, Henry inherited the bulk
of his father's estate following the early death of his brother Richard of
Charlwood. Henry added to this property in his lifetime, providing a
foundation for family wealth for the Ewell line. Henry saw to the building
of Savoy Hospital and is buried there according to his wish. About 1485, he
married Joan Lepton (c1466–1519) of Kipwich, York, with issue:

1.   William (see E16)

2.   Nicholas (c1488–1549). The eldest son of Henry, Nicholas married
     about 1513 Joan Iwardby, daughter of John and Senchia Carew Iwardby
     (c1485–p1549) and widow of Sir John St. John. Issue of Nicholas and
     Joan were as follows:

     1.   Joan, who married Richard Bray (–1559), builder of Ewell Chapel,
          having nine children, some of whose issue may have emigrated to
          Virginia. Joan later married William Tyrell.
     2.   Ursula, who married —— Hungerford, a Wiltshire family once
          in possession of the Manor of Buckland.
     3.   Joyce, who married —— Woolcock, a marriage that may have
          inaugurated the close association of the Saunders and Woolcocks
          in Wales, following the line of Erasmus Saunders.

3.   Agnes (c1501–c1530), who married Richard Keyes in 1518, having sons
     Thomas (1523–1571) and Edward.

4.   Margaret (c1504–), who was underage in 1517 and unmarried in 1519.

5.   Cornelia (perhaps), who married Peter Gilles of Norfolk and
     London, merchant of Antwerp and friend and publisher of the
     famed Reformation humanist Erasmus, who visited England on three
     occasions.

E16 William Saunders (c1502–1571).

William was educated in the law and was treasurer of Calais, later a
receiver of taxes for Surrey and Sussex, a receiver for augmentation and
commissioner of the peace, and cofferer for Queen Mary. He became
knight of the Shire for Surrey and rose to the defense of the queen with

Sir Thomas Saunders during an armed uprising. About 1530, William married Joan Marston (–1539), widow of Nicholas Mynne of Norfolk. Her eldest child John Mynne (1519–) became the ward of William Saunders. Issue of Joan and William were:

1. Erasmus (see W17). Erasmus was the second son from William's first marriage.

2. Nicholas (see E17). The eldest son.

3. Mary (c1536–p1613). The eldest daughter, Mary married Nicholas Lussher (c1537–1566) about 1557, having five children.

4. Urithe (c1538–1600), who married John Palgrave (1531–1611) of Norfolk. A John Palgrave of Norfolk and London was a friend of the Reformation scholar Erasmus and an acquaintance of Peter Gilles of Antwerp, who married Cornelia Saunders.

Following the death of Joan Marston Saunders in 1539, William second married about 1544 Joan Gittons, widow of Thomas Gittons, citizen and vintner of London. Joan previously may have married into the Spelman family of Norfolk. She died in 1580 and was buried at Narborough, Norfolk. Sons from the Gittons marriage were named in her will. The children of William and Joan Gittons Saunders were as follows:

5. Frances (c1545–1622), who married Henry (1525–), son of Sir John Spelman of Narborough. Frances lived at Congham in Norfolk and her sons were Sir Henry Spelman (1562–1641), antiquary, who married Eleanor LeStrange of Sedgeford, and Erasmus Spelman (c1565–), father of Henry Spelman, a linguist in Virginia who was slain by the Indians.

6. Francis (c1545–1613). Francis inherited lands in Kent, animal rents in Puttenham purchased of the Lusshers, and the lease of Somerset in Ashsted. He lived at Congham and in his will, administered by his nephew Richard Saunders, he included the young Virginian Henry Spelman.

7. Catherine (c1547–p1613) who first married Edmund Carvell (Kervill) of Surrey about 1562, second married John Spelman in 1571, and third in 1582 married Miles Corbett, Kt. (–1607).

8.   Elizabeth (c1549–p1613), who had three marriages. She first married Roger Castell of Norfolk before 1570 and second William Forthe (Ford). Elizabeth third married Thomas Garneis (–1652).

E17 Nicholas Saunders (c1532–1587).

Nicholas was twice married, first in 1560 to Isabel Carew of Beddington, daughter of Sir Nicholas Carew, who in 1521 was Lieutenant of Calais and who later was a court favorite of Henry VIII. Carew later was executed for his part in a Catholic plot along with Courtenay. Isabel's sister married a Throckmorton, and a granddaughter of that marriage was Elizabeth (Bess) Throckmorton, wife of Sir Walter Raleigh (1552–1618). Issue of Isabel and Nicholas were the following:

1.   Nicholas (see E18)

2.   Henry (1570–1632). Henry entered the Inner Temple in 1589 for the study of Law and in 1611 received a bequest in the will of Sir Francis Carew. Henry is thought to have had seven children.

3.   Anne (c1565–), who in 1590 married Henry Whitney, Jr.

4.   Mary, who married —— Bevil.

5.   Jane, who in 1589 married Luke Ward, a sea captain and gentleman of London. She second married Sir Alexander Clifford.

6.   Frances, who died at an early age.

Nicholas second married Margaret, daughter of Nicholas Bostock of Newington, Surrey, whose wife was the widow of Justice Fisher. William Cecil, Lord Burghley, was executor for the estate of Nicholas in 1587 and oversaw the future of his son Nicholas.

E18 Sir Nicholas Saunders (c1565–p1613).

Nicholas was knighted in 1603, and he married Elizabeth, daughter and sole heir of Richard Blount of London. He acquired property in South Petherton, Somerset. Their issue:

1.   Carew, who died after christening.

2.   Dorothy (perhaps) (–a1613)

3.   Henry (c1605–a1679). Henry married Frances Watson in 1636 and
     sold Battailes in 1659.

4.   Dame Isabel (c1610–1655). In 1635, Dame Isabel married Sir Roger
     Twisden, antiquary, of Royden Hall, East Peckham, Kent. Sir Roger's
     parents were Sir William Twysden (–1629), investor in the Virginia
     Company, and Lady Ann Finch (–1638), Countess of Winchelsea. Lady
     Ann's brother Sir Heneage Finch was acquainted with grammarian
     John Hoskins, and his daughter Ann was Viscountess Conway (1631–
     1679), who published philosophical works. Isabel and Roger had six
     children, among whom were William, Roger, and Charles Twysden.

5.   Frances, who married Edward Wareham of Devonshire.

6.   Elizabeth, who married John Napier of Devonshire.

ASTON (A)

A16 William (c1475–)

William evidently inherited Courtenay property at Aston, Oxfordshire,
and raised his children there. He also held property in Surrey or returned
there in later years. His issue were the following:

1.   William (c1500–). Often called William of Aston, he married Elizabeth
     Mynne (see E11), who later joined her exiled daughters in Europe.
     Claim is sometimes made that William was high sheriff of Surrey, but
     an equal case can be made that this was his cousin William of Ewell.
     The issue of Elizabeth and William of Aston numbered twelve in all,
     including:

     1.   Dr. Nicholas (1527–1581). Often called the Infamous Traitor,
          Nicholas studied under Jesuit influence in Rome and travelled
          widely in Europe on church affairs. Nicholas wrote pro-Roman
          Catholic treatises and books on the schism between the English
          Church and Rome. In his time, Nicholas was regarded as the
          leading Roman Catholic figure of England. Nicholas died
          in Ireland a hunted man, having travelled there under papal

sanction to abet a Spanish plot to overthrow English authority there.

2. Margaret (c1530–1576), who about 1550 married Henry Pitts of Alton, Hampshire. Margaret was a nun of Syon Abbey and spent years in Belgium and France, eventually dying an exiled Syon sister in 1576.

3. Elizabeth (c1540–1607), married John Pitts of Oxford and became a nun of Syon Abbey. She spent years in exile and returned to England before 1580. In that year Elizabeth was brought to inquiry by the bishop of Winchester for possessing "lewd and forbidden" Jesuit documents and was jailed for five years. Elizabeth then left England again, living some years in exile in the Syon Abbey community, in France, Spain, and Portugal, where she died in 1607.

2. Thomas (see D17)

DERBYSHIRE (D)

The Saunders settlement in Derby dates to 1524 when Thomas Saunders migrated to Derby following his service in the War of Flanders, having served under John Gresley. Thomas settled at Lullington, Derbyshire probably having married into the Gresley family. Subsequently added to family holdings through marriages were the Manors of Caldwell and Little Ireton in Derbyshire, and Collingwood and Barton in Staffordshire.

D17 Thomas Saunders (c1500–1558)

Thomas evidently married into the Gresley family and seems to have acquired Lullington in Derbyshire.

D18 Thomas Saunders (1548–1627)

Of Little Ireton in Derby, Thomas in 1575 married Alice Toone of Lullington, having one daughter:

1. 1. Alice (c1576–)

He second married Marjory Collingwood, having four daughters and either five or eight sons:

2. Collingwood (1578–1653), who inherited the manors of Caldwell and Ireton, Derby. He married Elizabeth, daughter and sole heir of Edmund Sleigh, a London Vintner, of Little Ireton, with issue:

    1. Margaret (1608–1654), the first child, who married John Rowe of Windlehill, Derby, having daughters Elizabeth, Mary, and Margaret.
    2. Elizabeth, the second daughter, who married Thomas Frost of Derby.
    3. Alice, the third daughter, who married Adam Chapman of London.
    4. Sir Thomas (1610–1695), known as the celebrated Roundhead for his role in the Parliamentary cause under Cromwell. He married Elizabeth, daughter of Henry Goring of Kingston, Stafford, with issue:

        1. Samuel (1641–1688), who thrice married.
        2. Thomas
        3. Isaac
        4. Elizabeth
        5. Mary
        6. Tryphena, who first married Richard Hill and second married John Jekyll (1611–1690) of London.

    5. Daniel (1620–), the second son, of Branston, Stafford, who married Mary, daughter of Robert Clark of Burton-on-Trent.
    6. Joseph (1626–1691), the third son, of Barton-under-Needwood, Stafford, who married Katherine, daughter of Humphrey Baker of Bishton, Stafford, widow of John Clark of Burton-on-Trent. Katherine died in 1658, and Joseph second married Mary, daughter of Samuel More of Linley, Shropshire.
    7. Henry, the fourth son, who married Isabel, daughter of Francis Sherman of London and Stapenhill, Derbyshire.
    8. Edmund
    9. John

3. Henry (1592–1666). Major Henry Saunders was a silkman of London
   and at one point Captain of the Cripplegate Ward Company. He
   married Susanna, daughter of Christopher Alleston, having issue:

   1. Thomas, who was a factor for the East India Company and who
      died at Bantum.
   2. Daniel (1620–), a silkman who died at Stockerton.
   3. Henry, a silkman of London.
   4. George, who settled in New England.
   5. Christopher, who settled in New England.
   6. Susanna, who thrice married, to Robert Mellor, Simon Ash, and
      Thomas Woodcock.

4. Peter, who was Clerk in the Enrollment Office.

5. Mary, who married Henry Gilbert, rector of Clifton, Camville, Stafford.

6. Frances, who married Thomas Mold, rector of Appleby, Leicester.

7. Katherine, who married John Bludworth of London.

8. Alice, who was baptized in 1576 and who married Richard Sleigh, a
   vintner of London who apprenticed Alice's brother Joseph.

9. Joseph (c1598–p1640), who was a vintner of London. He apprenticed
   under Richard Sleigh and received free admission to the Vintner
   Company in 1623. Joseph owned two ships, the *Flower de Luce* and the
   Bonny Bess, which regularly traveled to Virginia and Rotterdam during
   the 1630s. The *Flower de Luce* may have been named after a property
   once in the hands of Henry Saunders of Charlwood. Joseph married
   Anne, daughter of George Smyth of Micham, Surrey, and formed
   a partnership with William Smith for a warehouse at Accomack in
   Virginia. Roger Saunders, mariner, gentleman, and Virginia burgess,
   and Edward Saunders were also involved in this business venture. Anne
   and Joseph reportedly had a son Joseph (–1634) who died without
   issue, and Joseph is said to have married second into the Grindall
   family of Micham, Surrey.

WALES (W)

The presence of the Saunders family in Wales may date from the thirteenth and fourteenth centuries. Records indicate that the Saunders "originally from Surrey" were established in Wales by 1527. Erasmus Saunders is the first of the line described here to have established permanent domicile in Wales. He arrived in Wales about 1568 and lived in Pembrokeshire, acquiring a variety of properties, many former Barrett holdings, in his lifetime, and passing these on to the family line now known as the Saunders of Pentre.

W17 Erasmus Saunders (c1534–1603)

Erasmus is the first known of the line described here to have established permanent residence in Wales. He entered Oxford University about 1556 and completed the study of Law by 1563, when he took up professional life in London. In early records, Erasmus is described as "of London, gentleman." Erasmus traveled to Wales about 1568 as an appointed justice of the peace and was bailiff of Tenby, Pembrokeshire, in 1572. He was mayor of Tenby in 1577, and in that position was accused of collusion with Welsh pirates. He was listed in Recusant Roles, and for this Erasmus was arrested several times. He first married in London about 1563, but the name of his wife is not known. She died early, but they had a son:

1. Richard (1565–p1613), who was named executor of the will of Francis Saunders and who inherited family properties in Congham, Norfolk, Cliff in Kent, and at Ewell in Surrey.

Erasmus second married Jenet (c1550–1628), daughter of William Barrett and Ann, daughter of Thomas Lougher of Tenby, having issue:

2. Nicholas (c1571–1636) was born at Ewell and was the first son of Erasmus and Jenet. Later of Newton in the parish of Laugharne, Nicholas married Mary Massey, with issue:

    1. Francis (–c1630)
    2. Mary, who married Lewis Eaton of Llanddowror.
    3. Elizabeth, who married Thomas Davies of Newton.
    4. Temperance, who married James, son of Jason Lewis.
    5. Catherine, who married Jenkin, son of Rev. Rowland Lewis.

3. William (c1573–p1635). William married Florence Wlcot (as recorded, probably Woolcock) and resided at Pendine, Carmarthenshire. He inherited a variety of former Barrett properties in southwestern Wales. Their issue:

  1. Erasmus, who went to England.
  2. Henry, who went to England.
  3. Hugh
  4. Jane, the eldest daughter, who married Devereux Hammond of Tenby.
  5. Florence, the second daughter, who married Thomas Price of Pendine.
  6. William (c1600–1668). The second son, William married Jane Barrett (–1683) who previously had married —— Stevens. The issue of Jane and William were the following:

     1. William, who married Lettice Thomas of Eglwyscymmin.
     2. Charles, who married Sarah Thomas of Laugharne.
     3. Tobias (–1719) of Cilhedyn, Pembrokeshire, who married Lettice Phillips of Penboyr, Carmarthenshire.
     4. Jane
     5. John. It is said that John "went to travel."

4. Erasmus (c1574–1612)

5. John (c1576–1612), who was bailiff of Tenby in 1607. He may have had a son Thomas, whose guardian in childhood following his father's death was Thomas Griffiths.

6. Philip (c1578–c1625) (see W17).

7. Devereux (c1580–).

8. Elizabeth (1582–1655), who married Harry Davis.

9. Henry (c1584–1636), gentleman and bailiff of Tenby, who died without issue in Pendine, Carmarthenshire.

10. Ann (c1586–1613), of Eglwyscymmin, Carmarthenshire.

11. Jane (c1588–1613), who married Robert Fulford.

W18 Philip (c1578–c1625).

Philip is referred to as "of Pembroke, gentleman." Philip first married Jane Adams in 1603, she the daughter of Henry Adams and relict of John Knethell of Castlemartin in Pembrokeshire. The Adams owned a twelve-ton boat *Anne* and Nicholas Adams, Jane's uncle, was vice admiral for Pembroke. In later years, Philip evidently worked in England, where he was referred to as "Philip Saunders, mariner, of Abbots Leigh, Somerset." Issue of Thomas and Jane were the following:

1. Thomas (see G19).

2. Thomasine, who married Thomas Owen.

3. John (perhaps).

Between 1612 and 1615, Philip second married Alice, daughter of John Edwards of Tenby. Alice had previously married Howell Philpin and Saunders Barrett (–1611). No issue from this marriage are known to exist.

GLOUCESTERSHIRE (G)

Thomas Saunders, perhaps with a brother John, is the first of the line of Erasmus Saunders of Wales to live in Gloucestershire. Following an apprenticeship in Bristol, Thomas Saunders, son of Philip of Wales, took up residence in Wotton-under-Edge, marrying there in 1629, and he resided principally in Gloucestershire until his death shortly before 1653. Thomas may have died in Virginia where he worked during the 1640s. Nathaniel Saunders, son of this Thomas, moved from Berkeley, Gloucestershire to Bristol as a young man apprenticed in 1653 to Thomas Stratton, merchant and mariner, and later was master of the *Golden Lion*, plying trade between Bristol and the Caribbean. Numerous other family members remained in Tetbury and Wotton-under-Edge.

G19 Thomas Saunders (c1607–a1653).

Thomas arrived in Wotton-under-Edge in the late 1620s, following a period of apprenticeship in Bristol, and married Elizabeth, daughter of Anthony Webb, in 1629 in nearby Kingswood. In 1640, he second married Marjory Lewis (née Webb) in Tetbury, she the sister of Gyles Webb of Virginia. Thomas worked in Virginia during the 1640s, acquiring land there that remained in the family and, in his later years, was a merchant in Berkeley,

Gloucestershire, dying before 1653. The issue of Elizabeth and Thomas were as follows:

1. Nathaniel (see G20).

2. Thomas (c1632–1679), of Virginia and Barbados, married Elizabeth —— and had a son John.

3. Sarah, married John Clarkson (–p1682) and lived in St. Philip's Parish, Barbados, having daughters Alice and Elizabeth.

4. Mary, married John Hutchinson and lived in St. Philip's Parish, Barbados.

5. Samuel (1636–1686). Samuel was a mercer of Tetbury and married Catherine —— (–1682). He purchased land to form the estate of Upton Grove in 1680 and 1686. Known issue of Catherine and Samuel were as follows:

    1. Catherine (–1672).
    2. Margaret (1677–1750), who married —— White.
    3. Catherine (–1679).
    4. Samuel (1675–1746), a mercer of Upton Grove who passed this estate to his son Samuel (–1787). The latter Samuel left Upton Grove to Thomas Saunders (–1819), probably his nephew and heir, and finally the property was sold in 1849 by Thomas's son, Samuel Albin Saunders.

G20 Nathaniel Saunders (1634–1695)

Following his father Thomas Saunders's death, Nathaniel Saunders was apprenticed in 1653 to Thomas Stratton of Bristol. He became master of the *Golden Lion*, sailing that ship to Barbados at least three times during the 1670s. Later he was commander of the Globe, sailing for the London firm of Micajah Perry.

In 1658, Nathaniel sold a Barbados indenture to William Tukey, a former Virginian and relative of John Tukey, who held the Virginia headrights of John and Philip Saunders. Nathaniel traveled to Virginia by 1689 and managed his father's land in King and Queen County that his son Nathaniel eventually settled by 1702. In 1665, Nathaniel married Mary

Stratton (–1700), she the daughter of Thomas Stratton and his wife Mary, to whom Nathaniel was originally apprenticed, at St. Michael's Church in Bristol, with known issue:

1.   1. Nathaniel (see KQ21).

2. Mary (1666–1668).

3. Thomas (1668–1671).

4. Nathaniel (c1670–1672).

5. Thomas (1672–1708). Thomas traveled to Virginia by 1689, married Jane Blanton, and died there in 1708.

6. A son, name unknown (1674/5–).

7. Mary (1677–1682).

8. Elizabeth (1679–). In 1701 and again in 1704, the headright for Elizabeth Sanders was claimed by James Boughan of Essex County, Virginia.

9. Alban (1682–).

NEW WORLD LINEAGE
ACCOMACK (Ac)

Settlement at Accomack was among the earliest permanent English colonizations in Virginia. Sanders family members established a warehouse and trading connections at Accomack that facilitated additional family migration. A key early Virginian was Edward Saunders who arrived in Virginia in 1619 and witnessed the troubled early years of the colony. His sons eventually followed him to Virginia and took up residence in Northumberland County in the 1650s and afterward.

Ac20 Edward Sanders (1595–1639)

Edward Sanders was originally of Charlwood. He arrived in Virginia about 1619 and lived through the Massacre of 1622. In 1623, he was in London attesting to conditions in the colony described in the document, "The Unmasked Face of our Colony in Virginia as it was in the Winter of the

Year 1622." Edward returned to Virginia in 1635 on the *Safety* with his two underage sons, Thomas, age thirteen, and Edward, age nine. In 1637, Edward shipped goods on the *Flower de Luce*, a ship owned by his relative, London merchant and vintner Joseph Sanders. Edward died at sea in a 1639 Atlantic crossing on one of Joseph Saunders' ships. The guardianship of his sons, still underage, was assumed by John Pettit, a vintner, a chirurgeon, and a British alien, who was to have an important influence on the lives of Edward's sons. Edward's wife is unknown, but his children were the following:

1.　A daughter, who Edward transported to New England in the 1630s.

2.　Thomas (1622–1681). Following the death of his father, Thomas must have been taken to England since he was in 1648 granted free admission to the London Vintner Company under the sponsorship of John Pettit. About this same year, he married Grace, the daughter of Thomas Anscombe of Merstham in Surrey and returned to Virginia with Grace in 1652. Grace must have died later in that same decade because about 1661, Thomas married the widow of Thomas Dunkerton, who had lived near Thomas's brother Edward in Northumberland County. There is considerable uncertainty about Thomas's children, but these are thought to be:

    1.　Thomas (c1650–1681), whose headrights are found consistently in conjunction with John Richardson. Thomas is thought to be the father of two sons:

        1.　Thomas (c1678–), who sold land in Stafford County at Acquia Creek in 1698.
        2.　William (c1680–1727), who married into the Remy family of Westmoreland County.

    2.　Edward (c1665–c1705) (perhaps), whose issue were:

        1.　John
        2.　Thomas, who moved to Maryland in 1709
        3.　Edward, Jr. (–1729) of Northumberland County

    3.　William (c1665–1704) (perhaps), who may have lived in Maryland.

4. John (c1665–) (perhaps), who had a son William (1699–) and who may have lived in Maryland.

5. Another son, who may have lived in Maryland.

3. Dr. Edward (1625–1672). Edward Sanders, chirurgeon, returned to Virginia at about age thirty in 1655 and acquired a large land holding in Northumberland County. He married Mary Webb Hudnall, daughter of Gyles Webb. Edward authored his Will in 1669, which was proved in 1672. His wife Mary, who thereafter married William Thomas, was named guardian of their children, who were the following:

1. Edward (1663–1736). He lived in St. Stephen's Parish and is frequently referred to in the Northumberland County records as Captain Edward. In 1702, he was named coroner of that county and is said to have married Elizabeth ——. Of the many records for Captain Edward, not one appears to shed light on this marriage or children. Interestingly, one Lancelot Bathurst was named co-coroner of the county during Edward's tenure in that position. A Charlwood relative, Thomas Saunders, had in about the year 1600 married a daughter of Lancelot Bathurst, alderman of London.

2. Ebenezer (1661–1693) of Northumberland County. Records conflict as to whether he married Priscilla Presley or Elizabeth Phillips, daughter of Edward Phillips, or both. His issue:

    1. Elizabeth (1686–), who about 1702 first married Samuel Downing and second married Charles Nelms. Records for offspring have not been found.

    2. Edward (1686–p1744), who married Winifred Stevens and perhaps lived in St. Stephens Parish by 1720. In later years, he lived in Wicocomico Parish along the Northumberland-Lancaster County boundary. Their issue, perhaps subject to some debate, were as follows:

        1. Thomas, of Stafford County and later Charles County, Maryland, who married Judith ——.
        2. John, of Stafford County
        3. William (1718–1779), whose will is extant.
        4. Edward (1723–), whose descendants are known.

KING AND QUEEN (KQ)

For the family of Thomas Saunders, settlement was generally confined to the area of old Rappahannock County, on both the north and south sides of the Rappahannock River. For this part of the family, permanent settlement can be dated to the late 1650s, when John and Philip Sanders are known to have been in the colony. Both John and Philip Sanders lived originally on the south side of the Rappahannock in what was later to become Essex County, Philip taking up his first claim in 1665. At about the same time, Hugh Sanders arrived with his family to take up lands in Isle of Wight County, claiming his land in 1664, and another more distant relative John arrived about 1669.

Nathaniel Sanders appears in King and Queen County records of 1702, following his father and brother's visit in 1689 and 1690. In their lifetimes and the generation that followed, many of these family members deserted the Virginia Tidewater for lands in the Virginia interior.

KQ21 Nathaniel Sanders (1681–1731)

Nathaniel Sanders arrived in King and Queen County before 1700 and acquired two hundred acres of land in King and Queen County before 1704. Of Planter status, Nathaniel engaged in tobacco trade, owned an ordinary, and bought and sold a variety of properties in his lifetime. He acquired two thousand six hundred acres of New Land in Spotsylvania County in 1728 and dispersed all his holdings to his sons and a Humphrey Bate through his Will of 1731. About 1703, he married ——, daughter of Ann and Thomas Watkins of Essex County, with known issue:

1. Hugh (see KQ22).

2. Thomas, who lived in Spotsylvania County and mortgaged his possessions to open a racetrack near Port Royal in his later years.

3. John, probably John Wynell Sanders, who is said by some to be the eldest son. He served at sea as master of trading ships and lived later in Fauquier County, Virginia. His known issue:

    1. John
    2. James
    3. Nathaniel
    4. Robert, of Fauquier County, Virginia
    5. Polly, who married Adams Jones and moved to South Carolina.

4. Philip, who apparently was not named in Nathaniel's will of 1731 but who otherwise is cited as a son of Nathaniel. In some records, he is referred to as of King and Queen County, and he is found in Caroline County records through the 1760s. He married Mary ——, with known issue:

    1. Frances (1740–1832), who married John Sale in 1762 and died in Amherst County.
    2. Clara, who before 1772 married Thomas Sale, brother of John, and died in Amherst County.
    3. Mary, who may have resided in Essex County in 1750.

5. Nathaniel, who inherited four hundred acres of Spotsylvania County land but lost this for failure to maintain the property, probably because he migrated to North Carolina. He owned land in Northampton County, North Carolina and married Rosanna, daughter of Robert and Abigail (Lewis) Davis. A known son is Thomas William Maximilian Sanders.

6. Sally, who married Robert Coleman and had nine daughters and a son.

7. Fanny, who married Daniel Brown and had land in Culpeper County, Virginia, near property purchased by her brother Hugh.

KQ22 Hugh Sanders (1709–1781)

Of Spotsylvania County, Hugh inherited the bulk of his father's estate and in 1737 married Catherine Hoskins (c1719–p1793), daughter of Samuel and Mary Brereton Hoskins and descendant of the "ancient planter" Bartholomew Hoskins who arrived in Virginia about 1616. Their issue:

1. Nathaniel (see K23)

2. John (1738–1805), who married Jane Craig about 1762. John was an original settler of Ghent, Kentucky. Their issue:

    1. Polly (1763–), who married Joseph Bledsoe, having six children.
    2. Betty (1765–), who married James Smith, having eight children.
    3. Lydia (1768–), who married Hugh Sanders Gatewood, having at least two children.

4. Nathaniel (1771–), who married Sally Sanders, his cousin, daughter of Nathaniel and Sally (K18.0), with issue:

    1. Lewis (1796–), who married Margaret Price.
    2. Bennett
    3. Barizilla, who died at age sixteen.
    4. Samuel
    5. Nathaniel

5. John (1774–), who married Nancy Samuel, having one son, Samuel (1801–1873), who married Felicie Gex.

6. Samuel (1777–), who married Nancy Smith in 1804, with no children.

7. Lewis (1781–1861), married first Anne Nicholas in 1807 and second Adelaide Dumesnil in 1843. With Anne, Lewis resided at Grass Hills, Carroll County, Kentucky, and had issue:

    1. Mary Nicholas (1808–1841), who married Samuel Smith.
    2. John (1810–1858), who married Maria Dallas Wilkins.
    3. George Nicholas (c1812–1873), who married Anna J. Reid.
    4. John Barlett (1814–1814)
    5. James Weir (1815–1816)
    6. Samuel (1817–1836)
    7. Margaretta Galbraith (1819–1862), who married W. B. Lindsay.
    8. Joseph Hawkins (1824–1892), who married Mary Eliza Lathrop.
    9. Jane Craig (1827–1831)

8. Catherine (1784–), who died young.

3. Robert (1753–1805), who settled in Georgetown, Kentucky, and married Nancy Wharton, with issue:

    1. Tolliver, who never married.
    2. Valentine Long Wharton, who never married.
    3. Thomas Livingston, who never married.
    4. Benjamin Wharton, who married —— Flumoy.
    5. Lucy, who died young.

6. Nancy, who married Edward B. Bartlett.
7. Walter, who married Louise Flumoy.

4. Charles, who settled on the Ohio River near McCool's Creek in Gallatin County, Kentucky and married Nancy Blunt, with issue:

1. Hugh, who never married.
2. Abner, who never married.
3. Betsy, who married John Sanders Bledsoe.
4. Gabriel Madison, who never married.
5. John Lewis, who married Sally Remy (Ramey).
6. Sally, who married Jacob Shank.
7. Nancy, who married William Russell.
8. Robert, who never married.
9. Charles, who married —— Whitehead.

5. Sally, who married Peter Gatewood.
6. Elizabeth, who married Lewis Craig.
7. Molly, who married Francis W. Lea.
8. Mildred (Millie), who married James Jones.
9. Ann, who married John Pattie.
10. Catherine, who in 1782 married Henry (Harry) Brock.
11. Abigail, who married Peter Hargate.
12. Rosie, who married Constant Perkins and Charles Hammond.

KENTUCKY (K)

The decision to leave Virginia for Kentucky involved the wife and children of Hugh Sanders and was motivated largely by a desire for religious freedom, although opportunities for land acquisition were also important. Hugh is said by some, perhaps incorrectly, to have been of the Church of England, but other family members were devoutly Baptist. Although Hugh's will left his family and heirs amply cared for with Virginia lands, his family left Virginia six months after Hugh's death, some joining a Baptist group in the migration. Several family members set out with a large group of Baptist migrants from Craig's church in Spotsylvania County in the spring of 1782 in what has been called the "Traveling Church." The odyssey is well chronicled. By the summer of 1782 the group had arrived at Bryant's Station near Lexington and in August endured an Indian attack that claimed the life of one family member.

The sons of Hugh Sanders settled at different locations—Robert at Georgetown on Scott County, where he prospered as a racetrack and tavern owner; John at Ghent in Gallatin County, where he is named as an original settler; and Charles near John, on a farm at McCool's Creek in Gallatin County. The other son, Nathaniel, resided in frontier Virginia at an early age and purchased six thousand acres of land on Floyd's Fork near Louisville during the Revolution. He served in the Revolutionary War and later settled at the Forks of Elkhorn near Frankfort, Kentucky, assuming responsibilities for road building and settler safety. He later purchased substantial acreage on Eagle Creek in Gallatin County and moved to that location about 1804. His family and descendants remained at this location, now known as Sanders, Kentucky, until the twentieth century.

K23 Nathaniel Sanders (1741–1826).

A character of somewhat legendary proportions, Nathaniel is said to have run away from home at an early age and lived with the Indians for seven years, in adulthood to have been an Indian spy and Revolutionary War soldier, witnessing the surrender of Cornwallis at Yorktown in 1781. In Kentucky, he took some responsibility for settler safety, was named a commissioner raising funds for the first state capitol, was responsible for seeing to the building of a road from Frankfort to Cincinnati, and helped establish a Baptist church. In later years, he moved with his family to Gallatin County. Local legend claims he is the father of the famed Mexican general Santa Ana who attacked the Alamo in Texas, a claim given some credence by published reports and historical events surrounding Santa Ana's capture and removal to Kentucky.

Nathaniel with his brothers are the first of the line described here to have lived permanently in Kentucky. In 1776, he married Sallie, daughter of James Pattie of Caroline County, Virginia, having issue:

1.   Robert (see K24)

2.   Catherine (1779–), who married Thomas O'Neal.

3.   Hugh (1780–1832 or 1844), who married Nancy Moxley.

4.   Sally, who married Nathaniel Sanders, son of her uncle John, having eight children.

5. James (–1834), who married Elizabeth Moxley, having four children.

6. John (1789–), who married Sally Moxley.

7. Nathaniel (1791–1840), who married Mary (Polly) Craigmile.

8. George Washington (1798–), who first married Caty (Kitty) O'Neal, his niece (K18), and second married Eleanor Hixon, having four children. The town of Sanders, Kentucky is named in his memory.

K24 Robert Sanders (1794–1850)

In 1815, Robert of Gallatin County married Nancy Blanton (–1837) of New Liberty, Kentucky. Their known issue:

1. Elizabeth Craig, referred to as Aunt Craig, married Frank Sandford, who administered the estate of Robert Sanders in 1850.

2. John (c1823–), who died by suicide.

3. Robert L. (c1828–c1864), who was killed in an ambush returning from the Civil War.

4. Pritchard M. (c1831–c1908), who married Mary Jett.

5. Anna B. (1835–1911), who married her cousin Edward J. Sanders (–1910), son of Nathaniel (K18.7). Anna died near Hunniwell, Kansas and Edward died at the Peewee Valley Confederate Home near Louisville, Kentucky.

6. Agnes (1837–), who died of cholera.

    In 1839, Robert second married Mary (Polly) Lindsay, she the widow of Matthew Thompson (1795–1835) whom she had married in Dearborn County, Indiana in 1831. From her first marriage there were two children, Margaret and Nicholas. The issue of Robert and Mary (Polly) were:

7. Elijah Lawson (see K25)

8. Sarah Ella (c1841–)

Leaving The Land

9. Mary (1843–1922), who in 1861 married Solomon McDanell.

10. Martha Ann (1843–1864), who married William Wheatly.

11. William O. (1848–)

K25 Elijah Lawson Sanders (1845–1925)

Elijah was of Sanders, Kentucky, and in 1867 married Mary (Molly) Mullen, with issue:

1. Arthur Lee (see K26)

2. Ella (1868–)

3. Walter (1869–), who worked on the Ohio River.

4. Ernest

5. Everett Brown

6. Omar Thomas

7. Gertrude (1889–1966), of Cincinnati, Ohio. In 1909, she married V. Veith (1888–1960) and again married in 1922 to E. Bruns (1891–1975). Issue of the Veith marriage was:

    1. Anna Dorothy (1910–2001), who in 1928 married J. Schwertman, with issue:

        1. Dolores Gertrude (1929–), who in 1950 married W. Lemming (1923–1976).
        2. John (1932–1932)
        3. JoAnn Dorothy (1934–), who in 1956 married R. Book (1934–).

K26 Arthur Lee Sanders (1872–1957).

Born in Sanders, Kentucky, Arthur worked in Cincinnati as a streetcar motorman as a young man. He returned to Newport and in 1924 moved to Ft. Thomas, Kentucky. In 1897, he married Henrietta (1875–1968), daughter of Eugene Kroth, with issue:

1. Ralph Lee (see K26)
2. Eugenie (1900–1917)

K27 Ralph Lee Sanders (1906–1987)

Born in Cincinnati, Ohio, Ralph was raised in Newport, lived later in Ft. Thomas, Kentucky, and moved to Erie, Pennsylvania, following his marriage in 1937. He married Dorothy (1913–1999), daughter of William and Lauretta Grizzel Poate of Newport. Their children:

1. Margaret Lee (1938–), who married Charles Van der Heide of California, with issue:

    1. Jennifer Carole (1965–), who in 2003 married Alexander Escobar of La Dorada, Caldas, Colombia, with issue:

        1. Zara Meg (2004–)

    2. David Charles (1967–), who in 1995 married Lori Annette Putnam of Rochester, Minnesota, with issue:

        1. Emma Elizabeth (1997–)
        2. Claire Margaret (2000–)
        3. Mia Frances (2002–)

    3. Rebecca Anna (1971–), who in 1998 married Robert Galuska of Antigo, Wisconsin, with issue:

        1. James Charles (2006–).
        2. Gia Rose (2009–).

2. Carole Jean (1939–), of Erie, Pennsylvania and Ft. Thomas, Kentucky.

3. Ralph Allan (1941–), who in 1976 married Nancy, daughter of Harold and Florence Wertman Gustin, of Elmira and Manlius, New York, whose children from a previous marriage are as follows:

1. Shawn Wayne Hammond (1967–), who in 1996 married Terri Ann Hillock (1970–) of Farwell, Texas, whose child from a previous marriage, later adopted by Shawn, is as follows:
   1. Jeremi David (1992–)

   Issue of Shawn and Terri are the following:

   2. Taylar Paige (1997–)
   3. Hunter Andrew (2000–)
   4. Rylee Mackenzie (2002–)

2. Dawn Lee Hammond (1968–), who in 2003 married Martin, son of Otto and Margaret Sammet, of Lowenstein, Germany, with issue:

   1. Ben August (2006–)

Issue of Nancy and Ralph are the following:

3. Lucas Lee Sanders (1979–), who in 2011 married Julia Wheeler.
4. Matthew William Sanders (1981–).

APPENDIX II

RECORDS

The following records for Sanders and a few other families have not been published previously. They are taken from sources in the western part of England—from Bristol, Somerset, and Gloucestershire—mainly for the late seventeenth century. This area was a key source area for migrants to the new world at that time.

BRISTOL
St. Augustine, Bristol, Baptism, Marriage & Burial Register
1635–1700:

1674/5 Jan 21 (blank) s/o Nathaniell/Mary SANDERS, Baptized
1677 Aug 11 Mary d/o Nathaniell/Mary SANDERS, Baptized
1678/9 Feb 06 Elizabeth d/p Nathaniell/Mary SANDERS, Baptized
1681 Mary 12 Nathaniell S/O Nathaniell/MARY Sanders, Baptized
1682 Aug 07 Allban s/o Nathaniell/Mary SANDERS, Baptized

St. Augustine, Bristol, Appendices to above register
List of Sidemen & Waywardens 1680–1700:

1681–168-2 Nathaniell SANDERS – Sideman

List of Contributors towards the building of St. Pauls Cathedral, London:

1678 Oct 29 Mr. Nathaniell SAUNDERS/-(one shilling)

Moneys collected for French Protestants June 21–24, 1686:
Nathaniel SANDERS 1/ - (one shilling)

St. Nicholas, Bristol, Baptism register 1665–1675
No SANDERS or SAUNDERS entries
St. Nicholas, Bristol, Baptism register 1630–1645
No SANDERS/SAUNDERS or STRATTON
St. Nicholas, Bristol, Marriage register 1665–1667
No Nathaniel SANDERS & Mary STRATTON
St. Michael, Bristol, Baptism register 1665–1690
1666 May 01 Mary d/o Richard/Mary SANDERS
1666 MAY 01 Mary D/O Nathaniel/Mary SANDERS
1667/8 Jan 09 Joseph s/o Thomas/Ellinor SANDERS
1668 Aug 18 Richard s/o Richard/Sarah SANDERS
1668 NOV 1 Thomas s/o Nathaniel/Mary SANDERS
1671 May 28 John s/o Richard/Sarah SANDERS
1672 Nov 29 Thomas s/o Thomas/Mellin SANDERS
1672 DEC 19 Thomas s/o Nathaniel/Mary SANDERS
1673 OCT 05 William s/o Richard/Sarah SANDERS

St. Michael, Bristol, Marriage register 1665–1667
No entry for Nathaniel SANDERS & Mary STRETTON
St. Michael, Bristol, Burial register 1665–1700
1667/8 Mar 05 Mary d/o Nathaniel/Mary SANDERS
16700/1 Feb 20 Mary d/o Thomas/Elinor SANDEERS
1671/2 Jan 15 Thomas s/o Nathaniel SAUNDERS
1671/2 Mar 01 Nathaniel s/o Nathaniel SANDERS
1674 June 30 Thomas s/o Thomas SANDERS
1674/5 Feb 26 Thomas s/o Thomas SANDERS
1676 Dec 4 Sarah wife of Richard SAUNDERS
1676 Dec 20 Sarah wife of Thomas SAUNDERS
1676 Dec 20 Richard SAUNDERS
1676 Dec 22 William s/o Richard SAUNDERS
1677 Jul 21 Nathaniel s/o Thomas SANDERS
1678 Jul 31 Rebecca SANDERS
1682 May 18 Mary d/o Nathaniel SAUNDERS
1693/4 Feb 14 Matthew SANDERS
1695/6 Jan 24 Nathaniel SAUNDERS
1700 Apr 19 Mary SAUNDERS

St. Michael the Archangel, Bristol City

Earliest register 1653 – a note in 17[th]seventeenth century
hand says "Register 1637–1650 lost"

St. James, Bristol, Marriage register1665–1667
No Nathaniel SANDERS & Mary STRATTON

Bristol Marriage Licence Bonds 1637–1700
1662 Apr 23 William BALDWIN, Castle, Bristol, gent & Mary THRUPP,
St. Stephen, Bristol Bondsman: Thomas CHOCKE, Keynsham, Somerset,
gent. Marriage at St. Stephen

1665 APRIL 19 NATHANIEL Saunders, St. Nicholas,
Bristol, sailor, & Mary STRATTON, St. Nicholas,
Bristol, Bondsman: Thomas STRATTON, Bristol, sailor,
marriage to take place at St. Michael, Bristol
1687 Nov 13 Robert EDWARDS, Bristol, draper, & Joyce STRATTON,
St. Augustine, Bristol. Bondsman: Thomas CLARKE, Bristol, gent.
Marriage at St. Augustine.
Bristol Burgess books 627–1628; 1652–1662

1628 June 23 Thomas SAUNDERS mariner is admitted to the Liberties of
City, for that he was the Apprentice of William ROACH

1662 August 08 Nathaniel SANDERS mariner is admitted to the liberties of the
City, for that he was the apprentice of Thomas STRATTON, a freeman.

Bristol Apprentice registers 1616–1624

1616 May 15 Thomas w/o Thomas SAUNDERS late of Bristol, embroiderer
deceased, bound Apprentice to John SHARPE of Bristol, barber surgeon &
Susanna his wife, for 8 years

1620/1 Jan 20 Thomas s/o Philip SAUNDERS mariner of Abbots Leigh,
Somerset, bound Apprentice to John MINE of Bristol mariner & Martha his
wife, for 7 years. His father bound in L20 for his son's service and
truth.

Bristol Apprentice books 1650–1655

1649/50 Jan 29 William NICHOLAS s/o William NICHOLAS of Berkeley, Co.
Glos yeoman, bound apprentice to Thomas STRATTON of Bristol mariner &
Joan his wife, for 7 years.

1653 May 12 Robert NICHOLAS s/o William NICHOLAS of Clapton* Co.Glos
husbandman and Nathaniel SANDERS s/o Thomas SANDEERS of Berkeley

in the County aforesaid merchant deceased, bound apprentice to Thomas STRATTON mariner & Joan his wife, for 7 years. (*Clapton in Upper Berkeley Hundred)

Genealogical Abstract of Will of Thomas STRETTON of Bristol, mariner

"To my eldest son Thomas STRETTON my messuage called the Grange in Olveston parish, Co.Glos... to my son William STRETTON . . . to my son John STRETTON . . . to my daughter Mary SAUNDERS . . . to my daughter Joyce EDWARDS, Wife of (blank) EDWARDS of Sudbury, Co.Glos., yeoman . . . William, John and Richard sons of Mary daughter of my said son Thomas STRETTON . . . to my said two daughters Mary SAUNDERS and Joyce EDWARDS my messuage called the Glass House in Redcliff Street, St. Mary Redcliff parish, Bristol . . . to my daughter Mary SAUNDERS one silver beaker . . . my daughter in law Elizabeth STRETTON, wife of my son William STRETTON . . . to the Churchwardens & overseers of the Poor of St. Michael parish, Bristol f25 (various other legacies to the Poor follow) . . ."

Will made 1687 Dec 24. Signed by Testator, witnesses Peter ROSEWELL, Azariah WODHAM, Edward HORTON, Proved BRISTOL 1690 Jul 12. Executors:
William STRETTON and John STRETTON, sons of the deceased

Miscellaneous will reference

Ann STRATTON of Bristol, widow (1692) and her son William STRATTON of Bristol, tanner (1695).

SOMERSET

Genealogical Abstract of Will of Nathaniel SAUNDERS

"I, Nathaniel SAUNDERS of Wotton under Edge, Co.Glos. clothier . . . my son Samuel SAUNDERS... my son in law Thomas VINES . . . my son John SAUNDERS . . . my grandson John SAUNDERS . . . my grandson Nathaniel SAUNDERS . . . my granddaughter Deborah SAUNDERS . . . my granddaughter Hannah SAUNDERS . . . my grandchildren Thomas VINES, Samuel VINES, Isatt VINES, Sarah VINES and Elizabeth VINES . . . my grandson Samuel SAUNDERS . . . my sister Mary KNIGHT . . . my sister Deborah FFATHORNE . . . my nephew William RUGG . . . my daughter Mary, wife of Thomas VINES . . ."

Will made 1716 June. Signed by Testator, witnesses Elizabeth VINES,

Elizabeth THOMAS, Proved GLOUCESTER 1718

Holy Trinity, Abbots Leigh, Somerset Parish registers

Baptisms 1656–1670: no SANDERS OR SAUNDERS entries
Marriages 1656–1670:
1657 Jun 23 John SAUNDERS, seaman, & Elizabeth LUCKES,
spinster, both of this parish, by banns
1661 Aug 05 Edward SAUNDERS & Elizabeth GEORGE
Burials 1656–1667:
1657 Sep 24 John SANNDERS of Rownham
1658/9 Mar 11 Marie SANNDERS of Rownham, widow
1661 May 01 Francis SANDERS
1663 Oct 7 Grace d/o John SANNDERS
1665 Apr 14 John SANDERS
1665 Apr 21 Henry SANDERS
1665 Dec 9 Fillip SANDERS

Easton in Gordano, Somerset

Baptism register 1600–1640

1602 Apr 11 Elizabeth SAUNDERS
1604 Jun 24 Thomas SAUNDER
1606 Nov 16 Abraham s/o Philip SAUNDERS
1613 May 19 Benjamin s/o William SAUNDERS

Marriage register 1600–1640

1601 Jul 16 Philip SAUNDERS & Elizabeth FROGMAN
1612 Aug 17 William SAUNDERS & Katharine FROGMAN

Burial register 1600–1640

1614 Oct 11 Thomas SAUNDERS
1617/18 Feb 2 Katherine SAUNDERS widow & late wife of William SAUNDERS

Berkley, Somerset

Marriage register

1601 Jul 16 Philip SAUNDERS & Elizabeth FROGMAN

1612 AUG 17 William SAUNDERS & Katharine FROGMAM

Burial register 1600–1640

1614 Oct 11 Thomas SAUNDERS
1617/18 Feb 02 Katherine SAUNDERS widow & late wife of William SAUNDERS

Berkley, Somerset

Baptism register 1590–1654:

1590 Mar 4 Elizabeth base born d/o Mawde SAUNDERS
1593 Jun 22 Jane base born d/o Mary SAUNDERS of Fayroke
1597 Jul 24 Edward s/o John SAUNDERS
1604 Nov 30 Ann d/o John SAUNDERS
1606 Mar 30 Nathaniel s/o Thomas/Mary SAUNDER
1608 Mar 28 Jane d/o Thomas/Mary SAUNDERS
1610 Nov 18 Thomas s/o Thomas SAUNDERS
1615 Nov 24 Robert s/o Thomas SANDERS
1619 Dec 12 Mary d/o Thomas SANDERS
1648 May 30 Mary base born d/o Mary SAUNDERS

Marriage register 1580–1654:

1596 Oct 15 John SAUNDERS & Joane PALMER
1602 Nov 07 Nathaniel SAUNDERS & Edith WEAVER
1606 Jun 02 Christopher PALMER & Ann SAUNDERS, by licence
1632 Nov 19 Thomas CRABBY & Jane SAUNDERS
1635 Aug 24 Thomas WARD & Mary SAUNDERS
1650/51 Jan 28 George SWARTH & Mary SAUNDERS

Burial register 1590–1654:

1590 Feb 02 Mawde SAUNDERS widow
1593 Jul 12 Thomas SAUNDERS being an olde man
1594 Apr 12 Mary SAUNDERS
1594 Apr 30 Jane d/o Mary SAUNDERS
1596 Nov 07 Agnes SAUNDERS of Fayroke
1597 Oct 13 Margarett late wife to Thomas SAUNDERS
1608 Feb 12 Nathaniel s/o Thomas SAUNDERS
1609/10 Feb 23 John SAUNDERS
1634 Oct 22 Thomas s/o Thomas SAUNDERS of Standerwicke

1639 Jun 04 Thomas SAUNDERS
1653 May 16 Nathaniel SAUNDERS

Somerset Record Office: DD/SAS C/795 (A) P.D.80
Survey of Abbotts Leigh, Somerset, taken in 1668 – Leases

"Henry SANDERS held by Indenture of Lease bearing date of 20th day of
October in the 13th year of the Reigne of King James (1615–1616), one
Messuage or tenement with the appurtenances, a garden & orchard, and
Six closes of meadow & pasture containing 6 acres, situate in
Abbotts Leigh, for 99 years, if John SANNDERS aged 33 years or
Thereabouts, Grace BULLOCK aged 49 yeas or thereabouts, son &
daughter of the said Henry, or either of them, shall so long live.
By and under the yearly rent of 40 shillings, and 3 pence yearly for
common fuel, 2 pence yearly for custom works, and one couple of fat
Capons at Easter yearly, herriot the best beast or 40 shillings at
election, a Covenant for reparations taking sufficient estovers to
be spent upon the premises without waste, making a proviso if the
rents be unpaid by the space of one month being lawfully demanded
and no sufficient distress. Of if the said premises be demised
without licence, that then a reentry a Covenant for quiet enjoying,
Consideration L13 pounds. By the demise of Samuel HORTON Esq &
George NORTON Esq. worth per annum (sum omitted)"
Survey of Abbotts Leigh, Somerset, taken in 1668 – Copyhold

"John SANDERS holdeth by Copy of Court Roll bearing date the XVth
day of April in the 7th year of the Reigne of King Charles (1631–1632), one
messuage or tenement containing 28 acres of land meadow &
pasture, situate in Abbots Leigh, with the appurtenances, for the
natural life of the said John SANNDERS aged 55 years or thereabouts.
By & under the yearly rent of 20 shillings and 8 pence and two
Capons yearly at the birth of Our Lord, and a herriot when it shall
Happen, and other burdens works customs & services, fine L40 pounds.
By he demise of Arthur HORTON Esq. Worth per annum (sum omitted)"

GLOUCESTERSHIRE

St.Mary, Tetbury, Glos, Parish registers 1631*-1660
*start of earliest surviving register

Baptisms 1631–1660:

1633 Apr 07 Ann d/o Morgan SAUNDERS
1646/7 Feb 14 John s/o John SAUNDERS
1649/50 Mar 07 John s/o John SAUNDERS
1656 Aug 11 Catherine d/o John SAUNDERS

Marriages 1631–1660

1627/8 Feb 22 Henry STOKES & Sara SANDERS
1640 May 31 Thomas SANDERS & Margaret LEWS
1654 Apr 06 John HAYWARD & JOANE SAUNDERS

Burials 1631–1600:

1637/8 FEB 27 Robert SAUNDERS
1642/3 MAR 25 Agnes SANDERS
1653 JUN 30 Morgan SAUNDERS
1657 Jul 03 Robert SAUNDERS

St.Mary, Tetbury, Glos. Bishop's Transcripts (Baptisms)

1618 Oct 01 John s/o Morgan SAUNDERS
(Checked 1616, 1618, 1621–1625. 1627–1629)

Ralph Bigland's "Gloucestershire Collections" – Memorial Inscriptions

St. Mary, Tetbury: In the Church

Samuel SAUNDEERS died 1686 Jul 17
Catherine his wife died 1682 Jun 14
Catherine d/o the above died 1672 Mar 26
Also Mary d/o Samuel & Sarah SAUNDERS died 1739 Dec 03
Here lyeth the body of Catherine d/o Samuel SAUNDERS died 1679 Jun 05
Nathaniel SAUNDERS died 1757 Jul 26 aged 55yrs
Three of their children died in infancy

On Tablet on West wall

Sacred to the Memory of Maria the wife of Samuel Albin SAUNDERS
Formerly of Upton Grove in this parish, Esq,
Who was born 1808 Age 11 and died at Hastings (Sussex) 1853 May 28

Also of their children,
Samuel Albin SAUNDERS born 1847 Mar 23, died 1848 Nov 01, and
Rosa Maria SAUNDERS born 1848 Apr 27, died London 1850 Apr 25

Samuel Albin SAUNDERS died Tetbury 1856 in the sixty-fourth year of his age

West Cloister on a Tablet:

In a Vault underneath lie several of the SAUNDERS, late of this parish.
Particulars he Last Day will disclose
ARMS: Per Chevron Sable and Argt. Three Elephants, Heads erased, two &
one counter charged

On Tombs:

Margaret relict of John WIGHT, daughter of Samuel & Catherine SAUNDERS
Died 1750 Jan 25 aged 73

Genealogical Abstract of the will of Henry SAUNDERS of Co. Glos

"I give to my son Daniel SAUNDERS ten pounds, also all my working tools . . .
to my grandson John BARND my old gun. I make my wife Sarah SAUNDERS
my whole Executrix of all that I may not have disposed of . . ."
Will made 1670/1 Feb 17. Mark (X) of Testator, witnessed Nathanial HAYWARD,
John BARUND. Proved 1671 May 06. No parish mentioned in the will.

(No will proved in Gloucestershire for Samuel SAUNDERS of Tetbury who
died 1686)

St.Mary the Virgin, Olveston, Glos.

Marriage register for the period 1650–1696 is missing. No Bishop's Transcripts
to cover the gap

St.Mary, Wotton-under-Edge, Glos, Baptism register 1665–1680

1667/8 Jan 06 Samuel s/o Nathaniel SANDERS
1668/9 Mar 07 Sarah d/o Nathaniel SANDERS
1669 Aug 21 Mary d/o Joseph SANDERS
1670/1 Jan 01 Samuel s/o Nathaniel SANDERS
1671 May 16 John s/o Joseph SANDERS
1672 Oct 23 Mary d/o Nathaniel SANDERS

1674 Nov 18 Sarah d/o Nathaniel SANDERS
1686 Apr 08 Nathaniel s/o Nathaniel SAUNDERS

St.Mary, Wotton-under-Edge, Glos. Marriage register 1698

1698 Aug 26 Nathaniel SAUNDERS & Deborah FOWLER

St.Mary, Wotton-under-Edge, Glos. Burial register 1710=1718

1711 Aug 04 Deborah wife of Nathaniel SAUNDERS
1717 Nov 17 Nathaniel SAUNDERS

Berkeley, Glos, Baptism register 1630–1645

1634 Aug 20 Mary d/o William NICHOLAS of Clapton
1635 Nov 28 William s/o William NICHOLAS of Clapton
1637/8 Feb 07 Robert s/o William NICHOLAS of Clapton
1640 Apr 15 Thomas s/o William NICHOLAS of Clapton
1643 Nov 09 Matthew s/o William NICHOLAS of Clapton
(no SAUNDERS or SANDERS entries found)

Berkeley, Glos. Marriage register 1620–1645

1633 Oct 04 William NICHOLAS of Clapton & Alice STRATON of Berkeley
(no SAUNDEERS or SANDERS found)

Berkeley, Glos. Burial register 1620–1653

1653/4 Jan 4 William NICHOLAS senior of Clapton
(no SAUNDERS or SANDERS)

Wotton-under-Edge, Glos. Baptism register 1630–1645

1634 Dec 10 Nathaniel s/o Thomas SAUNDERS
1636 May 06 Elizabeth d/o Morgan SAUNDERS
1636/7 Jan 19 Samuel s/o Thomas SAUNDERS
1638 Oct 21 Samuel s/o John SAUNDERS
1640 Sep 21 Thomas s/o John SANDERS
1642 May 30 Nathaniel s/o John SANDERS
1643/4 Feb 03 Anne d/o John SAUNDERS
1645/6 Jan 30 Joseph s/o John SANDERS

<u>Wooton-under-Edge, Glos. Marriage register 1620–1634</u>

1628 Oct 23 Thomas OSBORNE & Rebecca SANDERS

<u>Wooton-under-Edge, Glos. Burial register 1636–1653</u>

No SAUNDERS or SANDERS

<u>Kingswood near Wotton-under-Edge, Glos. Baptism register 1630–1633, 1637–1643</u>

No SAUNDERS or SANDERS

<u>Kingswood near Wotton-under-Edge, Glos. Marriage reister 1629</u>

1629 Dec 15 Thomas SANDERES tooke to wife Elizabeth the daughter of Anthony WEBB

<u>Kingswood near Wotton-under-Edge, Glos. Burial register 1637–1643</u>

No SAUNDERS or SAUNDERS

<u>Gloucestershire wills index 1650–1660</u>

No Thomas SANDERS or SAUNDERS, no William CLAPTON

<u>Schedule of Berkeley, Glos. Records at Gloucestershire Record Office</u>

1665. 17 Charles II Fine between Nathaniel SAUNDERS, Giles MACHIN & Ursula MACHIN, William MARGRETTS & Alice his wife, of 2 messuages, 2 gardens, in Berkeley, Glos.

<u>Ralph Bigland's "Memorial Inscriptions of Gloucestershire"</u>

Kingswood near Wotton-under-Edge:

Persis, the daughter of Anthony WEBB, who died 1659 Apr 17 (on a Monument – Arms: Or, on a Bend Sable, Three Escallops Agent, for WEBB) Berkeley: no Thomas SAUNDERS or SANDERS found

<u>Gloucestershire wills index 1636–1649</u>

No relevant SAUNDERS or WEBB

Prerogative Court of Canterbury, Wills indexes 1620–1660

1629 Anthony WEBB, clothier, Kingswood, Wiltshire
1652/3 Jan 12 Elizabeth NICHOLAS of Stone, Berkeley, Gloucestershire,
widow
1657 Alice NICHOLAS of Beverstone, Berkeley, Gloucestershire
1660 John SAUNDERS of Wotton-under-Edge, Gloucestershire, mercer

Genealogical Abstract of the will of Anthony WEBB, clothier, Kingswood,
Wilts.

"My daughter Mary L100 . . . my daughters Prudence, Elizabeth, Sara &
Rebecca L100 each . . . their under John WEBB . . . William TANNER my
grandson
L20 . . . Joell & Joane GAYNER my grandchildren L10 each . . . Thomas WEBB
son of my daughter Persis L10 . . . Thomas WEBB my son in law L10 . . . Joan
my wife . . . my son Samuel . . . my sisters Margery and Annis, Jane and Joan
40 shillings each . . . my brother Christopher 20 shillings . . . I appoint my wife
Joan Executrix of this my will . . ."
Will made 1629 May 02. Signed by Testator, witnesses William TANNER,
John WEBB, Thomas WEBB. Proved LONDON 1629 Nov 06

Genealogical Abstract of the will of Alice NICHOLAS, widow, Berkeley,
Glos.

"My son Ralph NICHOLAS . . . my daughter Anne PARTRIDGE . . . my daughter
Elizabeth BALLENDEN . . . my daughter Jane THOMAS . . . my daughter
Mary . . . Thomas NICHOLAS my son and Mary NICHOLAS my said daughter
to be sole Executors
of this my will . . . my brother John NICHOLAS and Nathaniel WAIGHT to
be my
Overseers . . ."
Will made 1656/7 March 17. Mark of Testatrix, witnesses John DRIVER,
John NICHOLAS. Proved LONDON 1657 Jun 10

Genealogical Abstract of the will of John SAUNDERS, mercer, Wooton-
Under-Edge, Glos.

"My son John SAUNDERS L5 . . . my son Samuel SAUNDERS L5 . . . my son
Nathaniel

SAUNDERS L20 . . . my son Joseph SAUNDERS L20 . . . my son Achilles
SAUNDERS L20 . . . My son Benjamin SAUNDERS L20 . . . my daughter Anne
SAUNDERS L30 . . . my daughter Mary SAUNDERS L30 . . . my daughter
Damaras L30 . . . my daughter Deborah SAUNDERS L30 . . . my wife Margery
SAUNDERS . . . my friend Nicholas HESKINS, my brother inLaw Jonah OATES
and John SMYTH to be my Overseers . . ."
Will made 1660 Aug 17. Signed by Testator, witnessed Jonah OATES,
N. HESKING, John SMITH, Thomas SAUNDERS. Proved LONDON 1660
Nov 21

Kingswood, near Wotton-under-Edge, Glos. Burial Register 1629

1629 May 26 Anthony WEBB was buried

Berkeley, Glos. Burial Register 1654–1657

1654/5 Jan () John NICHOLAS of Clapton was buried

Wotton-under-Edge, Glos. Burial Register 1660

1660 Aug 30 John SANDERS was buried

Gloucestershire marriage index

1628 John SAUNDERS & Joan HAINES, at Henbury

Holy Trinity, Westbury on Trym, Glos. Marriage register 1625–1637

No relevant entries

Wotton-under-Edge, Glos. Marriage register 1628–1638

1628 Oct 23 Thomas OSBORNE & Rebecca SANDERS
1638 Nov 06 Jonas OKES & Dorothy WALLINGTON

Kingswood, near Wooton-under-Edge, Glos. Marriage Register 1628–-1638

1629 May 29 Thomas WALLFORD took to wife Prudence the daughter of
Anthony WEBB
1629 Nov 19 Robert BIDDLE took to wife Mary daughter of Anthony WEBB
1629 Dec 15 Thomas SANDERES took to wife Elizabeth daughter of Anthony
WEBB

Gloucestershire Record Office. Accession D7115 vol. 2, p. 70

Names of soldiers who ran away from Sir Charles Berkeley's Company
(inter alia):Nathaniell SAUNDERS of Tetbury, no date

Tetbury, Glos. Marriage register 1627

No further detail in the register or the Bishop's Transcript for the
Marriage of Henry STOKES and Sara SANDERS

Kingswood,   near   Wotton-under-Edge,   Glos.   Baptism   register
1600–1629,1634–1636

1613 Oct 24 Sarah d/o Anthony WEBB
1616 Sep 24 Rebecca d/o Anthony WEBB

Kingswood, near Wotton-under Edge, Glos. Burial Register 1630–1638

1638/9 Jan 17 Joane wife of Anthony WEBB

Ralph Bigland's "Monumental Inscriptions of Gloucestershire

Kingswood, nr Wotton-under-Edge:
Inscription in the church, on a Monument –

Arms: Or, on a bend Sable, Three Escallops Argent, for WEBB
In memory of his dear father Thomas WEBB late of Kingswood, son of
Richard WEBB of Wotton-under Edge gent, who died May 24, 1674, aged 84
His obsequious son Richard WEBB set up this monument & in memory of his
Virtuous Mother Persis, daughter of Anthony WEBB, who died 15 years before,
viz. Apr 17 1659

(No THRUPP entries in Bigland's monumental inscriptions index)

Gloucestershire Marriage Index 1526–1675

1662 Mary THRUPP & William BALDWIN, Bristol marriage bond

Prerogative Court of Canterbury wills index 1600–1619

1604 Anthonie WEBBE, yeoman, Goodrington, Bishops Cleve parish,
Co.Glos. (87 HARTE)

1613 Reginald NICHOLAS, gent, Prestbury, Gloucs (87 CAPELL)
1617 John THRUPP, vintner, Bristol, Gloucs (35 WELDON)
1617 George WEBBE, clothier, Old Sodbury, Gloucs (8r WELDON)

Gloucestershire Record Office card index

1613 John THRUPP of Doynton, vintner (D2957 p/798 110 [6])

D2957 p/798 110 (6)

1613 Mar 06 assignment of property

(1) Anthony HUNGERFORD Esq of Garson, Co. Wilts
Thomas Morgan vicar of Minety, Co. Wilts
John Bradshawe parson of Creedwell, Co. WILTS
Christopher MYLL alias BUTLER of Doynton, Co. Glos. Yeoman &
Grace his wife

(2) William WEBB gent of Marshfield, Co. Glos
Thomas CLEMENT soapmaker of Bristol
John THRUPP vintner of Bristol
Roger RADBORNE of Doynton, Co.Glos
Close of pasture called the Ham (10a) also one Close of arable
Adjoining called the Little field

(2a); note of Assignment of property to Henry WEARE of Hinton,
Co.Glos, 1663, endorse
Rent: a couple of capons
Terms: residue of 500 years
Witnesses: Robert LANCASTER, John DAVIS alias TAYLOR, John TYLLEY,
William OSBORNE, John TYNT, William PESTER

Gloucestershire Record Office card index

1657 Wick, Berkeley – Prerogative Court of Canterbury will (vol. 8 folio
143) of William NICHOLAS, yeoman (in PCC calendar as William NICHOLS)

Chipping Sodbury, Glos. Bishop's Transcripts 1607–1635

1607 Dec 24 Johane wife of (?) EDWARDS, buried
1609 Illegible
1618, 1620, 1622, 1628, 1629, 1632: no relevant entries

<u>Little Sodbury, Glos. Bishop's Transcripts 1602–1635</u>

1602, 1605, 1618, 1620, 1626: no relevant entries

<u>Old Sodbury, Glos. Bishop's Transcripts 1605–1635</u>

1605–1609, 1612: no relevant entries
1613 Aug 10 Roger s/o Alice SAUNDERS, buried
1617, 1620, 1621, 1623, 1625, 1628–1629: no relevant entries
(Note: earliest surviving parish registers as follows –
Chipping Sodbury 1661, Old Sodbury 1684, Little Sodbury 1754)

<u>Gloucestershire Apprentice registers 1595–1646</u>

Checked 1616—1624: no SAUNDERS entries

INDEX

A

Abigail (wife of Peter Hargate), 294
Adams, Jane, 180–81, 183
Aldhagh, 85, 109, 122, 151
Alexander the Great, 11–12, 21, 116
Alfred (duke), 13, 22–25
Alfred the Great, 22–23
Alisaundre, John, 12
Alisaundre, Robert, 12–13
Arnold, Benedict, 305–6, 314,
    331, 333
Arundel, Thomas, 222, 390
Athelfleda (wife of King Edgar),
    12, 23–24, 42

B

Bacon, Nathaniel, 233
Baldwin, William, 420, 431
Barrett, James, 167, 182
Barrett, Jenet, 167, 177, 179, 186
Barrett, John, 182
Barrett, William, 167
Bartlett, Thomas, 287, 292
Bartlett, William, 279, 292
Basset, Alan, 30, 44, 53, 56, 66
Basset, Gilbert, 30, 34–35, 51, 53,
    55–56
Basset, Thomas, 29–30, 34, 44, 46,
    50–51
    sons of, 34, 44
Bate, Henry, 265–67, 275

Bate, Nathaniel, 265, 267, 275
Battailes manor, 86, 109, 116, 118,
    120–22, 124, 133–34, 137,
    150, 153, 156, 158, 160–61,
    188–89, 394
Battle of Fornham, 29, 31
Battle of Renfrewshire, 10, 16
Beddington manor, 83, 120
Berkeley, William, 217, 247, 255–56,
    276, 355
Bermondsey Abbey, 25, 98, 123
Big Bristo (slave), 284, 295
Blackhall manor, 9, 14
Black Patch War, 370, 381
Blanton, Jane, 265, 274
Blanton, Thomas, 259, 265, 272, 274
Blanton, William, 327, 345, 348
Bocland, Hugh de, 29, 39
Bonny Bess, 209, 211, 401
bookland, 23
Brittany, 5–7, 10, 13, 32, 34, 40, 67,
    127, 238, 385–86
Bromley, Thomas, 104, 146–47, 149
bubonic plague, 72, 75, 81, 87,
    132, 235
Buckland manor, 154, 395

C

Cardens manor, 134, 141, 146–
    47, 169
Carew, Francis, 91, 397

Carew, Isabel, 148–49, 157, 161, 397
Carew, Joan, 82–85, 87–88, 90,
  96, 98, 100, 106–7, 109, 113,
  115–16, 120, 148
Carew, Nicholas, 82, 84–85, 90–91,
  101, 108–10, 115–16, 156
Carew, Thomas, 84, 90, 115, 389
Catholics, 136–37, 142, 164, 171,
  175–76, 179–80, 187, 189, 256
Cecil, William, 96, 147, 149, 165,
  171, 397
Charlwood manor, 75, 117, 393–94
Charlwood Place, 70, 75, 79, 84,
  101, 117, 144–45
Chertsey Abbey, 19, 61
Church of England, 99, 139, 145,
  160, 180, 285–86, 412
Clandon Regis manor, 25–26, 28,
  45–46, 55
coats of arms, 3–5, 13, 26, 33, 40,
  49, 81, 87, 178, 208, 379, 391
  Bolyn, 33
  bulls' heads, 3–5, 26, 33–34, 38,
    71, 82
  elephants' heads, 4–5, 13
  Sanders, 5, 33
Coleman, Robert, 263, 269, 293
Collenden, William, 59, 61, 70, 388
Combe manor, 27, 45, 50–52
Constitutions of Clarendon, 25, 38
Cooke, John, 96
Cope, Stephen, 96
Cope, William, 96
Courtenay, Agnes (Mrs. John
  Carew Saunder), 90
Courtenay, Agnes (Mrs. Richard
  Saundre), 100–101, 103,
  105, 154
Courtenay, Joane, 101
Courtenay, Margaret, 100–101
Courtenay, Peter, 101, 127, 154
Courtenay, Thomas, 100

Courtenay, William, 101
Covington, Richard, 263
Covington, William, 263, 272
Craig, Elizabeth Sanders, 346
Craig, Lewis, 286, 288, 295, 297,
  315, 333, 346
Creuses manor, 25, 48, 62, 108,
  134, 391
Croc, Robert (father), 10, 386
Croc, Robert (son), 10, 14, 46
Croshaw, Joseph, 216, 230, 232–
  33, 235
Crusades, 15, 35, 41
Crusades, Third, 35, 41, 49

D

Dammartin, William, 58
David (king of Scotland), 8, 13, 386
de Cumba, Richard, 28, 46, 49–56,
  59, 67–68, 387
de Dene, Ralph, 50, 52, 54
de Dene, Richard, 54
de Dene, Robert, 50
de Icklesham, Ralph, 52
de Icklesham, Robert, 49
de la Pole, William, 77
de Lega, Leonard. See de
  Sanderstead, Leonard
de Montfort, Hugh, 13
Dene, Sybilla, 49–50, 52, 54, 56,
  64, 387
de Pappeworth, Ralph, 41, 54,
  56–57, 61, 68, 387
de Pappeworth, Robert, 387
de Pappeworth, William, 55–56
de Sanderstead, Beatrice, 19, 27,
  29, 44, 46, 55, 58, 64
  death of, 47
  dower properties of, 26, 45–46
de Sanderstead, John, 48–49,
  69, 387

de Sanderstead, Leonard, xiii, 3–4,
8–10, 15, 26, 32, 38, 44, 47,
50, 55, 62–64, 71, 387
  birth of, 15
  children of, 28
  coat of arms of, 4, 32, 35
  death of, 35, 44
  family of, 45
  knighthood of, 16
  knight's crests of, 4, 32–33
  marriage of, 31
  position of, 3, 27, 34
  symbol of, 4, 26
  will of, 45
  work of, 27–29
de Sanderstead, Leonard,
  Wallingford stewardship,
  30–31
de Valletort, Ralph, 19
de Valognes, Philip, 16, 36
Dol, 6–7, 9–10, 67, 385–86
dower land, 26, 38, 52, 262, 295,
328, 348, 351, 354, 356,
359, 367
Downe Manor, 26, 28, 46, 48, 387
Dunstanville, Alice, 29, 46, 64
Dunstanville, Beatrice (Beatrice de
  Sanderstead), 17, 19, 27, 62
Dunstanville, Reginald, 8, 17–19,
28–29, 31, 34, 36–37, 39, 66
Dunstanville, Walter, 29, 49, 64

E

economy, 11, 86, 92, 166, 199, 207,
217, 224, 251, 277, 284, 294,
300, 355, 358, 369–70
  modern, 11
  traditional, 11
  world, 224
Edgar (king of England), 12, 23
Edmondson, Thomas, 262–63, 266

Edward I (king of England), 59
Edward III (king of England),
74–75, 82
Edward IV (king of England), 93,
95, 97–98, 100–101, 107, 111
Edwards, John, 182, 192, 251, 404
Edward VI (king of England), 142,
144, 147, 391
Elizabeth I (queen of England),
14, 137, 141, 165, 170, 175,
179–80, 189
English Channel, 6–7, 24
Erasmus, Desiderius, 128, 130, 132,
136, 163
  influence of, 128
Eschyna (wife of Walter FitzAlan),
10–11, 14–15, 17, 386
Ewell Manor, 138, 140, 147, 176

F

Fernand Braudel, 11, 219, 224
FitzAlan, Walter, 8–10, 13–14, 17–
18, 30, 34, 36, 50, 384, 386
FitzFlaad, Alan, 8, 384, 386
FitzRichard, Mabel, 19
FitzWalter, Alan, 14, 35
FitzWalter, Leonard, 19, 387
Florio, John, 149–50
Flower de Luce (house), 222, 390
Flower de Luce (trading vessel), 209–
11, 390, 401, 407
Floyd, John, 304, 332
Floyd, Robert, 318, 324–25
folkland, 23
Ford, Richard, 86, 108, 110, 238
Forks of Elkhorn, 313–15, 320–21,
324, 327, 329, 339, 344–
46, 413
Forks of Elkhorn Church, 336–37,
342, 353, 365

Foxe, Richard, 119–20, 127–28, 130, 132–33, 136, 155
Frogman, Elizabeth, 422

G

Gist, Nathaniel, 302, 331
Gittons, Joan, 140, 146–47, 158–59, 396
Gittons, Thomas, 140–41, 396
Globe, 241–44, 258, 405
Gloucestershire, xiii, 165, 197, 199, 201, 203, 205, 207, 209–17, 219, 223–25, 229–32, 247–48, 253–55, 404–5, 429
Golden Lion, 237–41, 244, 249–50, 271, 404–5
Great Depression, 376
Gresly, John, 207–8, 227, 391

H

Harwood, Thomas, 219, 230, 238, 244, 246, 271
Hayman, James, 240, 262
Hayton, Agnes, 84
Hayton, Thomas, 76, 83–84, 108
Henry I (king of England), 8, 17–19, 25, 27, 29, 387
Henry II (king of England), 17–20, 24–25, 27–30, 34–35, 37, 44, 49–51, 64, 113
Henry III (king of England), 12, 44, 54–55, 66
Henry VI (king of England), 77, 81, 111, 128
Henry VII (king of England), 119–20, 127–28, 130, 132
Henry VIII (king of England), 33, 99, 101, 104–5, 118, 124, 127–28, 130, 138–40, 142, 144, 151–52, 158, 160, 163, 172–73
Hill, Leonard, 263

Holgill, William, 132–33
Honour of Wallingford, 28–30, 33, 35, 39, 52
Hort, Frances, 224
Hoskins, Catherine. *See* Sanders, Caty (Catherine)
Hungate, Alys, 144, 389
Hutchinson, John, 233, 243

I

Iwardby, Joan, 90, 152, 394–95
Iwardby, John, 110, 152–53

J

James I (king of England), 179, 198
Jefferson, Thomas, 265, 269, 301, 356
John (king of England), 30, 34–35, 44, 49, 51, 55

K

Knethell, John, 180–81, 404
knight's fee, 20, 38, 50
Knights Templars, 35, 41
Kroth, Henrietta, 370, 374, 381, 383, 416
Kroth, Sarah, 370, 381

L

Lane, John, 233, 248
Lane, Thomas, 241
Lane, William, 240–41, 245, 248
Leigh, Henry, 222, 390
Leonard (son of Leonard de Sanderstead), xiii, 2–21, 23–41, 43–51, 55, 58, 62–65, 71, 379, 386–87
Leonard of Nabloc (saint), 15, 36
Leonard's Lee (place), 26, 45, 47
Lepton, Joan, 123, 395
Lepton, John, 124

Lepton, Ralph, 128, 132–33, 154
Lewis, Andrew, 314, 316, 336
Lewis, William, 316, 336
Lloyd, John, 112
Lodge Manor, 58–59, 61–62, 387
Lougher, Thomas, 167, 402

M

Magna Carta, 44
Manor of Purley, 25, 110, 153
marriage arrangement, 20, 36,
    46, 234
Marston, Joan, 138, 148, 156–
    58, 193
Marston, William, 138, 151
Martin, John, 201–2
Mary (queen of England), 105, 143,
    145, 158, 164, 395
Matilda (daughter of King Henry
    I), 8, 18–19
Maubanc, Philippa, 34, 46, 52
Maubanc, William, 46, 55–56
McDannell, Mary, 360–61, 367
Middle East, 31, 35–36
More, Thomas, 130, 139, 151
Morgan, Daniel, 304–5, 309,
    314, 332
Mullen, John, 359, 366
Mullen, Mary, 359
Mynne, John, 138, 157, 182–83, 197,
    212, 223, 396

N

Nicholas, William, 213, 216, 230,
    246, 420, 427, 432
Normans, 24, 32, 40
    conquest of England, xiii,
        141, 231
    rule in England, 9, 102

O

Olney, John, 92, 114, 124, 394
Oswestry, 7–8, 29, 50
Owen, Thomas, 183, 193
Owen, William, 193
Oxfordshire Manor, 30

P

Paisley Abbey, 9–10, 34
Palgrave, John, 130, 158, 396
Parker, Anna V., ix–x, 191, 257,
    260–61, 271–72, 292,
    331, 364
Pattie, James, 307, 333–34, 413
Pattie, Sally, 307, 312
Pendell Manor, 106, 126, 133–34,
    137, 154, 172
Perrot, John, 170–71
Perry, Micajah, 241–42, 244, 258,
    263, 405
Pettit, John, 243, 407
Philippa (daughter of Edward
    Gage), 392, 394
Philips, William, 269
Pirle, Nicholas, 52
Pitts, Henry, 173–74
Poate, William, 376, 382
Poate, William Richard, 382
Prior, William, 225
Protestantism, 136, 142, 145, 171,
    173, 180, 186, 236

R

Richard, 28–29, 41, 48–57, 59–65,
    67–68, 70–71, 80, 96, 100–
    105, 111, 117, 165, 192, 204,
    284, 387–90
Richard I (king of England), 35,
    51, 64
Richard III (brother of King
    Edward IV), 97–98

Roach, William, 183, 193, 213, 420
Roman Catholicism, 99, 160, 171,
    179, 207, 236
Roman Empire, 6, 22, 67

S

Sackville, Geoffrey, 52, 54, 65
Salomon, Roger, 57–62, 67, 387
Sanderby, Thomas, 225–26
Sanders, Abigail (daughter
    of Hugh Sanders of
    Spotsylvania), 282–83, 287,
    294, 412
Sanders, Alexander, 204
Sanders, Ann, xi, 265
Sanders, Arthur Lee, 63, 224,
    369–70, 374–76, 378–79, 381,
    383, 415
Sanders, Catherine "Caty," 279–80,
    282–85, 287–88, 290
Sanders, David, 204
Sanders, Dorothy, 376–78
Sanders, Edmond, 201–2, 205
Sanders, Edward (of Accomack),
    205–6, 210, 212, 216, 222–23,
    253, 406
Sanders, Edward (son of Edward of
    Accomack), 205, 254, 408
Sanders, Elizabeth (aunt of Robert
    Sanders), 272, 406
Sanders, Elizabeth Craig (daughter
    of Robert Sanders), 346–47,
    363, 414
Sanders, George (of Archer's
    Hope), 204
Sanders, George (of Barbados), 204
Sanders, George (son of Lewis
    Sanders), 337, 349, 365
Sanders, Henry, 202–3, 224,
    422, 424

Sanders, Hugh (of Isle of Wight),
    13, 16, 29, 67, 254, 258, 260–
    61, 269, 271–72, 276, 278–88,
    291–98, 310, 361, 409–10,
    412–13
Sanders, Hugh (of Spotsylvania),
    254, 260–61, 272, 276–77,
    279, 282–83, 286–87,
    310, 325
    death of, 287, 296
    early years of, 278
    estate of, 294, 298
    farmstead of, 283
    lands of, 269, 278–79, 292
    livelihood of, 281
Sanders, John, 254, 256, 270–72,
    297, 329, 335
Sanders, John Wynell, 260, 268
Sanders, Lewis, 332, 337, 349–
    51, 362
Sanders, Nathaniel, ix, 243–44,
    253–54, 257, 259–60, 266–
    68, 273, 301, 303–4, 309,
    316–18, 329–30, 342–43, 409,
    418–20, 426–27
Sanders, Nathaniel (of Gallatin
    County), 338, 342
Sanders, Nathaniel (of King and
    Queen County), 276, 409
Sanders, Nathaniel (of Spotsylvania
    County), 301–4, 307, 309,
    312, 329, 413
    home of, 326
    last will of, 327
Sanders, Nathaniel (son of
    Nathaniel of Spotslvania
    County), 329–30, 342
Sanders, Omar Thomas, 359, 367
Sanders, Philip (brother of Henry
    Saunders), 183
Sanders, Philip (mariner of Abbots
    Leigh), 224

Sanders, Philip (of Essex County), 261, 264–65, 271, 409

Sanders, Philip (of King and Queen County), 273, 275

Sanders, Polly Lindsay, 356–57, 359

Sanders, Ralph Lee, ix, 374, 378, 416

Sanders, Richard, 204–5

Sanders, Robert, 343–44, 363, 414

Sanders, Roger, 206, 211

Sanders, Samuel, 298, 354, 366

Sanders, Sarah Ryly, 265–66, 269

Sanders, Thomas (brother of Nathaniel Sanders), 265, 340

Sanders, Thomas (of Gloucestershire), 210

Sanders, Thomas (vintner), 243

Sanders, Thomas E. (of Louisville), xii

Sanders, Thomas William Maximilian (son of Nathaniel Sanders), 267, 410

Sanders, Virginia, 253

Sanders, Walter, 260, 273

Sanders, William, 81–83, 108–9, 183

Sanders Christian Church, 360

Sanders family, iii, 3–6, 8, 10, 12, 14, 16, 18, 20, 22, 58–60, 70–72, 190–92, 242–44, 272–74, 378–79

Sanders Family of Grass Hills, The (Parker), ix, 191, 271, 331

Sanders Genealogy, 12, 36, 57, 273, 384

Sanders Place, 61, 70–71, 75, 79, 81, 83–84, 120, 388

Sanderstead, xiii, 3–5, 8–13, 15, 20–25, 27–29, 34–35, 38, 41–50, 54–58, 61–64, 69–71, 83, 106–8, 378–79, 387

   ancient, 21–22, 41

   etymology of, 21, 80

Sanderstead Manor, 20, 24–25, 38, 44–47, 107

Sannders, John, 422, 424

Santa Anna. *See* Sanders, Nathaniel (son of Nathaniel of Spotslvania County)

Saunder, Henry, 90, 120, 127–28, 130, 132, 152–55

Saunder, Nicholas, 63, 90–91, 118, 133

Saunder, Richard, 90, 103, 127, 172, 207

Saunder, Thomas, 117, 422

Saunder, William, 71, 78, 82, 123–24, 127, 148, 151, 156, 172, 207

Saunders, Collingwood, 208

Saunders, David, 190, 192

Saunders, Edmund, 205, 210, 227, 392–93, 406, 422

Saunders, Elizabeth, 160, 172, 174, 180, 192, 249, 259, 422

Saunders, Erasmus, 130, 163–65, 167, 169–71, 176–77, 179–80, 183, 192, 225, 249, 404

   brothers of, 171, 184, 188, 191

   children of, 168, 184, 187

   father of, 169, 184–85, 194

   marriage of, 165, 184, 192

Saunders, Francis, 181, 184, 191–92, 220, 225, 402

Saunders, Henry (of Abbots Leigh), 183, 223–24, 270

Saunders, Henry (of Charlwood), 401

Saunders, Henry (of Ewell), 91, 135–36, 394

Saunders, Henry (silkman of London), 209, 401

Saunders, Jenet Barrett, 182–83

Saunders, Joan Carew, 394–95

Saunders, John, 185, 187, 192, 215, 336, 422–23, 425, 427, 429–30

Saunders, Joseph, 200, 206–7, 209–12, 216–18, 220, 223, 228, 244, 251, 390, 407

Saunders, Katherine, 422–23

Saunders, Mary, 233, 245, 419, 423

Saunders, Morgan, 425, 427

Saunders, Nathaniel, 215, 224, 229–32, 234–35, 237–40, 245–51, 253, 257, 298, 404–5, 419, 421, 423–25, 427–28

Saunders, Nicholas, 110, 130, 133, 144, 148–50, 152, 156–57, 161, 171–75, 179, 189–92, 194, 389, 394, 397

Saunders, Nicholas (eldest son of Nicholas Saunders and Isabel Carew), 149

Saunders, Nicholas (of Charlwood), 133, 144, 148

Saunders, Nicholas (of Ewell), 110, 130, 192, 397

Saunders, Philip, 166, 177–79, 181–83, 187, 191–93, 197, 212–13, 223, 235, 243, 404–5, 422

Saunders, Richard (of Banbury), 194

Saunders, Richard (of Charlwood), 117, 226, 389

Saunders, Richard (son of William and Marjory of Banbury), 109

Saunders, Robert, 425

Saunders, Roger, 206, 210, 228, 401

Saunders, Samuel (son of Nathaniel Saunders), 421, 425–26

Saunders, Samuel Albin, 405, 425–26

Saunders, Sara, 215

Saunders, Thomas (of Bristol), 80

Saunders, Thomas (of Charlwood), 105, 128, 143–44, 159, 162, 172, 194, 391, 393, 396

Saunders, Thomas (of Derbyshire), 399

Saunders, Thomas (of Gloucestershire), 219, 232, 404

Saunders, Thomas (of Little Ireton, Derby), 399

Saunders, Thomasin, 181, 183, 191, 193, 215

Saunders, Thomas White, 205, 221, 392

Saunders, William (of Aston), 172

Saunders, William (of Banbury), 94

Saunders, William (of Charlwood), 11, 389

Saunders, William (of Ewell), 104, 135–39, 141–43, 147–48, 163, 191

Saunders, William (of Surrey), 228

Saunders, William (of Welford), 393

Saundre, Henry, 104–6, 109, 123–24, 128, 132, 148, 166

Saundre, James, 74–75

Saundre, Joan, 109–10, 115–16

Saundre, John, 78, 80, 96, 109

Saundre, Matthew, 75, 388

Saundre, Nicholas, 97–98, 104, 110, 115, 123, 137

Saundre, Ralph, 57–59, 61, 67, 343, 387

Saundre, Richard, 59–60, 62, 70–71, 78, 80, 95–96, 100, 105, 109, 115, 117, 387

Saundre, Stephen, 28, 48–49, 63, 75–76, 88, 96, 98–99, 108, 115, 388–89

Saundre, Thomas, 76, 78–79, 83, 388
Saundre, William, 62, 71, 74, 83–88, 91–93, 95–100, 106, 108–10, 113, 115, 117, 120–21, 124, 151, 388
Saundre, William (of Banbury), 91, 98, 113, 117
Saundre, William (of Charlwood), 71, 84, 88, 96–100, 106, 109, 115, 120–21, 124, 388
Saxons, 21–24
  royalty of, xiii, 22, 25
Scott, John, 324, 339, 348–49, 351
Sende, 44–47, 50–52, 54–56, 62, 65, 81, 387
Sende manor, 44–47, 49, 51, 53–55, 57, 59, 61, 63, 65, 67, 69
seneschal, 6–7, 9, 386
Shakespeare, William, xi, 149
Sherland manor, 158
Smith, John, 200, 218, 220, 430
Southwark, 85–86, 91, 97–98, 104, 110, 121–23, 127, 133, 135, 139, 151–52, 165, 184, 389
Spelman, Clement, 159
Spelman, Erasmus, 159, 200, 396
Spelman, Henry, 159, 191, 200–201, 220, 396
Spelman, John, 159, 396
Spencer, Joan, 95–96
Stephen (king of England), 8, 18
Stephen (son of Leonard de Sanderstead), 28, 46, 48–49
stewardship, 10, 17, 28, 30–33, 35, 39, 53
Stockholm Codex Aureus, 22, 42
St. Peter's Abbey, 23–25, 38, 42, 47
Stratton, Joseph, 230, 241
Stratton, Mary, 231, 234–35, 246, 257, 419–20
Stratton, Richard, 230, 235

Stratton, Thomas, 230, 234, 241, 245–48, 251, 405–6, 420
Syon Abbey, 99, 116, 130, 172–73, 194–96, 389, 399

T

Three Crowns Inn, 97, 123–24, 126, 135, 228
Throckmorton, William, 210, 393
Toone, Alice, 208, 227–28
Traveling Church, 288, 290, 297–98, 313, 315–16, 346, 412

V

Vintners Company of London, 86, 206, 254

W

Walsingham, Katherine, 162, 208
Warlingham, 25–26, 28, 38, 45, 47–49, 62–63, 69, 85, 108, 110, 134, 387
Warlingham Manor, 25, 38, 69, 108
Warwickshire, 5, 48, 95, 161, 387, 394
Watkin (son of Leonard de Sanderstead), 28, 47–49, 63–64, 108, 387
Watkins, John, 260
Watkins, Thomas, 245, 258–59, 262, 272, 409
Webb, Anthony, 214–15, 404, 428–29
Webb, Elizabeth, 214–15, 230
Webb, John, 429
Webb, Thomas, 429
Wellys, Richard, 116
Wessex, 22, 255
William (king of Scotland), 16–17
William the Conqueror, 7–8
Williton Manor, 148

Willoughby, John, 158
Winchester, bishop of, 101, 121,
    127–28, 132, 399
Winterbourne Manor, 56
Wogan, Hugh, 183, 213
Woodford, William, 285, 302,
    304, 307
Woodmanstern manor, 85, 109
Woodstock, 27, 50, 57, 64–65
Wynell, John, 260, 263

Printed in Great Britain
by Amazon